D1277585

For
Reference
Use Only

SELBY PUBLIC LIBRARY
1331 FIRST STREET
SARASOTA, FL 34236

AUTHORS SERIES · VOLUME VIII

THE NORWEGIAN–AMERICAN HISTORICAL ASSOCIATION

LAWRENCE O. HAUGE, *President*

Board of Publications:

ODD S. LOVOLL, *Editor*

ARLOW W. ANDERSEN

CARL H. CHRISLOCK

JON GJERDE

TERJE I. LEIREN

DEBORAH L. MILLER

TODD W. NICHOL

JANET E. RASMUSSEN

COURTESY CHICAGO HISTORICAL SOCIETY

"A Pageant of All Nations"

AUTHORS SERIES · VOLUME VIII

The Western Home

A Literary History of Norwegian America

by ORM ØVERLAND

1996

PUBLISHED BY
The Norwegian American Historical Association

DISTRIBUTED BY
The University of Illinois Press

SELBY PUBLIC LIBRARY
1331 FIRST STREET
SARASOTA, FL 34236

Copyright © 1996 by the
NORWEGIAN-AMERICAN HISTORICAL ASSOCIATION
THE UNIVERSITY OF ILLINOIS PRESS
ISBN 0-252-02327-7

3 1969 02232 1169

The figure that appears on the cover and title page of this book is one of the twenty-four letters in the older Germanic runic alphabet used in the Scandinavian countries from about 200 to 800 A.D. In addition to representing the sound "m," approximately as in modern English, it also has a name, meaning "man" or "mankind." It thus serves here as a symbol for the humanities.

Foreword

Waldemar Ager once expressed his conviction to his fellow author Ole Buslett that if the Norwegian people should in time disappear in the larger American society, the literature they had created would become the yardstick for Norwegian-American culture, "because it is art and history all in one." Like other imaginative literature, immigrant fiction reflects the society and the circumstances in which it was created. This literature was produced in America and thus by definition constitutes American belles-lettres. It was the need to explain and to define their changed existence in America, as well as memories of a painful departure from the homeland, and even a yearning to transcend their experience as an immigrant people in the making of a new society, that led to an amazing flourishing of ethnic writing. Because they were formulated in the Norwegian language, these varied immigrant narratives are, however, accessible to most readers only when translated into English.

In his history of these works of literature, *The Western Home: A Literary History of Norwegian America,* Orm Øverland paints a compelling portrait based on a meticulous and critical reading. It is the first comprehensive scholarly treatment of Norwegian immigrant fiction. There is a sensitive portrayal of the literary artists, those men and women who contributed to the development of creative writing in the immigrant communities in America, and an insightful discussion of the wide range of subjects they treated as well as a careful appraisal of their literary careers, mainly as amateurs while making their living in other professions and occupations. We are pleased to publish this major treatise as volume eight in our Authors Series.

Orm Øverland is a professor of American literature at the University of

Bergen. He earned his doctoral degree in American Studies at Yale University in 1969; his dissertation on James Fenimore Cooper was published in 1973. It is only one of several works he has written or edited. He is currently co-editing a multivolume edition of America letters.

The Association is grateful to the Norwegian Research Council for a subvention in support of publication and to the University of Illinois Press for serving as marketing agent.

Circumstances relating to my own leave of absence and research obligations have left much of the responsibility of preparing the manuscript for publication in the capable hands of my editorial assistant Mary R. Hove. I thank her most cordially and also the staff of the Association, in particular the assistant secretary Ruth Hanold Crane, for expeditious and efficient services. As in past publications, Mary Hove is responsible for the index.

ODD S. LOVOLL
St. Olaf College
University of Oslo

Contents

Preface

This is a history of American literature. It aims at presenting the literary history of one of the many groups who have entered this country, those who came from Norway. For more than a century a significant portion of this group continued to use the language of their European past even as they were exploring and building their American future. Most histories of American literature, however, are based on the theory that Americans did not really become Americans until they forgot the languages they had brought with them and expressed not only their practical concerns but their reflections and emotions in English. The American mind functions in English only and American culture is expressed in this language. Such a theory dismisses the fact that throughout American history majorities have naturally spoken, written, and read other languages than English for periods in the life of many cities, towns, and rural areas. But the dismissal naturally follows from the theory: those who use other languages are foreigners or at least not yet Americans. And, as Nina Baym has observed, "we never read American literature directly or freely, but always through the perspective allowed by theories" (1981, 123). In this book American literature is the literature of those who are American by choice or by birth regardless of language.

To the extent that immigrants appear in American literary histories, they do so as silent and huddled masses. They are occasionally glimpsed from above and afar, much in the way Basil March in William Dean Howells's *A Hazard of New Fortunes* observes the immigrants in New York from the elevated railways of that city. In Howells's novel, however, this is not so much the recommended point of view as a recognition of the actual distance between the protagonist and his new compatriots and an implied criticism of the inability or unwillingness of the Anglo-American to approach Americans of other origins on their own disparate terms. One reason for this inability is the language barrier. In many immigrant cultures language is the main unifying force. It is, however, also what makes these cultures silent and inaccessible to most American literary historians. Abraham Cahan was long unable to find a publisher for an English version of his novel *Yekl*. When Howells was told that he had published it in Yiddish instead, his first reaction was distress that this would keep Cahan away from the English-reading public. But then he realized that what had happened had no significance and expressed his relief: "It means that the book hasn't been published" (Chametzky 1972, 64). If Cahan reacted to this affront, it has not been recorded. This book does not accept the Howellsian definition of American publication. Moreover, it invites readers to step down from the elevated seat of Basil March and observe an immigrant literary culture from the inside, how it came into being, grew, and was eventually discarded for the more enticing literary culture of the dominant language, a development urged by some, warned against by others.

To my knowledge nothing quite like this literary history has been attempted. There are books and essays on aspects of American literatures in other languages, in particular German and the Scandinavian languages, but there is no complete narrative of an American non-English literary culture. It would not have been possible to complete this one without much and generous assistance.

Grants from the Norwegian Research Council, the United States–Norway Fulbright Foundation for Educational Exchange, the Meltzer Foundation, and the University of Bergen have enabled me to visit and spend time at archives and libraries in the United States and Norway. St. Olaf College and the University of Washington have provided work space and services during two full-year sabbaticals as well as shorter visits. This work would not have been possible without the archives of the Norwegian-American Historical Association and its dedicated archivists, Charlotte Jacobson and Forrest Brown, and secretary Ruth Crane. In Norway the most important repository of Norwegian Americana is the University Library in Oslo, and here the knowledgeable and generous Johanna Barstad offered invaluable assistance far beyond her duties as librarian and curator for this special collection. Her successor, Faith Ann Sevilä, has continued this tradition and has always responded to requests for assistance. Other institutions with relevant collections where I received friendly and expert assistance are the libraries of Luther College, Pacific Lutheran University, the University of Washington, the University of Wisconsin, the University of Minnesota, the Minnesota Historical Society, and the Historical Society of Wisconsin. My work at the University of Bergen would have been impossible without the expert help of the staff of the library's division for inter-library loan. Maya Thee, reference librarian for American literature, has been of great help in suggesting material relevant for my work. Albert E. Anderson, director of the then Augsburg Publishing House, kindly invited me to make use of their archives and gave me freely of his time. My participation in the multilingual American literature project of the Longfellow Institute in the Department of English and American Literature and Language at Harvard University was an invaluable inspiration during the concluding stages of my work.

Over the years I have benefited from the interest other scholars have shown in my work. My long-standing interest in historicist literary study has been nourished by my early and close relations with three fine scholars, Sigmund Skard and Norman Holmes Pearson, to whom I very much would have liked to show this book, and Jay Martin, whose advice I continue to enjoy. My interest in Norwegian-American literature was awakened in the course of several years of service as outside examiner for Dorothy Burton Skårdal's seminar on Scandinavian-American literature and culture at the University of Oslo in the 1970s and early 1980s. She is one of the earliest advocates for the study of American literature in other languages than English. Dorothy Skårdal has also kindly read a version of my manuscript. My first steps in searching and researching the field were taken with the generous and expert advice of Lloyd Hustvedt, professor emeritus of Norwegian at St. Olaf College. His knowledge of Norwegian-American literature is unequaled and his critical acumen combined with his uncanny sense of where it might be a good idea to look for information stood by me when I first came to him at St. Olaf College as a novice in the field. I could not have moved far beyond my state of ignorance without his generosity. Odd S. Lovoll, publications editor for the Norwegian-American Historical Association, has given me invaluable encouragement in many and long conversations, and this book owes much to his and his editorial assistant Mary Hove's expert editing. Gerald Thorson, whose pioneering study of the Norwegian-American novel has been an inspiration, read drafts of what has become chapters two, three, and four, John Higham read an early version of the first chapter, and Øyvind T. Gulliksen and Werner Sollors have read versions of the entire manuscript. I am grateful for their advice and kindness.

This work has taken many years and would not have been possible without the support and encouragement of my wife, Inger Øverland, to whom I dedicate this book.

ORM ØVERLAND
University of Bergen

Note on Usage and References

The language of the writers presented in this book was Norwegian. Except where the context makes clear that the original language of a quotation is English, quotations are in translation. When first mentioned, titles are given in Norwegian and set in italics, with English translation following, italicized only if the translation has been published. When a title is repeated usage may vary. In cases where there has been a published translation, the title of this translation is generally used; in other cases the original or a translation may be used depending on whether the context makes clear what text is referred to.

In older Dano-Norwegian usage, nouns were capitalized. Such capitalization has been omitted in this text.

References follow the author-date system and refer to the two lists of primary and secondary sources. A list of abbreviations is placed first in the bibliography section of the book. In the bibliography all titles are in the original language. When a text has been translated the two years of publication are separated by a virgule (1921/1933).

Where no reference is made for correspondence, the source is always the collection of papers of the recipient in the archives of the Norwegian-American Historical Association.

for
Inger

"What land is this?" asks Jacob of his sons.
"It's Goshen," answers Judah. "Here the land
 Has beauty as the land that was my fathers's.
 Behold, this is to be your home." The old
 Patriarch looks out upon the land.
"Here you'll be filled with longing, father!"
 Says Benjamin. — "Why should that be, my son?"
"Because there are no memories." — "There were
 No memories before we built our homes
 In that land from which we now have come.
 Our land is where we make our memories
 Or wherever we are led by life."
"I cannot understand. Please, father, did not
 God give us the home we've left behind?"
"He did, my son, but this, too, is our gift
 From God."

JON NORSTOG (1918)

As Americans, we feel that the literature of this country is our
literature, expressing and interpreting our common American life;
but as Americans of Norwegian descent, having our own peculiar
characteristics, history, traditions, institutions, and problems, we
need also a literature of our own.

ANDERS M. SUNDHEIM (1920)

PART ONE

Introduction

Vesterheimen:
A Marginal and Transitional Culture

Migration from Norway to the United States began in 1825 with the arrival in New York of the sloop *Restauration* with fifty-three people on board. Although the next emigrant vessels did not depart from Norway until 1836, letters from the first group of emigrants, as well as from individual immigrants, created a growing interest in the possibilities offered by the availability of land in the United States. This interest in America spread so rapidly that it was soon seen as a threat to social stability and was labeled a disease— the America fever. As early as 1837 the Bishop of Bergen, Jacob Neumann, found it necessary to publish a pastoral letter of admonition to the farmers in his diocese who had been struck by this contagion. He appealed to their Christian faith as well as to their patriotism and countered the glowing reports in the many letters circulating among them with accounts of illness and disasters. But neither the bishop nor the many others of his class who spoke and wrote against emigration could stem the tide.

The emigrants left an outlying country in the northwestern corner of Europe. Up to 1814 it had for several centuries been a province of Denmark; then it became the inferior partner in a dual monarchy with Sweden. In spite of a long period of growth that had begun in the late eighteenth century, mid-nineteenth-century Norway was an economically under-developed country compared to most of western Europe. It was essentially rural. Of a total population of 1,328,471 in 1845, only 161,875 lived in towns, only two of which had more than 20,000 inhabitants. Although Norway's constitution was the most liberal in Europe at mid-century, traditional class barriers as well as trade regulations limited social mobility, and religious life was controlled through the Lutheran State Church.

Reasons for emigration were many and varied. An important factor in the spread of the America fever in the 1830s and 1840s was the population growth in the first half of the century coupled with a scarcity of arable land: there was an almost 100 percent increase in population between 1815 and 1865. The first million mark was passed in 1822, the second in 1890, and these figures must be seen in relation to an emigration that in relative numbers was surpassed only by that from Ireland. After the first shipload in 1825, relatively few came for religious reasons, nor was political repression a reason for many to emigrate. Immigrants who later stressed the repressive social system as a reason for emigration acknowledged that they would not have left but for the promise of "improved economic prospects . . . in the rich and sparsely populated America, with its mild climate and fertile soil" (Langeland 1888, 25). Material motives for emigration were dominant.

The majority of the early immigrants were either of the landowning farmer class or cotters (*husmenn*) and other members of the rural proletariat. With the significant changes in Norwegian society in the course of the nineteenth century, there was an increasing urban component in the composition of the immigrant group. One consequence of the social, economic, and cultural developments in the old country was a sense of alienation felt by many immigrants who returned to visit scenes of childhood and youth. The immigrant culture was necessarily conservative; preservation of a way of life in foreign surroundings was its main *raison d'être*. Many of its spokesmen were strangers to the intellectual trends that had become dominant in the changed society of the land they had left behind. Waldemar Ager, who will figure prominently in pages to come, was painfully aware of the cultural discrepancies between Norwegians and Norwegian Americans when he wrote in 1905 that "We are not at the same stage of development as our relatives across the ocean . . . Modern Norwegian literature is an empty book for the greater part of our people. Not because it is inaccessible, but because in the mass we lack the comprehension to understand and appreciate it" (Lovoll 1977, 47).

The first attempt to establish a Norwegian settlement in America was in New York, on the shores of Lake Erie, in 1825. After a few years, however, the majority of the "Sloopers" (as they have come down in history) were persuaded by their guide and trailblazer Cleng Peerson to move west to Illinois, and the first permanent Norwegian settlement was established in La Salle county, north of the present city of Ottawa, in 1834. When the next group arrived two years later, the Midwest was already established as the Promised Land for Norwegian immigrants, and in the course of the nineteenth century an identifiable Norwegian America, *Vesterheimen*, with its own transitional yet distinctive culture, was ensconced in an area largely made up of Illinois, Wisconsin, Iowa, Minnesota, and the Dakotas, with the Pacific Northwest as a far-flung subsidiary.

Vesterheimen, which in the original Old Norse meant "the Western World," but which was used in the sense of "our Western Home," was introduced in 1875 by American-born Rasmus B. Anderson in an article in the Chicago newspaper *Skandinaven*, where he recommended that Norwegian Americans adopt this Icelandic word for America (23 Feb.). The term *Vesterheimen* caught on and soon acquired the meaning of a specifically Norwegian America; it was used by Norwegian Americans as a fond epithet for their own vaguely defined and unstable ethnic niche within the larger, multi-ethnic Western Home. *Vesterheimen* was for instance the name of a Minnesota newspaper. The popular Christmas annual published by Augsburg Publishing House from 1911 to 1957 was called *Jul i Vesterheimen* and *Vesterheim* is the name of the Norwegian Immigrant Museum in Decorah, Iowa. In the present book *Vesterheimen* is used in two related senses. It designates the Norwegian-American social and cultural community rather than individual Norwegian Americans. It is also used to designate the dream that gave life to this community, the idealistic vision of a vital and lasting Norwegian-American culture within the larger American culture. Although *Vesterheimen* now is both literally and metaphorically speaking a museum, it was once not merely the transitional home of many Americans but the main inspiration for their cultural and intellectual endeavors.

Norwegian Americans are a relatively small group. The census for 1850 shows 12,678 Norwegian born; for 1860, 43,995. By 1880 the number of Norwegian-born Americans had grown to 181,729, jumping to 322,665 during the next decade and remaining fairly stable up to the eve of the Second World War. Many of the children of these immigrants were also part of the population of *Vesterheimen*, and the 1890 figure for both first—and second-generation Norwegian Americans is 606,316, almost twice that for the first generation alone. By 1920 their number had grown to more than a million. The geographic concentration of *Vesterheimen* may be illustrated by some other figures from the 1890 census: while the Norwegian-born were only 3.49 percent of the total population, their percentage in the north-central states was 6.99 and in the western states 2.63, with less than one percent spread over the rest of the country. The importance of concentration can be seen in the 1850 figures for Wisconsin, the state where the first Norwegian-American publications appeared in the 1840s and 1850s. While there were only 12,678 of Norwegian birth in the United States, 8,651 of these were in Wisconsin, where they ran fourth behind those born in Germany (34,519), Ireland (21,043), and England (18,952) (Thernstrom 1980, 1050, 1059–1060).

Reflecting on the question "whether the frontier broke with or continued eastern customs and traditions," Wallace Stegner has observed that the intention of settlers coming "to make a home in the West" seemed to be "to transplant the old one to the new place." He illustrates his point with the experience of a cousin of his Norwegian grandfather. On a visit to Norway Stegner had met this ancient relative who told him of his experience as a farmhand in the United States around 1890: "He had worked, he said, on sixteen different farms during his five or six years in Minnesota, North Dakota, and Iowa, and he had never worked on the farm of anybody but somebody from the town of Ulvik. This is concentrating your old life in the new place with a vengeance" (Stegner 1990, 146–147). Indeed, the reader of Norwegian-American journals, memoirs, or novels from the decades before and after 1900 may have the impression of a largely Norwegian-speaking Midwest; for the tendency of Norwegian Americans (and other immigrants) to group together in settlements or city wards and live their social and religious lives in institutions of their own making further strengthened the cultural cohesiveness made possible by the concentration of Norwegians in the Midwest. This concentration and cohesiveness was a necessary condition for *Vesterheimen*.

Another statistical fact should be considered in order to appreciate that so many Norwegian immigrants could envision a lasting literary culture in America in their own language. Although English was the *de facto* official language and although English-speaking inhabitants made up the largest group in the midwestern states, English was nevertheless a minority language in many areas with concentrations of immigrants. German was dominant in parts of Wisconsin, and even a small group like the Norwegians could have the experience of living in a largely Norwegian-speaking community. Americans did not have to be nativists to see this linguistic situation as a threat to American culture; the spokesmen for the many thriving immigrant cultures, however, saw their language as a gift to their new land.

The proportion of immigrants in the Midwest in the late nineteenth century may give a misleading picture of their cultural, social, or political influence, for they were never a unified group, not even politically and certainly not culturally. Even the closely related Scandinavian groups, the Danes, Norwegians, and Swedes, did not as a rule have common social or

As this cartoonist in the Norwegian-American newspaper suggests, the Norwegian-American press performed an important role in bringing the immigrant group into America.

religious institutions in the United States. Individual Danes were prominent in the Norwegian-American community in the earliest period; there were, at times, synods or church organizations that had members from more than one Scandinavian group; occasionally Danes and Norwegians were members of the same dramatic society; and a Danish-American publisher like Christian Rasmussen also published Norwegian books, while N.Fr. Hansen Publishing Co. in Cedar Rapids, Iowa, was a Dano-Norwegian husband-and-wife team. The rule, however, was that each small group jealously kept to itself in spite of their cultural and linguistic similarities.

Norwegian-American publications often called themselves Scandinavian, especially in the early decades. Thus, despite its name, *Skandinaven*, founded in Chicago in 1866, was almost exclusively a Norwegian-American newspaper. A common written language for Danes and Norwegians made it convenient for their publications to try to address a common readership. Although Sweden and Norway were united under one king, there was less intermingling between these two groups than between Norwegians and Danes. One reason was that the Swedes were numerically strong and formed their own communities. Another was that their publications were not interchangeable: While Norwegians and Danes used black letter in their publications, Swedes used Roman type (called "English letters" by

Norwegian Americans) and written Swedish was distinctly different from Dano-Norwegian. When the publishers of *Skandinaven* sent a circular letter to local public officials in 1874 requesting their help in making an "announcement to the Scandinavians of the North-West," they asked for "the names and addresses of . . . Norwegians and Danes (not Swedes)" (JAJP).

Norwegians, Hungarians, Swedes, Bohemians, Finns, Germans, and other immigrant groups in the nineteenth century developed their own immigrant cultures in their own languages. The same process may be observed in the large immigrant groups that continue to pour into the country today. These cultures all have a basic common characteristic in being transitional, in the quite specific sense of being a movement from one culture to another. Indeed, this constant process of transition has become an important aspect of American culture as a whole.

An immigrant culture is transitional in two important ways. The Norwegian immigrant culture was transitional in that it began with the first arrivals in the 1820s and then grew and developed until it underwent such significant changes with the end of mass immigration in the 1920s that it gradually became an integrated American ethnic culture rather than a separate, transplanted immigrant culture. Norwegian has ceased to be an American language but a Norwegian-American identity survives in family lore, traditions, festivals, and organizations. While schools like Luther College and St. Olaf College are no longer Norwegian-American immigrant institutions, they remain American institutions with strong ethnic roots.[1] Although it no longer publishes in Norwegian but in English for an American church whose membership includes many ethnic groups, Augsburg Publishing House, now Augsburg Fortress, has its ethnic history. Indeed, most nineteenth-century immigrant churches, once transplanted European churches, have merged with others to become American institutions with their history as the only tie with the immigrant past. *Vesterheim* today is an American museum in Decorah, Iowa.

The immigrant culture, with its language, institutions, myths, and traditions, may, then, be seen as a transition from the culture of the home country to a more or less ethnically flavored American culture. This is a process where the new roots the culture set down in America gradually and almost imperceptibly become more vital conduits of life than the old and withered ones. All services in Norwegian-American Lutheran churches were held in Norwegian at the turn of the century. By 1917, the year three synods united to form the Norwegian Lutheran Church in America, 73.1 percent of the services were in Norwegian. By 1925 more than half were held in English and in 1928 English was adopted as the official language of the church (Haugen 1953, 267). Finally, in 1946, the full step into America was symbolized in the decision to strike the reminder of the institution's immigrant origins from its name: the Norwegian Lutheran Church in America became the Evangelical Lutheran Church.

The stability of the immigrant culture depended on a steady influx of new individuals to make up for the loss of individuals who were moving out and becoming integrated with the larger American culture. Consequently, the historian must distinguish between those who were merely Norwegian American by descent and those who were also assenting inhabitants of that more amorphous nation within a nation here called *Vesterheimen*. When the Chicago amateur historian, versatile hack writer, and journalist, David M. Schøyen, was planning to write "The Saga of the Norse Nation in *Vesterheimen*" after he had completed his three-volume American history in 1876, he complained to Rasmus B. Anderson in Madison about the difficulty of getting support for his project: "the older settlers have considerable property but are without literary interests or national feeling—they cannot speak or read Norwegian and harbor no friendly feelings for their more recently arrived countrymen" (17 Sept. 1877, RBAP). Thus the immigrant culture may have a great degree of continuity at the institutional level and at the same time be characterized by a constant turnover at the membership level, as individual immigrants moved into the dominant Anglo-American culture or as second- or third-generation Americans felt estranged from the culture of their parents. An immigrant newspaper could survive for several generations, but with a shifting readership.

The immigrant culture was a halfway house for individuals in transit, for some an isolating cultural and social ghetto, for others a supportive system during their process of Americanization. It attracted some and repelled others. The parents of Andrew and Thorstein Veblen came from Valdres in Norway to Nerstrand in Rice county, Minnesota. Both brothers became prominent academics in their different fields. Andrew, however, a physicist, lived much of his social and emotional life within Norwegian-American organizations, while Thorstein kept a greater distance from his ethnic group. Victor F. Lawson, who had inherited his part ownership in *Skandinaven* from his immigrant father in 1872, sold out four years later in order to become owner and publisher of the Chicago *Daily News*. Peer Strømme, Wisconsin-born of immigrant parents and a graduate of Luther College, was a gifted writer in two languages and served on the editorial staff of the *Minneapolis Times*, but he chose to live his life and have his career in *Vesterheimen*.

This is a book about people who not only lived in but created *Vester-heimen* through their literary and other cultural efforts. They were, of course, a minority among the Norwegian Americans, many of whom lived for a period of their lives within the bounds of *Vesterheimen* while others took the full step into America on arrival. Orm Øverland, who became Tom Overland on immigrating in 1881, began his American career as jour-nalist and editor in Norwegian-American newspapers in Minnesota, but by the end of the decade he was editor of an English-language labor paper in Duluth and never returned to the Norwegian language press. His sister, Martha Ubø Øverland, did not even try to enter *Vesterheimen* after immi-grating in 1888 and eventually became a corporation lawyer in New York. Her main published work, *A Manual of Statutory Corporation Law*, was not noticed by the book reviewers of *Vesterheimen*.[2] Their younger brother Hans stayed in Minnesota his first year after arriving in 1887 and then went west to Montana Territory. After seven years of occasional and seasonal labor, in hotels, on ranches, and on the railroad, he wrote home to his father for return fare back to Norway. There were no rules or patterns for immi-grant behavior or careers and there were as many experiences of transition as there were immigrants.

Vesterheimen was nevertheless real and tangible in its many religious and secular institutions; it had businessmen as well as artists who worked mainly within its limits; saloons as well as churches catered to its inhabitants; and it offered a full range of services to its members. It had no official status, and the immigrant lay preacher would hardly have accepted the immigrant saloonkeeper as co-inhabitant of a united nation within the nation. Indeed, lay preachers and theologians were often more preoccupied with excom-municating each other than with claiming a common culture. In this they were expressing one of the characteristics of the culture of *Vesterheimen*, strife, and also, paradoxically, were underlining its basic cohesiveness. For as in any national culture, its members as well as its spokesmen were more fre-quently engaged in conflict than in proclaiming a family fellowship they took for granted.

Vesterheimen was as much a theoretical concept as it was a transitional real-ity. For many of its writers and leaders the vision of a vital and lasting Nor-wegian America was at the center of their lives. In this they were at odds not only with the necessarily transitional character of their culture but with its equally necessary condition of marginality. Indeed, in their dedication to the creation and preservation of an American literary culture they were implic-itly acknowledging the threatened and marginal status of such a literature.

The literary culture of *Vesterheimen* was marginal from most points of view. It was marginal for the group that was its basis in that Norwegians did not emigrate to America in order to create a new culture and a new literature on American soil but to create a better living for themselves and their descendants. Their motives for emigration as well as their goals as immigrants were material rather than idealistic. David Schøyen, who complained to Rasmus Anderson about the lack of interest in culture among those who had been in Chicago for several decades, was equally pessimistic concerning the newly arrived, "who, especially during the recent economic depression, have their minds concentrated on breadwinning or, for diversion, on picnics and balls."

A literature in Norwegian was necessarily marginal in a country where Norwegian was a foreign language. As a literature of and for the Midwest it was also marginal from the point of view of a national literary culture whose centers were in the urban East. For the immigrant settler on the prairies and plains, the heartland of America was a hard-won home. The archetypal Norwegian-American story is about this homemaking process. By contrast, the archetypal story of the American writer escaping a stifling rural and small-town America for the cultural Meccas of the East is a central myth in the standard version of American literary history. The different attitudes to the western settlements in Anglo-American and Norwegian-American fiction become obvious when any Norwegian-American novel about the winning of a new home in the West is compared to a western novel such as E.W. Howe's melodramatic *The Story of a Country Town*. Howe's narrator constantly wonders why anyone would want to settle in such a place: "I became early impressed with the fact that our people seemed to be miserable and discontented, and frequently wondered that they did not load their effects on wagons again, and move away from a place which made all the men surly and rough, and the women pale and fretful" (1927, 2). Faced with the ignorance of the common people, the narrator's attitude is fashionably negative: "I was surprised to learn that the people of Fairview were satisfied, and that they were well pleased with the change" (9). In the context of such dominant attitudes to the West among establishment intellectuals and those who vied for their approval, an American literary culture that has the real-life equivalents not only of Zenith but also of Gopher Prairie as its cultural and intellectual centers can hardly have a recognized existence — regardless of language.

The inhabitants of *Vesterheimen*, however, were often equally ignorant of the concerns of mainstream America and its cultural and intellectual centers. In his *Life Story*, Rasmus B. Anderson tells of a meeting with the Norwegian writer Bjørnstjerne Bjørnson on his first visit to the country of his parents in 1872. When Bjørnson opened his mail and showed his visitor a letter and a copy of *Leaves of Grass* from Walt Whitman, Anderson was embarrassed: "I was an American and here was an American of whom I had never heard even the name before." Thinking that it perhaps was a book on botany, he ventured that "the opinion in regard to Walt Whitman's merit and standing was divided." Bjørnson immediately realized Anderson's ignorance and became furious, roaring that "we Americans did not appreciate our greatest men." So Anderson confessed, but promised to read Whitman on his return. In Madison, however, he was unable to get a copy of *Leaves of Grass* in any bookstore (1915, 160-162).

The culture of Vesterheimen retained its marginal and isolated status throughout its history. Indeed, isolation was in many ways the condition of its existence. One of the emblematic meetings in American literary history took place in Northfield, Minnesota, in 1926, a meeting emblematic not only of the marginality of immigrant cultures in the United States, but of their transitional quality. The writer Lincoln Colcord was visiting Minneapolis when he learned that a professor at St. Olaf College had recently become a literary celebrity in Norway. His curiosity led to a meeting with Ole Edvart Rølvaag and he wrote from Minneapolis to Eugene Saxton of Harper & Brothers on March 9 about "a few of the facts and impressions which I gained." To Colcord, "by far the most important" of these facts was that the two novels he had sent to Harper were not Rølvaag's first literary efforts, but that he had already had four other novels published in Norwegian in Minneapolis: "I have come away from the meeting greatly sobered. I feel that I have had an insight into a life of creative genius, of lonliness [sic] and adversity, and of unswerving fidelity to an artistic ideal. The books which antedate the ones that have made a name for him, are the more intimate revelations of his own spiritual experience ... At any rate you will see from all this that there is a formidable background to the present picture, and a body of work already in existence sufficient to make or break a literary reputation. He tells me that never before in his life has he been met on just this ground, or felt himself in touch with the publishing profession in America. Doesn't this seem incredible? Such is the lot of the alien in our midst. He simply has had no contacts ... " (OERP) Rølvaag's loneliness was only from the outsider's point of view, for few American writers have lived as closely with their readers, been on such intimate terms with their fellow writers, and had such a sense of belonging to their culture as Rølvaag, whose roots in *Vesterheimen* were essential to his identity as an artist. His relations with the "publishing profession" were also probably better than for most American authors: the head of Augsburg Publishing House, Anders M. Sundheim, was a close friend. The inhabitants of *Vesterheimen* were not more lonely than most Americans; the loneliness Colcord wrote about with such feeling was the isolation of the immigrant culture as a whole in America.

Rølvaag, however, was as isolated from the cultural centers of Norway as from those of America and access to publishers in Oslo was as difficult as to those in New York. In the 1920s Norwegian intellectuals were discovering new American writers like Sherwood Anderson, Louis Bromfield, and Ernest Hemingway and had no interest in what Norwegian immigrants might be doing in their new land. Most Norwegian immigrants had been socially marginal before departure. To the Norwegian elite, their cultural life in America was scarcely of even marginal interest. David Schøyen's sister, Elisabeth, who had published a drama about Joan of Arc in 1870 when only eighteen, and who came to America in 1882 intending to make a living from readings of her plays, soon returned in despair. "It is quite impossible for me to find anything to interest me in these half-civilized Scandinavian colonies, and I long for the East as for light and sun," she wrote 6 August to Rasmus Anderson, whom she had visited in Madison. "Had I been among the Hottentots in South Africa there might have been something new and strange that could have given food for later reflections, but what I find here has neither the poetry of savagery nor the progress of culture, but is something in between, something completely without character and boring to the death." In desperation, she begged a free ticket from one of the steamship companies and was in Liverpool by 17 September when she again wrote to Anderson, explaining that her free ticket was for the 2nd class, "but when I had been there for one hour I went up to the captain and asked if I could go first and pay the difference on arrival in Denmark, since staying with all the dirty people made me sick" (RBAP). This, surely, was not the stuff *Vesterheimen* was made of.

Elisabeth Schøyen's reaction was extreme only in that she had the opportunity of a direct response. The cultural elite in Norway, to which she so quickly returned, simply ignored the possibility of a culture among the Norwegian immigrants in America and would not accept that there could be a literature there worth considering. In the Christiania newspaper *Nationen* for 19 June 1919, an essay on Norwegian-American literature by Matti Aikio was given the subtitle "Why It Does Not Exist."

The instinct to survive is ingrained in most human beings and the will to survive is an integral and central aspect of a culture. For the writers who used Norwegian in America, linguistic survival was essential to the survival of the group, and for a language to survive it must live and develop, and for this it must have a literature. Such was the conviction of a small group of writers and intellectuals in *Vesterheimen*. However marginal and however transitional their efforts necessarily were, they left behind a legacy that they themselves regarded as their contribution to American culture.

The roots of Norwegian-American literature were nourished by the liberating force that lay in the process of emigration. Throughout the century-long history of an American literature in Norwegian there are writers and would-be writers whose efforts are inspired by the destruction of the social and cultural barriers that had set the limits for what the individual could aspire to in the old country. People who had broken away from the only way of life they had been able to imagine, weathered the many weeks of the Atlantic crossing, found their way across enormous stretches of a strange continent, and made for themselves a business or a farm with an acreage and a quality of soil undreamed of in the old country would also be able to say to themselves: perhaps I can write, too. As late as the 1920s, Rølvaag was receiving letters from men and women with vague ideas of spelling and syntax but with a strong urge to publish fiction, asking for his advice and encouragement.

On 15 April 1853, *Emigranten* had an article signed by "A Norwegian Farmer in Illinois," that began: "Even though I am of lowly origin and have little education, I assume that *Emigranten* will accept these lines . . . therefore I must ask you, Mr. Editor, to correct what there could be of mistakes in language and style." The three-column article is an attack on the competing journal *Friheds-Banneret* in Chicago, and in praise of *Emigranten*, both of which, the Illinois farmer tells us, have been "visitors in my simple log cabin." It was no small step for him thus "for the first time to stand before the public," and what may strike us today as an overly meek and submissive tone was in fact revolutionary: in spite of my social shortcomings, my voice, too, can and shall be heard! Few farmers, smallholders, or cotters in the old country would have dared *assume* that the editor of a newspaper would publish whatever they submitted. Among the immigrants, however, such an assumption quickly became so widespread that editors came to regard the many communications in prose and verse from readers who wanted to be writers as a problem. "We are being *flooded* with communications from all parts of the country," Victor Lawson wrote (in English) to Wisconsin industrialist John A. Johnson, at that time a fellow publisher of *Skandinaven*

(11 Feb. 1873, JAJP). "Much of it is of no interest and much of it requires so much doctoring that it is worse than writing it entire. But of course all is perfect in the eyes of writers, and they take offense if it is not inserted." It would be a grave error to assume a correlation between the primitive material conditions of the majority of the homesteaders and their intellectual life. A well-informed article in the Minneapolis newspaper *Budstikken* (6 Aug. 1879) on the legal issue of literary copyright is signed: "Written on the prairies of Nebraska in a sod house."

The history of the literature of Norwegian immigrants and their descendants, written and published in Norwegian by Americans and for an American audience, is the subject of this book. As would be true of any literature, most of this literature is of historical interest only and has little life independent of its context. However, all Norwegian-American writers, publishers, book dealers, newspaper editors, book reviewers, and, perhaps most important of all, readers made up an American literary culture that did produce a handful of writers who should be taken into account whenever the American literary canon is reconsidered. This book is a contribution to such reconsiderations.

NOTES

1. Karen Larsen (1929) has observed that "in the usually accepted sense of the word, Luther College in the [eighteen] sixties and seventies was certainly not an American college." The curriculum as well as the teachers were Norwegian, as was "the language of instruction and even of the playground ... " And yet "it was unlike anything that could be found in the Old World" in that "the students, coming as a rule from the pioneer farms, belonged to a social group whose cousins in Norway" were largely excluded from a higher academic education (9). Thus the social revolution inherent in the immigration process quickly changed the character if not the contents and formal structure of a transplanted immigrant institution.

2. New York: The Ronald Press, 1906. The copy I have seen is inscribed to the author's father in Norway.

PART TWO

Getting Started

Writing for a
European Audience

From the first stirrings in the 1820s, the transatlantic migrations from Norway stimulated literacy and created a new need for written communication. Cultural transmission of folk tales, ballads, and music as well as skills, knowledge, and ethics had traditionally been oral or by example. Little was known about the outside world beyond what was narrated by the few who had returned from it. In the new settlements of Illinois and Wisconsin much of the traditional lore did not apply; new conditions required new skills and a new freedom required new knowledge to fulfill new responsibilities. Reading became more necessary than before and was no longer reserved for religious instruction and the perusal of homilies.[1] The radical ruptures of emigration made letter writers of members of a social class unfamiliar with the use of pen and paper.

Personal letters, the communications between individuals, may seem to have little relevance for the history of literature, a body of texts addressed to a public audience. But many early immigrant letters should be regarded as pamphlets and their writers as pamphleteers. By the 1860s there is a marked shift in the content as well as the function of the America letters; their dominant concern has become the private sphere. The earliest letters from America to Norway, however, mark the beginnings of an American literature in Norwegian. Taken as a whole, the body of early letters is a folk literature, but from it emerge a number of individual writers who acquired a reputation in their time. These writers addressed themselves to a readership that was not only potentially American but that to an amazing extent actually became American, often encouraged by their letters. If one measure of the quality of a literary text is its potential to move readers, the America letters deserve our attention.

The letter was the obvious genre for these writers. The process of publishing was beyond their ken; nor were newspapers and books frequent guests in the homes of those they were trying to reach. The authors wrote as spokesmen for the vanguard of immigration and those who received their letters made use of the two means of publication available to the rural community: the letters were read aloud and were copied by hand and distributed, often far beyond the island or valley of the addressee. Some letters also found their way to newspapers and entered the public debate on emigration. While most representatives of authority, whether temporal or ecclesiastical, warned against emigration, the letters functioned as an underground literature which was effective precisely because it was not distributed through official channels. The writers spoke directly to the interests of their readers, who paid little attention to the strictures of better educated critics.

Several letter writers became known for their role in influencing public opinion and convincing large numbers to migrate, among them Gjert Gregoriussen Hovland, who emigrated with his family in 1831. In America he joined the pioneer Kendall settlement in northern New York. The first known group of letters from Hovland is from the spring of 1835, and by 1838 the first book by a Norwegian immigrant mentions Hovland's importance as a writer and his influence on Norwegian emigration (Rynning 74). Accounts by contemporaries agree on the role played by Hovland's letters and on how they were "transcribed in hundreds of copies and passed from house to house, and from parish to parish" (Anderson 1895, 82). Several have come down to us in the versions that were printed in newspapers. "I cannot neglect my duty to write," he began a letter in 1838, "reminded as I am of my old native country Norway and my friends there." Although by this time he is aware of the impact he has had, he acknowledges his lowly beginnings: "Since my childhood, I have been very deficient in education, but as I hope that this letter will reach you safely, I take occasion to write with the hope that those who have more intelligence than I will take my humble contribution in good part" (Blegen 1955, 44). Contemporary claims of his influence may seem hyperbolic, but the letters are evidence of his artless skill and sense of strategy. The earliest preserved letter, written 22 April 1835 on the eve of the collective move from Kendall to Illinois, may serve as illustration of his authorship (Blegen, 21–25).

The opening sentences are designed to put natural anxieties about life in

The early immigrant letters were the first Norwegian-American literature.
Courtesy Norwegian National Archives.

a strange world to rest. They tell not only of "the best of health" and satisfaction, but also about speedy integration and acceptance: "Our son attends
the English school and talks English as well as the native born." Hovland
then turns to a question of importance to his readers: His income from his
work is far greater than in Norway and he is sure of earning a living for a
growing family "so long as God gives me good health." This faint suggestion of insecurity is only entered to highlight the advantages of America:
"such excellent plans have been developed here that, even though one be
infirm, no one need go hungry." Hovland describes a social welfare system
in some detail and takes care to observe that "no discrimination is shown
between the native born and those from foreign countries." Hovland may
appear to be boasting, so he insists: "These things I have learned through
daily observation." Such letters were persuasive because they spoke with the
voice of experience of common men as opposed to the warning voices of
authority; and, as if in recognition of this advantage, Hovland describes a
democratic society free from the restrictions of class and trade regulations.
Again, however, he is aware that he must allay his readers' anxieties. America is a free society, but not an anarchistic one: "Everyone is permitted to
engage in whatever business he finds most desirable, in trade or commerce,
by land or water. But if anyone is found guilty of crime, he is prosecuted
and severely punished." Hovland concludes the first part of his letter advis-
ing those who are poorly off in Norway and "willing to work" to come to
America, "for even if many more come, there will still be room here for
all." There are, he knows, moralistic arguments against emigration: "It is as if
they thought that those who move to a better land, a land of plenty, do
wrong. But I cannot find that our creator has forbidden us to seek our food
in an honorable way." Of course he misses friends in the old country and
would like to visit with them, "but we do not wish to live in Norway. We
lived there altogether too long."

Now that he has made his argument in terms of principles and general
conditions, Hovland turns to his personal experience. The dates of departures and arrivals for the stages of his journey to the Kendall settlement
would help his readers understand the distances involved. He is specific
about how long he had to work for wages before he could buy fifty acres of
land and about when he and his family could move into the house he had
put up. He gives information on seeding and harvest for the first year, the
market value of his produce, and the prices for some common commodi-
ties. Even though these first four years in America have given him good returns for his labor, Hovland announces that the settlement is about to move

to even more promising land "farther west in the country to a place called Illinois." He explains the availability of public lands to all for $1.25 an acre and extols the quality of the land. Details about the sale of his farm and the amount needed to buy 160 acres in the West again serve to enable his readers to make their own assessments. Still, there are fears to be addressed: "Law and order exist here, and the country is governed by wise authorities." Moreover, the settlement at Kendall is not breaking up, it is merely moving to a new and better location, "for they prefer to live near each other, although many of the natives are people just as good." Hovland rounds off his description of conditions in America with another eulogy of American freedom, especially from excessive taxes, and a brief account of an American natural wonder: trees that yield sap that "makes sugar, syrup, ale, and vinegar." He concludes with personal greetings and devout reflections. Even the convention of concluding a letter with religious sentiments, however, is made part of Hovland's overall argument. He observes that the churches of Norway are not the only places where God can be sought: "Wherever we may wander in this earthly sphere, let us seek Him who is the true light and life, and follow His voice which calls to our hearts, no matter where we go or stand."

Hovland, like so many of the writers in this book, was indeed "deficient in education," but his letter is an effective and persuasive text. There can be no doubt of its actual impact. In 1837 the dean in charge of parishes in the district of Hardanger sent a report on emigration to the local police authorities that not only described the general influence of Hovland's letters but also included a copy of this one. Written the year before the second shipload of emigrants was to leave Norway, Hovland's text, moreover, is an outline of the major concerns of Norwegian-American culture: education; integration vs. segregation; success in the new world vs. longing for friends and places in the old; American freedoms vs. Norwegian restrictions; social equality vs. class society; westward migration and the acquisition of land; and the importance of a Christian faith.

Few letter writers acquired the reputation of Hovland and not all wrote with his sense of responsibility. One who gained a reputation for sending misleading accounts was Gunnul Vindegg. Among his contemporaries in Wisconsin there were "numerous stories in circulation about the contents of his America letters," Svein Nilsson reported in *Billed-Magazin* in 1869. "Many newcomers evidently discovered that the reality did not measure up to expectations; and Vindegg, who had advised them to emigrate, has on occasion been blamed for letting his friends in Norway see the new world in altogether too rosy colors" (Nilsson 1982, 94). The unrealistically positive letters, however, are not representative. Most give precise information, taking care not to instill exaggerated expectations nor to advise immigration. Indeed, a sentence in one of Hovland's 1835 letters, "I will not advise anyone to come or not to come here," became a standard phrase, repeated in letter after letter in the next two decades (Øverland 1992, 33).

Some complain of the miserable conditions offered the immigrant and express regret at having left Norway. Such a writer was Sjur Haaeim, who had left in 1836. In 1839 he wrote to the bishop of Bergen complaining that Hovland's letters had misled the people. Haaeim returned to Norway and in 1842 he published a little book, *Oplysninger om forholdene i Nordamerika* (Information on conditions in North America), a sad account of the tribulations of pioneer life, similar to an earlier book by another failed immigrant, the tinsmith Peter Testman, in 1839. The bishop had the letter published, voices of authority promoted Haaeim and his views, and newspapers reprinted his pamphlet. But all this simply weakened the credibility of Haaeim and similar writers. "One investigator reported that the farmers regarded the writings against America much as they had regarded the earlier outpourings of officialdom against the election of farmers to the Storting" (Blegen 1931, 156). While the American Hovland could become a spokesman for his class in Norway, Haaeim, by returning and warning against America, was regarded as a renegade.

By the 1840s the letter was no longer the only mode of literary expression for the immigrants: the first books had been published before the decade began. One of the best known letter writers of the 1840s is a transitional figure, with an unfinished book to his credit in addition to his many letters. Ole Trovatten had acquired the little education required of a schoolteacher and sexton before he emigrated in 1840, apparently driven by accusations of counterfeiting money. Regardless of the suspicions of the authorities, Trovatten retained the confidence of the people of his region, becoming their most important source of information about the New World. One of Nilsson's informants recalled that the "sexton's eulogies of America exerted a tremendous influence . . . 'Ole Trovatten has said it; that's what he writes': this phrase became the refrain of all the stories about the Land of Wonder, and for several years he was the most talked-of man in the whole district of Upper Telemark" (114). Outward manifestations of the respect and trust he enjoyed were the offices of sexton and teacher in the Koshkonong settlement in Dane county, Wisconsin. Trovatten's American career also illustrates that intellectual gifts, public service, and hard work do not necessarily spell material success: his life here was largely characterized by mishaps and disasters. In this he was representative of many immigrants. What made him exceptional was that his personal troubles did not interfere with his vision of the promise America held for his people. The uncompleted journal that he probably wrote in 1842 is a story of hardship and illness, theft of all his savings, and passing despondency; but it is full of hope and inspired by the conviction that immigration was the answer to the poverty and lack of opportunity of Norway: "Up to now my fortune in the New World has been rather varied, but generally I have been bowed down with hard work in order to provide for my family and myself. I believe, however, that the future will gradually ease my burdens. I feel assured that the laboring man can do well here because America rewards her workers far better than Norway is able to do" (1956, 156). His journal is evidence not only of Trovatten's continuing sense of responsibility to keep those who still lived in Norway informed about conditions on this side of the Atlantic but of his ambition to move beyond the role of letter writer: that the manuscript was written with publication in mind is obvious from its practical advice on farming.

A less likely candidate for achieving the publication that eluded Trovatten than Ole Nattestad can hardly be imagined. In 1836 he and his brother Ansten heard the name America for the first time. The consequent experience of breaking away from home the next year, crossing the Atlantic, the city of New York, trains and canals, and of the journey to Detroit made such an impression on Ole Nattestad that he took the unprecedented step of committing his wonderment to paper, and his *Beskrivelse over en reise til Nordamerika* (*Description of a Journey to North America*) was published in Norway in 1839. Blegen observes that "One can find nowhere a more illuminating picture of the attitude of the shrewd and honest peasant from the interior of Norway as he reacted to the new environment of America. Unconscious humor, gullibility, and astonishment are apparent on every page of the book" (1931, 105). Nattestad's *Beskrivelse over en reise til Nordamerika* is a naive account of personal experience and the author seems unable to make the step from the many details that catch his attention to any general view of the country. When the author's brother, Ansten, visited Norway in the spring of 1838, however, Ole's journal was not the only manuscript he brought with him. Later that same year there appeared in Christiania another book, which was modest in size but was to have a greater impact on early immigration than any other publication: *Sandfærdig beretning om Amerika, til oplysning og nytte for bonde og menigmand (True Account of Amer-*

The brothers Ole and Ansten Nattestad were among the earliest Norwegian settlers in Wisconsin, in 1838–1839. Some months before they immigrated in 1837 they had never heard of America, yet, when Ansten visited Norway in 1838, he brought with him a book manuscript by his brother Ole. Beskrivelse over en reise til Nordamerika *was published there in 1839.*

ica for the Information and Help of Peasant and Commoner). The title page had no name but the "Preface" was signed Ole Rynning and the dateline was Illinois, February 13, 1838.

As the son of a clergyman, Ole Rynning was of the influential civil servant class. He had a degree from the University of Christiania and several careers would have been open to him. It may be that his reasons for immigrating were personal, but he recognized that he was part of a social movement of great significance for the common man. He was readily accepted as a leader by those who met him. In spite of the disastrous end of the Beaver Creek settlement in Illinois where the book was written—Rynning and most of his followers died of malaria before the end of 1838—his reputation grew to superhuman proportions among his contemporaries. Ansten Nattestad's estimate, as reported by Nilsson, is representative of the popular apotheosis of Rynning: "I have never known another man who based his life on such noble principles and was so thoroughly altruistic. His character was as genuine as gold, and a sincere desire for the welfare of his fellowmen was the inspiration for all his acts ... A good and great idea was the central

Sandfærdig Beretning

om

Amerika,

til Oplysning og Nytte for Bonde og
Menigmand.

Forfattet af

En Norsk, som kom derover i Juni
Maaned 1837.

.Christiania.

—

1838.

Ole Rynning's Sandfærdig beretning om Amerika *(True Account of America)*, though written in Illinois, was aimed at a Norwegian audience. Because of the impact of this book many of its readers became immigrants and Americans.

fact in all his thinking: to find a happier home on this side of the Atlantic for the oppressed and poverty-stricken people of Norway "(57-58). Rynning's *True Account* is adapted to his intended readers' frame of reference, yet informed by the author's perspectives and insights in a way that made it effectively popular without being ostentatiously learned. While Ole Nattestad wrote a naive account of personal experiences, Rynning's writing was governed by a vision of America as a future home for the lower classes of Norway. Indeed, one of the remarkable aspects of Rynning and his book is the extent to which he was able to see beyond his acute misery to the possibilities of America. Ansten Nattestad's account to Nilsson of how the book was written is a fitting introduction to a reading of the text: "I remember very well when he came home once after a long inspection trip. Frost had set in while he was traveling; the ice on the swamps and the snow-crusts had cut through his shoes. When he finally returned to the settlement, his feet were badly frozen and bloody. They were a terrible sight and all of us were confident that he would be crippled for life. Only he remained confident and never complained. It was while in bed after this injury that he wrote his *True Account of America* . . . As he finished sections of the work, he read them aloud to us and we expressed our opinions" (58). From one point of view the circumstances were ideal: he could try out his book in progress on critics whose comments and queries would anticipate those of the audience he was writing for.

In his preface, addressed to "Dear countrymen—peasants and artisans," Rynning puts forth his qualifications as well as his purpose, and what he does not say is as worth noting as what he does. He makes no reference to his background or education; it is only in experience that he is better qualified than his readers: "I have now been in America eight months, and in this time have had an opportunity to learn much in regard to which I vainly sought to procure information before I left Norway." He had not merely experienced how difficult it was to immigrate "without a trustworthy and fairly detailed account of the country," but had discovered "how great the ignorance of the people is, and what false and preposterous reports were believed as full truth. It has therefore been my endeavor in this little publication to answer every question that I myself raised, to make clear every point in regard to which I observed that people were in ignorance, and to refute the false reports which have come to my ears ." His method and style are admirably suited to this purpose. The readers he had in mind were little used to reading. One book they all had been exposed to, however, was Luther's *Little Catechism,* and Rynning makes this book his model. Each of his short chapters consists of one or more specific questions followed by straightforward and practical answers. The style is simple and, without condescending, Rynning assumes no prior knowledge on the part of his readers. The first chapter is headed with guileless simplicity: "In what general direction from Norway does America lie, and how far away is it?" In later chapters Rynning addresses himself with the same seriousness to the "general belief among the common people" that America had been "depopulated by a plague, leaving cultivated farms with furnished houses that immigrants could move right into"; the "silly rumor . . . that those who wished to emigrate to America were taken to Turkey and sold as slaves"; and the threat posed by the system of slavery and the insistence on states rights in the South: "there will in all likelihood soon come either a separation between the northern and southern states, or else bloody civil disputes."

The nature and quality of Rynning's *True Account* may be more clearly seen in comparison with a better known book on America of the 1830s, *Democracy in America,* by Alexis de Tocqueville. He was a visitor with a liberal yet upper-class European perspective. He had access to the mansions, public and private, of the land, and addressed himself to an educated European audience disinterestedly curious about the New World. Rynning wrote from the point of view of the immigrant in a primitive pioneer cabin and for a peasantry whose interest in America was not only practical and personal but whose eventual choices and decisions would commit them to the new country. Granting its more modest scope, Rynning's "America book" may tell us as much about how America of the 1830s appeared to the poor immigrant as de Tocqueville's work does about the upper-class intellectual visitor's view.

Another major difference is that Rynning was not only describing a new country but actually writing the history of a Norwegian America to which he belonged. In 1825 the first group of immigrants had settled on the shores of Lake Ontario. Not until 1834 did most of them resettle in the Fox River Valley southwest of Chicago. While *Vesterheimen* was scarcely more than a few pioneers on the Illinois prairies and a handful of laborers in Chicago, however, Rynning was already dealing with it as an idea. When in his second chapter—"How did the country first become known?"—he gives an account of the Norwegian experience in North America, he not only sounds the central theme of history in Norwegian-American writing, but also shares an underlying purpose of many writers who were to follow: that of staking a claim for his people in what a Second World War journal devoted to the celebration of American ethnicity was to call the *Common*

Ground. The opening paragraph of this chapter explains that "the credit for the discovery of America is now given to *Christopher Columbus*" but devotes more space to the saga accounts of the Norse settlements in North America in the tenth century, implying that his countrymen had a long history to connect them with the New World. He then tells the story of the scouting tours of Cleng Peerson in 1821 and 1824, the party of fifty-two who made the adventurous journey from Stavanger to New York in 1825, the taking of land in Kendall, the important role of the letters of Gjert Hovland, and the coming of more groups in 1836 and 1837. In chapters five and six Rynning elaborates further on the *Vesterheimen* theme by addressing the questions "In what part of the country have the Norwegians settled? What is the most convenient and cheapest way to reach them?" and "What is the nature of the land where the Norwegians have settled?" Here Rynning gives an account of "Illinois and the other western states" with specific information on how to go about acquiring land. Chapters three and four give a general description of the United States and deal with the questions of possible overpopulation and immigration restriction. He assures his readers that there would be land enough for another fifty years and that though there was no danger that immigration would be prohibited, there was a reasonable head tax on all who arrived. The questions he addresses in the following chapters mirror the concerns of prospective immigrants and the experience of Rynning and his fellow pioneers: "What kind of religion is to be found in America? Is there any kind of order or government in the land, or can everyone do as he pleases?" "What provisions are made for the education of children, and for the care of poor people?" "What language is spoken in America? Is it difficult to learn?" "Is there considerable danger from disease in America? Is there reason to fear wild animals and the Indians?" "For what kind of people is it advisable to emigrate to America, and for whom is it not advisable?" "What particular dangers is one likely to encounter on the ocean? Is it true that those who are taken to America are sold as slaves?"

Ansten Nattestad, who had brought Rynning's and his brother's manuscripts with him to Norway, was without experience in literary matters and placed the responsibility for the editing of Rynning's text with a Norwegian clergyman who "deleted the chapter about the Norwegian clergy, who were accused of religious intolerance and of taking a do-nothing attitude toward social improvements and popular enlightenment" (Nilsson 56). Even in its censored form, Rynning's *True Account* was a revolutionary text: no other book of that period had as radical an impact on the lives of the "peasants and artisans" of Norway, and none had so strong an influence on the early making of *Vesterheimen*.

There were several other books around 1840. One of the party that followed Ansten Nattestad to America in 1839 was Knud Knudsen, a blacksmith who published an account of his adventures in 1840. He shared Ole Nattestad's sense of wonder and gave it expression in verse, one poem inspired by the "mechanical wonder" of a train, another "by my wonderment over America's varied accomplishments." Knudsen gives detailed and practical advice for the passage and concludes with a sentence that echoes the dominant message of the early letters: "We have everything we had longed for, and are convinced that we will find what we are looking for." Knudsen's booklet is a reminder of how misleading it would be to make a sharp distinction between the early books and letters: it was addressed to his "friends both in Drammen and in the surrounding area" and written as two letters also signed by other members of the emigrant party. Letters, on the other hand, were not only copied and distributed by hand, but were also published in newspapers. Immigrants in America referred to Hovland, Rynning, or Trovatten indiscriminately as having influenced their decision to emigrate. Meanwhile, in the two decades after the arrival of the first shipload of immigrants in 1825, so many had followed that they began to be perceived as a more important audience for immigrant writers than those they had left behind.

NOTE

1. In the culture they had left, a "reader" (*leser*) meant a pietist, one who spent much time reading the Bible. The pioneering edition of immigrant letters is Blegen 1955. The multivolume edition by Orm Øverland and Steinar Kjærheim (1992-) will include all letters in the Norwegian National Archives.

The First Newspapers

In his slanted survey of the Scandinavian press in America in *Emigranten* (20 May 1853), Adolph C. Preus (as "A") discusses six newspapers and two church monthlies. This is an impressive display of journalistic effort only six years after the appearance of the first newspapers, *Skandinavia* and *Nordlyset*.[1] It is in the pages of these unassuming and poorly printed weekly newspapers that the genesis of a Norwegian-American literature must be traced. Knud Langeland's observation in *Democraten* (10 Aug. 1850) on their literary importance in the absence of books remained valid for another twenty-five years. As Arthur C. Paulson explained in 1932, "in those days *Emigranten* served the immigrants and their children in the same way that our daily newspapers, literary magazines, and a goodly share of our books put together serve us today. It was one of the greatest agencies for molding the Norwegian-American consciousness which was at that time developing rapidly."

Two precursors of the newspapers are the organized correspondences from Chicago and the Muskego settlement in Wisconsin. In 1848 immigrants in Chicago organized a correspondence society with the purpose of writing monthly letters to refute hostile criticism of America (Fletre 1979). The executive committee was in effect an editorial board, selecting both the themes and the writers for the letters that were sent in the name of the society. In 1845 a group of settlers in Muskego sent a statement on conditions in America to a Christiania newspaper (Blegen 1931, 209–211). Iver Lawson, one of the leaders in the Chicago group, in 1866 became co-founder of *Skandinaven*, which was to become one of the most successful newspapers and publishing houses, while one of the initiators of the "Muskego Manifesto," Even Heg, was a co-founder of the first weekly newspaper, *Nordlyset*, which made its appearance in 1847 from a press set up in Heg's log cabin. It was too early, however, for a newspaper to succeed. The first Norwegian settlers in Wisconsin had arrived in 1838 and the few potential readers of *Nordlyset* were still in the phase of clearing the land and living in primitive huts and cabins. In his memoirs Knud Langeland, who edited both *Nordlyset* and its successor, *Democraten*, has a list of the subscribers to the two newspapers. It totals 280 (1888, 99–106).[2]

The practical problems of running a press under pioneer conditions may be difficult to appreciate. On 11 January 1856 the editor of *Emigranten* explained that there was no news from Europe since the cold had hindered the mail and made printing difficult: "Regardless of how much fuel we burn in these expensive times to keep the print shop warm, the paper nevertheless freezes into one lump. The form is frozen to the stone, the ink and the roll have coagulated, and the press operates at half its normal speed. The wind whistles through doors and windows and tempts the workers to take turns standing at the oven and at the compositor's bench, and the quality of pioneer architecture is given its due." For several years *Emigranten* was delayed once a month: there was not enough type to set both the church monthly and the newspaper at the same time. The black letter or gothic type required was not easy to come by, and the printer at times had to resort to roman type. These problems were compounded by the lack of skilled compositors and printers.[3]

Such conditions, however, were not the only challenges to publishers and editors. Looking back at the problems of pioneer publishing, Langeland observed that "the first immigrants were mostly from rural areas where few were used to other reading than their religious books, and many even regarded the reading of newspapers as a sin" (98). Consequently, the education of immigrants was an important editorial aim. The first issue of *Nordlyset* (19 July 1847) offered its readers translations of the Declaration of Independence and Daniel Webster's orations. Later issues included translations of presidential and gubernatorial messages and sketches of the lives of well-known Americans. This educational policy became even more pronounced when Langeland took over *Nordlyset* late in 1849 and then let it continue as *Democraten* from 8 June 1850 till he was forced to give it up on 29 October 1851. From the very beginning, however, *Nordlyset* also sought to entertain its readers: education involved more than the strictly utilitarian areas of politics and agriculture.

From its third issue *Nordlyset* averaged a poem every other week, mainly

Nordlyset

No. 42.   Thorsdagen den 8de Juni 1848.   1ste Aarg.

FRIHED og LIIGHED.

Nordlyset,

(tryk af N. Ole, 419 og Compagni, og redigeret af J. D. Reymert)

Landbodrift.

Byg.
(Fortsat.)

Maadeholdssagens Fremskridt.

(Af Svend Janson.)

Emigranten.

8ᵈᵉ Aargang.

No. 2.

Et uafhængig demokratisk Blad.

Løbende No.

344.

Udgivet af den Skandinaviske Presse-Forening.

Fremad til Sandhed og Oplysning!

Redigeret af C. Fr. Solberg

Madison, Dane Co., Wisconsin, Onsdagen den 12te Januar 1859.

The first newspaper, Nordlyset, *which began publication in 1847, never had more than 300 subscribers.* Emigranten, *which began publication in 1851, was quite successful and played an important role in the development of a Norwegian literature.*

verse written and submitted by subscribers. The first of these poems, the anonymous "Emigrantens tilbageblik" (The emigrant looks back), is by far the most interesting. In relatively well-wrought verse the poet gives expression to the dual loyalties of the immigrant and presents a resolution to the conflict that was to remain a central theme in early Norwegian-American literature:

> Farewell Norway! God bless you.
> You were always hardhearted and stern,
> But I still honor you as a mother
> Even though you often cut my bread thin . . .
>
> Another land now offers me
> Independence,
> A return for my toil,
> And a bright future for my family.
> This you did not offer me, Norway,
> Filled as you were with wealthy men.
> You were governed by the power of the rich
> And shackled in bondage.

Thus the poet explains why he has "steered my course away from you." Then he contrasts the poverty as well as the lack of freedom in Norway with his new country, where

> I shall take part in the growth
> Of a nation that is great and yet young.
> There the flame of freedom burns
> And freedom of trade has a home.

In the concluding stanza he not only expresses his love for the old country, but prays that it, too, will soon become free:

> I repeat: Farewell Norway.
> I will bless you till I die.
> You were, after all, my parent in childhood
> And you gave me many sweet joys.
> I will always remember you
> Under the many changes fate may bring
> And always pray that you will be able to throw off the chains
> That embittered my life.[4]

There is surprisingly little nostalgia in the literature of this early period. When sentimental expressions of longing appear they are generally, as here, tempered by the liberal conviction that the United States offered freedom from the class barriers and restrictions that kept the Norwegian rural population in poverty.

Most of the poetic attempts are embarrassingly crude, but the editor evidently tried to encourage his subscribers' creativity. To one brief poem in praise of the newspaper and its supporters he added an editorial note: "It is with the greatest pleasure that we publish this poem from our subscriber Miss R. Wigeland. It gives as great credit to her heart as to her poetic genius and bears witness to a warmth of feeling and power of expression that does not require much circumstance to develop her points" (23 Sept. 1847).

Prose fiction was regarded with suspicion. The first stories, translations from English, were published in October, 1849. One reason for the late appearance of fiction in *Nordlyset* may be seen in the essay "Tag dig iagt for slemme bøger" (Beware of bad books) by O. Olson (2 March 1848). All fiction except the most obviously didactic and moralizing tales belonged in the category "bad books," and it should not be surprising to find this early nineteenth-century view of fiction repeated on the mid-century frontier. Although he, too, was suspicious of fiction, Langeland used stories in a deliberate attempt to enlarge his audience. In his first editorial (23 Feb. 1850) he promised to publish useful and edifying family reading, and early issues had biographies as well as travel accounts. The fiction he presented, however, was contrived and sentimental and when an installment of "Den smukke kone" (The pretty wife) filled the first and part of the second of the four pages of *Nordlyset* on 23 November, he evidently felt he had betrayed his own editorial principles: an editorial note insists that he disapproved of such fiction, but found it necessary to satisfy less fastidious readers.

The only story in *Democraten* that is at one with the liberal policy of the editor is "Naadig fruen" (Her Grace, 11, 18 Jan. 1851). Its plot may be as sentimental and melodramatic as that of the others, its style as wooden, but it is an explicit critique of the class structure of rural Norway, more specifically of the *husmann* or cotter system: "Our penal institutions are as Paradise compared to such an existence." The story is reprinted from a Norwegian source, but marks the first appearance of an important theme in early Norwegian-American fiction, the evils of the cotter system and class barriers in Norway, culminating in 1885 with H.A. Foss' *Husmands-gutten* (*The Cotter's Son*).

Literature in the present limited sense did not figure prominently in

Langeland's list of priorities. For him, the newspaper as a whole was literature and the aim of literature was didactic. "The enlightenment of the
people," he later wrote in his memoirs, "was my hobbyhorse" (1888, 218).
He had been an exceptionally gifted and frustrated member of the peasant
class in Norway, and in Wisconsin he was a pioneer farmer before and after
he edited *Nordlyset* and *Democraten*. For Langeland immigration was not
merely a geographical migration but a social revolution, and the solidarity
of the immigrant group would determine how much progress they would
make. Newspapers played a crucial role in maintaining the national identity
and language: "No one can deny that the time has come for the Norseman
in the West to let his voice be heard and to say whether he will excommu-
nicate the brother tongue and the family spirit from the western hemi-
sphere for all time; the time has come for him to decide whether the language of the North shall forever be stilled and the spirit of the North no
longer live in our hearts." In this bombastic editorial in the first issue of
Democraten (8 June 1850) Langeland is not advocating a separate Norwegian
nation in North America. On the contrary, his concerns as well as his loyalties were American from the very beginning. When he argued for a more
systematically organized migration and concentrated settlements (10 Aug.),
nothing could have been further from his mind than bringing the Norwegian class society to America. On the contrary, readers found Langeland too
critical of Norway and its institutions. The issues for 14 and 21 September
presented poems and articles that reflected a leftist working-class view of
Norwegian society and caused so much reaction that he defended himself
in an editorial on the 28th, insisting that the radicalism readers had reacted
to merely reflected American ideals: he wished to make *Democraten* "American in spirit and policy."

Langeland's aim was to help bring the Norwegian Americans into
American society as an enlightened and influential group. This goal must
have seemed distant when he wrote his last editorial for *Democraten* (29 Oct.
1851). But even though he had failed in his first two publishing ventures, a
new one was being organized, and Langeland hoped "that the patriots who
have come together to work for the survival of the language of our fathers
in this distant continent" would succeed and that their efforts would "be to
the honor of our beloved Scandinavian literature." These "patriots" had recently met in Koshkonong to discuss the organization of a publishing association as proposed and outlined by pastor C.L. Clausen in *Democraten,* 18
September 1851. It was decided to hold a constitutional meeting the 15th of
November. The different venues for these two meetings, the first in the

Claus L. Clausen (1820–1892) ministered to the first Norwegian congregation in Muskego. Courtesy Norwegian-American Historical Association.

home of the anti-authoritarian Ole Trovatten, the second in the parsonage at Luther Valley, the home of Georg F. Dietrichson, a recently arrived university graduate and member of the social elite of his home country, are symbolic of a shift in power among the Norwegian immigrants that was to have far-reaching effects on the culture and politics of *Vesterheimen* (Øverland 1986). A group of young ministers, graduates of the university in Christiania and ordained in Norway, had come to work in the pioneer settlements. They were conservative in theology as well as in their social views and had a class-based confidence in their own authority. In 1852 they took over the one-year-old Norwegian Synod presided over by the American-ordained Clausen, as in 1851 they had taken control of the Scandinavian Press Association and gradually set aside Clausen, making it a different undertaking from that envisaged by the liberal Langeland.

The Press Association was formally a secular institution and laymen had a majority of the shares, but clergy were dominant on the Board of Directors that was responsible for management, finances, and the running of the press. A church monthly, *Maanedstidende*, was edited by the Synod clergy, while the editor of the weekly newspaper, *Emigranten*, was appointed by the Board. The Board also selected books for publication.

Clausen reluctantly accepted the position of editor and immediately collided with the Board when he published his editorial program and, in English, made an appeal for support from the Anglo-American community (28 Jan. 1852). The Board objected to Clausen's English editorial, in particular to his comments on "the indifference generally entertained by our people toward newspapers of any description." Clausen had elaborated: "To keep [that is, subscribe to] a newspaper was a luxury never thought of by most of them in Norway; they were too poor for that, and perhaps we may add, they did not care, because they were compelled and accustomed to trust everything to others, and had too little self-reliance to utter any thoughts of what was right and what was wrong in public matters, and would therefore remain ignorant thereof." Clausen was neither the first nor the last to make such observations, but his university-educated colleagues read his editorial as a slur on *their* Norway. Their rebuttal (7 May) explained that the editor's misrepresentation was due to his ignorance, since he had formed his opinions "principally from what he has seen of the Norwegians in this country, and likewise, from his apparent desire to misrepresent our condition in order to please you and awaken your sympathies." Implied is the plea that Norwegians should not be judged by the kind of people that made up the majority of immigrants, and that those who remained at home were of a better sort. In his reply Clausen professed his inability to understand the views of his colleagues and a few months later, on 27 August, he retired, referring to his disagreement with the Board on important political issues. Clausen was in far better touch with the views and sensibilities of the immigrants than his colleagues. Until Langeland again became an influential editor with the founding of *Skandinaven* in Chicago in 1866, the press was largely dominated by editors who had a condescending attitude toward the majority of their readers.

Clausen was as committed to a serious program of education and as suspicious of fiction as Langeland. He serialized a history of the United States on the front page. Introducing this feature Clausen wrote that he had been advised to follow the example of "American" editors and have light reading on the front page. His ambition, however, was that "the newspaper could be filled with something better . . . We do not see it as our duty to write or translate light reading for our compatriots but rather to contribute to the spreading of useful knowledge" (20 Feb. 1852). Under the influence of the new editor, Carl Riise (later Charles Reese), a young student recently arrived from Denmark, translated fiction was featured on the last page. Then, on 25 February 1853, he dropped the serialized history and announced his decision to present "short fiction of common interest or original contributions, correspondence, etc." on the front page. He started with a story translated from the French. Riise, however, did not remain long in the editor's chair, and a more sober style is evident after January, 1854, when Knud Fleischer edited the newspaper under the supervision of the Board of Directors. When Adolph Preus addressed himself to the question "What should we Norwegian readers wish and expect of our Norwegian newspaper Emigranten?" (5, 12 May 1854) he criticized the newspaper for not giving priority to "useful and entertaining reading" for the young, but made it clear that he did not want a return to the "fiction and love stories that Riise gave us in such liberal fashion."

Preus took his responsibilities as a member of the Board seriously and was a frequent contributor of essays on a wide range of topics in 1853–1854, appearing as "A" except when he was engaged in polemics or wrote on an issue of concern to the church. His academic style marked the cultural gap between the university graduate and the pioneer farmers who made up the majority of the readers. In a brief comment on the first installment of "A"'s essay on what should be expected of the newspaper, the editor observed that readers often complained that "'A''s articles were too learned and too difficult." His ponderous style is evident in his essay "Om historien og de kilder hvorfra den haves" (On history and its sources, 15 Sept. 1854), submitted as an instance of what he believed would make the newspaper more popular with young readers. Regardless of age, however, readers did not expect frivolity in their newspaper, and the essay, on political and philosophical as well as aesthetic themes, was the genre in which early writers excelled. Many of these writers hid behind pseudonyms and most made single appearances.

Several, however, stand out as essayists of some ability and contributed articles over a relatively long period. One of the first is P.L. Mossin, who made his living as an engraver in Milwaukee. The sophisticated level of his political reasoning and his familiarity with the contemporary American debate demonstrate the important role of the immigrant newspaper in acculturation and the speed with which members of the immigrant group be-

came involved in the concerns of the larger society even though they continued to function primarily within *Vesterheimen*. But Mossin's ambitions
outgrew his abilities, and he became increasingly and not very interestingly
philosophical (for example, 4 April, 2 May 1856). Toward the end of the
decade he disappears from the pages of *Emigranten*, and an editorial note explains that a refused essay by Mossin was "far too abstract and, so it seems to
us, without aim and purpose" (12 March 1859). For Chas. Erickson's 1858
almanac Mossin wrote brief biographical sketches and an account of Ole
Bull's failed colony, Oleana. Mossin was also a prolific contributor of verse
and his poems continued to appear in *Skandinaven* in the 1860s and 1870s.
More urbane in style and with a more solid education than Mossin was the
newly arrived Dane, Ferdinand Winslow, who in 1854 and 1855 sent a series
of essays to *Emigranten* from New York, first entering its columns 13 October with reflections on immigrant attitudes. Other pieces have titles such as
"Et glædeligt nytaar" (Happy New Year, 29 Dec. 1854) and "Sproget" (Our
language, 12 Jan. 1855).[5]

From 1857, when *Emigranten* moved to Madison and C.F. Solberg took
over as editor, it has a distinctly brighter tone. This is to no small degree due
to the contributions of Frithjof A. Meidell, a humorist and satirist whose
light touch still makes him delightful reading. Meidell, brother of the Norwegian journalist Ditmar Meidell who wrote the popular ballad "Oleana,"
immigrated in 1852 and lived for some years in Springfield, Illinois, before
moving to California in 1858.[6] During this period Meidell submitted a series of sketches to the Norwegian *Aftenbladet* as well as to *Emigranten*, where
he used the pseudonym Terje Terjesen Terjeland. Sketches such as "Running for æn Office" (23 Sept. 1857), and "Terjes brev fra Kansas" (Terje's letter from Kansas, 4 Oct. 1858) satirize the immigrant's difficulties with the
English language. American politics seen through the innocent eyes of the
newcomer is the theme of both sketches. In the first, a satire on the violence
of Kansas politics on the eve of the Civil War, Terje's employer tells him
that he is "running for æn office todæ," and suggests that Terje should work
hard for him. Terje is given an unusually bountiful breakfast and some shots
of whisky, but believes that he has been encouraged to cut as much wood as
he can. As he works other members of the family come and encourage him
to help at the polls. But while Terje is uncomprehending, they on the other
hand show but little interest in his person. They are ignorant of his name
and all simply call him "Tjan" (John). When his master comes and says he
was beaten, Terje is again unable to understand, since his face is unbruised,
but he appreciates that he was beaten by fifty, since he would have been too

strong for one man alone. In this sketch the two languages are so intermixed that the essay would be incomprehensible for a Norwegian without American experience, and it was written exclusively for *Emigranten*.

Some of Meidell's satirical sketches are elaborate fictions of the narrator's experiences in the New World. In "Onkel Jim" (24 Feb. 1858) the narrator, in the manner of the frontier tall tale, tells of how a vegetarian family insisted, in spite of all his protests to the contrary, that he was their expected cousin Jim from England. The next day, after the misunderstanding has finally been accepted and after he has promised not to reveal that he has been kissed by the ladies of the family, he receives a letter from one of the daughters who explains that the others will be off at a camp meeting and asks him to visit her alone, bringing meat and a cookbook purchased with the enclosed five dollar bill. The family come home unexpectedly and are horrified at the sight of meat on their table. Frithjof Meidell is the first Norwegian-American writer of fiction. His dialect satires, which seem to have inspired many followers, and his narratives are far more sophisticated fictions than those attempted by his contemporaries. As a satirist he was unrivaled until the appearance of Ole S. Hervin ("Herm. Wang") in the Minneapolis newspaper *Budstikken* in 1880.

From 1857 fiction appears with greater frequency in *Emigranten*, even though the intensity of the slavery debate does not often allow space to mere stories, some from Norwegian sources, most translations from American journals and newspapers. On 22 November 1858 the first installment of an extended original narrative, "Brudstykker af Jens og Oles hændelser paa vestsiden af Mississippi" (Fragments of Jens and Ole's adventures on the west bank of the Mississippi), appears on the front page. The story is about two friends who live near Beloit and who decide to take a look at the land to the west of the Mississippi in 1849. In a wooden and unimaginative style that tries to be funny we are told of their journey up the river by steamboat and their two-year residence among Indians, whom they help in their war with the Winnebagos. They depart for further adventures, and although the narrative is promised to be "continued," there are no further installments. Whether the anonymous author wearied of his project or the editor decided that the quality was too poor is not revealed. Nevertheless, the aborted narrative is evidence that before the Civil War an unpracticed writer was toying with the ambition of writing an American novel in Norwegian.

The only other piece of original fiction in *Emigranten* before its merger with *Fædrelandet* in 1868 was a tediously didactic story, "Een mand eet navn" (One man one name, 27 Oct. 1862) by a writer who signed himself

"Adopted Citizen" and whose purpose was to warn against the tendency among immigrants to change their names. But by then the newspaper had published fiction that was to prove a more important contribution to the development of a Norwegian-American literature than the attempts by the immigrants themselves. Bjørnstjerne Bjørnson's *Synnøve Solbakken* (1857), which quickly became one of the most popular of contemporary works of Norwegian fiction, was serialized in the first weeks of 1859, and by the spring of 1862 two more Bjørnson novels, *En glad gut* (*A Happy Boy*) and *Arne*, and the short story "The Father" had also been presented. These stories had a rural setting and were mildly critical of the class barriers that most immigrants had turned their backs on. More importantly, the young Bjørnson was becoming a leading spokesman for the growing liberal and national trends in Norwegian culture and society and this, too, contributed to making his fiction popular among immigrants. Increasingly, *Emigranten* published fiction by well-known Norwegian writers, an improvement on the poorly translated magazine fiction of the early years.

When the editor of *Fædrelandet og Emigranten* wrote an apologia for fiction in 1869, his views were significantly different from those of Clausen and Langeland two decades earlier: "It has long been assumed in aristocratic Europe that journals that were to please the great masses . . . would have to lower themselves to flatter their wanton desires. As a consequence of this view, all countries are filled with novels and serials that no father of a family should have in his house." "The great English author" Bulwer-Lytton is the editor's authority for the view that while the aristocracy may be able to afford frivolity, the people need practical knowledge. Nevertheless, the people also need lighter fare to create an "entertaining counterbalance" to the dull realities of life, and for this purpose the editor promises serialized novels as a regular feature. Since they will be literature that should be "an adornment for any family's library, the installments will be printed so that they may be cut out and later bound as a book." In this manner subscribers could acquire useful and pleasing books without any extra cost, the editor concludes (14 Jan.). Installments designed for subsequent binding had been presented by the Danish *Fremad* some months earlier and were to be a standard feature of the newspapers for several decades. In the 1860s the printing and selling of books, often after prior serialization, was an increasingly important part of the business of newspaper publishing, both as an additional source of income and as the most frequently used "premium" to subscribers who paid for a year in advance. With the growth of a book trade, newspapers also gave more space to book news and criticism in their columns.

NOTES

1. His pseudonym is identified in *Den norske Amerikaner* 22 Sept. 1855. Preus omitted the New York *Skandinavia* (1847) and *Afholdenhedsvennen*, a temperance journal published by P. L. Mossin in Racine in 1852.

2. Contemporary accounts of *Nordlyset* are Bache 1951 and Ræder 1929. Nothing came of the plans of a group of lay preachers in LaSalle county, Illinois, to publish a Chicago newspaper, "De norskes opmærksomhed," with a constitution committed to "liberty and equality" (Ræder 179).

3. An editorial 30 Jan. 1852 is set in roman type and toward the end the compositor has run out of "v"s and has had to substitute them with "w"s.

4. "Emigrantens tilbageblik": "Farvel Norrig! signet være; / Haard og stræng du stedse var, / Som en moder jeg dig ære / Om mit brød, du knapt mig skar . . . // Andre egne mig tilbyder / Uafhængighedens aar; / Gjengjeld for min møie yder / For min slægt saa blide kaar / Norrig—dette du ei bød mig / Norrig—fyldt med herremænd / Stormands magt alt styred i dig / Tvang var bunden om din lænd. // . . . // . . . Hvor jeg hjelpe skal at svulme / En nation vel ung, men stor / Der vil frihedsilden ulme / Der hvor næringsfrihed boer. // Jeg gjentager, Farvel Norge / Jeg dig signer til min død, / Du var dog min barndoms værge / Du gav mangen glæde sød / Stedse vil paa dig jeg tænke / Under skjebnens mange kaar / Stedse bede: løs den lænke, / Som forbitret mine aar!"

5. Winslow, who wrote above the signature "F.W." or "W," was a successful banker in Chicago until the great fire brought about his ruin. He was angel for the short-lived Danish newspaper *Fremad* in the late 1860s and also played a prominent role in the Scandinavian Lutheran Education Sociey 1869–1871. His career came to an ignoble end in 1877 when he was found guilty of financial irregularities in Washington.

6. See Øverland 1992 for Meidell's letters.

The Genesis of Commercial Publishing
1847–1876

The first publishing venture was symptomatic of how early immigrants viewed the prospects for linguistic survival. Elling Eielsen was a lay preacher who immigrated in 1839. Traveling among the pioneer settlements he soon came to believe that while the lack of texts was a serious obstacle to the religious education of immigrant children, the newly arrived parents appeared unwilling to have their children taught in the language of the country they had left behind. Consequently, Eielsen had an English translation of Luther's Small Catechism printed in New York in 1841. But when Eielsen the following year had another cornerstone in a Norwegian Lutheran education, a text by the Danish Bishop Erik Pontoppidan, printed in New York, he seems to have realized that his translation effort had been a panic reaction. He kept the Dano-Norwegian language of the original, even insisting on black letter type that had to be brought from Philadelphia (Nelson and Fevold 1960, 77–78).[1]

By the time the Scandinavian Press Association was established in 1851, the use of Norwegian was taken for granted. The policy of the association reflected its ecclesiastical base. Clausen's program had called for the printing "of such books as are most needed here, especially hymnals and school books, first of all ABC's and catechisms, of which there is a sore need." As Eielsen had realized a decade earlier, the immigrant settlements could not rely on a supply of texts from Europe. This perception was matched by the immigrants' developing interest in reading and purchasing books. For immigrants in business, books were one potentially profitable commodity. *Nordlyset* advertised books from the first issue, mainly religious titles. Beginning 18 November 1847, L.J. Fribert ran advertisements reminding the public that he had German and Norwegian books in his store in Watertown, Wisconsin, and later announced plans to open a bookstore in Milwaukee. Books were also advertised by Berendt Frøiseth in Cambridge, Wisconsin, who submitted poems to *Nordlyset*. Most issues of *Democraten* have an advertisement for an English bookstore in Racine and there are notices from clergymen who have religious books for sale. Though there was a market for Norwegian books in Illinois and Wisconsin, it was not yet large enough to make printing and publishing an attractive commercial venture. The first publishing project, a popular book of homilies, announced by *Nordlyset* 16 September 1847, suggests some of the problems involved. Since the press did not have sufficient type for such a large undertaking, they had to ask for subscriptions, and the plan was not realized. By the end of the year the publishers advertised their first book off the press: an almanac. Langeland played with the possibility of publishing *Guldbergs Psalmebog*, the main hymnal in Norway, as a way of raising money, but it was still too early for commercial publishing, even of religious books (*Democraten* 25 June 1851).

The two main motivations for publishing were the same as for the early journals: politics and religion. While the latter prompted the reproduction of Lutheran texts from the old country, politics was inspired by the new environment. By 1848 several anti-slavery pamphlets had been translated into Norwegian and were advertised in *Nordlyset* 6 April. Other instances of political publishing were also Whig-inspired. Ole J. Hatlestad, who published a competing church monthly, *Kirketidende*, printed translations of the campaign biography of General Winfield Scott and Horace Greeley's "Why I am a Whig" in 1852. *Emigranten*'s attack on these publications (8 Oct. 1852) was in line with majority opinion among the Norwegian settlers, who were still inclined to be Democrats, albeit of the Free Soil persuasion. Since Hatlestad's monthly supported Pierce, it seems obvious that the Scott biography, the first secular book (except almanacs) from a Norwegian-American press, was not initiated by him, but paid for by supporters of the disintegrating Whig Party. *Emigranten* noted, somewhat maliciously, that the Norwegian edition did not have the illustrations of the English and German versions.

When the Scandinavian Press Association announced their first books, an ABC and Pontoppidan's edition of Luther's catechism, early in 1853, they were fully aware of the importance of their undertaking. While the books were still in the press an editorial (24 Dec. 1852) explained that "The publication of *Emigranten* and *Maanedstidende* is a subsidiary matter even though it is . . . a necessary step in making the Norwegian common people here more enlightened than they usually are when they arrive; the main aim of this Association is to publish the school books and religious books that the Norwegians have a desire to own and use regularly." During its eight years the association was able to publish and keep in print about ten such books. The costs involved made book publishing a financial burden. The main difficulty, however, proved to be the attempt to combine the conflicting interests of a secular newspaper and Synod publishing, and when the association was formally dissolved in 1860 this was mainly because the joint venture had become unattractive as well as impractical for both parties (30 Jan. 1860). *Emigranten*, which along with the press had been moved to Madison in 1857, thrived under private ownership until it merged with *Fædrelandet* in 1868.

The Scandinavian Press Association dominated publishing in the 1850s. Other press societies with a basis in other Lutheran factions did not have much more than a paper existence, with two titles published by the clergyman Ole Andrewson in Leland, Illinois, in 1854 and 1856. The market was too limited to encourage competition. It took Elias Stangeland more than two years to plan and print his ambitious edition of Luther's homilies by late 1857 (*Den norske Amerikaner* 7 July, 15 Dec. 1855, 13 Dec. 1856). In spite of the enmity between the pietistic layman and the Synod clergy, *Emigranten* gave his volume a favorable review along with an itinerary of his sales campaign (20 Jan. 1858). Even so, Stangeland was unable to make ends meet and he had to announce a price reduction. His accompanying lament on the immigrants' lack of interest in books was repeated in various forms by most of those who were to try their hand at creating a Norwegian-American literature (*E* 18 Oct. 1858).

Although they mostly reprinted books from Norway, the immigrant presses from the beginning also produced original work. *Nordlyset* published an almanac, no mean effort in 1847, and a group of laymen, apparently with Trovatten as a prime mover, had a polemical pamphlet, *Nogle ord til de norske i America* (Some words to the Norwegians in America), printed in Buffalo in 1854. The first of many immigrant memoirs, the pamphlet *Erindringer fra min reise over Atlanterhavet* (Memoirs of my journey across the Atlantic), was written by O.O. Østrem and printed on the press of Ole Andrewson in 1858. Another pre-Civil War publication illustrates the need a new land created for new knowledge: farming in the Midwest required new techniques and raised unfamiliar problems not met by experience transferred from Norway. Christian Krug's *Dyrlægebog*, a veterinary handbook for the immigrant farmer, was published by *Nordstjernen* and advertised in *Emigranten* (29 Aug. 1859). It was the first of many such books.

That their children would need an education that was not a replica of that offered by school and church in the old country was not quite so obvious. On 5 May 1857, however, the Scandinavian Press Association announced a prize for the best manuscript for an ABC or beginner's reader. The main requirement was that the book be "fit for use in schools under our present conditions." No one responded to the call, so the directors turned to Adolph Preus, president of the Synod. He complied, and his *ABC eller første begyndelsesgrunde til læsning for børn* (ABC or the foundation of reading for children) was published in August. Since the price had been set at ten cents, Preus had to limit himself to sixteen printed pages. In *Emigranten* Preus discussed his pedagogical intentions and explained why he had departed from the methods and texts used in the current Norwegian ABCs (26 Aug.). His modest pamphlet marks the beginning of a textbook tradition that culminated with the three-volume *Norsk læsebok* (Norwegian reader) by P.J. Eikeland and Ole Rølvaag (1919-1925). These readers were motivated by the realization that "our present conditions" made the texts used in Norway unsuitable for American children and young people acquiring skills in the language of their parents and grandparents.

On 20 January 1858, *Emigranten* reviewed three books. One was Stangeland's Luther edition. The other two illustrate how publishing by the end of the 1850s had grown to include a variety of genres. Johannes Johannessen, a bookbinder in Madison, had published a translation of the Swedish Esaias Tegnér's popular epic poem *Frithjofs Saga*. The reviewer noted that all who have read the book will now be pleased to learn that they may experience the epic again "here in prosaic America." The third book is an instance of how *Vesterheimen* was acquiring a history as well as a literature. *Norsk Folke Calender*, an almanac, has a blend of Scandinavian, American, and Norwegian-American reading matter that became typical of this genre. It includes an essay on "Life in Ole Bull's Colony," the violin virtuoso's ill-famed Oleana. Placed among pieces on the American Washington and the Danish hymnist and bishop Thomas Kingo, the essay on Oleana signals that *Vesterheimen* already had its own distinct lore.

When the Scandinavian Press Association began in 1851, publishing had been a mission. When it ceased in 1860, publishing was an expanding business. The scale was still modest. The first editorial in *Emigranten* for 1858 observed that "the Norwegian newspapers in this country have hardly more than 3,000 subscribers." But advertisements in *Emigranten* for five firms sell-

ing Norwegian books in Madison alone suggest that there was a profit in
books by the late 1850s (Øverland 1986, 188–189). The book trade prolifer-
ated in the 1860s. In 1861 Ole Monsen in Madison, a printer with *Emigranten*, began advertising his bookstore, followed the next year by Anders
Gulliksen in Decorah, Iowa, and C. Amundsen & Co. in Winona, Minnesota. By the mid-1860s there are advertisements for several booksellers in
Chicago and the founding of *Skandinaven* in 1866 marked the dominance
of that city in the Norwegian book trade in the 1870s and 1880s. The first
advertisement (*E* 9 Jan. 1865) for B. Tobias Olsen's *Noget om den Christelige
børneopdragelse og undervisning* (On the Christian upbringing and education
of children) lists sixteen places where it can be bought and by 6 February
thirty-four are listed, in Wisconsin, Iowa, and Minnesota. Even though
many of these addresses were clergymen or parochial-school teachers who
served as agents, the number speaks not only of the availability of books but
of the possibilities authors had for distribution of their products.

Vesterheimen was spread over a large area and the location of a bookstore
mattered less than advertisements in the newspapers: most trade was by mail
order. The increasing volume and changing nature of the book trade is evident from the variety of books listed for sale. In an advertisement for Fleis-
chers Boghandel (*E* 11 July 1859) most items are devotional books and
school texts, but under the heading "Children's Books etc." some fiction is
listed, for instance Bjørnson's *Synnøve Solbakken*, which had just been serialized in *Emigranten*. When Ole Monsen began to advertise his bookstore in
1861, he had titles on history, some moralistic fiction, and three books by
Eilert Sundt, a pioneering sociologist, in addition to the two dominant categories of religious books and school texts. By 1864 his list of 101 titles had
54 devotional and theological books while the second largest category was
fiction, with 18 titles, closely followed by school texts with 14. The trend
toward a more diversified stock is evident two years later in the advertisements for Anders Gulliksen's bookstore in Decorah. His list is divided into
the categories "Homilies and Devotional Books," "School Texts and Children's Books," "History and Geography," "Hymnals," "Language," "Handbooks," "Novels and Stories," "Books of Various Content," and "The Latest
Poems." The first category is still the largest, with about one fourth of the
titles, but immigrants could by now acquire a fairly varied and balanced collection of books in their old language as their new country gave them the
material conditions that made such acquisition possible.

In the course of the 1860s the basic patterns for publishing were established. There were three main kinds of publishing even though distinctions

between them were not always clear cut: private publishing by the author; commercial publishing, often in connection with a newspaper and a bookstore; and church-related publishing. That so many books were published by the author was no doubt partly because they were unprofitable for commercial or church publishers, but frequently private publishing was preferred because it offered a greater net profit. Author publishing remained important throughout the history of *Vesterheimen*. It is often difficult to determine the mode of publication from the title page alone since publishers would use "published by" and "printed by" as roughly synonymous. *Skandinaven* did not distinguish in their advertising between books they had published and those they had merely printed. Nor is the distinction between commercial and church publishing always clear, since the two kinds of publishers published similar books.

While advertisements made it possible for publishers and booksellers to reach the many settlements in *Vesterheimen*, the author-publisher could also use the press to speak directly to his potential readers. In 1861 Søren Hansen, a doctor in Madison, wrote a polemical book, *Menneskelighed og orthodoxi* (Humanity and orthodoxy), criticizing the doctrines of the Synod. His first advertisement (*E* 5 Aug.) gave an estimate of size, date of publication, and price, and asked for subscriptions at twenty-five cents a copy. He did not expect people to take such a step blindfold: copies of the first sheet had been printed and were sent to potential subscribers free of charge. The doctor, however, was unprepared for the response he got. He presented his problem in an advertisement: "When I first proposed my plans for this book I had in mind readers of a class who are more used to different kinds of reading than the common class . . . Consequently, I made use of several uncommon words and terms." But the response had made him realize that there was a far broader interest in his project than he had first thought, so he would "adjust his style" to a broader public. For readers who might find the already printed first pages difficult, Hansen promised a list explaining some of his terms (2 Sept.). Although writers continued to complain of their public for the next seventy years, the intimate relationship that Dr. Hansen experienced with his audience in 1861 was not uncommon in *Vesterheimen*.

In 1863 the recently arrived Johan Schrøder demonstrated an enterprising approach to publishing. Schrøder had traveled in Canada and had begun a survey of the settlements in the United States in preparation for a book. He submitted some extracts from his manuscript to *Emigranten*, where they were published in three issues in October, 1863, as "En bog for nordboerne hjemme og i Amerika (A book for Norwegians at home and in America).

An introduction explained that the subtitle "From Schrøder's American Diary" indicated "that it is a modest work, collected and written during his travels." The series concluded with the announcement that the book would be available that year from *Emigranten* and other bookstores in America and Norway. But then Schrøder became co-editor and publisher with Frederick Fleischer of a competing newspaper, *Fædrelandet*, from January, 1864, till he resigned in the early fall of 1865. Newspaper work was not the only reason why Schrøder's book was delayed till 1867; his ambitions had grown and he now aimed at a comprehensive survey of all Norwegian settlements. To collect information he tried to set up a network of informants through an open letter to Scandinavian clergymen requesting specified information about their settlements (*F* 11 Jan 1866). As editor, however, Schrøder had so antagonized the clergy that he had little response to his request. Undaunted by this cold shoulder, Schrøder addressed his second appeal for assistance "To the Norwegian People in America" (*F* 22 Feb. and *Marcus Thrane's Norske Amerikaner* 25 May). The attempt to involve as many correspondents as possible in his project was also a marketing device; Schrøder had already placed an "Invitation to Subscribers" in *Fædrelandet*, offering to list their names in the book for an extra twenty-five cents (14 Dec. 1865). Eventually 443 seem to have paid for this honor. The financial success of Schrøder's book was further secured by the soliciting of advertisements that take up eighteen pages in the completed volume, more than half of this space bought by railroads. To the editor of *Emigranten*, Schrøder's "Invitation" seemed inexcusably bombastic. Ironically, the sentence Solberg found most offensive was: "Let us show our countrymen in the old country that the Scandinavians in America have the strength and ability to publish books that the old country must take home from America to be informed." Schrøder's *Skandinaverne i de Forenede Stater og Canada* (The Scandinavians in the United States and Canada) was published not only in La Crosse, Wisconsin, but in Christiania and, in Swedish translation, in Stockholm.[2]

Knud Henderson, a successful author-publisher who started out in the 1860s, was a more representative immigrant than Hansen or Schrøder. He came with his parents from Voss in 1849 at the age of thirteen. They settled in Wisconsin, and after two years Knud was sent to Chicago to learn a trade. Since he had a good voice and the church he attended had no trained organist or choir leader, Knud was helped on the way to a rudimentary music education (Henderson 1928). In 1865 he published his *Koral-Bog* or hymnal with harmonizations that were considerably simplified compared to those in the authorized Norwegian hymnal and thus better suited for use in immigrant congregations. Henderson was his own publisher and had successfully sold three editions of the hymnal before he let it go to *Skandinaven* in 1873. The popularity of Henderson's *Koral-Bog* did not suffer from the negative criticism of specialists. On the contrary, their attacks may even have enhanced its attraction with populistically inclined immigrants. It was success rather than failure that drove Henderson into the hands of a commercial publisher, who also published his *National—og selskabssange* (1876). Both of Henderson's books remained in print through the first two decades of this century.

The two main competitors in the book trade of the 1860s were Anders Gulliksen in Decorah and Ole Monsen in Madison. Monsen had the advantage of being a printer for *Emigranten* and could make good use of this connection for the production, marketing, and distribution of his books. His first publishing venture in 1865 was a broadside ballad capitalizing on the recent assassination of President Lincoln. He continued with popular literature, in particular the autobiography of the famous robber and escape artist of early nineteenth-century Norway, Gjest Baardsen. This book was to become a staple of Norwegian-American publishing, often mentioned as the only secular book in a homesteader's cabin. Monsen was the first commercial publisher of any note, with at least eight titles in 1866 and 1867.

Gulliksen was primarily a bookseller. He had started off rather modestly in a corner of a general store in Decorah where he worked as a clerk, but his business expanded and for a time he had branches in Winona, Minnesota, and Manitowoc, Wisconsin. The one book that carries his imprint, *Haandbog, eller Hver mands brev-, skrive-, og regnemester* (Handbook or everyman's letter, writing, and arithmetic teacher, 1865), gives examples of letters in both languages for different occasions, demonstrates how to draw up contracts and legal documents, and has a variety of tables. A shorter version appeared in 1873. Reviewing a third edition of a similar book, O.M. Peterson's *Fuldstændig norsk-amerikansk brev—og formularbog* (Complete Norwegian-American letter and document book), in 1876 *Skandinaven* noted that the sale of two editions in less than one and a half years was evidence of "a real need" (3 Oct.). Gulliksen was the first to see the commercial possibilities for books of this kind; in his preface he explained that handbooks produced in Norway were of little use for immigrants in America. Nevertheless he seems to have lifted much of his material from a book recently published in Norway, judging from a complaint in *Emigranten* (11 Dec.). In *Fædrelandet*, where the book had been printed, he was praised for having done his fellow immigrants a great service, as evidenced by the large sale (4 Jan. 1866). Pirat-

*Rasmus B. Anderson (1846–1936)
was professor of Scandinavian languages
at the University of Wisconsin,
1869–1883. Courtesy Norwegian-
American Historical Association.*

ing was characteristic of Norwegian-American publishing and essential for securing a varied supply of books at affordable prices.

Alongside commercial ventures and church-related publishing in the tradition of the Scandinavian Press Association, there was also an idealistic motivation for publishing: the desire to keep Norwegian language and culture alive in the New World. The organization of a Scandinavian Lutheran Society for Popular Education in 1869 demonstrated that while the conflict between secular and ecclesiastical interests was still very much alive, the balance of power had shifted. Knud Langeland, now editor of *Skandinaven*, and C.L. Clausen, whose earlier project had been taken over by the young conservative churchmen in 1851, were now successful in holding their own against Herman Preus, president of the Synod, who tried to dominate the inaugural meeting in Madison 4 March. Clausen was elected president, and other prominent members of the society were the Madison businessman John A. Johnson and the young scholar Rasmus B. Anderson. The Society for Popular Education achieved little beyond the adoption of an ambitious program but is nevertheless an interesting manifestation of cultural concerns. While schools and education were the most important issues on the agenda, the society also "called for a wider interest in Norwegian history and literature and in establishing good libraries throughout the Norwegian communities" (Blegen 1940, 259). In August, 1870, Johnson, who had been elected to succeed Clausen as president, received a draft of a new program for the Society (JAJP). It was essentially a program for a publishing society; an elaborate organization for distribution and an ambitious publishing project are outlined in fifteen paragraphs. The program is based on knowledgeable estimates of printing costs, but assumes an interest in culture and literature that was hardly shared by the majority of immigrants. The successful publishers of *Vesterheimen* provided what the public were eager to buy rather than what they ideally should have wanted.

Publishers of popular fare, however, were by no means ensured success. In 1866, when Brynild Anundsen, a printer in La Crosse, launched *Ved Arnen*, a popular monthly with light fiction as a main ingredient, *Skandinaven* observed that "the experience we have had of the possibilities for a Scandinavian literature in America is not of a kind to create an excessive optimism" (15 Nov.). The market was growing rapidly, both because immigration was picking up again after the Civil War and because the proliferation of newspapers made it possible to advertise in the extensive region of Norwegian settlement from Chicago to Minneapolis. Nevertheless, *Skandinaven*'s pessimism proved justified: by 1870, two years after he had moved his business to Decorah, Anundsen had to acknowledge defeat. Four years later, however, he was back again with the longest-lived publishing business in *Vesterheimen*, *Decorah-Posten*, which appeared weekly or biweekly from 1874 to 1972. *Ved Arnen* was resurrected as the newspaper's literary supplement and became the main purveyor of poetry and fiction in many immigrant homes.

Skandinavisk Billed-Magazin in Madison had a very short life, from 1868 to 1870. In spite of the experience of the publisher, Bertel W. Suckow, and the editor, Svein Nilsson, the enterprise proved too ambitious: the cost of printing a liberally illustrated monthly on good paper could not be met by the small number who were willing to pay. *Billed-Magazin* is nevertheless a milestone in Norwegian-American publishing because of Nilsson's series of articles on the early migration and life in the Norwegian settlements. Nilsson, who later succeeded Knud Langeland as editor of *Skandinaven*, made an effort to publish original contributions and *Billed-Magazin* has more such material than either *Ved Arnen* or the third family journal of this period, *For Hjemmet*.

The year Anundsen and Suckow gave up their projects, three professors at Luther College began to publish *For Hjemmet*, a family magazine with higher literary pretensions than those aspired to by Anundsen but produced on cheaper paper and with fewer illustrations than *Billed-Magazin*. The editors' dedication to their vocation as teachers at a church college showed up

Skandinaven *building in Chicago. Courtesy Norwegian-American Historical Association.*

in the tone and contents of their "Journal of Useful and Entertaining Reading." The essays on travel, popular science, and history, as well as the fiction
and poetry are mainly from Dano-Norwegian, English, and German
sources. From the first issue poetry was translated by the editorial assistant
Knud Throndsen, who had worked as a journalist for both *Emigranten* and
Skandinaven and had taught part time at Luther. He was editor from 1876
till he had to give up the journal in 1887. The increasing number of newspapers and journals featuring essays, verse, short stories, and serialized novels
were a stimulus for immigrants with literary ambitions. *For Hjemmet* had
original contributions in prose and verse and in 1874 it brought one of the
earliest Norwegian-American novels, Nicolai Hassel's "Alf Brage," to its
subscribers.

The most important event in early publishing is the founding of *Skandinaven* in Chicago by John Anderson, Iver Lawson, and Knud Langeland in
1866. *Skandinaven* not only became one of the most influential and successful newspapers in *Vesterheimen.* but also developed a publishing business that
became the largest venture of its kind. John Anderson was a printer by trade

John Anderson (1836–1910), founder and publisher of Skandinaven *in his editorial office. Courtesy Norwegian-American Historical Association.*

and soon began to print books on his press in addition to the job printing that was always a significant part of his business. But he was cautious and did only a few books in the late 1860s. The foundation for the publishing the firm was to thrive on was laid when Langeland and Lawson broke with Anderson in the spring of 1872 and established a competing newspaper, *Amerika*, with the active support of a new partner, John A. Johnson of Madison. The three decided to publish a volume of Norwegian folk tales and stories edited by Rasmus B. Anderson, the professor of Scandinavian languages at the University of Wisconsin. Although *Amerika* had merged with *Skandinaven* by the time the book was ready for marketing as *Julegave* or Christmas gift, it nevertheless bore the imprint "Amerika's Forlag."

The volume is a modest one, yet for Anderson it was an important cultural event: "When I have visited Norwegian families . . . I have almost always found a lack of Norwegian books, and especially books that contain light reading for children and young people," he wrote in his preface. "If we are to maintain the Norwegian language in this country we will have to supply our bookshelves with some of our fatherland's literature and try to awaken a taste and interest for the mother tongue in our children." The growth of the book trade had made him optimistic: "Ten years ago we had hardly a single Norwegian bookstore in America. Now there is a considerable Norwegian book trade in Chicago, Decorah, La Crosse, etc. and some Norwegian libraries have had considerable growth." The number of newspapers, church journals, and literary magazines had also increased. Nevertheless, he continued, "hardly any Norwegian books that are not specifically religious have been published in this country with the exception of serials ... Is it not time that we begin to publish historical works, collections of stories, poetry, and folk tales? I think it is. The Germans in America have already published the literature of their country with good results, and even though the Norwegian public is small compared to the German one, I still believe it is a worthwhile experiment." At first the publishers demonstrated little faith in the project and did not even bother to advertise the book. It nevertheless sold well from the very beginning and became one of *Skandinaven*'s many popular successes, remaining in print for about thirty years, with the eighth and last edition published in 1900.

By this time two other Chicago firms were doing a prosperous trade in imported books: I.T. Relling and Fritz Frantzen, for a time close neighbors on Milwaukee Avenue. They were joined in 1874 by the successful publishing business of Christian Rasmussen. David Schøyen's 1874 series in *Skandinaven* on Scandinavian-American businesses included bookbinders and printers as well as booksellers and he saw the flourishing businesses of Relling and Frantzen as "telling and encouraging proof of the fact that a taste for literature and culture is growing among our nationality" (24 Feb.).

Skandinaven established a bookstore division, Skandinavens Boghandel, in 1876. The two main reasons for their interest in the book trade were to find a profitable use for the excess capacity of their printing press and to strengthen their growing newspaper, which by the mid 1870s had weekly, tri-weekly, and daily editions as well as a special European one for distribution in Norway and Denmark. In October, 1873, *Skandinaven* began the publication of *Husbibliothek*, a monthly subtitled "A Journal for Entertaining Reading," making novels, stories, and poems available at low prices. The advertising theme was that a subscription would make it possible for immigrants to build up a library that would have been unavailable to them in the old country. It was an immediate success: "Husbibliothek will bear some 'brag,' even '*much*,'—I think," Victor Lawson wrote, as always in English, to Johnson on 6 December. "We have now 900 subscribers—fully 700 have paid 1 year in advance" (JAJP). A few months later, in 1874, the publishers launched a venture that was intimately linked to circulation-building: on 24 March *Skandinaven* offered a new two-volume history of the United States as a premium to all of the 13,000 subscribers who paid for one year in advance. This eventually became the three volumes of David Schøyen's *Amerikas Forenede Staters Historie* (1874, 1875, 1876 and many later reprints). The marketing campaign seems to have paid off: on 21 February 1876 Lawson wrote to Johnson about the logistics of distributing 10,000 copies of the second volume (JAJP). This would have been a respectable first printing for any American book in the mid-1870s, but it is quite remarkable considering an estimated population of about 150,000 Norwegian Americans.

Books could be used to increase newspaper circulation and a newspaper could advertise a book and give it favorable reviews. This practical combination of printing press, newspaper, journal, publishing, and bookstore proved so successful that other Chicago booksellers followed suit. The two most successful ones were I.T. Relling, who began to publish the weekly newspaper *Norden* in 1874, with reviews of books available from his bookstore as a prominent feature, and the Dane Christian Rasmussen, who, after beginning on a modest scale in Chicago in 1874, moved his publishing business to Minneapolis in 1887, probably to get out from the shadow of John Anderson. At the time of incorporation in Minneapolis in 1887 his capital was $40,000 and after a few years the firm employed about fifty people (Søderstrøm 1899, 430–432; Wist 1914, 175–177).

One reason publishing could prosper in the face of competition from Norway and Denmark was the cost factor. The competitive price of books produced in America was from the very beginning an important marketing theme, as when *Emigranten* (25 Jan. 1866) observed that while the price for Henderson's *Koral-Bog* was $1.00, an imported book of the same kind would cost at least $2.00. The tariff, which imposed high import duties on books, protected the growth of publishing. However, as Erik L. Petersen observed in the Minneapolis newspaper *Budstikken* (15 Feb. 1881), the tariff had an adverse effect on writers since it not only made European books unnecessarily expensive but tended to encourage pirating and deprived authors on both sides of the Atlantic of their income.

It is difficult to assess the volume of the book trade in these years, since sales figures are seldom available. In a letter to R.B. Anderson 28 July 1880 (RBAP), Louis Pio, who had arrived from Denmark three years earlier, presents a list of his literary accomplishments in America. Several of the books he had edited or translated had been published by the Chicago Methodist

This photograph of Milwaukee Avenue in Chicago was taken in 1890. The Norwegian-American newspaperman I. T. Relling published the newspaper Norden *here, operated* Skandinavisk Boghandel, *a steamship agency, and a bank in the same building.*
Courtesy Gladys Geerling Nieman Collection.

publisher Christian Treider and the sales figures he gives for two of these are 1,500 and 1,000 copies. His translation of F. W. Günther's best seller, *The Little American*, had sold 6,000 copies and a history of Chicago 2,500. The figure he gave for a legal handbook published by Rasmussen in 1879, 1,500 copies, may also throw light on the business volume of *Skandinaven*, which had published a competing book by Schøyen in 1878 that was reprinted four times by 1884. The importance of the book trade for newspapers is evident in *Skandinaven* for 20 October 1874, where the front page has two columns advertising books available in the newspaper's bookstore. An editorial note suggests the publisher's sense of mission: "The books advertized here are entertaining, educational, and in other respects useful, and deserve a place in the bookcase of any intelligent man. We would like to admonish our readers that in this country, where one does not count every penny as we did in Norway, it will be wise for parents to supply their family with good books in order to make the home a pleasant place for the young, some of whom will acquire a love for books. You will discover that money spent on books bears interest." Two of the eight books were Scandinavian reprints; six were Norwegian-American products. Two were in English: Hjalmar H. Boyesen's *Gunnar* and R.B. Anderson's *America Not Discovered By Columbus*; the others were the first volume of Schøyen's United States history, Henderson's *Koral-Bog*, O.M. Peterson's *100 Timer i Engelsk* (100 lessons in English), and Anderson's *Julegave*.

Two weeks later, in a review of Peterson's textbook, Anderson commented on the literary awakening among the Norwegians in America and concluded that he "would appreciate having more Norwegian-American books to review in the near future" (3 Nov.). Anderson was at this time seeing such a book of his own through the press, *Den norske maalsag* (The Norwegian language question), published by *Skandinaven* some weeks later. Two reviewers noted that Anderson's book was a sign of an important development in Norwegian-American culture. In *Skandinaven* "B.T." observed that "a more active interest in better and more wholesome reading may be observed among our people. The reasons this development has been so slow should be obvious to all who have studied the growth of our people here. We have lacked the intellectual as well as the material resources . . . For even though there may have been intellectual powers hidden away in some corner, our material conditions have kept books from publication . . . the barrier has been so great that it must often have broken the courage of those who may have had the ability to produce good books" (18 May). The reviewer speculates in romantic terms on the "sparks" that glow in the masses, some of which may burst into flame, and on the signs of an awakening. Books were beginning to appear, "and the publishers of *Skandinaven* deserve our gratitude for their recent initiative in book publishing, through which they have opened the way for the development of an independent Norwegian-American literature." In *Budstikken* (25 May 1875) E.L. Petersen offered much the same observations on the conditions for a Norwegian-American literature, and he, too, pointed "to the publishers of *Skandinaven*; they are men with great financial resources and they also seem to be inspired by a will to further all that can be to the honor and usefulness of our people. Men who wish to appear as authors could now perhaps have hopes of a helping publisher's hand in Chicago."

Two would-be novelists had already acted on such hopes. Tellef

Homesteading in Dakota. Much of the potential audience for the publishers and authors of Vesterheimen *lived under such conditions. On the shelf above his table the Norwegian-American homesteader has a selection of books. Courtesy Norwegian-American Historical Association.*

Grundysen, a cotter's son from Telemark, had sent the manuscript of *Fra begge sider af havet* (From both sides of the ocean) from Fillmore county, Minnesota, to *Skandinaven*. Lawson had realized the potential interest of an original novel and sent it on to Anderson in Madison on 20 May, asking his "opinion as to advisability of publishing it." Bernt Askevold, an ambitious young immigrant in Decorah, Iowa, had already signed a contract with *Skandinaven* for a novel he had recently completed.

R. B. Anderson, though always surrounded by controversies, largely of his own making, held a position of prominence in *Vesterheimen* that should not be underestimated. As professor of Scandinavian languages at the University of Wisconsin he was the only inhabitant of *Vesterheimen* outside the conservative Synod with fully respectable academic credentials. Moreover, he was a born and bred American. When Askevold, a teacher who had immigrated in 1873 and was employed by Anundsen as editor of *Decorah-*

B. Anundsen (1844–1913)
founder of Decorah-Posten.

Posten, completed his first novel, it was natural for him to send it to Anderson for approval. Anderson, who was indefatigable in his support of new talent, recommended the novel to *Skandinaven.* The partners discussed the project with Anderson breathing down their necks, and Lawson had to assure him that they were working on the matter. The reply came to Askevold in the form of a contract dated 15 May 1875: "If we print the book we will have an edition of about 1,000 copies. When 400 copies at $1 are sold our expenses will be about covered, counting the unbound 600 copies. If you can get 400 subscribers for the book at $1, we will print it and pay you 10% of the sale price of all copies sold in addition to the 400, but nothing for the 400, so that if 1,000 are sold at $1 per copy you will receive $60 . . . You may advertise free of charge in *Skandinaven* for six months, not using more than 3 inches of a column each week, excepting reviews, etc. . . . When the book is printed you shall have 30 free copies for distribution or sale as you decide. The copyright is ours. If you find these conditions satisfactory please sign this letter as 'accepted' in your own hand and send us a

The first issue of Decorah-Posten, Saturday, September 5, 1874.

copy. It will then be a valid contract . . . Sincerely, Johnson, Anderson & Lawson" (JAJP). The conditions may appear stringent, but were similar to those offered R. B. Anderson for his book on the Norwegian language, and he, too, had advertised for subscriptions in the fall of 1874. Askevold responded immediately, buoyed by the interest and support of all he had approached. His employer in Decorah let him advertise in his name, thus giving his stamp of approval to the project as well as a dependable address for the subscription campaign. The first advertisement for the forthcoming novel *Ragnhild* appeared in *Skandinaven* 1 June 1875. What followed must have dampened the spirits of the young novelist. Despite several months of advertising and a personal appeal from the author (*Sk* 17 Aug. 1875), few responded. On 31 August R. B. Anderson appealed: "Will not the Norwegian people in America take part in encouraging and supporting a Norwegian-American literature?" Only one hundred had subscribed and when Anderson wrote again on 5 October, forty-four names had been added to the list, still far below the initial optimistic expectations. The advertisements continued for more than a year, the last one on 22 August 1876. By then the conditions of the contract were finally met, and the publication of the novel was announced 17 October.

Even when it flourished, publishing in *Vesterheimen* was a successful business in relative terms only. On 6 November 1875 Lawson wrote rather pessimistically to R. B. Anderson, "We are selling *very* few books of any kind now, — and yours are about as 'few' as the rest." The sales figures he gives for the last three months for the four books by Anderson they have in stock vary from three to eight copies. All books, however, were not equally poor properties and Lawson could give nice figures for O.M. Peterson's practical guide to writing letters and contracts, published in April: "We have sold since that date 184 copies, and we shall probably sell 100 more this winter, notwithstanding that there are half a doz others selling it."

However unsuccessful the first attempts to publish original fiction and belles lettres were from a business point of view, *Skandinaven* and other publishers felt it was their cultural responsibility to include such titles on their lists. From 1876 original fiction, poetry, and drama were regular features of Norwegian-American publishing for half a century. Moreover, the establishment of publishers among the immigrants was a precondition for a literature: the availability of outlets for poems, essays and stories, as well as for books, was the impetus needed for literary efforts. In an undated essay "Lidt skandinavisk-amerikansk literaturhistorie." (A little Scandinavian-American literary history) the aging Knud Langeland looked back on the history in which he had played such a central role and commented on the changes that had taken place during the 1870s and early 1880s "in what we may call Scandinavian-American literature. Before this time the works by Scandinavian writers in America could be counted on the fingers of one hand, and the books read by our compatriots were either homilies or books like *Gjest Baardsen*. Because of the work of several publishers we now have a public that is able to appreciate the importance of good books and there is good reason to believe that this improved taste may gradually lead to the creation of an independent literary culture in our mother tongue in our new homeland." Although the commercial publishers were not quite as idealistic as Knud Langeland here makes them appear, and *Skandinaven* thrived on the publication of numerous editions of *Gjest Baardsen* and similar popular fare, the Chicago newspaper and publisher did perform as midwife at the birth of a Norwegian-American literature.

NOTES

1. Books for Norwegian immigrants were also produced outside the small group itself. The first American Bible Society publication in Norwegian was a Bible in 1848, and the American Tract Society distributed translations of *A Pilgrim's Progress* (1852) and other edifying books. Contemporary accounts of such publishing activity are in *Democraten* 4 Jan. and 8 Feb. 1851.

2. For an account of the context of Schrøder's book and a translation of the chapters on Canada, see Øverland 1989.

PART THREE

A Literature Takes Shape
1865–1880

Bearing Historical Witness

Recording their people's history was an important motive for immigrant writing. The spokesmen of the seventeenth-century colonists of New England were convinced that they were the vanguard of a migration of momentous religious and historical import. Those who gave voice to the thoughts and feelings of the early immigrants from Norway were similarly conscious of being a vanguard, even though their vision of the historical significance of their undertaking was a secular one. In 1838 Ole Rynning included a chapter on the history of immigration in his *True Account of America*. In 1847 an editorial in *Nordlyset* informed readers that "it would be of historical and statistical interest both now and in the future to receive brief descriptions of the different settlements." A history of our own, explained the editor, would create a sense of community and "give us the importance and influence in this country that we, as a united class, deserve" (9 Sept.). Clausen made a similar appeal in the second issue of *Emigranten* in 1852. In 1853 Adolph Preus wrote a history of the press for *Emigranten*. In 1873 a young immigrant in Chicago planned to write "a lengthy literary and cultural historical dissertation on 'The progress of Norwegian-American literature from its first days and to our own time.'"[1]

Throughout his career Knud Langeland worked to foster a sense of cultural and political identity among the immigrants. His goal was the forging of an American ethnic group that would preserve the best traits in the Scandinavian character and acquire the best traits in the American. By preserving and developing our identity, he wrote in his first editorial in *Skandinaven* (1 June 1866), "we may be able to place our small contribution to the outcome of the great migrations of the nineteenth century on the altar of

Svein Nilsson (1826–1908), prominent editor of Billed-Magazin *and* Skandinaven. *Courtesy State Historical Society of Wisconsin.*

our adopted fatherland with the conviction that though our contribution may be small compared to that of other nationalities, it may yet in quality be the equal of any." History was crucial to Langeland's vision: "No people can claim to be civilized unless it leaves behind testimonials to its history. A people's literature is the best, although not the only witness to its cultural level."

The first comprehensive history after Rynning's survey in 1838 was Svein Nilsson's series on "The Scandinavian Settlements in America" in *Billed-Magazin,* based on written communications and interviews with early settlers (1868–1870). *Skandinaven's* review of the first installments remarked on Nilsson's tendency to present slanted personal accounts as objective history (29 Dec. 1869), but the personal flavor makes for a lively anecdotal narrative. His main theme is the success of the migration movement. Of individual after individual we learn that he became prosperous and had a large farm or had left large farms to his descendants: "Both are farmers in Cottage Grove, live in easy circumstances, and are highly respected men" (161) is the concluding sentence of the series. Pride in Norwegian-American achievement is a central theme for most amateur historians from Nilsson to Olaf Norlie's *History of the Norwegian People in America* (1925); it found succinct expression in the title of O.N. Nelson's *History of the Scandinavians and Successful Scandinavians in the United States* (1893). The line between national pride and prejudice is not easily drawn. Nilsson exalts the virtues of the Scandinavians, who "the Yankees declare" are the nationality who, "in relation to their number, are of the greatest service to this country. Their industry makes them excellent clearers of land and their frugality creates prosperity. They are loyal and willingly obey the laws. They have a natural feeling for orderly behavior and there are few criminals among them." By contrast, the Irish "prefer town life, and many of the cities in this country are rimmed by several rows of Irish shanties which surround the business district like a frame. Here the sons of Erin live in complete harmony with the habits of their forefathers" (79). Filiopietism is the dominant mode of the early historians of *Vesterheimen.*

Nilsson wrote with a sense of urgency brought about by his awareness that "one after another of the fathers of emigration are leaving us. Before many years have passed there will not be anyone left among the living who can give eyewitness accounts of the first Norwegian emigrants' departure from the homeland—about their longings and hopes, and their fate on this side of the mighty ocean" (105). A similar sense of the need to create the historical record before the deeds of the past were forgotten is also seen in John A. Johnson's compilation, *Det skandinaviske regiments historie* (1869), the first of several histories of the 15th Wisconsin Civil War infantry regiment.[2] He requested information in *Emigranten* and *Fædrelandet* (12 Feb. 1866) and the editor of the latter reminded his readers that there "would be reason to fear that the Regiment's Scandinavian character" would not be stressed by American historians. It proved so difficult to collect the necessary material, however, that the project Johnson thought would be completed by spring took him three years.

During the 1870s and 1880s the need to collect sources and write immigration history was often discussed within a circle of individuals connected with *Skandinaven.* The first result was the formation of a "Norwegian Pioneer Society" in 1873 with the aim of "collecting and preserving for later generations the history of Norwegian immigration." The bylaws outlined an ambitious publication policy. Johnson and Anderson were elected president and secretary but no more is heard of the society after a brief notice in *Skandinaven* 28 April 1874. A new project was discussed in correspondence

*Knud Langeland (1813–1888),
prominent newspaperman, co-founder
and first editor of* Skandinaven.
*Courtesy Norwegian-American
Historical Association.*

between Schøyen and Anderson in the winter of 1877. Schøyen had included a brief history of Norwegian immigration in the second volume of
his *Amerikas forenede staters historie* (History of the United States) and an account of the Wisconsin 15th in his third, and he now hoped to spend two
years on "The Saga of the Norsemen in *Vesterheimen.*" "It is high time this
work be done ... " he wrote in December, 1876, " any delay will greatly increase the difficulties in getting reliable accounts of the earliest times." He
promised more detailed plans in a later letter, but hack work kept him busy
and he did not write again until September, 1877.[3]

Hindsight suggests that the problem was not that the earliest history was
slipping into oblivion, but that the time was not yet ripe: there was no
repository of source material. In Chicago, Schøyen claimed, "there is no
collection of the older volumes of *Skandinaven,* and only some issues of the
most recent years of any other paper. Now that Pastor Krogness has left the
city, I have not found anyone with a substantial collection of the older
church journals."[4] In 1879, an essay on "Two Fathers of Norwegian Immigration" (*Sk* 9 Sept.) revived Schøyen's interest and he made a call for a
Scandinavian-American Historical Association in the September issue of *Illustreret Familieblad*: "The new civilization that is being created here in
America will not merely be a product of external natural and cultural con-

ditions, but of the original characteristics of each of the major nationalities . . . in this racial amalgamation process the Scandinavians must play their
role and have their historical impact on one of the most powerful and influential societies in the world." The responses in journals in Chicago and
Minneapolis led to nothing.[5] Schøyen continued to collect material but did
not have sufficient stability in his life to complete his ambitious project. He
gave it up on becoming editor of the short-lived *Skandinavisk Tribune*
(1887–1888) in Madison, and passed on his notes to his twenty-three-year-
old assistant, Johannes B. Wist. Wist set to work immediately and published
two chapters as a pamphlet in 1888, *Den norske indvandring til 1850* (Norwegian immigration before 1850), claiming that the rest would soon be
printed. Wist's youthful enthusiasm soon wore out, however, and no more
came of the project. When he revised his pamphlet some years later he admitted that neither he nor Schøyen was near completion of their history.[6]

The idea of a historical society continued to live in *Vesterheimen* but did
not enter public debate until 1884, when a new initiative was taken by S. M.
Krogness, a Lutheran minister in Chicago, in *Skandinaven*, urging Johnson
to organize "a society to collect material for a history of the Norwegian
people in America" (15 Jan.).[7] Johnson declined the honor but presented
his list of potential historians, including pioneers like Nilsson, Schrøder,
Anderson, Clausen, and C.F. Solberg. His list, however, is topped by Langeland, who was "unpartisan" and "the best man in the country to write such
a history" (*Sk* 5 Feb.). Johnson and Langeland had been corresponding on
the subject earlier that winter after Langeland had urged Johnson, his
brother Ole, and Anderson to get together and collect material for a "Scandinavian history of Imigration [sic]."[8] Thus Krogness' initiative was a welcome opportunity for Johnson to go public with his attempts to get his old
friend to write, and his hyperbolic insistence that Langeland's memoirs
alone would make all other sources superfluous is a response to Langeland's
excuse that he was too old and infirm to collect any new material. When
Johnson characterized his friend as "unpartisan," however, he knew better.
He had just had a letter from Langeland, who had insisted on the importance of a history written from the point of view of "laymen" and not of
the conservative Synod clergy. Indeed, Langeland had claimed that it was
because the "Norwegian clergy, who for a long time were the only representatives of an intelligentsia among us, are my bitter enemies" and would
attack his work without mercy, that he had decided not to publish a history.
"Consequently," he wrote to Johnson, "I hope that men with ability and
strength will do something about it; for in our time it would be shameful if

our historians, in the manner of Snorre Sturlason, would have to rely on a many hundred years old popular oral tradition. But I want this work to be done by laymen. When we farmers went to America, the clergy prophesied that we were going to Hell; when they followed us here, they came to live, rule, and consume, not to build the country, not to create progress, but to restrain us, suppress us, and tax us. They should not write the history of the rough Scandinavian farmers in this country; it would scarcely receive the correct coloring in their hands" (30 Jan.). Although Langeland had been re-tired for some years on his farm in Racine county, Wisconsin, the pressure to take up the pen again had been strong and constant. In spite of misgiv-ings because of his failing health, Langeland began to organize his historical notes that spring assisted by his son James. It was common knowledge that he already had a manuscript autobiography, and his former partner, John Anderson, now the sole owner of *Skandinaven*, was eager to publish.[9] "John Anderson has been to see me twice about getting my manuscript," Lange-land wrote in English to Johnson 10 May 1884, asking his advice.

Langeland's *Nordmændene i Amerika* (The Norwegians in America) was finally published in 1888, shortly before his death on February 8th. On the 16th James wrote to Johnson (in English) of his father's appreciation of Johnson's review of the book in *Norden* and added, "When at work on his book he often expressed regret that he had not begun it sooner when he was stronger mentally and physically." With all its faults it is one of the most valuable literary documents of nineteenth-century *Vesterheimen* because of the concluding autobiography, "An immigrant's memoirs of life in Norway and America." The first part of the book is basically a compilation of notes, but remains a useful source in spite of Langeland's tendency to stress the success theme.

Langeland's story is of a youth from the bottom of rural society and his struggle for knowledge and an education. His antagonists are the represen-tatives of power in a rigid class structure who seem to be parties to a con-spiracy to keep the lower classes in a state of ignorance. Within this system the school appears an institution designed to keep the people in bondage rather than to enlighten them. Young Langeland learns to write on his own, laboriously copying letters left by his dead father. In Bergen a teacher at a common school accepts him as an unofficial apprentice, but when his pres-ence is discovered by a clergyman inspector, he is dismissed: "Off with you, young man, we don't teach farmers how to become teachers here!" (169) A few years later Langeland reveals his intention of going to England in order to improve his English to a book dealer: "What do you want to do in England? A Norwegian farmer in England—learning English! Your impudence has taken you too far. Stick to your catechism and your hymnbook, they are sufficient for the likes of you." Langeland adds, "I am giving you some of the many incidents of this sort that I encountered during my thirty years in Norway and that had considerable influence upon my attitude to life and my later career" (194-195). Langeland's memoirs present his account of why so many emigrated from rural Norway and of the opportunities given to him and his countrymen in their new country.

Langeland's career in America is best understood against his Norwegian background: "The education of the people became my hobbyhorse," he explains (218). This is seen not only in his work as editor but in his strong support of the American common school against the attempts of the Synod clergy to keep children in parochial schools under their control. When Norwegian clergy began to arrive in America around 1850, Langeland experienced their work as an attempt to establish the old class system in the new republic. Adolph Preus, who in attitude and bearing must have appeared the very image of the clergymen who had tried to keep the young Langeland in his proper place and position in Norway, wrote condescendingly in his 1853 history of the press in *Emigranten*: "judged in the light of the education Mr. Langeland had for editorial work, we must admit that the newspaper was not edited without some suggestion of talent . . . But in other respects Mr. Langeland demonstrated indecision and inconsistency as well as lack of discretion, which had its harmful effects then as later. He had poor control of his columns and all too often there were articles that should not have seen the light of day." The university-educated clergyman found particular pleasure in pointing out the stylistic infelicities of Langeland and other editors with similar lower-class backgrounds.

From his retirement Langeland wrote to *Skandinaven* (28 March 1882) on "the liberty of the press and its proper use," explaining his belief "that we Norwegian farmers in America needed some awakening and development in order to do our duty as citizens of equal standing in the great democracy of the United States. I believed that the reading of newspapers and participation in current debates on the important questions of the day would be a useful school for us where we could make up for some of our lost opportunities." In his dedication to his educational and democratic goals Knud Langeland is one of the important builders of *Vesterheimen*. In his vision of history and literature as essential to a people's civilization, his contribution to the foundation of a Norwegian-American literature cannot be overestimated.

NOTES

1. John W. Arctander to John A. Johnson, 14 Feb. 1873 (JAJP). Arctander became a successful lawyer in Minneapolis.

2. Others are Dietrichson (1884), Janson (1887, fiction), Buslett (1894) and Ager (1916). A German history of the Civil War, *Die Deutschen im amerikanischen Bürgerkriege* (Munich, 1911), calls this regiment predominantly German and Swedish and lists Heg as a German officer (510).

3. Schøyen to Anderson 15, 21 Dec. 1876 and 17 Sept. 1877. Schøyen had been a lawyer in Christiania before emigrating in 1869. *Skandinaven* noted his arrival and announced his free-lance connection with the newspaper 1 Sept. 1869. Among Schøyen's books are a legal handbook (1878) and potboilers on the murders of Lincoln (1880) and Garfield (1881). For short periods he was editor of *Verdens Gang, Vort Land* (Chicago), *Skandinavisk Tribune* (Madison), and *Normannen* (Stoughton). He died in a railway accident in Wisconsin in 1896.

4. The collections Schøyen refers to were lost in a fire, according to a letter Krogness wrote to Anderson 12 Feb. 1880, asking that Anderson either organize a historical society or collect the material and write the history himself.

5. Schøyen's proposal was reprinted in *Budstikken* 28 Oct. Respondents were Luth Jæger in *Budstikken* 28 Oct. 1879, reprinted in *Illustreret Familieblad* 1 (Oct.-Nov.), 86; the New York clergyman R.B. Andersen in the December issue; and Professor Anderson in the January, 1880, issue of the same journal.

6. Wist's *Fragments of the History of Immigration* was reprinted in 1906. A note explains that it had first appeared in a "Folkekalender" (Popular Calendar) published by Christian Rasmussen; internal evidence suggests a date before Schøyen's death in 1896.

7. Krogness outlined his plans for a historical society in greater detail in a letter to Johnson 4 March 1884. Earlier letters to Anderson urging him or Langeland to collect material and write a history are 12 Feb. 1880 and 18 May 1881.

8. Langeland's letter (29 Dec. 1883) is in English. Tellingly, he had first written "Emigration" and then crossed out the "E" and added an "I": the perspective should be American, not European!

9. Luth Jæger had been given permission to use Langeland's manuscript for a biographical essay he wrote for *Illustreret Ugeblad* 28 July 1882. Langeland had probably written it in 1872, when for a brief period he was unemployed after *Amerika* merged with *Skandinaven*.

A Pattern of Verse

Verse was the genre closest to the hearts of rural immigrants and most familiar to their ears through folk songs, ballads, and hymns. As soon as newspapers began to appear, immigrants tried to express themselves in halting rhythms and faulty rhymes and sent their efforts to the editors. The many innocuous to bad poems in the newspapers, however, are only a selection of those that were submitted, as suggested by an editorial note in *Emigranten* 5 March 1859. Some years later the editors added a note to "A Ballad Against Liquor": "The title is not very poetic, nor is the song a great work of literature, and on the whole we are opposed to publishing the attempts at verse in which our compatriots are so inclined to give vent to their sorrows, desires, and longings. But regardless of its weaknesses, this song has some good points, and on the urging of the contributor, a respected farmer in Koshkonong, who thought that the poem was as good as an editorial against the liquor devil, we have published it" (1 Feb. 1864). The editors of *Fædrelandet* were threatened by a would-be poet whose verse had been returned: "we receive a disproportionately large amount of poetry and verse, which often has no interest for the majority of our subscribers. We cannot fill our paper with such ballads" (27 Aug. 1865). But many immigrants did cherish these poems and preserved them in scrapbooks. Some contributors of verse, such as the editor of *For Hjemmet* Knut Throndsen (1830–1910), felt encouraged to present their work in a volume. In his preface to *Ørkenblomster* (1890, Desert blossoms) he explained: "We hope the honorable reader will agree that what is written for the people is part of their spiritual property and treasure and should be preserved if it is not without all value; but if it is not retrieved from newspapers and journals where it often lies buried and forgotten, it is lost for posterity and even for the present."

Although the earliest attempts at poetry may be part of the "spiritual property" of *Vesterheimen* there is little reason to retrieve most of this amateurish verse from the pages of the immigrant newspapers. One exception is the anonymous "Emigrantens tilbageblik" (The emigrant looks back) in the third issue of *Nordlyset* in 1847, an interesting expression of the political and nationalistic attitudes of the early immigrant, thinking fondly of the old country even though it kept the poor in bondage and was governed by the rich, and expressing loyalty to the new country that offers freedom and opportunity. There were many variations on this theme, for instance P. L. Mossin's redundantly titled "The Emigrant's Emigration" (*E* 4 June 1852), where emigration is the answer to the problems of the old country, and the freedom of the new home is extolled.[1] On the last day of the year Mossin had a poem "Would You Be Strong and Free?" that combines the themes of temperance and American freedom:

> Remember that if you desire to be free
> Then be free entire and whole.
> For a government you no longer slave;
> Why then slave for the glass and bowl?

With less pretension than most would-be poets, and using the four-line "stev," a stanza used for improvisation in rural Norway, Iver J. Jaastad wrote "Looking Back to Norway" (*E* 21 Jan. 1861). On "the wings of imagination" the poet returns to Norway, not to sentimentalize but to tell his friends and family that they, too, should emigrate, at least if they are poor. In the early poems there is little of the nostalgia that characterizes the later sentimental immigrant songs, epitomized by the still popular anonymous "Kan du glemme gamle Norge?" (Can you forget old Norway?). An exception is J.M.C. Wærenskjold's "A Norseman's Longing for Home" (*E* 19 March 1856). Wærenskjold was educated and belonged to a social class that set him apart from the average rural emigrant, and this is reflected in his more refined and genteel, but no less cliché-ridden imagery and diction.

   The poetry of the early decades is by no means limited to reflections on the immigrant experience. There is much occasional verse, such as poems in praise of the newspaper in which they appear,[2] poems for political candidates,[3] obituary poems,[4] religious verse, and, of course, 17th of May poems in abundance.[5] The emotional and social upheavals of the immigrant experience are factors that may explain why so many people from all stations in life were moved to write poetry and try to have it published.

Emigrant ballads were more current in the old country than in the new one and some of those published in the United States are of Norwegian origin, as for instance "The Emigration to America" (*E* 23 Feb. 1855), or the most widespread of all emigrant ballads, "Farvel du Moder Norge," of which one version may be found in *Budstikken* 11 May 1887.[6] While the representative *emigrant* ballad concentrates on the experience of leaving and on what is left behind, there are also some *immigrant* ballads on the experience of settling in a new country. One such ballad that was widespread in *Vesterheimen* and acquired the status of a folk ballad was "Korlejdes dæ gjek" (How things have gone), also frequently called "Wisconsin-Visen" or the Wisconsin Ballad, apparently written by Syver Holland of Moscow, Wisconsin, in 1873 (and translated by Einar Haugen):

> At the start we had troubles a-plenty
> When we stepped on this far-away strand;
> We heard only a meaningless babble
> When our ears caught the speech of the land.

"Again and again people of various dialect backgrounds learned his poem by heart, and wrote it down without regard to the spelling norm which he had in mind when he wrote it, unconsciously shaping it over into their own forms," Einar Haugen concludes his account of the ballad (1949, 18–19).

Although most poetasters appear only once or twice, some published verse over several decades, suggesting that they took their vocation seriously. One such poet with a long and prolific career was the doctor Johan C. Dundas (1815–1883) in Cambridge, Wisconsin, who first used the name Dass, after the Norwegian baroque poet with whom he claimed kinship and whose meters he sometimes employed. Dundas published verse from his arrival in 1850 to his death, in such journals as the short-lived New York *Skandinaven* (1851–1852), the equally short-lived Chicago *Friheds-Banneret* (1852–1853), *Emigranten*, *Skandinaven*, *Husbibliothek*, *Heimdal* (Chicago), *Den nye tid* (Chicago), and others. While his sense of the formal aspects of poetry, his diction, and his occasionally successful metaphors place him above most contemporaries, his poetic ambition is countered both by a lack of clarity and by a polemical bent that led him into constant controversies. His single separate publication, *Tre digte* (1882, *Three Poems*), demonstrates his weaknesses as well as his moderate gifts and gives instances of the three genres that he mostly employed: nature poems, polemics, and philosophical verse. Some years earlier he had made attempts to have a volume of about

540 pages published by *Skandinaven*, but in spite of the assistance and intervention of R.B. Anderson, Dundas never came to an agreement with the publisher (RBAP). Dundas had studied at several European universities and must have led a lonely life in Cambridge as the village freethinker and rationalist, but among his friends he counted the violinist Ole Bull, in whose praise he wrote many poems.[7] When Ludvig Lima compiled his anthology of Norwegian-American poems in 1903, Dundas was the oldest poet of those whose works he culled from forgotten newspapers.

Rasmus O. Reine (1846–1871) came as a child to America and after elementary school he farmed in Waupaca county, Wisconsin. He was a serious-minded young man with bookish interests, and in the spring of 1868 his poems began to appear in *Fædrelandet*, which later that year merged with *Emigranten*. His first efforts are a poem against alcohol, a nature poem, and a campaign song for Grant. That fall Reine had an intense religious experience and found his true vocation as a writer of hymns and religious verse. "A Christian's Struggle and Victory" (*FogE* 3 Dec.) is a testimony to his conversion; in the few years that remained of his life he published regularly in the newspaper and the Synod monthly, *Kirkelig Maanedstidende*. Reine had to work his farm all day, but would "at dinner and in the evening write down what he had composed for his own edification behind the plow or on the road," the Reverend A. Mikkelsen observed in Reine's obituary in *Kirkelig Maanedstidende*. He was evidently popular and by 1870 he was averaging a poem in each issue of the newspaper. On receiving a new batch of poems the editor assumed "that this will be good news for our readers, for Mr. Reine's poems distinguish themselves now as earlier in being better than the other poems we publish" (25 Aug.). *Fædrelandet og Emigranten* was eager to publish a volume, the preparation of which became the main occupation of the bedridden Reine during his last months.

In his preface to *En liden samling af psalmer og religiøse digte* (1871, A small collection of hymns and religious poems) Reine is appropriately modest: "I am fully aware that these poems are simple and naive and that they can not be compared to the glorious hymns of an earlier age; but I find comfort in that they do not contain more than is taught by the word of God and thus are in harmony with older hymns. I believe that the Church . . . should sing for their Lord with those talents and gifts the Lord gives them, confess his name to the world and celebrate and praise him for his great mercy and grace." Several poems are on the theme of death, judgment, and the after life, as may be expected from a pious man's deathbed:

> Behold the grass is swiftly shorn,
> Its flowers fall to earth,
> For all of us to death were born—
> Of age or close to birth:
> As grass to earth so swiftly falls,
> So God our soul to Heaven calls
> When He our spirit touches. (No. 17)

Reine frequently contemplates the fate of those who meet their Judge and Maker unprepared: "Too late to the door they came, / Knocked on the frame, / Were sent to their eternal shame" (No. 14).[8] With a few exceptions, such as the joyous No. 46, "On a Spring Morning," the message of Reine's late verse is a rather grim and forbidding rendering of the "bright light of pure doctrine" (No. 18) as professed by the Synod. In spite of their quality, the limited scope and harsh doctrine of his hymns do not invite a widespread use in Lutheran congregations today. Indeed, his hymns were not included in contemporary collections and Reine was soon forgotten. His harsh doctrine may be one reason for his neglect, but his disappearance from memory is also an illustration of the transitional character of the immigrant culture.

In the following decades there are several volumes of hymns and religious songs, most by clergymen or lay preachers, such as Andreas Wright's *Turtelduen* (1877, The turtle dove).[9] None, however, has the freshness of the stanzas by the young Wisconsin farmer Rasmus Reine, nor will they be considered in the following pages. Erik L. Petersen's review of Lund and Hoyme's *Harpen* (1880), will do as characterization of them all: "The present collection has a content that is virtually indistinguishable from the many other Harps. As in most volumes of religious songs there is little or no thought of real poetry and formal structure. On the contrary, the material is presented in all its nakedness, and if one is able to rhyme 'hat' with 'cat' and 'door' with 'floor,' it is always possible to assemble some sort of verse which passes for religious poetry. That in the process, all kinds of platitudes, pleonasms, and other rubbish are produced is only to be expected. But then the volume is supposed to serve piety and not taste, so all is as it should be, I must imagine" (*B* 23 Aug. 1881). Happily for compilers and versifiers as well as publishers, the public did not share Petersen's exacting sense of quality and cultivated taste.

While Reine's doctrine may have made his poetry unpalatable, Ulrikka Feldtman Bruun's verse on lofty themes may occasionally invoke risibility.

She began to produce verse on all kinds of occasions soon after her arrival in Chicago in 1874, much of it published in *Skandinaven*, but did not publish her 442-page volume until 1920. On a visit to Norway in 1886 she composed "Farvel til Amerika" (*Sk* 1 Sept.), an interesting expression of an experience shared by many immigrants on departing from their new land. After some stanzas on the gratitude felt to this "haven of freedom" and on the fond memories of America "engraved in our hearts," she wrote: "And now as Norway's coast in all its beauty / For longing eyes arises from the blue, / We realize our love for you is constant / And thank God for our mothers two." Verse was merely one of several weapons in Bruun's lifelong battle for the causes of temperance, women's rights, and pietistic Christianity, and in her versified preface in 1920 she asked that her efforts not be judged by "the measuring stick of art." Surely it would be meaningless to belittle her role in the WCTU and her work as courageous organizer and leader of Hope Mission in Chicago because she was an amateurish versifier.

The most ambitious of the early poets is Nils Kolkin, born in Minnesota of Norwegian parents. He completed his first book manuscript in the spring of 1878 and wrote to Rasmus Anderson from the small Minnesota town of Christiania on March 22: "You may still remember my name. I have fought poverty ever since I last saw you. Now I have been so stupid as to write a verse narrative, like *Fridtjofs Saga*, based on the Dakota legends about Winona. I don't know whether I should have it published. May I send it to you so that you could give me advice?"[10] One should not be misled by his apparent humility: Kolkin's comparison with Tegnér's epic poem is indicative of his ambition. *Winona* was published by *Skandinaven* at the end of the year.

In his introduction Kolkin hopes that "since large numbers of Scandinavians now have settled in Minnesota and Dakota . . . this poem may be a worthy memorial among them of a people on whose land they now live." His slim volume is unique in the literature of *Vesterheimen* as the only book devoted entirely to the Native American. In a series of poems, divided into four books and in a variety of meters, the legend of the Dakota princess Winona is narrated in the conventional nineteenth-century American tradition of sentimentalizing the vanishing Indian. When Kolkin wrote to Anderson on 6 December, asking him to review *Winona*, he added that he was hard at work on a new project. "I am borrowing books from the University of Minnesota and reading all I can come upon in preparation for the work I have mentioned." He had no doubt done similar research for

Winona. Compared to the sentimental Indian portraits and narratives of Freneau, Sarah Wentworth Morton, Bryant, and Longfellow, Kolkin's is no mean achievement. Not only does he handle narrative, characterization, and description well, but he also has a more professional grasp of the craft of poetry than his Norwegian-American contemporaries. Erik L. Petersen criticized him for not using one meter throughout the book, but whether Kolkin in youthful exuberance was trying to demonstrate his mastery of prosody or whether he deliberately wrote a cycle of poems rather than the epic Petersen assumed he had failed to achieve, the result is quite successful. Kolkin's rendering of the legend of the brave warrior Wabasha and his beloved Winona may be in a manner long gone out of style, but it is evidence both of the literary aspirations and the talents of a second-generation American on the agricultural frontier, and of the strength of an immigrant culture capable of attracting a native-born American, giving him the ambition to create poetry in the language of his parents. The limitations of an immigrant culture, however, must be kept in mind when evaluating its achievements. Kolkin's awareness of his potential readers' limited sophistication is suggested by a passage in his introduction: "Since this is a story, I must admonish my friends . . . that they must not leaf through it in search of something to sing, thus doing away with all suspense in content or fancy, but that they should read through it as they would a story. I hope that readers who do not need such an admonition will not take offense." While Kolkin had immersed himself in American as well as Norwegian poetry, he was writing for a public whose main literary fare was homilies and "Harps."

Even though few copies were sold, *Winona* received considerable attention in the press. Anderson hailed it as the first major work of Norwegian poetry in *Vesterheimen* and compared it to *Fridtjofs Saga*: "Had it been written in English rather than in Norwegian, it would have given the author a high status among the poets of this country" (*Sk* 31 Dec.). His praise is a complement to Kolkin's bombastic dedication of *Winona* to Anderson as "friend of Brage" (the Norse god of poetry) but was surely not occasioned by it, for in the 1870s and 1880s it was Anderson's program and inclination to support and encourage all Norwegian-American literary efforts. Petersen, however, had an entirely different view of how a critic should best serve the culture of *Vesterheimen*. Petersen was an enlightened intellectual, conservative (he could not stomach Zola or Dostoyevsky) in some respects, liberal (a staunch supporter of Ibsen and Norwegian realists) in others, and he always insisted on the same high standards for Norwegian-American writers as for others. His review is condescendingly positive: "Mr. Kolkin is not without talent. His verse is pleasant and, with a few exceptions, correct. He has a good ear for rhythm . . . His efforts are praiseworthy, and there is no doubt that given time and diligent studies he will be able to produce better work than this youthful attempt" (*B* 26 Feb. 1879). But most of the review consists of scathingly sarcastic remarks on two side issues. To the academically trained and urbane Petersen—who had pursued a theater career in Norway, had been a Roman Catholic theologian and priest, and now was an Episcopalian minister in Faribault, Minnesota—the intellectual and scholarly pretensions of Anderson, like Kolkin the son of an immigrant farmer, were illustrative of the state of culture and learning in the undeveloped American West. So he ridiculed the innocent and well-intentioned Kolkin for lavishing praise on a mere "accomplished compiler and not unsuccessful translator." But the urbane conservative reserved his sharpest barbs for Kolkin's attempts to reform the Dano-Norwegian literary language, making fun of usage that strikes a present-day reader as good Norwegian, and treating ironically the apotheosis of common, lower-class idioms into poetic language. The fact that hindsight shows both that Anderson played a central role in *Vesterheimen* and that Kolkin's attempts at language reform were in keeping with trends that were to carry the day could not possibly cushion the heavy blows of Petersen's critical sledgehammer. Kolkin was too independent-minded to be easily swayed and politely held his ground in his reply, thanking Petersen for his criticism (5 March), and Petersen, taken in by Kolkin's apparent humility, wrote a new, and decidedly more friendly comment on his work (19 March). Kolkin must have regretted the dedication of his book, for in the long debate that followed, Anderson's status became the main issue, and Kolkin and *Winona* were only an excuse to praise or attack the professor in Madison.

Kolkin's promise came to naught; his intellectual ability was countered by an unbalanced mind. On completing *Winona* he was already at work on a crackpot project involving electromagnetic fluids and the functioning of the brain. His behavior became increasingly odd, he was hospitalized, and then made an unsuccessful attempt to homestead in Dakota Territory.[10] When he again opened correspondence with Anderson, then American minister to Denmark, in the spring of 1888, he had been pondering on *Winona*, which he was convinced *Skandinaven* had reprinted and was profiting by. He sent Anderson a long essay on literary theory and the interpretation of poems, using *Winona* as illustration. He also sent him a new "preface to Winona" where he is still preoccupied with the dedication and the critical debate it had led to. As manuscripts of fiction, scientific experiments, and mystical philosophy, some in English, some in Norwegian, piled up in his sod house and as he brooded on the reception of *Winona*, his homestead remained untilled and was foreclosed for nineteen dollars.[12] Kolkin's contribution and promise were forgotten and he is not referred to in surveys of Norwegian-American literature.

NOTES

1. Revised as "Udvandringen" (The emigration), *Sk* 30 March 1870. Another poem on this theme is H.J.K., "Til Fædrelandet," *Friheds-Banneret* 12 Feb. 1853.

2. For example, B. A. Frøiseth, "Til Nordlyset" (9 Sept. 1847); J.A., "For Emigranten" (30 April 1852), where the would-be poet in conclusion explains that he "is not a poet, merely a farmer"; and the clergyman A. Wright, who presented his versified views on the Norwegian-American press in *Skandinaven* (14 March 1867).

3. "Scandinavian Song for the Coming Presidential Election" (*E* 17 Oct. 1856); "The Battle for Freedom and Equality," a campaign song for James Buchanan (*Den norske Amerikaner* 16 Aug. 1856); D. M. Fuglestad, "On the Occasion of the Presidential Election" (*S* 24 June 1868); Hans Mornes, "For Grant (*S* 8 July 1868).

4. Frøiseth, "Our Little Loved One" (*Nordlyset* 9 March 1848); "Engel Philippa Dietrichson" (*E* 22 Sept. 1854).

5. The first recorded attempt to celebrate the 17th of May in verse was for festivities in Boston in 1856 (see *E* 6 June) and the second was written for soldiers of the Wisconsin 15th, who celebrated Norway's constitution day on 10th Island, Tennessee (*E* 28 July 1862). A third, "Fra en Skandinav i 15de Wisconsin Regiment," is in *F* 7 April 1864.

6. Blegen 1936 and Amundsen 1975 are the two standard collections of Norwegian emigrant ballads. "Farvel du Moder Norge" also exists in Danish, Finnish, and Swedish versions, but seems to be Norwegian in origin (Wright 1983, 11). Another version is in *Husbibliothek* 17 June 1896. "Amerikafeberen" (*S* 20 July 1880) seems to be of Norwegian origin; a different song with the same title is in Amundsen.

7. See, for example, *Sk* 9 Dec. 1868 and 23 March 1870.

8. The originals read: "Se græsset skjæres hastig af, / Dets blomst til jorden falder, / Det minder os om død og grav / I hver en tid og alder: / Som græsset falder ved vor haand, / Saa giver kjødet op sin aand, / Naar herrens aand det rører." And "At du ei skal ved døren staa / Og banke paa / Og bort med evig skjændsel gaa."

9. Wright is also the author of the pious allegory *Gjenløser blandt syndere* (1881, Redeemer among sinners).

10. (RBAP) Kolkin had been Anderson's student at Albion Academy in 1868–1869. In the fall of 1869 he was enrolled in the preparatory class of Augsburg Seminary. See Helland 1920, 44, 57; Hustvedt 1966, 84–85.

11. Kolkin claimed to have been published in a French scientific journal, and in an article on his experiments in *Skandinaven* 11 Sept. 1883, he refers to an article in the *Electrical Review* 25 Nov. 1882. There is a brief note in *Budstikken* 30 March 1887 on

his arrest as he ran down Cedar Avenue in his nightshirt: "During the night he had had a fit of insanity, rushed out of bed, jumped out the window, and right out on the street." The copy of *Winona* at NAHA has a MS note by Skordalsvold on Kolkin's scientific projects, his poverty, instability, and hospitalization.

12. Letters to Anderson 20, 26, and 30 April and 4 May.

7

Staging the
Immigrant Scene

When Erik L. Petersen responded to Nils Kolkin in *Budstikken* (19 March 1879) he observed that his book was especially welcome since so few literary works had yet appeared among the Scandinavians in America. His short list includes Dundas, a volume of verse by the Danish immigrant J. Valdemar Borchsenius, and some "poor plays" by "the artist Anker-Midling, a Mr. Heinse, and Mr. Sommer." Two of these "poor plays" had been hailed by *Skandinaven* as inaugurating a new literature that "at one and the same time represents both American and Scandinavian conditions and ideas." Immigration had reached a stage where an "independent literature" could be supported, and "the special conditions of our life here have already had such influence on us that our nationality may be said to have developed in directions that are different from those of our brothers in our home countries" (30 Nov. 1875). In their different ways, both Petersen and *Skandinaven* were aware that a new literature, including drama, was manifesting itself in *Vesterheimen*.

Neither drama nor the theater was familiar to the majority of immigrants. The theater is an urban institution and most immigrants came from and settled in rural areas. Some, however, settled in cities, and Chicago, followed by Madison, Minneapolis, and St. Paul, soon had sizable Norwegian communities. Churches were their first institutions but these soon had to share the ground with secular societies of various kinds: political, charitable, literary, athletic, musical, and theatrical. There were sporadic attempts to organize theatricals in the 1850s and the earliest recorded dramatic performance was 30 October 1853 in Boston, where a group of amateurs performed a Danish vaudeville in the Boston Theater for an audience of five

Den norske
Dramatiske Forening.

Præsident:—E. S. Howland...Regisseur:—E. Meyel.
Secretair:—J. Warnejs.......Kasserer:—R. Antersen.

Förste Forestilling

gives i

GERMAN HALL

Lørdagen den 28de Marts, 1868.

Til Optorelse kommer:

En Hallingdøl, som Prolog,

udføres af.......... ....Hr. E. Meyel.

Derefter:

Den graae Paletot,

Vaudeville i 1 Akt af Erik Bøgh.

Personerne:

Jægermester v. Scytel............... Mr. Svereland
Holger hans Broersen......... ... .." Warnejs.
Vilhelm Valberg.................... " Meyel.
Clara Holmgaard.... ....Miss Gjertsen.
Assesor Sievert .... Mr. Møller.
Peter, Holgers Oppasser. . ... " Howland.
Melchior, en Jøde................. " Berg.
Strattermester Jesperson.............. " Rojs.
Anette, Claras Pige............. ... Mrs. Warnejs.

Til Slutning:

Soldaterløier,

Sangspil i 1 Akt af Hostrup.

Personerne:

Lange, Godseier.....................Mr. Howland.
Emilie hans Datter................Mrs. Svereland.
Prokurator Barting......... ....Mr. Berg.
Magister Glob, h. Broersen........, ..." Rojs.
Anker, Landskabsmaler .... " Meyel.
Leitnant Vilmer.......................... " Warnejs
Mads Gaartskar........ .... " Møller.
Handlingen foregaar paa Langes Gods.

Program of the first performance of the Norwegian Dramatic Society. Courtesy Norwegian-American Historical Association.

Marcus Thrane (1817–1890).
Courtesy Norwegian-American
Historical Association.

to six hundred Scandinavians (*E* 27 Jan. 1854). In Madison two plays by the Danish J.L. Heiberg were performed in 1859, but with the Civil War such frivolous activities seem to have been suspended. After the war, amateur theatricals became a regular feature of urban immigrant communities. Dramatic societies were organized in Chicago and Minneapolis and these occasionally toured with their productions. Some were commercial theater companies, such as Skandia Theater Company of Chicago, which advertised in the Minneapolis *Budstikken* (for example, 10 Aug. 1892), recommending their productions to Scandinavians who were planning to visit Chicago. A majority of the theatricals advertised in the press, at least outside of Chicago, are ad hoc events. Light comedies and vaudevilles were the main fare.

The first attempt to establish a theatrical company was the Norwegian National Theater organized by Marcus Thrane (1817–1890) in Chicago in 1866–1868.[1] Thrane, a labor leader who came to America in 1864 after serving a prison term in Norway for his political activities, led a restless life in his new country, never concentrating on a single endeavor for any length of time. He started a newspaper in May, 1866, and when he sold out to

Skandinaven by the end of the summer it may be that he wished to give more time to the Norwegian National Theater, which had its first season that fall. For a couple of years Thrane was the manager, director, and playwright of this company. An early notice of the company (*Sk* 15 Nov. 1866), probably penned by Thrane or one of his associates, welcomed it as one of several signs "of the progress of enlightenment and cultivated society among our countrymen." Of the thirty-two plays performed, five were written by Thrane, and he translated and adapted others.

Most of his plays were slight farces, but Thrane also used the theater to present his social views, as in *Skydsskiftet i Hallingdal* (The posting station in Hallingdal), which "used emigration as a theme, but in a nostalgic, sentimental tone" (Leiren 1987, 73). Our only information on *Syttende Mai* (The 17th of May), which dramatizes the immigrant experience as well as Thrane's personal experience of having been rejected by his country, is the reviews in *Emigranten* (25 May 1867) and *Skandinaven* (23 May 1867). The play seems to have been an indictment of the old-world class society in the first act while the second was made up of several improbable love plots. In the first act the conflict grew out of the landowner's opposition to a *husmann* or cotter's determination to celebrate the Norwegian constitution day, the 17th of May, and concluded with the *husmann*, played by a son of the playwright, deciding to emigrate with his family. The reviewer in *Skandinaven*, conscious of the reputation of Thrane as a radical, suggested that the play did not so much criticize "the faults of the [Norwegian] constitution itself as its misuse and neglect." For Carl Solberg in *Emigranten* Thrane's play was a scurrilous attack on "the old mother country." The reviews have little comment on the part of the play set in the United States and Thrane does not seem to have had much to say about the society he lived in apart from suggesting the beneficial effects of immigration to America, for instance by having the one-time *husmann* and his family appear with their faces washed. Their dress as well as their "yankeefied" appearance were further signals of their success.

Several years later Thrane again turned to the theater, inspired by his anti-clerical and rationalistic outlook, with "Holden," performed in Chicago in 1880. Thrane called his play a "Synod Opera" and its satire is vicious, especially considering the fact that everyone in the audience knew who was being satirized. For "Holden" lays bare a current domestic scandal involving the Reverend Bernt J. Muus, whose congregation was in Holden, Minnesota, and his estranged wife Oline. The play's subtitle, which may be translated "Be Patient!" was one of the often quoted tidbits from the well-publicized court proceedings in Minneapolis.[2] Thrane recognized the symbolic significance of the scandal: the theme of his light comedy is the liberation from authoritarian strictures and the breaking down of barriers both within and surrounding the immigrant community. Oline (Thrane bars no holds and uses the real proper names) leaves her husband in defiance of doctrine, and the obligatory young lovers of vaudeville—Ola Nauteby, who to begin with speaks no English even though he is a native of Goodhue county, and the daughter of the German saloonkeeper—are married by a justice of the peace. "Holden" is more a series of loosely connected episodes and songs than a carefully structured play: the character of a newspaper reporter from St. Paul, who to begin with represents an outside point of view on the farcical goings on in Holden, simply disappears from the play.

Neither a summary nor, indeed, the full text can do justice to a Thrane play, which was as much a musical as a dramatic experience. Thrane, whose uncle Waldemar Thrane was a composer, was responsible for the musical scores. His audiences, who were served refreshments during the play and afterwards danced to the music provided by the theater orchestra, seem to have enjoyed themselves. After the first performance of "The 17th of May," *Skandinaven* observed that it was "of great interest for us as Norwegian Americans, and when we consider that the actors still must be regarded as beginners, our readers will probably agree with us in our judgment that the production as a whole was very successful." The Swedish-American journalist Ernst Skarstedt, a close friend of Thrane, reports that "Holden" "in a lively and devastating manner" made fun of "hypocrisy and self-righteousness," and that it had "several entertaining duets with light and catching melodies" (1914, 178).

When Thrane's company ceased in the late winter of 1868 it was succeeded by the Norwegian Dramatic Society, which was active for five years (Wilt and Naeseth 1938). By then theatricals were an established feature of the urban communities of *Vesterheimen*. In Minneapolis the Scandinavian Society, established in 1869, produced many plays, most of them in Norwegian, in the course of its four years. The Scandinavian Dramatic Society of Minneapolis was established in 1870 and produced plays in all three Scandinavian languages in its early years. These dramatic societies had many successors (Skarstedt 262–271).

The quality of the Norwegian-American theater is reflected in the few original plays that were published. One of the efforts referred to by Petersen in *Budstikken, Lidt forstyrrelse paa farmen* (1875, Confusion down on the farm), is a musical comedy by the Danish-American journalist John Heinse; the characters are specified as both Norwegian and Danish, thus requiring a mixed group of actors. The setting is a farm in Wisconsin where several characters, for more or less plausible reasons, are visiting from Chicago. The simple plot is based on mistaken identities and the farmer's prejudice against doctors. Although many novels may be equally inept, they usually relate more meaningfully to immigrant life than the work of Heinse and other early playwrights. One might have expected more of Heinse's contemporary, Julius Anker-Midling, who had had a career on the stages of Bergen and Christiania and been secretary to Henrik Ibsen before he emigrated in 1868. His farce *Under election eller valglivets mysterier* (1875, . . . or the mysteries of political life) makes fun of the political pretensions of a cobbler in Chicago, but does not bear comparison with its model, Ludvig Holberg's eighteenth-century comedy on the same theme, *Den politiske kandestøber* (1723, The political tinker). Even though Anker-Midling's play has few qualities that would interest audiences today, it was a success when produced in 1875, no doubt helped by its thinly disguised references to contemporary events. "Those who are acquainted with the political situation . . . in Chicago," wrote the reviewer for *Skandinaven*, "will recognize the characters" (30 Nov.). A decade later, in Minneapolis, *Budstikken* advertised the production of a new play, *Under Election or Campaigning in Minneapolis* (16 March 1886). The brief description makes clear that this is Anker-Midling's Chicago farce in new and updated local dress even though no acknowledgment is made.

That apparent qualifications from the old world did not necessarily lead to success in the new is also illustrated by another play ridiculing political pretensions, *Politiske røvere* (1885, Political bandits) by Edward Larssen, who had been editor of *Bergens Tidende* before he emigrated in 1868. To Erik L. Petersen, Larssen's play was "immature hodgepodge and senseless trash" (*B* 18 Aug. 1885). Both Larssen and Anker-Midling had been active in the Norwegian Dramatic Society, a fact that may suggest the artistic level of that company in particular and amateur theatricals among the Norwegian immigrants in general.

A third play mentioned by Petersen, *Et sognebud* (1887, A sickbed visit), by a clergyman, Ole Amble, who used the pseudonym "Samuel Sommer," was a verse drama not intended for stage production, attacking the alleged inhumane dogmatism of the Synod. In the play, a doctrinaire clergyman refuses to administer the last sacrament to a dying layman who will not subscribe to the doctrines of the Synod, and a reviewer (*Sk* 2 Oct. 1877) in-

In 1891 L. O. Michelsen, an
actor at the National Stage in
Bergen, performed at Scandia Hall.
Here he plays the title role in the
fourth act of Ibsen's Brand.

sisted that though the situation might seem incredible, it was easily recognizable by those who knew the Synod in Wisconsin. Petersen was as usual primarily concerned with aesthetics and observed that "Mr. Sommer has little understanding of the practical arrangements in a theater" (*FogE* 28 Nov. 1877).

The attempts to move the theater out of the sphere of mere entertainment were few and isolated. What seems to have been the first American Ibsen production was a performance of *Ghosts* by a Dano-Norwegian company in Chicago in May, 1882. *Ghosts* had been published in Copenhagen the year before and *Skandinaven* (30 May 1882) had a long review, placing the play in the context of both literary naturalism and Ibsen's earlier work. The review presents a balanced and intelligent view of Ibsen, especially when compared to the New York reviews when *Ghosts* finally got to that city twelve years later (Øverland 1968). But although the reviewer believed that the theater should show up the faults of society by holding up a mirror before it, he concluded that *Ghosts* was a failure because it did not give "an image of society as a whole but merely presented an example of a situation that, happily, is an exception." There were no other productions of Ibsen or comparable fare in the following seasons. The limitations set by the modest resources of amateur companies should be kept in mind. The production of *Ghosts* must have been a prodigious venture for the clerks, artisans, and professionals who came together after work to rehearse a major dramatic work that even enlightened New York a decade later would find too avant-garde.

Ambitious productions were seldom successful, as may be observed in the brief history of the Norwegian Dramatic Society in Minneapolis in 1878, which Ernst Skarstedt compared to "a blazing rocket that falls down and kills those who launched it" (264). Their attempt to open with a tragedy by the Danish Adam Oehlenschläger proved disastrous and quickly led to the demise of the society. In the fall of 1875 Anderson was asked by Kristofer Janson to be American agent for his new play, *Amerikanske fantasier* (American fantasies), soon to be produced in Bergen. Anderson sent the manuscript to Hallvard Hande, editor of *Norden*, who responded that "it would be a pity to let him out on Chicago's Scandinavian stage, considering its low level. Nor do I think it would be able to give him any royalties worth mentioning, since it is said that they can barely get by from day to day without paying fees to dramatists" (18 Nov. RBAP). Hande was not alone in his low opinion of the immigrant theater: when Petersen reviewed Bjørnson's new play *Geografi og kjærlighed* (*Geography and Love*) (*B* 10 Aug. 1886), he observed that it was beyond the artistic resources of the Norwegian-American theater. Some years later, in a review of Ibsen's *Hedda Gabler*, the Chicago correspondent for *Budstikken* reminded readers that "Last week we expressed the view that the director, Mr. Jacobsen, would hardly be wise in including *Hedda Gabler* in the repertoire of his company, and we believe that the current production demonstrates the correctness of our evaluation of the company's resources" (2 Nov. 1892). For the intellectual challenges of Ibsen and Bjørnson *Vesterheimen* had to depend on publishers like *Skandinaven*, which brought out at least four of Ibsen's plays, and newspapers, where Ibsen and other writers were discussed.[3]

The theater advertisements and brief reviews do not say much about what it may have been like to attend immigrant theatricals. While some were relatively sophisticated affairs for a small urban social elite, most were more like the shows to which Pete brought the wondering Maggie in

Bjørnson's The Newlyweds *performed by the Norwegian Literary Society of Chicago, 1926. Courtesy the Norwegian Literary Society of Chicago.*

Stephen Crane's 1893 novel. In either case they were as much social as cultural events. Most advertisements were for "Theater and Ball." After the actors had taken their bows there was dancing, often far into the night. Indeed, as if this were not sufficient affront to refined sensibilities, refreshments, beer and sandwiches, were served during the performance. This was not a tradition peculiar to *Vesterheimen* but an institution that flourished in the American cities in which they settled. The short-lived Scandinavian Theater Society in Minneapolis (1882–1885), a dedicated group that performed fifty different plays in the course of three years, was no exception to this practice. A reviewer in *Budstikken* (28 March 1883) complained about the custom and concluded: "The society should have too much respect for itself and for its audience to run such a catering business on the floor as well as in the galleries and thus create a disturbance that drowns out all sound from the stage."

The only description of an immigrant theater performance in Norwegian-American fiction may help to explain both why drama did not become a prominent genre and why the intellectuals of *Vesterheimen* never took the theater seriously. Astrid Holm, the unhappy heroine of Drude Janson's *En saloonkeepers datter* (A saloonkeeper's daughter) (1889), longs for a meaningful life in her sordid surroundings in Minneapolis and forms a theater company with some friends. Against their advice she insists that they play Bjørnson, whose name vied with that of Ibsen. Before the curtain rises in Turner Hall one evening after Christmas she understands the skepticism of her friends and the folly of her idealism: for on the other side of the curtain is not an eagerly expectant audience, but a rowdy, boisterous crowd, drinking beer and waiting for the dance to begin. Janson's description of the audience is vicious. She evidently despised this crude and uncultivated society: "At long last the curtain rises. The actors are met with a roar of applause. They begin but they cannot be heard over the laughter and clapping. They start afresh—the same laughter and clapping—and then they continue the play as if unconcerned. Those in the front rows stand up in order to hear; children and women stand on the tables so that they can see over the backs of those who are standing, occasionally throwing angry glances at the disturbers of the peace in the rear. Finally there is a sufficient lull for those close to the stage to hear some of the dialogue" (76). As the curtain rises on the second act, a voice is heard: "We don't understand any of this!" And another responds: "Yes, but the women are pretty." There is jeering when the hero takes the heroine in his arms. As soon as it is over the audience makes the hall ready for dancing: there are no curtain calls.

Drude Janson was not alone in assigning the theater a low status in the immigrant community's intellectual and cultural life: the pulpit, the book, and the newspaper were far more important means of expression than the stage. Since the theater had a setting that was an affront not only to the many who were organized in the largely pietistic churches but also to the small minority with literary and intellectual aspirations, it is not surprising that the theater did not attract many writers and that the few plays that were published were either crude entertainments or, like Amble's effort, intended for reading and not for actual production. The theater notices in the newspapers suggest that a considerable number of vaudevilles and one-act farces were written, only to be forgotten after a few productions for audiences whose critical attention was diverted by the available refreshments and the expectation of the dance to follow. Though dramatic societies and theatricals were a prominent feature of Norwegian-American life in the urban Midwest, they belong more to the social than to the literary history of *Vesterheimen.*

NOTES

1. Leiren 1987 has a chapter on Thrane's work for the theater and gives plot summaries of several of his plays. The MSS of some of Thrane's Chicago plays are in the University Libraries of Bergen and Oslo.

2. The Muus case may be followed week by week in *Budstikken* from 20 Jan. 1880 through 1881, and in scattered later issues. An account of the case is in the memoirs of Mrs. Muus's lawyer, Andreas Ueland 1929, 40–43.

3. Paulson and Bjork 1940 give an account of a literary debate on Ibsen's *A Doll's House* in *Norden* in 1880, two years before the first performance in Milwaukee and ten years before it appeared in Boston and New York (Øverland 1968).

8

Immigrant Fictions:
On Both Sides of the Ocean

Verse was published as soon as the first printing press began to function and original plays were produced as soon as the first amateur theater companies began their activity after the Civil War, but immigrants were more hesitant about writing stories and novels. Newspaper fiction was mostly translated or copied from Norwegian and Danish sources. Not until 1867, when *Fædrelandet* serialized "Pleiedatteren" (The foster daughter) by Julius Monson, the first American novel in Norwegian, did the aborted novel in *Emigranten* in 1858 have a successor.[1]

Monson's narrative technique in "Pleiedatteren" is primitive and naive, but his story about Aagot, the gentle, intelligent, and beautiful daughter of poor parents, who is brought up in the wealthy family of M, and the love between her and the youngest son of the family, Lucidor, and all the complications that arise from this breach of class barriers, has many of the ingredients that were staples of popular fiction in general and immigrant fiction in particular. After Lucidor, home from the sea, has declared his intentions, it is clear that the family cannot accept a union: "Aagot, the poor girl, daughter of the madam's own servant, was more than the sensitive and aristocratic lady could stomach." So the young lovers decide to emigrate even though it is difficult for the gentle Aagot to leave the country where her "blessed mother lies buried." But alas, their plans are not as secret as they believe and as soon as Lucidor has left, expecting to be joined by Aagot, she is whisked away to a family in Trondheim. As might be expected, M fails in business and, further weakened by illness, he relents and tells his son, who now lives in Chicago, where to find Aagot. From Trondheim, however, Lucidor gets the news that Aagot has drowned. We know better, for Aagot has devised a plot by which in secrecy she is able to get passage on a vessel bound for the New World. Here she settles in Chicago and as governess in a wealthy Chicago family she is confronted with her long lost lover and faints in his arms as he exclaims, in English, "Can it be possible, my lost Fostersister from Norway, in Amerika, my God, my God, this is more than I ever expected." His surprise can only be explained by his apparent unfamiliarity with the conventions of popular fiction. The last installment has a postscript: "To be continued in the story of the refugees on Pilot Island, Lake Superior," but nothing came of this, perhaps because the editors preferred to take their stories gratis from Norwegian sources. A few months later, an essay on "Encouragement to Read Good Books and Journals" (5 March 1868) by N.P. Lang, a frequent contributor, warned against "overwrought, poor novels, and reading to pass time," and recommended the autobiography of Benjamin Franklin. But, as the editors of *Fædrelandet og Emigranten* observed 14 January 1869, people needed lighter fare as an "entertaining counterbalance" to the dull realities of life, and Monson's story and similar products served such a purpose.

Monson's novel had little impact on the development of Norwegian-American literature and was soon forgotten. The first separately published novel, the anonymous *Aarsager hvorfor Jens Jensen og hans familie udvandrede til Amerika* (Reasons why Jens Jensen and his family emigrated to America), had a similar fate: even though it had at least two printings, in 1870 and in 1871, there is no reference to it in contemporary sources. Whether this sixty-six-page booklet served its purpose is therefore difficult to judge, but it is safe to say that its purpose was not literary, nor was it to create an "entertaining counterbalance." The full title continues: "Containing Much Useful Advice on How One Leaves Home and the Journey to the United States and Information for Persons who Plan to Settle There." The title page further informs us that the book is "Published for the guidance and benefit of emigrants by a fellow countryman and friend of humanity." *Aarsager hvorfor Jens Jensen og hans familie udvandrede til Amerika* is a promotional pamphlet for the Anchor Line disguised as fiction. Not only does the story demonstrate the advantages of this steamship company over its competitors in the Atlantic trade but the pamphlet includes advertisements, mostly for the Anchor Line but also for the Union Pacific railroad and its Nebraska Land Commissioner.

There is no reason to assume that Monson's story influenced the anonymous writer of the story of Jens Jensen and his family. Shared popular conceptions of fiction and a common immigrant experience made for a narrative formula available to the unlettered writers of *Vesterheimen* from the very beginning. Plot elements that recur in early immigrant stories are the restrictions of a rigid class society, often expressed through a love story; the lack of economic opportunity in the old country; taking leave; the Atlantic crossing; the confusion of arrival (in Quebec or New York's Castle Garden) and the journey to the interior; settling; the experience of a free society, and, usually, social and economic improvement. Not surprisingly, considering the many migrations over vast distances, a favored plot element is the loss and miraculous rediscovery of family members or a lover. These plot elements not only echo the experiences of the audience but were ingredients in many immigrant letters.

Jens Jensen, a farmer, has fallen upon hard times and can no longer support his family. In a conversation with the local storekeeper that reflects the current public debate on emigration, he is advised to sell his farm and leave. A public meeting where the schoolteacher lectures on America is a fictional device for the presentation of twelve pages of practical information. The agitation for emigration causes a conflict with the local officials of state and church and members of the propertied classes but the farmers and cotters are not to be stopped by the voices of officialdom, nor are they, for that matter, duped by the agent for another steamship line, especially after a visiting Norwegian American has talked of his experience. When Jens, his family, and many of their neighbors leave, "the Norwegian family tree lost one of its strongest branches." Agents of the Anchor Line are at hand everywhere and smooth their journey all the way to Wisconsin where they help them to find good land. A young couple who have been separated are joined after the youth had been given up for lost: instead of using the Anchor Line he had gone by sailing ship via Quebec and spent two months crossing the Atlantic! Land is broken, farms are built, and in conclusion Jens writes home encouraging friends to follow.

Before judging this thinly disguised promotional pamphlet too harshly, it would do well to consider that it was written for a semi-literate class of readers. The editors of *For Hjemmet* had a more ambitious editorial policy. Their family journal was aimed at the small group of middle-class immigrants and the growing number who realized that their material success in the New World had created new opportunities for their American children. "Published under the auspices of the Norwegian Synod" (Halvorsen 1903, 225–226), *For Hjemmet* was reviewed favorably by J.A. Ottesen in the Synod's monthly, *Kirkelig Maanedstidende*, in 1871 and recommended for its "wholesome Christian spirit" as well as its educational and entertaining contents. When the editors decided to publish two novels submitted by a parochial-school teacher, Nicolai Severin Hassel, in 1874, they may have been prompted by a sense of responsibility for Norwegian-American literature or they may simply have recognized the potential popularity of an original novel about immigrant life.

Hassel's "Alf Brage; eller skolelæreren i Minnesota" (Alf Brage, or the schoolteacher in Minnesota) and "Rædselsdagene; et norsk billede fra indianerkrigen i Minnesota" (The days of terror: A Norwegian narrative of the Indian wars in Minnesota) are a continuous narrative of the adventures and spiritual development of the hero. The story begins, as do most early fictions, in the Old World, where Alf Brage, after failing to become a merchant in Christiania, decides to emigrate. His life in Norway, his migration, and his first two years in Wisconsin and Illinois are perfunctorily dealt with and then, one November evening, he is presented as the peripatetic "schoolteacher in a Norwegian Lutheran congregation" on "one of the vast prairies of Minnesota" (5). The first novel has two intertwined plots: the machinations of the miserly Eivind Haakensen and the love between Alf Brage and Emma Johnsen. Haakensen is too ridiculous to evoke much fear in the reader and it is also difficult to get emotionally involved in a love story in which Alf proposes by reading aloud the letter where his parents in Norway give him their permission to marry: "'Yes,' she whispered, and he could see that there were tears in her eyes" (84). The narrative, however, is clearly secondary to the author's main purpose, the propagation of the Synod's views on theology, education, and church polity. Blatant improbabilities of plot, like the sudden appearances of a lost uncle, now both wealthy and redeemed, are of less consequence than the edifying lessons they illustrate. The lovers are finally united with the help of his wealthy uncle. Alf is encouraged to seek the ministry, but decides he would serve his fellow immigrants best as a parochial-school teacher.

"Alf Brage" has no conclusion. Indeed, the last chapter, in the traditional manner of serial publication, suggests a new plot and introduces a new character, both to be developed in the sequel, "Rædselsdagene." Hassel improved with practice and the complex plot of the second novel, blending fiction and fact, is relatively well handled. As in "Alf Brage," however, many episodes are pretexts for a discussion of "pure doctrine," and among the less palatable themes is the presentation of the Sioux uprising in 1862 as God's fatherly chastisement of true Christians and His unrelenting punishment of the ungodly: there are remarkably few fatalities among the Lutheran Norwegians while New Ulm, the home of German freethinkers, is devastated.

Hassel's view of God's purpose with Norwegian immigration to America is expressed in a conversation between Alf Brage's uncle and an unnamed Norwegian immigrant: "'Yes,' uncle said, 'when I contemplate how strongly the Norwegian nation is represented here in Minnesota I cannot but regard it as a miracle from God that so few Norwegians have lost their lives during the terrible blood bath we had here ... And I believe that it should encourage us to cling to the pure word and never let go the Word of God and the doctrine of Luther.' 'No,' responded the man, 'neither do I believe that it would benefit us in the long run to exchange the doctrine we were taught as children and our naive faith for the trash of rationalism ... we must hold on to ... our simple Lutheran doctrine and our Norwegian earnestness, our honesty, simplicity and other qualities that we have brought with us from home. Should we let go of this, our children and our descendants will one day hold us responsible and the Lord will have no more use for us here.'" (264) The Puritans were not the only group to come from Europe with a sense of mission.

In "Den gamlesjøulk" (The old tar), serialized in *Fædrelandet og Emigranten* in 1876, Hassel is less concerned with the propagation of doctrine than with telling a tale. The theme of this story of a seaman who appears before his ailing wife in a Norwegian coastal town the moment he is swept overboard in a storm off Scotland is the shortcomings of rationalism in the face of the many inexplicable happenings in human experience.

Educated readers reacted against the awkward narrative as well as the harsh theology of Hassel's novels, and in contemporary debates they were used as evidence that a Norwegian-American literature could not be taken seriously. In 1874, a polemic in *Skandinaven* was more important than Hassel's fiction for the development of cultural self-awareness in *Vesterheimen*. Sven Oftedal had been called from Norway to a chair at Augsburg Seminary in 1873 and immediately become involved in doctrinal as well as cultural disputes in the immigrant community. In a "Public Declaration" (29 Jan. 1874) he and a colleague attacked the Norwegian Synod so severely that even critics of the Synod took offense. Undaunted by the storm he had raised, Oftedal followed up with an attack on Norwegian-American culture (10 March), blaming the sterility of the doctrinal disputes and the "spiritual tyranny" of the Synod for the lack of cultural and political progress among the immigrants. Although Oftedal was repeating views voiced by Rasmus B. Anderson, the American-born Anderson took offense at the supercilious tone of the newcomer and responded on 14 April with a list of Norwegian-American successes—"Figures do not lie!"—concluding that Oftedal "demonstrated a definite contempt for all that has been done for the advancement of the Norwegian-American people." Many joined the fray on both sides and although much of the debate consisted of *ad hominem* rhetoric, there were some valuable contributions to an understanding of the nature of the immigrant culture, notably a two-part essay by Peter Iverslie (21, 28 July) pointing to the gap between the dialects spoken by the immigrants and the language of their churches and schools in America. From a literary point of view, the contribution by the recently arrived Jørgen Jensen (9 June) is of particular interest. He ridiculed Anderson for pointing to church buildings, a college in Iowa, and newspapers as measures of a people's cultural level and explained that the accepted criterion for cultural achievement was the quality of art, science, and literature. Among Norwegian Americans art was non-existent, science was limited to the practical question of how to increase the wheat harvest, and the existence of perhaps one well-edited newspaper could hardly be an indication of cultural achievement. There was, however, actually an "original Norwegian work that is . . . a striking example of what may be published and here we may find a true expression of the spiritual life of our people." He was referring to Hassel's two novels and insinuated that this "terrible botch" was evidence of the editors' low estimation of their readers. After an anonymous contributor had defended *For Hjemmet*, explaining that readers indeed did not have a well developed aesthetic sensibility and that there was little point in having "aesthetic criticism" of magazine fiction because it "merely laid claim to an ephemeral place in literature" (30 June), Jensen returned to clarify his view (18 July): *For Hjemmet* held a high editorial standard and by publishing such poor fiction the editors were doing their uneducated readers as well as literature a disservice.

Critics were justified in their strictures against the poor quality of the literature of the 1870s. It was nevertheless the naive enthusiasm of Anderson, who in the most inept verse and fiction saw evidence of the gestation of a literary culture, that made it possible for him to play the role of midwife. When in 1876 he castigated the readers of *Skandinaven* for their lack of interest in Bernt Askevold's novel *Ragnhild*, Anderson was again met with the argument that a literature represented by the "choleric nonsense" in *For hjemmet* was not worthy of anyone's support (21 Sept.). Anderson did not refer to Hassel, but insisted on a shared responsibility for the encouragement of Norwegian-American literature. When C.M. Hvistendal, a Synod clergyman, wrote favorably of *For Hjemmet* in *Fædrelandet og Emigranten* (10

Feb. 1876), no mention was made of Hassel. Nor did his name appear again in the pages of *For hjemmet*.

For hjemmet also presented the first attempts at fiction and poetry by Bernt Askevold (1846–1926), who was to pursue a modest literary career for the length of his active life, with four novels, some volumes of theology and other non-fiction, short stories, poems, and essays. Askevold, who had emigrated in 1873, was encouraged in his literary ambitions while a student at Luther College in 1874–1875. The editors, who also were his teachers, accepted some poems and stories, and Brynild Anundsen hired him as the first editor of *Decorah-Posten*. Askevold, however, had a vocation for the ministry, taught parochial school in addition to his editorial duties, and was eventually ordained in 1882.[2] His first novel, *Ragnhild* (1876), is a story of his home region in West Norway in a style derived from Bjørnson's popular stories of rural life from the late 1850s. Askevold never seems to have committed himself to America. He planned to move back to Norway as early as 1878,[3] visited several times, and eventually retired there in 1922. While *Trang vei* (1899, The narrow path) is based on his American experience, his two other novels (1888 and 1893) were set and published in Norway.

Ragnhild is the conventional story of the cotter's son, Ola, who falls in love with Ragnhild, the well-to-do farmer's daughter. Unlike the hero of the most popular novel in this genre, H.A. Foss's *The Cotter's Son* (1885), Askevold's hero does not rise by emigrating to America, but by going to school, and the rich farmer is convinced of the hero's worth when he hears him extemporize on the theme of religious belief at a wedding. Askevold's novel was not reviewed and sold poorly, and this cool reception suggests that his story was not of a kind to fire the imaginations of his Americanized countrymen. Nor would *Trang vei*, his only novel with an American setting, endear him to most immigrants: it is a poorly disguised autobiographical jeremiad on parishioners who do not appreciate their pastor. But although Askevold failed to take up the challenge of expressing the immigrant experience in fiction, he must be given credit for writing narratives that were superior in style and structure to the efforts of the other writers of the 1870s. While *Trang vei* is an artistic failure because of Askevold's lack of distance from his material and the sentimental posturing of his hero, it has suggestions of a sophisticated approach to narrative technique that is rare in *Vesterheimen*.

The success of Tellef Grundysen's *Fra begge sider af havet* (1877, From both sides of the ocean) illustrates that even an elementary grasp of narrative technique is not necessary for popular appeal. In spite of its muddled

plot and stilted dialogue, the novel not only got public attention and sold
well for at least two decades, but the author has been hailed as "the first to
break the soil" for a Norwegian-American literature (Larson 1934, 17).
Grundysen came to Fillmore county, Minnesota, as a seven-year-old in 1861
and had no education in Norwegian beyond the few summer weeks in
parochial school. In 1873 he attended a business college in Madison, Wisconsin, and after graduation he was employed for two years in a drugstore in
Decorah, where he and Askevold, unknown to each other, both completed
their novels by the spring of 1875. While Askevold sent his manuscript to
Professor Anderson, Grundysen was a stranger to academia and merely aspired to serialized publication in *Skandinaven*'s new supplement, *Husbibliothek*. It was Anderson who recommended book publication.

As his title suggests, Grundysen, like Monson and the anonymous promoter of the Anchor Line, begins his story in Norway, has his characters
emigrate, and describes their life in the New World. While the two earlier
writers bring their stories to a conclusion after they have brought their
characters across the ocean, Grundysen's descriptions of life in Setesdal and
the ocean crossing function merely as an introduction to the American
plot, which covers two generations. Askevold wrote with nostalgia of life in
his childhood valley, but Grundysen, who could only have had faint memories of the valley he had left as a small child, gave his account of life there a
flavor of the exotic that was tempered by his parents's stories of their difficulties in feeding their growing family. Anne, the heroine, or at least the
main contender for this role in a narrative that often is muddled beyond
comprehension, and Gunnar, the man she marries, are both of the cotter
class. The title also suggests a central theme in the novel: although material
conditions differ, life is essentially the same on both sides of the ocean and
little is gained by the transplantation. The weak, like Gunnar, remain weak,
the evil remain evil, and the good remain good but benefit as little from
their honesty and gentleness in the United States as in Norway. Anne's family is not overly successful in the New World even though her son, who
holds center stage in the concluding chapter, becomes a doctor. His life is
lonely and Anne remains unhappy: the closing sentence shows her
"mourning every day, reflecting on the many and strange events of her life."

A main strand in the American plot evolves from a conspiracy by members of her own family to defraud Anne of her inheritance from her
brother, a casualty of the Civil War. In his preface the modest author had
disclaimed all pretensions of having written a work of literature (*digterværk*)
since he was aware of having committed "too many errors in style as well as

in execution of theme. It may therefore have its greatest value and interest in being based on an actual event." Resenting the praise of Grundysen and his novel in a report from "Red River and Dakota" by K.J. Romland (*Sk* 10 Sep. 1878), Ole A. Lien expressed surprise that anyone from Setesdal "could honor the author of a book where people from Setesdal are described as dishonest people. Here in Fillmore county we still regard ourselves as honest even though the book shows the opposite. Young as well as old intensely dislike these descriptions of the national character since they give a completely false image of the truth, as any person from Setesdal will affirm" (1 Oct). Grundysen's descriptions of life in Setesdal raised the ire of some fellow immigrants, but the main reason for the polemic, which continued in *Skandinaven* for almost a year, was his use of a local scandal in Fillmore county. In his preface Grundysen had, after all, referred to "an actual event." Romland came to his defense (19 Nov.), explaining that Grundysen had not described the people of Setesdal but specific characters. "Here Mr. Grundysen is regarded as an honorable man, a skilled pharmacist, teacher, public speaker, and author ." Moreover, he was now "at work on a new novel in English that would be far superior to his first book." But Lien was not to be daunted so easily, and had eleven of his neighbors sign a statement (31 Dec.) concluding that only the desire to make money could explain why Grundysen wrote the book and *Skandinaven* published it. Later installments in this sub-literary debate did not advance it to a higher level of sophistication. But it serves to illustrate some reasons why Grundysen's awkwardly written novel could attain popularity. Surely the main point is not that he publicized a current scandal, but that he wrote about a world his fellow immigrants recognized and reacted to. The initial motivation for publishing Askevold and Grundysen was the encouragement of a Norwegian-American literature. The success of *Paa begge sider af havet* and the poor sales figures for Askevold's novel may have suggested that profitable publishing of original fiction would depend on the extent to which this fiction addressed itself to the immigrant experience.

NOTES

1. A letter to R. B. Anderson (9 Feb. 1899) from Monson's adopted son Torkel Monson reveals the identity of the author. The letter was found in the issue of *Fædrelandet* at Luther College with the first installment of Monson's story. For information on Monson, see Bagley 1916, 524.

2. Hausberg 1977; Norlie 1922, 436, 447; Wist 1914, 71.

3. See letters to Laur. Larsen June 1878 (LC).

PART FOUR

ᛤ

The Confident Years
1880–1914

Vesterheimen was never very populous. By 1866 — when there were competing newspapers in Chicago and Wisconsin, when commercial publishing
was attempted in Madison, LaCrosse, and Chicago, when books were available in all settlements by mail or colporteurs, when Thrane had formed his
theater company, and when a few idealists were talking of an American literature in Norwegian — fewer than 100,000 Norwegians had entered the
United States. But the rate of immigration was increasing and more than
15,000 had come in 1866 alone. In 1880 the census reported that 181,729
people born in Norway were living in the United States. By then a recognizably Norwegian-American literature had been established: original
works in a variety of genres had appeared, reprints of Scandinavian books
and translations had been published, magazines and newspapers were outlets
for those who wrote verse and fiction or wished to have their views
printed, and reviewers were taking Norwegian-American books for
granted. In the following decades the growth of this literary culture coincided with a peak in immigration. Lovoll has observed that in the fourteen
years between 1880 and 1893, "On the average, 18,900 Norwegians left an-
nually, or ten of every thousand inhabitants," giving "Norway one of the
highest rates of emigration in Europe, surpassed only by Ireland. It culminated in 1882 with 28,804 travelers to America, a number that exceeded the
natural population increase" (1984, 23–26). In 1900 the census reported that
334,388 inhabitants of the United States were Norwegian-born.

In assessing the importance of these numbers, the emigration rate is
not the least important factor. In the towns and rural settlements of the
Midwest, Norwegian immigrants rubbed shoulders with relatives, friends,

and acquaintances from home; in addition to their identity as Norwegian Americans, many felt primary ties to their valley or region of origin. A newspaper like *Visergutten* (1895–1944), first published in Iowa, later in South Dakota, could cater specifically to immigrants from the county surrounding Stavanger in southwestern Norway, and one of the strongest movements for cultural cohesion in *Vesterheimen* was the *bygdelag* movement, beginning around the turn of the century and organizing Norwegian Americans according to the district from which they or their parents came (Lovoll 1975). Because so many left, the ties between the home communities and the midwestern settlements were strong. Although Norwegian Americans were few compared to, for instance, German Americans, their relative strength compared to the sparsely populated home country could strengthen their sense of importance. *Vesterheim* centers in Chicago and Minneapolis were small compared to the considerably larger German-American communities, but not as small and insignificant as Christiania compared to Berlin.

Immigrants returning from visits to the old country brought a sense of achievement and pride in being Norwegian American rather than merely Norwegian back to their midwestern farms. Comparing their spreads with the small holdings of those who had stayed behind and comparing their middle-class comforts and opportunities with the poorer and smaller world of their relatives, they saw no reason to feel inferior. Soon community buildings began to appear in Norwegian valleys financed by the efforts of those who had emigrated. In 1884, when a parliamentary "revolution" in Norway brought about a system like the British, with cabinet ministers responsible to parliament rather than to the king, the main contributions to the budget of the new Liberal Party were from *Vesterheimen*. In their own eyes Norwegian Americans were a successful group and their self-esteem was bolstered by the knowledge that they were growing rapidly.

While growing numbers, concentration in the Midwest, the high emigration rate, and a sense of success were essential conditions for the growth of a Norwegian-American culture, *Vesterheimen*, like all immigrant cultures, was based on pride in roots and devotion to the language, religion, and traditions of the old country. In an article on "The Importance of a Newspaper Literature" in *Budstikken* 18 April 1876, the editor, Paul Hjelm-Hansen, expressed views that were shared by the cultural and intellectual elite of *Vesterheimen*: The future of America depended on "the preservation and development of the vital core imported from abroad. The immigrants must not sever their spiritual ties with those fatherlands they have left behind . . .

The more noble characteristics a nationality has, the greater the loss for America if the immigrant casts them off." Hjelm-Hansen gives equal importance to two kinds of endeavor: preservation and development. At this early stage, however, the majority of immigrants with literary interests would stress the connection with the cultural life of the homeland. The most influential promoter of an American literature in Norwegian in the 1870s, Rasmus B. Anderson, was, it should be noted, a native of Wisconsin.

Gradually the possibility of a literature based in America and not necessarily in harmony with that of Norway was taken for granted, as when B.A. Schmarling concluded a series of two articles on literature (*B* 6 June, 5 July 1876): "We Norwegians in America have not yet advanced beyond the point where we should take our homeland's literature as a model; but that does not mean that we should fail to see its faults. A careful use of the literature of our fatherland is one of the main conditions for a Norwegian-American literature." The implication is that Norwegian literature may not necessarily be in keeping with the cultural development of *Vesterheimen*, and it should be no surprise that Schmarling's cautionary note is a conservative reaction to contemporary realism in the land of Ibsen and Bjørnson.

In correspondence, book reviews, general essays, and editorials the idea of a Norwegian-American literature was taking hold by the end of the 1870s, and the first major statement on the conditions and future development of such a literature was by Bernt Askevold (*B* 14, 21 Nov. 1876). He observed that though the earliest immigrants were few and poorly educated and improvement of their material conditions was their motivation for emigration, the situation had now changed. Not only was the number of Norwegians in America increasing but there were many among them "with knowledge and education and a love of their own nationality." Askevold also noted that communications between the two countries had improved. Consequently there was much greater interest in Norwegian culture. Even though Askevold was atypical in that he was less committed to his new country than most spokesmen for *Vesterheimen*, he nevertheless stressed the importance of a strong ethnic cultural identity in "achieving importance in this country and having some influence on the larger development of America." It was this growing commitment to a Norwegian-American identity that gave Askevold "faith in the possibility of a Norwegian-American literature written in the Norwegian language." While the first few immigrants had had no reason to believe that their language would be able to withstand the pressure of English, the radical increase in immigration from several European countries in the decades that followed made linguistic survival seem not only a possibility but a probability to many by the 1870s. Askevold admitted that the Norwegian language might be entirely displaced by English by the end of the century, but he also found it "not improbable that the Norwegian language could be sustained for centuries, particularly if the Norwegian book trade . . . Norwegian newspapers, associations, societies, schools, libraries, etc. will continue to thrive." When he suggested, however, that the English language in the future would be limited to certain regions of the United States, and that the country would be divided into linguistic regions much like Europe and with German ("the world's foremost civilized language") as a dominant American language, the editor commented in a footnote that "this would probably remain a *pium desideratum.*" Askevold's somewhat fanciful speculations on the linguistic development of the United States, however, are a useful reminder of the optimistic view of language retention in many immigrant groups in a period of increasing immigration. For the inhabitants of *Vesterheimen*, an American literary tradition in Norwegian was no longer merely a possibility but a developing fact.

Many Were Called

The mere availability of printing, publishing, and distribution facilities cannot alone explain the rapid growth of a homespun literature in a culture of transplanted peasants. That so many immigrants should feel called to express themselves in fiction and have their efforts published is an indication of the liberating force of the process of migration. The ambitious Ulrikka Feldtman Bruun (1854–1940), who arrived in Chicago at the age of twenty, is a case in point. She spent a year in college, experienced a pietistic conversion, and found her vocation as a worker and writer in the cause of temperance. After early widowhood she founded Hope Mission in Chicago in 1888, adding to it some years later a home and employment office for Scandinavian working girls. Her active life, constantly on the road campaigning for Norwegian-American temperance societies as well as the WCTU, gave her little time for a sustained literary effort and she would jot down occasional poems on the train or after having retired for the night.[1] Her first book, in 1879, was a tract-like tale of the evils of alcohol, *Menneskets største fiende* (Man's greatest enemy).

Whether because she was ignorant of Chicago publishing or because the community she had left behind still seemed more important than the one she had recently joined, she sent the manuscript to her mother for publication in Norway. To the reviewer in *Illustreret Familieblad* she "demonstrated an uncommon literary talent in describing situations and characters" (July–Aug. 1879). A critic less biased by the desire to encourage talent in the immigrant community would have found little to recommend in this tract that warns its readers not only of the consequences of drinking but also of going to parties and the theater and of taking part in politics. The

Ulrikka Feldtman Bruun
(1854–1940).

inexperienced author is unable to develop a story, and the first part is a series of short admonishing character sketches on the wages of sin and the
power of faith. The second and concluding part concentrates on Rolf
Berge, who is tempted first by a worldly companion and then by the love of
a passionate actress. Brought to his senses and to the faith of his parents, Rolf
announces on Christmas day that he will become a missionary. Bruun's
next effort, *Lykkens nøgle* (The keys to happiness), was published in Chicago
the following year and according to a friendly reviewer in *Skandinaven* this
second novel by "a young servant girl whose only school has been that of
independent thought and experience" was "far superior to the first in both
style and content" (5 Dec. 1982). *Illustreret Familieblad* was enthusiastic, recommending it for its "lively and entertaining style" (Jan. 1880).

Her third and last novel is an interesting illustration of the uneasy relationship in the WCTU between conventional Protestant piety and radical
feminist politics. *Fjendens faldgruber* (The enemy's pitfalls) was published in
Chicago by C. Rasmussen in 1884. In the story of the poor but gifted Karl
who is in love with the equally poor and gifted heroine Ragna, the popular
success story of the cotter's son who rises in life and marries his loyal
beloved is reversed. For while Karl longs to make a good wife of Ragna and
belittles her ambitions because they are unbecoming to a woman, Ragna
rebels against both the individuals and the society that would tie her to

woman's conventional role: "If I am to be chained to the pot, the wash-basin, and the crib," she exclaims, "these mountains shall at least not witness it!" (13) Clearly Karl, who means so well, is in the wrong, and he emigrates. In a society where, as Ragna's mother explains, women are excluded from public life and fathers have no concern for the education of daughters (19), women must rely on each other. After a year at a "folk high school," paid for with her mother's hard-earned savings, Ragna still finds all doors closed to her and she, too, emigrates. Again she is offered the haven of marriage, this time by a Norwegian-American farmer she meets on the boat, but again Ragna refuses a suitor, baffling the well-intentioned farmer with a lecture on the value of independence and freedom (52–54). In Chicago all her endeavors are met with defeat and after several years she is still a housemaid. Then the wealthy wife of a prominent doctor offers to see her through medical school after she had served as their housekeeper for two years at half pay (89–92). But just as Ragna sees life opening up for her, she is struck by illness. In the hospital she is "born again" through the kind ministrations of a woman who brings the word of God to hospital patients. By the time Ragna embarks on her new life as housekeeper for Dr. and Mrs. Pomer and is finally on her way to the education she has longed for, her views have mellowed. She still speaks warmly of women's rights but also of the value of making a good home. Meanwhile, Karl has succeeded in fulfilling his dreams and comes to Chicago as a university professor, where he, as is to be expected, unexpectedly meets Ragna, who discovers that the one-time peasant has also changed his views on the relations between the sexes: in spontaneous verse over three pages Karl speaks of the rights of woman and equality in marriage. Inevitably, they marry and the feminist message boils down to the importance of finding an understanding husband. As Ragna jesuitically explains to the disappointed Dr. Pomer, imprisonment can be freedom (183). In spite of the ambiguity of its conventional conclusion, Bruun's third novel is remarkable for its feminist theme.

Clearly, Bruun was not a literary artist; her novels are tracts and her verse doggerel. Her songs were nevertheless sung at temperance meetings all over the Midwest and *The Enemy's Pitfalls* would have been useful and encouraging reading for young immigrant women of the 1880s. In 1928 she planned to republish her three novels in one volume (Bruun 1928) but she changed her mind, perhaps because she realized that her early novels had become outmoded and would not have been kindly received. If she was at all aware that the literature of *Vesterheimen* had left her behind, she could have comforted herself with having been one of its pioneers.

Although it may be difficult to imagine two writers as different as Ulrikka Bruun and Lars Andreas Stenholt (1850–1911), both came to America
in the hope that their frustrated dreams might be realized. Growing up on a
small tenant farm in the southern section of the same county as Bruun, he
attended a teachers' training college in Tromsø and taught school in the
North until he was fired, whether for political reasons or for some other
kind of scandalous behavior is not clear. He then returned to his home region and tried to make a living as a journalist and author in Ålesund, where
he published two small books in 1880 and 1881. The second, a biography of
the self-taught Sivert Aarflot, is evidence of Stenholt's vision of America as
a land of opportunity: "had he but lived in America, his name would have
shone alongside that of a Franklin, a Washington, a Lincoln, or a Horace
Greeley. It cannot be denied that one of the most attractive aspects of the
American political system is that they are able to utilize talent whether it is
found in the peasant or the estate owner, whether it is housed in the palace
or the cabin" (5). He then moved to the capital and his main project prior
to emigration was a history of Norway in the nineteenth century. Convinced of the high quality of this work, he bitterly accused conservative
academics of conspiring to bar its publication.[2]

In 1882 Stenholt entered the land of Franklin and Greeley, where he became the most prolific, probably the most read, and certainly the most despised writer in Vesterheimen. He lost no time establishing himself as a man
of letters; a few days after his arrival his account of the journey appeared in
Skandinaven (5, 12 Dec.). He contributed articles to newspapers, at times
raising the ire of conservative editors (No 23 Aug. 1883). In order to further
his career he ingratiated himself with Professor Anderson in Madison in
1883, and Anderson, still eager to promote new talent, let him enter the lecture circuit on his coattails. Stenholt supplemented his meager earnings as a
lecturer by contributing notices on the places he visited to Budstikken, signing himself "Spektator."[3] The traits that emerge from the lectures, newspaper articles, and letters of these years are characteristic of the rest of his career: his pretentious claims to learning, his hatred of old-world class
barriers, his time-serving tendency to present whatever view seemed most
advantageous, his unscrupulous use of slander, and his unswerving dedication to a literary career. He lectured on Bjørnstjerne Bjørnson, Henrik
Wergeland, and Sivert Aarflot, on Norwegian history, and on social and political issues. In Decorah, Iowa, he gave pious and ostentatiously learned lectures on temperance, at the same time that "Spektator" was satirizing the
liquor restrictions there in Budstikken (27 Jan. 1885).

His lectures were the point of departure for his first two American books, in 1887: *Mod drik* (Against drink) and *Bjørnstjerne Bjørnson*. Their publication is emblematic of the shift in Stenholt's alliances and career expectations after his first years of vying for acceptance by *Vesterheimen*. The first, a modest volume on temperance in Stenholt's hyperbolic, pretentious style, mildly criticizing the Synod for its opposition to prohibition and praising the Knights of Labor for their support of temperance, was printed by the respectable *Decorah-Posten*. The second was published by the disreputable Waldemar Kriedt, who on arriving in Minneapolis in 1883 had started business as a saloonkeeper before he opened a printing shop and saloon on Washington Avenue in 1885. Two years later he moved next door to *Budstikken* (30 March).[4] Danish by birth, Kriedt, who had been in the book business for some years in Christiania, was the American publisher of the many editions of Stenholt's approximately forty titles, while his brother or cousin in Christiania, Sophus Kriedt, published most of those that appeared in Norway. Waldemar Kriedt, J. Leachman & Son, and Capital Publishing Co. specialized in providing cheap literature to Scandinavian immigrants in the Midwest, distributing their books through newsstands, tobacco shops, and railway vendors. The language of the book would frequently be displayed on the spine: SWEDISH, NORWEGIAN. These books were bought and read by farmers and workers and the business was surely profitable: in several advertisements Kriedt boasted of having sold 40,000 copies of a Stenholt book. But Stenholt made little money from his literary efforts. His changing addresses are in working-class neighborhoods and suggest a social decline in his later years (Andreassen 1977, 14–15).

Stenholt's books may be classified as fiction, popular journalism, popular history, and satire, but these categories may blend and merge in any given book, history being fictionalized, fiction being derived from newspaper stories, and a heavy-handed satire permeating all. In his 1888 *Chicago anarkisterne* the many references to Norwegian-American newspapers suggest that the author still had to rely on information available in Norwegian. While Stenholt seems to sympathize with the accused anarchists, his attitude tends to shift with his sources. Other titles that popularize current events are *Sitting Bull* (1891), subtitled "Scenes from the last Indian war," *Pullman, Debs og Coxey* (1895), *Amerika's kamp med Spanien* (1898, America's war with Spain), *Præsident Wm. McKinley* (1901), and the posthumous *John F. Deitz* (1912), with the long subtitle, "The battle of Deitz and his family against the lumber kings for the property rights to the Camron Dam on the Thornapple River in Wisconsin: A contemporary drama from Wisconsin."

A glance at two books in this genre will illustrate Stenholt's general sympathies. In *Fra farmergut til millionær* (1893, From farmer's boy to millionaire) the biography of Jay Gould is framed by opening reflections on inequality and concluding, moralizing remarks in the vein of: "Would that the children of America could draw a lesson from this life, so rich in banditry but poor in great and noble traits" (97). Stenholt seems to have moved to the left toward the end of his career, but it is difficult to determine whether the shift reflects his own convictions, his assumptions of what would sell, or the nature of his sources. Compared to his early book on the Chicago Anarchists, his 1908 book on class conflict, *Arbeidets martyrer samt deres bødler . . .* (The martyrs of labor and their hangmen James McParland and Orchard & Co), subtitled "A historical account of the tragedy in Boise, Idaho," has a marked leftist stance. Stenholt may appear pretentious in his preface, but this is typical of his style and does not necessarily reflect on his sincerity: "I have never been as involved in the writing of a book as with this one. The foul deed of the capital interests against the three innocent men ignited a flame in my soul that only death will be able to quench." His heroes are Charles Moyer, William Haywood, and George Pettibone, and his villains the Pinkertons, the tools of capital; he is quite militant in his concluding remarks in Chapter 10 on the growth of American capitalism and the consequent unavoidable class war.

When evaluating Stenholt's crude novelistic technique, his sententiousness, and his naive references to sources, the large and unlettered audience of these books should be considered: for many immigrants Stenholt was their only introduction to American affairs and the closest they ever came to literature. It is more difficult, however, to point to redeeming qualities in Stenholt's many attempts to cash in on current scandals and criminal cases. The earliest, *Dr. Cronins mord* (The murder of Dr. Cronin) (1890), is typically prefaced by remarks on the value of the jury trial system, while the account of a violent murder and sensational trial wallows in detailed and gory descriptions. 1895 was a good year for murder cases and the newspapers provided Stenholt with material for four books published the following year: *Durrant* (subtitled "A true narrative of the terrible double murder in the Immanuel Church of San Francisco"), *Hayward og Blixt* (subtitled "A historical account of the murder of Katharina Ging"), *Harry Hayward's bekjendelser* (Harry Hayward's confessions), subtitled: Written and dictated by himself just before he was hanged, and *Massemorderen Holmes* (Holmes the mass murderer). A later book on celebrated criminal cases departs from the usual wallowing in gore: *L.A. Stenholt's politihistorier* (1903, Police stories), a slightly fictionalized account of corruption in Minneapolis, is a call for action against corrupt politicians and has a pretentious concluding chapter where he discusses the American constitution and the possibility of reform.

Although Stenholt often urges integration with American society, he never achieved mastery of the English language and remained preoccupied with life in *Vesterheimen*. This preoccupation can surface in the most unexpected contexts, as in his book on the James and Younger brothers where he somewhat speciously links the bandits with the conservative theologians of the German Missouri Synod and the Norwegian Synod who argued that slavery was not a sin.[5] His ranting against these theologians, based on a dispute that was buried long before he himself had arrived in the United States, may seem out of place in a popular book about bandits, but is typical of the tone and approach of his many books that satirize and scandalize his fellow Norwegian Americans, in particular the clergy. For instance, *Præsten Erik* (1889, The Reverend Erik) and *Præste-historier* (1893, Tales of the clergy), make merciless fun of the well-known story of a Christiania schoolteacher who duped the professors of Luther College and was ordained by the Synod. A pamphlet published in 1900, *Prest Erik Jensen: Den forenede kirkes arvefiende* (The Reverend Erik Jensen, the arch-enemy of the United Church), shows that Stenholt had discovered an 1882 satire by Marcus Thrane, *The Wisconsin Bible*; the following year Stenholt published *Minnesota-bibelen for 1901* subtitled A sequel to the Wisconsin Bible. But even though they may have seemed clever to a contemporary audience, the humor and wit of both Thrane's and Stenholt's "biblical" works depend too closely on intimate knowledge of long forgotten issues and personalities to be much enjoyed today. In his most vicious exploitation of ecclesiastical scandal *Falk og jødinden* (1901, Falk and the Jewess), a thinly disguised narrative based on allegations of misconduct against the popular Minneapolis clergyman M. Falk Gjertsen, Stenholt writes with greater success than usual. The clergy were the most frequent butts of Stenholt's satires, but he also paid his compliments to medical practitioners (1905) and dishonest businessmen (1907) in the immigrant community. His 1908 book on Rasmus Anderson, *Paven i Madison* (The pope in Madison), is no harsher in tone than the frequent polemics by his querulous subject, and Stenholt gives a fair survey of Anderson's career and changing alliances.

Stenholt's historical books are his most ambitious works, but even the friendliest appraisal reveals them to be mere potboilers, compilations from various sources, as for instance *Nordmændenes opdagelse af Amerika* (1893, The Norsemen's discovery of America). Stenholt was always quick to respond to current events and his account of Norway's declaration of independence from the Swedish monarch in 1905, *Det frie Norge*, appeared that year but is marred by his crude fictional devices and anti-Swedish prejudices. No less prejudiced is his 1897 history of Norwegians in America, *Norge i Amerika*. He has hardly researched his topic, and pontifications and digressions serve to space out an otherwise thin account. The introduction claims the "common man" to be his main theme as historian, but there is no consistent ideology in the book: throughout, he gives vent to prejudices, airs pet ideas, and talks about himself. The same criticism could be made of his biography of the Minnesota senator Knute Nelson (1896). The opening pages are an essay on immigration and class antagonism, and a self-defense against accusations that he has cast dirt on his people. The second chapter ("In the cabin in Voss") is a pastiche of the popular *Husmands-gutten* by H.A. Foss, the well-known fiction supplying the clichés through which "reality" is rendered, and the recorded "facts" of this particular case explaining the popularity (and realism) of the fiction. In the story of Knute Nelson Stenholt evidently saw a parallel to the story of his own rise from obscure poverty in Norway to becoming a writer in America. As biography it is superficial work: Stenholt had little source material at his disposal and the many digressions are necessary padding.

There is little to admire in Stenholt—his vituperative personal attacks, his prejudices, his crude style, his hackwork posing as scholarship—and it is difficult to like the strident and pretentious personality revealed in his style. Yet, the sheer force of his ambition to become an author, the forty or so titles he wrote in twenty-four years, makes some demand on our attention. A few books suggest that given other conditions, Stenholt might have become a better writer than he appears in most of the books he set his name to. One is *Fangen paa Djevleøen. Alfred Dreyfus. Et billede af nutidens største sørgespil* (1900, The prisoner on Devil's Island, Alfred Dreyfus: A scene from the greatest tragedy of our time), which seems a sincere attempt to write a compassionate account. Like all his documentaries, this one, too, makes use of novelistic techniques and constructed dialogue, but with considerable success.[6]

Stenholt's best book, and with 352 pages also his longest, is the novel *Tyve aar paa farten efter lykken* (1905, Twenty years in search of success), subtitled "An interesting and didactic tale of the remarkable adventures of Karl Johnson and his tempestuous career in search of happiness." The protagonist's one great principle in life is never to work for others, only for himself (292). Starting out in his teens, Karl's career as an itinerant salesman and trader is a series of modest successes and major disasters. His travels take him through most of the Upper Midwest, and while horse-trading is an avocation that usually leaves him empty-handed, his own brand of furniture polish helps him through hard times. His rhetorical gifts get him out of more than one tight spot, and he makes several appearances as an auctioneer. After the disastrous end of each episode he returns home, where his mother is furious and his stepfather full of understanding and ready to give him a helping hand for a new start. Eventually he achieves modest success and sufficient capital to set himself up in the wholesale jewelry business in Minneapolis, whereupon Karl Johnson and his family live happily ever after. Many episodes are in the tradition of the Western tall tale, but Karl also has traits in common with the Ashlad character of Norwegian folk tales. *Tyve aar paa farten efter lykken* is an intelligent and entertaining parody of the American success story and concludes with the expression of pious gratitude to his parents and ironic platitudes on how hard work and diligence are the only road to success. It is unique among Stenholt's books and probably the only one worth resuscitation.

A subplot, with the protagonist as colporteur of Norwegian-American books, is set among the elite of *Vesterheimen* and is a vehicle for Stenholt's disgust with the pretensions and aspirations of Norwegian-American culture. The medical profession is again up for attack in the character of Ole Winge (146), but most of Stenholt's venom is reserved for the writers of *Vesterheimen*, many of whom are parodied. Special ridicule is piled on the amateur historian Martin Ulvestad (in the character of Ole Bjørneby) and jibes are made at Peter Hendrichsen (as Paul Krabbe, who writes books on "farming and animal husbandry although he had never touched a plow nor milked a cow"), Wilhelm Pettersen (as Professor Wilhelm Lynne), Peer Strømme (as the "brilliant" Per Krake), Ole A. Buslett (as Truls Poulsen, "the great wise man in the Wisconsin forest"), and R.B. Anderson (as "the famous intellectual giant, Rasmus Kvelve," 179–210, 299–308). Stenholt could safely attack his colleagues since it would have appeared to him that they had conspired never to review him or even to mention his name in print. While the most inane published pieties were given attention in the press, and the faintest suspicion of a lurking talent brought forth encouraging praise, Stenholt seldom saw a review of his work. In literary history, the voice of the people, however good for sales, has a less godlike ring than the voice of the critic.

In his 1908 book on R.B. Anderson he refers to himself as "a minor writer" (104). He takes issue with Anderson for having tagged him "a Bohème writer," an epithet he does not deserve. "I must admit, however, that I have been a razor.[7] In my modest way I have castigated what is wrong, hollow, and empty, and I must also admit that my books have gained acceptance among our people" (105). Not among his peers, however. Waldemar Ager wrote condescendingly of Stenholt in an essay on Norwegian-American literature where he observed, not without resentment, that he was the only writer to make a living, albeit a poor one, by his pen: "More copies of his books were sold than of all the other Norwegian-American authors put together. It must be said in defense of Stenholt, as he lies in his cheap coffin, that he tried to write proper books but that neither his public nor his publisher would have them" (Wist 1914, 296). Buslett, in a polemical exchange in December, 1922, with John Heitmann in *Duluth Skandinav*, used Stenholt as an instance of the lowest depths to which the culture of *Vesterheimen* had stooped, suggesting that he practiced blackmail, scandalizing in print those who would not pay him or befriend him.[8] Such is also the vicious portrait of Stenholt as Bolwarius Lyvenfelt, in Johannes B. Wist's satirical novel of immigrant life in Minneapolis, *Nykommerbilleder* (1920, Newcomer sketches), who sits with his beer and writes myopically in the rear of the print shop of Franz Jeppesen. Lyvenfelt is portrayed as a man without any principles, who will libel anyone in writing if he is only paid properly. In order to get the most recent scandal off the press as quickly as possible, the writer and the printer work hand in hand (70–73, 90–93). The only contemporary voice heard in praise of Stenholt belongs to a writer who also had an uneasy relationship with the cultural establishment of *Vesterheimen*, Knut Teigen. In the Swedish-American journal *Forskaren*, he called Stenholt "the most hated, despised, and persecuted by the elite, but also the most read and loved Norwegian author in America among common people. This I know because of my travels far and wide last summer. In the cabins of small farms, in the residences of large farms and cities, almost everywhere I found one or more of Stenholt's popular works." Indeed, when he had tried to present the establishment view of Stenholt as "Waldemar Kriedt's corrupt hack and day laborer" people had protested because they loved him, "not so much for his style and literary artistry, but for his sincere and all pervasive hatred of hypocrites and liars as well as for his moral courage in telling all refined rogues the unvarnished truth" (April 1909, 140).

His death 31 December 1911 in the Minneapolis City Hospital was barely noticed. *Skandinaven* had a thirty-five-word obituary that did not identify him as an author (10 Jan.), and *Decorah-Posten* observed that "he has also written several books that he peddled himself and that therefore were read by many" (9 Jan.). Ager in *Reform* was more generous and noted that Stenholt's books "will always have a place in our history" as "illustrations of how far we had come in our cultural development in the first decades of the twentieth century. For it is a fact that these books sold while books of considerable literary value remained unsold." Ager's obituary portrays Stenholt as a literary talent whose growth was stunted by the cultural level of his society (9 Jan.). Now that the cheap paper of the few remaining copies of his books is brittle and the establishment view has prevailed, it may be time to remember Stenholt as one of the most dedicated and diligent workers in the literature of *Vesterheimen*.

An underbrush of books and magazines that are quickly forgotten is perhaps necessary for the growth of more substantial literary timber. While a retrospective view tends to take in that select group of authors and titles that make up the canon of a culture, the forgotten ones are often those that were most visible and most read in their own time. For the literary historian it is therefore important to place the Bruuns and Stenholts in the total picture. And there were many such calling for the immigrants' attention. That so many clergymen, lay preachers, and temperance workers used fiction to attract followers and exhort them is further evidence that the reading of fiction was widespread by the end of the century. A representative work in this category is *Billeder fra Dødens Dal* (1899, Scenes from the valley of death) by the itinerant temperance agitator Engebret Løbeck, who also had a volume of sentimental songs, *Forglemmigei* (1894, Forget-me-not), which he would sing to the "mild and soft harmonies of the guitar," as he put it in one of his songs (3). As could be expected, the novel holds forth on the evils of alcohol.

A genre all to itself is the story of the clergyman and his congregation, for instance the previously mentioned *Trang vei* (1899) by Bernt Askevold, *Unge Helgesen* (1911, The young Helgesen) by Peer Strømme, and Waldemar Ager's *Kristus for Pilatus* (1910, *Christ Before Pilate*), the best novel in this genre. Minor contributions are Bernt B. Haugan's *Et besøg hos presten* (1895, A visit to the minister), where a major issue in the congregation is prohibition, favored by the young and a succession of young clergymen, and opposed by the old-line lay leaders; Ole Shefveland's *Pastor Gram* (1899), a moralizing tract on a pastor's conflicts with his congregation and his final apotheosis; and Mons Pedersen Gjerde's *Kamp og seier* (1900, Battle and victory), another tract on the awakening of a congregation and the power of prayer.[9]

Pietism or, more particularly, an anti-authoritarian religiosity with roots

in late eighteenth-century Norway and the work of the lay preacher Hans
Nielsen Hauge was a motivating force behind much immigrant literature.
The work of Ulrikka Bruun was merely one of many examples. Marie
Bang's *Livets alvor* (1901, The solemnity of life), with most of its melodramatic action set in Sogndal, Norway, has an implied liberalizing message
simply by being a novel by a rural woman writing for her peers. A male
character of the educated upper classes turns out to be the villain, doing his
best to corrupt and seduce the heroine, who eventually comes to her own
people in Minnesota, where she teaches in a parochial school and experiences a conversion. *Livets alvor* departs from the expectations of sentimental
melodrama in having the heroine place piety above love and reject the
young man she has loved for many years because he does not share her faith.

The blend of populism and pietism is more pronounced in two novels
by Knut Birkeland (1857–1925), who had completed teachers' training college before emigrating in 1882 and then served a few years as a clergyman.
In *Han kommer* (1895, He is coming) and its sequel *Farlige mænd* (1896, Dangerous men) emigration is a response to class conflict, and liberalism, populism, and pietism are closely related. In the second volume this affinity is
recognized by an avowed freethinker who turns to religion but retains his
liberal politics and his opposition to the state church. In Minnesota the social conflict from home is continued in the congregational conflicts between adherents of the Synod and the Free Church, with which the author
was affiliated. In spite of its obvious weaknesses—characters who are introduced only to be forgotten and unbridged gaps between the Norwegian
and Minnesotan plots—Birkeland's novels are interesting documents of
how some saw their exodus as a socioreligious movement. A populist interpretation of immigration is also implied in Embret Martinson's *Sigmund
Framnæs* (1895). Although the last page promises a sequel taking the hero to
America, it never materialized. A more pietistic version of this populist
view of immigration is suggested in the popular juvenile novel, *Taale Tangen*
(1892), by the clergyman Ole Nilsen (1844–1933), where the young hero,
who has the call to become a missionary, finds that for such as he there is no
possibility of education in Norway, and emigrates. "It is strange," said Taale.
"Once more it is as if the doors close on me here at home, and once again
America is suggested to me" (56), implying that immigration is God's will.
The preface underlines this theme, explaining that the book will first show
young readers "life in the homeland as seen by your father and mother" and
then take them "to your own blessed America." The populist objectives in
these works are achieved by immigration.

More politically explicit and sophisticated, and also critical of the social system of his adopted country, is Lars Heiberg, who emigrated in the early 1880s and became a clergyman in the low-church Hauge Synod. In one of several letters to O. A. Buslett in the fall of 1893 he describes himself as a pietist, conservative in religion but socialist in politics (24 Oct., OABP). In the spring of 1892 he had been active in both roles, agitating in North Dakota for the populist Independent ticket and preaching on Sundays in the local Hauge church (Foss 1922, 62–63). Although he could be a perceptive critic (19 Sept., OABP), there is a striking disparity between the sentimental platitudes of his verse and fiction in *Brogede blade. Et socialt-kristeligt agitationsskrift* (1893, Multicolored leaves: A book of Social-Christian agitation) and the sophisticated arguments of his essays on social and political issues that make up most of the book. With titles like "Liberty, Equality and Brotherhood," some essays point to Christianity as a liberating political force and in "Christianity and Politics" he quotes at length from the social gospel theologian George D. Herron. Heiberg discusses major reform issues of the day: "Women's Rights," "Prohibition," and "Pacifism." Although most immigrants would concur in a moderate criticism of the social and political system of the country they had left, they did not readily find fault with the country they had chosen in order to improve their lot. Writing to Buslett 24 October 1893, Heiberg complained that he had sold only 700 copies of his book and still owed a couple of hundred dollars on it, blaming the newspapers for their silence and the clergy and politicians for their attacks. Ironically, the one theologian who praised his book and wrote in support of his political views was the Unitarian Kristofer Janson, who held Heiberg's book up as an example for other Lutheran clergymen in his journal *Saamanden* (Aug. 1893), but refrained from commenting on his pietism.

Two writers who shared Heiberg's political views published their work through Waldemar Kriedt and were thus outside the sphere where the views of clergy or other establishment figures mattered. Albert Jacobson's *Fremskridtets kamp: Eller, indgangen til "det tusindaarige rige"* (1896, The battle for progress. or, the entrance to the millennium) is surely one of the strangest of Norwegian-American books, with enough stories and plots for half a dozen or so novels. Except for the introductory chapter, where the manuscript of the book that follows is found in the Yukon, the novel is set in a northern county of Norway. While the concoction of plots is difficult to follow, the political, moral, and religious ideas for which the plots are vehicles are coherent and intelligently developed. The essence of these ideas is presented in a dream vision of the future narrated by an ancient and dying

prophet, and it is in particular this section, obviously inspired by the futuris-
tic fantasies of Ignatius Donnelly and Edward Bellamy, that makes Jacobson's *Fremskridtets kamp* a representative American novel in spite of its Norwegian setting.

Less concerned with political ideology, but no less populist in spirit, is
Gunnar Kleven's *De splidagtige* (1898, The contentious). The author subtitled his book of four stories "A contemporary novel from both sides of the
ocean" and he may have had ambitious intentions of thematic coherence.
Two stories have the same narrator-protagonist, an independent-minded
farmer, and are set in Norway. In the first, "A disastrous horse trade," the
complicated series of trades is quite entertainingly told and brings to mind
the relish with which William Faulkner could let similar plots unfold. In
both stories the protagonist is taken to court but gets the better of his opponent while the representatives of authority appear ridiculous. A good sense
of humor permeates the third, one of the few instances of fantasy fiction:
"Talatta's most beautiful adventure. Or an expedition to the North Pole in
the beginning of this millennium. Told in the manner of a fairy tale."[10] The
fourth story brings us to this side of the ocean: an account of the adventures
of Ole and Martin, who, after being cheated by several Intelligence Offices
(that is, employment bureaus), make their way as tramps from Arkansas back
to Minneapolis. Social criticism is integrated in an entertaining narrative;
the exploitation of the poor is exposed and those in power shown to be
cold-hearted and cruel, but there is no sentimental moralizing, not even in
an episode called "The whore in St. Louis."

Storytelling was Kleven's main objective, and this desire to write fictions
and present them to their fellow immigrants was shared by many from different walks of life. But few would have seen it as a way of making a living:
best sellers were rare in *Vesterheimen*. When one did appear, such as Allan
Sætre's popular 1883 narrative of the good Marit Kjølseth and her adventures in Chicago, it is difficult to say whether the author or the publisher
profited from its twenty-four editions.[11] Sætre was a journalist with *Skandinaven* and had translated several books. In 1882 he concocted a dual language
*English and Scandinavian Conversationalist. A Collection of Familiar Words,
Phrases, Sayings, Dialogues &c. Especially Adapted to the Use of the American
Housewife and the Scandinavian Servant as a Book of Reference*. Here both servant and housewife could supposedly communicate with the assistance of a
collection of phrases ("Is breakfast ready?" "No? Well hurry up.") and a series of imagined dialogues—such as "Between a Lady and a Girl Wanting a
Place" and "Between Mistress and Servant Girl." These sketches, revealing of

the servant-master relationship encountered by so many immigrant women in American cities, may have appealed to Sætre's sense of the ridiculous and inspired him to write the comedy of the good-hearted Marit Kjølseth who leaves her family farm in Wisconsin to help her niece and her family who have fallen upon hard times in Chicago. There she is exposed to the puzzling ways of the city but comes out right in the end, thanks to her benevolence and common sense, and brings her niece's family back to the farm.

The popularity of Sætre's work is underscored by the attempt of Gudbrand Hagen, editor of the newspaper *Vesterheimen,* to cash in on it twenty years later with *Per Kjølseth, eller Manden til Marit* (1903), or "Marit's husband," subtitled "The funniest book since Marit visited Chicago." In *Smuler,* Ole S. Hervin claimed that the main blemish of the book, apart from its language, which "was not really Norwegian," was the author's need to "preach an artificial and old-fashioned Populism which is out of place in a book designed to entertain" (Nov. 1903). Hagen's political satire takes over and he is unable to reproduce Sætre's naively entertaining and low-keyed narrative style. Per eventually gets to Washington where, as a loyal Republican, he has a standing invitation to visit the President, and on his return home, his political future is ensured and the book concludes with his election to Congress.

Another comic novel from this period deserves mention for its style, Sever Severson's *Dei møttes ved Utica* (1892, They met near Utica), a series of episodes previously serialized in the Wisconsin newspaper *Normannen* and subtitled "A description of life in the older Norwegian-American settlements based on personal observations."[12] Severson (1840–1897) was two years old when he came to Muskego in 1842 and did not begin writing for publication until he was about fifty. Yet he claims to write a "pure Telemark" dialect, spurning *Landsmaal* as a constructed language. His dialect, however, was rooted in Wisconsin and abounds in Americanisms.[13] In a succession of brief episodes calamities are piled on Per, but he and his friends survive unscathed by the tragedies, conspiracies, and mishaps they are exposed to, not unlike the characters in the comic strip "Han Ola og han Per" by Peter Rosendahl in *Decorah-Posten.*

Comic novels that take their American setting for granted and do not ponder what it means to be a Norwegian American are evidence of the Americanization of *Vesterheimen.* A similar adaptation to the American setting may be observed in the melodramatic stories in the Danish-American Carl Hansen's *Præriens børn* (1896, Children of the prairie) and is particularly pronounced in novels that are far removed from the world of *Vester-*

heimen, as for instance Emil Hirsch's *Jagt og rejseeventyr i Montana* (1886, Hunting and travel adventures in Montana), a comic western with a greenhorn narrator. Even further afield is the work of Olaf T. Kvam, who published his novel of Alaskan adventure, *En fremsynt* (A clairvoyant), in San Francisco in 1892. The author seems inspired by Jack London, without being much affected by his style or narrative technique. The plot hinges on the suspicion that the Norwegian-American hero has murdered the half-brother of the Norwegian-American-Russian-Indian heroine, and bliss follows a melodramatic revelation of confused identities. But such an easy and unquestioning acceptance of an American existence with no backward glance at the old country was not shared by the majority of those who sought expression through fiction, and the both-sides-of-the-ocean story remained typical of the fiction of this period.[14]

The anonymous *Fagerlierne* (1888) has chapter titles emblematic of the immigrant experience. The first three tell the story of emigration and settlement: "At Home," "The Outward Journey" and "Out There." The concluding two suggest the process of acquiring new roots: the chapter about a return to what was "home" in the first chapter is called "In the Old Home," and the place first thought of as "Out There" eventually becomes "The New Home." Both homes have the name Fagerlien; thus the title *Fagerlierne* (The two Fagerliens). The novel opens with an attack of the America fever in a rural community. Among the many who leave are the two heroes, Einar, who is serious and hardworking, and Knut, who is lively but lazy; they are engaged to two sisters who have promised to wait. Melodrama is ensured by a cast of characters that includes a minister, a self-righteous lay preacher, a devious moneylender, a thief, and an escaped murderer. But this motley crew are also used to illustrate what it takes to make it in the New World and what kinds of characters are welcome future citizens of America: America needs all who are willing to do manual work and will reward them well! In addition to the standard ingredients of the immigrant novel (taking land, working on threshing teams and for lumber companies, battling a snowstorm on the plains), *Fagerlierne* also has the makings of a Western: a mysterious deputy sheriff (who turns out to be the escaped murderer) bent on tracking down a gang of horse thieves (among them the Norwegian thief), who have a secret hangout with an underground passageway and stable. There is much riding, posses on the trail, gunfights, a lynching, and a tar-and-feathering before the bad are either killed or have to return to Norway, realizing that America is not for them. A snowstorm has cured the lay preacher of his self-righteousness and chastised Knut, who loses a leg and an arm but acquires the attitude necessary to success. When the two heroes finally return to Norway to get their brides they can bring them back to a flourishing farm and mill in Minnesota: now there is a "Fagerlien" on both sides of the ocean.

A more ambitious and didactic but less entertaining instance of the both-sides-of-the-ocean genre is *Mor Hansen* (1900) by A.B. Pedersen. Here, as in Foss's celebrated *Husmands-gutten*, America is mainly where you prove yourself; most of the action of this rural novel of manners is laid to a Norwegian valley, to which the hero and his beloved return. In affirming the new land as home by describing it in the language of the old, the majority of the writers of *Vesterheimen* were involved in an undertaking better represented by *Fagerlierne* and the protagonists' pride in their new home in America than by Pedersen's appeals to nostalgia.

NOTES

1. An account of her work in the field is in Foss 1923. The WCTU was in effect nativist, and Bruun was accepted in a limited role as a worker among immigrants. In *The Union Signal* she was condescendingly commended for toiling "in the midst of the foreign population . . . in a part of the city that swarms with saloons and every other iniquity" (Lovoll 1988, 126).

2. 10 Feb. 1885 he wrote a spiteful and bombastic letter to R. Monrad, a teacher at Luther College, placing the main blame on his father, the influential professor of philosophy Marcus Monrad. "But when I am dead my manuscript will be placed in the [Oslo] University Library and will remain there as evidence of what Professor Monrad . . . understands of history" (Ole Glesne Papers, NAHA).

3. Letters to Anderson 17 May, 13 and 30 Nov. 1883 (RBAP). Two notices in *B* 21 Oct. 1884, one of them by Stenholt himself, give accounts of two lectures he had given in Rushford, Minnesota, the second on a program where Anderson was the main event.

4. The Minneapolis city directory gives information on the changing addresses of Kriedt and his businesses.

5. *To banditter. James og Younger brødrenes bedrifter* (1897). In 1905 he added a supplement on the Younger Brothers, also published separately in 1906 as well as bound with two other books as *Tre udvalgte fortællinger* (n.d.). The comments on theologians are in this supplement.

6. The Dreyfus book seems at odds with the anti-Semitic jibes that turn up in Stenholt's work, but a mindless anti-Semitism was very much a part of his cultural context.

7. The Norwegian "Ragekniv," meaning razor, is a misinterpretation of the similar-sounding English word "rake" as in "muckraker."

8. Clipping in OERP. In earlier years Buslett had been more kindly inclined, as may be seen in *Rolf Hagen* (1893, 105).

9. Shefveland (1863–1933) published a second novel on a similar theme, *Marit Gjeldaker*, in 1924. Rølvaag, whose review was not accepted by *Lutheraneren*, reacted strongly to this plotless tract promoting a self-righteous, conservative Lutheranism. This sub-genre has been identified and described by Hustvedt (1990).

10. Except for the work of Buslett, there is only one other comparable text, Ole Hustoft's collection of fantasy fiction, *Taktmesteren og andre eventyr* (1916). His style has an oral, folk-tale quality. The best story is "The Rusty Key," where an apparently valueless key is rejected by a series of important people until a youth listens to its voice and returns it to the King, where it is discovered to be the key to peace and love.

11. *Bondekonen Maret Kjølseths erfaringer i Chicago*. The narrative of a woman ignorant of the mysteries of city life and her adventures during a brief stay in the Garden City, was published by *Skandinaven*. Although it was reprinted many times—the 1918 edition claims to be the twenty-fourth—Sætre may not have benefited from his popularity. He had neglected to acquire copyright and it was claimed in 1894 by Sealand Publishing Co., perhaps spurring the author to get it for himself for the 1899 edition.

12. Dating is problematic. While the title page has 1892 and the preface is dated that year, the concluding biographical essay on the author mentions his death in 1897. The print type changes toward the end of the book, suggesting that although printing may have begun in 1892, it was completed later.

13. As in the opening sentence: "Han Ola o han Per dei møttes i Utica, som æ ein Krosveg, den eine bærte te Staaten aa den andre te Edgerton." The phonetic spelling of "Staaten" for Stoughton is also typical of Severson's style.

14. Indeed, a number of fictions concern themselves entirely with life in the Old World, for instance Amund Jensen's two stories based on his memories of his native region, Hedemark: *Kommersraaden* and *Greven*. His book was sold, the cover tells us, in "Mrs. A. Jensens Restaurant, Elizabeth, Minn. eller i Johnsons Apothek, Fergus Falls, Minn.," suggesting some of the unconventional ways in which books were distributed.

Ole Amundsen Buslett:
Romantic Idealist from Wisconsin

"He has seen more and larger visions and has dreamt more and wilder
dreams than anyone among us."

(PEER STRØMME 1923, 341)

Ole Amundsen Buslett's (1855–1924) literary gifts were not commensurate
with his ambitions.[1] Nor were his gifts cultivated and his critical intellect
systematically trained. He had four years of rural elementary school in Norway before coming with his parents to Iola, Wisconsin, at the age of thirteen, where he immediately began to work, on farms and in lumber camps.
He read what he came upon, laying the ground for that blend of idiosyn-
crasy and stubborn conviction so often the hallmark of the autodidact.
Buslett was twenty-six when a lecture by Professor Rasmus B. Anderson inspired him to become a writer; he sold the boardinghouse he and his wife
had started the year before and went to Madison in the spring of 1882 to
work for a few months on the University grounds and receive tutelage from
the encouraging professor who also served as go-between when *Skandinaven* printed his first manuscripts.[2]

Looking back on his life in 1922, Buslett dates his intellectual awakening
to that summer when he wrote his first books. His young imagination was
fired by the romanticized version of Norse mythology taught by Anderson,
by the romantic poetry of Henrik Wergeland, by the early work of Ibsen
and Bjørnson, by a sentimentalized nationalism that had grown from the
memories and dreams of his Norwegian childhood, and by an inflated vision of the poet's calling: "The sacrifice of poetry, which I have thrown to a
materialistic people, was no sacrifice. To sacrifice my life and my time in

Ole Amundsen Buslett
(1855–1924).

this manner was my desire and my delight," Buslett wrote in 1922 (*Buslett's* 1: 3–4). He made little effort, however, to address himself to the immediate concerns of his "materialistic people." Nor did his early work have qualities that would have excited the rare experienced reader. Even the enthusiastic Anderson was restrained in his praise of Buslett's first volume of verse (1882): "The contents are so good that it is my duty to tell you that you must make a careful study of versification, rhyme, etc., so that the poems may also be perfect from a formal point of view" (OABP). Buslett had written these poems before he came to Madison; a short novel, *Fram!* (1882, Forward), and a narrative poem *Skaars skjæbne* (1883, Skaar's fate), were written that summer; a verse drama, *De to veivisere* (The two guides), was written in the fall but not published till 1885, the same year as *Øistein og Nora*, written in 1883. Even though these books are slim, they represent an impressive burst of creativity for a young lumberjack and boardinghouse keeper.

Fram! has a plot with potential popularity: the son of the poor cotter loves the unattainable daughter of the wealthy farmer. When the hero goes out into the world, she promises to wait. The evil machinations of an undeserving suitor bring her family down in life. Meanwhile the hero acquires a fortune in America and returns just in time to purchase the mortgaged farm and marry his faithful loved one. The story is well-known among those familiar with *Vesterheimen*—not because Buslett wrote it in *Fram!* but because H.A. Foss wrote it, four years later, in *Husmands-gutten*. Foss's novel became an instant and long-lasting success, while Buslett's had little impact in spite of an encouraging review by Erik L. Petersen, who hailed him as "a future Norwegian-American writer" (*B* 21 Feb. 1883). Anderson was enthusiastic, urging "all who have any interest in the cultural development of Norwegian Americans to give him a friendly hand" (*Sk* 9 Jan.). But there is good reason why Foss achieved popularity with his version while Buslett did not. Both concocted improbable plots, both wrote wooden dialogue and both, influenced but barely inspired by Bjørnson, gave their characters poorly written verse to sing at inappropriate times. Buslett, however, shows no interest in character: in his seventy-five pages, compared to Foss's 278, he merely gives a rough outline, telling what happened to his characters rather than letting his readers get to know them so that they could take interest in them. The basic theme of both is America as a land of success for the diligent and lucky, but while Foss's transcending message is one of social criticism, Buslett's is one of romantic idealism: his hero is a model for youth who want to go "Forward."

Buslett's idealism as well as his bent for melodrama is evident in the narrative poem about the fate of Einar Skaar, a young immigrant who has just cleared a few fields in the Wisconsin forest, married and had a daughter when he volunteers to serve in the Wisconsin 15th at the outbreak of the Civil War. He shows great bravery, is promoted, survives heavy wounds, and escapes from the horrors of Andersonville, but on returning home he finds his fields unkept, his cabin burned, and a dying wife who expires in his arms. He lives out the rest of his years caring for his farm and his daughter.

His Civil War narrative is also a vehicle for a nationalistic romantic idealism that is at the center of his next two works. In a letter to Anderson 29 January 1884 Buslett describes *Øistein og Nora* as an allegorical poem and his concept of allegory is suggested in his 1922 reflections on his early years where he explains that he had written "what he saw and what he thought between the lines of *Øistein og Nora*" (3: 6). It is one of Buslett's pet conceits that he wrote between the lines, but his intended allegory is not expressed in the imagery, characterization, or narrative of *Øistein og Nora*; there is no objective correlative in the text. Nora may be intended as a personification of Norway and Øistein of the Norwegian patriot, with Øistein eventually

returning to a Nora free of her oppressive and conservative clergyman father (the civil servant class) as well as of her devious and foreign bride-
groom (the Swedish monarchy), but the melodramatic text lends little support to such a reading.

Buslett's message in *De to veivisere* is less obscure. The action is set on and
near a mountain, a sort of Norwegian Olympus, on which the son of
Brage, Old Norse god of poetry, resides in a grove with his council of six
women and six men. The valley below is controlled by the representatives
of materialism, corruption, and a dead religion. Attempting to climb the
mountain is Jørgen, the idealistic poet, urged on by Idun, the no less idealistic woman who often stands on higher ground than that achieved by Jørgen. Voices offer comments on Jørgen's climbing as he slides and falls because of his poor judgment, wavering faith, and inclination to take short
cuts. In the central third act of *De to veivisere*, Jørgen, who has married Idun
but given up getting to the top of the mountain, has settled for a village
cabin and the role of social critic. Digging among boulders, he finds the
skeleton of a king, and Idun, urged by a mystical voice, tries to convince
him to let the bones be. Despite Idun's constant admonitions Jørgen goes
about his lowly ways, becomes a drunk, and writes his magnum opus, "The
King," an example of what Buslett thought of as decadent naturalism.
When Jørgen is arrested and stands trial for writing disrespectfully of king
and country, his defense is partly that of poetic license and partly the claim
that the criticism of social ills is the main aim of poetry: "For vice is simply
a device / To stop the spread and growth of vice; / A mirror where we all
may see / And fear our own depravity." Digging up the skeleton is thus emblematic of the naturalist writer's program. In *Sagastolen* (1908, The saga
seat) the narrator is told he is blind if he does not see that "we have dug up
what was hidden in the night of history," and responds: "You may have dug
up skeletons but what of the spirit?" (89) After prison Jørgen continues on
his self-destructive path with only faint attempts to heed the voice of the
still loving Idun and eventually he dies, expressing remorse, in her arms.
The last act concludes with the apotheosis of Idun: her wedding with Brage
who has pronounced that love of man and of nation must be the true basis
for poetry. Anderson, then American consul in Copenhagen, piled immediate and lavish praise on the author: "I hope that all educated Norwegians in
America will take the trouble to read your book" (24 Aug. 1885). But most
of the 1,000 copies printed (21 July 1884, OABP) remained unsold.

In the meantime Buslett had published two verse dramas, a comedy and
a tragedy (both in 1890), and a volume of poetry (1891), and in 1892 he

began his short and unsuccessful career as newspaper publisher and editor, first of *Varden*, then, in 1893, of *Folkevennen*, and, finally, of *Normanden*, the first two in La Crosse, the third beginning in Stoughton and concluding its brief history in Madison in the spring of 1896. Although it left him disappointed, his newspaper experience brought him out of his self-imposed isolation and, as suggested by Hustvedt, the obligation "to write for an average reader" may have had a beneficial influence on his prose style (1980, 139). His 1893 novel, *Rolf Hagen*, first serialized in *Varden*, seems designed for a popular audience, with murder, theft, false accusations, gypsies, intricate family relations, a commune with free love and, of course, a happy ending promising bliss for hero and heroine. The only other work he completed during his three newspaper years is a voluminous history of the Wisconsin 15th Infantry Regiment (1894).

Buslett had begun work on an ambitious novel inspired by midwestern politics and the many utopian fictions of the time, but with the demise of *Normanden* in March, 1896, he ceased to function as a professional writer: "he broke down and wept and pledged that never again would he leave his beloved north woods" (Hustvedt 1980, 138). When he made his first efforts to break out of his isolation in 1900, it was Waldemar Ager who provided the main encouragement. When Buslett wrote to Ager complaining that he had been forgotten by the inhabitants of *Vesterheimen* who, moreover, looked down upon all attempts to create an independent literature, Ager tried to wake him from his despondent state, affirming his own faith in "the health of our people" and welcoming Buslett as a contributor to his weekly newspaper *Reform* (13 Feb. OABP). Buslett's awakening found expression in ideas for a writers' association, a literary journal, and a publishing society, but mainly in contributions to *Reform* and, to a lesser degree, *Skandinaven*. The years 1904 and 1905 were a turning point. Not only was there a marked increase in his contributions to *Reform* and other newspapers, but Buslett was invited to contribute to several new journals, among them the monthly *Vor Tid*, edited by Peer Strømme. Here Buslett announced that Norwegian-American literature was entering a new age and was "ready for the art of bards and for men in the saga seat" (1904, 104). He had literally left the "saga seat" nine years earlier when he had shelved his projected novel and published a fragment as *Torstein in nybygden* (1897, Torstein in the settlement). Now he took his place there again: on 2 May 1905 *Reform* began the serialization of "A chapter of 'In the saga seat,' an unpublished novel by O.A. Buslett." But it took him another three years to complete the novel. *Vor Tid* had wanted more from his pen, and Buslett complied with a series of sketches of pioneer life (Nov. 1906 to Feb. 1907). He also completed the satirical poems "Frelserne" (Our saviors) for O.S. Hervin's monthly, *Smuler*. "Just give us publishers and critics and a literature will not be far behind," Buslett had concluded his 1904 essay on "The conditions for a Norwegian-American literature," and with the many requests for contributions it would seem that the first prerequisite was about to be filled. *Skandinaven* and its supplement *Husbibliothek* accepted whatever Buslett submitted, and Ager solicited a story for the first volume of *Kvartalskrift* (22 Nov. 1905, OABP).

Finally, in 1908, his long-delayed novel, *Sagastolen* (The saga seat), subtitled "A novel of Norwegian North America," was published by *Skandinaven*. The publishers, however, were not quite sure what kind of book they had on their hands. "Who shall we ask to review it?" they wrote to the author. "Couldn't you give us an anonymous review or write a somewhat more extensive explanation of the book's content and theme than the present preface?" (2 Feb. 1909) The preface admits that the book was not of the kind mostly read by Norwegian Americans: "The book has an ideological purpose [is a *Tendensskrift*]; under the narrative form lie social issues that are becoming more and more important in our time" (5). Buslett was again practicing "writing between the lines," and he evidently confused his publisher as well as most of his readers.

The novel has three very different parts. The first, Buslett claims in his preface, is about "those aspects of Norwegian-American life that he knows best and, in part, has experienced himself." In the opening pages the narrator, Olav Busterud, zooms in on the landscape and people of a central Wisconsin Norwegian settlement and on the character whose story is the focus of the first part, Torstein Aasen. This is essentially a story of faithful love, concluding with the marriage of Torstein. Influenced by the utopian fictions in vogue in the late nineteenth century, the novel then departs from realism and turns into an anti-utopian narrative, describing the organization of a revolutionary association among young farmers (the Red Club) and their attempt to establish a socialist colony, "Bygdom" (The settlements). Here the narrator's son and Torstein's stepdaughter play central roles, the former admitting: "I, too, was a socialist . . . Now . . . I am an individualist; no more of *Bygdom* for me" (189). The brief concluding part begins with a vision of a future utopia. Gigantic cuts through the Rocky Mountains have changed the climate of the arid West, where an ostrich-like electrical contraption serves as a universal carrier and tractor on land and in the air and where each township has a public temple at its center for all communal functions. The family is universally respected and the individual farmer has the highest status in society. This vision, however, wanders off in a repetitive, verbose essay presenting a romantic vision of the universe, God, man, and creation. While the first part illustrates the values that are destroyed by Buslett's negative version of socialism in the second, the concluding part presents Buslett's metaphysical foundation for the ethics propounded in the first two. It is not so difficult to see the author's intentions, but *Sagastolen* is nevertheless a rambling and cranky book.

Ager praised *Sagastolen* as "a valuable contribution to our literature" (*Kv* April 1909), pointing to the descriptions of pioneer life rather than the story of political conspiracy and the utopian visions. A reviewer in the Chicago *Idun* is full of respect for Buslett as one of the fathers of Norwegian-American literature but regards this "careless and flawed" novel as a product of a defective literary culture: such an author "must be an autodidact whose contemporaries have not even paid him sufficient attention to lend him a helping or chastising hand" (164).

A poet is the central character and the poet's vocation the main theme of Buslett's next work, *I Parnassets lunde* (1911, In the groves of Parnassus), a strange, fairy-tale-like story, with spirits and trolls. The plot is the conventional triangle: Jakob, the hero, is torn between the dark lady, Sylfie, and the light lady, Konvallen (Lily of the Valley), and he is first ensnared by the sexuality of the former. However, as Sylfie is ennobled by motherhood, Konvallen is corrupted by her father's schemes. The spirits of Jakob's dead parents keep watch and Jakob and Sylfie are finally united as their son plays music on their wedding day. The allegory suggests Buslett's recognition of the life-denying impulses of his earlier idealism, which set pure spirit above a more earthy realism, and his new awareness of the need to merge the ideal and the material, the spirit and the flesh. Ager did not make much sense of the book: "Your poetic offspring fly rather high for the Norwegian American" (8 March, OABP).

The synthesis suggested by *I Parnassets lunde* seems to have been his intention with his next novel, *Benedictus og Jacobus*, which he sent to *Skandinaven* in August, 1911. The initial response was positive, but after the publishers had read the manuscript, subtitled "A story of some Norwegian citizens of Wisconsin who have been influential in private and public life," they decided not to touch it because of its slanderous attacks on recognizable individuals (25 Aug. 5, 8, 9 Sept. OABP). Buslett, long active in local politics, had become more ambitious and had been elected state representative in 1909. When he ran for the state senate the following year, however, he was defeated and left politics, as he had left newspaper publishing, convinced that his failure was due to the machinations of others. The novel in which Buslett took revenge on his political enemies was eventually published in 1920 by Ager's *Fremad*, but may as well have been kept in the author's files. The two parts, the one on Benedictus, the clown turned idealist-poet-film director-preacher, and the one on Jacobus, the scoundrel forger-swindler-conspirator-politician, are not integrated and do not function as portraits of contrasting characters since neither is sufficiently developed to gain the reader's interest.

Buslett's next venture into utopian political fiction was *Glans-om-Sol og hans folks historie* (1912, Splendor-of-Sun and the story of his people), a companion piece to *Sagastolen*. While the earlier novel was set in the Midwest of the present and near future, *Glans-om-Sol* is fantasy fiction: Buslett has created an alternate world with its own history, religion, and culture, with a family as bearers of apparently long-forgotten Judeo-Christian ideals. The basic message of the novel, however, is about the Midwest of the 1890s: the populist conviction that the gold standard is the root of social evil. Ager, ever supportive of the efforts of his colleagues, wrote encouragingly to Buslett, but doubted that many readers in *Vesterheimen* would be able to understand his new novel (14 May, OABP). Jon Norstog in *Eidsvold,* however, had no problem in seeing that the society of *Glans-om-Sol* is "a mirror of our gold-thirsty and spiritually impoverished age."

John, his wife, and his daughter are shipwrecked on the shores of a primitive society where gold, in the figure of an immense golden ox — Splendor-of-Sun — is worshiped and where all effort goes into the mining of gold and the manufacture of golden objects given as gifts to Splendor-of-Sun and his priests and used for the purchase of women. Widowed, John and his daughter are exiled to an island off the coast because their Christian faith makes them a threat to social stability. Eventually, a successful revolution topples the power of the priesthood and destroys Splendor-of-Sun. A utopian society is established on agrarian and egalitarian principles according to the advice and teaching of Old John (78–90). Central to the new society is a year of jubilee, and as Book Two opens, the first fifty-year period of the new society is nearing its end and there is much agitation for a return to gold mining. While the older worship of Splendor-of-Sun was religiously inspired, the present movement is based on a self-serving worship of gold. The coup fails, but the country becomes a subject outpost governed by a powerful nation referred to as the "homeland." Or, to read "between the lines": the United States, weakened by internal strife, is dominated by Britain. As in some of his other books, women are bearers of value and tradition. In Book

Three the people rise, inspired by the vision of the old prophet and led by his granddaughter Agate and her daughter. Eventually, the people are victorious. But there can be no final victory over the evil represented by the golden calf. The author's postscript concludes: "No terrible destruction has yet defeated him; no prophet has yet won over him; Splendor-of-Sun haunts the world, will always haunt the world!" For once, a summary cannot do justice to a Buslett novel: the plots are well managed and the characters engaging, and the ideas are rooted in both. Not only is there suspense to compel the reader to keep turning the pages, but the descriptions of the changing economic and political systems of this imaginary world are in themselves essential to a reader's enjoyment of the novel. *Glans-om-Sol* not only compares favorably to other turn-of-the-century utopian and anti-utopian fictions, but is an interesting contribution to fantasy fiction.

That it should take thirty years for Buslett to produce a satisfactory work of fiction speaks more of the conditions under which he worked than of his potential as a writer. Not only was he without any formal training, but he was seldom met with constructive and informed criticism. Writing in 1904 to Kristian Prestgard in *Decorah-Posten*, Buslett thanked him for the careful criticism he had offered of a poem he had submitted to the newspaper: "This is the very kind of criticism we need in this country. What we get is either bland praise or ignorant attacks." Without criticism, he concluded, "we will not have a real literature."[3] In response to some deserved criticism in *Smuler* June, 1911, Buslett responded in August: "this is just what we Norwegian Americans lack." He had needed more than the few summer months of study with Anderson to learn the writer's trade, but toward the end of his career Buslett wrote works that make his long period of gestation worthwhile. One of these, *Veien til Golden Gate* (The road to the Golden Gate), was published in 1915.

In 1913 he had submitted " —Og de solgte ut" (—And they sold out) to Augsburg's Christmas annual, *Jul i Vesterheimen*. The editor, Anders Sundheim, found it both "interesting and suitable" (6 June 1913, OABP), and asked for a contribution for 1915 (18 Feb. 1915). Buslett had two stories, a conventional tale of an immigrant unfit for life in America, and an allegory on multi-culturalism. Sending the latter to Rølvaag, Buslett received both the encouragement and the constructive criticism he needed: send it to Sundheim, Rølvaag concluded his long letter (10 May 1915, OABP). Sundheim, however, felt forced to prefer the alternative, "Butt og Bøle" (Bucket and chest.). "I liked your story," he wrote to Buslett. "This is the pure, unadulterated truth and I wish I could have used it in *Jul i Vesterheimen*. But

I cannot! It would have been useless suicide" (10 June). He explained that the Augsburg board would have regarded it as "an obvious misuse of my position. I have published a few with a similar theme, but your account is so devastatingly powerful, in spite of its beautiful and engaging style, that I fear it would cause a terrible storm."

Veien til Golden Gate is a response to the pressures of Americanization and a clear statement of the cultural program of transitional pluralism that Buslett shared with his younger contemporaries, Waldemar Ager and Ole Rølvaag. It has the typographical appearance of a story but is in the dramatic mode favored by Buslett. The opening stage set has "a sunny day and bright skies over Vesterheimen" with settlements and towns suggested to the right, the western prairie to the left, and a road in the foreground going past "a small log cabin built in Norwegian style and protected by a grove of large firs."[4] This is the road from Castle Garden (which for earlier immigration is the equivalent of Ellis Island) to the Golden Gate, from one end of the continent to the other but also into the Promised Land. Walking westward on the road are Rosalita, the protagonist, and her father, who is about to leave his daughter on the doorstep of the small house, the home of Kristiane Hellevei and her son Haakon. Rosalita's father is one of the Norwegian Americans Buslett had castigated in " — Og de solgte ut": he has acquired the Yankee's restlessness and sold one homestead after the other, constantly moving farther west, leaving his wife and two children behind in graves in as many states. Rosalita is an idealistic and steadfast character like Idun in *De to veivisere*, and in Haakon she finds a no less staunch and clearminded companion, one who can give her instinctive conviction that "no one should sell his home" an ideological underpinning.

The dramatic conflict is created by three road commissioners who want to redirect the road that runs past the Hellevei homestead. As Haakon explains, it is not merely the piece of road that runs through their farm that is at stake: their aim is to "change the direction of our entire road — all the way from Castle Garden to the Golden Gate!" Not only will the projected road bypass all that the immigrants have built in America, "the churches we have raised . . . the crosses on our graves, and all our dear and bitter memories for which we have paid so high a price," but it will lead right into the "Yankee Slough" where it will sink. The swamp is Buslett's version of the melting pot, the place where all ethnic characteristics will disappear, and the commissioners are the ethnic spokesmen for integration. Rosalita suggests that they may become Yankees by entering the Slough, but Haakon responds, "They'll all become alike." Of course, Haakon explains, "All the people of *Vesterheimen* are Americans," and he accepts that some of his people may become Yankees. But he is as opposed to any pressure to redirect "the road that my forefathers have constructed and traveled on" as he is to the nostalgic dream of the road back across the ocean, which his mother points to. In their attempts to convince the three of the inevitability of the new and straight road from Castle Garden to Golden Gate, the commissioners appeal to Haakon's interests and reason, to the dignity of his mother, and to the love and devotion of Rosalita. Haakon, however, insists that all they will achieve by straightening the road is "to get to the Golden Gate a few days before those of us who travel along the road used by our fathers." The two alternatives, as put by the commissioners, are the old French, German, or Norwegian roads and a common road for all nationalities that will go right through the Yankee Slough. After the commissioners have left, Rosalita and Haakon climb a hill close to the road where they study the swamp and the land surrounding it through a pair of binoculars, observing the beauty of the Norwegian road and land as well as the German and French lying close to the borders of the swamp. One day, Haakon foresees, the swamp will be filled, and it will be a land wonderful beyond conceiving, but it will not be a "Yankee Slough": "many have property rights that extend into the slough and the settlements will expand on their waste deposits." From the hill, they see the road commissioners disappear in the swamp and they pledge their love and their decision to "go together on our old road— to the Golden Gate."

Reviewing the story, Ager found it difficult to understand (*Kv* Jan. 1916). Rølvaag, on the other hand, had advised Buslett to delete all explicit statements in the text, letting the symbols of "road" and "slough" speak for themselves. While Buslett's two colleagues may have been far apart in literary sophistication, they were in full agreement with the cultural program outlined in Buslett's allegory. Along with Ager's *On the Road to the Melting Pot* (1917) and Rølvaag's *Their Fathers' God* (1931), Buslett's *Veien til Golden Gate* is a major fictional statement on the ideology of multi-culturalism in the literature of *Vesterheimen.*

Throughout his more than forty-year career as a writer Buslett aspired to be a poet. He used verse in narratives as well as in drama and the collection of poems he published in 1891 was a large volume of 279 pages. His preface, however, speaks modestly of his efforts, admitting that "The poems, if I may use such a resounding name for these rhymes and songs, are defective in style and form and many of them should have been excluded." While the quality of his prose writing improves with time, his verse remains lifeless and has unintended comic effects, bathos, and inappropriate metaphors and symbols. While he seems to have had no ear for rhyme or rhythm in poetry, his ear for Norwegian-American speech rhythms, however, is evident in the prose of his later years.

In his 1891 volume there is a poem, "The Wisconsin River," that attempts to call to life his youthful experience as lumberjack and raftsman, and one reason for his failure as a poet may be the attitude revealed when he refers to the physical labor of the logging camps as "naked prose / A life without calling and poetry." Later in life Buslett began to revise this volume and to the poem about the Wisconsin River he added a line to the effect that though many of those he then knew are dead, "memories and dreams remain."[5] Happily he did not try to express these memories in verse but in prose, and the result is his crowning achievement: the autobiographical novel *Fra min ungdoms nabolag* (1918, From the neighborhood of my youth). In 1917 he wrote to Ager offering his novel in progress for serialization in *Reform*: "It is light in manner and will not be difficult to read—and since it is in all respects a realistic novel with a dreamer as the main character, I believe that it will be interesting" (4 Sept. WAP).

Two central themes, the immigrant experience and the lumber industry in Northern Wisconsin in the 1860s and 1870s, are evoked in the opening paragraph: "In the beginning of August, 1868, a little wheeler steamed up the Little Wolf. The boat butted against the current among the drifting logs on their way to the sawmills in Oshkosh" (3). On board is the family of Erik Larshus, bound for Iola. Soon the oldest son, Olaf, emerges as the protagonist, and with him two other themes: the making of an artist and romantic love. While Buslett's earlier work is marred by a lack of interest in character as well as story, this one succeeds because of its specificity—its attention to place, to character, and to the details of daily life. *Fra min ungdoms nabolag* is an account of growing up in post-Civil-War northern Wisconsin. Anecdotal episodes give life to the immigrant community around Iola: local politics, class differences, successes, and failures. The narrative voice is a speaking voice; the oral quality of the style with its deliberate use of dialect and code switching is an essential aspect of the novel's success. The author's romantic attitude to art is evident in the account of the artist-protagonist and his secret hiding place in a cave, where he keeps his books, sculptor's tools, and other cherished objects in a chest he calls "Our Heritage." No less romantic are the narrator's vision of the face of a beautiful young woman that he strives to recreate in marble, and the inevitable equation of art and the feminine ideal: "The spirit of art was the loved one of his soul" (60).

It becomes evident that America could not turn Olaf's likable but weak-willed father into a hard worker. Both parents are lovingly evoked in the story of how Erik spent the winter after the panic of 1873 making raft grubs, wooden pegs used to build rafts of logs for floating down the river, and of how he goes off to Stevens Point with a neighbor to sell them and returns empty-handed after several days of drinking: "He got his cream porridge, but it was old now and heated in milk. He also got something else, a sermon so earnest that for once he kept his mouth shut and accepted it" (70–71). At the age of twenty-one the protagonist leaves home; he hides his chest in the secret place and goes to work in the logging camps. His first job is "to raft lumber and run the river,"[6] the very work that the young Buslett had characterized as "naked prose." Now, however, his careful attention to detail in evoking the nature and quality of this work makes the account of the rafting process, from the building of the rafts at Stevens Point to the sighting of St. Louis ("Ho, there, mate! Won't you wake up? Here comes the Missouri with a full load of Red River dirt! We're in the middle of the Big Bend–Can't you see Saint Louis?"), the best writing of his long career (72–91). For the young Buslett poetry was exalted and idealistic, and the result was wooden verse; at his best, the mature Buslett could write prose evoking the poetry of plain facts and experienced life.

Meanwhile, Olaf has seen the face of the ideal woman of his dreams in a young girl of the logging camps and he returns to declare his love and marry her. On the day of their marriage two explosions are heard from the hill where Olaf had hidden his treasure chest: he has blown up the visions and dreams of his youth. His concluding words, however, make explicit the implicit message of the novel: "Yet—They were dreams, yes—But life, beautiful life, is at one with delightful dreams" (121).

Julius Baumann, who had been reading the installments of the serialized version in *Reform*, wrote to Buslett praising his work: "There are so many original phrases and so much pure gold that I have to take it up again and again. Yes, you have remained 'young' while the other people of the 'neighborhood' became 'old'" (5 Dec. 1918, OABP). Peer Strømme, hoping to have a selection of the best Norwegian-American literature published in Norway, wanted to include Buslett's *Fra min ungdoms nabolag* (23 Feb. 1921, OABP). Buslett, evidently not the best critic of his own work, preferred the vindictive and chaotic *Benedictus og Jacobus*. By this time, moreover, Buslett was more interested in preserving what he had written than in the creation of new work. The first issue of *Buslett's*, a journal devoted to the publication of a revised collected edition with critical and autobiographical introductions by the author, appeared in 1922. Of the projected thirty issues, however, only four were published before Buslett's death in June, 1924.

The critics and writers of *Vesterheimen* were unanimous in their respect for Buslett; none, however, as Hustvedt observes, followed in his footsteps (1980, 155). His occasional crankiness was a function of his isolated life. He was deeply influenced by the romantic idealism of mid-nineteenth-century Norwegian literature and much of his work can hardly be said to address itself to the concerns of his fellow immigrants. But then *Vesterheimen* was always more a place of the mind than the actual daily home of an American ethnic group, and book by book, Ole Amundsen Buslett was one of the builders of *Vesterheimen*. Although much of his work will be read by only a few diligent scholars, some of it has historical interest for anyone wanting to understand Norwegian-American history. A few texts, including *Glans-om-Sol*, *Veien til Golden Gate,* and *Fra min ungdoms nabolag* should be read by anyone claiming a good knowledge of American literature—no mean achievement for an uneducated immigrant starting off as a backwoodsman and lumberjack.

NOTES

1. The translation of the quotation from Strømme is in Hustvedt's excellent biographical-critical essay on Buslett (1980).

2. Buslett to Anderson 21 Sept. 1883 (RBAP) and Sk to Buslett 26 Sept. 1883 (OABP). References to correspondence to Anderson and to Buslett in this chapter are to these two collections.

3. Prestgard's letter of 1 March is in OABP, Buslett's reply, dated 15 March, in LC.

4. Quotations are from this author's translation in a forthcoming dual-language anthology edited by Marc Shell and Werner Sollors.

5. The copy of *Digte og Sange* with the author's revisions is in the University of Minnesota Library. He did not revise beyond the poem about the Wisconsin River (16). The revisions were probably intended for his projected collected works.

6. Code switching is essential to the charm and historical value of the novel. The quoted phrase reads: "rafte Lumber og rende Røvern"—with the conjunctive "og" (and) as the only Norwegian word.

Hans A. Foss:
Populist

Among the readers of *Buslett's* in 1922 was Hans Anderson Foss, a grain merchant in Minot, North Dakota, and author of the most popular Norwegian-American novel, *Husmands-gutten* (1885, *The Cotter's Son*). He ordered twenty copies of the first issue and bought extra copies of the following issues for distribution among his friends and business associates.[1] Foss had never met the complaint that his fictions were difficult to understand. There was no need to read between the lines in order to find his message, and in writing to entertain, he could not be accused of lowering his literary standards: he wrote not only the best but the only way he knew. Ever modest about his achievements, he reminisced in *Decorah-Posten* about a visit to Luther College after the publication of his second book, when he had confessed to an admiring student "that my writing was based on emotion, not intellect. For this reason my narratives were often defective or, rather, unnatural." He concluded on a similarly self-deprecating note: "Even though my insignificant stories did not become recognized as real literature and most reviews, particularly in Norway, were not very encouraging, they seemed to be well received among the laity and were accepted as popular reading" (5 Sept. 1924).

Like so many aspiring writers, Foss had his first manuscript turned down. He had sent *Husmands-gutten* to the Chicago publisher Relling, in whose newspaper, *Norden*, he had published a poem on the evils of alcohol (18 March 1884). Happily, he did not despair, but sent it to another publisher, Anundsen, in the little Iowa town of Decorah. Anundsen was in financial straits, but he nevertheless offered what Foss later characterized as "a relatively generous honorarium" for serialization in *Decorah-Posten* and sug-

*Hans A. Foss
(1851–1929).*

gested that the plates be used for subsequent book publication. It may be, as Wist suggests, that the astute Anundsen actually saw a potential lifesaver in the unpretentious manuscript; in effect it turned out to be just that and more. *Decorah-Posten* had a surge of new subscriptions because people wanted to read the new novel, and Anundsen graciously acknowledged Foss's contribution by doubling his honorarium (Wist 1914, 76, 125–126; Foss 1924).

Husmands-gutten is popular fiction in the true sense of the word, written by an uneducated amateur, with stilted dialogue, inept description, and melodramatic plot, yet with a strong appeal to a mass audience. Briefly told, it is the story of the son of a poor but kind-hearted cotter, born, christened, and confirmed on the same days as the daughter of a wealthy and cruel farmer. Inevitably they grow up loving each other but, equally inevitably, class differences keep them apart. The hero finally emigrates, and after years of vicissitudes and hard work, failures and eventual success in America, he returns to the valley of his youth and love. Here he finds the wealthy farmer wealthy no more; drink and his own machinations have brought him down, and the farm is slated for auction. As would be expected, the auction is held on the day the hero arrives and he buys the farm—for himself and the loved one who has faithfully waited for his return.

It is not difficult to understand the appeal of *Husmands-gutten* on both sides of the ocean. When Gjert Hovland wrote his letters in the 1830s, he tried to convince readers that it would be to their advantage to emigrate. Foss's novel was addressed to those who had made the move and demonstrated that it had been a wise one. Readers in the United States found reassurance that their choice of country, regardless of sacrifices, had been the right choice: this was a country where you could reap your deserved reward for your hard work. Lower-class readers in Norway found evidence that they were as good as, perhaps somewhat better than, the propertied classes, and that it was a deficient social and political system, not deficient character, that kept them in poverty. The focus is more on Norway than on the United States, both in the sense that more space is given to the Norwegian than to the American action and in the sense that the hero merely visits America to make his fortune and returns home to enjoy the fruits of his American years. The literary context is also primarily Norwegian: the setting, the characters, and the plot are derived from Bjørnson's trend-setting stories of rural life. But in the novel's emphasis on success as the just reward for faithfulness and hard work, American culture may be seen to have had its effect on the immigrant writer. It did not take long before Foss was involved in American politics of a more radical bent than was suggested in his first book.

In 1886 Foss published two novels. First he wrote *Livet i Vesterheimen* (Life in the western home), which he later characterized as a "monstrosity" and Anundsen found "unsuitable for serialization." Instead, Anundsen suggested that he write a novel "of the same innocent nature as *Husmands-gutten*" (Foss 1924). Foss complied and *Kristine* was serialized in *Decorah-Posten*. While neither qualifies as a masterpiece, the "monstrosity" is of more interest than the "innocent" *Kristine*, which is Norwegian in setting, thematic concerns, and style. But through the incongruous elements and convoluted turns of the gothic-flavored plot of *Livet i Vesterheimen* comes an American story of the stresses and hardships of immigration: madness and amnesia, arson and murder, capitalistic exploitation and ecclesiastical suppression, Indian captivity and the evils of alcohol are some of the ills that the characters have to suffer as the progress of westward migration and settlement takes them from Norway to Wisconsin and on to the Red River Valley. One way of making sense of the melodramatic confusion is to read it as an allegory of passage into America. The hero Christian Vold (=Christian Rampart) and his wife are separated under violent and tragic circumstances and he disappears. The positive values in the novel are represented by Troberg (=Faith-Rock) and his son, while the negative forces are imbedded in the characters Thomas Vanterud (a name implying lack of faith), Svingen, who wavers back and forth as his name (Swing) suggests, Mikkel Aagre (=Foxy Usurer) and the Synod pastor, X.Y. Babel, who are all introduced with comments on the implication of their names. The evils of capitalistic exploitation, drink, and a repressive and priest-ridden church are not American; they are found within the immigrant community itself, in corrupt individuals. They also exist in two institutions with European roots: the conservative Synod, an offshoot of the Norwegian state church, and the saloon. The saloon may be no more a Norwegian institution than an American one, but it is essential to Foss's strategy to portray it as one of the old-world evils that the immigrant must slough off in order to enter America. By voting for prohibition you prove your Americanism. Eventually, under the leadership of Christian Vold and Johan Troberg, the evil forces are vanquished and with a democratic church and a strong temperance society the immigrants can progress and win the respect of their fellow Americans.

With his next novel, *Den amerikanske saloon* (1889), Foss took a further step into America. At first glance this prohibition novel may not seem so different from *Livet i Vesterheimen*. While the latter was exclusively concerned with strife within the immigrant group, however, the central issue in the 1889 novel was also the major political issue in North Dakota that year: the debate on whether the new state constitution should enforce prohibition. Foss used his novel to demonstrate the need for political action through a third party.[2] Prophetically, it also hailed the success of such political action; on 1 October 1889 the prohibition article in the North Dakota constitution was ratified with a narrow margin.

In order to appreciate *Den amerikanske saloon* it is necessary to see that the author's strategies were dictated by political rather than literary aims: to strengthen the Norwegian-American community culturally, politically, and socially; to forge an alliance between Norwegian Americans and Anglo-Americans; and to bring about political reform, specifically prohibition. As in *Livet i Vesterheimen*, drink is one of the old-world evils that the immigrant must cleanse himself of in the new.[3] Again, Foss sees both the Synod and the saloon as foreign elements in a free republic; and again the Synod is criticized for its opposition to the cause of prohibition. Foss, however, takes care to demonstrate that his is a Christian cause: a low-church clergyman becomes a leader of the prohibitionists. While *Den amerikanske saloon* also demonstrates that the way to American acceptance is through the rejection of negative aspects of the Old World, it also stresses the importance of maintaining those Norwegian values that are in harmony with the ideals of a democratic republic. And this is best done in co-operation with the in-heritors of the founding values of the new country, the descendants of the New England Puritans. Thus the Anti-Saloon League is initiated by Norwegian immigrants who then find allies in a select group of Anglo-Americans, among them the town's one honest attorney and its principal merchant. The forces of evil, on the other hand, are represented by the town's three saloonkeepers: one Irish, one German, and one Norwegian. By joining forces with "the best" in the American tradition against the evils of European origin, the immigrants achieve both recognition and reform. With reform understood literally as getting rid of old-world evils, the strat-egy of furthering reform is intimately related to the two other strategies— strengthening the Norwegian-American community and forging an al-liance with Anglo-America.

Reviewers were condescendingly friendly, recognizing that though the novel had little literary value, it made a strong statement for social progress: "We believe that temperance is a good cause and therefore believe that this book should do some good. But we do not believe that it may be character-ized as a great work of literature," Peer Strømme ironically concluded his review of "A Strange Book" (*No* 16 April 1889). Kristofer Janson made much the same point in *Saamanden*, regretting, however, that Norwegian immigrants showed so little discipline that it was necessary to abolish the sa-loon in certain areas (April 1889, 217). The reading public of *Vesterheimen*, however, seemed more in agreement with the reviewer in *Decorah-Posten*, quoted with tongue in cheek by Strømme, who hailed the book as the *Uncle Tom's Cabin* of the battle against alcohol. Foss later remembered that "as soon as it was off the press there were so many orders from booksellers and other agents that the first printing of several thousand copies was quickly sold and gave the author a considerable income" (Foss 1922, 32–33). Like all his novels, *Den amerikanske saloon* was also published in Norway and it was the only novel Foss saw translated into English. As *Tobias: A Story of the Northwest* (1899), it was distributed by the Minnesota Anti-Saloon League.

The back cover of Foss's next novel, *Hvide slaver. En social-politisk skildring* (1892, White slaves: A socio-political narrative), has an advertisement for the publisher, the author's North Dakota newspaper *Normanden*, "the only Norwegian newspaper for reform in the Northwest that has not bent knee

Hvide Slaver.

En social-politisk Skildring.

—AF—

H. A. FOSS.

Normanden Publishing Company.
GRAND FORKS, N. D.
1892.

Hvide Slaver, *Foss's final novel, is a populist attack on "Plutocrats and Whiskey Barons."*

for either money power or liquor power, but has fought steadfastly for the cause of temperance and for improved conditions for farmers and workers." The publisher's political as well as literary sympathies are further suggested by the two books the newspaper offered as premiums to new subscribers: Edward Bellamy's *Looking Backward* (1888) and Ignatius Donnelly's *Caesar's Column* (1891), both in Norwegian translation. Just as Foss's anti-saloon novel had addressed a major political issue in North Dakota of 1889, his 1892 novel was a contribution to the North Dakota political campaigns triggered by the organization of the populist Independent Party in 1890.[4] Again Foss wrote a novel that predicted victory for the forces of reform, and again he was vindicated, at least partly, by the turn of events: the Populists carried the state in 1892 but then went into decline. It is evident from his "Socio-Political Narrative" that Foss was radicalized along with the Farmers' Alliance and the Prohibitionists after 1889. The white slaves of his title, a figure of speech in keeping with the colorful and fiery imagery of the Populist orators of the 1880s and 1890s, are the victims of capitalism, and Foss saw no solution for America short of revolutionary reform based on the People's Party platform.

As Foss was moving into the mainstream of American politics, he also moved into a mainstream of American fiction. Reflecting the widespread sense of social crisis, one of the popular genres of contemporary fiction was the utopian or anti-utopian novel, works that explored alternative future solutions or that presented apocalyptic visions of the outcome of the present crisis. The two most popular examples of such fiction were the two novels that Foss offered his subscribers in 1892. They were also widely read in Europe, but it was not only there that translations were necessary for a broad popular appeal: in order to reach a wider public, Donnelly's Chicago publishers did three translations, German, Norwegian (1892), and Swedish, for the domestic market. Foss was obviously aware of the close affinity between his *Hvide slaver* and *Looking Backward* and *Caesar's Column*, but the difference between them is nevertheless striking. Bellamy (who was unable to imagine a bridge between his sordid present and a utopian future) and Donnelly (who imagined apocalyptic destruction as the outcome of the social strife of his day) both present a basically pessimistic view of the prospects for their society. *Hvide slaver* is an optimistic work inspired by faith in American ideals and the American system of government. This difference reflects the different backgrounds of the authors; *Hvide slaver* is as much about the immigrant's need to belong to American society as about his desire to reform it.

The novel begins in Norway in the 1850s where the radical views of
Knut Rolfsen have cost him his job as a teacher. With his wife Aagot he
goes with great expectations to America, the land of freedom. The Civil
War breaks out soon after their arrival in Wisconsin and Knut and many
others are conscripted. Three prominent citizens of a nearby town, however, Mr. Pluto, Mr. Shylock, and Mr. Monopolio, buy substitutes. With Mr.
Bull from England they enter a conspiracy to profit from the war, which
they appear to have instigated. As the conspirators amass riches and power,
Knut is taken prisoner and sold as a slave by a corrupt confederate officer to
work in the coal mine of a northern capitalist. Back in Wisconsin, a son is
born to Aagot. Alone, she is unable to protect the farm from the capitalists,
and she lives with her child in extreme poverty until she is thrown into
prison accused of theft. The efforts on her behalf by the radical German-
American lawyer Hartman are in vain, and her young son Rolf is on his
own. Both immigrants are now literally slaves of capitalism. The Pluto, Monopolio, Shylock Bullion Co. of America and England controls the government as well as the courts, and the partners strengthen their hold on the
country by buying representatives of the press, the church, and the universities, as well as the two bigwigs in the service of Uncle Sam, Republiko and
Democratio. After they have forced Uncle Sam to throw out silver, the
three successfully corner all the gold in the nation and weather the mo-
mentary setback of the Black Friday of 1869.

Rolf grows up, and aided by Hartman and the Knights of Labor he succeeds in tracking down his father. In a grand showdown the owner of the
coal mine is forced to set his white slaves free, and Rolf and his parents join
the surging westward movement to begin a new life in the Red River Valley
of the Dakota Territory. The banks and railroads, however, soon get the
upper hand, driving the hard-working farmers into debt. After the first
elections it becomes evident that the capitalists have the state legislature in
their pocket. The farmers realize that they will have to organize, and the
Farmers' Alliance is born. At a state convention several threads in the melodramatic plot come together in ways that may be disturbing to the aesthetic
sensibility but which make beautiful sense from a political and ideological
point of view. Knut Rolfsen receives letters from his aging parents in Norway who forgive him the unruly ways of his youth. Then the Norwegian-
American family and an Anglo-American family are joined in the marriage
of son and daughter, with the ceremony performed on the stage of the convention hall by a clergyman excluded from his church because of his support of the Populist cause. The message is clear: in his struggle for reform,

Knut Rolfsen acts in accord with the best traditions of the old country and with the blessing of his parents. Moreover, the immigrant who stands up for progressive American ideals gains acceptance as a member of the American family. While the church as an institution may be against progress, the best spokesmen of the church are with the people. In joining the Populist cause the immigrant claims his Norwegian heritage and makes his adopted country his true home. The convention demands a speech and Knut Rolfsen shares his vision with his audience: "I see, in my mind's eye, the mountains rise from the sea . . . as I and Aagot, our son and daughter . . . sail towards the coast of Norway to go home and kneel and receive the blessing . . . of the old ones. Once more I can see the dear hills and the mountain tops . . . the whole rocky land lies there smiling and friendly and dressed for celebration, ready to accept us. But America is now our new home; here we have a responsibility to take care of; I have forsworn all loyalty to the king of my motherland and sworn loyalty to the American flag. I have risked my life for the Union and have been poorly paid. But now the page is turned, now the dreams of my spring are about to be realized. I will fight with the weapons of the mind and will give all I have for the salvation of this Republic. My text shall be the story of my life; my reward shall be the liberation of the people from the tyrant's grasp" (187–188). The convention is jubilant and Foss no doubt hoped that his readers would be exhilarated as well; such would be their reception if they, too, joined the Populist cause.

At this point the novel moves into the future, showing what could become their reward. In spite of a Populist victory at the polls, the Eastern capitalists remain entrenched in their power. Amid growing frustration the farmers and the workers, the Alliance and the Knights of Labor, form a national organization and plan for military as well as political action. Evicted farmers fight back. There are pitched battles between Populist and Pinkerton forces. The Populists gain control of Congress and pass laws designed to weaken the power of the capitalists, but to little effect until the Senate, led by the younger Rolfsen, now "completely Americanized" (234), finds ways to take over the railroads and do away with the gold standard. The planks in the Populist platform are made law and the novel ends in a vision of the final goal: Socialism. Old Knut Rolfsen, the one-time slave at the bottom of Shaft 9, is given the last word: "'Now we can die knowing that our lives have had a purpose and that the white slaves of America will be liberated.' Then the sun set—to rise again in the morning."

A vision of the new morning and a version of one of the central myths of *Vesterheimen* are given by the German-American Hartman in a speech to a summer meeting of the Populists. There are Norwegian and American flags in the wind, and after relating his vision of the future, he thanks the Norwegians for their contribution to "the liberation of our country. One day history will tell that the people who set her leaders on the English throne, who gave new lifeblood to the enfeebled French people, and who erected Norman towers in France, also were a powerful factor in the liberation of this, their land of Leif Erikson" (246). In effect, the Norsemen were not only the first Europeans to come to the New World, but the United States, founded by the English, whose land was governed by and according to the ideals of the descendants of the Normans, who were Norwegian immigrants in France, was the natural home of its Norwegian immigrants: it was "their land of Leif Erikson." Foss did not write to scare his readers, like Donnelly, or, like Bellamy, to present a theoretical and impossibly distant utopia. He wrote with the optimism of the practical reformer to persuade his fellow immigrants to make common cause with the People's Party. His main strategy was to argue that they had a stake in their new land and that by fighting for their own threatened interests shoulder to shoulder with other Americans they were true to their own traditions and were serving their new country. The Populists were the true Americans—as were the immigrants who joined them.

Foss and his partner Edvard Lund were discouraged by the political developments in North Dakota in 1893 and sold a majority share in *Nordmanden* for $10,000. The opposition was not sparing in its use of invective. To *Afholdsbasunen,* a conservative North Dakota temperance weekly, Foss "lacked the courage to help carry the Populist corpse to its last resting place" (May 10). Republican *Skandinaven* branded him a traitor to his cause, suggesting that the new owners were in the pocket of "Jim Hill or some other plutocratic power" (May 17). Piqued by such insinuations, Foss and Lund began a new newspaper, *Nye Normanden,* in Moorhead, Minnesota, in 1894, taking it to Minneapolis the following year, where it moved further to the left under a succession of socialist editors until it ceased to exist in 1904. Foss became involved in the grain business, first as chief clerk of the Minnesota Grain Inspection department in Duluth in 1899 and later as North Dakota representative of a large firm of grain commission merchants (Wist 1914, 124–127; Sandvik 1977, 72–73). He continued to write occasional pieces, and kept his hand in publishing, both through the Foss and Lund Publishing Company and from 1905 as editor, later co-editor, of *Kvindens Magazin* (The woman's journal), until Nils N. Rønning took over and in 1916 merged it with a religious monthly, *Ungdommens Ven* (The friend of youth), to become *Familiens Magazin*. After his 1894 short story, "4000 Bushels Hvede" (4,000 bushels of wheat), which expressed a Populist view similar to that of *Hvide slaver*, his politics become more moderate, as might be expected in a man increasingly involved with the buying and selling of wheat rather than its production.

As Foss became an American businessman, he also became more concerned with *Vesterheimen*, much like the old farmer in the 1916 short story "Nybyggerens Jul" (The settler's Christmas), who often retreats with his wife to the original log cabin still standing on their farm because things have changed so much that he does not feel at home in his own house. His 1921–1922 series of articles on Norwegian-American authors, "Saamænd paa vidderne" (Sowers on the plains), in *Nordmands-Forbundet* is an act of devotion. The most explicit expression of his interest in *Vesterheimen* and his concern for its future is the reminiscence "Gamle Minder" (Old memories) in a multi-volume history of immigration from the region of his birth.[5] Here he tells of a visit to a couple he had known from childhood in Norway, now retired on their North Dakota farm, mourning the loss of a son in the war and embittered by having their Americanism made suspect because of their love of their Old-World heritage. Their home bears witness to their interest in the countries of their birth and choice: on the walls are portraits of Norwegian writers and statesmen as well as of Washington and Lincoln, and the bookcases have volumes on Norwegian and United States history. A daughter is a teacher in the local school and the children come and serenade the guests with "The Star-Spangled Banner" and Norwegian songs. The old friend speaks of the war that had to be fought and the sacrifices that had to be made: " ... it is even demanded of us who have survived that we should sacrifice our precious inheritance on what they call the altar of patriotism! During the war the word patriotism became distorted to mean that we should think, speak, and write in only one language, and that if we know two languages, then we are only half Americans and half patriots. I have nothing to boast of, since I have merely done my duty as a citizen. But have not Synnøve and I given evidence of our love and loyalty to our adopted country by wearing ourselves out in the little war of the farmer in clearing and developing a large farm; by assisting in the building of schools, churches, courthouses, bridges, and roads; in serving our country in public office in county and state; in knitting and sewing for the Red Cross and giving money to all war-time charities; in lending all the money we could to our government by purchasing Liberty and Victory Bonds; in giving our country four strong sons and three daughters, of whom all but one live and will continue to work for land and people when we depart—and in our dear son Thorvald's death on the battlefields of France . . . have we not given the costliest pledge of patriotism that may be requested of a father and mother?" (1921, 309) In his last letter their son had written that two things made him happy to take part in the war: "First, that I am a citizen of the great American Republic . . . who in the name of humanity and liberty came here to slay German militarism and sever the chains of the autocrats so that people might govern themselves and live their own lives. Second, that my father and all our dear family . . . might through my sacrifice for my country be accepted by their fellow citizens as loyal and perfect American citizens" (310–311). Here Foss had the theme, setting, and story for *Valborg*, published in 1927, two years before his death.

When Foss turned to writing as soon as retirement had freed him from "the treadmill of commercialism," as he put it in a letter to Kristian Prestgard in *Decorah-Posten*, he had thought of something "along the same lines as *Husmands-gutten*, except that I now have more experience and will be able to avoid the many and partly naive flaws" of his first novel. A few days letter he wrote again, giving a plot summary that he had worked on over several years on his "travels by train and by automobile" and promised that it would include "many exciting love affairs and intrigues": "I am sure that the book would be interesting, were I only able to describe the prairie, the landscape, realistically as a backdrop, [but] my intellect is somewhat enfeebled" (23, 30 August 1926, LC). Foss's theme of the ethnic group threatened from without by the anti-hyphen hysteria of American nativism and from within by the natural process of acculturation was a timely one, but in execution *Valborg*, written as if nothing had happened in the literature of *Vesterheimen* since the times of *Husmands-gutten*, struck most of the already dwindling number of readers, and certainly most reviewers, as a throwback.[6]

Valborg is a tale of two immigrant families. It begins in the 1880s when they meet on their way west from Wisconsin to homestead in Dakota Territory. There are many similarities to the basic plot of *Husmands-gutten* and the reader realizes that two members of the American-born generation of the two families are destined for each other according to the laws of popular fiction: Valborg is the baby in one of the wagons, Thorleif in the other. The two families are among the first to settle in the area north of Minot, the North Dakota home of the author, and the growth of the settlement and the making of a community is a central theme. The two families remain close to each other and prosper, and a subplot demonstrates that the social distinctions of the old country are invalid in the new. As in Simon Johnson's novels of the 1920s, the First World War and the strident nativism that followed in its wake become testing grounds for the characters' true worth. The war sends Thorleif to the front while Valborg interrupts a promising career as a singer and goes to France as a nurse. Meanwhile Thorleif's father, Torger, who has bought bonds for $10,000 and given large sums to the Red Cross, is accused of treason, but the court finds him innocent. Thorleif, long believed to be missing in action, and Valborg finally marry and on their wedding night listen patiently to a lecture on the value of their Norwegian heritage. Indeed, to be good in this novel is tantamount to respecting and holding on to the culture, language, and religion of your parents. The dangers in store for those who do not share the ideals of Thorleif and Valborg are demonstrated in the characters of Thorleif's two sisters: one prefers ragtime to Norwegian folk songs and the other marries an Irishman!

In his last novel Foss has come to terms with the American establishment of which he wrote with such skepticism in *Hvide slaver*. Yet the differences between his late and early work should not be exaggerated. True, the two families whose story is traced from the 1880s to the present now prove themselves through their solid conservatism and their material success, but they, too, prove their Americanism by living up to American ideals. While the ideals may have changed, the need to win approval remains much the same. As the good immigrants in *Livet i Vesterheimen* win the approval of the representatives of Anglo-America, and as the son of Knut and Aagot in *Hvide slaver* wins approval through marriage, the American approval of the two families in *Valborg* is expressed through the friendship bestowed upon them by the scion of a wealthy Boston family, who is hopelessly in love with the heroine. Although *Hvide slaver* is an expression of American radicalism and *Valborg* expresses conservative American ideals, all of Foss's novels, from *Husmands-gutten* in 1885 to *Valborg* in 1927, give fictional expression to the shifting dominant concerns of the Norwegian-American Midwest.

NOTES

1. Foss to Buslett Jan. 1922-Dec. 1923 in OABP. Sandvik 1977 is a useful study.

2. In his history of the temperance movement in North Dakota Foss writes about the political campaign for prohibition (1922, 25–31). For an account of the constitutional convention of 1889 and prohibition see Robinson 1966, 208–211.

3. Misuse of alcohol was a scourge of the lower classes in nineteenth-century Norway. In an 1892 article on "The Scandinavian in the United States" in the *North American Review*, Hjalmar H. Boyesen observes that "their national vice, at home, is

drunkenness" but that although they bring this vice with them to America, "the rise of the temperance movement among the Scandinavians in the West has been a major influence for the good" (528–529).

4. Foss played a central role in the Independent Party and was a reluctant candidate for Congress. The party organ, *The North Dakota Independent*, co-edited by Foss, was housed and printed by Foss's *Normanden* (Foss 1922, 57–69, *Sk* 17 May 1893).

5. *Utvandringshistorie fra Ringerikesbygderne*, edited by Ole S. Johnson in four volumes from 1919 to 1930. Foss's contribution is in the second volume (1921).

6. In his obituary in the Chicago literary magazine, *Norden,* 1 (October, 1929), 29, Ager commented on the reception of *Valborg:* "but the public is not the same now as it once was, and the book was not a success. The reading Norwegian America had changed, while the author had remained the same."

The Minneapolis Interlude
of the Jansons

In their points of departure, Hans Andersen Foss and Kristofer Janson offer
a study in social and cultural contrasts. When Foss wrote in a popular vein
he wrote the only way he knew, presenting melodramatic plots in a stilted
bookish language that he and his readers associated with "literature." When
Janson wrote in a popular vein he did so deliberately. Foss came to America
with no education, no prospects, and empty pockets. When Janson, a theologian whose liberal views had led him to break with the Lutheran church
and become a Unitarian, arrived in the United States in the fall of 1881 he
was a respected author in his homeland, one of the first four writers to receive an annual stipend from the Norwegian parliament in 1876. Janson's
maternal grandfather, Jacob Neumann, bishop of Bergen, had published a
pastoral warning against emigration in 1837, but his grandson gave evidence
of quite contrary attitudes to the United States several years before he decided to settle there himself. He not only shared with Foss a view of America as a liberal alternative to the conservative and priest-ridden class societies of Europe, but Janson's American experience also led him to identify
"the enemies of the people," in his short story of that title, as the saloon and
the Synod: "The one drains the life force from the body, the other from the
soul" (1885, 2: 33).[1]

Janson was primarily a novelist and short-story writer, but he also tried
his hand at other genres. In 1875 he wrote a play about life in the United
States—of which he had little knowledge and no experience—appropriately titled *Amerikanske fantasier* (American fantasies), and decided to have it
published in Chicago. His awareness of the possibilities offered a Norwegian writer in the United States may have come a year earlier when he re-

Kristofer Janson (1841–1917).

ceived news that R.B. Anderson would include one of his stories in his book on the new dialect-based version of Norwegian (*landsmaal*). The book was published by *Skandinaven* in 1875 and Janson soon became Norwegian correspondent for the newspaper, his first contribution appearing 22 February 1876 just as his play was coming off the press.

Amerikanske fantasier is a success story that sets the American ideal of self-reliance against the European obeisance to family and class. Henrik Hald, a young upper-class Norwegian, is first seen as a spoiled idler in San Francisco, sponging on the wealthy father of his fiancée, Mary. When Mary's father suffers failure in business, Henrik determines to prove himself capable of providing for Mary on his own, and Mary promises to await his return. Henrik begins his new life as a common laborer but advances through hard work and good luck to become the wealthy owner of a gold mine. The distance he has travelled from his old-world background is brought out in his confrontations with David Bing, a conservative tourist who sends slanted reports about the United States to newspapers in Norway. Henrik wins his Mary by practicing American ideals and fulfilling the success myth.

Reviewers read the play through political glasses. In *Budstikken* (11 April) and *Illustreret Familieblad* (Jan. 1879) it was praised for its realistic portrayal of American life, while the conservative *Fædrelandet og Emigranten* (16 March 1876) and *Norden* (6 April) found the play badly executed fantasy. Indeed, *Norden* warned that it would break down its readers' sense of literary value and thus harm the growth of a Norwegian-American literature. In *Skandi-naven* R. B. Anderson trumpeted the book as harbinger of what was to come, insisting that the future of a *Vesterheim* literature depended on the success of *Amerikanske fantasier* (7 March). Janson was used to such disparate reactions and was no doubt as encouraged by conservative attacks as by liberal support. Urged by Anderson he soon began to plan a lecture tour of *Vesterheimen*.

Janson's second book about life in the United States, no less appropriately titled *Amerikanske forholde* (American conditions), was based on observations during his lecture tour in the fall and winter of 1879–1880. By the time it was published in Copenhagen in 1881, the author had already decided to emigrate. On his visit he had noted the radical transformation of the docile and subservient Norwegian peasant into the independent and self-reliant American farmer, a confirmation of his belief in the superiority of American institutions. He had also noted, however, that the conservative Synod had a repressive effect on immigrants with its insistence on a literal interpretation of scripture. Having declared his departure from the doctrines of the Lutheran Church, in particular those concerning the Trinity and damnation, he sought service in the Unitarian Church and was ordained in Chicago in November, 1882. He then went on to Minneapolis to begin his ministry among his immigrant compatriots. Although he returned to Norway eleven years later, in 1893, the dozen books, more pamphlets, and numerous items in newspapers and journals that he published in the United States were a significant contribution to the literature of *Vesterheimen*.

Janson's literary labors during his first two years in Minneapolis were mainly related to his ministry. Attacked by the orthodox establishment as a freethinker, Janson responded not only with polemics but also with expressions of his Christian faith.[2] Reviewing one of Janson's theological-polemical pamphlets, *Helvedesbørn* (1884, Children of Hell), E. L. Petersen exhorted his clerical brother to "return to the writing of novels" (*B* 10 Feb. 1885). By then, however, Janson had already written his first American fiction. Five stories were published in three volumes in 1885 with the common title

Præriens saga (The saga of the prairie). Two short novels, *Femtende Wisconsin* (The fifteenth Wisconsin) and *Vildrose. Fortælling fra indianerudbruddet i 1862* (Wild Rose: A novel of the Indian uprising in 1862), followed in 1887, and another short novel, *Et arbeidsdyr* (A beast of labor), was published in 1889.

A dominant theme of Janson's early American fiction is women's rights or, more specifically, the plight of immigrant women in the West. Consistently, the main obstacle to their liberation is European conservatism, in particular Lutheran fundamentalism. The theme of women's rights is part and parcel of Janson's larger theme of how the Lutheran churches enthrall the minds of the immigrants and keep them from assimilating to American life. Since the author was such a controversial figure in his homeland, *Præriens saga* received more attention in Norway than usual for literary products from *Vesterheimen,* and these reviews, reprinted in the immigrant press, became the occasion of polemics here as well. The public debate, however, began in advance of publication. Janson had conducted readings of the most controversial of the five stories in Chicago and Minneapolis, and an English translation, "Wives Submit Yourselves Unto Your Husbands," had been serialized in the monthly journal *Scandinavia.*[3] In this story Emma, the daughter of an impoverished widow of a civil servant, falls in love with an uneducated but handsome *husmann.* The two emigrate, marry, and homestead in Minnesota, where their troubles soon begin. The harsh conditions bring out their incompatibility; she is gradually worn down by hard work and lack of intellectual and emotional stimulation as he turns into an ignorant, materialistic tyrant who in his insistence on absolute mastery in the home has the full support of the Synod pastor. Emma's awakening to her plight as well as to her alternatives comes with the chance visit of an American woman. Driven to the edge of insanity, Emma escapes to her brother in Minneapolis and here she experiences a few days of freedom, gains new strength, and even attends a feminist meeting. The pastor tracks her down, however, and Emma is brought home to her gloating husband. That night she drowns herself and her baby daughter in a pond, and the pastor finds her the next day on his way home from church where he has just given a sermon admonishing wives to submit themselves to their husbands: "Washed up on the sand, so that half the body still lay in the water, was Emma. A green tortoise had become entangled in her hair, a slimy snail had crept up on her bosom. But her wan, pinched face was turned toward heaven, as though to call down vengeance; one hand clutched her infant, the other was clenched toward the priest." No less controversial was "En Buggy-Præst" (*A Buggy Priest*), where the pastor, unnamed as are the other characters, freezes to death in his buggy while making notes for a theological dispute, his death emblematic of his frozen religion, "the great icehouse of orthodoxy" (81). In this story, too, the uncompromisingly orthodox clergyman drives one of his flock to his death. He also drives his own wife to near despair. She, however, has miraculously been set free by a white man who has married an Indian woman, a "squaw man"—who turns out not only to be a Norwegian with a degree in theology, but to have been in love with her mother—and she is planning to leave her husband as he dies.

In Norway, liberals and conservatives found confirmation of their prejudices in Janson's stories, but it was difficult for the inhabitants of *Vesterheimen* not to see them as an attack on the entire immigrant group. To no avail did the editor of *Scandinavia* observe that it would be as wrong to generalize from one story to a whole people as to judge "the English or the American nations from their social novels." Most readers probably agreed with P.P. Iverslie, who concluded his scathing review in *Norden* with the wish that "our conditions could be dealt with in fiction by someone in sympathy with our people" (29 June 1886). Iverslie was not alone in finding Janson lacking in such sympathy: "It occurs to me that Kristofer has a special talent for misunderstanding the ordinary Norwegian American," Dr. Knut Hoegh wrote to Anderson in 1888 (Draxten 1976, 365). At work here are the sensitive defense mechanisms of spokesmen for an ethnic group who know all too well that the majority culture tends to find confirmation of its stereotypes in the behavior of individuals.[4]

The most successful story in *Prœriens saga* is, as Iverslie claimed, "En bygdekonge" (A settlement king). Here, as in "Kjærlighed paa kofangeren" (Love on the cowcatcher), Janson aims at comedy. He keeps up his verbal assaults on the Lutheran churches, but at the center of the story is his portrayal of the local despot, an immigrant farmer in Goodhue county, Minnesota, who finds true enjoyment in lording it over all the others and who makes use of the bitter enmity between Lutherans of different orthodoxies to manipulate the pastors as well as their flocks. With the settlement continually at war, he is in full control.

Janson's two historical novels, *Femtende Wisconsin* and *Vildrose*, are slight works compared to the short stories in *Prœriens saga*. Janson apparently wanted to present the history of the Fifteenth Wisconsin through popular fiction, but neither the occasional footnotes nor the incorporation of letters in the text makes his book convincing history, and his mixture of slapstick humor and folk comedy with sentimental melodrama is unconvincing fiction. Compared to Waldemar Ager's use of the regiment in *Sons of the Old*

Country (1926/1983), Janson's Civil War story is an embarrassing failure, as is his story of the 1862 Sioux War in Minnesota, *Vildrose*, where incredible turns of plot compete with wooden characters in turning away even the most sympathetically inclined reader. Even though buried in muddled fictions, Janson's feminist theme may be seen in the characters of the Irish-American Kate, who goes to battle with the 15th Wisconsin disguised as a man, and of Vildrose, the daughter of a Norwegian immigrant, brought up among Indians on the Minnesota frontier, who rides and shoots as well as any Annie Oakley and who finally gives her life so that others may live.

As Janson was moving out of the narrow Norwegian-American world and attempting the broader American themes of the Civil War and the Indian frontier, his wife had already shown the way. Although Drude Janson was an unknown beginner, her first novel, *En saloonkeepers datter* (1889, A saloonkeeper's daughter), is an advance on her literary mentor's American fiction.[5] Her style may be more stilted than that of her more experienced spouse, but her didactic feminist story is not marred by his melodramatic exesses. One measure of its popularity, in part ensured by its reputation as a *roman à clef*, is its four American editions by 1894. In *Budstikken* E.L. Petersen had reviewed *Geography and Love*, the latest play by Bjørnstjerne Bjørnson, not only the most popular Norwegian writer of his day but a liberal activist with all of Europe as his stage (10 Aug. 1886). Drude Janson, who had been Bjørnson's model for the play's heroine (Draxten 147), must have read the review with interest and, preoccupied with thoughts of her own projected novel, she would surely have noted Petersen's observation that plays such as Bjørnson's were beyond the artistic resources of the Norwegian-American theater. From this germ and the author's frustrations with the limited world of the Norwegian colony in Minneapolis grew the story of Astrid Holm.

As a young girl in Kristiania, Astrid is full of love for her good but consumptive mother, a one-time actress, and fearful of her cold and distant father, a merchant. Readers of nineteenth-century fiction would not be surprised by the death of the good mother nor by the bankruptcy of the bad father, who flees the consequences of his failure by emigrating. When Astrid and her two brothers join him in Minneapolis a year later, she discovers to her dismay that he runs a saloon. Astrid cannot but reflect on how her life is governed by her insensitive father, who in Norway had denied her his permission to become an actress and thus bring shame on her family, and here forces her to live a degrading life above a saloon. She wonders whether he "would have dared do it if she had been a man" (53). Surpris-

Drude Krog Janson (1846–1934).

ingly, when Astrid and some acquaintances plan to organize a theater company, this meets with approval from the saloon-keeping father; only later
does Astrid realize why he was so encouraging. While Astrid thinks of the
theater as a means of bringing the enlightened ideas of Bjørnson before her
fellow immigrants, her father sees it as an occasion to improve his business.
Before the curtain rises in Turner Hall she understands the folly of her idealism: on the other side of the curtain is not an eagerly expectant audience,
but a boisterous crowd waiting for the dance to begin and drinking beer
catered by her father.

Astrid's fragile dreams are smashed: "Now she could look forward to the
life that offered itself to her in all its frightening reality. She was the saloonkeeper's daughter, neither more nor less—would never be anything else"
(111–112). In her despondency she is first victimized by a seedy ne'er-do-
well, then by a successful but insensitive lawyer. Unable to resist the latter's
entreaties, she becomes engaged, against her own better judgment. Just in
time, however, she is inspired to break away from her fiancé, who is already
speaking of her as his future property. Inspiration comes from the great

Bjørnson himself, who actually had used Minneapolis as a base on his American lecture tour and stayed with friends of the Jansons. Astrid asks his advice and he lectures her on women's responsibility for taking their lives into their own hands and suggests that the ministry might be a calling where Astrid could realize her idealistic ambitions. Not the kind of minister known to the Norwegian church, he explains, "but the kind of whom there are many here in America, mild and loving men and women who preach peace on earth and . . . have a burning faith in the triumph of good and in eternal progress, who do not stress faith, but life, as do the ministers of the liberal persuasion" (185), like, we may add, Kristofer Janson. Read the works of John Stuart Mill and Herbert Spencer, he exhorts the young immigrant. But Astrid Holm is now alone in the world. Where can she go? Men, except for the demi-god Bjørnson, have been shown to be faithless, brutal, or stupid. In Minneapolis, however, working among the poor, is a dedicated doctor, Helene Nielsen, and she offers Astrid her home, her support, and her friendship. After an unsuccessful attempt as a temperance speaker, Astrid, with the support of Helene and the prominent Unitarian minister of St. Paul, William Channing Gannet, enters a Unitarian divinity school and in the novel's concluding pages she is ordained in Unity Church, Chicago. The two women will live together, both working for the good of mankind, the one as a doctor, the other as a minister.[6] Astrid realizes, however, that her own people are not yet ready to receive her; she will have to find an American congregation. Drude Janson's novel places hope in the America most immigrants were aspiring to enter. The main targets of her criticism are Norwegian conservatism and an immigrant society dominated by a pretentious but uneducated middle class. It should be noted that Bjørnson does not encourage Astrid to return to Norway but to become a part of America. The European liberal, clearly speaking for the author, realizes that the New World offers greater opportunities for the independent woman than the old one. On the other hand, Astrid has not been so discouraged by her experience with *Vesterheimen* as to turn her back on it entirely; she looks forward to a time when she can work among Norwegian Americans and other kinds of Americans, all members of one congregation.

Kristofer shared Drude's feminist views and his Unitarian journal, *Saamanden*, had columns for the causes of both feminism and labor. While Drude lets Astrid Holm develop to shape her own career, however, his female characters tend to be victims of male oppression. Perhaps influenced by his wife's success, Kristofer Janson chose an urban setting and demonstrated a similar interest in American themes for his next novel, *Bag gardinet*

(1889, Behind the curtain).[7] Janson's working title was "Mysteries of Minneapolis" and the novel is in the tradition of Eugène Sue's *Les Mystères de Paris* (1842–1843), as made explicit by one of his characters, the wealthy Frank Plummer: "We are out looking at the mysteries of Minneapolis," he explains when visiting seedy establishments with a fake French count (68). Janson's title has the same implications: "There is much in Minneapolis that happens behind the curtains. The newspapers say that evil has been eradicated, but it has only been moved—behind the curtains. And the city proudly bares its virtuous and pretty face for all to see, as virtuous as an American Sunday, but no one talks of what happens—behind the curtains" (65–66). The reviewer in *Budstikken* was fully aware of this literary context, observing that the novel "was similar to other mysteries in that it dealt with the corruption of high society" (12 Feb. 1890). In *Saamanden*, Janson had advertised his novel as "a glove thrown at all public and private corruption over here. It will become a book for the working class" (Sept. 1889).

The mysteries of Minneapolis are recounted through the lives of four families and the alcoholic Linner. The upper reaches are represented by the nouveau riche Plummers, who are first seen at the apex of their social acceptance as the hosts of a servant posing as a French count, and in the end are despised by the establishment, as represented by the philanthropic Walters, modeled on Thomas B. and Harriet Granger Walker.[8] Mrs. Pryts, a widow, and her daughter Agnes move from genteel poverty to a comfortable middle-class status thanks to Agnes's recognition as a music teacher. Another immigrant family, the Nilsens, represent the working class, with the widower Daniel as an uncompromising spokesman for the rights of labor and protector of his son, Arne, and daughter, Dina. At the very bottom of society is Linner, once a feared and respected lawyer and a fine musician, now an alcoholic who fiddles for room and board in a saloon on Washington Avenue, but who is allowed a brief return to court, as Dina's lawyer in her successful first suit against Frank Plummer, before his death in a scene dripping of Dickensian sentimentality.

The opening chapters of social comedy, with the ignorant but wealthy Plummers at the center, are overdone and clash with the over-all somber tone of the novel. This opening, however, serves an important purpose and represents a new departure for Norwegian-American fiction in that the immigrant characters are gradually introduced in their relations to the Plummers and thus are seen as part of the social structure of Minneapolis and not as an isolated group: the visit of the false count is the occasion that makes it possible for Agnes Pryts to take the step from maid in the Plummer household to independent professional woman; Dina Nilsen succeeds Agnes as maid, is raped by Frank Plummer, and eventually takes her life in spite of the kindness of Edith Walter; her father, Daniel, has broken his health working for the Plummers and finally hangs himself at their door; Linner is first seen playing his violin in a saloon visited by Frank Plummer and the false count. *Bag gardinet* is a story of Minneapolis where most of the characters happen to be Norwegian immigrants. The novel has three main thematic concerns. The plight of labor is brought out in the stories of the three Nilsens, and the surviving Arne confides to Agnes that he plans to study engineering and then "continue father's work and do something for the workers and the weak" (242). The theme of women's rights is expressed through the stories of Agnes and Dina, the one as a positive lesson, the other as a victim of male brutality and social prejudice. In Linner, his actions as well as his admonitions to young Arne, the theme of the dangers of the misuse of alcohol is expressed. The large gallery of characters and the many crossing plot lines lead to superficial portraits of the individual characters, but the constant moves back and forth between different levels of society and different parts of the city belong to the "mysteries" genre. The painfully extreme melodrama of the concluding pages, however—the frozen corpse of Dina presented to a crowd by her frenzied father, his body found hanging at the entrance of the Plummer residence, and the discovery of the body of Frank Plummer lying across the grave of Dina after his suicide—is Janson's hallmark. The funeral of the two Nilsens is one of the many images of social and cultural acceptance in Norwegian-American literature. The Walters have mobilized their friends and the procession is headed by "a long row of elegant coaches with some of the city's most prominent families . . . After this row of coaches came the various labor organizations with their solemn banners in an unending procession . . . One of the city's respected liberal clergymen and one of the best known labor agitators gave orations at the grave . . . Daniel Nilsen and his unhappy daughter could not have had greater redress" (244–245). While the powerful Plummers may despise Norwegian immigrants, they are in turn despised by Americans of all classes, the wealthy friends of the Walters as well as the trade unionists, who turn out to show respect for Daniel and Dina Nilsen.

While the social criticism of *Bag gardinet* was obfuscated not only by the extremes of melodrama but also by rather abstract and secondhand accounts of labor conditions, *Sara* (1891), the last novel he completed in America, takes us on a tour of the sweatshops of Chicago. Janson's indignation in his descriptions of Sara's attempts to make a living by selling her labor and not her body affects his style, giving the reader a sense of the stenches, the misery, and the pain of the factories and tenements. His indignation is informed by several contemporary studies of the condition of female workers, in particular Helen Campbell's *Prisoners of Poverty*, which had been reviewed by Drude Janson in a Norwegian feminist journal when it appeared in 1887.

Sara is a young woman suffering under the strictures of a low-church Lutheranism in an immigrant settlement. All knowledge of the world is regarded with suspicion and the Bible and devotional texts are the only books permitted in the home. Sara's awareness of the outside world has been awakened through visits to a well-read and liberal-minded tailor with her childhood friend, the rebellious Peter, who later runs away from home while Sara is forced into a marriage with an older, sanctimonious pastor. Numbed into submission, Sara's next awakening comes with a visiting artist who beguiles the clergyman with flattery and tempts his wife with an enticing aesthetic view of life. When she burns all bridges and takes the train to Chicago to join the artist at his hotel, his shock is ample demonstration of the folly of her illusion. Her struggle to survive in the urban jungle is an occasion for Janson to survey the working and living conditions of the Chicago poor. In these chapters, where stark reality offers more than sufficient material for the elicitation of emotional response, Janson is more sparing than usual with his stock of sentimental and melodramatic trappings and, consequently, achieves the best prose fiction of his American years. But while two younger contemporary masters, Crane and Dreiser, allow their Maggie and Carrie to be carried along by a convincingly inexorable succession of events, Janson again resorts to improbabilities and the interference of a fairy godmother character at the nadir of Sara's exposure to the horrors of working-class Chicago. She becomes the companion of the kind and wealthy Mrs. King, reads the works of the great authors, travels in Italy, and is finally joined in marriage with Mr. Brown, a proponent of the Social Gospel.

This brief summary fails to do justice to the melodramatic improbabilities that crowd Janson's pages, as when Sara's clergyman-husband is killed in a railway accident just after Sara has sent a telegram to Mr. Brown referring him to Mrs. King for the explanation of why she will never be able to marry him and just in time for her to send a new telegram—"I am free, I am yours!" (398). It is more important for an appreciation of Janson's development, however, to note that this novel is his most thoroughly American one. Its main characters, including Sara and Peter, are American, its plot takes the heroine not merely out of the Norwegian settlement and into the larger American world of Chicago, but into the same Europe that American authors were using as a setting for their characters, the Italy of artists and American tourists, rather than the fjords and valleys of Norway, a country that exists only as a distant memory of tales told by Sara's parents and as a cultural presence represented by the works of Ibsen as appreciated by the intellectuals of Chicago. But although *Sara* is an American novel and although its author was an immigrant, apparently committed to the service of his Minnesota congregations, *Sara* never became a part of the literature of the isolated American land of *Vesterheimen* but was published only in Kristiania and Copenhagen and was not reviewed in this country. As Drude and Kristofer Janson were seemingly showing affinity in their literary work and increasing involvement with the concerns of their adopted country, they were actually drifting apart and also growing disenchanted with the United States. With the break-up of their marriage in 1893 they returned to their native land. Their Minneapolis interlude, however, demonstrates the viability of the literary culture of *Vesterheimen*: Kristofer, an established Norwegian author, could live eleven years in the United States without interrupting his literary career; Drude could return to Norway to continue a literary career begun in the United States.

NOTES

1. Draxten 1976 is a well-researched biography of Janson's American years.

2. Although his theological position was Unitarian, he cherished a near mystical love for Jesus that found expression in some of the hymns he published in *Budstikken* in 1883. After a mystical experience of a visitation of Christ in 1891, Janson composed his emotional *Jesus-sangene* (1893).

3. 2:1–4 (Jan.–April 1885). The quotation below is in April 1885, 103. Janson's story may not be as extreme as critics claimed. In 1896 O. Odson had a similar story, "Went Out of Her Mind: How a Norwegian Farmer's Wife Lost Her Senses," in *Husbibliothek* (19 Feb.).

4. In Janson's 1889 novel, *Bag gardinet*, Frank Plummer's mother will not permit him to associate with an immigrant woman and when Frank asks her whether Scandinavians are not as good as others, she responds: "So that's what you think? ... Don't we see them come in loads to this city and fill the depots so that proper people cannot enter them? Their clothes smell, as do their chests of food, and flocks of dirty children hang around them. They are the ones who sweep the streets, who go down into the sewers, who do all the lowliest work; they are the ones who fill the saloons and the penitentiary. And you want to take the likes of such people into the house of Plummer?" (97).

5. It was first published in Copenhagen in 1887 with the bland title *En ung pige* (A Young Girl). The Danish publisher had apparently not liked the Americanism of *En*

saloonkeepers datter, which she used for the 1888 serialization in *Illustreret Ugeblad* as well as for the 1889 edition, both published in Minneapolis by Christian Rasmussen (Draxten 161, 177). Her husband wrote a preface for the first edition, recommending his wife's first literary attempt to the public and insisting that "The descriptions of Minneapolis are rendered with photographic accuracy."

6. The careers of the two women were unusual, but not improbable. In the 1870s there was a Norwegian woman practicing medicine in Minneapolis (see advertisement for Milla C. Svanøe in *Budstikken* 6 July 1875) and there were female clergy in the Unitarian Church, notably the Reverend Marie Jennie, who married the novelist Frederic Howe.

7. *A Beast of Labor,* also in 1889, is mainly the work of Amandus Norman, then a student, later Janson's successor as minister in his Minnesota congregations. Again the main female character is a victim and her situation is changed when her husband learns to appreciate her and the position of women.

8. While Thomas B. Walker is primarily remembered for his contributions to the art collections of Minneapolis, Harriet G. Walker gave much of her time to the Sisterhood of Bethany and Bethany Home for the care of "erring women." In the novel, Edith Walter devotes her time to the same category of women, her "chickens," as she calls them, and has founded "Bethany Home." The Minneapolis lawyer Andreas Ueland was a close friend of the Jansons. In the novel a judge named Ueland is friendly to Linner.

Knut Teigen and Peer Strømme:
Natives of Wisconsin

For the Jansons, Norway remained the home to which they eventually returned. For Knut Martin Olsen Teigen (1854–1914) and Peer Olsen
Strømme (1856–1921), home was Wisconsin. So strong, however, was the
pull of *Vesterheimen* on these native-born Americans that it remained their
main culture of reference throughout their lives. Teigen's relationship to
Vesterheimen was troubled and difficult; Strømme became its most popular
man of letters, fondly referred to as the Norwegian-American Mark Twain.

Knut Teigen was born in Koshkonong in Dane county, Wisconsin, one
of the first Norwegian settlements and a founding congregation of the
Synod.[1] His parents selected Luther College as the educational institution
for their talented son, but he left this church institution and got his BA degree from the University of Wisconsin. His eventual break with the church
of his childhood did not come easily; before he decided to become a doctor, eventually graduating from the medical school of New York University
in 1882, he studied for the ministry at Luther Seminary in Madison. For
twelve years he practiced medicine in North Dakota, where his statewide
involvement in professional matters and politics and his contributions to
Normanden, the weekly newspaper edited by Foss, won him recognition and
the Independent Party nomination for Congress in 1892. Teigen did not
run, however, but withdrew from the race when the Democratic Party en-
dorsed the Independent ticket with the exception of himself. Teigen had
contributed articles to medical journals as well as to *Normanden*, but it was
in Minneapolis that he awoke to the pursuit of a literary career. His first
book, *Ligt og uligt i vers, skisser, humoresker og smaaskildringer fra livet blandt de*

norske i Amerika (A bit of everything in verse, sketches, humoresques, and short stories about the life of Norwegians in America), appeared in 1899.

Teigen had an uncommonly sensitive ear for language, writing not only in the Danish-derived *riksmaal* and the alternative written form, *landsmaal*, but having his characters speak in a rich variety of dialects, often with a liberal blend of Americanisms, one aspect of the code switching characteristic of immigrant speech. From this point of view his childhood in Koshkonong was an advantage: no single locality in Norway would have given him such an opportunity to hear so many varieties of his mother tongue or to develop such an open and non-judgmental attitude to them all. A fine example of his linguistic versatility is the short story "Værkefingeren" (1899, The infected finger), where one after another of the narrator's neighbors gives advice on how to cure his badly swollen finger, each in his or her recognizable dialect. "One is surprised as well as puzzled by how it has been possible for this poet, born and bred in *Vesterheimen*, to acquire this linguistic versatility in Norwegian," Julius Baumann wrote in his review (*Smuler* Nov. 1905) of Teigen's *Vesterlandske digte* (Poems of the western land).

Koshkonong was Teigen's point of departure and to Koshkonong he returned, in verse and in prose, to praise it, poke gentle fun at it, or simply record his memories in fond veneration. The first section of *Vesterlandske digte* (1905) is called "Patriotic Songs." The opening one, "Vesterlandet," is a paean to the United States, but the most "patriotic" is "Koshkonong," where he hails his childhood region as "the jewel among the settlements of the West" and praises it as the "wonderful and loving mother / of Vesterheimen's ancestral blossom from the North." Teigen can write with humor about his childhood settlement, can even satirize his people, but his stories of Koshkonong do not have the bitter undertone of so many of his other texts. Whether they are presented as fictions, like "Paa sellebreisjen" (At a celebration), or as personal memories, like the account of Christmas customs among the immigrants in "From before Christmas to after the New Year," Teigen's Koshkonong texts are a rich store of insight into rural life in Wisconsin in the 1860s and 1870s.

When Teigen wrote about AMNOR or USONA, however, his satire could be vicious.[2] The most frequent targets of his satire were social pretensions and the retention of an obsequious respect for old-world class distinctions. Teigen resented the condescension of colleagues with European degrees as well as the ingrained respect of immigrant farmers for the Norwegian educated classes, and in some stories and poems he vents his chagrin by exposing the character of Bombastus Blæhr to ridicule.[3] In the stories

"Værkefingeren" and "From home" Blæhr is a medical doctor who had barely been able to get his Norwegian degree but who makes good money on easily fooled immigrants who admire him for treating them as he would the peasantry of the old country. He has the support of Lutheran pastors who look down upon their American-educated brethren: "It may indeed be doubted whether real theologians can be educated here in America. These farmer youths from Decorah [that is, Luther College], Augsburg, and St. Olaf may be good enough in their way . . . but real learning, ability, and inspiration . . . that is something entirely different" (1899, 64–65). In the narrative poem "Bombastus Blæhr" (1899, 132–144) the title character does not have a medical degree, since a sexual scandal has forced him to leave Christiania in a hurry. After a few years of sponging on whoever is impressed by his old-world manners, he gradually sinks to the bottom of Chicago society, his body eventually turning up in the anatomy room of a medical school. Such texts are evidence of the powerful counter-integration forces at work in the immigrant community. The second-generation son of immigrant farmers, with degrees from the University of Wisconsin and New York University, may be a man of standing in American society, but in *Vesterheimen* the sons of immigrant farmers are ranked below the Bombastus Blæhrs. In revenge Teigen places the skeleton of "the fine Christiania snob" in a display case where it can gather dust as later generations of immigrant sons pursue their professional studies.

The Blæhr tales and his most ambitious story, "An everyday tragedy" (1899), are set in Kaksville, Iowa, his fictional version of Decorah, home of Luther College and the administrative center of the Synod. In Teigen's language *kakse* is a prominent member of society and Teigen's Kaksville ("Bigwigton") is dominated by shopkeepers and professionals whose pretensions and sense of importance are punctured by their laughable antics in scrambling for positions of authority and respect. The inanities of Kaksville society fawning for the attention of a visiting Norwegian statesman, and the risible pretensions of a group of businessmen discussing the interpretation of a phrase in a play by Ibsen—these are some of the comic situations in which the would-be social elite of *Vesterheimen* is exposed to ridicule.[4] "En hverdagstragedie" ends with the deaths of two pillars of Kaksville society, Pastor Kleven and Hans Tippen, the wealthy pharmacist, after it has been revealed that the former is the natural father of the latter's only child. In its explicit treatment of sex, for instance in the episode revealing the size of Tippen's penis, the story is daring for its time and place.[5] But it is far from lurid sensationalism and simple pastor-bashing: both Kleven and Tippen are rounded characters and the text moves from satirizing them to accepting the humanity of both. A reading that merely sees the sterility of Tippen as an emblem of the cultural and intellectual emptiness of *Vesterheimen*'s striving middle class or the peccadillos of the Lutheran pastor as an indictment of the Synod would close our eyes to a complex literary text.

Teigen's laughter is more often friendly than derisive, as in the portrait of the frontier pastor in "Hunting and spiritual guidance" (1899), who has to resort to his gun in order to care for his stomach as he sees to the spiritual needs of his far-flung flock. But few of the leaders of the cultural life of *Vesterheimen* had the insight to laugh with Teigen. He felt hampered by the strictures of his immigrant society as did Hilda Houg, the protagonist of "The Seamstress" (1899), who is driven from home by the pietistic moralism of her father and his church. Although she achieves success as an independent businesswoman she is eventually brought down, literally killed, by the strictures of American fashion: the corset and a debilitating diet. Her American beau runs off with her money and she comes home to die.

Teigen, who started out as an American nationalist, grew as impatient with the United States as with AMNOR. Although he toyed with the ambition of writing a novel, as evidenced by the 1908 fragment "I slatten østom Svartekulpen" (Haying east of Black Pond), the closed texts of satires and epigrammatic verse largely replaced his open fictions. In the expanded second edition of his first book, *Ligt og uligt*, in 1907, the new texts are either reminiscences of Koshkonong or satires on the inability of the people of *Vesterheimen* to work together for a common goal. His contributions to the monthly *Smuler*, beginning in the first volume in 1901 and continuing through 1910, are increasingly bitter and acrimonious. His early satires on religion and the servants of the Church had been the friendly jibes of a close bystander; his later attacks on all religion in the Swedish-American atheistic journal *Forskaren* are bitterly negative. The United States, praised in the 1905 poem "Vesterlandet" as the home of freedom, has in *Some Popular American Paranoias at Large* (1911) become the home of "monophobias" such as "Ontophobia—fear of naked truth" and "monomanias" such as "Hæmatomania—blood lust." In the series of critical essays on Norwegian-American culture and society in *Forskaren*, "Usonas vikingestamme" (1909, The Viking tribe of USONA), he is still literally on speaking terms with *Vesterheimen* but in 1911 he lashes out in English against immigrants and unassimilated Norwegian Americans suffering from Anglophobia, "a provincial endemic mental aberration characterized by linguistic illusions, religious or military hallucinations and financial, political , or literary delusions" (26). Three years before he and his wife took their own lives, Teigen was attacking what had been the foundation for his own intellectual and spiritual life and recommending that immigrants who insisted on the "lunacy" of "trying to build a little Ireland, Finland, Norway, Sweden, or even a miniature Germany or American France, over here" should be put in "a strait-jacket" and shipped to Halifax (28–29).

When he published his last volume of verse, *Amnorske digte*, in 1913 he was still addressing the people of the "little . . . Norway" he had put so much effort into building in the United States, but he announced on the title page that he had moved out of its narrow confines by presenting himself as a member of the "American Materialist Association, the Secular Union and Freethought Federation, the London Rationalist Press Association, the University press Alliance of Europe, &c, &c." None of these poems is as interesting as the best ones in *Vesterlandske digte* and Teigen's resignation is expressed in the concluding "The scald's evening sigh":

> Hear, powerful God of Light with heart afire
> Show me before I go to rest
> How you melt the layers of ice on lakes and land
> And bring seeds to aspire and grow.
>
> How does your light enter the kernels
> And awaken the grey plains to the life of spring?
> Dear Sun, lend me a little power to thaw frozen minds!
> Teach me the art of reaching hearts!

In 1902 O.S. Hervin wrote rhymed couplets to "The rising poet of USONA," suggesting that greatness was yet to be achieved (*Smuler* Jan. 1902). By then, however, Teigen had written his best work. Most of his creative effort had been dedicated to the preservation and development of *Vesterheimen*, but his last years were embittered by the conviction that this effort had been wasted and that the melting pot and not multiculturalism was the American way. The concluding essay in his 1909 series on "Usonas vikingstamme" is called "I Usonas smeltedigel" (In Usona's melting pot), with the Button Molder's judgment on Ibsen's Peer Gynt as motto: "He has set at defiance his life's design; / Clap him into the ladle with other spoilt goods."[6] Taking his cue from Ibsen and Zangwill, Teigen proclaims that "A lot of slag must be boiled out of Jews, 'Christians,' Vikings, and the rest before the precious metal in each nationality is sufficiently purified to be molded into the crown of Queen Columbia" (342). Teigen, however,

Peer O. Strømme (1856–1921).

never quite made the long and difficult course from Koshkonong through the melting pot: a comparison of his 1911 book of essays in English with his last volume of poetry (1913) can leave no one in doubt as to which language was closer to his heart and more obedient to his will.

Peer Strømme wrote English with greater ease than Teigen, indeed he insisted that "it is obviously most natural for me to write in English,"[7] yet he never seriously considered leaving the small world of the Norwegian-American press for the greater challenges and potentially larger rewards of Anglo-American journalism. Indeed, whether we look to his two autobiographical novels or to his memoirs for evidence, none of the choices Strømme made seem to have cost him much struggle; these books are remarkable for their absence of inner conflict. He did what was expected of a bright boy in a Wisconsin Norwegian settlement; he went to Luther College at the age of thirteen and after completing the six-year course he went

on to study theology at Concordia Seminary in St. Louis. In due time he
was ordained and served for some years as a minister, first in Minnesota and
then, briefly, in Wisconsin. Although he resigned from the ministry, he
never broke with the church, unlike Teigen.

In an appreciative essay on Strømme in *Symra* (1905) Johannes B. Wist
took exception to Strømme's claim in his novel *Halvor* that the early Norwegian settlers had "founded the new Norway, that we have inherited and
know and love as the best of a hundred lands" (1893, 6), explaining that the
view that "we should actually have founded a *new Norway* over here" was
"based on a misconception," since "we are lacking in all prerequisites" for
such a society.[8] Nevertheless, Strømme persisted in giving his allegiance to
this "new Norway" and in his obituary (*DP* 23 Sept. 1921) Wist regretted
that Strømme had not chosen to express himself in English. His preference
for Norwegian "was evidence of how closely he was bound to Norwegian
America, of how deeply he felt at one with the cultural beginnings that
have emerged among our people and of the faith he had in their continued
growth." In his memoirs Strømme writes of his first visit to Norway in
1890 that it was then he "became Norwegian and in a way found myself. It
was then I began to understand that if I were to develop I would have to
experience my relationship with my own people; that I would suffer spiritual starvation if I did not have my roots in the land of my fathers" (1923,
278).

This love relationship with his people in America was reciprocal:
Strømme's popularity in *Vesterheimen* as journalist and lecturer was unequaled. And he achieved this popularity against considerable odds. He was
an active Democrat at a time and in a region where Norwegian Americans
almost to a man were Republicans. During his ministry theological strife
seemed the central concern of the several Lutheran churches and many
congregations of the Synod, to which he belonged, were torn apart. But
even though he constantly campaigned against Norwegian candidates, was
involved in polemics with fellow journalists, and even broke with the majority faction of his Synod before he left the ministry, there was seldom any
rancor and friendships remained intact. The newspapers he was involved in
had limited circulation and were frequently on the verge of failure. But
whatever he wrote in one paper would be reprinted in or quoted by others,
so he had readers throughout *Vesterheimen*, and when he was billed as a lecturer people would flock to listen. It was certainly not his few and hurriedly
written books that made him popular; rather, it was his popularity that sold
his books. Glimpses of his engaging personality may still be had in his

memoirs (1923), which he wrote during his last illness, hoping that the royalties would provide his widow with a pension.

After he left the ministry in 1887, Strømme moved from one job to the other in order to support himself and his family until he finally found a relatively stable source of income for the remaining years of his life in the Grand Forks, North Dakota, newspaper *Normanden* in 1909. He taught briefly at St. Olaf College and, as principal, at an academy in Mount Horeb, Wisconsin; he was editor of the small but prestigious Chicago newspaper *Norden*; he edited and published the failing Wisconsin newspaper *Superior Posten*; he edited the ambitious literary monthly *Vor Tid*; he was political correspondent and associate editor of the English-American, as he called it, *Minneapolis Times*; he sent contributions to a wide range of Norwegian-American newspapers; he campaigned for the Democratic party; and he did literary hack work, translating books, mostly popular fiction, for *Skandinaven* and other publishers, and writing a textbook on church history. This did not leave him much time for his own writing and he scribbled down the chapters of *Halvor* (1893/1960) as the weekly installments appeared in *Superior Posten*. He had set out to emulate H.A. Foss, but although he claimed that the serialized novel generated a thousand or so new subscriptions, it could not save the newspaper. Relieved of his editing and publishing responsibilities, Strømme found time to do a few hasty revisions, add two concluding chapters, and have the novel published. It apparently sold very well, but Strømme claims that because he was never good at bookkeeping he did not make much money from his bestseller (1923, 321–322, 335).

Like *Husmands-gutten*, *Halvor* is a success story, but there all similarity ends. *Halvor* is a fictionalized retelling of his own childhood and youth and in its descriptions of life among the early settlers of central Wisconsin and its accounts of Luther College and Concordia Seminary in the 1860s and 1870s it is a valuable documentary text. It has little interest as a novel, however, partly because the documentary takes over and partly because the characters do not come alive. Halvor leaves home at the age of thirteen without any but the most superficial qualms, he studies theology and is ordained without any religious reflection, and he presumably falls in love and is married without any disturbing emotions. All of this is as Strømme felt it should be; in his memoirs he twice makes a point of explaining that "to reveal the heart's most secret thoughts of a sacred nature" to the public would be to "violate what I regard as a proper sense of spiritual modesty" (1923, 7, 220). This may be an acceptable position for most private uses but spells disaster for the novelist or autobiographer.

While *Halvor* had presented life among "the older generation of Norwegian Americans," its sequel, *Unge Helgesen* (Young Helgeson), Strømme explains in his preface, is about "the new generation in a settlement in the Red River Valley that is an offshoot of the old one." Indeed, many characters in *Unge Helgeson*, who are making new homes on both sides of the Minnesota-North Dakota border, are the sons and daughters of the pioneers in the Wisconsin settlement described in *Halvor*. The most interesting sections of Strømme's novel are those describing the often violent politics in northwestern Minnesota that gave the Fifth District the epithet "bloody." But his accounts of political strife fall short of the superior achievement of Johannes Wist's later trilogy. Strømme may not have had the ability and certainly did not take the time to create living characters and an integrated plot.

Strømme's third novel has little in common with any other work of fiction to come out of *Vesterheimen*. It may seem strange that a man of Strømme's presumed sunny disposition, whose most popular piece of writing was the often reprinted poem "Solsiden" (The sunny side, 1920), should write so dark a novel as *Den vonde ivold* (1910, In the clutches of the evil one).[9] But then he made every attempt to distance himself from his book and never acknowledged its authorship. The book is catalogued by the Library of Congress under the name of its fictitious narrator, Halfdan Moe; a Peer Strømme look-alike character in the novel, Ole S. Benson, is the fictitious writer of the novel's preface who explains that the manuscript was entrusted to him by Halfdan Moe before he died; Benson has in turn given the manuscript to Peer Strømme, whose name appears on the title page as translator. Strømme began serialization in *Eidsvold*, a journal he co-edited, but after the first installment (Feb. 1910) reactions were so strong that the publisher fired his co-editor and promised that his journal would not publish such "swinish literature" in the future. The arbiters of literary taste in *Vesterheimen* were no more open to the decadence they saw prevalent in Europe than were their English-speaking colleagues in the Midwest. To no avail could Strømme have tried to argue that *Den vonde ivold* was a moral work. Indeed, he had tried to argue this case some years earlier when he explained in his first editorial in *Vor Tid* that the journal would not touch anything "that sensible and informed people would call immoral literature." However, he added, the Norwegian literature that had been thus characterized "had preached that the wages of sin is death, and a book that does this cannot really be called immoral be it ever so shocking and ugly" (1904). That the wages of sin is death could indeed have been set as motto for the novel he published six years later, but the guardians of morality had made clear that this was no excuse for portraying sordid depravity. In *Evangelisk Luthersk Kirketidende* the editor had reviewed the first issue of *Vor Tid* with special attention to the editorial and its alleged defence of immoral literature: "Has a man who has been a minister in the Norwegian Synod and presented fine testimonials against filthy literature really come so low that he absolves all the indecent filth that in Norway was called bohemian literature from the judgment of immorality so long as it preaches that the wages of sin is death, which presumably it has generally done?" (31: 882–883). No wonder the one-time clergyman tried to disclaim authorship of *Den vonde ivold*.

The novel tells the story of two young men, Nils Holmsen and Halfdan Moe—the latter the narrator, a malformed consumptive, the former the one who from an early age believes himself to be in the clutches of Satan—from their years in grammar school and at the university in Christiania to Chicago, where they come in halfhearted pursuit of careers in journalism: "If it won't work, I've heard that it is an easy matter to fall off a bridge there and drown" (39). Since he had only secondhand information on the low life of Christiania, Strømme is more convincing in the Chicago chapters, which are informed by his own newspaper days there. One focal point of the novel is the Story Club (a fictional version of the Chicago Press Club), to which the two main characters are introduced by Ole S. Benson, who, like the author, is an American-born journalist in both languages, attends church, is temperate, and has an interest in Democratic politics. The publisher they go to for employment is obviously John Anderson of *Skandinaven*, and Halfdan Moe, like his author, makes a kind of living by translating popular novels for him.[10] Holmsen never becomes the diabolic character Strømme intended. He is given to pronouncements on free love and the respect owed to prostitutes, and develops a self-destructive attitude that drives him to the suicide with which the novel opens. Before the physically and spiritually infirm Moe dies in a state institution, he talks with the understanding pastor Hansen and gives his manuscript to his faithful friend Ole Benson. His last words are those of the remorseful publican, "God be merciful to me a sinner."

Hardly a great novelist, Strømme was a great traveler, finding his true vocation in 1890 when he ventured for the first time outside the Midwest and visited the land of his parents as well as Sweden, Finland, and Russia. Wherever he traveled he wrote reports for a newspaper and it was with these articles that he gained the attention and won the hearts of the inhabitants of *Vesterheimen*. Reports of a journey round the world in *Normanden* were reprinted as a book (1911) and some travel essays are preserved in *Jul i Vester-*

heimen (1915, 1921), but most of his travel writing is in the pages of newspapers from which they are unlikely to be excavated.

Strømme also wrote poems, in English and Norwegian. These are also
for the most part hidden in newspapers (for example, *Reform* 3 and 24 April
and 15 May 1900), but marked by his final illness, he selected a handful for a
slim volume (1920), among them "Solsiden" and his declaration of love to
his wife, "Til min hustru." His verse is inferior to his prose, as is evident in
"A Dark Night," where the speaker is related to the narrator of *Den vonde
ivold*, and "The Norwegian America" and "Song for Sons of Norway,"
which give voice to banalities compared to his prose on the same theme.
Whatever their defects, his poems were popular, and a few months after the
volume had been published by Augsburg, Strømme was asked to prepare a
new edition. It may be, as he explained to Buslett, that the sales amounting
to $500 in royalties were due to the "many acquaintances and kind friends
who have heard that I have been ill for a long time and needed the money"
(26 Feb. 1921, OABP), but the popularity of his poems is also evidence of
how well he was attuned to the people he wrote for.

As the end was approaching, Strømme was involved in two projects, one
an exercise in nostalgia, the other an effort to promote Norwegian-American
literature. His memoirs (1923) were a farewell to the people and places of
his beloved *Vesterheimen*; the delightful account of his many and varied experiences at times takes on the appearance of a catalogue, as he enumerates
the names, families, and even genealogies of the many people he had met on
his way through life. It has been suggested that his motive for listing so
many names was the hope that many would buy a book in which they were
mentioned. Be that as it may, the effect is more that of taking farewell than
of mercenary promotion, and the land he takes leave of, the broad expanses
of the Midwest, takes on the appearance of a land peopled largely by Norwegian Americans, Strømme's "new Norway."

Before he was forced to accept the inevitable outcome of his last illness,
Strømme had planned yet another visit to Norway in the summer of 1921.
Some years earlier he had been elected chairman of the virtually defunct
Norwegian-American Writers' Association and on 3 February 1921 he
wrote to Rølvaag: "Aren't you the secretary of our writers' association?"
(OERP). Strømme had been in touch with the chairman of the Norwegian
Writers' Association, Johan Bojer, who had expressed interest in coopera-
tion between the two associations, and Strømme had immediately made
proposals for the Norwegian publication of a representative selection of
Norwegian-American texts. In his letter to Rølvaag he claims that publish-

ers in Christiania were interested in such a venture and suggests that he could negotiate on behalf of the Association since he is going to Norway anyway. At this point he thought of including Rølvaag's *To tullinger* (1920) and his own *Halvor*, and by 23 February, when he wrote to Buslett, he had a longer list: "Poems by Baumann and Wilhelm Petterson, something by Buslett, a story by Simon Johnson and one ditto by H.A. Foss, *To tullinger* by Rølvaag, Kirkeberg's *Minder fra Valdres*, Mengshoel's *Mene Tekel*, Rødvik's 'Stories from Canada', an expanded edition of my 'Poems' and *Halvor* etc." A few days later he specified *Fra min ungdoms nabolag* as the Buslett novel he would prefer (OABP).

Up to the time he died, Strømme was actively engaged in the building of his "new Norway" and confident that it would continue to thrive. In a farewell letter, published in many newspapers and included as the preface to his memoirs, Strømme regretted that he would be unable to see the outcome of "the battle to reinstate a democracy with full freedom of speech and thought. But our country will manage this, too, without my help" (1923, 7). By the time his memoirs were published, however, it had become clear that immigration restrictions would be permanent and that the "new Norway" Strømme had devoted his life to would soon become history. When Waldemar Ager reflected on the contrast between the two Wisconsin writers, the embittered Teigen and the optimistic Strømme, he suggested that Teigen's despair may have been a consequence of his genius: Strømme "was spared Teigen's fate and retained his good spirits because he was wiser and less gifted" (Wist 1914, 298).

★   ★   ★

Optimism had been simpler around the turn of the century, when the growth of the population of *Vesterheimen* had coincided with its cultural growth and a significant Norwegian branch of American literature seemed in the making. Reviewing Teigen's *Vesterlandske digte*, Julius Baumann admitted that the book had its imperfections but that this was not the time to meet literary attempts with negative strictures: "Let us give this literature a home. Let us as gardeners lovingly weed away the stultifying growths that cling to it and cut off the sick and crippled twigs. Should it bleed, then let us apply the wax of tolerance to the wound. When it is cleaned and watered, let us place it in the sun. Let us then say proudly and encouragingly: 'Here is "your" work and here is "his." It is good, but it could and should be better. Now you will have to compete and see who will do best'—and we shall see that some time in the future some 'Foss,' 'Strømme,' 'Ager' and 'Teigen' will stand forth as a Bjørnson, an Ibsen, a Lie, and a Garborg on American Soil" (*Smuler* Nov. 1905). Baumann was not alone in looking forward to a future when the literature of *Vesterheimen* would be recognized as the equal of that of the old country. In 1876 Bernt Askevold had believed it possible to retain Norwegian as an American language for several centuries, and the growth of immigration had bolstered such heartening visions. The institutions, publishers, journals, bookstores, libraries, and reading societies were firmly established. Novels, plays, volumes of verse and short fiction, and belles lettres of all kinds appeared regularly. The year before Baumann had looked forward to the arrival of an Ibsen or a Bjørnson in *Vesterheimen*, Buslett had made a similarly prophetic statement. Looking back, he saw the literary efforts of the previous decades as merely the foundation and preparation "for the art of bards and for men in the saga seat." As the following chapters will demonstrate, such optimistic faith in the future of a Norwegian-American literature was widespread and not without grounds. But by the time the writers that Buslett and Baumann had looked forward to had appeared, their reading public was in decline. As the growth of publishing and book distribution had been key factors in the birth of an American literature in Norwegian, its coming of age coincided with the erosion of the basis for such institutions. Events were to show that Strømme was right in his belief that Norwegian publishers were ready for Norwegian-American books, but, paradoxically, by then authors had to depend on publication in their old country because publication of fiction in Norwegian was no longer profitable in their new one.

NOTES

1. Biographical information in the Ludvig Hektoen Papers, NAHA.
2. USONA is an acronym for the United States of Norwegian America and AMNOR is American Norway. Both have adjectival forms.
3. Bombastus Blæhr has the pretensions suggested by the bombast in his first name while his family name gives associations both to the actual civil servant-class family name of Blehr and to conceitedness: *blære* means bladder and *blæret* or "bladdered" is a common adjective meaning conceited.
4. The Norwegian politician Viggo Ullman visited the United States in connection with the Chicago World's Fair in 1893. The discussion of the interpretation of a line from Ibsen's *Brand* (239) is probably suggested by Ibsen's response to Peer Strømme's farfetched interpretation of a line from that play (*B* 6 Jan. 1892).
5. Another story that would have shocked the delicate sensibilities of most editors is "The Christmas Guest" (1899), which begins as the standard sentimental story of

the unexpected guest on Christmas Eve and ends with the daughter sending her unwed mother to bed with the guest, who has turned out to be her natural father.

6. The translation is by William Archer in the fourth volume of Scribner's collected edition of 1907. The first American production of Zangwill's *The Melting Pot* was Oct. 5 1908, and it was published in 1909.

7. Editorial, *Vor Tid,* 1:1 (1904), 2.

8. This quotation from *Halvor* is the conclusion of a sentence that begins: "They were heroes, the Norwegian settlers who in those days had the courage and the love to leave their impoverished homes between the mountains and seek bread for themselves and their families in what appeared to be a totally strange world and . . . " This sentence is not included in the edited English translation of 1960. Two chapters, one on the attractiveness of the saloon to the early settlers and one on congregational strife, are also omitted.

9. *Den vonde ivold* was inspired by a Norwegian novel by Hans Jæger, *Fra Kristiania bohemen*, which had been confiscated on its publication in 1885. The preface to Strømme's novel claims that the original manuscript had the title "Chicago bohemen" (The Chicago Bohemians). As if to counter accusations of plagiarism, Strømme has his narrator show his first chapters to a clergyman who claims it is merely a warmed-up version of Jæger.

10. The Press Club and the editorial offices of *Skandinaven* are also described in Strømme's memoirs. The novel's Richard Otis is a portrait of Opie Read, the friend most fondly remembered by Strømme from the Press Club, some of whose novels he translated into Norwegian.

PART FIVE

Culmination

Celebrations, Controversies, and Appraisals:
1884 · 1905 · 1914 · 1925

Many Norwegian Americans still celebrate the 17th of May, the constitution day of their country of origin, but there are no similar manifestations of ethnic consciousness among such close relatives as Americans of Danish or Swedish descent. Neither do the English celebrate their ethnicity, while descendants of immigrants from neighboring Ireland do display theirs on St. Patrick's Day (joined by many others simply for the fun of it all). One shared characteristic of the Irish and the Norwegian immigrants is that they came from countries where nationhood could not be taken for granted.

Although Norway had declared its independence from Denmark in 1814, it had to accept the role of minor partner in the double monarchy of Sweden and Norway. But it retained its liberal constitution and throughout the nineteenth century the history of the growth of democracy is also the history of the movement toward complete independence. With a monarch insisting on his sovereign prerogatives and a *Storting* or parliament equally insistent upon its authority based on popular sovereignty, it was unavoidable that the conflict should also be regarded as a national one, between a Swedish monarch and Norwegian institutions. An important battle was won in 1884 with the beginnings of parliamentary government that had a galvanizing effect on the ethnic consciousness of Norwegian Americans. They rallied to the support of the new Liberal Party, collecting funds that financed the party in its early phase.

The conflict was not resolved until the *Storting* dissolved the union 7 June 1905. Support was unanimous in the Norwegian-American newspapers. In *Skandinaven* Peder Langbach hoped that "the example from Norway would have an awakening effect on us who are in this country," and

Seventeenth of May parade in Ballard, Seattle, Washington, 1994. Courtesy James Vatn.

suggested that the 7th of June be celebrated among Norwegian Americans (10 Jan. 1906). But the 17th of May was already established as the day for the manifestation of bonds between Norwegian Americans and their country of origin, and newspapers could report that in 1906 these celebrations attracted greater participation than ever before. In one of the many speeches on that day, the audience was reminded that "Since we last celebrated the 17th of May many and great things have happened ... If we as Norwegians had reason before to be proud of our fatherland, our traditions, and our people, we now have all the more" (Hougen 1906, 3). *Decorah-Posten* noted that churches had been involved in the celebrations for the first time (22 May), and *Skandinaven* reported that for the first time the day had been given official recognition in the United States: in North Dakota it had been celebrated in Grand Forks under the auspices of the state university and in Chicago the governor of Illinois had been a speaker (18 May). Reflecting on the implications of 1905 in *Kvartalskrift*, Johannes B. Wist noted that Americans in general had "discovered Norway" and that Norwegian Americans had acquired a new pride in their national origin (Jan. 1906).

    This pride was further bolstered by the celebration of the centennial of the Norwegian constitution in 1914. Two committees had very different demonstrations of national pride in mind. One set about organizing a "memorial gift" to the home country, the other began to plan a gathering of

Norwegian Americans from all over the country in Minneapolis and St. Paul. While the contributions to Norway in 1884 had been politically motivated and partisan in spirit, the 1914 gift had no suggestion of any party affiliation. But it proved difficult to unite Norwegian Americans behind a single national cause. The cathedral in Trondheim, where King Haakon VII had been crowned in 1905, seemed a fitting recipient of a centennial gift but many immigrants objected to giving money to a project in a region to which they had no ties. Consequently, it was decided to create a fund for the victims of calamities or poverty (*DP* 16, 20 Jan. 1914). The primary bonds of many immigrants were to their home valley or region and the subscription lists in *Decorah-Posten* reveal that more money was collected in 1913 and 1914 for local projects in Norway than for the nationwide "memorial gift," which eventually grossed the equivalent of 250,000 *kroner* (*DP* 23 June 1914). There were hardly any dissenting voices, however, to the three days of celebration in Minneapolis and St. Paul, and an important reason for the support for these festivities was that they incorporated the local as well as the national interest and were organized and sponsored by the joint council of the *bygdelag*, societies organizing Norwegian Americans with roots in a specific district or *bygd*. Approximately 50,000 people took part in the two processions and in the many meetings, reunions, and entertainments on the Minnesota state fairgrounds 16–18 May 1914. Lovoll has noted how this celebration took on symbolic value, demonstrating both the strength and the contributions of Norwegian Americans to American society (1975, 120; 1984, 183).

The beginning of the *bygdelag* movement in 1901, the organization Det norske selskab (The Norwegian Society) in 1903, and other cultural and social associations in the early years of the century, the merging of the main Norwegian Lutheran churches into one Norwegian Lutheran Church in America in 1917, the many ambitious journals that were launched in the early years of the century, and the celebrations of 1905 and 1914 — these were all expressions of a sense of being not simply Americans and certainly not Norwegians, but of proudly being not ethnic, since the term was yet to be used, but hyphenated Americans. In *Decorah-Posten* a contributor noted that "both native-born Americans and immigrants prefer to place a nationality indicator followed by a hyphen in front of the noun when speaking of naturalized Americans . . . Norwegian-Americans should do the same and follow the others in cultivating their national heritage." The recently formed Norwegian Society was recommended as a step in the right direction (13 Nov. 1903). In any account of the social and cultural life of Norwegian Americans the *bygdelag* movement must have an important place, while the avowedly elitist Norwegian Society may be dealt with in a few sentences. A *bygdelag* was typically a strong and vital organization for three to four decades; the Norwegian Society, the proclaimed protector and promoter of Norwegian culture in the United States, never had more than a few hundred members and after a brief active period became only a paper organization. Yet it stimulated some of the more important literary debates in *Vesterheimen* and was the main battleground for the two opposed views of the nature and aims of a Norwegian-American literary culture.

Rasmus B. Anderson, the one-time champion of Norwegian-American literature, now turned ultra-conservative, almost succeeded in killing the society at its birth. In his newspaper *Amerika* he insisted that only *bona fide* Lutherans should be accepted as members. The Norwegian Society in America was nevertheless duly constituted in Minneapolis 28 January 1903 after Anderson had walked out of the assembly. The society immediately bent over backward to assure skeptics and doubters of its conservative credentials. Noting that the society was to work for the preservation of the Norwegian heritage in the United States by "disseminating good Norwegian literature," O. S. Hervin observed that the interpretation of "good" would be the major "stumbling block": "Since the committee consists of three clergymen and one professor of theology . . . and a doctor who is probably included as an ornament, we should be able to foresee that 'good' literature will be devotional books, Sunday-school tales, and biographies of more or less modern saints" (*Smuler* July 1902). Hervin was unfair, however, in concentrating his satire on the clergy. Norwegian-American culture as a whole was more conservative than that of Norway, both because an immigrant culture tends to preserve a tradition rather than develop it and because this particular one was also a part of the culture of the conservative Midwest.

At the banquet after the first general assembly Professor Julius Olson of the University of Wisconsin was the main speaker and he attempted to assure skeptics within the church that the Norwegian Society was not in conflict with their moral views. The professor of Scandinavian literature explained that the society would not approve of realistic literature for an uneducated audience: "Although I believe that the works of our greatest authors may be read with benefit by educated and mature men and women, I am also convinced that the majority of these works are not suitable reading for a peasant-born commonality, such as the majority of our people in this country . . . *A Doll's House*, which is so obvious and transparent to an educated person, a play where egotism is relentlessly lambasted and where equality between spouses is championed with the most fine-honed weapons, is not at all obvious and transparent to an uneducated or undeveloped person" (*DP* 8 Sep. 1903). The professor's way of eating his cake by insisting that he did not intend to share it with the *hoi polloi* would not have brought his predecessor, Anderson, or the conservative clergy over to his side. For them most contemporary Norwegian literature, including Ibsen and Bjørnson, was dirty or "swinish."[1] It is not easy, however, to see the difference between the views of Anderson and the writers with whom he was in constant disagreement. For they not only claimed that Norwegian-American literature was purer and more wholesome than that of Norway, but would, as Buslett did in *Skandinaven*, dismiss much of the latter as "bedroom literature." But the difference between Norwegian and Norwegian-American literature went deeper than the treatment of sexual matters. Our literature "is foreign to them—just as Norwegian literature is foreign to Norwegian Americans, except for a few educated ones" (28 Sep. 1923).

Buslett's views were shared by Waldemar Ager, whose main statement on the negative development of Norwegian literature is a series of three articles in *Kvartalskrift* in 1910. In *Smuler* Hervin observed that *Kvartalskrift* had so few readers that it could hardly be taken seriously (Sept. 1910), but the impact of the written word does not depend only on how many you reach but on whom you reach, and Ager must have been gratified when he received a letter from the manager of *Skandinaven*'s bookstore in Chicago, thanking him for his advice on what books should not be sold by them (25 Oct. 1911, WAP). *Skandinaven* was the largest secular bookseller in *Vesterheimen*; its ecclesiastical counterpart, the Augsburg Publishing House, would not have contemplated distributing any of the books Ager wrote about. Wist was also impressed by Ager's survey of current Norwegian literature and asked him to write a revised version of it for the prestigious journal *Symra* (1911). Ager, as usual, wrote with a certain flair: "Hate became evil and was called realism; boldness became shamelessness—and it was realism; spontaneity became brutality—and it was realism; love became lewdness— and it, too, was realism." Ager was not without sophistication and explained that books could be "raw and offensive without having to be immoral," but it was nevertheless Ager's sensationalist message, that explicit sex was dominant in contemporary Norwegian literature, that received attention: "Virtually all love relations in this literature are on their way to the bedroom" (*Kv* Jan., July 1910). The squeamishness of Norwegian-American culture was natural to most of its writers but increasingly an uncomfortable restriction

A representative assortment of Norwegian-American newspapers and periodicals.

on some. Even Ager loosened up as he developed, and for Rølvaag the prudery of *Vesterheimen* had become unbearable by the time he wrote his most important work.

But the main literary dispute in *Vesterheimen* in the early decades of the century was not so much concerned with the purity of Norwegian-American literature as with its very existence: was there such a thing, could there be such a thing, and if so, was it worth having? Such discussions had been introduced in the first newspapers before the Civil War and were given new impetus by the founding of the Norwegian Society. In the 1903 yearbook of Det norske selskab Johannes B. Wist agreed that the society's aim to preserve the Norwegian language in America could be fulfilled only by having a literature. And he insisted that this literature could not simply be a transplanted Norwegian literature—just as American literature could not be a transplanted English literature. A Norwegian-American literature will have to give us "recognizable characters from the life that surrounds us. We must attempt to reconstruct in literature the life of our people, in work and in thought, in views and in actions, in way of life and in our peculiar context" (1904, 86–87). But on further reflection he became more skeptical: Norwegian-American literature is "the result of Norwegian impulses and American only in the sense that it more or less happened to be written while a writer was in this country" (*DP* 5 Jan. 1904). A few months later he arrived at the view that was to rankle colleagues like Buslett and Ager: the basic conditions for an independent literature did not exist and the work to keep a Norwegian literary culture alive in the United States must concentrate on the promotion of literature from Norway: "Norwegian literature in America is only conceivable in connection with the literature of the homeland and the little we may be able to contribute will never be more than a shadow of what has already appeared full-bodied on the soil of our fathers" (10 May).

Wist was the main speaker at the banquet in Dania Hall in Minneapolis following the second annual meeting of the Norwegian Society. He repeated the views he had developed in his 10 May essay, and claimed support from the American literary establishment. William Dean Howells had, according to Wist, "recently declared that as yet not a single truly American novel has been written . . . the national setting as a whole has not yet developed anything culturally typical which could be mirrored in the country's literature."[2] So how could one dare to "hope that a small Norwegian population . . . will be able to create an independent literature or contribute to source material for an original intellectual life" (Lovoll 1977, 40, 41). As a people that culturally speaking are "wandering, nomads in transition from one nation to another," it is to the mother culture that Norwegian Americans must look for nurture until their descendants "have become assimilated, and, as an integral part of the nation, can more exclusively nurture themselves on its cultural fruits" (39). Consequently, the main obligation of the Norwegian Society was "to build bridges and maintain the bridges which already exist between the fatherland and its emigrated children" (45). Ager was so incensed by Wist's speech that he improvised a counterstatement, taking his cue from Wist's closing image. He "had little faith in 'bridge building' between Norway and the emigrants" because the people there had no interest in those who had left. Consequently, "we had better make do with what we could create ourselves" (*DP* 6 Sept.). As editor of the society's quarterly, Strømme could not but publish Wist's speech in the first issue, but his heart was with the other side and he invited Ager to submit an essay presenting his views in the following issue. Ager soon succeeded Strømme as editor of *Kvartalskrift* and until it ceased to exist in 1922 he used it to propagate his views. Ager accepted Wist's view of a people "in transition from one nation to another" but insisted that a literature would ensure that "our saga will . . . be written in a way to indicate that we have left independent cultural traces which mirror our own lives, our own struggles" (Lovoll 1977, 47), words that echo Knud Langeland's first editorial in *Skandinaven* (1 June 1866) where he had explained that "No people can claim to be civilized unless it leaves behind testimonials to its history."

Ager's main argument for cultural independence is that the culture of Norway was no longer the culture of the Norwegian Americans and that its literature is "as strange to us as is American literature" (48). His attacks on realism in Norwegian fiction in 1910 were not merely the squeamish reactions of a conservative prude but part and parcel of his view of the separate paths the two cultures had taken because of the radical differences between the experiences on the two sides of the ocean. Rølvaag was to develop this view in essays and fiction without sharing the prudery of Ager and Buslett. It is expressed in his first novel, *Amerika-breve* (1912, America letters): "When we severed our ties with our Fatherland, we became not only strangers among strangers, but we were cut off from our own nation and became strangers to our own people. Our pulse no longer throbs in rhythm with the hearts of our own kindred. We have become strangers; strangers to those we left, and strangers to those we came to" (1971, 126).

When Strømme wrote to Buslett 28 September 1903, a few weeks after the annual meeting in Minneapolis, requesting an essay "on the conditions for an independent Norwegian-American literature" for his new literary monthly *Vor Tid* (OABP), he was obviously asking for a response to Wist. Buslett lifted his title, "Om betingelserne for en norsk-amerikansk skjønlit-eratur" (1904, On the conditions for a Norwegian-American literature) from the editor's letter, and in an unintended refutation of the laments on the lack of materials for an American fiction by James Fenimore Cooper and Henry James, but in deliberate rebuttal of Wist, he presented his list of the material available to the writer. Here he includes "a unique pioneer life in the forest and on the prairies," "a unique development in church organi-zation and education as well as in politics," "a special tone in human rela-tions," the peculiar Norwegian-American language, "the newcomer," in particular the educated one and "the student from Karl Johan [the main street in Christiania on which the University had its buildings] with his fan-tasy aspirations and his sarcasm about life among us, the letters home," the wild tales told about us in newspapers in Norway, and "the longing for home that already has its peculiar yet insipid poetry." The inhabitants of *Vesterheimen* are neither Norwegians nor Americans, he explained, as had Ager, but Norwegian Americans. "And it is as such that we must work out our lives, our art, and our literature."

Despite the aggressive tone and occasional bombast of these polemics the relations between the participants were far from acrimonious. It was Wist who had nominated Ager to succeed Strømme as editor of *Kvartal-skrift* and when he reviewed Ager's new volume of short stories (*DP* 30 Sept. 1904) he was positive in spite of his misgivings about their didactic character: "It may yet be that Waldemar Ager (or someone else) in time will produce something that from a purely aesthetic and cultural viewpoint will provide evidence for his theory that the Norwegian-American soil is sufficiently fertile for a future independent and original literature." Indeed, it would seem that Wist gradually came around to at least wishing that Ager and Buslett were correct in their predictions. In a review of Ager's 1913 volume of short stories he pronounced the stories "accurate depictions of Norwegian-American life, and if such literature could thrive amongst us . . . it would be possible to speak of a real Norwegian-American litera-ture, a literature that is both a fruit of the life our people have lived in this country and a signpost on the road that leads into the future. Our public will determine whether the books by our authors will achieve this aim" (*DP* 8 Jan. 1915). Judging from the brief life span of *Vesterheimen*'s many lit-erary and cultural journals and magazines in the early years of the twentieth century, however, it was no easy matter to get the support of the public.

Kvartalskrift may appear to be an exception, running from 1905 to 1922. But this was due only to the dedication of Waldemar Ager—and even he was able to give the quarterly only a faint semblance of life in its last years. By the time of the 1923 annual meeting of the Norwegian Society twenty-six members had paid their $1.00 dues.[3]

Light and satirical where *Kvartalskrift* was heavy-handed and straight-forward, idiosyncratic and iconoclastic where *Kvartalskrift* was ideological and constructive, *Smuler*, which appeared with 32–34 page monthly issues from 1901 to 1910 and then with increasing irregularity until its demise in 1916, had little in common with *Kvartalskrift* beyond being the product of an equally dogged journalist, Ole S. Hervin. At the end of his third year he claimed fewer than 800 subscribers, barely enough to cover his expenses (Dec. 1904). By the end of 1909 so many of the then 3,000 subscribers had not paid that there could be no issues for the two first months of 1910 (March 1910). Among the contributors to *Smuler* were Buslett, Teigen, often as MOT, and Julius Baumann, who signed himself Julius Apostata.

More concerned with the cultural politics of the old country was *Norrøna*, whose editor, Peer Storeygard, proclaimed it "The First Journal in the Norwegian Language in Vesterheimen." For Storeygard the Norwegian language was *Landsmaal,* and *Norrøna* advocated its use in Norway as well as in *Vesterheimen.* The eight pages of each monthly issue in 1900 offered the subscribers less to read than an average issue of most weekly newspapers, and since it had only four pages a month in its second year, it is not surprising that it ceased publication by the end of 1901. In 1914 it was revived and had a new run of two years with a maximum of about 1,000 subscribers (Lovoll 1970, 91).

The main impulse behind *Kvartalskrift, Smuler,* and *Norrøna* was idealistic. *Vor Tid*, published in Minneapolis 1904–1907, was born as a business venture. The former clergyman B.B. Haugan had experience from publishing and other business and his partner, Olaf Huseby, had been a publisher in Christiania before emigrating. They offered Peer Strømme a decent salary in order to secure an editor with experience as well as a large potential public.[4] In an ambitious editorial, Strømme announced that he would give priority to "articles by our own people, by Norwegian Americans" (1904, 1: 2). In the second issue the publishers claimed more than 2,000 subscribers, and 17 January 1905 *Vor Tid* had more than 3,000. Haugan insisted that he needed 10,000 to break even and in the February 1906 issue he claimed almost 8,000 and now set 25,000 as his goal. According to Strømme, who left the editor's chair after five issues, it was a hand-to-mouth operation: "Regardless of how much money came in to *Vor Tid*, there was never cash in the register" (1923, 291). It held to a high editorial standard, however, presenting fiction, criticism, and general essays, and 8,000 subscribers is an impressive figure.

Subscribers who missed *Vor Tid* after its demise did not have to wait long until three other publishers presented journals with similar cultural ambitions. In Minneapolis Laurits Stavnheim remade his weekly socialist newspaper *Politiken* into the monthly *Ny Tid* in 1907. Although he presented a varied literary fare in addition to essays on politics and social issues, his politics alienated many who had enjoyed *Vor Tid*. The North Dakota *Eidsvold* (1909–10), however, was in the mainstream tradition of *Vor Tid*. Before he died in 1911, Kjetil Knutsson, assisted first by Jon Norstog and then for a short while by Strømme, edited and published two volumes where Norwegian-American writers such as Norstog, Foss, Simon Johnson, Strømme, Hjalmar Rued Holand, and Kristian Prestgard appeared along with Georg Brandes and Knut Hamsun. In June 1912 Hans Jervell started a journal with the same title in Fargo but did not achieve the editorial quality of his predecessor. In spite of ten or more pages of advertisements in each issue and Jervell's last-ditch attempts to associate his journal with the growing *bygdelag* movement, *Eidsvold* ceased with the issue for June 1913. In 1908 the Northern Book and Music Company in Chicago subtitled their new monthly, *Idun*, "Journal for Literature, Music, etc." To Haldor Hansen, the publisher and editor, *Idun* must have seemed a sound business undertaking since it also functioned as an advertising medium for his music publications and bookstore. But by April 1909 *Idun* ceased to appear monthly and it came to an end in May 1910.

A few publications outside the Midwest also catered to the literary interests of *Vesterheimen*. Indeed, *Skirnir*, published in Tacoma from December 1895 to November 1897, was a pioneer effort, attempting to realize the same ambitious editorial aims as the later *Vor Tid*. Another western attempt was *Varden*, edited by Josef Straaberg and Christian Johannessen in Salt Lake City, 1910–1911, and featuring such Norwegian-American writers as Ager, Fridthjof Lunde, Rølvaag, and Strømme. Paradoxically, the large Norwegian-American community in New York was more isolated from the cultural centers of *Vesterheimen* than were Salt Lake City and Tacoma. The immigrant community in New York maintained closer relations to Norway than to the Midwest, much as the urban culture of the east coast in general tended to face Europe rather than the heartland of America. This may be observed in the only Norwegian-American novel to be published in New

York, Helge Amundsen's *Hjemløse fugle* (1910, Homeless birds), where most of the characters are back in Norway by the time the series of unrelated and awkwardly structured plots has come to an end. The author, who for a brief period edited *Norges-Posten* (Wist 1914, 159), frequently makes negative observations on American society and clearly does not identify himself with the country he is living in.[5]

Not until 1926 did a journal with literary pretensions appear in New York, and its character speaks both of the different nature of the New York community and of a later type of immigrant. In his first issue of *Symra*, the young Karsten Roedder, editor-to-be of *Nordisk Tidende*, appealed to the recent urban immigrant, alienated from the traditional culture of *Vesterheimen*, who either did not read Norwegian-American publications or found them "decrepit, reactionary, and obtuse, without other intellectual interests than a worn phrase that has long been a comic fiasco—the preservation of our heritage." Attempting a sophisticated urban style, reviewing Broadway shows and opera and paying little attention to Norwegian America, Roedder was an outsider to the cultural centers of *Vesterheimen*. The fourth issue (21 Oct.), which had a short and innocuous essay on Ager, commented on Norwegian-American literature, explaining that no suitable work had been found for serialization: "As far as we know, no modern literary work [in Norwegian] has appeared in America since *Under Vestens himmel* [1918], which was about animal rather than human life." When he made fun of *Decorah-Posten* (No. 4) and *Minneapolis Tidende*, which had characterized the New York magazine as provincial (No. 5), the editor further demonstrated his ignorance of *Vesterheimen*. After seven issues no more was heard of the Brooklyn *Symra*.

The name, meaning anemone, a flower of early spring in Norway, had been used as a title with symbolic implications by the Norwegian poet and creator of *Landsmaal*, Ivar Aasen; but while Roedder was aware of this antecedent he was ignorant of the *Symra* edited and published in Decorah by Wist and Prestgard in 1905–1914, probably the most ambitious and certainly the most voluminous periodical publication in Norwegian in the United States. That this distinction should fall on the small Iowa town of Decorah rather than on New York is emblematic of the character of Norwegian-American culture. *Symra* was Wist's response to the concluding statement in his own banquet speech in 1904 on bridge building, and in their subtitle the editors addressed themselves to "Norwegians on both sides of the ocean." Norwegian-American writers and scholars appeared alongside prominent contributors from Norway; immigrant reminiscences interpreted the experiences of an older generation for the more recent ones, and literary essays gave critical assessments of writers such as Strømme, Ager, and Norstog. Blegen considered it "the best literary magazine that the Norwegians in America ever published" (1940, 552). But it depended on the support of B. Anundsen, publisher of *Decorah-Posten*, and the dedication of its two editors, and by 1914 it had become clear that it did not have enough subscribers to continue publication.

Although few periodicals were able to publish for more than a few years, their number suggests not only a large potential readership but optimistic publishers. In his historical survey of the press, Wist considers the question why periodicals were less successful than newspapers and observes that while the newspapers were alone in bringing news from Norway and the immigrant communities, the periodicals competed with the many journals in English for readers with literary and intellectual interests. Moreover, the newspapers themselves served many of the functions of journals, printing reviews of Norwegian and Norwegian-American books as well as also articles that made it possible for "their readers to keep up with intellectual developments in the home country" (1914, 181–182). The supplements of *Decorah-Posten* (*Ved Arnen*) and *Skandinaven* (*Husbibliothek*), which had popular articles on a variety of topics as well as serialized novels and short fiction, continued publication for several decades after Norwegian books and more serious literary journals had in effect ceased to appear in the United States, as did the independent popular journal *Kvinden og Hjemmet* (The woman and the home), founded and edited by Ida Hansen and published by her husband in Cedar Rapids, Iowa, which lived for sixty years, from 1888 to 1947, when it was still printed in the antiquated black letter type that had gone out of use in Norway by the middle of the nineteenth century.[6] Any survey of publications that omitted the newspapers, the popular journals, and the plethora of religious publications would misrepresent both the size and character of the readership in the early decades of the twentieth century.

One journal that bridged the gap between church and literary publications is the Christmas annual *Jul i Vesterheimen* (1911–1957) published by the Augsburg Publishing House of the United Norwegian Lutheran Church and, after the merger of three churches in 1917, of the Norwegian Lutheran Church in America (NLCA). The immigrant churches, mainly Lutheran, were the single most influential body of institutions for linguistic and cultural preservation. But while language preservation was central to the cultural ideology of writers such as Ager, Buslett, and Rølvaag, the churches

Augsburg Publishing House, early 20th century.

were necessarily pragmatic in their language policy. This pragmatism was spelled out in an editorial in the church weekly, *Lutheraneren*, in 1922: "The church has nothing to do with promotion of language preservation or Norwegian culture. The church has nothing to do with language change or Americanization. The church is not a servant of the languages; the languages shall serve the church, and the church shall serve the people—with one or several languages as the occasion demands" (1104). By the end of the nineteenth century warnings were heard that if the churches did not adopt the English language they would lose the younger generations. In 1896 the managers of Augsburg urged the Annual Meeting of the United Church to start work on an English version of the hymnal: "That time is not far away when these words must be written above every Norwegian church door in our Association: 'The English language or death.'"[7] In urging a switch to English at this early date, however, the management of Augsburg was jumping the gun. Norwegian was still the preferred language of the overwhelming majority of the congregations and the press had little success with ventures in English. The first English hymnal, in 1898, was printed in only 2,000 copies compared to the 33,000 copies of the Norwegian version.

With its readiness to adopt English, Augsburg did not seem a likely candidate for a major role in cultural and linguistic preservation. As church publisher, its main responsibility was to provide books and pamphlets for

Anders M. Sundheim (1861–1945) at his desk in the 1920s.
Courtesy Augsburg Fortress, Minneapolis.

congregations, schools, and domestic devotions. There was a slight change in the publishing pattern before the turn of the century and by the end of the first decade of the next one Augsburg was not only publishing pious books for general reading but their bookstore was advertising fiction by Ager and Strømme. In 1911 and 1912 two events suggest a change in policy: the appearance of a lavishly illustrated Christmas annual, *Jul i Vesterheimen*, and the publication of *Amerika-breve*, a novel without any discernible Christian message, by a Paal Mørck, later revealed to be a young professor of Norwegian at St. Olaf College named Ole Edvart Rølvaag. *Jul i Vesterheimen* was from the start the pet project of Anders M. Sundheim (1861–1945), a printer who had advanced to assistant director in 1904 (Sundheim 1957). Until it ceased publication in 1957, *Jul i Vesterheimen* was an important outlet for short fiction and poetry for Norwegian-American authors.

Sundheim saw no conflict between his duties as a servant of the church and his conviction that the future of his people in America depended on the preservation and cultivation of the Norwegian language. In 1912 he contributed to a publication of Concordia College in Moorhead, Minnesota, where he observed that the college had a dual responsibility, one "religious," the other "national" and cultural: it should "lead our youth into a Lutheran Christian life and Norwegian culture" (Reite 70). Sundheim's ascendancy at Augsburg is evident in the twenty-fifth anniversary report in 1915, which for the first time commits Augsburg to this dual responsibility: "Without exaggeration it may safely be said that our book concern has become a factor of great importance in the religious, literary, and cultural development of our people in this country." In hoping that Augsburg will not only "continue to be a blessing to our Church" but be "a means of ennoblement among our people," the report implies that Augsburg had a cultural responsibility that included all Norwegian Americans, not merely the members of the United Church.

After the 1917 merger, Sundheim became the new director of a consolidated Augsburg. His report to the NLCA in 1918 includes a policy statement that was to be a source of contention for the duration of his term of office: "It is also the aim of the publishing house to publish books both of a religious and of a purely literary character in order to encourage literary efforts among our people. It is important that people who are endowed with natural talents should be given an opportunity to reach the public. Such people are more numerous than we are apt to think. They should be helped and encouraged. Both as a people and as a Church we need it for our own good. Our spiritual and cultural strength as a Church is judged by the books we publish, and our literature is an indication of our spiritual life" (Skordalsvold 1931, 742). Sundheim's report justifies secular publishing in ecclesiastical terms. A secular argument is presented in English in his essay, "A Literature of Our Own," in the *Augsburg Publishing House Bulletin* 1: 3 (Jan. 1920): "As Americans, we feel that the literature of this country is our literature, expressing and interpreting our common American life; but as Americans of Norwegian descent, having our own peculiar characteristics, history, traditions, institutions, and problems, we need also a literature of our own."

Sundheim's policy could not but be controversial. Not only did the shift in policy take place when xenophobia was at its height during and immediately following the First World War, but it ran counter to the usual policy of a church publisher. By 1928 his position at Augsburg had become untenable and his resignation was accepted in January 1929. From the perspective of a church historian, Sundheim's policy resulted in "a conspicuous fringe of non-religious titles" that was uncharacteristic of the dominant trend in American Lutheran church publishing of the time. The new manager, Randolph E. Haugen, redirected the "publishing enterprise in a single-minded effort to serve the church" (Ozolius 1972, 206, 232–233). The implied criticism of Anders Sundheim, however, is unjust. He, too, was a servant of his church and saw all his efforts at Augsburg as directed to this service. But Sundheim had a broader view of the role of the church and, consequently, of the role of its publishing house than his critics. The NLCA was by default the institution that represented the largest number of Norwegian-speaking Americans; to Sundheim his work for a Norwegian-American literature and his work for the church were not only compatible but inseparable.

The front lines between the proponents of language retention and of Anglicization had hardened during and after the First World War. Wist, who in 1904 had spoken of the transitional character of the immigrant culture, now seemed a preservationist compared to those who questioned the patriotism of any American who used a foreign language. The new church formed in 1917 had identified itself as "Norwegian" but wartime nativist pressure led to a resolution (533 voting yes, 61, no) at the first biennial convention in 1918 to drop this adjective. The resolution had to be confirmed by a second biennial meeting, and the opposition mobilized, forming a society, For Fædrearven (For our ancestral heritage), with the purpose of keeping the church "Norwegian." The prime mover and secretary was Rølvaag. In a newspaper in Canton, South Dakota, *Visergutten*, he wrote a series of articles and edited a debate on Norwegian-American culture (3 Feb. 1921–15 June 1922), eventually publishing his contributions in 1922 in *Omkring fædrearven* (On our ancestral heritage). As nativist sentiment subsided with the end of the war and a disruptive debate on a non-theological issue was foreseen, leaders of the church themselves recommended that the convention reverse its position in 1920 (Chrislock 1977, 220–221). The spokesmen for "our heritage" had won the battle against what had seemed significant odds. Indeed the ground swell of sympathy for the preservationist stance not only demonstrated a reaction to the experience of near persecution of minority cultures but seemed to augur a revitalization of *Vesterheimen*. The Norwegian Society had never gained popular support in the early years of the century; For Fædrearven could boast annual meetings with several thousand participants (Rølvaag 1922, 17).

In the first of the three essays in his 1922 volume, "Naive reflections on our heritage," Rølvaag develops a theory of ethnicity and describes the traits and characteristics that Norwegian Americans may contribute to their new country. While this essay presents the most complete statement of the preservationist views shared by Ager, Buslett, Johnson, and Strømme, the

TELEPHONES:
GENEVA 8338
GENEVA 8394

A. M. SUNDHEIM, MANAGER

Augsburg Publishing House

PUBLISHERS & IMPORTERS ~ PRINTERS &
BOOKBINDERS

MINNEAPOLIS. MINN.. Oct. 30, 1922.

Prof. O. E. Rølvaag,
St. Olaf College,
Northfield, Minn.

Kjære Ven:

Tak for brevet.

Jeg sender efterspørsel angaaende læseboken til
alle skoler som har nogen forbindelse med vort samfund,og likeledes til Frikirkens og andre institutioner.

Det er umulig for mig at gjøre noget overslag over
hvor mange eksemplarer vi kan avhænde av boken, "Omkring
Fædrearven." Som arrangementet nu er, har du fuld fri-
het til at utsende cirkulærer og virke for salget av
boken selv. Jeg gjør regning paa, at største delen
vil bestille direkte fra dig, og saa er der ogsaa mange
andre ting som spiller ind. Jeg tror at boken vil faa
gode anmeldelser, da det ligger i norske blades selv-
interesse at boken faar utbredelse, og jeg tror at det
vil være retfærdigt mot dig, at der sættes i forbindelse
med anmeldelserne at boken erholdes hos Augsburg Publishing House og hos forfatteren, Prof. O. E. Rølvaag,
osv.

I vor egen avertering derimot sætter vi selvfølge-
lig bare Augsburg Publishing House, og da det er bedst
for begge parter at boken holdes paa lager "in commission,"
saa spiller det ikke nogen rolle hvor mange eksemplar vi
tar om gangen.

Venligst,

AUGSBURG PUBLISHING HOUSE.

AMS:EE   Ved *A. M. Sundheim*

*Letter to Rølvaag from A. M. Sundheim, Augsburg Publishing House, in regard to
marketing Rølvaag's collection of articles, Omkring fædrearven
(On our ancestral heritage).*

other two essays are more polemical in tone and add little to the theory or the rhetoric of the first. Nostalgia for the Old World has no place in Rølvaag's reflections; he speaks as a Norwegian American, not as a Norwegian. In keeping with the terminology of his day, Rølvaag speaks of "race" where we would speak of ethnicity and he may at times seem to suggest that national traits are not merely cultural but are transferred genetically. Nevertheless, his message to his readers is less concerned with what they are than with what they must do. His appeals to ethnic pride must be understood in a context where the ideologues of Americanism were suggesting that the traits of immigrants were not only undesirable but inferior. In his conclusion to the first essay he speaks to the heart of the matter, the *"sancta sanctorum*: our emotional relationship to the land we have become citizens of and where our children will live and build after us." He asks how someone with a "Norwegian soul" may become a good American citizen, and replies: "let us hold high our heritage; then our emotional relationship to America will be *all right*. For this land needs human beings, not merely creatures" (107–108. Italics are Rølvaag's.).

His implied antagonists are the spokesmen for the melting-pot ideology, who appear to be near relatives of Ibsen's Button Molder. In the last act of *Peer Gynt* the Button Molder explains that since Peer had failed to realize himself in life, he would go neither to hell nor to heaven but would be melted down by orders of a "thrifty" Master who "throws out nothing as irreparable / That still can be used for raw material." Peer protests that even "the old-time judgment" would be better than "simply to disappear / Like a mote in a stranger's blood, to forswear / being Gynt for a ladle-existence, to melt—/ It makes my innermost soul revolt." But he meets little understanding from the Button Molder, who points out that "Yourself is just what you've never been—/ So what difference to you to get melted down?"[8] Literate Norwegian Americans were preconditioned to react negatively to Israel Zangwill's vision of America in *The Melting-Pot* (1909), and Rølvaag merges Ibsen's metaphor of the "melting ladle" with Zangwill's "melting pot": "We cannot be reconciled to the doctrine that it would benefit our country if all its inhabitants become identical, molded in the same ladle, with all dissimilarities ground away. We believe this would impoverish us as a people" (1922, 22).

The "For fædrearven" debate was not an isolated phenomenon triggered by the name controversy in the NLCA, but an episode in a debate where preservationist and integrationist views had been argued from the very beginning. In many respects the arguments remained unchanged throughout

The Norwegian-Danish Press Association of America, 1927.
Courtesy Norwegian-American Historical Association.

the history of *Vesterheimen*: in 1913 Luth. Jæger argued for a transition to English and rapid assimilation in *Symra* in much the same way as he had in *Budstikken* in the 1870s.[9] While Norwegian-American literature grew in quantity as well as quality, criticism did not follow suit. Indeed, few later reviewers rivaled the intellectual sophistication and breadth of knowledge of E.L. Petersen in the 1870s and 1880s. Rølvaag wrote professional reviews, as did a handful of others, but they were conscious of writing for an uneducated immigrant audience. The weekly and semi-weekly newspapers, some purely local, others like *Skandinaven, Decorah-Posten,* and *Minneapolis Tidende* with subscribers all over *Vesterheimen*, were the main vehicles for literary and cultural criticism. Thus the 1904 Norwegian Society controversy was revived in *Decorah-Posten* in 1916–1917 when D.G. Ristad, Julius Baumann, Buslett, Rølvaag, and others responded to the proclaimed "realism" of Wist.[10] The "For fædrearven" discussions were conducted by Rølvaag in the South Dakota newspaper *Visergutten* and a similar literary debate began in *Duluth Skandinav* in 1921, when this newspaper reprinted parts of a polemic from *Visergutten* (see Rølvaag 1922, 111–122). Both newspapers increased their subscriptions because of the interest generated by the controversy, which was reprinted in other newspapers.

The debate in *Duluth Skandinav* picked up after John Heitmann ("Bjarne Blehr") had criticized Norwegian-American writers for drawing negative portraits of their people. His example was Wist, who had given his 1922 satirical novel *Jonasville* the subtitle "A social portrait": "It should rather have been called a caricature—a caricature of the writer's own mind," Heitmann pontificated. "For there is not a single honest person in the book, not a single sane character" (16 Oct. 1922). In the installments that followed, "Bjarne Blehr" criticized "Our Authors" for being overly concerned with the dark aspects of life (5 Dec.). His praise is reserved for Foss, who alone among these pessimists "spoke to the hopes and dreams of the people" (29 Dec.). The pontifications of "Bjarne Blehr" may appear the products of the kind of mind satirized in *Main Street* or *Babbitt*, but he was a deliberately created persona. In letters to Rølvaag, a close friend from the same northern island in Norway, the sophisticated Heitmann writes about the taking on of roles. Typical of his sly wit is his response to Rølvaag's solemn exhortations in *Omkring fædrearven*. Try to imagine, wrote Heitmann, a young man recently engaged and filled with love for his fiancée and hope for his future life with her, who is admonished to love his mother! (8, 20 Dec. 1922, OERP).

Love and loyalty to the land of their choice as well as an abiding interest in the bonds to the land of their mother and father were central to the writers of *Vesterheimen*. This dual set of emotions surfaced on all occasions when immigrants reflected on their achievements or their commitments and was a common denominator in their responses to the Norwegian events of 1884 and 1905 and in their annual 17th of May celebrations. Norwegian Americans, however, also had festive occasions of their own when they met to celebrate their American pioneer past. Such gatherings gained momentum with the growth of historical awareness in the 1870s, and on 5 July 1875 many came to Turner Park in Chicago to celebrate the fiftieth anniversary of Norwegian immigration to the United States. Among the songs was one by R.E. Schei (*B* 13 July) where all joined in singing that immigration was borne by "the flame of freedom" and "powerful ideas" that "liberated" the Norwegian "as from a prison" to "longing for the land far in the West," to which they followed in the footsteps of "the brave Leif and Thorvald" (brothers who on different occasions visited North America in the late tenth century). Although they proclaimed that their material success and their freedom had been won by leaving the prison of Norway, the immigrants in Turner Park in 1875 sang not only of appreciation of their present home but of pride in their origin. Such were also the main themes of the far greater celebrations of the immigration centennial in 1925. But by then the affirmation of American roots set down firmly and deeply in the course of a century was also expressive of a need to refute the still lingering stigma of hyphenation.

As in 1914, the centennial celebration was organized by the Council of Bygdelags, but there were revealing differences between the two. In 1914 Norwegian had been the main language of the various festivities; in 1925

English was dominant. The lone Norwegian voice in the handsomely printed 96-page souvenir program was that of Ager, winner of the essay contest on the theme "Why We Celebrate." For him the significance of the Centennial lay not merely in reminding Norwegian Americans of their achievements but in "underlining the importance of preserving our racial characteristics in order to make contributions of value to the cultural life of the nation" (1925, 13). But to most participants Ager's was a voice of the past. The 1925 Centennial was in many respects "the last rally" (Lovoll 1975, 145) and in spite of a record participation of 100,000 at the main event, the vast majority of these participants were in their daily lives strangers to the *Vesterheimen* of Ager and his dwindling band. The most highly acclaimed speaker at the festivities, President Calvin Coolidge, spoke not of Norwegian Americans preserving a separate identity but of their having entered American life: "You have given your pledge to the Land of the Free. The pledge of the Norwegian people has never yet gone unredeemed." According to a syndicated reporter, "The great roar that rose from Nordic throats to Thor and Odin above the lowering gray clouds told that the pride of the race had been touched" (Lovoll 1975, 167). No less enthusiastic was the response to the President's endorsement of Leif Erickson as the first European discoverer of America, a symbolic gesture of welcome to an integrated ethnic group.[11]

The dominant mode of 1925 was retrospective, and out of this retrospection the Norwegian-American Historical Association was born. Rølvaag became its first secretary and gave much of his valuable time to building up an institution for the preservation of the records of a culture. One controversial issue at the founding was the question of language and it was decided that all publications should be in English in order to address Norwegian Americans as well as the general community of scholars. To Ager, this was tantamount to betraying the cause and he withdrew his initial support for the society, comparing it "to the old man who believed that he would soon die and now wanted to get his papers and affairs in order." Ager was of course correct in seeing NAHA as a recognition of the end of an era. To Lars W. Boe, president of St. Olaf College, "Whatever interest we have in things Norwegian after this will have to be as it is in the NAHA, connected with the laying of the foundation of American life" (Hustvedt 1971, 304).

Although the 1925 festivities did not mark the end of a Norwegian-American literary culture, they came at a time when it was clear that the end was approaching. Year by year fewer congregations were using Norwegian, the newspapers had a dwindling number of subscribers, books had fewer buyers, and Augsburg was ceasing to be an outlet for novelists and poets. Rølvaag was about to publish in Oslo and New York as was his friend Ager. Norstog, Johnson, Dorthea Dahl, and others ceased to publish, while those who kept on wrote for the few remaining newspapers and journals. But before Norwegian-American literature ground to a halt in the 1930s it lived through a brief but intense period of fruition.

NOTES

1. "Griselitteratur"—swinish literature—was a common term. In all fairness to the two professors it should be remembered that in 1903 the drama critics of New York were still having difficulties with Ibsen plays like *Ghosts* and *Hedda Gabler* (Øverland 1968).

2. This runs counter to Howells's published statements on American literature. In a review of Wendell's *A Literary History of America* he insists that American literature was so radically different from English literature that it would fail "so far as it was like English literature, just as English literature would show itself inferior where it was like American literature" (*North American Review* 172 [April 1901], 639). In "A Possible Difference in English and American Fiction" he antedates Richard Chase: "To put it paradoxically, our life is too large for our art to be broad. In despair at the immense variety of the material offered it by American civilization, American fiction must specialize, and turning from the superabundance of character it must burrow far down in a soul or two" (*North American Review* 173 [July 1901], 135).

3. Minutes in Det Norske Selskab Papers, NAHA. *Kvartalskrift* for 1920 had only one 32-page issue and a final issue of this size made up volumes 17 and 18 for 1921–1922.

4. Huseby later published the journal *Vesterland* in Morris, Illinois, which had nine issues in 1915. The first editorial does not mention Norwegian-American literature, and although Huseby wrote to Buslett about a Christmas issue featuring Norwegian-American authors (6 Sept. 1915), it was not realized. At the time, Huseby's main business was the *Grundy County* (Illinois) *Gazette*. Ironically, Buslett had unsuccessfully submitted a manuscript to Huseby in Kristiania in 1888 (24 April 1888, OABP).

5. Amundsen's *Hjemløse fugle* has, characteristically, not been located in any library in the Midwest or West, while copies exist in several libraries in Norway. Wist's history of the Norwegian-American press has twelve pages on North Dakota; little more than two are devoted to "Norwegian newspapers in the East" (1914, 132–144, 157–160).

6. Ida Hansen was assisted by her sister, Mina Jensen, a self-taught typographer. From 1901 the subtitle was in English: "A Monthly Journal for the Scandinavian Women in America." By 1905 the circulation was given as 82,645, a figure that includes the Swedish edition which began in 1893. An English version, *Woman and Home*, was attempted in 1907–1908.

7. Skordalsvold's compilation of translated reports on the Augsburg Publishing House (1931) is in the Augsburg archives. This quotation is on p.345. For a more

complete discussion of the role of Augsburg as publisher of Norwegian-American literature see Øverland 1993.

8. Quoted from Rolf Fjelde's translation, New York, 1964.

9. *Symra* 9: 171–173; *Budstikken* 3 April, 29 May 1878.

10. The debate was initiated by Wist 13 Oct. 1916 and concluded by Rølvaag 9 Jan. 1917.

11. The view that there was a radical change in the nature of Norwegian-American culture in the mid-1920s has been questioned by April Schultz, who argues for a continuing ethnic culture (1991). At issue here is the importance of language in an ethnic culture.

A Broadening Base: Non-fiction
1900–1930

One measure of the vitality of the literary culture of *Vesterheimen* at the turn of the century is its broadening base. The structure of this base had been developed in the nineteenth century. Newspapers—weeklies, some bi-weeklies, and two dailies—continued to play a crucial role as outlets for would-be writers and in the production, publishing, distribution, marketing, and reviewing of books, while monthly and quarterly journals of various kinds were a relatively new feature. Religious books were a significant part of the total production of printed pages, as may be expected in a culture where the churches played such a dominant role. Within the broad genre of religious publications the sub-genre of internecine theological quarrel virtually disappeared as popular reading, while a very different genre, practical handbooks for farming, housekeeping, health, law, language, and other areas of life, more than held its ground.[1]

Johannes O. Liabøe's ambitious four-volume history of religion (1910–1916) did not find many readers in spite of lavish praise in *Kvartalskrift* by Ager, who claimed that the second volume was "one of the most interesting books I have ever read" (Jan. 1913). The success of the gifted amateur historian Hjalmar Rued Holand (1872–1963), however, speaks of a shift in interest from the theological to the secular. Organized by settlements in a chronological order that corresponds to the geographical movement from east to west, his *De norske settlementers historie* (1908, A history of the Norwegian settlements) combines detailed information and narrative sweep. Holand has a novelist's gift for description, characterization, and the revealing anecdote, and, rare in an amateur historian, he frequently allows a glint of humor to slip in and enliven his account. Whether in appreciation of its literary quality or out of interest in their own history, many bought the book. Holand was his own publisher and the first printing had an inexpensive binding, but when a third printing in 1909 made for a total of 9,000 copies, Holand felt safe to use not only more expensive paper and wider margins but a leather binding. In 1912 *Skandinaven* was confident that there was yet a larger market for his book and published a fourth edition. Holand continued to write after the Norwegian-American Historical Association had brought new standards of professionalism to immigrant history, and his 1930 volume, *Den siste folkevandring (The Last Migration)*, was published in Oslo. Rølvaag found it "a unique work in Norwegian literature," comparing it to the medieval Icelandic *Landnámabók (Norden* 1930, 3). Holand, however, had realized that there was a diminishing American public for books in Norwegian and that publication in Norway would not be a natural solution for an American writer. He switched to English, and *Old Peninsula Days* (1925) recaptures some of the narrative qualities of his best work in Norwegian. But he soon devoted himself to the championship of the Kensington Rune Stone and strove to prove that medieval Vikings had roamed in Minnesota.

Thor Helgeson (1842–1928), a Wisconsin parochial-school teacher, was a gifted collector of historical and folkloristic material. While he, too, demonstrates narrative skill, he did not, as Einar Haugen has observed, give his material a coherent structure (1970, 25). His books about pioneer life in the area of central and northern Wisconsin that Norwegian settlers called "Indilandet" are invaluable sources for the lore and everyday life of early Wisconsin. Helgeson is more concerned with life's comedies than its tragedies, and in their folksy humor his sketches provide a necessary corrective to the calamities that dominate much of immigrant fiction. In his first volume (1915 is Haugen's conjectured date) a chapter on "Diverse Trades" even allows a comic view of the whiskey trade, an anomaly in a literature that so often revels in tragedies blamed on the saloon. No less entertaining is J. Swanes's history of the northwestern halibut fisheries that were dominated by Norwegian immigrants (1934).

The work of Martin Ulvestad (1865–1942), farmer and amateur historian and linguist, is graced by neither the narrative gifts nor the sense of humor of Holand, Helgeson, and Swanes. They were writers of considerable skill, Ulvestad was an antiquarian and compiler of facts. His ambition and dedication led him to produce three monumental volumes packed with names and information (1901, 1907, 1913). These and other works were published at his own expense, but sales were disappointing and he became increasingly embittered by the indifference of the people he had set out to serve.

The *bygdelag* movement gave new encouragement to amateur historians. The most ambitious of the historical projects initiated by a *bygdelag* were the four volumes on immigration from Ringerike by Ole S. Johnson (1843–1935), a farmer in Spring Grove, Minnesota, whose other works include an 80-page polemic on socialism (1906). Another *bygdelag* project was the massive history of emigration from Voss (1930), a township east of Bergen, by Knut Rene, who had spent about thirteen years compiling and writing his more than 800-page volume. Other histories commissioned by *bygdelag* cannot compare in quality or volume with these two. K.G. Nilsen published his *Østerdølenes saga* (Saga of the people from Østerdal) in 1938, and a corresponding book about immigrants from Nordfjord by Lars M. Gimmestad appeared as late as 1940. Ager had feared that the *bygdelag* would break up Norwegian America into groups that cultivated a local rather than a national heritage. They were, however, not only the prime movers behind the rallies of 1914 and 1925 but continued to use Norwegian in their publications many years after most other literary activity had ceased.

Immigration and repatriation were also dominant themes in autobiographies and memoirs. Many, however, were also preoccupied with the spiritual life and were intended as guides to salvation as much as records of Americanization. While a good number of those who felt called to write about their lives were clergymen, as might be expected in a culture where they so often had leading roles in the community, the accounts written by their wives are often of greater interest to the reader of later times. The young clergymen who came to serve and lead their compatriots in the early decades of immigration were usually of a background very different from the members of their congregations. Their brides came direct to the frontier settlements from protected upper-middle-class homes in the few urban centers of mid-nineteenth century Norway, and their music lessons, balls, and polite conversation were not an ideal preparation for the society in which they were expected to play an important role. A fascinating account of the experience of a woman who was twenty-one when she came to Iowa with her clergyman husband in 1853 is the diary of Elisabeth Koren, of which an edited version was published in 1914 and a full text in translation in 1955. All her negative reflections on the coarse peasants among whom she had to spend most of her days were expurgated from the 1914 edition. But the full text speaks less of her class prejudices than of her adjustment to her new life. Less ready to adjust was Caja Munch, who came to Wiota,

Elisabeth Koren (1832–1918).
Courtesy Norwegian-American
Historical Association.

Wisconsin, in 1855 with her clergyman husband and returned with him to Norway four years later. Other women who wrote from this point of view were Lulla Preus (1911) and the latecomer Ragnhild Thinn Thvedt, who published her entertaining anecdotal memoirs in 1940.

By 1940, however, books of any kind in Norwegian were rare and the many who wrote memoirs and autobiographies of their immigrant or second-generation experience had turned to English, as for instance Andreas Ueland in *Recollections of an Immigrant* (1929), Nils Nilsen Rønning in *The Boy from Telemark* (1933), and Borghild Dahl in *I Wanted to See* (1944). Such books invariably speak of New World successes, often in the face of adversity. The memoir literature of *Vesterheimen* gives few reminders that the immigrant experience was not uniformly one of success; one that tells a story of misery and failure does so under a thin and not very convincing mask of fiction. John Harildstad's *Bondegutten Hastad under asylbehandling i den nye verden* (1919, Hastad the farmer boy and his treatment in asylums in the New World) is a pathetic account by a naive writer whose incoherence seems due partly to lack of education and partly to mental illness. That the author identifies himself with his protagonist John Hastad seems obvious from the confused preface. He immigrated in 1898 and was soon placed in a Minnesota mental hospital. After four harrowing years as a patient he is sent back to Norway. He returns but is thrown into prison and sent back again. But he is determined to live in America and immigrates to Canada where he becomes a farmer. Harildstad's book is a document of life in a mental hospital from a patient's point of view and of a patient's futile efforts to achieve justice and retribution.

Vesterheimen was a new society, founded mainly by uneducated rural immigrants, and it is little wonder that most critical writing was amateurish and uninformed. One exception was Peter Iverslie (1844–1921), who was only three years of age when he arrived and who, like his fellow Wisconsinites, Anderson, Teigen, and Strømme, chose to live much of his life within the confines of *Vesterheimen*. After two years at the fledgling Luther College in the early 1860s Iverslie turned to farming, first in Wisconsin and later in Minnesota, usually teaching primary school in the winter season (Paulson and Bjork, 1940, 2). Throughout his adult life he was an active man of letters, providing newspapers and journals with articles and book reviews and publishing three books on history (1899, 1902, 1912), one of them in English, and an English translation of a play by Ludvig Holberg (1910). Opinionated and solemn, traits no doubt enhanced by his isolation, he was often embroiled in controversy. But for all his quirkiness, Iverslie was an important contributor to the culture of *Vesterheimen*.

For novelists and poets the lack of constructive criticism was compounded by the reviewers' good intentions. Some lamented the absence of informed criticism and were aware of how essential criticism is to the development of a literary culture. Buslett, responding to justified criticism in *Smuler*, concluded: "To the attack! ye critics; it is criticism that we Norwegian Americans need" (Aug. 1911). As a group of writers with a professional attitude to their craft evolved, they also turned to the criticism of their colleagues as a natural part of their literary work, but since literary sophistication was rare and since most authors saw it as their main duty to be supportive, they seldom contributed criticism of much value. Waldemar Ager is a case in point. As editor of *Kvartalskrift* and *Reform* he felt a responsibility for the development of his culture but his many reviews suggest that he had little sensitivity to or appreciation of texts that went beyond his own conservative realism. Nevertheless, he felt duty bound to praise them. Ager was mystified by Jon Norstog and claimed he was unable to understand his *Landsmaal*, yet he faithfully recommended every book by Norstog that came his way. Rølvaag shared Ager's desire to support Norwegian-American literature, but his professionalism kept him from writing mere blurbs for his colleagues and friends. Authors were used to a sheltered life, however, and Rølvaag's honest criticism had a wounding effect on his friend the novelist Simon Johnson (Hustvedt 1976, 57). Among the reviewers who wrote with insight and understanding during the first decades of the twentieth century were the poets Julius Baumann, Ditlef Ristad, and Sigurd Folkestad. In *Decorah-Posten* the editors Wist and Prestgard on occasion wrote with intelligence and sensitivity about literature and the latter produced a monumental anthology of Norwegian poetry with a general introduction and brief essays on the forty-three selected poets (1906).

Some had critical ambitions that went beyond the occasional book review and it should not be surprising that it was American literature that received their critical attention. C.B. Christensen planned a comprehensive study of American culture but published only an introductory essay on the American assumption of cultural inferiority to Europe and some critical essays on Nathaniel Hawthorne under the ambitious title *Fra Amerikas kultur. Et aandslivs historie* (1898, On American culture: An intellectual history). A book on American civilization, *Amerika og amerikanerne*, had been published in 1887 by the radical journalist Anton B. Lange. His chapter on "Literature and art" claims Poe as the only poet worth noticing in the first half of the century and Howells and James as the only contemporary novelists worthy of comparison with other moderns. Lange dismisses American drama and declares criticism reactionary and prudish (117–119). In his scathing observations on the lack of literary interests in American society, on censorship, scandal-mongering newspapers, the "thick ignorance and proud stupidity" (130) of Mark Twain, and the theater as business, Lange strikes a tone that was echoed two years later in Knut Hamsun's negative portrait of American culture after his return to Scandinavia (1889).[2] In all fairness, however, it should be added that Lange was not more critical of American society and culture than he was of *Vesterheimen* (Wist 1914, 120), and when he writes of how American publishers made profits on pirated editions, prompted by the high import duty on books from Europe, he includes the immigrant presses, with special criticism of *Skandinaven* for its pirated and bowdlerized editions of Norwegian writers (141).

Such sweeping judgmental statements were far from the thoughtful and informed criticism of Oscar Gundersen (1861–1941), a bookkeeper in Chicago for most of his adult life, and probably the most gifted literary critic of *Vesterheimen* after E.L. Petersen, who died in 1887. While Petersen had a solid international education, including theological studies in Rome, Gundersen, who immigrated at the age of twenty-one, was self-taught. With a rigorous discipline rare in an individual seeking knowledge merely for its own sake, Gundersen mastered German, French, and sufficient Greek to read in the New Testament on Sunday mornings (Draxten 1966). He was a voracious reader and developed a habit of writing extensive notes on his readings, often in the form of essays (letter to Norstog 30 Dec. 1932, LC). He began to appear in the Minneapolis newspaper *Budstikken* in 1887 with well-informed philosophical essays on the theory of evolution and Darwinism (4 May, 1, 8 June). A story of unrequited love, "Fiskerens historie," some weeks later, demonstrated a sense of narrative and considerable descriptive ability. He continued to contribute essays and stories to *Budstikken, Minneapolis Tidende,* and *Skandinaven,* and from 1891 these contributions increasingly include poems. This burst of poetic expression, resulting in the volume *Stemningsbilder* (1891, Images of moods), may have been a response to the death of his first wife in 1890. His best poems show promise but he later disavowed most of them in a letter to Rølvaag as "beneath all criticism" (18 Dec. 1928, OERP). While his newspaper fiction is marred by sentimentality, his wide-ranging critical essays are still worth reading. In *Budstikken* he wrote with insight about Bjørnstjerne Bjørnson (9 May 1888), John Stuart Mill (17 July 1889), Matthew Arnold (16 July 1890), Edgar Saltus (8 July 1891), and Tennyson (26 Oct. 1892). Only rarely did he write about Norwegian-American literature, as when he reviewed Ager's first book, recognizing the young writer's talents and encouraging him to separate his writing from his efforts for the cause of prohibition (*B* 26 Dec. 1894).

Gundersen's best book is *Ralph Waldo Emerson* (1910). An early story (*B* 30 April, 7 May 1890) corroborates his claim in the preface that he had made his "acquaintance with the work of Emerson more than twenty years ago," and the book is ample evidence of his continuing interest. Although Gundersen was self-taught, there is little that is amateurish about his work, except in the literal sense that he indeed read and wrote with love for his literary vocation. Gundersen presents Emerson through translations and paraphrases of systematically selected key passages, interspersed with critical comments that are informed by a personal knowledge of German philosophy and the English Romantics. The introductory paragraph to his tenth chapter may give an indication of Gundersen's style and manner: "One who only knew Emerson as, I will not say philosopher since all he has written touches upon philosophy, but as metaphysician, psychologist, and moralist, may draw the conclusion that he had a tendency towards generalization, a disdain for limitations, that both negated critical analysis and rendered it impossible. For the strength of critical analysis lies in limitation, in creating a frame where the individual pregnant statement, the peculiar characteristic, and the dominant trait is at the center of attention. But there is nevertheless in Emerson's genius something that works counter to his contemplative soaring in the vague blue: his individualism and his interest in the individual. In addition there is his sublime and superior sense of humor that is always aimed at the individual and is thus a defense against the rigidity of abstraction" (86). Gundersen illustrates these general reflections with quotations from Emerson's characterization of Theodore Parker, followed by an informed evaluation. A similar look at Emerson's characterization of Lincoln then serves as introduction to a discussion of *Representative Men* and *English Traits* (88–125).

Gundersen continued his life of scholarship, but rarely shared his writing with the public. It may be that he recognized in himself the character of the protagonist in an early story with the longings but not the strength required of a poet (*B* 11 Dec. 1889). This sentimental portrait, however, is set off by a "humoresque" about an isolated and lonely poet looking for someone who will listen to his poem, perhaps the author's wry comment on his own isolation as a bookkeeper at the State Bank of Chicago pursuing his Arnoldian vocation as poet and scholar-critic (*B* 16 Sep. 1892). He sought fellowship in the 1890s in the Arne Garborg Club (Draxten 1966) and from 1925 in Det Litterære Samfund (The Literary Society), where a founding member recollects that he "was often asked to lecture on eminent authors or literary movements in Europe and U.S.A.,"[3] and for a brief period, from 1928 to 1933, he again wrote for the public in the society's journal *Norden.*. This activity brought him into correspondence with Rølvaag and Norstog, but his secluded life at his desk may be as much a reflection of his own personality as of the situation of the intellectual in an immigrant society.

While literary criticism was an esoteric genre in an immigrant culture, there was another prose genre, for which there are no traditional educational requirements, that attracted a large number of writers: the travel narrative. In writing and enjoying travel narratives Norwegian Americans were at one with other Americans: this was one of the more popular genres in the United States of the late nineteenth century, cultivated as an art by writers such as Bayard Taylor and spoofed by Mark Twain. Indeed, the travel narrative may be claimed as the oldest and the most widespread Norwegian-American genre, with the many immigrant letters describing the journey from the old home to the new and the many guidebooks, for example Schrøder's narrative of travel in Canada (Øverland 1989). For the early immigrants in the period of sail a return visit to the old country was virtually impossible, but as immigrants and their children in increasing numbers visited Norway, their impressions were published in newspapers, pamphlets, and books. The best travel writers, such as Peer Strømme (1911), express a simple love of adventure and the desire to share it with others. The lure of the exotic was made acceptable, indeed, recommendable in narratives that presented the experience of missionaries, such as for instance Carl Døving and Hanna Larsen's books about South Africa (1892, 1905), S.E. Jørgensen and Hans Sæterlie's books about Madagascar (1893, 1912), and O.S. Næstegaard's account of his experiences in Mongolia (1895).

Nehemias Tjernagel's account of travel on foot in Egypt and Palestine, published privately in Randall, Iowa, in 1897, may not have reached many readers, but after two more books of travel in English (1913, 1917), Augsburg eventually brought out a handsome second edition of his first book, obviously banking on the popularity of the genre. B.B. Haugan traveled in the 1890s as correspondent for *Ungdommens Ven*. In 1897 he collected his writings in a book he called *Over land og bølge. Reiseskildringer fra Orienten og de europeiske lande* (Over land and billow: Travel narratives from the Orient and Europe). Further evidence of the popularity of the genre is *Bibelens lande* (The lands of the Bible) by the Wisconsin businessman Halle Steensland (1832–1910). Published in 1898, it sold so well that he not only could print two further editions that year but had Augsburg market a significantly expanded edition of 557 heavily illustrated pages (up from 211) with expensive paper and a fancy binding in 1900. Yet another indication that the readers of *Vesterheimen* were no less eager to buy books of travel than those in English-reading America is that Osmun Johnson, who published *Johnson's Journey Around the World* in Chicago in 1887, published a Norwegian edition in the same city three years later.[4]

One admirably suited to write of adventurous travel, but who entered the field too late to cash in fully on his talents, was Ola Særvold (1867–1937), singled out by Ager in his brief 1929 survey of the travel genre in *Norden* as the author of "the best of that kind that I have read." Særvold seems to have been a restless soul. Immigrating in his late teens, he sailed for a few years on the Great Lakes before attending Luther College. After graduation in 1895 he became a correspondent for the Chicago newspaper *Inter-Ocean* (OJSP). His literary ambitions were first expressed in lame English blank verse in *Erling: A Tale From the Land of the Midnight-Sun* (1898). Evidently, he decided to reenter *Vesterheimen* and spent a decade as a free-lance journalist and public speaker, offering the illustrated lecture "Land of the Midnight Sun" in English as well as Norwegian. After a Norwegian interlude of eight years he again returned to the United States and to journalism, as traveling corre-

Ola Johan Særvold (1867–1937).
Courtesy Norwegian-American
Historical Association.

spondent for *Skandinaven* and, after 1925, as a free-lance journalist, with a three-volume account of his travels (1926) based on his newspaper corre- spondence as his major work. The first volume is devoted to travel in Scan- dinavia and Central Europe, the second to the Near East, and the third to Italy and the French Riviera. The accounts of landscapes and monuments, cities and villages combine extensive research with personal impressions; some of the many photographs are exclusive to these volumes and, as does the text, they occasionally place the author in an exotic environment. Sær- vold was his own publisher and had hoped that his handsomely bound and printed set would be found under many a Christmas tree in 1926, but the Augsburg printers evidently needed more time than he had foreseen and the work was not available until January, when he immediately sent copies for review to newspapers and prospective reviewers.[5] He had invited sub- scriptions at a pre-publication price of $3.00 and, judging from his own records, he had more than 500 subscribers before he began printing. By the end of 1929 he had sold more than 2,200 sets, only about 150 of these through bookstores (OJSP). Considering the diminishing market for Norwegian books in America in the late 1920s this is an impressive sale for a three-volume work, but it was achieved only through extensive correspondence and travel, and both author and *Vesterheimen* were too well along in years for a sequel.

Særvold had appealed to his public's interest in Norway and, as may be expected, many travel books were about visits to the ancestral home, occasionally, as was the case with Wilhelm Pettersen (1911) and Erik Johnsen (1918), including accounts of travel in other European countries. Olav Bøhmer (1924) included an account of youthful adventures on the Amazon, and the American-born Carl Roan (1921) added some descriptions of travel in the United States. While many accounts of visits to Norway are both crude and sentimental, such as the unpretentious books by Jacob Berven (1850–1927) in 1916 or Laura Bratager (1862–1934) in 1921, some, as for instance Nils Rønning's (1870–1962) *A Summer in Telemarken* (1903), Pettersen's *Fra Bjørkeskog og granholt* (1911, From woods of birch and fir), and Prestgard's two-volume *En sommer i Norge* (1928 — translated in 1938 as *Fjords and Faces*), have considerable charm and may still be enjoyed.[6] Another book that still has interest is Luther Nelson's account of his experiences in France during the First World War (1917). Nelson begins with his senior year at St. Olaf College, but quickly moves on to Paris where he joins the Morgan and Harjes Corps at the front. His book gives an account of the work of an ambulance driver and concludes on 20 March 1917 with his hopes of joining the air force should the United States enter the war.

Hjalmar Sunde's *Vagabonden* (1903, The vagabond) is a refreshing reminder that *Vesterheimen* was not quite as genteel as the publications of the immigrant establishment suggest. Indeed, when Ager wrote his survey of Norwegian-American travel literature in 1929, he smugly explained that while narratives of tramping life were in vogue in Norway, as was so much other questionable literature, they had not appeared "in books or newspapers over here . . . Perhaps because here those who have lived in such a manner are ashamed of it and try to keep it hidden. It remains difficult to see anything brave or daring in being a blind passenger, being kicked off trains, knocking on kitchen doors, or slouching around as an offense to people who work for their living" (6).[7] Sunde's book, published by the Minneapolis socialist newspaper *Nye Nordmanden*, is similar in content and appearance to those published with such success by Waldemar Kriedt,

books that Ager thought a blot on the reputation of *Vesterheimen.* Sunde's
message, however, is not so much of socialism as of faith in America. His
narrative begins in North Dakota where discouragement leads him to give
up homesteading and return to Norway. He gives accounts of life at the
bottom of society as he moves through Chicago, New York, London, and
Christiania, his home town. At one point he reflects on the foolishness of
people who buy such books as "The Mysteries of London and the ditto of
Paris" (60). Nevertheless, the "mysteries" genre is the one that comes to
mind in reading Sunde's account of low life in these cities. He seems as
conversant with members of the police force as with criminals, and his account of visits to doctors and popular healers demonstrates the differences
in medical aid available to those at the top and the bottom of the social
scale. Disgusted with the class society of his old country, the protagonist sets
off again. Traveling sometimes as seaman, sometimes as steerage passenger,
he goes from London through the Straits of Gibraltar and the Suez Canal
to Ceylon, where he jumps ship, and then on to Bombay, Java, Hong Kong,
and Australia. He is obviously well read, makes frequent literary allusions,
and at times gives conventional accounts of the sights on his way. In Australia he confronts a society that combines the hated class structure of Europe with the rawness of the American West and after many discouraging
experiences he realizes that he is filled with longing for "the Land of the
Free" and Uncle Sam's Star-Spangled Banner. Indeed, the flag is a dominant symbol in Sunde's book in much the same way that it serves to express
the message of Americanism at the conclusion of Jacob Riis's *The Making
of an American.* He waves the American flag to his friends on leaving Christiania and sings its praise in verse (138–140). In the Mediterranean he feels a
surge of emotion when they pass a steamer flying the flag of Norway but
recognizes it as sentimentality (158–159). It is his vision of "Old Glory" flying from the mast of a steamer he is on that brings home to him the lesson
of his long journey: it is his own country, the United States, that offers the
best possibilities to achieve the happiness he had searched for all over the
world (313). Seeing the flag again as they approach the Golden Gate, he recognizes it as "the greatest and most beautiful flag that has ever flown over a
free people" (318).

Sharing Sunde's social attitudes and political views but not his dedica-
tion to America is Albert Houeland, whose *Stavangergutten* (The boy from
Stavanger) was printed in Minneapolis in 1917 on the press of Emil L.
Mengshoel's socialist newspaper, *Gaa Paa.* After jumping ship in New York,
Houeland wanders across the continent, trying a series of jobs on his way,

experiencing the evils of capitalism, and talking to people about the need for socialism. But while Sunde's book moves from disenchantment to a renewed faith in America, Houeland's ends in Norway where it had begun fifteen years earlier and where the loved one is still waiting faithfully, much as in Foss's *Husmands-gutten.*

Such books provide a necessary corrective to the dominant genteel mode of the travel literature of *Vesterheimen.* Yet another perspective on this isolated literary culture may be had by considering that while many books about travel in Norway were being published for a small immigrant group in the Midwest, far more books of Norwegian travel were published for a national public and were probably as little known to the people of *Vesterheimen* as theirs were to the general public.[8] In an important sense these two sets of books were about the same country in name only. To the writers and readers of *Vesterheimen*, the exotically primitive and distant northern corner of Europe described in so many English and American travel books was the home of their fathers and mothers.

NOTES

1. Some examples from the genre of popular medicine may illustrate this. In the 1870s and 1880s there were several translated medical handbooks, as for instance the 1879 premium for subscribers to *Norden* and John Kellogg's *Household Manual* published by the Adventist press in Battle Creek, Michigan, in 1882. In 1890 *Decorah-Posten's* premium was the first of several editions of *Before the Doctor Arrives,* by Fredrik Mohn, who wrote a regular column for the newspaper. In 1895 *Decorah-Posten* printed *The Healthy and the Ill Human Being* by Mathias Johnson. In 1914 the American-born Carl Roan began a medical column for *Kvindens Magasin* and his *Illness, Health and Well-being* was published by the magazine in 1916. Roan continued his column in the succeeding *Familiens Magasin* and it was so popular that he published an expanded edition through Augsburg in 1924. His work competed with a translation by J.J. Skordalsvold of F.M. Rossiter's substantial and handsomely produced *Practical Guide in Health and Illness* (1913), a church venture, published by the Pacific Press. Roan's third medical handbook, *Home, Church and Sex* (New York, 1930), was in English.

2. Edited and translated by Barbara Gordon Morgridge as *The Cultural Life of Modern America* (Cambridge, Massachusetts: Harvard University Press, 1969).

3. Birger Osland to Beulah Folkedal 26 July 1961, OGP.

4. At the turn of the century the immigrant market was attractive to American publishers. The German, Norwegian, and Swedish editions of Donnelly's *Caesar's Column* have been mentioned. In 1895 Harper and Brothers published a German translation of Lew Wallace's *Ben-Hur.* The printers of Johnson's books of travel, Rand McNally & Co., were equipped with the type necessary to produce a book in black letter, which suggests that this was not the only work they did for a Norwegian, Danish, or German market.

5. Letters to Prestgard (19 Jan. 1927, KPP), Rølvaag (22 Jan. 1927, OERP), and Ager (23 Feb. 1927, WAP). A scrapbook in OJSP includes reviews of *Reisebreve*.

6. Other such travel narratives are P. Grønfur (1912), Arthur Olsen (1914), Anton A. Nybroten (1922), and Johannes O. Sæter (1929).

7. Two books on tramping were published in Norway by returned immigrants: Harald Hansen, *Landstrykerliv i Amerika* (1918) and Olai Aslagsson, *Trampliv* (1922).

8. Selected titles are John Caton, *A Summer in Norway* (Chicago, 1875), Katharine Tyler, *The Story of a Scandinavian Summer* (New York, 1881), Hetta Hervey, *Glimpses of Norseland* (Boston, 1889), Thomas Steele, *A Voyage to Viking-Land* (Boston, 1896), M.S. Emery, *Norway Through the Stereoscope* (New York, 1900), W.S. Monroe, *In Viking Land* (Boston, 1908), W.S. Monroe, *The Spell of Norway* (Boston, 1923), Robert McBride, *Norwegian Towns and People* (New York, 1923), and Samuel Beckett, *A Wayfarer in Norway* (New York, 1936).

16

A Mixed Chorus
of Singers

On 29 January 1895 Olav Kringen wrote to Buslett asking his advice about a poetry anthology (OABP). The Swedes had an anthology, he wrote, wondering whether "the Norwegians could not do it too." He gave only two names, "Prof. Pettersen, John Benson, and some others," adding "that they each have their circle of readers who would buy such a work at a reasonable price," and that this "would ensure a financial success for the publisher." Buslett must have expressed a skepticism born of several decades of frustrated attempts to sell his books to farmers, laborers, and artisans in Wisconsin. The two met in St. Paul at the founding convention of the Norwegian-Danish Press Association early that summer and when Kringen wrote to Buslett on July 30, he made no further mention of the project.

A few years later, a medical student at Hamline University in St. Paul was hard at work between classes and clinics collecting poems for an anthology, and he, too, wrote to Buslett for advice and assistance. By the end of June 1902 Ludvig Lima (1877–1948) had collected what he found "of value" by reading the available books, corresponding with poets, and searching the files of newspapers (23 June 1902, OABP). In the spring of the following year he had a manuscript with poems by forty-five writers that was accepted in the fall by the publisher of *Ungdommens Ven*, reorganized in 1905 as the K.C. Holter Publishing Co. Lima is conventionally apologetic in his brief preface, observing that "the Norwegian people in America are a pioneer people more busy with the ax and the plow than the pen."

Before he made his selection, Lima must have skimmed through mountains of doggerel. Norwegian Americans continued to express their emotions and experiences in verse and, as might be expected, much of it is sentimentally nostalgic, as suggested by the titles *I ensomme stunder* (1899, Lonely hours) by Peder Smedsrud, who was not found worthy of inclusion by Lima, and *Ensomme frivagtstunde* (1900, Lonely off-duty hours) by Franklin Petersen, who was. Petersen, a journalist and editor of several New York publications, among them *Nordisk Tidende*, pursued his literary interests throughout his life, publishing fiction in *Decorah-Posten* as late as 1938. His verse appeared in newspapers and journals and in a second volume, *Siv i strømmen* (Reeds in the current), in 1907. Petersen's first volume has themes that are representative of much of the poetry produced by immigrant versifiers. There is the nationalistic paean to the Viking explorers of Vinland, "Leif Erikson" (Yes, we Norsemen are proud, because we today / Can stand free on Leif Erikson's strand), the nostalgic "Emigranten," and the tear-dripping "The Cradle is Empty," where the doggerel all but ridicules the poet's heartfelt emotions on the death of his child. Petersen's 1907 volume fills in the thematic register of immigrant verse with further sentimental poems of mother, Christmas, and the seasons.[1]

Much verse is frankly utilitarian—unpretentious poems intended for song in the service of God or the cause of temperance or to be enjoyed by readers whose critical faculties were as aesthetically uneducated as those of the poets themselves. It would be beside the point to criticize the meter or metaphor of the religious songs of the clergyman Nils Minne (1900) or the temperance songs of Syver Rodning (1907). Such volumes brought pleasure to an unlettered public and served the causes for which they were intended. They did little harm and probably some good.[2] Potentially harmful to the aesthetic development of their readers, however, were those who took themselves seriously as poets and whose lofty sentiments dressed in doggerel were foisted on innocent readers as literature. Anders Neppelberg introduces his second volume of verse (1911) with rhymed apologies for his own inadequate skills but he also pretentiously displays his learning (acquired at Augsburg Seminary) in the long "Ode to Woman," and his own lack of self-criticism in ridiculously bombastic poems like "The Poet's Calling" and "The Poet." Less ridiculous, but in a romantic manner that has degenerated into cliché, are sentimental narratives such as "Little Kari," about the innocent rural girl misled and misused by the urban artist.

Equally amateurish but less misguided by learning, hence more refreshing, is K.K. Rudie, an immigrant from Valdres, who devoted his spare time to letters, writing verse, and running a small publishing business from his Minneapolis home. In the preface to his first volume of poems (1903) Rudie admits that many early poems "should probably have been omitted.

But I could not make a selection and wanted to include them even though they appear in simple everyday dress, for I have lacked both time and opportunity for the work they deserve." Ole S. Hervin, always ready to point out the ridiculous in places high and low, observed that Rudie should have quit poetry when he began it—in his youth. But in this instance time has not dealt well with Hervin's prejudices: he reacted primarily to the *Landsmaal* Rudie used in many poems, a language Hervin claimed he could not understand (*Smuler* Oct. 1903). Now, however, these are among the more readable of Rudie's poems. He writes on many of the central themes of immigrant verse—parents, the old home, Norwegian landscapes, and the seasons—and he also has religious verse and some on the evils of drink. Rudie is not just nostalgic about the Old World: "A Landowner: An Idyll from a Mountain Valley 1882" is an ironically titled story of class conflict. Rudie also sings of American landscapes and places and of the working man and woman in the new world. Among the individuals to whom he dedicates poems are the socialists Olav Kringen and Emil Mengshoel.

Thorstein Rogne is also refreshingly unpretentious. The title poem of *Ole paa prærien* (Ole on the prairie), published about 1930 in Alberta, is a rambling and anecdotal poem about the settling of the Midwest, progressing from Wisconsin to Minnesota and on to North Dakota. Saturday night dances and fights as well as toil and tribulations are celebrated. Most themes of prairie narratives are touched upon: cyclones, blizzards, fires, sod houses, the oxen and the primitive cart called the *kubberull*. He may indulge in nostalgia, as in "The Journey to America," in patriotism, both Norwegian (23) and Canadian (10), and in celebrations of the Viking past, but he also calls on labor to organize (6). Some of his poems are in his Valdres dialect and his verse is often striking in imagery and idiom.

Rudie's and Rogne's verse may be crude but it is never cloyingly cute and simperingly sentimental like the popular books of verse by Lise Hommefoss (1916, 1917, 1920) and Laura Bratager (1910, 1912), which appeared in several editions. Bratager, who also wrote reviews and Christmas stories in addition to her cultural and social activities in Minneapolis, wrote to Ager for advice and encouragement before she published her first book. He responded with a request for poems but even this accommodating editor apparently did not find any of them worthy of his journal (19 May, 20 July 1910, WAP). Her popular successes, however, gave her the confidence to keep her head high in spite of the condescending tone of her male critics. As she observed in a letter to Rølvaag shortly after she had been ridiculed in *Superior Tidende*, "I have sufficient confidence to claim that what I have done for Norsedom in speech and writing weighs as much as the work of most men, even though I lack a higher education." She suggests that her male critics do not "understand the mission" of her books because they are too involved with their exclusively male concerns and self-promoting societies (3 Feb. 1922, OERP). Bratager may have had some reason for her resentment; the cultural institutions of *Vesterheimen* were as male-dominated as those of the United States, but her just anger does not improve the quality of her verse. Nor were her critics as misogynist as she suggested. When Hervin wrote of the verses of Anna Marie Holter (1914) that they contained "more piety than poetry" (*Smuler* Jan. 1905) he reacted to her pious sentimentality, not to her femininity. Holter's reviewer in *Vor Tid* saw the appearance of woman writers as "a good sign" (1905, 327), and both Bratager and Holter were included in Lima's anthology.

Besides the many amateurish writers of poor verse, however, there were a handful who pursued their muse with such dedication and skill that they deserve the name of poet. Wilhelm Mauritz Pettersen (1860–1932) had spent several years at sea before he followed his parents in 1881 to North Dakota, where they had settled a few years earlier (Ager 1908). He studied at Augsburg Seminary and the University of Minnesota and then taught at the former institution until 1910, after which he served several congregations. Throughout his life he followed a literary vocation, with stories and essays in journals and newspapers, a novel and a volume of critical and philosophical essays (both 1927), a book of travel (1911), and a biography (1921). But first and last he was a poet, much called upon for occasional verse and with a reputation based on a large output of lyric, narrative, and dramatic poetry. C. Rasmussen published his first book of poetry in a handsomely bound and illustrated volume in 1891. Most poems are in chronological order, the oldest from 1884. The volume opens with an ostentatious display of learning: a motto by Correggio in Italian, a dedication in Latin, and an introductory lyric in German. The other two introductory poems probe aspects of the immigrant experience in interesting ways. In "Proscenium," an allegorical dramatic dialogue between father and son wandering in the mountains in trackless snow, the son, convinced that his father is on the wrong road, parts ways and they both disappear in the storm. "Amerika" is an homage to the masses from Europe who have built the country: "He entered here and cleared a road, / The uncultured plebeian of Europe. / He cleared the ground for you and me, / He gained for us what we have."[3] The poems that follow, however, have as little to do with the American experience of the 1880s and 1890s as much of the polite neo-romantic poetry in English of Pettersen's contemporaries. Many are derivative. The main influence is Ibsen, and the master's presence can be painfully obvious, as in the narrative poem "Hope." His few hymns echo well-known models; some religious poems are vaguely pantheistic and others are conventionally Lutheran. Pettersen's poems are uneven, his voice may shift in a poem from high seriousness to heavy irony and he may waver between sing-song and rough rhythms. His ambition, however, is evident in his postures and themes and the overall scope of his volume. That a book profuse in classical references and with quotations in several languages could hardly appeal to Pettersen's fellow immigrant, the "uncultured plebeian of Europe," was underscored by *Skandinaven* (5 Aug. 1891). With ill-concealed delight and considerable aplomb the reviewer makes fun of the multilingual confusion of the opening pages. But in spite of Pettersen's "foreign phrases and the linguistic vanity with which he apparently wishes to impress schoolboys and the uneducated," the reviewer saw promise in his work: "We offer him our hand from a full heart and wish him welcome, saying: 'Continue on your way as soon as you have pressed some water out of your arteries.'"

The promise was not fulfilled. *Naar juleklokkene ringer* (1922, When Christmas bells are chiming), which includes verse of several decades, is not an improvement on his first volume. In 1908 he published a volume of verse in English, *The Pilot's Christmas and Other Poems*. Even his weakest poems in Norwegian are superior to the ineptitudes of these poems where the violence of a winter storm is described as "Grim ghastliness galore" (5). His most ambitious work, *En ny slægt* (1895, A new generation), is a verse drama where the influence of Ibsen is obvious in the Brand-like character of Hansen, an idealistic theological student, in his fiancée Marie, a strong and independent-minded woman, and in several allegorical episodes reminiscent of *Peer Gynt*. Pettersen's intentions are didactic and his message is directed at the future servants of the church, such as his own students at Augsburg Seminary who helped raise money for publication. In a perceptive critical essay Ager observed that Pettersen does not succeed in revealing what "the new generation" stood for. To Ager, Pettersen was an instance of how difficult it is to realize literary and intellectual promise in an immigrant culture (1908).[4]

Less presumptuous and more in touch with his immigrant audience was the Wisconsin clergyman Ditlef Ristad (1863–1938), whose literary interests had long been evident in the book reviews and essays he had contributed to newspapers and journals before his first book in 1922. Its title, *Fra det nye*

Normandie (From the new Normandy), announces both that his poems are American and that they are in a long tradition of Norwegian migration and nation building. Normandy, the ancestral home of the English lords who created the Magna Charta, was a medieval Norwegian settlement, and Ristad's subtitle, "Kvad," meaning songs or poems, a word derived from an Old Norse word for speaking or making verse, invokes both the world of the "Old Normandy" and a tradition in which to sing of the New. In his review of Ristad's second and last book, *Kvad. Fra det norske Amerika* (1930, Songs: From the Norwegian America), an expanded and revised version of his first, Rølvaag declared, "These are songs that truly sing of you and me." In the title poem, "Det nye Normandie," "the land we won under the western sun" was first found and settled by "Leiv . . . Thorfinn, Thorhall, and Gudrid," but it was a later generation of immigrants who discovered their "inheritance" that lay beyond "Helluland, Markland, and Vinland." When we defend this land, "built with law and equality" by "Washington's strong courage," where "freedom and security for the citizens has been written with Lincoln's blood," "we are also defending our Norwegian heritage"; "As we lift the free Star-Spangled Banner / We are again building a Normandy" (1930, 13–14). Several poems in narrative as well as lyric modes sing of the experience of immigration and settlement, and others commemorate the contributions of the scout for the first immigrants in 1825, "Kleng Peerson" (1922, 1930), the commanding officer of the Wisconsin 15th, "Oberst Hans Heg" (1922, 1930), and the writers Baumann (1922), Wist, Anderson, and Rølvaag (1930). In his best narrative poems, such as "Missionspresten," about the pioneer pastor who has grown old and wasted in the service of his congregation on the plains, and "The Sharp Shooter," on the contrast between the hero's welcome of the returning soldiers and their memories of the trenches, Ristad combines the compressed language of poetry with a compelling story. Ristad speaks with the conviction of a prophet to his people. His best poems, could later generations but have read them, could have been cherished as their songs of the making of the Western Home.[5]

Ristad had bestowed the title of the poet of Norwegian America, the *scald* or singer of *Vesterheimen*, on Julius Berg Baumann (1870–1923) on the appearance of his first volume of poems in 1909. Baumann, who immigrated in 1889, was born near Vadsø in Finnmark, the most northern of Norway's counties, where he grew up learning to speak Finnish and Russian. During his first years in the United States he worked as a farmhand in North Dakota and in lumber camps and sawmills in Minnesota and Wis-

*Julius B. Baumann (1870–1923).
Courtesy Augsburg Publishing
House.*

consin, where he was given positions with increasing responsibility and was in 1907 transferred to Cloquet, Minnesota, where three years later he became register of deeds of Carlton county, a position he held until his death (Heitmann 1924; 1949). A man of wide intellectual interests but little formal education, Baumann had written verse regularly since his early teens, and in 1896 he had his first poem in *Skandinaven*. While working in Minnesota in the early winter of 1896 he sent a story to *Reform* in Eau Claire. Ager published "Lap Jon" (4 Jan. 1897), and wrote encouragingly to the unknown writer. It was his move to Cloquet in 1907 that gave Baumann the time, stability, and confidence he needed to realize his literary ambitions, but it was not at all obvious in what direction these ambitions would take him. For while his lyrics mostly speak of a sunny disposition, warmth of feeling, and conventional attitudes, his early contributions to *Smuler* and his correspondence with close friends speak of a bleakly atheistic outlook. In the lyric mode he wrote finely crafted poems of family, spring, and Christmas, in terse aphorisms he wrote of his belief in an empty heaven.[6] His "Blind tro" (Naked truths) by "Julius Apostata" are as conventional in their moralistic rationalism as the lyrics under his own name are in their more acceptable sentiments, but there is little commerce between them. "Julius Apostata" may observe that "Nothing is 'ugly' in nature. A slimy snake is just as beautiful as a gold and silver speckled trout" (July 1906), but no slimy snakes are admitted into Baumann's lyrics.

Baumann's poems, first collected in *Digte* (1909, Poems), then in *Paa vidderne* (1915, On the range), and finally in the 1924 posthumous collected edition, do not go deeper in their different ways than his rationalistic statements but they radiate warmth, sensitivity, and compassion whereas the aphorisms appear cold and unfeeling in their absolute ideological stance; the lyrics are the products of a poet, the aphorisms the cerebrations of a self-taught moral philosopher. Baumann the lyricist was not dissimulating when he wrote poems that were published by Augsburg and loved and cherished by people who would have abhorred the rationalism of "Julius Apostata." Love was a motivating force in his life, and he expressed his love in poems to his wife, children, friends, and, above all, his mother. The theme of love is struck in the first poem of his first volume (in Heitmann's translation): "Could I but light in the hate-filled heart / Sparks of the love that redeems and releases, / Songs I would sing with the poet's art, / Sing love songs till hatred ceases."

Baumann explored and exploited a few basic themes throughout his career. In his first volume, four poems are to or about his mother, eight celebrate spring and two summer, while the seasons are rounded off with five reflections on fall and two on winter. Christmas held special meaning for Baumann—he was born on Christmas day and consequently named Julius (*jul*=Christmas)—and his first volume has three Christmas poems and one for the new year. There are eleven poems on his wife, home, and family and the rest may be classified as poems of ideas, narratives, and impressions of his Finnmark childhood and youth. At this point in his life the vision of *Vesterheimen*, of an American literary culture in Norwegian, had only just begun to play a role in his intellectual and emotional life. The concluding stanza of "Norwegian-American Literature," however, demonstrates that he was thinking along the same lines as Ager, Buslett, and Rølvaag: "Then the pregnant seed that lies concealed in Vinland will flower. It will spread the blossoms of summer so that the scent will reach the island of our fathers and our saga will never be forgotten" (163). Hervin called Baumann's first volume "the brightest, most beautiful and sunny Norwegian book ever printed in this country" (*Smuler*, April 1910), and he was by no means alone in his judgment.

The early poems are well crafted, yet with simple and uncomplicated meters and rhyme schemes. In the second volume there is a marked shift to longer poems and more complex forms, as evidenced in the repetitions, rhythms, images, and rhymes of the opening morning poem. A greater subtlety of expression may be observed by comparing his 1915 Christmas poem "Oh, then Chime, Chime!" with his earlier Christmas lyrics. In 1909 the Christmas poems naively celebrate both the family feast and the Gospel of peace on earth; in 1915 the title is the concluding response in each stanza to a series of questions that undercut a simple faith in the power of the Gospel of Christmas to change the world. By 1915 the Midwest has taken a stronger hold on his imagination than the memories of Northern Norway: in "Norge" the images are seen "through dimmed eyes" and "through the flame of memory" (181) and Christmas is now "Vesterheimen's Norwegian Christmas Eve." He can be sentimental, as in the narrative "Too Late," which uses the device of the double to explore the theme of the immigrant's "divided heart," and the poems that celebrate *Vesterheimen*, in particular those that evoke the medieval Viking settlements, may be embarrassingly nationalistic in their claims. In his otherwise positive review in *Reform* (1 Feb. 1916) Rølvaag singled out one of these, "Vinland," for its false tone. The collected edition of 1924 adds poems to the two previous volumes but little to Baumann's reputation as a poet.

Reviewing Baumann's 1915 book, Hervin had congratulated him in rhymed tercets on making such beautiful and pious verse "that Augsburg could safely publish it" and leading some to believe "that you had become conservative" (*Smuler* Aug. 1916). Although Baumann may not have become conservative, he became more attuned to a vaguely defined religiosity and consequently distanced himself from the iconoclastically atheistic "Julius Apostata." In return he was taken into the hearts and minds of the people of *Vesterheimen* like no other writer before him. Few poets in any language have died as did Baumann with the assurance that an entire people loved him. On his last Christmas Day, in 1922, he sent a letter of acknowledgment to *Duluth Skandinav* and other newspapers. Here he wrote of how Christmas had always held a dear place in his heart since his childhood, when he was always at the center of attention because it was his birthday. Now, however, this was even more the case, since he had received greetings "from my own people all over the entire land, where my songs have been read and my name has been made known in all these years . . . Had I not known it before, I then realized that the most beautiful dream of my life— to be permitted so long a life and to be gifted with sufficient spirit and warmth to be able to sing my way into the hearts of my own people—has become real" (Scrapbook, JBBP). By popular acclaim, Julius Berg Baumann was the poet of *Vesterheimen*.[7]

There had been at least one dissenting voice, however, that of the poet-novelist-dramatist Jon Norstog, who wrote a scathing review of Baumann's first book: "Mr. Baumann is a fine and distinguished gentleman, in his Prince Albert coat, shirt cuffs, glacé gloves, silver-headed—or maybe it is gold-headed—stick and patent-leather shoes—or perhaps boots. Graciously and formally he moves around—enters the rooms, does not make a mess, does not break furniture or window panes, no, he moves in formal and distinguished fashion through the rooms, into the kitchen to the ladies, lays aside his gloves and stick, formal and distinguished, then begins to speak, formal and distinguished, brings it to a finish, formal and distinguished, gets up, formal and distinguished, then walks to the nursery, formal and distinguished, pets and kisses the children, formal and distinguished, speaks to the nurse, formal and distinguished, and then departs, formal and distinguished, walking on the well-worn paved road, keeps all the time to the road, stops now and then and looks at nature, formal and distinguished, and at last disappears on the well-worn paved road—formal and distinguished" (*Eidsvold* Feb. 1910). Norstog, a poet of passions where Baumann is a poet of emotions, a poet of cosmic conflicts where Baumann is a poet of domestic sentiments, may be grossly unfair, but he is also perceptive in pouncing upon the antiseptic quality not only of Baumann's verse but of the culture of *Vesterheimen*. Indeed, in order to fully appreciate Baumann and many of his fellow writers it is necessary to make the concession that they often appear to belong to the generation of their fathers and mothers rather than that of their contemporaries in the United States and Norway. One who at his best may be read as a poet of his own generation, however, is the clergyman and journalist Sigurd Folkestad (1877–1963).

Folkestad came to New York in 1902 to work for the Norwegian Seamen's Mission after first having tried his fortune in London and Norway. In New York he soon turned to journalism and edited the newspaper *Den norske amerikaner* from 1906 to 1908. Then he decided to prepare himself for the ministry, graduated from Luther Seminary the following year, and served as pastor in Strum, Wisconsin.[8] Most poems in his first book, *Paa kongevei* (1911, On the royal road), were written before he emigrated and the concluding section of American poems is appropriately titled "In a foreign land." In his effusive review, Ager remarked on the narrative structure suggested by the four chapter headings "Night," "At dawn," "Day" and "In a foreign land," especially when read with the overall title in mind (*Kv* April 1911). In the same journal Wilhelm Pettersen commented on the lyrical-narrative form of the few powerful poems in an otherwise flawed and lackluster volume (July 1911). A letter Folkestad wrote to Buslett 14 June 1911 is also suggestive of a narrative bent of mind: "*Paa kongevei* is a search for the inner beauty and an attempt to show where it may be found. It is a journey through life as I have lived it and fought it" (OABP). His second book, *Flytfugl* (1916, Migratory bird), is a sequence of lyrics that form a novel-like narrative. Although the poems are uneven, Folkestad is more successful than in his first volume; he attempts a semi-free form of verse with irregular rhyme and also experiments (as he had in 1911) with the alliteration of Old Norse verse. His ear, however, is not quite good enough for such departures from the beaten track and there are too many rough lines to make the reading uniformly enjoyable. In its overall structure as well as in its individual poems, however, Folkestad's *Flytfugl* is *Vesterheimen*'s most ambitious and perhaps most successful long poem.

The two opening poems, "Babylon" and "The morning hours," describe the life and surroundings of the protagonist, Oskar, a bum in New York. On awakening, he has a vision of home in spring, and after a sequence of eight lyrics on familiar scenes and moods, he concludes: "I will go home, I will go home to Norway" (22). On returning to his small coastal home town he finds that his father, a wealthy but hardhearted businessman, is dead and that he is the sole heir. After a vision of his dead mother, which leads to his conversion and the decision to change his life, he gives a large party in his old home, described in the five-poem cycle "The great party in the Knagen mansion," where he announces that he is giving his former home to the town for an orphanage. Oskar, however, cannot forget a young woman, Gudrun, who had visited him when he was ill in a New York hospital. His return to the underworld of New York is described in a cycle of eight poems where Oskar finds a drunk and suicidal childhood friend, coaxes him back to life, and gives him the fare for passage home, only to discover that he is then killed for the money and thrown into the river. The poem that concludes this sequence, "On the suspension bridge," points forward to Hart Crane's "Proem" in imagery that contrasts the beauty and mystical qualities of the bridge with the busy life of the big city:

A morning song is played
on the bridge's harp of steel . . .

The powerful strings vibrate
under the pressure of a thousand footsteps
and wagons that spark and rush
on like a nightmare
high over the receding roofs
and the long-stretching hands of the docks
that embrace the ships' loins
in the black-blue sheets of coal smoke
and the whistling white of the steam winch.

It vibrates, the strong arch
of steel that stands against the sun breeze,
and sings in the day-white flame
of a merciless spring for the people . . .

And Babylon's skyscraper mountains
and the canyons that are seen in the distance
are filled with human dwarfs
with a glowing energy of life.
And the mountain sings and glitters
of brightness and lightning sparks,
and the unrest exults to heaven
with a strength that emerges from the throng:
This is the bridge's song of steel (123–124).[9]

After a melodramatic concluding sequence, Gudrun and Oskar are joined
and it is suggested that they will live a life in the service of God and man.
The migratory bird has found his home in the New World.

Folkestad's last book of poems, *Fra utflytter-kampen* (1919, From the battle
of emigration), is a disappointment, aesthetically as well as thematically. The
two dominant modes are sentimental nostalgia and angry polemics, the one
fixed on the true home across the Atlantic, the other lashing out in blind
fury at the integrationists. In order to understand the shift in emphasis from
the acceptance and affirmation of the American home in 1916 to the embittered defense of an extreme isolationism three years later it is necessary
to recall the attacks on immigrant groups in America after the country entered the First World War, the repression of languages other than English,
the censorship of the immigrant press, and the insistence that a hyphenated
American could not be a true patriot. In his polemics, Rølvaag, when an-

gered, chastises as a loving father chastises wayward children; the uncompromising hatred of Folkestad, however, suggests that he had turned his back on
Vesterheimen. He returned to Norway in 1920.

Unlike his protagonist Oskar, Folkestad was unable to let go of the old
country and come to terms with his new one. In this he was hardly unique:
a significant number of immigrants from most European countries eventually returned to their homelands. The move was made easy for Folkestad,
since the education and the experience he had acquired in America opened
Norwegian doors that earlier had been closed to him. Agnes Mathilde
Wergeland (1857–1914), like so many immigrants before and after her arrival
in 1890, had found doors closed to her in Norway—and, since she was a
woman and an academic, they remained closed in her lifetime. Unlike most
of the characters in this narrative, Wergeland did not enter America by way
of *Vesterheimen.* Indeed, she seems to have been unaware of the existence of
a Norwegian America for the first twenty of her twenty-four years in
America.[10]

Agnes Mathilde Wergeland was from a gifted family. Her granduncle
had been a member of the Constitutional Assembly in 1814 and Henrik
Wergeland and Camilla Collett, his son and daughter, are key figures in
Norwegian history. In spite of their impoverished beginnings, Mathilde and
her brother Oscar, the survivors of six siblings, both had remarkable careers.
The brother as a painter, the sister as the first Norwegian woman to achieve
a doctorate. When she attended a private school for women in Christiania
in 1878, however, women were still barred from the University. She was
drawn to the study of music and art as well as the writing of poetry, but
eventually history became her chosen field and with meager stipends she
went abroad twice in the 1880s for study, first in Munich and then at the
University of Zurich, where she was awarded her doctorate in 1890 for a
thesis on medieval legal history. That fall she came to the United States as
a graduate fellow in history at Bryn Mawr. She was at the University of
Chicago from 1896 to 1902, but even though she published substantial
scholarly articles in the *Journal of Political Economy* and was a regular contributor to *The Dial* she was denied tenure, since "the president of the university
did not favor the appointment of women professors" (Semmingsen 1980,
118). In 1902 she accepted a position as professor of history and French at
the University of Wyoming in Laramie, where she lived and worked for the
rest of her life with her close friend Grace R. Hebard, of whom she wrote
lovingly in "Your Hand": "And I would gladly kiss these elegant flower
stems / Almost entirely hidden in lace and silk, / And I would gladly hold

Agnes Mathilde Wergeland
(1857–1914).

in mine / The warm hand that reveals your beautiful mind" (1912, 53).[11] She continued to publish scholarly work and kept up her close ties with *The Dial*, but she also returned to her early love of poetry, writing these more intimate communications in Norwegian: "I wrote in German and in English, flexed my muscles — / But my greatest need was for the quiet power of my mother tongue" (1912, 29).[12]

In 1911 she submitted an article on the European political situation after Italy's invasion of Tripoli to *Symra,* and Wist, recognizing the quality of his new contributor, asked her to submit more. After seeing some of her poems (*Symra* 1912) he arranged to have a substantial volume of her verse published by *Decorah-Posten. Amerika og andre digte* (1912, America and other poems) is unique in the literature of *Vesterheimen* in that it does not feature any of the conventional themes of immigrant poetry such as nostalgia for the old country, pride in the Viking discoveries, or the celebration of *Vesterheimen.* Wergeland writes as a well-educated European woman who has found a new home in the West and not as a member of an immigrant culture. The title poem, "America Magna," takes its motto ("America is another name for opportunity") from Emerson, uses the *Mayflower* of 1620 rather than the Norwegian *Restauration* of 1825 as its image of the storm-tossed ship crossing the Atlantic to the New World, pits despotic Russia rather than a rural class-ridden Norwegian valley against the free and welcoming United States, and has "the youth of America" rather than the immigrants of the Fifteenth Wisconsin "dying for the cause of the slave." This ambitious poem, however, also reveals her weaknesses as a poet: it has inversion and tortured syntax, it has limping meter, poor rhythm, and questionable rhymes, and after a broad sweep of history and ideas, it concludes rather lamely with platitudes on the respect shown to labor in America: " 'Work! Work' " This is our answer, / . . . Nowhere was labor as respected / Nor idleness as deeply scorned / As in this new world: / It is new in every fiber" (22–23).[13]

She writes about western landscapes and changing seasons, about friendship, flowers, and her beloved home. In the poem to her summer home, "The hermitage," she writes of her happiness in her seclusion while sensual, even erotic imagery speaks of the intimacy of the sharing of this seclusion. But her seclusion in no way isolates her from the world. In "My home," she writes of her deep joy in being able to close her own door behind her, but also of a home that is open to the world: "And when I sit here in my green rocking chair / And read those that I love the most, / the ancient Greeks, Virgil, Vigny, Shelley, / My dear American singers, / My living room is also a meeting place / for infinite, great, and powerful ideas, / . . . all lives here / In wonderful, inspiring power . . . " (184–189).

Wergeland was gifted, and she must also have had a remarkable strength of will and determination. Nevertheless she selects the archaic lyre, an unfashionable instrument with a delicate tone, as emblem of her character, and not only sets it up against more powerful instruments of brass, but contrasts its aristocratic qualities with "this orchestral / Democracy's bold collective song" (1912, 24–25). With her lyre she nevertheless sings the cause of democracy, in particular of the downtrodden, as in "The Indian blanket," "Blessed are the meek," and "When the Japanese arrived" (1912), the second a political poem that specifically addresses itself to the plight of women, the third in praise of the Japanese immigrant for his culture and tradition as well as for his hard work and frugality. In Chicago she had become a friend of Thorstein Veblen, and among her contributions to *The Dial*, which he edited from 1896 to 1905, is a 1905 review of his *Theory of Business Enterprise*. "Finery" (1912) opens with an irritated dismissal of the leisure class ("Phew! Our age desires finery, / It is simply finery-crazed . . . ") but quickly turns to a socioeconomic analysis of the relationship between the buyer of finery and the "miserable beings who have sewn each stitch, / Tried to earn their bread, / Tried to fool starvation." While the impover-ished laborers do not receive sufficient wages for producing these luxury items, the wearer boasts of his good bargain. The poem concludes: "These are tears that glitter in between the snowy lace, / This is blood that you, you fool, have covered yourself with."

She could easily have been discouraged by the reception *Vesterheimen* gave her poetry. Most reviews were negative and few copies were sold. One reviewer who complained that the poems were too difficult was Simon Johnson, who later (1914) recalled that a letter from Wergeland was the be-ginning of their correspondence and friendship. Ager, too, found her poetry difficult: "She is learned and plays with words and expressions that common people must admit with shame they have never heard of before" (*Kv* Jan. 1913). In *Reform* he embellished this point, characterizing Wergeland's book "as a foreign fowl among us. It is only natural that we should sniff some-what reluctantly at it. It has been nurtured on foreign foods and has feathers that are a stark contrast with our own common gray and black ones" (17 Sept. 1913). But he praised the beauty of specific poems and Wergeland re-sponded by reaching out to him as a fellow writer. She was hurt by the lack of understanding she was met with. To Johnson she had written, "Now it has been killed. It takes so little to kill such a thing," and Johnson, who himself was easily hurt by negative reviews, smarted with the memory of her words as he wrote of her after her death. By patiently responding to critics who evidently were strangers to the world of learning she had lived in for so long, she became accepted as a colleague by the virtually all-male group of recognized authors in *Vesterheimen*. Reviving his appeals for a Norwegian-American writers' association, Buslett specifically urged that "the Wergeland Diana in the West" be included (*Reform* 28 Oct. 1913). Wergeland's need for fellowship with writers in her own language may be seen in the eagerness with which she responded to this proposal and her en-deavors to realize it. She wrote an appreciation of Norstog's *Tone* for *Symra*. To Ager she not only sent poems for *Reform* and *Kvartalskrift* (all included in her posthumous volume), but also a letter with critical observations on the short stories and novel he had sent to her (2 April 1913, WAP). Simon Johnson she referred to as "the Auerbach of the plains" and after reading a chapter of his projected novel in *Reform* (23 Dec. 1913) she immediately wrote to the editor urging him to publish more (30 Dec. WAP). The last notes she wrote on her deathbed were addressed to Ager.

Wergeland's intense involvement with the writers of *Vesterheimen* is reflected in the new thematic concerns of her last poems. In "The book" (1914) she reflects on her situation as an American poet using Norwegian and in "Silence" she addresses her fellow immigrants, "My people over here," complaining that they do not appreciate poetry. In "A word" she admonishes them to honor their motherland by using her language, not by sending her money: "The money you send her, the gold you bring with you / Only diminish your homeland. / No, let us honor her in another fashion / By spreading her language! / Let us stand together as in former times, / Renew the praise of our mother tongue in song and speech / And thus prevent our downfall." "The greater Norway" expresses themes similar to Buslett's "Amerika-Paul," which Wergeland read as it was serialized in *Reform* (from 12 Aug. 1913). She, too, writes of a Norway changed by hydroelectricity, industrialism, and capitalism and holds up the old values that have been lost. She even has a conventional immigrant poem of nostalgia, "Longing for home": "Could I only go barefoot / And pick blueberries! / I exchanged freedom for bread; / Now I am filled with remorse until my death."

Such, then, was the strength of the literary culture of this untutored flock of immigrants that Agnes Wergeland, whose intellectual powers and ambition had made her too large for the confined and conservative society of her homeland and who was more than qualified for acceptance in the intellectual centers of Europe and the United States, eventually sought the fellowship of writers such as Ager, Buslett, and Johnson. Wyoming had recognized her academic achievement. It was *Vesterheimen* with all its provincial limitations that helped her realize her youthful ambition of becoming a poet.

NOTES

1. Other writers of pedestrian verse include Gustav Melbye (1892), Zacharias Ødegaard (1907), M.H. Woldhagen (1909), Helge Amundsen (1910), Halvor Odden (1910), Hedvig Knudsen (1914), Johan Ovren (1915), Einar Hilsen (1915, 1916), Johan Selnes (1918), Johan Egilsrud (1926), Christian Bentsen (n.d.), Frithjof Werenskjold (n.d.), Bertha Buan (1937), Marcus Tellevik (1938) and Peter Hansen, whose 1923 volume contains many of the themes of popular immigrant verse, including the opening disclaimer that he is not much of a poet. He has a conventional poem about loving and honoring the country he left behind and a complementary one on gratitude to America, as well as a poem on "Our language."

2. Some writers of religious and/or temperance verse are Olaf Mathison (1907), John Morthensen (1914), Ola Rise (1908), Gustav Sand (*Adam*, a philosophical and

dramatic poem, 1918), Olav Refsdal (1912, 1916), and the immensely popular Ole S. Sneve (1896, 1899, 1904, 1912).

3. "Han slap herind og hugged vei, — / Europas raa plebeier. / Han rydded grund for dig og mig; / han vandt os, hvad vi eier" (18).

4. In the verse drama *Bjarne* (1926) Eldor Hanson presents an uncompromising and idealistic hero, related to Ibsen's Brand, who speaks for the author's low-church views. The slight plot is a flimsy excuse to present interminable discussions of church issues, and the play is obviously not intended for performance. Most plays of the twentieth century are light farces for amateurs: Sverre Sieverts (1925), Christian Bentsen (1926), Syver S. Rodning (1926), Olaf J. Ihme (1929), Herman Baalson (1929), and Reidar Haugan (1893–1972), a journalist who succeeded Grevstad as editor of *Skandinaven* in 1940, a year before it ceased publication.

5. Ristad's images and themes of a "New Normandy," of Viking settlements, pioneer exploits, and heroic sacrifice are typical of the "home-making myths" developed in most European immigrant groups to demonstrate that they have a special right to an Amerian home. See Øverland 1996.

6. To Buslett he wrote 2 Jan. 1916: "I don't waste the Sunday by going to the village church. There is only death, no progress, no evolution, only old and moldy dogmas" (OABP). In 1922 he was offered a job with the monthly *Norsk Ungdom*, but turned it down, he wrote Rølvaag, because he did not want to appear "as an orthodox Lutheran." (21 Sept. 1922, OERP). He had little patience with Jon Norstog and his religious themes, referring to his work as "biblical nonsense" (2 April 1916, OABP).

7. Ole Sneve had a similar experience on his deathbed. A major effort was made during his last illness to publish a collected volume of his poetry, and far more than the required 400 copies were subscribed to in a relatively short time. For reactions to his death see *Reform* 10, 17 June 1913.

8. Biographical information in Ager 1918 and *Nordmanns-Forbundet* 56 (April 1963).

9. "Det toner et morgenkvæde / i hængebroens harpe af staal . . . // . . . De dirrer de sterke strenger / under trykket af de tusinde skridt / og vogne, som gnistrer og sprænger / afsted som et mareridt / høit over de vigende tager / og dokkernes langstrakte lænder / i kulrøgens blaasorte flager / og dampvinchens hvæsende hvidt. // Den dirrer, den sterke bue / af staal, som imod solvinden staar / og synger i den daghvide lue / om en folkets hensynslöse vaar . . . // Og Babylons skyskraberbjerge / og kløfterne, som blaaner deri, / de fyldes med menneskedverge / med en tindrende livsenergi. / Og det synger i bjerget og knitrer / af funker og lynglimt, som glitrer. / Og uroen jubler mod himlen / med styrke, som stiger i stimlen: / Det er hængebroens staalmelodi."

10. The main sources on Wergeland are Michelet (1916) and Semmingsen (1980).

11. "Og jeg vil gjerne kysse disse smekre blomsterstilke / som dølges næsten helt av kniplinger og silke, / og jeg vil gjerne holde den i min, / den varme haand som viser os Dit skjønne sind." Also translated in Michelet 1916, 94–98.

12. From "Akvareller": "Jeg skrev paa tysk, paa engelsk, øved mine kræfter — / men mest jeg kræved modersmaalets stille kraft" (1914, 29).

13. "Arbeid! Arbeid! er vort løsen, / . . . Ingensteds var arbeid saa høiagtet, / lediggang saa dypt foragtet, / som i denne nye verden: / Ny i hver en fibre er den."

They All Had Stories
To Tell

One indication of how many of the inhabitants of *Vesterheimen* wrote for publication is the number of their newspapers and journals. Contributions from subscribers, mostly farmers, artisans, and shopkeepers, made up a significant part of the more than sixty periodical publications available in 1910. There were brief notices of life in the settlements, reports on the meetings of associations and church assemblies, and contributions to the many controversies—political, theological and cultural—on which these journals thrived. Many also tried their hand at creative writing, and while verse had the strongest appeal in the early years, fiction was the more popular genre in the twentieth century.

With so many who published, there must have been many more whose efforts remained in manuscript. One would-be novelist wrote to Rølvaag from Iowa that *Reform* had accepted one of her stories. Her ambition was to be a writer and translator, but she had no training in Norwegian beyond what she picked up from her grandmother and for her confirmation. Would it be worthwhile for her to pursue a writer's career and would it be possible to have someone help her to correct her mistakes? (7 Nov. 1919, OERP). Rølvaag's reply is not available but he surely wrote as comfortingly and as positively as he could to his aspiring colleague, as Buslett likely did to a similar correspondent in Alberta: "I have such an infinite desire to write and I can write poems in a few minutes that my friends insist are quite good." She, too, is aware of her poor education and needs someone to correct her manuscripts. Would Buslett please give her advice? (1 Feb. 1923, OABP). There is little reason to assume that the unpublished efforts of such would-be writers were of less value than some that were printed.

While most short stories in the newspapers and journals around the turn of the twentieth century may not be worthy of notice as individual texts, it is nevertheless necessary to take them into account if an assessment is to be made of the breadth of the fiction published in *Vesterheimen*. Some writers were quite productive, as for instance Thorvald Gransted, who published stories and poems in *Skandinaven* and *Husbibliothek*. More ambitious in its literary aspirations, *Vor Tid* published Fridthjof Lunde (1904), Erik Quam (1905), Martin Heir (1906), Thomas Vetlesen (1906), and the anonymous writer of a delightful serialized account of life in an early settlement (1906). Other writers sought a public through *Symra*, such as Ola Andreassen and M. Sørensen (1912), *Kvartalskrift*, such as Ragnhild Thinn Thvedt (1917), the Salt Lake City journal *Varden*, such as Josef Straaberg (1910), and *Jul i Vesterheimen*, such as Anna Dahl (from 1922). Of these only Lunde (1908) and Straaberg (1921) eventually published books, which may suggest the limited ambitions of the others, considering the easy access to printing and publishing. From the many presses, a thriving underbrush of fiction spread through *Vesterheimen*.

Popular Minneapolis publishers like Waldemar Kriedt and Capital Publishing Co. continued to profit from cheap entertainments such as the anonymous *Rivalinderne: eller heltene fra Kamphaug. En roman fra vestens prærier* (1908, The female rivals: A novel of the prairies of the West), where a series of plot complications and comic exaggerations climaxes in a double wedding ceremony in a balloon at the St. Louis World Fair. In the 1920s, as the era of a Norwegian-American literature was drawing to a close, there were novels that are no better than the awkward attempts of the 1880s and 1890s, such as another anonymous western, *Paa sporet* (On the trail), probably by J.A. Førde and published in Decorah in 1924. Its primitive narrative technique intersperses ridiculous plots and wooden characters with pretentious reflective and descriptive passages. As a story of the western frontier where the hero is a frontiersman who seeks the loneliness of the wilderness rather than take part in a new community, the novel is untypical of the Norwegian-American novel of the farmers' frontier. Neither the superman hero, first observed as a boy sleeping under the open sky with his pet deer and later, during his years at Luther College, working summers as guide and leader for a train of pioneers across the plains, nor the narrator, a U.S. Army colonel, and his loyal half-breed scout are commonly met with in the fiction of *Vesterheimen*.

Then as now, the crudely popular had a wide appeal. One writer who made a career of popular fiction was Oscar Ødegaard (1889–1965), who, after some years of study at Concordia and St. Olaf colleges and as a teacher in parochial schools in North Dakota, turned to journalism and various business enterprises. In his own eyes he was a writer and, judging from his successful sales, he was also highly regarded by his readers. Beginning in 1921, Ødegaard traveled for more than thirty years as an agent for the North Dakota newspaper *Normanden*. When he entered a home or spoke with people wherever they congregated, he would also peddle his own books and books by other authors that he sold on commission. His most popular novel, *Naar det blomstrer i husmandsstuen* (1914, When the flowers bloom in the cotter's home), eventually sold 10,000 copies. Ødegaard wrote with great confidence to his less popular colleagues, at times giving them freely of his professional experience. To Buslett, for instance, he suggested that *Veien til Golden Gate* might be too deep for common readers and recommended his own books even though "they may be rather light reading." Jon Norstog, he added, "writes well, but agh! His books smell. He also forgets ... that we are not all professors or pastors." But as so often, Ødegaard's main business is business: he wants Buslett to recommend his books in the press and would like to sell Buslett's books if he could have them at an advantageous price (6 Jan. 1916, OABP). To Rølvaag he wrote that he was sure the Norwegian edition of *Giants in the Earth* would be a success, since "it is rather direct and crude" (20 Dec. 1924, OERP).

Ødegaard's popularity must have been an embarrassment to both Buslett and Rølvaag and it is difficult to see how his 1914 pastiche of Foss's *Husmands-gutten* could have been enjoyed by those who were acquainted with its model. Ødegaard includes false letters, a drinking *bonde,* and many of the other ingredients, but adds the different twist that the two lovers depart for North Dakota and even more success and happiness in the end. Success was as appreciated by Norwegian-reading as by English-reading Americans, and Ødegaard exploited this theme in most of his little books, for instance *Fra visergutt til millionær* (1917, From errand boy to millionaire). Mostly his stories are harmless affairs, such as *Skyttsengelen* (1932, The guardian angel), where big city corruption is contrasted with small town values, but at times Ødegaard gives vent to popular prejudices: the short story "Klara Fager-lien" from the collection published in 1924 wallows in the most primitive anti-Irish and anti-Catholic bias.

Neither entertainment nor profit was the main aim of most who wrote fiction. Many immigrants had a story to tell and their books probably had a limited distribution in the author's county or among subscribers to the newspaper that did the printing. Others used fiction as a vehicle for their messages to the people of *Vesterheimen*. But the message may be rather vague, as it is when Ole E. Hagen introduces his novel with a pretentious, quasi-philosophical preface (1904). G.A. Skugrud's *En banebryter. En norsk guts levnedløb* (1899, A pioneer: The life story of a Norwegian youth) takes its readers through a naive and incoherent narrative back and forth several times from Minnesota, to Texas, California, Oregon, Washington, Idaho, back to Texas, and Idaho. Its concluding message is unrelated to the preceding narrative: hypnotism as the solution to the world's problems!

No more likely to appeal to readers of a later time are the many religious novels which point out the right path to salvation. Among them are Olav Refsdal, *To konfirmanter* (1902, Two candidates for confirmation), a juvenile; John N. Kildahl (1857–1920), *Naar Jesus kommer ind i huset* (1906, *When Jesus Enters the Home*); George A.T. Rygh, *Morgenrødens vinger* (1909, translated as *The Shadow of a Wrong*); D.J.O. Westheim, *Fra aandens slagmark* (1910, From the battleground of the soul), a contrived story with a second-generation hero by a second-generation author; Anders Tangen, *Skjulte kræfter* (1918, Hidden powers), a tract-like tale with a rare Baptist message; Ole Shefveland, *Marit Gjeldaker* (1924), where the slight story is an excuse to preach a self-righteous, conservative Lutheranism; and Olaus Rinde, *Forandringen paa Stone Hill* (1934, The change on Stone Hill), which like Shefveland's novel has the ingratitude of a congregation towards its good pastor as a central theme.[1] Nils N. Rønning, who played a central role in *Vesterheimen* as editor, publisher, and author, contributed to the genre of pietistic Lutheran fiction with *Gutten fra Norge* (1924, translated as *Lars Lee, The Boy from Norway*), which shares several plot elements with Foss's *Husmands-gutten* as well as the conviction that America offers opportunities to those on whom Norwegian class society had closed its doors. To Ager, Rygh's novel *Morgenrødens vinger*, which apparently sold quite well, was evidence of the undeveloped literary taste of *Vesterheimen*: "It is Stenholt and *Morgenrødens vinger* that shall live," he wrote in a bitter mood to Buslett, "the one presumably assisted by . . . Satan, the other by the church" (5 March 1911, OABP). But there is little point in applying literary criteria to these pious books. They were written to comfort and strengthen believers in their faith, and their popularity suggests that they fulfilled this need with many readers.

Nor was Ager in a position to be overly critical of the religious novels of other publishers since he himself published and recommended books and stories of no more literary merit where the message was temperance. One such novel, however, *I ørneskyggen* (1907, In the shadow of the eagle), suggests that the author, A.H. Mason, might have gone on to write far better things had he not been killed in the First World War. In *Smuler*, Hervin dismissed the book as "an ugly temperance dream" (July 1908), but Gerald Thorson's favorable assessment (1957, 247) is the more balanced judgment. Mason's novel begins as a naive, tract-like, and moralizing temperance story, but gradually Mason seems to become more interested in his characters and his story improves. Toward the end the novel turns into a detective story, featuring Sleipner, one of the rare detectives in Norwegian-American fiction. A descriptive talent is also evident in some of Mason's poetry, in particular the humorous narrative "Hyrekaren kvæder" (The hired man sings).

Palma Pedersen, who made her first appearance with a collection of poems, *Syrener* (Lilacs), in 1911, was as serious in her intentions as the writers of didactic fictions. Her poor grammar, idiosyncratic spelling, and distorted syntax, however, are at odds with her effusively pretentious poetic persona. She, too, lacked elementary training in Norwegian, but had neither the modesty nor the timidity of those who wrote to Rølvaag and Buslett about their linguistic shortcomings. Yet, Palma, her *nom de plume*, was taken seriously by *Vesterheimen*. Hervin poked fun at her lyrical transgressions in *Smuler* (Aug. 1911) and in *Duluth Skandinav* Rølvaag observed that her second novel, *Ragna* (1924), had as little to do with art as a wax figure with a human being (27 Feb. 1925), but she was praised by others and the Norwegian Society awarded her its annual prize for her first novel, *Under ansvarets svøbe* (1923, Under the lash of responsibility). For all her faults and pretentiousness, Palma Pedersen is not so easily dismissed as the surface quality of her books might suggest. She had the courage—after an impoverished childhood spent partly in an orphanage—to immigrate alone at the age of fifteen in 1894. She lived with a grandmother and attended public school before she struck out on her own, coming to La Crosse as a maid in a family named Pedersen. When the wife died shortly thereafter, Palma eventually became Mrs. Pedersen and took on responsibility for three children. There could be no more time for education, hardly even for reading, but her poems began to appear in newspapers all over *Vesterheimen*. By the age of forty-one she was widowed and she lived the rest of her life with her unmarried stepson. She had considerable faith in her own powers—artistic genius is one of her main themes—and she responded to negative reviews with letters of appreciation, as when she wrote to Rølvaag after his devastating review of *Ragna*: "Thank you greatly for your review . . . You do not know Palma at all well if you believe that she cannot stand rough treatment—a real whipping. No other author writing in Norwegian has had such rough treatment and so many lashes as she, and yet she survives and has more courage and desire to live than ever before" (9 March 1925, OERP). Her novels are marred by linguistic infelicities but they are nevertheless memorials to a brave woman, who in a male-dominated culture created female characters of extraordinary moral and spiritual strength.

Her first heroine, Gudrun in the 1923 novel, is given a background of miserable poverty much like the author's, and like the author she rises above this background with her high ideals and moral convictions. After a muddled series of plot complications, disasters, and deaths, Gudrun on the last page is married to Ole Skjoldhammer, an idealized male character. Both have had dreams of becoming artists, but now they must bow under the lash of responsibility. Their responsibility is the three children of Ole's dead sister, and in *Genier* (1925, Geniuses) Palma tells of their loves, sorrows, and successes. While the artist heroine of *Ragna* is a painter, Gudrun is a writer working on a novel called "Gifted People." In *Skandinaven* Rølvaag had much fun with Palma's geniuses—Ideus, who becomes the most celebrated architect of New York, Ole Skjoldhammer, who retires from his bank to devote himself to his many inventions and finally is killed in the wreck of an airship constructed with a metal of his own invention, Charlotte, self-taught singer, pianist, and composer, who miraculously cures herself of a fatal disease—and was cruelly blunt: "The most revolting aspect of her book, however, is its sentimentality—it is simply awful!" (10 July 1925). Rølvaag had taken the trouble of sending her a letter with detailed criticism, in particular of her style, and Palma Pedersen realized that the coming review might not be what she had hoped for: "if it is in harmony with your rebukes in your last letter it will surely be a death sentence for my continued work as an author" (7 July). The review hurt: "I can at least not make myself believe that you harbor so much evil as you there pretend: for if so—then I must pity you and yours." But she is as resilient as ever, refuses to be discouraged, and begs him to continue to criticize her work (16 July). This letter is also a revealing document in regard to the problems immigrants had with language retention. She justifies some of her linguistic errors, insisting that this is the way she remembers her mother speaking, and she is unable to see some of her anglicisms even after they have been pointed out. Gudrun has the same aspirations and the same limitations as her creator. She, too, sends poems to newspapers, in particular to *Amerika*, edited by R.B. Anderson, and as Palma regarded the real Anderson as her mentor and wrote him frequent letters (RBAP), the novel quotes liberally from Gudrun's fictitious correspondence with Anderson and equally imaginary exchanges with a critical and ironic Strømme and a more friendly Baumann as well as fictitious reviews and letters by Lunde, Ager, and Folkestad.[2] As the other characters go from success to success, Gudrun understandably has bouts of self-doubt, recognizing that her "products occasioned more laughter, criticism, and derision than recognition and praise . . . Perhaps . . . she only imagined that she had literary gifts?" (111). A low point is reached when her manuscript is returned from *Skandinaven* with a letter that is as harsh in its judgment as any criticism received by Palma herself (125–6). But on the last page, along with Charlotte's miraculous cure and the marriage of three happy couples, Gudrun rises unconsumed from her critical cremation like the Phoenix for which Ole's exploded airship was named: her new novel, "Gifted People," is met with acclaim and the genius of its author is recognized.

Palma Pedersen continued to write and to correspond with other writers. Newspapers printed her poems, but her novels were not so readily accepted. The novel *Skandinaven* returned to Gudrun was in part set in Russia, as was Palma's unpublished novel "Battles of the soul" (5, 14 Oct. 1927, OERP). Another novel, "Det rette valg" (The right choice), was first turned down by the editor of *Decorah-Posten*, Kristian Prestgard, who then helped her with the necessary revisions (24 Nov. 1934, LC).[3] When it eventually appeared in the February and March issues of the supplement *Ved Arnen*, Palma Pedersen was overjoyed. Although she received no honorarium, she felt that for the first time an editor had given her the advice and corrections she needed. Not only had Prestgard introduced her novel with kind words about the author, at a meeting of the Bjørnson Literary Society in La Crosse Palma had read the first installment and been met with a standing ovation. She expressed her gratitude to Prestgard in several letters, explaining that "nothing in the world is so dear and so important as to be able to express the gift that God has given me" (24 Nov. 1934, 20 Feb., 4, 5 March 1935, KPP).

Palma Pedersen was not alone in being the butt of ridicule among other writers. On Christmas day in 1915 Rølvaag wrote in holiday spirit to Buslett recommending Gulbrand Sether's *Fjeldbygdens datter* (1915, The daughter of the mountain valley): "It is about the funniest thing I have seen—and probably will ever see—in print" (OERP). Sether's novel is a fantastic tale of the odyssey of Agnes Jordan from the mountain valley of her birth not only through the cities of Christiania, Berlin, Paris, and Nice and then back to Christiania and Bergen but also through all levels of society, the low life of the whorehouse as well as the world of the fantastically rich. Through it all Agnes retains her innocence, and after more than average portions of adversity and luck she becomes both incredibly wealthy and the bride of her long lost first love. Rølvaag had good reason to write as he did to Buslett.

Although Sether (1869–1941) and Pedersen share a preoccupation with genius and although they both revel in incredible plots, Sether knew far more of the world he wrote about than did Palma. Sether's path from his childhood in rural poverty to limited success as a painter of landscapes in Chicago was both rocky and winding, leading to Christiania, where he was an apprentice baker when he became the protege of Fritz Thaulow, to Paris, where he studied at the Atelier Julien, and to London, where he was near starvation before he sold enough paintings to pay his ticket to the United States in 1898 (Ager 1913). His first novel, *Stræv* (1912, Struggle), a first-person narrative of a young artist's spectacular adventures in London and Paris, ending with his arrival in New York, is based on the author's own struggle to become an artist.

These two novels, published by the author, sold well and *Skandinaven* was no doubt happy to publish his next one, *Sønnen paa Hofstad* (The son from Hofstad), in 1917, selling three printings in a few months. Thorvald, the son of the proud and wealthy farmer of Hofstad, is dissolute and finally emigrates in shame, leaving behind a natural son who grows up with his poor maternal grandparents. In New York Thorvald goes from bad to worse and a large inheritance merely speeds him on his downward path of alcohol and shady deals. After his marriage ends in divorce, he loses all contact with his wife and son and the account of his life as a derelict in New York and Brooklyn is central to the novel. Meanwhile, in Norway and New York, both his sons are hardworking and successful, the Norwegian accepted by a relenting paternal grandfather who gives him Hofstad, and the New Yorker, a bank clerk, welcomed into partnership as the husband of the banker's daughter. After the New York son discovers that an old bum is his lost father, all ends in bliss and Thorvald lives out the rest of his days at Hofstad. The family fortune is divided between the two sons and while one carries on the Hofstad tradition in Norway the other does the same in the United States. The wounds of immigration are healed and the family's two branches are bound together by love and tradition. Sether's fourth and last novel, *Bernt Myrstua* (1920), is not redeemed by any such symbolic plot. For all its sanctimonious sentiments about the need *Vesterheimen* has for good writers (69–70), the slight frame narrative of the author-narrator Bernt Myrstua is merely a thin excuse to present a series of disconnected adventures that have the same basic structure as the episodes in his earlier work: good luck followed by catastrophe.

Emil Mengshoel (1867–1945), who regarded political journalism as his main calling, wrote two novels that are head and shoulders above the other works of fiction considered in this chapter.[4] His first extended literary work was an 1898 translation of one of the period's many utopian novels, Frederick Upham Adams' *President John Smith: The Story of a Peaceful Revolution* (1897). His first novel, *Øen Salvavida* (The isle of Salvavida), was published in 1904 in Girard, Kansas, where Mengshoel and his wife Helle had come the year before on the invitation of John Wayland to edit a socialist journal, *Gaa Paa!* (Forward!), for Scandinavian immigrants. It turned out that Wayland was not prepared to take on the publishing responsibility, but Emil and Helle Mengshoel decided to give it a try nevertheless. It hardly made sense to remain in Girard, however, if your audience was in *Vesterheimen,* and shortly after *Øen Salvavida* was off the press, the publishers brought the novel and the journal back to Minneapolis.

The setting of Mengshoel's utopian fantasy, the salon of Madame Blawatskaja, seems as out of place in working-class Minneapolis as in Wayland's Girard. The narrator, a Norwegian sailor, discovers that the famous mystic is in Le Havre and he goes to her for a demonstration of psychic phenomena. He is well received and as they talk he reveals his conviction that egotism and self-interest are the cornerstones of civilization. She offers him a vision but warns that it will change his life and the narrator accepts the risk. In his supervised trance the narrator is aboard the ship *Sociedad,* wrecked on Salvavida, a South Pacific island, during a violent storm. All but the captain survive and the crew and a group of immigrants manage to get ashore with their belongings. The first mate takes command and also claims ownership of the island, based on documents proving that he is descended from their Spanish discoverer. Assisted by the pious sailmaker, who becomes his bishop, and a few armed crew members, he takes possession and sets the others to work. All opposition is quelled and a feudal system with land grants to some of the loyal assistants is installed. Unhappy and restless, the narrator and his educated friend find another island to the southwest and plot a successful mass migration that leaves the proprietor of Salvavida alone in his glory. On the new island a socialistic republic—"Fridland"—is established, an ideal society based on moral rather than legal right. As all are celebrating their achievement, however, the narrator sits by himself troubled by his realization that he can remember nothing before the point when he was awakened just before the shipwreck. He is awakened a second time, now by Madame Blawatskaja, and goes out into the real world with his eyes opened to the inequities of western civilization and to the fact that the cruel regime

of Salvavida dominates the world. "But out there in the breakwaters of the
future Fridland is already rising up to meet us. There lies the course of society's hope."

   This confidence in the future is not evident in *Mené Tekél*, subtitled "A
Norwegian-American labor novel from the end of the nineteenth century"
and published in 1919. Its melodramatic plot provides settings in which the
violent and self-destructive anti-hero, August Varberg, is tried and shown to
be not only a failure but a danger to the socialist cause.[5] Mengshoel was a
social democrat, convinced that education and the ballot were the most important levers for social change. "*Gaa Paa* rejected the idea of direct action
and sabotage advocated by elements within the radical and syndicalist Industrial Workers of the World; in industrial conflicts the newspaper embraced the nonviolence plank adopted by the Socialist party in 1912" (Lovoll 1990, 93). August, an artist whose biography is strikingly similar to that
of the author, has been introduced to socialism before coming to the
United States, where he continues his education, reading John Wayland and
Edward Bellamy. But August does not share the sober approach of his men-
tors and is governed more by his emotions than his intellect—in politics as
in his private life. As the novel opens August is digging a ditch and kills the
foreman in a fit of rage. In his flight he again responds with violence when
provoked and kills a railway guard. Also other situations in the novel serve
to underline his violent streak as well as his inability to work steadily at a
project with future goals in mind. He is an artist, and as he leaves Minneapolis and his beloved Valborg Sand he learns that his ambitious allegorical painting "Mené Tekél" has been sold by a dealer. When he eventually
returns after many adventures he discovers the identity of the wealthy yet
progressive patron, Sir Aylcroft, and is commissioned to paint another allegorical picture. Another influence on his life, however, is a Polish nihilist
who speaks of suicidal action for the benefit of mankind. When a rich
young man discovers that August is wanted for murder he blackmails Valborg into marrying him. August, misinterpreting her action, responds in nihilist fashion, throwing a homemade bomb in the cathedral during the
wedding ceremony that brings down the entire structure killing all, including himself. In an "Epilogue" the Polish nihilist and the wealthy Sir Aylcroft
stand side by side looking at the rubble, which the Pole speaks of as a good
piece of work while Sir Aylcroft is dismayed, asking if he, too, is mad. "He
gave them their Mené Tekél, all right!" responds the nihilist while Sir Aylcroft agrees but observes that "with this mad terrorist action he again wiped
out the writing on the wall . . . For every such act of madness you strike a

shaft through the hope for a just society." These are the closing words of the novel and Sir Aylcroft speaks for the author in warning against the revolutionary violence of the anti-hero. In *Mené Tekél* the writing on the wall is as much directed against the violence-prone left as against the capitalistic system that the author sought to change.

Another writer who shared Mengshoel's socialist convictions was Olaf Berild, a contributor to *Gaa Paa* who also wrote several books. One of these, a novel with the uninformative title *Glimt av Norge og Amerika* (Glimpses of Norway and America), was published in Seattle in 1924. But Berild had neither Mengshoel's literary skills nor his intellectual understanding of politics and his novel, intended as a vehicle for a socialist critique of Norway and America, is a poorly written melodrama. Berild's other books, a pretentious socialist-evolutionist essay (1917) and a simplistic farce (1931), are of even less interest.

Progressive in its message rather than socialist, *Harald Hegg* (1914), by M. Falk Gjertsen (1847–1913), is an interesting document, less for its literary value than for its views on American politics and Norwegian-American culture.[6] Writing in Southern California after retirement, Gjertsen was evidently preoccupied with the future of his group as well as his country and his young characters are three second-generation Norwegian Americans and an Anglo-American woman. Gjertsen trumpets the value of the Norwegian heritage no less loudly than did preservationists such as Buslett, Simon Johnson, and Ager, but he moves his characters out of the narrow confines of their immigrant group and into the larger American society, thus pointing to integration rather than isolation as the path for his people. Both the pastor's son Karl Holm and the farmer's son Harald Hegg are educated at a Norwegian-American college and study law at Yale. It is Karl's sister who introduces Harald's Anglo-American future wife to classic American literature and Harald is the novel's spokesman for American ideals in his war against political and financial corruption. He is an idealistic young lawyer who takes on cases involving corruption, racism, and the misuse of economic power. The real power, however, is the "System"—a conspiracy of the capital interests. Consequently, the problem needs a political solution and Harald enters politics and wins a seat in the state legislature. In the end, the progressive forces achieve victory, passing a law regulating the railways. America, presumably, is on the right track. But Gjertsen's narrative technique is amateurish and, as Ager observed in his review, the recent appearance of new novelists like Simon Johnson and Paal Mørck had "raised the expectations for a Norwegian-American novel" (*Kv* Jan. 1915).

Ager responded less favorably to a far better book some years later in a letter to Buslett, explaining that although it was written in Norwegian it had "no importance" as Norwegian-American literature: "It has not the slightest thing to do with us" (18 Dec. 1918, OABP). Reviewing Olai Aslagsson's *Under vestens himmel* (1918, *Under Western Skies*) some weeks later, he apparently contradicted himself, claiming it was "one of the best books written in the Norwegian language in America" (*Kv* Jan. 1919, 32). But there was no more contradiction here than in Rølvaag's positive review in *Lutheraneren* that insisted that "it is only Norwegian in the sense that it is written in Norwegian" (Dec. 25, 1918). While both could not but be happy to see good books published in *Vesterheimen* they were not quite sure about how to react to such books when they demonstrated no interest in *Vesterheimen* or, indeed, in immigrant themes. The narrator of the three longest of Aslagsson's western stories is by implication a Norwegian American (1918, 61, 147) but his ethnicity is never an issue. *Under vestens himmel* is simply a book of well-executed stories influenced by the Jack London of *The Call of the Wild* and *White Fang*. Aslagsson was already planning his return to Norway, where his first book was reissued and where he had a long career as an author specializing in books set in the wilderness and with animal protagonists.

Fictional works with themes and settings that go outside the narrow confines of *Vesterheimen*, whether in the manner of Mengshoel and Gjertsen or in the apolitical manner of Aslagsson, are not representative. And the many amateurish novels suggest that time may appear to have stood still in *Vesterheimen*. But themes and concerns that may seem irrelevant to outsiders could nevertheless be of great importance to the writers and their intended audience. Thus Kristofer Dalager's sketchy novel of 1925, *Jordens skjød* (The bosom of the earth), yet another naive story of homesteading and the growth of settlements in the West, turns into a didactic tale of the quality of orphanages, a vital issue in a society where premature deaths left so many children without parents. While Dalager's story is roughly contemporary, J.K. Moen's *Knut Langaas*, which was published by K.K. Rudie in 1926, is about an orphan who comes to the Midwest in 1844. Through hard work, sharp wits, and a lot of good luck, the poor immigrant becomes a wealthy and progressive farmer and governor of his state. Even more of a throwback to the mode of an earlier period is Ole Nilsen's *Dalrosen. Fra virkelighetens verden paa begge sider av havet* (The rose of the valley: From real life on both sides of the ocean), which though published in 1928, would not have raised an eyebrow had it appeared fifty years earlier. Similarly archaic are the novels by Thorvald Bakke (1927), John Christopherson (1928), and John

Bangsberg (1929). In Bangsberg's novel the first section, set in Norway, is a disconnected series of moralistic episodes, while the briefer concluding section, set in North Dakota, is the conventional tale of the growth of a new settlement.

It is against the background of all this pedestrian rehashing of old modes and old stories that Rølvaag's extremely positive review of Hans Rønnevik's *100 procent* in 1926 should be appreciated: "For despite ... major faults, this book is perhaps the best first novel that has ever seen the light of day among us" (*Sk*; clipping in OERP). Rønnevik was a farmer in Carlisle, Minnesota, who spent his evenings trying to master the art of fiction and had occasionally published stories in newspapers. In 1925 a manuscript novel, "Toward a new day," had been going the rounds of editors and publishers, to Torkel Oftelie, editor of *Telesoga*, to Augsburg Publishing House, to Waldemar Ager, and to Rølvaag, to whom he wrote explaining that he would not be able to rewrite it along the lines he had suggested. Nevertheless, Rølvaag's letter had given him much food for thought: "I am merely a common farmer who toils with the soil, cattle, and much debt. It is hard work all year, you see, heavy work that taps my strength ... " (6 Feb. OERP). He has decided to lay aside the manuscript that had met with such discouraging response, since he has completed another novel that he is publishing at his own expense and that he hopes Rølvaag will like better.

This correspondence must have predisposed Rølvaag to be sympathetic to the well-meaning farmer, but he also approved wholeheartedly of Rønnevik's message that the best way to be an American patriot was to cultivate your immigrant heritage. As the novel opens it presents a second-generation hero who has gone against the current and reversed the common tendency to Anglicize Norwegian names: Lewis Olson takes the name Lars Holte on reaching maturity in 1912, much to the consternation of his father and neighbors. Two episodes follow which demonstrate his dual allegiance, his patriotic love of his country and his strong interest in the cultural tradition of his forebears: he raises a flagpole on his father's farm and flies the flag on the Fourth of July even though there is no precedent for such behavior, and on the boat he has inherited from his grandfather he sets the sails that his grandfather had so often talked about having used in the old country. Ironically, he is sent away from the farm by his father and in town he has a series of confrontations with the three main enemies of his immigrant heritage: the minister who tries to avoid using the language he was born to, the banker Pete Harmsen (earlier, Peter Hermandsen), who "was Norwegian with the Norwegians and farmer with the farmers, but also

American among Americans and urbanite among the townsfolk" (15), and
Edward Stone, publisher and editor of the local newspaper, who manipu-
lates both minister and banker.

Two political upheavals disrupt life in this small Minnesota community—the agitation of the Nonpartisan League and the chauvinist hysteria that followed America's entry into the First World War. Lars registers for
military service, but is not called up because of the nefarious machinations
of Stone. He is both attracted by the NPL platform and active in organizing
a society for Norwegian culture; on both scores he becomes an easy target
for his enemies. Lars, a loyal patriot, is convicted of treason and sits in prison
till the end of the war, and Guri, a widow who has lost three of her sons at
the front, comes under attack for her interest in Norwegian culture. The
greatest loss, however, is suffered by the country itself, for disheartened by
their experience, the little flock of true patriots, Lars and his family, Guri
and her invalid son, and another Norwegian American who has suffered on
active duty, return to the land of their forebears. In Rønnevik's novel the
good are righteous and the bad are stupid and mean. His main fault, wrote
Rølvaag in *Skandinaven*, is his indignation and anger. The wartime idealism
that had swept the nation "was so naive and childish, that . . . it became
ridiculous. Consequently, anger does not work, especially now so many
years later; laughter, however, would have smarted." Within a few months of
publication Rønnevik had "sold about 230 books, perhaps 25 in the mail
and the rest direct—*peddling* . . . The most difficult thing is to get reviews,"
he wrote to Rølvaag, concluding, "Well, I won't bother you any more
now—it has been a good lesson—and I also had fun doing it" (30 Oct.
1926). He continued to write and published stories and verse in *Jul i Vesterheimen*, but no more novels.

Indeed, by the late 1920s few Norwegian-American novels were published except at the author's expense. Augsburg had been a major publishing outlet in the early 1920s, but by the time Sundheim resigned in 1928 the
writers he had helped had either ceased to publish or were relying on publishers in Norway and New York. As *Vesterheimen* ceased to offer a market
for novelists, however, many new writers, most of them women, were appearing. Newspapers were still an outlet for fiction, and the main provider
of light reading by and for *Vesterheimen* in the 1920s, and until it ceased publication in 1972, was *Decorah-Posten* and its supplement *Ved Arnen*.

The most interesting serialized fiction in *Decorah-Posten*, however, was
not a novel but a comic strip by Peter J. Rosendahl, "Han Ola og han Per,"
about the adventures of two Minnesota farmers and their families, friends,

The popular cartoon series "Han Ola og han Per" which appeared for many years in Decorah-Posten was created by the Norwegian-American farmer P. J. Rosendahl from Spring Grove, Minnesota. It is here reprinted with English translation in a collection of his cartoons edited by Joan N. Buckley and Einar Haugen, Han Ola og han Per (University of Oslo Press, 1984).

and neighbors. Rosendahl was a unique artist and his disaster-prone characters continue to entertain the readers of *Decorah-Posten*'s successor, *Western
Viking*. The strip is also available in two volumes edited by Joan Buckley
and Einar Haugen (1984, 1988), who have written excellent introductions,
the first placing Rosendahl in the history of the American comic strip, the
other analyzing his linguistic skills. While it could be claimed that a study of
the American comic strip would be incomplete without notice of
Rosendahl, such a claim could hardly be made for the place in American literature of the group of writers who had their novels and stories published
in the same newspaper. The fiction of Antonette Tovsen, Ruth Fjeldsaa,
Karin Berg, Johannes Eriksen, Signe Solheim, or Emma Bonhus is not
likely to attract many readers to the microfilm on which it is now available.
If some of these stories seem quaint and old-fashioned, it should be considered that Tovsen and Erikson did not begin to write for publication until
after retirement. If most seem overly simplistic and sentimental, it should be
remembered that their authors did not belong in the literary world of the
Hemingways and Faulkners, but in the very different world of pulp ro-
mances.

Popular with her readers was Antonette Tovsen, who had been a bookkeeper in her brother-in-law's drugstore in Brooklyn and who wrote the
novels and short stories she sent to faraway Decorah and other midwestern
addresses in her home in Hampstead Gardens, Long Island, after retirement
(Fjeldsaa 1943). Her first story, "Blaaveis" (Blue anemone), was serialized in
1920. She was awarded first prize in a *Decorah-Posten* fiction competition in
1924 for "Naar strengene brister" (When the strings break), published the
following spring (letter from Prestgard 22 April 1924, LC). Recognition
seems to have kindled her ambition: she also sent stories to *Skandinaven* and
Jul i Vesterheimen and, beginning with "Rebecca" in 1929, her last five contributions to *Decorah-Posten* are full-blown novels, the last appearing after her
death in 1942.

Another popular writer in the 1920s was Karin Berg, who then lived in
Minneapolis but later returned to the country of her birth (Thorson 1957,
350). Five of her novels were serialized in *Decorah-Posten* from 1922 to 1929;
one of them, "I Bakkehuset" (In the Bakke home), was awarded second
prize in the 1924 competition. *Oberstindens pleiedatter* (The ward of the
colonel's wife) was published in 1929 by N. Fr. Hansen in Cedar Rapids,
publisher of the women's magazine *For kvinden og hjemmet*. This novel is an
updated version of the old "on-both-sides-of-the-ocean" genre, archaic in
style yet set in twentieth-century Montana. The heroine, a bright, lively, and

impulsive orphan, is brought up by her aristocratic aunt and uncle to become a cold-hearted and pretentious aristocrat. Their fortune is lost, however, and emigration is the heroine's last resort. In America successive failures leave her with no alternative but to marry a Norwegian-American Montana homesteader. The marriage appears doomed to be a disaster, but the heroine gradually learns the ways of the West and a visit to Europe opens her eyes to the fact that she, too, has come to share the democratic values of her husband and her new country. She returns to the West where love and happiness are waiting. Although the settings are different and a heroine has replaced the hero, Berg's 1929 novel has much the same message as Foss's *Decorah-Posten* novel of the 1880s: dear reader, immigration was a wise choice.

Attracted by the competition in 1924, Ruth Fjeldsaa submitted a manuscript to *Decorah-Posten* that was serialized as "Guld og glans" (Gold and glitter). She won third prize and was further encouraged when a story was purchased by *Skandinaven* in 1925. More importantly, the competition made her aware that near her home on Long Island lived a kindred spirit, Antonette Tovsen, and the two often met to talk about their shared interest in literature (Fjeldsaa 1943). Like the older Palma Pedersen, Ruth Fjeldsaa preferred to appear under a pseudonym, "Jutta," and like her she also needed careful editing, as may be seen in the correspondence with Prestgard about "Stækkede vinger" (Stunted wings), eventually serialized in 1927 (LC). Indeed, Rølvaag's critical review of Palma Pedersen's *Genier* in *Skandinaven* in 1925 also had a sobering effect on Fjeldsaa, who had been encouraged by her successes in *Skandinaven* and *Decorah-Posten*, but now decided not to publish her most recent effort as a book (To Rølvaag Oct. 1925, OERP). Fjeldsaa, too, wrote about the artist and the artist's sensibility, as in "Hans ungdoms borg" (The fortress of his youth), serialized in 1933–1934. As *Vesterheimen* was becoming more urbanized, so was its fiction and for Fjeldsaa Brooklyn was a natural setting. Here, at long last, a son finds his lost father, Harry Brown, born Hans Brun, after searching for him for ten years. Hans Brun had come to America in order to realize his dream of becoming a poet: "Now he told his son about his life in America, of his difficult struggle to achieve his goal and of all his vain efforts to have a book in Norwegian published here. Newspapers were eager to accept stories and poems as well as novels, but they paid so little that no one could make a living as a writer" (12 Dec. 1933). Consequently, he had accumulated large piles of manuscript. After this interesting sidelight on the working conditions of Ruth Fjeldsaa and her author colleagues in the 1930s and 1940s, the novel rapidly disintegrates into an abundance of complications and misunderstandings that seem to have the primary function of stretching out the story. Ruth Fjeldsaa loved the sea and eventually moved from Long Island to Key West, where she continued to write for a diminishing audience. Throughout her career she had sent poems to newspapers and journals and in Florida she finally published a book of verse.

One of the journals to which Fjeldsaa had sent her verse was *Norsk Ungdom*, a monthly youth magazine that combined a pietistic outlook with an interest in cultural preservation. *Norsk Ungdom* frequently had editorials or contributions in verse and prose on the value of using Norwegian in America; indeed English was associated with secular distractions, the "questionable entertainments that tempt our youth, indolence and lack of seriousness and initiative in the cause of the Kingdom of God" (Jan. 1932, 2). Although the magazine published verse as well as essays on literature, it shied away from fiction. In response to requests, the editor explained that they could not afford to pay for new stories and that "Many stories and books written in Norwegian today contain so much that is crude and indelicate that we are not willing to fill the magazine's columns with such matter" (Jan. 1926, 9). In 1926, however, the editor received a manuscript that fulfilled his requirements for a "pure literature": "Kaffekjelen" (The coffee pot) ran for two full years (Sept. 1926 to Sept. 1928), brought many new subscribers to the magazine (see Oct. 1927), and proved so popular with readers (see Sept. 1928) that the editor promised yet another story from the writer only known as "Elisabeth."

It is tempting to dismiss this sentimental and implausible story of a coffee pot and ascribe its popularity to the lack of literary sophistication of its readers. An historian of small-town Middle America in the 1920s, however, may be advised to give it some attention. For Elisabeth's mild and gentle criticism of the conservative and orthodox clergyman married to the female protagonist, as well as her modest but insistent urging of a more meaningful role for women in church and family were important issues for the subscribers. That she thus spoke to the concerns of her readers is a more likely reason for her popularity than her implausible plots. The cultural interests of the subscribers to *Norsk Ungdom* should not be underestimated. In 1927 it gave readers the first publication of the fascinating 1839–1847 diaries of Søren Bache, an important source for the early history of Norwegian immigration. A few years later, in 1932, it published four essays by Kristine Haugen that constitute the earliest assessment of the contribution of Ole Edvart Rølvaag. Indeed, on his success with *Giants in the Earth*, Rølvaag's realism seems to have been forgiven: "We heartily congratulate Rølvaag. May his pen long interpret the desires, mind, and behavior of the Norse people" (July 1927, 104).

The culture of *Vesterheimen* was of one cloth, though dyed in many colors and used to dress a wide variety of attitudes and activities. The most ambitious attempt to revive the waning cultural and intellectual life of *Vesterheimen* grew out of Det Litterære Samfund, a literary society in Chicago that attracted young recently arrived academics, such as Aaslaug Berger (later Aileen Berger Evanson), who had come to the United States as a student at the University of Minnesota in 1921, as well older Chicagoans such as Oscar Gundersen. In 1928 the society subtitled their new literary magazine, *Norden*, "Journal for Norwegian America."[7] Although *Norden* had a secular, urban, and elitist cultural orientation while *Norsk Ungdom* was pietistic and popular, they shared contributors such as Sigrid Hakstad, librarian in the Scandinavian section of the Chicago Public Library. The fiction published in *Norden* is frequently no better than the popular fictions of *Decorah-Posten*. One *Norden* writer, however, deserves special mention for the way in which she brings the new educated urban immigrant woman into the fiction of *Vesterheimen*. The female perspective of Aileen Berger Evanson's fiction in *Norden* is evident in "Bumpens land," a sketch of a young woman in Chicago who longs for her old home but who finally decides not to visit Norway for Christmas because she realizes that America is her child's home—Bumpen's land (Feb. 1930). Her most ambitious fictional effort, the novel *Slekt i Amerika. Chicago fortælling* (Family in America: A Chicago story), is undated but was probably published after the demise of *Norden* in 1933, and is interesting for the way in which it integrates old structures with modern urban elements. It begins, like the "on-both-sides-of-the-ocean" story, in Norway, but in upper-middle-class Oslo rather than in a cotter's hut in a rural valley. Kate, the protagonist, who has taken her university entrance exams and is the stepdaughter of a successful lawyer, is invited to visit her unknown relatives in Chicago, where she was born but from where her mother had taken her back to Norway after the mysterious death of her father. Although the story thus gives an account of the urban migration of the 1920s and 1930s, which was very different from the migrations of the 1870s, some of its motifs are strikingly similar to those of earlier novels. For example, when she meets the poor Chicago painter Knut Ellingsen, the contrast between American democracy and Old World class distinctions is illustrated through the reception given him by the Crosbys, Kate's wealthy and illustrious Chicago family. They treat him "entirely as an equal," Kate notes in surprise (13). Also as in earlier fiction, however, old-world cultural values are contrasted with New World materialism (15), and Kate gradually learns to see behind the facade of the powerful Crosby family. The male protagonist, Olai Andell, works in a bank, has ambitions of becoming a writer, and sends essays to the Norwegian-American press, much in the manner of the older real-life Oscar Gundersen. Kate and Olai are obviously destined for each other, but this can come about only after many turns of the melodramatic plot and after Kate comes to terms with the violence and evil in her American mother's past and accepts her inheritance from her Norwegian stepfather. Kate weathers the Depression and Olai returns to Chicago after attempts to study theology in the West. They are reunited and decide to study sociology at a university in Chicago and live "A modern life!" — Kate's concluding words.

Meanwhile, there was little desire for a modern life in the fiction that continued to be published in *Decorah-Posten* in the 1930s and 1940s. In her retirement in Key West, reflecting in 1943 on the death of her friend and colleague Antonette Tovsen, Ruth Fjeldsaa could not but note that her "own little world" was getting to be "rather empty." "The few authors we have had have in a shockingly brief span of time recently laid down their wanderer's stave . . . we remember with a sense of loss names like Ristad, Rølvaag, John Benson, Waldemar Ager, Jon Norstog, and now, most recently, Antonette Tovsen. But let us cling to the hope that all who love the Norwegian language will rally in support of what remains so that our Norwegian-American press may yet for a long time enrich us and please us with poems and novels in our beloved Norwegian language." *Decorah-Posten* was to live yet another thirty years. *Jul i Vesterheimen* appeared for the last time in December 1957. In the last decades of the twentieth century newspapers such as *Minnesota-Posten* (1956–1978) in Minneapolis and *Western Viking* in Seattle continued to print the work of the few remaining American writers using Norwegian, such as Eyvind J. Evans (Torvik 1982). But in effect, as a literary culture with a variety of publishers and journals and with reviewers as well as a sufficient number of book buyers to make it all economically feasible, *Vesterheimen* had ceased to exist by the early 1930s. Traditions and languages, however, die hard and as late as 1969 a sixty-five-year-old poet in Tacoma, Washington, Arnfinn Bruflot, sent the manuscript of the first of his five volumes of poems to a publisher in Oslo. The title of his only novel (1980) aptly sums up the story of what had happened to *Vesterheimen* — *Inn i Amerika* — it had been absorbed into America.

NOTES

1. Novels with a religious message were not necessarily Lutheran or even Christian. In Helen Storjohann Egilsrud's *New Day* (1932) the pedestrian story is an excuse to present long conversations on Eastern mysticism and Theosophy.

2. While most literary references in *Genier* are to *Vesterheimen*, Gudrun's favorite writers are Elizabeth Allen and Edgar Guest. In her 16 July letter to Rølvaag, Palma praises the work of Ella Wheeler Wilcox.

3. In a 15 Oct. 1925 letter to *Minneapolis Tidende* Palma mentions yet another novel: "*Labor Omnia Vincit*" (MTCP).

4. Studies of Mengshoel are Granhus 1988 and 1992 and Lovoll 1990.

5. His names suggest both imperial authoritarianism and the dangerous instability of the werewolf (*varulv*), the latter also suggested by his joined brows. Other names are equally suggestive: August thinks of the heroine, Valborg Sand, as a Valkyrie; he is constantly jealous of her, while her last name means "true"; an exploiting farmer is named Cheetam; Dr. Wayupp is a wealthy proponent of social Darwinism.

6. For a biography of Gjertsen see Draxten 1988.

7. *Norden* was a continuation of mimeographed literary journals, *Forum* and *Nota Bene*, produced for the society's members.

PART SIX

Six Authors

Simon Johnson:
Poet of the Prairies

Simon Johnson (1874–1970) came to North Dakota at the age of eight and grew up with an idealized image of the country of his birth. While he derived his sense of values from a heady reading of nineteenth-century Norwegian literature, however, he had his sense of natural beauty from the plains and prairies of his childhood and youth. In verse and prose he sang of the landscape in which he was rooted, the "blessed place" of his 1906 poem "De nye hjem" (The new homes). A third influence on his character was his great respect for the writers of New England, "Longfellow, Emerson, Holmes, yes, even Owen Wister," who gave him a no less idealized image of the United States.[1] With his conservative values and deep-seated patriotism, few were hurt more than Johnson by the nativist excesses and xenophobia of the First World War. In his contribution to a history of the North Dakota Temperance Association, Johnson insisted that by being loyal to his traditions the immigrant would also be most loyal to his country: "As *Americans* . . . they tried to realize their best ideals in public service; as *Norwegians* they based their work on their own cultural values . . . They were, in other words, faithful to the best interests of their state. Should such behavior be the occasion of the insinuations of 'disloyalty' that now are so commonly heard?" (Foss 1923, 116).

Studious rather than adventurous, the young Johnson was not one to strike out on his own and he worked faithfully on the family farm near Hillsboro until he was offered modest employment as secretary of the North Dakota Temperance Association at the age of twenty-six. During the seven years he served the association Johnson not only took up a homestead farther west, near Minot, but also began his literary career, submitting

Simon Johnson (1874–1970).

news items and verse to *Reform*, for instance a poem inspired by the naval battle at Santiago and the insobriety of the losing Spaniards (4 June 1901). He soon left such propagandistic verse behind and turned to personal themes (1904), to contemplation of the Dakota prairies and to the immigrant experience. Two of the early poems on the latter themes, in 1906, suggest that the aspiring author is beginning to acquire greater confidence: they mark his first appearances in literary journals, *Vor Tid* and *Kvartalskrift*. The next year he published his first novel.

Et geni (A genius) has a promising opening, but the story of the gifted inventor Sigurd turns into a crude prohibition tract and concludes with the hero, ruined by alcohol, giving his beloved "her freedom." There can be no hope for people like him, he declares, so long as saloons are permitted to exist. In *Kvartalskrift* (Oct. 1907), Ager praised Johnson's landscapes and his sense of life on the prairies and made comparisons with Ibsen, Zola, and Hauptmann in defense of the young author's way of ending his first novel. But even as he publicly praised Johnson's descriptive powers, Ager had private doubts about his lack of realism as well as his ear: "Norse girls don't speak that way" (Thorson 1957, 264). Strømme, who had found *Et geni* a "monstrosity," written to convince people that they should become members of the local temperance society, pronounced that Johnson's next novel, *Lonea* (1909), was a "real novel of the prairies" (*Eidsvold* 1910, 82). In 1912 it was awarded the Norwegian Society's new prize "for the best book recently written in Norwegian in America" (*Kv* Jan. 1913).

Like no novelist before him, Johnson in *Lonea* expresses a deep love of the land of North Dakota in his descriptions of the many faces of the prairie and the emotional responses of his characters to their landscape. The settlers have worked hard to make the land theirs. But the land is not possessed by toil alone. They will have to cultivate their traditions and history as well as the soil before the land can become their home. "I cannot imagine that a healthy people will populate these plains if their memories are not honored and preserved," a recently arrived immigrant tells a meeting called to consider an "Old Settlers Celebration" (36). The diaries of Franz Fagervold are a store of such memories. He is the long dead uncle of the young heroine, Julia, or Jul as she is called, suggesting her great value whether in the Norwegian sense as Christmas or in English as "jewel." Jul inherits her uncle's estate and the manner in which she is found worthy of this inheritance is emblematic of Johnson's idealism.

Jul is the daughter of a hardworking but unlucky farmer. Surrounded by success made manifest in the brightly painted frame houses of their neighbors, the Fagervolds still live in a modified sod house. Jul is the ugly duckling, bent over by constant hard work, but, as we might expect, she grows up to be a beautiful swan. Her greatest reward, however, is the recognition she receives from Miss Parley, whose home is a museum of New England traditions, and the banker, Mr. Young, also from Massachusetts, who had been a good friend of Franz Fagervold and who, advised by Miss Parley, passes his legacy on to his niece. As in the fiction of Foss, those who uphold "Norwegian values" are recognized by those who represent "American values." And Jul embodies the values of both Johnson's idealized Norway and New England: dedication, love of family and homeland (that is, North Dakota), hard work, goodness of heart, and an undaunted spirit. Jul is "Lonea," the fantasy name her beautiful but sickly friend Jenny has given to a lonely and exposed mountain flower in one of her books. All this may be too much of a good thing, but the novel also offers descriptions of life in the Upper Midwest that make it a valuable source for the social historian: an account of a day in a country schoolhouse, a sketch of an itinerant lay preacher, descriptions of meetings both secular and religious, glimpses of the drudgery of a marginal existence—all add up to a book that may be read with interest in spite of its sentimentality.

The friendly reception of *Lonea* was encouraging, but Johnson's next novel did not come easily. "I seildugsvognen" (In the prairie schooner), about a pioneer journey from Wisconsin to North Dakota, presented in *Reform* (23 Dec. 1913) as a fragment of a novel in progress, suggests that at least one draft was left uncompleted. Other indications that he was at work on a narrative of greater complexity than his first two are poems in *Kvartalskrift* (1911, 1912) and a brief sketch of the hardships of pioneer life in *Symra* (1914). Finally, in 1914, he published *I et nyt rige* (In a new kingdom, translated in 1916 as *From Fjord to Prairie*), a novel with a narrative scope and historical sweep new in the fiction of *Vesterheimen*. Where others had interpreted the individual immigrant experience, Johnson's aim in *I et nyt rige* was to dramatize the history of settling the North Dakota plains. Although it cannot but suffer in comparison with Rølvaag's *Giants in the Earth*, the boldness of Johnson's conception should be acknowledged.[2] In *Kvartalskrift* and *Reform* (1915), Ager heaped lavish praise on his colleague: "There is probably not a better prairie novel in the English language."

I et nyt rige is a collective novel about a settlement from homesteading days to an established rural society. The novel opens with Bernt Aasen alone against an alien landscape seen through the conventional image of the sea. But the image is not merely one of appearance; it symbolizes the pioneer's sense of alienation: "they are all as if lost at sea, drifted away from the rest of the world and surrounded by a yellowing waste of grass that in all directions stretched out to the horizon" (1914, 6). For a landscape that might offer a feeling of home as well as aesthetic pleasure he resorts to his imagination: "The mighty mountains crowned with snow, the clear lake between them, mirroring mountain, glacier, and sky—and at the center of all this beauty, the boat with the bridal party! The vision warmed his heart. God, how beautiful it was" (12).[3]

Through the device of a party at the Eng homestead, the characters are presented and characterized as Bernt brings invitations to their homesteads. There is no single protagonist but some characters are assigned specific roles: Bernt as observer and messenger, Tore Eng as practical leader, and his father, Old Eng, as prophet and seer. Alfred and Signe, representatives of the second generation, have the symbolic roles of prince and princess of the new kingdom. In the early years of settlement, when hardships are common to all and rewards are meager, solidarity is as natural as it is crucial to the survival of the embattled group. Frans Fykjarud feels this as he listens to the talk of his neighbors at the party: "There was a sense of fellowship. He understood that the others were interested in him and he on his side was glad that the others existed and were all to be found in this cabin" (33). This sense of fellowship finds practical expression when the neighbors realize that the Brovaags do not have money for the winter provisions they are going to town to buy. "The expedition concerned them all: they had talked about it and looked forward to it. And it was a danger for them all—for those who went as well as for those who stayed behind." And it was not only important for their material needs: "Through this journey to town they would again establish some sort of connection with the world" (43).

The first and longer of the novel's two parts shows how the community survives the hardships and catastrophes of the early years, the second shows how success and progress threaten to tear it apart. The seeds of evil are within the community. All are upset when it is discovered that Dreng Hagaard mistreats his wife. When a neighbor comes with advice, speaking on behalf of "we," Dreng responds through clenched teeth: "We! Here it is I not we" (162). But urban technology and values are more dangerous threats to the community, and after the first piece of machinery, a mowing machine, is introduced, the garden never regains its innocence. The members of the community nevertheless move forward to reap increasing rewards for their struggles. When the leader of a threshing team boasts that he has not seen such yields in the thirty harvests he has taken part in between there and Chicago, they are confirmed in their faith in the land: "What riches! Just a little elbowroom and a few years—what riches! Tore had stopped once that fall faced with this vision. He saw the entire plains broken by the plow—one unending field heavy with harvest to the last square inch" (206).

When Bernt, who has been in Norway, returns with a bride from the old country, the prosperous settlement is in a sad state. The once homogeneous community has been disrupted by the inroads of "Yankee" settlers, and the railroad and the town with its unavoidable saloons have brought further corruption. The old prophet is ailing, but before he dies Old Eng shares his fears and hopes for the future with Bernt. He sees the prairies in forty to fifty years filled with "people of Norwegian blood" still perhaps not truly rooted in their new home, and he asks Bernt to take responsibility for the education and guidance of young Alfred. Old Eng's mantle falls on Bernt, who was in Norway during the years when the pioneer community was corrupted and has returned pure and uncontaminated. Such were Johnson's sentimental notions of the land he had left as a child.

The novel fittingly ends as it began—with a party. The neighbors are gathered in the new home of Frans Fykjarud where there is plenty and where the host is anxious that his guests be fully aware of his prosperity.

Bernt finds the atmosphere stifling and longs for his modest cabin. Alfred and Signe, however, make use of the occasion to confess their love and make their promises as Alfred reveals his plan to go to school before settling down in what has become their home: "And the dark autumn night of the prairie closed in over them." The positive process of making a home of what first had appeared an alien waste and making the depressing evening sky of the opening sentence into the protective cloak of the closing one underlies the more ambiguous movement from poverty to material comfort in the novel.

Johnson's idealism also informed his politics, and "Vaarstunder" (Spring-time), in the 1917 volume of four short stories, is his response to the success of the Nonpartisan League in the elections of 1916. Johnson wrote to Ager that the story "deals with questions that became important for me during the political revolution in the state. I no longer feel at home in North Dakota. That the thoroughly conservative prairie farmers could surrender hand and foot to a political boss who we have seen is no less than a cheat of the most dangerous kind—who could have believed it? I sincerely hope that the man will prove to be better than rumors and events make him out to be, because this revolt is actually as a breath of spring air over the state—the only refreshing thing that has happened here since the battle for prohibition" (19 Feb, 1917, WAP). "Vaarstunder" is the story of how a prosperous farmer, Charley Knuteson, succumbs to the charisma of Owen Birkley, "the greatest speaker of the new movement" (1917, 77), and becomes a local political boss, a tyrant who terrorizes his family as well as the entire county into submission. Only the aging schoolteacher Tor Wilhelmsen and his neighbors in the "gravel bottom" refuse to follow. At a public meeting Wilhelmsen speaks against the materialistic aims of Birkley and his movement: "I, too, have hoped for a popular rising . . . but one concerned with the human spirit not just with the pocketbook" (156). But Knuteson declines into increasingly ab-horrent tactics and his public victory at the polls becomes his private defeat when his daughter turns her back on him. Wilhelmsen's concluding message echoes the author's fear of an encroaching urban civilization: "People must learn that city life is a curse . . . Even country people have their body in the country and the little imagination they have—their soul—in the city. This is aggravated by the cultural activities in the cities. The country is the home of culture . . . the farmers' movement is a cultural movement, but it must not in-corporate the evils of urban culture" (176).

Johnson was an unreconstructed romantic and from his first novel he es-tablishes a dichotomy of city versus country. When the protagonist of *Et geni* is in town: "There did not seem to be any bond between him and

them . . . Here the issue was not life and death but buying and selling"
(35–36). In *Lonea* Jenny insists on returning to the open prairie to die, and
in *I et nyt rige* the growing town of Fordville represents the forces that disrupt the rural community. This love of the land and distrust of the city is
basic to much of the literature of *Vesterheimen*. It is a premise for an early
work like Knut Hasberg's *Trapperens veileder* (1871, Trapper's guide), where
nature, "the great book we read solemnly and with a deep and quiet attention," is set up against the corruption of the city: "Come reader and fellow
Norwegian with us to Chicago. There we will visit the streets and alleys, the
saloons and boardinghouses where so many of our Scandinavian brothers
spend their lives. As we give thanks to Providence that we have been preserved from falling to such depths or entering into such a depraved and cor-
rupting life and company, we will return home to our beautiful Minnesota"
(47–48). But Johnson knew better than to blame the city for all the evil in
the human heart. The seeds of evil are in the pioneers of *I et nyt rige*, and in
his ambitious fourth novel, *Falitten paa Braastad* (The bankruptcy at Braastad), evil is in the proud and mighty farmer Jens Braastad himself.

Although it was written as early as 1914–1916, *Falitten paa Braastad* for
some reason did not appear until 1922.[4] The bankruptcy at the farm that is
the pride and glory of its owner and creator Jens Braastad is of the spirit.
Set in the countryside outside the town of Fordville, as was *I et nyt rige*, this
novel, too, warns against the corruption of success. And it does so with
much the same gallery of types as "Vaarstunder": a wealthy and hardhearted
farmer, Jens Braastad, his neglected wife Lisa, their idealistic and gifted
daughter Lovise and profligate son Henry, and the poor farmer's son, Olaf
Nelson, who eventually marries the rich farmer's daughter. The role of ide-
ologue, in "Vaarstunder" given to Wilhelmsen, is divided between two
characters, the mysterious Fele-Nils—Nils the Fiddler—and the family
doctor, Kvam, both of whom give set speeches on the author's cultural ideology. Other characters are Mary Aasen, who eventually helps to reform
Henry and then marries him, the Shay family, who provide both the arch-
villain, Jonathan, and comic relief in the antics of the socially ambitious
mother and two daughters, and, in a very minor role, pastor Langstad,
whose portrait is so vicious a caricature that it may seem strange that the
novel bears the imprint of a church publisher.

Driven by his childhood memories of poverty in Norway, Jens Braastad
has carved a small empire out of the one-time wilderness. But as his fields
and livestock thrive—"he could now fill a little freight train by himself if
called upon" (9)—his family disintegrates, his wife a near invalid, his son a

drunkard, and his daughter loyal yet disapproving. It is Braastad's thirst for more land and more power that motivates the melodramatic excesses of the plot. Since he has renounced all hope for his own son, he encourages the devious son on the neighboring farm, Jonathan Shay, in his designs on Lovise; their union will ensure that his descendants possess an even larger empire on the plains. But Lovise has given her heart to Olaf Nelson, who is attending college, and Jonathan's suit fails. In desperation, Braastad lets him know that everyone except Lovise will be away one day and that he has a free hand. Faced with "a fate worse than death," Lovise plunges through the screen of her second-story window. Now there are two invalids in the family, and as Lovise is taken to a hospital, her mother, unbalanced by her daughter's revelation of what has happened, is sent to a mental institution.

There are further complications of the melodramatic plot as well as some heavy-handed social comedy. Braastad lives in isolation on the large farm. With the help and support of the upright Olaf Nelson and the loving Mary Aasen, Henry Braastad becomes a responsible citizen. Dr. Kvam instructs Lovise in Norwegian music and literature (while the Shay daughter plays ragtime, Lovise plays Grieg!) and Fele-Nils inspires Olaf Nelson along the path of romantic idealism. Mary and Henry marry and live with their child in a modest white-painted house in town. Henry's mother lives with them, unknown to her husband, who is making a fool of himself courting the forty-years-younger Lucy Shay. Jens Braastad's sudden conversion comes on Christmas Eve when he arrives at the little white house and finds his family assembled for the holidays. He sees the folly of his ways and is reconciled with his wife and children.

Meanwhile Olaf, who has completed his college degree, has been spending his time as the author did in his youth: "Books were his only resource and his reading included many peoples and many conditions. The literatures that interested him most were the Norwegian, from Wergeland [a Romantic poet] to his own time, and the American from the richest period of the New England states" (435). His reading gives life to "his racial consciousness" and an awareness that "American life had never been more beautifully expressed than at the time when America had made up its differences with England and then set about seeking nourishment from its culture" (436). The result is a deeper love of his country reinforced by his pride in his Norwegian heritage. Olaf's widowed father has planned to return to the old country and live the rest of his days there, but when time draws near he realizes that his true home is on the prairie and offers his ticket to his son so that he can get to know the country of his parents. Thus

Olaf will share yet another experience with his author, who went on a similar pilgrimage in 1910–1911. The novel comes to a close as Olaf, joined by Fele-Nils, settles in his seat in the eastbound train as Lovise waves to them from her car. Clearly a sequel is called for.

Johnson's sensitivity and unworldly idealism made him unfit for the rough and tumble of politics in general and the xenophobia of the war years in particular. "I have been living under a cloud for a while now; I am tired and hurt," he wrote to Rølvaag (19 Dec. 1920, OERP). He was also dejected by Ager's negative review of the *Braastad* novel in which he had objected that Johnson's idealized characters had no counterparts in flesh and blood. Writing to Rølvaag, Johnson defended himself with references to Ibsen's idealized Brand and Solveig (16 Dec. 1922). But a year later he is still smarting from Ager's unkindness: "to me it seems stupid, almost disloyal to the interests that we authors are trying to promote" (14 Dec.). The issue of loyalty was central to the sequel he was working on, and in 1924 he responded to Sundheim's request for a contribution to *Jul i Vesterheimen* by lifting an episode from his novel in progress, dressing it up as a short story he called "Borgere" (Citizens). The youngest son of the elderly farmer couple Ole and Maren Norden is killed in action and his body is sent home to be buried with full military honors. The parent's request for a funeral service in Norwegian is turned down because the authorities permit public ceremonies only in English. In the evening, when the cemetery is empty, they go to their son's grave and pray the Lord's prayer in their own language. How much, the story asks, must immigrants sacrifice to be fully accepted as American citizens? *Frihetens hjem* (1925, The home of freedom) is set in a period when the values of the protagonists make them disloyal Americans in the eyes of their super-patriotic neighbors. As in "Vaarstunder," the opportunistic time-servers are organized in the "Farmers' Party," masterminded by Jonathan Shay, still governed by his hatred of the Braastad family. The main values of the protagonists are personal integrity and loyalty—to cultural roots and to the United States: "It is great to be a Norwegian American—to have building materials from a country like Norway and to use them in a country like the United States," Lovise exclaims to her husband after her return from her first visit to the land of her parents (1925, 107). This snatch of dialogue not only gives the gist of Johnson's message but also suggests why the novel fails: this is how Olaf and Lovise speak to each other throughout the novel. In his review, Rølvaag made derogatory comments on the flawless hero and melodramatic villains (*Sk* 11 Dec. 1925). Johnson, who had been hurt by Ager's criticism, was devastated by the ridicule of a man he considered a close friend (Hustvedt 1976). *Frihetens hjem* may be Johnson's weakest novel after *Et geni*, but it is also an interesting document, demonstrating, along with Foss's *Valborg* and Rønnevik's *100 procent*, the traumatic experience of World War I nativism among many loyal Americans in the Upper Midwest.

As the novel opens, the community has changed in character. Many settlers have sold their land and a new type of farmer without the roots and loyalties of the Braastads or the Nelsons has moved in. The newcomers are caricatures, Norwegians who have taken names like Marx Glibb Masterlee and Jerome Audubon Mostead and whose speech is as unrealistic as their names. Olaf Nelson is still on his pilgrimage and his letters to Lovise tell of how his love for America has been intensified in Norway: "The few times I have seen our flag my heart has beat faster and I have experienced as a fact and a vital joy that the Star-Spangled Banner is my flag. My sense of the fabulous adventure of taking part in building the world's greatest republic has been strengthened . . . But I have also come to appreciate the value of family ties as a constructive factor in human life. I believe that we, as immigrants and the descendants of immigrants in our new land, may serve its future best by giving attention to our own identity. In this there is growth— and if we grow as human beings our country will grow in and with us" (9). The novel describes a period of cultural growth in *Vesterheimen*: "Singers and poets addressed people in their mother tongue and had their attention, novelists embraced the people's deeds and desires and transformed them to narratives. *Bygdelag* and other societies were founded—all under the banner of Norsedom" (98). But trouble is brewing: at home the Farmers' Party becomes powerful through promises of material gains, and abroad the European powers clash in war. As the scheming Jonathan Shay increases his power, Olaf and Lovise continue their idyllic life, tilling the soil and reading Norwegian and American poetry to each other. With the Party's growing influence, "a new spirit is brought into the settlement. Traditional Norwegian honesty is no longer regarded as a virtue" and people are lured "by the poisonous locutions of the agitators" (213). When the United States enters the war, the isolationist Farmer's Party is on the defensive and Olaf is given positions of trust, both in organizing drives for Liberty Bonds and on the local draft board. Ever noble, however, Olaf does not use his authority to get back at his enemies. Not to be daunted, these enemies now concentrate their attacks on the treachery implied in the use of foreign languages. Eventually Olaf, his cultural values and his personal integrity at stake, steps down from his lofty position and does battle with the forces of hatred and prejudice. After the war Olaf achieves a public hearing chaired by a state commissioner, where he demonstrates not only that a Norwegian American is a true American but that America has more than one cultural tradition: "When an Englishman becomes an American citizen he is not attacked if wants to make English culture a part of his own. And why? because these cultural treasures exist in the same language as that used by the majority in this country. This is also true of the Irishman and the Scot—and for the same reason. If they attempt to transfer their cultural treasures to their children . . . their loyalty as citizens is not questioned. But when I make use of the same right, then I am made a target of suspicion and hatred . . . Is not American justice strong enough to give the same right to the descendants of the Vikings as to those of English immigrants?" (349). Her husband vindicated and his enemies proved to be either misled or scoundrels, Lovise proudly and lovingly embraces "my Norwegian American" (357).[5]

Frihetens hjem, the most explicit statement of his idealism and his faith in cultural pluralism, was Johnson's last published novel. He continued to write, but with the exception of his journalistic work for *Decorah-Posten* and occasional stories and poems, mainly in *Jul i Vesterheimen*, he ceased to publish. It may be that he felt that his literary sensibility was at odds with his time. It may be that he never regained his confidence after the unfriendly reception of his last novel. It may be that faced with the rapid disintegration of publishing and book distribution in *Vesterheimen* in the late 1920s Johnson was reluctant to step down from his status as author of hard-bound novels with the Augsburg imprint into the less prestigious world of Tovsen and Fjeldsaa and serialization in *Decorah-Posten*. He was encouraged to make use of this last outlet available to the remaining novelists of *Vesterheimen* by Kristian Prestgard, who had heard that Johnson had several novels in manuscript. Johnson responded cautiously that he could possibly send the typescript of a "large settler and prairie novel" for serialization "since it was not devoid of a romantic element." He had, however, written it "with book publication in mind . . . but conditions have changed . . . Augsburg's distribution, which was never very large, has now declined, and authors who have connections in Norway publish their work there." Johnson describes two other drafted novels that could be typed and a few short stories, but adversity and illness have tapped his strength and he complains that his situation is "like sitting in a desert. There is no response, no reply from those one writes for and for whose interests one tries to make oneself into a sort of spokesman. Heavy silence. But not a silence with peace and quiet. Only a vast emptiness" (8 Sep. 1928, LC). Although he did not serialize his fiction in

Decorah-Posten, Johnson, who had married in 1924, moved from Grand Forks to Decorah in 1929 to an editorial position with the newspaper and to many years of accumulating manuscripts of verse, short stories, and novels.[6]

NOTES

1. Johnson's typescript memoirs, "Opplevd," 114 (SJP). Useful studies of Johnson are Thorson 1957, Hustvedt 1976, and Rodgers 1979.

2. Johnson's story "An Outpost Skirmish" (1916) may have provided Rølvaag with the germ of his central marital conflict between two conflicting personalities: the extrovert husband who in the vast emptiness sees his vision of future progress and his wife who despairs of their isolation from "the human community."

3. The vision is of a painting, "The Wedding Procession in Hardanger," by A. Tidemand and H. Gude, who made five versions in the period 1848–1853. In 1849 it inspired a poem by Andreas Munch, set to music by Halvdan Kjerulf. Painting and song would be well known to Johnson's readers.

4. Ødegaard claimed that Johnson wrote the *Braastad* novel in 1914 (3 April 1923, OERP). In 1917 Johnson wrote to Ager that the long novel had been a challenge to his health (19 Feb., WAP).

5. Actually, the Nonpartisan League was the target of unwarranted accusations of disloyalty in North Dakota.

6. Johnson left his manuscripts—two collections of verse, four novels, several short stories, and an autobiography—to the Oslo University Library and the archives of NAHA.

Dorthea Dahl:
Poet of Everyday Life

In 1900, the year Johnson submitted his first notices to *Reform* on the war against alcohol in North Dakota, a slightly younger woman, Dorthea Dahl (1881–1958), began to send similar news items from South Dakota, the state to which she had come with her parents at the age of two.[1] Her first story (1901), a melancholy sketch of the recently widowed wife of a missionary who decides to remain on the mission field, is an expression of the author's youthful ambition to become a missionary. But her frail health did not allow her to spend more than a few weeks at St. Olaf College in 1902, and the next year her parents moved to the healthier environment of Moscow, Idaho, where Dorthea lived most of her life. Compared to the broad sweep of historical and social themes as well as landscapes in Johnson's best work, Dahl's fiction is one of close interiors. Granted the narrowness of her *donné*, however, Dahl is the superior artist of the two. From the minutiae of domestic life she creates characters more convincing than Johnson's idealizations and by playing out their conflicts and dreams on the stages of home and congregation she gives them greater credibility and, paradoxically, endows them with more compelling interest than the more wide-ranging characters of Johnson. Congregational strife was a regrettable factor in the life of *Vesterheimen* and many works of fiction were written to reveal the unseemly behavior of theological adversaries. In her best fiction, however, Dahl used the congregation, the social institution she knew best, to throw light on character, not to further particular views on church polity. For the reader able to accept that congregations and ladies' aid societies are as adequate settings for fiction as bars or locker rooms, Dorthea Dahl is a minor writer worth attention.

Dorthea Dahl (1881–1958).

The volume of her fiction from 1914 to the early 1930s suggests that writing was more important to her than her employment as a bookkeeper. She must have been encouraged by the positive reception of her first book of short stories, *Fra hverdagslivet* (From everyday life), published by Augsburg in 1915 and awarded the literary prize of the Norwegian Society in 1918, when another ambitious work, a commissioned series of four related stories, was serialized in *Lutheraneren.* The author wrote to relatives in Norway that she was working almost every night until midnight. "But it is wonderful work. If I could only reach the point where I could leave my job at the office and devote myself to writing so that it could amount to something; but with only a little time each evening even a single sketch takes a long time to finish" (Brungot 54–55). Translations of four previously published stories are among the six selected for her one book in English, *Returning Home* (1920). Throughout the 1920s and 1930s she contributed stories in English to Lutheran publications such as *The North Star, Our Young People, Lutheran Church Herald,* and *The Friend* as well as to *Jul i Vesterheimen.*

Indeed, in the late 1920s she wrote only in English until a new literary magazine in Chicago, *Norden*, spurred her to use the language of her parents again and write one of her best stories, "Kopper-kjelen" (1931, "The Copper Kettle"). Her last story, in English, was in *The Friend* in 1942.

Idaho was on the fringe of *Vesterheimen*. Added to her gender-imposed isolation from the male fellowship of the other writers was the geographical isolation of living far from the centers of the culture of which she was a part. With a more practical attitude to the question of language than Johnson, Ager, or Rølvaag, Dahl gradually turned to English with little regret. Indeed, living alone after the death of her last parent in 1925, she would have had little occasion to use any other language than English in her daily life. When she sent her first book to Rølvaag, he both praised her stories and promised to write a review. Dahl replied that she was particularly pleased by his kind words since she "had never had a single lesson in Norwegian grammar or ever made any proper study of the Norwegian language . . . I have read about all I could of Norwegian literature, but never *studied* a single book." She was not sure, however, whether she would continue to write books, not only because she had to work for her living but because she wondered whether "all my creative powers were spent in this attempt!" (3 Jan. 1916, OERP). Nor was her living all she had to work for. Her mother was ailing, and as she explained to Rølvaag when she wrote on 5 February, thanking him for his review in *Reform*, she was "busy with the thousands of things that must be done in a home in addition to taking care of medication, massages, and poultices and whatever needs to be done for a patient." For Dahl even more than for her male colleagues, time for writing had to be stolen in late evenings.

As she began to see herself as a writer, she also began to dream of a career in the larger world outside *Vesterheimen* where she would be paid for her work. Her fiction in English, however, did not give her a wider reach, since she wrote for the publications of the growing but nevertheless limited English-using section of the NLCA. As early as 1918 she was looking forward to writing for regular journals even though "not much has come of it yet. American magazines pay much more for manuscripts than our Norwegian ones, but then the best of them also demand so much more that I really do not feel that I am ready to tackle them yet" (Brungot 57–58). There may have been several reasons for her lack of appeal to the editors of the *Woman's Home Companion* and similar magazines in the 1920s and 1930s. Her English style bore the stamp of her small town life where she was surrounded for the most part by immigrant families and where there was little other intellectual stimulation than that provided by the public library. Moreover, if the stories she submitted to *Woman's Home Companion* were based on her own experience, they would hardly attract editors catering to a public with little interest in "ethnic" literature. Yet another obstacle may have been her acknowledged interest in character and setting rather than in plot. "I am not very interested in intrigues and complicated 'plots,' and it is therefore only natural that my own writing won't have much to offer along those lines . . . neither in the little I have written nor in what I may be able to write will there be anything for the reader who reads a story merely for the sake of the *story*," she wrote to Rølvaag (5 Feb. 1916). In "The Story that was Never Written" (*JiV* 1920) the protagonist, an unmarried writer of magazine fiction, realizes that her Christian faith is more important to her than the fame or money she may be able to achieve by writing the way worldly fashion dictates; she turns down a flattering offer to write for the Christmas issue of a magazine because the editor has ruled out "that over-worked child-in-the-manger theme." Thus Dahl defiantly makes a virtue of her failure to break out of the limitations set by church publications and gain acceptance by the major purveyors of secular short fiction.

The title of her first book, *From Everyday Life*, is a fitting characterization of all she wrote. In the opening story, "Kjærlighetsbudet" (The commandment of love), the protagonist is a college teacher eagerly looking forward to her summer vacation when she can concentrate on her book. She has turned down an invitation from her younger married sister, whom she has never forgiven for turning away from a career and settling for a conventional woman's portion in life, but writing does not go as easily as expected; thoughts of her sister's children keep interfering and the words she puts down on paper seem lifeless and insignificant. On a Sunday morning walk she enters a little church and her thoughts are set in motion by the sermon on "a life in service, a life given for others," just what she thinks she has been doing this summer by concentrating on her book (19). But as she sits in the church she understands that she is writing for "fame and honor rather than to help others" (20) and when she returns home she realizes that her book will have to be entirely different and decides to spend the rest of her vacation with her sister and her family. Dahl is not implying that her own work is of less value than that of a child-rearing and homemaking married woman. Rather, she is speaking directly of her own situation and her own values, writing a story that confirms that although she does not have the opportunity to devote herself fully to her work, the very demands made upon her are necessary in order for her writing to reflect life and speak to vital human concerns. For Dahl, the vital human concerns are personal ones revolving around the moral responsibility of the individual for family and community and for the preservation of the heritage of the elder generation.

Her most successful stories are less concerned with moral decisions or proclamations of faith than with entertainment through a low-keyed humor or gentle satire, as are two in the 1915 volume, "Agathe paa reise" (Agathe's Journey) and "Et fragment." In the latter, the protagonist is a neurotic housewife whose chores demand all her time. At the end of the story she is standing alone on the front stoop looking at the starlit sky thinking of her dreams that had come to naught. The reader may have been led to expect a decision to change her life, but instead: "Anna pulled her shawl more tightly around her shoulders and got up to go indoors. A wind was blowing up and she was tired and wanted to go to bed. Edward would probably not be home for a while yet. And little Tulla's dress was in the cupboard, not much more than halfway done."

Ironically, considering the moral seriousness of "The Story that was Never Written," her least successful stories are probably the many written for Christmas publications, such as "Englesangen," (1915, The song of the angels), where the poor girl gets her dress, there is food for Christmas Eve, and the Lord is praised as the formula requires. "The choir of the First Lutheran Church of Hancock had ceased to exist," is the opening sentence of one of Dahl's better stories in this genre, "Sangkoret i Hancock," first published in *Jul i Vesterheimen* in 1917 and then translated as "The Choir in Hancock" for *Returning Home*. It had proved impossible to keep choir membership steady. "Those who remained in the choir—unchosen—could never reconcile themselves to the fact that those who married and continued to make their home in Hancock would need to be lost to the choir, but experience proved that to be the case." The choir is missed, things are not quite the same without music, not even church picnics. When an old member of the congregation dies "shortly before Christmas" the congregation wakes up to how much church life has suffered, for his widow explains that "He did not seem to look forward to Christmas this year as he usually did . . . I think the reason was that we never get any songs from the choir any more. Andreas was always so fond of listening to the choir" (130). As required by the genre, there is a happy ending. Many come to realize "how their singing could be, unknown to themselves, a service to others. And so they took hold again and sang not only at the funeral and at the Christmas service soon following, but they determined to continue" (132). Old Andreas has not died in vain.

"Service to others" sums up one of Dahl's central themes. One of her 1918 stories about life in the congregation at Wauka Ridge, "Kirkeindvielsen," translated for the 1920 volume as "The Dedication," makes a similar statement, both in the well-executed comic frame story and in the main narrative. The pastor sends a ludicrously written article from the local newspaper about the coming church dedication to his onetime friend, a prominent natural scientist at one of the large universities in the East. He intends it as a joke but the scientist is moved to serious thought about his career rather than to laughter, for he has just "been offered a position as head of the science department at the very school that he and Jacob had attended together" (101). Because of the lowly status of the church college as well as the poor salary, his first thought had been that it was a misunderstanding, but now he begins to reflect on his friend's life of service. So he decides to travel out west to Idaho to visit him and be present at the dedication. As expected, the experience gives his life a new direction. After the ceremony he sends "two telegrams, one his resignation from the position he had held, the other an acceptance of the position that had been offered him" (1920, 120).

Dahl's stories of congregational life present a woman's perspective on the church. In interesting ways they offer a contrast not only to the many congregational settings in the fiction of *Vesterheimen* but to most accounts of the Norwegian Lutheran churches in America. The best Norwegian-American novel with a church setting may be Ager's *Christ Before Pilate*, yet Dahl's delightful sketches of the bickering and small power struggles in ladies' aid societies have more life and credibility than Ager's satirical account of how the women of the congregation organize a *lutefisk* supper. This is a function partly of Dahl's intimate knowledge of congregational life, particularly that of the women, and partly of her faith in the transcendent purpose of the church. The funniest of Dahl's satirical sketches of congregational squabbles is the chapter "The great issue" in her novel *Byen paa berget* (1925, The city upon a hill), where the women in a recently settled South Dakota town discuss the propriety of having a ladies' aid society in their new congregation and almost founder on the question of a regular meeting day. One is used to having such meetings on Wednesdays, another on Thursdays, but when it is suggested that Monday would be the most practical choice, this taxes the patience of Mrs. Thorkildson, who wonders when she then would be expected to do her washing, and makes another woman object that they then would have to eat bread baked on Saturday.

Much of the comic effect achieved by Dahl in this chapter, however, depends on the mixture of English and Norwegian spoken by the women, and again a comparison with Ager will bring out how different Dahl is from her male colleagues. When Ager has the women in *On the Way to the Melting Pot* (1917) mix languages it is to demonstrate his thesis of the cultural decline of people who do not hold on to their linguistic and cultural heritage. Dahl, on the other hand, simply tries to present the speech of her characters as realistically as possible and never suggests that code switching is deplorable.

Although Dahl did not share the extreme preservationist views of Johnson or Ager, she was no less concerned than they with the peculiar situation of the immigrant between two cultures. But where they primarily saw this problem from an ideological point of view, Dahl's interest was personal, in its impact on the life of the individual rather than on the future of *Vesterheimen*. Like Buslett, Rølvaag, and Johnson, Dahl often relates her characters' concern for their heritage to their attachment to the soil, in particular the land cleared and farmed by their parents, as in "Rotfæstet" ("Rooted"), a story first published in *Lutheraneren* in 1918 and translated for the 1929 issue of *Jul i Vesterheimen*. The elderly couple Birger and Marianne Engen have decided to sell their farm in northern Idaho. They cannot take care of it any longer and none of their children has demonstrated any interest in farming the old homestead. But as the sale becomes a reality, they realize how much they will miss their home and their neighbors. The denouement comes with a surprise party where not only their neighbors and the pastor take part, but their children turn up as well, and the single word "rooted" in one of the speeches sets off a series of reflections in Birger's mind: "Rooted, that was what he was. Rooted to the old home farm, the old friends. And if torn up at an advanced age, what would happen? There would be no more growth—plants and humans were alike." It turns out that the youngest son, Carl, has been thinking similar thoughts and before the party is over all has been arranged: Carl will take over the farm and his parents will stay there with him to the end of their days. A similar story is told in "Grandmother," first published in the 1915 volume and translated for *Returning Home*. While Buslett wrote an angry story denouncing the inclination to sell farms not only out of the family but out of the ethnic group (*JiV* 1913), Dahl wrote with understanding of individuals faced with having to make a decision.

In "Det gamle bokskap" ("The Old Bookcase"), first published in *Jul i Vesterheimen* in 1919 and translated for the 1920 volume, the relationship between two generations is affirmed even though the older one has passed away. The protagonist, Herman Diesen, is building up his legal practice in Seattle after his service in the World War and is infatuated with Edith, a caricature of a shallow society woman. Just before Christmas a telegram from Herman's childhood home in the Midwest brings the news of his father's sudden death and he goes home for the first time in many years. After the funeral he goes through everything in the old home, making lists of what to sell, what to give away, and what to discard as junk. In the last room he surveys there is an old bookcase: "Strange that his father had not bought a new bookcase in all these years. Really, it was too old to sell, or even to give away . . . What could be done with a pile of old books? Books no one would ever think of reading any more." He begins "to look them over. There was the old family Bible, which had belonged to his grandfather. Such things were customarily passed from father to son, but what could he do with it all?" Many of the books have "a distinctly theological appearance" and he begins "to feel dimly that there were values hidden in these books, not so much perhaps on account of the things they contained as for the reason that they had comprised his father's whole world." There are many other books, old and new—histories and biographies, but also "books of a more purely literary character." Some of these he recognizes from the collection of a friend who "prided himself on keeping in touch with the movement for saving the cultural inheritance of those whose fathers had come from another land and making it a part of the life in the new homeland." This is an excellent brief statement of the concern for what Rølvaag called "our ancestral heritage," and the protagonist ponders "how all this had existed outside of his own interests—this, which had meant so much to his father and which still meant so much to many others." As he sits alone among the paraphernalia of his father's life he realizes that he has not thought of Edith since he arrived in the Midwest and at the same time he sees that the empty life he lives in Seattle would never interest Margaret, the idealistic young woman he had met the day before in the parsonage, a nurse who had been a close friend of his father. Then, as he is about to leave, a book falls on the floor and he sees the words "To my son" written on the title page. Opening other books he finds the same inscription, and in a particularly well-used one: "To Margaret." "Evidently his father had had no intention of sending these books to the ones for whom they eventually were intended. What had been his dreams when he had been writing those names in his books?" Before the day is over decisions are made: Herman will take over the legal practice of an old friend of his father and he will share with Margaret the values left to them both in his father's old bookcase.

While the books in "The Old Bookcase" represent values that await discovery so that they may be made "a part of the life in the new home-land," two later stories provide a new twist to this formula. Here, old discarded objects are discovered to have value as antiques for a later generation. And as antiques, the objects remain objects, even though they may serve as memorials of a past tradition. Thus a tradition may be respected, even though its time has passed. "Julekvad" (Christmas song), in the December 1931 issue of *Norden*, is a Christmas story where the immigrant heritage rather than the Christmas Gospel is brought to the attention of the family of an old grandmother who has come to them from the farm after the recent death of her husband. It is Christmas Eve, and as she wonders at the lack of traditional preparations for the holiday, she is suddenly made aware that everybody has gifts for Christmas, a custom she is not used to. Dejected, she finds herself unable to take part in the festivities. At the last minute, however, her granddaughter, who knows no Norwegian, and who insists that grandmother must come since they have prepared such a great surprise for her, suggests that the grandmother's old books and other heirlooms from Norway would surely make everyone happy. While the grandmother protests that she could not possibly give away "the old junk she had been so stupid as to take with her from the farm," her granddaughter insists that old things are "very fashionable," and together they wrap some gifts. The big surprise is a traditional Christmas feast with porridge, *lefse* and *lutefisk,* and when the time comes to open the presents, and her son gets the "old Bible that had belonged to his father" and the others get "old books that would be collector's items, a Norwegian silver buckle, a piece of embroidery that had turned yellow with age" the grandmother realizes that her gifts have been truly appreciated.

Also the other story she wrote for *Norden*, "The Copper Kettle" (Dec. 1930), turns on the discovery that the immigrants' heritage may have a second life as a valued antique. On the farm, the simple but hardworking and warmhearted Anders is not appreciated by his wife, who has social pretensions after some years of service as a maid for a wealthy American family. To supplement their income they take in a boarder, a young and literally disinherited city woman, who needs to recuperate after a nervous breakdown. In the barn she discovers an old copper kettle dented and black with soot that Anders had brought with him from the old country in his youth. His wife has always despised it, so it has been left among other discarded objects in the barn. Their boarder, however, insists that it is an object of great beauty and value, and regrets that she cannot pay its true worth. Good-hearted An-

ders for once overrules his wife, who now wants to sell the kettle, and places
it in the hands of the woman who has pointed out its value. As the young
woman could see the kettle beneath the soot and dirt, Anders' wife now
comes to realize that her husband, too, has qualities she has not been able to
appreciate. So eventually both the kettle and Anders—both battered and
discarded contributions from the old country to the new—are seen in their
true beauty.

Thematically related to her short stories, Dahl's novel *Byen paa berget* am-
bitiously sets out to explore the nature of a life of service. While so many of
her stories merely lead their protagonists up to the decision to embark on
such a life, her novel ironically begins with the frustration of the protagonist's dreams to serve. Nor is this the only point of resemblance between the
author and her protagonist, for in her loving account of the lifelong marriage of her protagonist Frederikke and her storekeeper husband in a small
pioneer town in South Dakota there are echoes of Dorthea's own youthful
romance with a storekeeper in the same state (Brungot 15–16). The immediate reason for Dahl's decision to write a novel was *Decorah-Posten*'s literary
competition in 1924, which had also inspired Ruth Fjeldsaa and Antonette
Tovsen. Dahl's entry was not awarded a prize and though the editor offered
to serialize it, he made clear that revisions would be required (13 June 1924,
LC). Dahl's plotless and uneventful story of a marriage in a small South
Dakota town did not fit the format of the serialized novel. Augsburg, however, accepted it for publication the following year and most reviewers were
politely if not overwhelmingly friendly.

It has proved as difficult to assess the value of Dahl's novel as to see the
true beauty of Anders' battered kettle. In *Duluth Skandinav* John Heitmann
explained that Dahl should have cut away a fourth of the book, and Brungot, who finds it unfortunate that the author "lists too many details," agrees,
calling it "much too wordy" (1977, 132). To Gerald Thorson, *Byen paa berget*
is "a thin, sketchy, and imitative narrative, covering too large a canvas, with
little attempt at motivation or authentic characterization" (351). But lack of
focus may be in the eyes of the beholder. Brungot was mainly interested in
the extent to which the novel was "a faithful account of Dakota pioneer
days" (109), and for Thorson, "The most interesting feature of this book is
not the narrative, but the descriptions of the rivalries between the various
church synods and the church schools, of which there is a great plenty"
(352). But the center of the novel is in full view, like the city upon a hill, the
life and marriage of Frederikke Lervang, whom we first meet as a self-
centered and aspiring young woman fresh out of college and spending the

summer of 1883 on her parents' farm in Minnesota. To be sure, there is much talk of division between and within the various synods, but never a word on what it is that divides them, only how the disagreements invade private lives and families. To be sure, the reader is vaguely aware of the growth of settlements, but only as a sketched-in background to the uneventful life of Frederikke. To criticize *Byen paa berget* for paying so little attention to large social issues is like criticizing Frank Capra's *It's a Wonderful Life* for not sending George Bailey to Washington. The comparison is not fortuitous, for Frederikke's successes are not unlike those of George, as she comes to realize without the assistance of an interfering angel.

The slow-moving opening chapters—seven of the twenty-seven take us through a few summer months—set the stage for the courtship of Frederikke and Otto Lervang, a theological student at Augsburg Seminary. Both are Norwegian Americans, but from the two separate worlds of the Synod and the Conference; she feels a stranger to the culture she meets when she goes with him to the Conference congregation he serves as student assistant, and her family eye him with suspicion for harboring false doctrine. But faith, love, and charity take precedence over theology and church polity, and their engagement is reluctantly accepted by her family. Her vision of the future may not seem so grand to the sophisticated reader, but it nevertheless transcends the restricted world of the immigrant homesteader's daughter: "In her dreams she had always seen herself in a vicarage—now taking leave of Otto when he was off on a journey, now jubilantly welcoming him on his return. And at other times she would be with him on visits to members of the congregation, taking part in ladies' aid meetings, playing the organ at services while he was officiating at the altar." Her dreams are not entirely free from worldly ambition: "And always there was the unconscious thought that she as the fine and charming minister's wife would be as loved and respected as the minister himself" (74).

Such as they are, her dreams are crushed. Otto has to drop out of school because of an eye disease, and his apparent readiness to accept his fate and his satisfaction with his new and promising partnership with Thorkildson, a Minneapolis grocer who wants to establish himself in the Dakota Territory, is as disturbing to the high-minded Frederikke as is the door closing on her future as a minister's wife. There is some compensation, however, for now they will be able to marry; but when Otto writes that he cannot leave the business and come east for a wedding and that she will have to come west alone, "it did not seem possible that it was Otto who demanded this of her" (82). Off she goes with her belongings and her new wedding gown, chang-

ing trains from one frontier town to another, not to Drummond, where
Thorkildson and Lervang have established their new business, but to Lakeview, the county seat where there is a Norwegian pastor who can marry
them. Frederikke arrives safely, but without her baggage, and comes to her
makeshift wedding "in her dark brown traveling outfit and heard little of
what the pastor said or of the responses she gave mechanically to questions
she hardly heard. No organ music, no song, no veil, no flowers" (89). And
then across the plains in a cart pulled by ponies from the livery stable, "with
a sense of having been cut off from all that had belonged to her past" (92),
to Drummond, some elevators, a depot, and a few houses on either side of a
single dusty street, among them a two-storied structure displaying the sign
"Thorkildson & Lervang": "The rooms above the store were low and small,
and when Otto opened the door at the end of the stairs on the outside of
the building and let Frederikke enter first, he followed her face anxiously
for her reaction. But for her the rooms became large and light-filled cham-
bers and at his breast, with his arms around her and without having to manage the stubborn ponies and without having to think of nosy travelers, all
the world was forgotten" (100). But there is yet a dream to be crushed and
again the wedding gown is taken up only to be laid down again unused.
They decide to return to Lakeview for the baptism of their first child and
Frederikke plans to use the dress that she has not even had the heart to show
to Otto: "It was of blue silk and perhaps a little too fancy for the occasion;
but she was attracted to the notion that she was to wear the dress she couldn't
wear to her wedding for her son's baptism" (124). But the baptism, which
they perform themselves at home, is even more hurried and urgent than the
wedding: their son dies a few days after he is born. As the years go by and
Frederikke's thoughts of what should and might have been grow fainter, the
unused wedding gown, no garment for a pioneer woman, becomes a symbol of her unrealized dreams and ambitions. But in their love and support of
each other, in their care for their growing family, in their quiet and unosten-
tatious work for their community and congregation, their life is a success, "a
city upon a hill," as an old friend explains at their silver anniversary and as
one of their sons recalls when he writes to his widowed mother from the
front in France at the very end of the novel. When she was expecting her
first child, it was inconceivable to Frederikke that he should ever live in
Drummond as an adult. Now her oldest daughter is a physician in the town
and a son has taken over his father's business, while the son at the front has
decided to study for the ministry, the vocation his father had to renounce,
and Frederikke looks back on her failed ambitions and her achieved love.

Dahl wisely concentrated her novel on the early years, perhaps realizing that it is easier to create a convincing portrait of a woman faced with adversity than of a woman increasingly blessed with idealized children. The last five chapters present short-story-like sketches of a few significant events, their move from the rooms above the store to their own house, the war with Spain, their silver anniversary, and 1917, the year of the war, which takes the life of a son, and of the Spanish flu, which takes Otto's. It may be just to conclude that Dahl was a better short-story writer than a novelist, yet *Byen paa berget* is a remarkable achievement and a valuable contribution to the literature of *Vesterheimen*.

Dahl also provides a corrective to the more strongly voiced views of her male colleagues on the central ideological issues in *Vesterheimen*: the future of the language and the nature of loyalty. The stories in which she speaks most clearly on these issues are not among her best, but in their accommodating stance they reflect a practical and realistic approach in contrast to the romantic idealism of Buslett or Johnson. In "The Seventeenth of May," first published in *The North Star* in 1921, the "Language Question" threatens to break apart the congregation in Burch's Butte and the young pastor, trying his best to keep the two factions together, hits upon the idea of observing the Seventeenth of May, a celebration that "would in its very nature serve to appease the ultra-Norwegian faction, while the minister hoped that by using English almost exclusively at the program the other faction would be satisfied." All seems to go well until "the women became interested, and pandemonium broke loose" (222–223). On the question of whether ice cream or *rømmegrøt*, a traditional sour-cream porridge, should be served no compromise seems possible; neither side will consider taking part if the opposing side's menu is accepted. For the defenders of ice cream, like Mrs. Daniels (who had lost the two last letters of her name "when the family acquired a Ford and the oldest daughter was sent through business college"), their status as Americans is at stake: "'We had ought to remember that we ain't Norwegians no more,' she said with the air of one who has a message to bring," relating how her daughter had had to stand up for her Americanism when her employer had spoken of what a fine country Norway was: "she wanted her to know that she wasn't no more Norwegian than anybody else" (224–225). A younger member of the ladies' aid, however, saves the congregation from the impending disaster: not only are both ice cream and *rømmegrøt* served at the feast, but the opposing parties ladle out the other's dish and all ends in harmony and understanding. It is hoped that the people of Burch's Butte will continue to enjoy *rømmegrøt* and celebrate the Seventeenth of May as they unavoidably speak more and more English. Whether this can be explained by her female perspective, by her life on the outskirts of *Vesterheimen* or her pragmatism, the fiction of Dorthea Dahl gives a more balanced and more optimistic view of the situation of the immigrant—the individual and the culture—than most of the fiction by her male contemporaries in *Vesterheimen*.

NOTE

1. Hilde Brungot's thesis from 1977 is the main source for biographical information. An early contribution to *Reform* is "A Woman's Political Views" (27 Nov. 1900).

Jon Norstog:
Prophet in the Wilderness

Jon Norstog (1877–1942) had little patience with the idealistic sentimentality of Simon Johnson or the domesticity of Dorthea Dahl. Indeed, he had
little patience with anyone and insisted on saying so. Even though he had
"noticed that people are easily insulted . . . I like to speak out," he explained
to Rølvaag (1929? OERP). He can often appear insensitive, as when he
wrote to Ager refusing to delete some sentences on the ailing Rølvaag from
an article he had submitted to *Reform*: "I don't believe he is so ill that he is
too weak for criticism, and should it be so, then he has no right to live. You
and he are good friends, but never would I have a man as a friend who
bound me so that I lost my freedom; that is not friendship but slavery" (n.d.
WAP). But then he did not seek much society and lived mostly alone in a
cabin on his homestead in northwestern North Dakota, even after he married Inga Bredesen in 1919 and his family helped him build a modest house
on the outskirts of Watford.[1]

He seems to have been immune to criticism; perhaps because he could
say to himself, as he wrote to Rølvaag in 1917, "I am not a writer, nor do I
wish to be one! I am a warrior in the flaming army of the Lord!" (18 April,
OERP). He often, as in this letter, used "art" and "artist" pejoratively. Seeing
himself in the role of an Old Testament prophet, he justified his own work
with the rhetorical question, "Is there art in the Bible?" Although he made
a virtue of his self-reliance, publishing, printing, and binding most of his
books, Norstog made unsuccessful attempts to interest major Norwegian
publishers in his work. Late in his career, no doubt goaded by the New York
successes of Rølvaag and Ager, he also tried to arrange for an English translation of his trilogy *Exodus*.[2] When he submitted the manuscript of his bib-

Jon Norstog (1877–1942).

lical verse drama, *Saul,* to Aschehoug in Christiania, the poet, novelist, and dramatist Vilhelm Krag observed that "Jon Norstog is a writer who is inclined to take on the greatest of tasks," but that there was a "regrettable lack of self-criticism that made his drama uneven . . . Mr. Norstog should bear in mind that it is easy for a good writer to write verses; the difficult part is to delete them. When he has learned this, I would enjoy meeting him" (4 Jan. 1919, LC). But Norstog was above all advice and criticism. "Jack London was never allowed to publish his books the way he wrote them," he wrote to Rølvaag in 1929, "he simply had to cut as the publisher demanded. I have had the same experience but have always said: the book is to be published as written! I have my own printing press!" (OERP).

Accommodation was not for Norstog. A firm believer, he never joined a church; abstaining from alcohol, he never joined a temperance society. He did, however, make his beliefs and views known, in his books and through frequent contributions to the press. In religion he was pietistic and conservative, in politics he was liberal, giving his support to the Nonpartisan League and, later, to the Democratic Party. His self-reliance was fortified by his self-righteousness, an essential character trait for a prophet denouncing the laxity and materialism of his age. "Christianity is no longer Christianity as it once *has been* and *could* be. Only the name remains," he wrote to Ditlef Ristad in 1918. "Christ cleaned out the temple with a whip, a real whip. The Christianity of our time will have to be purified with a knotted whip! Churches and pastors and congregations, whip them, scourge them, flay them, to the bone! *Crush them!* Oh, how cold it becomes around us! There is no sun. Snow and ice wherever we look, endless white plains, snow, snow, snow—Nice churches, nice people, nice pastors, but only ice. Culture. Oh, how I long for the days that have gone. For the days of the prophets, when whips and sticks danced on high and low, chopped and cut and flayed so that rags of flesh would hang and bones shine and souls would twist and turn as in fire. For the days of Christ. When Christ went like a fire through the people of culture, the pastors, the kings, etc." (24 Nov. DGRP). This is the Christ of *Natten* (1915, The night) which Ristad had just reviewed, but Norstog could also write of the no less demanding Christ of love and charity, as in his narrative sequence of lyrics, *Tone* (1913). His mood could change from self-righteous anger to dejection. In 1918, the year before he married, he wrote to Ager that he was tired of the treatment he had received from Norwegian-American editors and was "through with America." He would sell his land and return to Norway: "I have thrown away fifteen years to no purpose and that will have to suffice—I cannot afford more" (22 March, WAP).

Norstog had immigrated at the age of twenty-five in 1902, the year his first book of poems, *Yggdrasil*, was dismissed by the critics. Unlike Johnson and Dahl, Norstog was at home in his language, which for him was not the established *Riksmaal*, but the *Landsmaal* based on rural dialects. As Norway seemed closed to the aspiring author, *Vesterheimen* was growing and offered an opportunity for a literary career. He came to an uncle who farmed near the small town of Joice in northern Iowa. But Norstog proved no fonder of farming in America than he had been in Norway, and turned to letters, publishing a modest journal, *Dølen*, also the title of a journal by the poet and essayist Aasmund O. Vinje, a first cousin of his mother. Here he presented brief essays on Vinje and romantic-idealist verse and prose sketches. He acquired a small press and began to learn the printer's trade as well as that of the binder, as he slowly and rather amateurishly produced the slender issues of *Dølen* himself.[3] The next year he tried to publish his journal in Minneapolis, but had to give up after one issue. In 1905 he moved to North Dakota where he first worked for *Normanden* in Fargo and then for newspapers in Minot until he homesteaded near Watford City in 1910, the year after his father, four sisters, two brothers, and their families had settled there (Williamson 68–69).[4]

Norstog's multifariousness—he wrote novels, lyric and epic verse, and prose and verse drama, and he used biblical, American, Norwegian, and international settings—may at first obscure his obsessive concern with a few themes and archetypes, in particular those of Christ and the Prophet, often merged into one figure, as in *Kain* (1912), and as prefigured in the story of the doomed Benoni in his first novel, *Paa heklemogen* (1903, On the stony clearing).[5] Three other early works, the novels *Haakon Sollid* (1906), with a Norwegian setting, and *Ørnerud* (1907) and the narrative sequence of lyrics *Svein* (1909), explore the theme of loyalty—loyalty to parents, to the land, both as country and as soil, and to the heritage with which his characters are entrusted—a theme dear to the heart of the immigrant Norstog, who had close emotional ties to the soil even though he had little inclination to farm it.

In his review of *Haakon Sollid* in *Smuler*, Hervin wryly calls it a "love story where the girl is of a somewhat (but not very much) finer family than the boy, but where they, after the usual portion of difficulties, eventually get each other. Consequently, it can hardly be said to be a really new story" (Aug. 1906). Ager, too, observed that Norstog's novel was "Bjørnson through and through. The characters are old and familiar . . . The very day the boy is born the reader is not left in doubt that he will be happily married" (*Reform* 19 June 1906). Ager, the city-bred realist, had as little patience with this style of writing as with its rural idealism, but had he listened more carefully he would have heard a message not essentially different from that of his own essays exhorting Norwegian Americans to remain loyal to their language and their cultural heritage. Far more interesting than the derivative plot is the typical Norstog character of Haakon Sollid, exceptionally gifted yet with a deep sense of loyalty to his parents and the small farm they have created. Not only will he remain a farmer like his father but at a public meeting he denounces "the sickness in the blood" of his generation, who seek education in order to avoid real work and who do not merely betray the home of their forefathers by going to the city but their country by going to America. "Sweep out this sickness," he exhorts his people in his peroration. "The land lies before us, beautiful in its bounty, and awaits us . . . Let us not make ourselves poorhouse inmates, exiles, traitors! Let us go to work!" (1906, 37). Such nationalistic fervor advocating a return to the soil and laying the blame for current ills on a sickness in the blood, effeminate aristocrats, work-shy intellectuals, and urbanization in general may smack too much of fascism not to create uneasiness in a present-day reader, but to wrench Norstog out of context would be to misconstrue not only him but much of nineteenth-century populism.

It is ironic that the immigrant Norstog should place a diatribe against emigration in the mouth of his hero, and he addresses himself more directly to this irony in *Ørnerud*[6] (1907), a novel about the making of an artist and, paradoxically, of an American farmer. While it is difficult to muster much interest in the uncommunicated love of Svein Ørnerud and Margit Storaasli, their story is nevertheless interesting as Norstog's transplantation of the nationalism of *Haakon Sollid* from Telemark to North Dakota, suggesting in the manner of Johnson and others that the best Norwegian is the best American. In the spirit of *Haakon Sollid*, the gifted Svein remains on the farm and does not go to college. From childhood he is attracted to the Norwegian past of his parents and to the two impoverished *husmann* lots of land they came from. As a young man he makes a pilgrimage to Norway, purchases Ørnerud, his father's childhood home, and builds a small house on the ruins of the former buildings. There he studies languages and literature and learns to write *Landsmaal* before returning to his true home in America where he puts his Norwegian experience into practice by making his father's renamed farm into a model for all to follow. Svein's family name in America, Lofthus, is that of the farm for which his father had worked as a tenant, not of his modest home, Ørnerud. In taking the name Ørnerud, Svein not only identifies himself with the lower classes rather than with the landowners and intelligentsia but also affirms the ties between the new home of Ørnerud in America and his parent's *husmann* past. Norstog's obvious message is that the way to put down roots and find true happiness in America is to cherish your own heritage. At the end of the novel the wisdom of Svein's choice of Margit rather than her rival Julie Bang (a name suggestive of upper-class origins) is made obvious when the two play the piano for a neighborhood party at the renamed Ørnerud farm: Julie plays popular waltzes, Margit plays Grieg and Chopin. On the last page Svein and Margit at long last express their love: "Then Svein took Margit's hand and pointed towards Ørnerud, where they could see the buildings, the flags, and their neighbors: 'There is our home, Margit, and there are our people!'" Norstog's romanticized view of all that is Norwegian ran counter to the sentiments of most of his fellow immigrants and this was the tenor of *Normanden*'s negative review: "We dare bet an old hat that it would be impossible to find an American youth, regardless of his Norwegian heritage, who would show so little appreciation for his own country and so much for

Norway, especially not an American as uniquely gifted as Svein Lofthus" (Clipping, NAHA).

Svein is also the name of the very different protagonist of the narrative sequence of simple yet effective lyrics, *Svein* (1909). While the Svein of *Ørnerud* is a winner, the other is a loser, one who betrays his heritage, his parents, and his country by immigrating, and who never is able to rid himself of his guilt. He longs for his old home and his lonely and aging father but eventually he dies in his new one, a sod house on the North Dakota plains. The conflicting stories of Haakon and the two Sveins reflect the complex response of Norstog to his own act of immigration.

Norstog's only book to receive a limited popularity was another narrative sequence of lyrics, *Tone*, first published by the author in 1913 and by Augsburg in 1920. It may be that this genre, which allowed him to concentrate on a succession of events and to explore their lyric potential, was ideally suited to Norstog's lack of interest in story and plot. From an aesthetic point of view, *Svein* and *Tone* are his most successful books. Tone, however, has little in common with the character of Svein. Indeed, she is more akin to his idealized Christlike characters. Superficially, the story of Tone is a variation on the Bjørnson-Foss story of the boy or girl from the lowly *husmann* family who marries the daughter or son of the wealthy and haughty farmer: in *Tone* this love is never consummated, at least not on earth. Moved to do so by what he sees as his duty to his family, and with the blessing of his beloved Tone, Tov, the farmer's son, marries for money and Tone lives a life of altruistic service until she dies in old age, filled with love of God and man, and wearing the ring Tov had given her in her youth on a ribbon around her neck. No other book by Norstog received so many unequivocally positive reviews. For Ager, this "song of the great resignation" was "perhaps one of the most wonderful poems ever written in Norwegian" (*R* 21 Oct. 1913). The most appreciative review was by Agnes Wergeland in *Symra*.

The same year as *Svein*, Norstog published another book of lyrics, *Glitretind*. The lyric remained an important mode of expression for the prolific Norstog, whose verse may be found in many newspapers and in the volumes *Fraa Audni* (1923, From the wilderness) and *Havet* (The ocean), his last book, published in 1938. *Livshorpa* (1927, The harp of life) is a narrative sequence of lyrics in the manner of *Svein* and *Tone*.

The homestead he acquired after completing *Svein* and *Glitretind* did not turn Norstog into a farmer; his main energy went into the making of a 324-page verse drama about the archetypal migrant, the cursed and landless Cain (1912), written in a basic meter of four stressed syllables and shifting rhyme patterns. In the following decade the Bible was to be Norstog's main source of inspiration: "There is only one book in the world. Its name is the Bible" was the motto for his next biblical verse drama, *Moses* (1914). *Kain* opens with the protagonist fleeing with a black cross marked on his forehead and speaking with dread of his evil deed. His mother, Eve, and his wife are full of love and forgiveness, but Cain, who is filled with longing for God and hatred of the Serpent, insists that he must fight his own battle with evil. At the end of the second act Cain is about to acknowledge his defeat and accept the dominance of the Serpent when a lion leaps into the fray, kills the Serpent, and makes Cain realize the omnipotence of God. In the third act Cain visits Paradise guided by his brother Abel. But their tour is interrupted when Cain, repeating his mother's primal fall, eats of the fruit of the Tree of Knowledge, and again he is lost. In the concluding two acts Cain takes on the mantle of a prophet, confronting the priests and other authorities in the city of Hanok, home of the descendants of Set and Cain. Scenes of confrontation alternate with scenes of Cain in the wilderness, communing with the spirits of his dead parents and Abel and reflecting on God's love and His divine design. Loving God and His creation and carrying the sins of mankind, Cain is a prefiguration of Christ. But he himself is cursed and can not bring salvation to himself or to the world. Before he dies he has a vision of the crucifixion of Christ, but Cain realizes that God's design of redemption does not include him and that he is forever damned. In the concept of Cain dedicated to the service of the God who has cursed him, Norstog has a grand design. *Kain*, moreover, has passages of lyrical beauty and dramatic power. Had Norstog been able to show greater restraint or had he had critical readers and, above all, had he been willing to take their advice, Norstog might have produced a more compelling series of biblical dramas and epics than the nine that came from the little press in his homestead cabin in the years from 1913 to 1923.

Moses (1914) is another drama of exile. Moses is a proud, easily angered, and violent young man, and the two first acts show his growth as a leader, called by God at Horeb, confronting Pharaoh, and leading his people out of Egypt. The next two acts focus on the faithlessness of the Jewish people, their dissatisfaction and complaints, and their many rebellions against Moses. No sooner is one of their false leaders struck down than others rise to take his place. Time and again the people of Israel are saved from the wrath of God through the intervention of Moses. One rebel, the artist Pallu, recognizes the greatness of Moses and becomes his faithful poet: "What is an artist, Pallu, an artist of the Lord?" he is asked and replies, looking at a candlestick of gold, "A candlestick that shines before the face of God" (279). The central themes in the long middle section are courage and faith as opposed to cowardice and disloyalty. While Pallu is the true poet, serving God through his art, there are many false ones who lead the people astray. The fifth and last act focuses on the Christlike character of Moses, who intervenes on behalf of his erring people. Toward the end of the drama Pallu sings his last song, prophesying Christ. Moses dies, and although the drama concludes with his apotheosis, its vision of the future for Israel is dark.

Norstog's ambitious epic of the people of Israel was continued in the verse dramas *Josva* (1916) and *Israel* (1917), the most impressive in volume with twelve acts and 885 pages. *Josef* (1918) is an epic poem in crude blank verse yet with occasionally powerful imagery. In forty-seven chapters of varying length Norstog retells the story of Joseph, stressing the theme of the chosen of God. In the concluding chapter, the narrative of Jacob moving to Goshen with his eleven sons is given added poignancy by the immigrant perspective of the poet and becomes a statement on the endeavors of Norstog and his fellow writers in *Vesterheimen*, their Goshen. Then follow the verse dramas *Kong Saul* in 1920, the two parts of *Kong David* in 1921 and 1923, and finally, the only one based on the New Testament, *Golgatariket* (The kingdom of Golgotha), about Saul/Paul, also in 1923.

Protagonists no less dedicated than Moses or Paul and no less consumed by their love of God than Cain are placed in vaguely contemporary settings in a novel and two plays influenced by Ibsen's verse drama about an idealistic and uncompromising young clergyman, *Brand*. Unlike Ibsen's plays, however, Norstog's loosely structured symbolic plays with a multitude of characters and rapid shifts of settings are as little fit for stage production as his biblical dramas. Norstog's first work with a Christlike clergyman protagonist is also his first attempt to use the dramatic form, *Tornekronen* (The crown of thorns), in 1908. In a series of symbolic and allegorical scenes the protagonist, Stig, is identified with Christ. Representatives of church and state place him, naked except for a loin cloth, on an altar, set a crown of thorns on his head, mock him to perform miracles, and immolate him in flames. Stig's last word is "Hallelujah!"—first coming from the flaming altar, then repeated in his voice from the ascending flame and a third time voiced by an "invisible choir" as the flame disappears in a cloud.

Tornekronen may appear preposterous in its allegorical scenes pitting Stig against abstractions in male and female guises. Norstog's next drama about a clergyman-Christ, *Natten* (1915, The night), at least places the protagonist in a recognizably realistic setting. The protagonist of *Natten*, Bjørn Borg, is a brilliant young clergyman with a promising career who antagonizes representatives of power, wealth, and culture by his refusal to compromise with the absolute demands of Christ. Righteous rather than compassionate, Borg nevertheless demonstrates his charity for the poor and weak as the first act is concluded. In the second, he is given a choice between mending his ways and losing his congregation. As he is about to resign, poor members of the congregation beg him not to forsake them. This leaves him open to temptation, and his father convinces him that he can achieve the most good through forgiveness and pragmatic compromise. As the act closes, a subdued Borg has accepted the conditions of the leaders of his congregation but vows to keep up his support of the poor in secrecy. The effect of his compromise is seen in the third act, where he is praised by the wealthy but has lost the power of faith. In the fourth act the consequences of his weakness are revealed: Borg is surrounded by moral decay, his wife has a lover, and his parents are divorced. Borg responds by giving more and more of himself to charity and he lovingly helps and supports the weak and the lowliest of sinners. The final act opens upon a party in honor of Borg. Intellectuals and theologians alike speak of the victory of reason and humanism over darkness, while Borg, without strength or conviction, tries to speak of the salvation of the soul. That same evening his assistant comes to reveal to him the failure of his charitable efforts: "You have been fooled by love," she tells him. "When you took off your armor, when you laid down your weapons, that was when you failed, pastor Borg" (128). Faced with the consequences—for himself and for those he wanted to help—of his substitution of loving humanism for a living faith, Borg, in the last scene, confesses his failure to his congregation before he consecrates himself to Christ at the altar and goes out into the world a beggar, forsaken by all.

Natten reflects Norstog's own inflexible character and his despair of institutionalized Christianity. The clergyman characters in his trilogy *Exodus* suggest that Norstog's views had changed in the intervening years, and this change is evident in the 1934 novel *Når elvane møtest* (When the rivers meet). His last work of fiction is in some respects a striking departure from all he had done before. While *Ørnerud* had seemed to insist that everything of value was of Norwegian origin, Norstog concluded his career with an Anglo-American protagonist, the Reverend Samuel Huntington, and an international setting. The title refers to a seascape lighted by the rays of a rising sun after a heavy storm that Samuel Huntington has above his desk. The ocean is where all the rivers meet and the painting is to Huntington an image of the Bible. The painting gradually takes on further symbolic implications and becomes an image of Huntington's religious, social, and international programs, which all have the ultimate aim of bringing God's light and peace to the world. The force that makes it possible to change the world is not only faith in Christ and the word of God as revealed in the Holy Bible but a full and uncompromising commitment to this faith, as Bjørn Borg discovers when he loses his strength and his ability to do good after his compromise.

In the two plays, the Christlike protagonists are rejected by their wealthy fathers. The senior Huntington, however, backs his son in all he does and helps him to realize his great projects for the glory of God. Instead of serving his denomination, Huntington builds his own magnificent church in a midwestern city after he has graduated from divinity school. Here he preaches his social gospel of peace, brotherhood, and the example of Christ. During the nationalistic fury of the First World War the pacifist Huntington not only refuses to support the war effort, but has the Luther—and thus German—hymn "A Mighty Fortress is Our God" played on the organ of his church. The church is destroyed by an angry mob and Huntington himself is sentenced to prison. Only a few of his followers and friends remain faithful and keep things ready for his return. Released from prison after the war, and with a rebuilt and even more magnificent church, Huntington gradually wins the support and loyalty of his former enemies. His first step toward political power is taken when he saves a failed bank and promises all the poor who have trusted the faithless banker with their savings that nothing shall be lost. As spokesman for a Christian socialism he is elected mayor of the city, restructuring it according to Christian principles. In this first part of the novel Norstog shows more interest than usual in telling a story. The pages are packed with the conventional novelistic intrigues of love, betrayal, repentance, and crimes and their detection. His interest in story lags in the second half of the novel, however. Here Huntington branches out from his local, midwestern base, first setting out to save the United States and then the world. As he travels from place to place giving sermons and organizing his movement, the narrative becomes repetitive and seems no more than an excuse to present his arguments for a new international order, a union of all nations of the world. The leaders of many countries secretly agree with him but cannot admit this publicly. He even preaches in the Soviet Union, drawing large crowds and winning the secret confidence of the dictator. The novel ends in Palestine, where Huntington has a vision of Christ, who encourages him to continue his good work.

The protagonist of *Tornekronen* is sacrificed by an angry and mocking crowd. In *Natten* Borg walks alone into a hostile world. Huntington, however, makes a success of his biblical crusade, perhaps suggested to Norstog by the evangelistic crusade of Frank Buchman, who was enjoying a limited international success in the years before Norstog published his novel. But the triumphs of Huntington are less convincing and certainly less engaging than the struggles and eventual failure of Sigbjørn Djuve, the immigrant artist who is the protagonist of Norstog's most ambitious work, the trilogy *Exodus* (1928, 1930, 1931). Migration is a motif in many of his biblical works, but he had not dealt with Norwegian-American themes except in brief lyrics in the twenty-odd years since *Ørnerud* and *Svein*. It may have seemed a paradox to Norstog that Ole Rølvaag in the 1920s had broken out of the narrow confines of *Vesterheimen* by limiting himself to this culture for his material, while he had been unable to attract the interest of major publishers. He may not even have tried to have *Exodus* published in Norway; the preserved correspondence from this period reveals only his futile attempts in 1931 and 1936 to interest Norwegian publishers in his last collection of verse, *Havet*, eventually published by himself in 1938.[7] But *Exodus* is Norstog's major statement on Americanization and the American experience and on the role and predicament of the artist in society, and his efforts throughout the thirties to have it translated show how important it had become for him to make a larger world aware of his work.[8] Today it seems unlikely that the trilogy will ever be available in English. Had Norstog but had an appreciative editor and had he but been able to take advice, he might have left behind a powerful novel of half the length of his trilogy.

The trilogy opens on the Wisconsin shore of Lake Michigan, where the recently arrived Sigbjørn Djuve lives in a simple log cabin left behind by a failed immigrant. Djuve is a sculptor, and among his sketched projects is "A nude man on his knees with pick and shovel at his side, staring into a ditch that he has just made. He stares and stares and is unaware that he is on his way into the ditch" (1928, 10). At the center of the first volume is Sigbjørn's lonely struggle with himself on his homestead in northwestern North Dakota. There he is visited by his doctor friend, who has moved with him from Wisconsin, and by a Lutheran clergyman, characters who function as teacher figures in the trilogy. He spends time, as did Norstog, helping his neighbors, he befriends a successful rancher, contemplates entering politics as well as marrying a wealthy widow, and goes hunting and fishing with the doctor and the clergyman. But in his art he is forced to face the conflict raging within himself, a conflict that concerns his religious as well as his cultural identity. For Sigbjørn has come to America convinced that here all the many nationalities must lay aside what divides them and become one nation: "All these nations will have to grow together and give the best of what they have brought with them to each other, flow together like brooks to a great river, running deep and mirroring earth and heaven" (14). The main spokesmen in the trilogy for a preservationist view are of Anglo-American stock, notably Ruth Hamilton, who not only urges Sigbjørn to recognize his cultural identity, but who for love of him learns Norwegian and studies Norwegian literature.

Alone in his cabin on the plains, Sigbjørn works on portrait sculptures of Ruth and his long dead mother as he continues to struggle with his major work, a group of writhing bodies emerging from the soil that appears to hold on to them as they stretch upward toward a mountain peak. The peak, however, "stands cold and empty" (159, 382, 399). During the long winter months he has periods of depression when he sees himself as Judas and periods of manic creativity when he works on his sculptures, realizing that he will have to come to terms with what they represent. Spring comes with renewal of life, but not of Sigbjørn's spirit. The two sculptures of his mother and of Ruth are finished, but the large group of figures who are striving to free themselves from the soil is incomplete. The figures stretch their hands up toward a mountain peak, but on the peak itself is a void. Unable to live with this void and unable to see how it might be filled, Sigbjørn leaves his cabin and contemplates suicide on the river bank. Enter, miraculously, Ruth, who drives up to the cabin in her car, discovers the sculptures, looks around in Sigbjørn's studio, and there, on a small table in a corner, swaddled in blue cloth, is "a child done in pure white marble," which she places on the mountain top: "Now the work of art was complete!" (409). She walks down to the river where Sigbjørn is still standing on the bank and together they walk back to the cabin where Sigbjørn stands staring at the changed sculpture. "Sigbjørn, this is what you have not found." And thus ends the first volume of the trilogy.

In the second, Sigbjørn's struggle with himself, his identity, and his art, continues. It, too, opens on the shores of Lake Michigan with the newly wed Ruth and Sigbjørn in the old settler's cabin. The action moves back to the growing settlement in North Dakota, the land that was the making of one great American, Theodore Roosevelt, and may yet be the making of another, Sigbjørn Djuve. At the thematic center of the second volume is the nature and process of Americanization. From an immigrant perspective this takes the form of the question how the Norwegian and the American are to be united, a union symbolically expressed in the marriage of Sigbjørn and Ruth as well as in the issue of this marriage, their daughter.

Religion is as central to their identity as is culture, and Sigbjørn discovers that in rebuilding and expanding his original cabin he has given their home the structure of a cross, to him an ominous symbol of death, to his wife a symbol of renewal and salvation. Mysteriously and inexplicably, the child of marble disappears from the mountain top and when their daughter is born Sigbjørn cannot free himself from the fear that she, too, may be lost. As in the first volume, Sigbjørn's struggle and search for an answer is expressed through his work, now an even more ambitious sculpture of a man trying to cross over a chasm as wild animals grasp, claw, and snap at him from below. On the other side is a lighted altar partly covered by a wild rosebush (1930, 72, 106). In this volume Norstog's tendency to rely on symbols and lengthy revelations of the striving of the soul is more pronounced. As he was revising his second volume he wrote to Rølvaag that he had enjoyed reading his latest book (*Their Fathers' God*) but that "It seems to me that you only see the outside of your characters" (undated, OERP). While Rølvaag reveals his characters through action and lets them develop with the story, Norstog's characters remain static figures, since their struggles are not revealed in action but through inner monologues and long conversations. Sigbjørn creates a sculpture of Cain and then decides that his great work is to be a sculpture of God; he spends much of the second volume searching for His image in the Bible until Christ is revealed to him when he eventually gets to the New Testament. All this may suggest that the protagonist is related to the author but it still does not bring him to life. The novel closes with the first public recognition of Sigbjørn's art, an article on his work by Ruth in a prominent journal, but also with the failure and breakdown of the relationship between Sigbjørn and Ruth after the death of their daughter and the destruction of their home in an unexplained fire.[9] For Sigbjørn this death leads to a defiance of God; for Ruth it leads to acceptance and a renewal of faith.

The third volume also opens in the cabin by Lake Michigan, where they have moved after the destruction of their homestead. Sigbjørn has become paranoid; he is convinced not only that Ruth is guilty of the death of their child but that she is playing the role of loving wife only to harm him: "She has sucked all my strength from me. She is the world's greatest vampire!" Such are his melodramatic musings as he works in his studio or wanders alone on the plains (1931, 118). When Ruth asks to go with him back to North Dakota to rebuild their home, his sick mind tells him to play the role of loving husband in order to take the life of his evil wife: "She had bereft him of his dearest possession! She had lain in waiting like a serpent for the right moment to strike with her venomous fangs! Oh, how slippery she had been! And now it was his turn! But that turn would never come! He would arrange for her illness and death! And he would be free! Free! Free! Then he would build! Build so that the towers would enter Heaven" (11). Thus Norstog resorts to a series of emotional exclamations instead of a representation or dramatization of a mental process. Indeed, much of *Exodus* is in the exclamatory mode.

In North Dakota, Sigbjørn is consumed by revenge; as Ruth, soon a mother for the second time, ever turns a loving smile to him as she works around the home and cares for their son Joshua, Sigbjørn seeks the company of other women. Again his sculptures function as symbols. He discovers the lost marble child in the ashes of his former home and hides it in a cave that he closes with a stone on which he carves a warrior with drawn sword. His new great work is of the Temptation of Christ, with Ruth as the model for Satan showing Christ all the glory of the world. But when he donates his sculpture as an altarpiece to the new church, his refined revenge on his wife backfires and brings her admiration. Through the latter part of the volume Sigbjørn is weakened by an illness he contracted one night when he slept on the grave of his daughter and he gathers his remaining strength for his final work of art, a mother fleeing in terror with a child in her arms (216). And much as when the crew of the Pequod give their interpretations of the image on the coin Ahab has nailed to the mast, friends and neighbors drop in to see his latest masterpiece and offer interpretations that reflect their characters. His work completed, Sigbjørn walks into the night with his hammer and chisel to the cave with the marble child. Here he erases the image of the warrior and cuts a new image of a slain warrior with a broken sword. A violent thunderstorm erupts as Sigbjørn walks up to the top of the hill, flings his tools over the precipice, and prays to the "unknown God" he has fought against throughout his life, asking that the people of the earth will be led to the flaming altar where the child will bless them. For himself, he asks for judgment, not forgiveness: "He fell in a heap. Lightning brightened his dimming eyes." Ruth and her child stand at Sigbjørn's grave on Easter morning. As the sun rises, "the child nudges his mother and points to the grave and to the sun and speaks words that no one can understand" (246–247).

A brief summary of three hefty volumes must necessarily strip away much of what makes them a novel rather than a sequence of symbols and symbolic acts, but for all its 979 pages *Exodus* deals mainly in abstractions, and despite all its exclamation marks it is pale for lack of blood. Norstog seems to have started his trilogy with the intention of writing a work about immigration, about the apotheosis or the tragedy—both are potential outcomes of the pronouncements as well as the action of the first volume—of those who had left mountainous Norway to people the great prairies and plains of North America. Indeed, the choice of name for his female protagonist—Ruth, the Moabite, who as a widow remained faithful to the people of her husband and who became the ancestral mother of David and his line—may suggest that what he then had in mind was the tragedy of an individual, Sigbjørn, but a potential future for Norwegian Americans as a group. Norstog may have had this design in mind when he named the mismatched couple's second child Joshua in the third volume, but Sigbjørn sees only darkness when he climbs his mountain peak to die, and a little child making incomprehensible sounds and pointing to a grave and the sun is hardly a sufficient reason to expect a promised land.

Reviewing the two first volumes in *Reform*, Ager observed that the title was inappropriate (20 Nov. 1930), and it seems obvious that the immigration themes of Johnson, Ager, and Rølvaag were not Norstog's burning concern. Much in the way of the elderly Ibsen, who confronted his career as artist in the symbol-laden *When We Dead Awaken*, Norstog turned the immigration trilogy suggested by his title into a personal confrontation with the artist's conflicting responsibilities to man and God. The importance of *Exodus* to Norstog, and, consequently, to anyone wishing to understand his complex character, is evident in the way in which so much of his earlier work enters into and informs his trilogy—Benoni in *Paa heklemogen*, the protagonists of *Svein, Tone,* and *Natten,* the theme of Norway in America in *Ørnerud*, and so many of his boldly drawn biblical characters, Cain, Moses, Joshua, and David, all of whom are extensively referred to in *Exodus*. Nevertheless, his major work is a failure: a three-volume narrative cannot demand to be interpreted as a series of symbols, nor may the characters request of us that they be understood in allegorical terms only.

Norstog had a touch of genius and ambition to go with it. Notwithstanding the occasional power of his biblical books, he lacked the necessary discipline to create a consistently great or even good book, with the possible exception of *Tone*. He also lacked the modesty of true greatness, a modesty that should have suggested his responsibility to his readers. Norstog, however, wrote with disdain for responsibility to anyone but himself when he accused Rølvaag of bowing to the reading public and his publishers and claimed that the only worthy response to any request for revision was "The book is to be published as written!" Norstog also lacked the critical faculty to distinguish the lofty from the silly, as Oscar Gundersen observed in his perceptive review of the trilogy in *Norden*: "Norstog apparently likes enigmas. His profundity is rather unfathomable and his brilliancy is at times indistinguishable from what the French call *niaiserie*" (Dec. 1932), that is to say, foolishness, nonsense.

Ager repeatedly admitted that he was not sure what to make of Norstog. Only to a certain extent was this due to the linguistic difficulties posed by his wide-ranging yet dialect-based vocabulary: "Norstog stands alone and prefers to stand alone because his nature demands it. And when his nature demands it, this is probably because he does not fit in, because he is not in harmony with our time. Even geographically he has isolated himself by settling in the sparsely populated northwestern corner of North Dakota. Linguistically he has also set himself apart . . . He is also a Romantic who wants to be a Realist, a Mystic, a Philosopher, and a Language Reformer—all at once—and this is a heady mixture. He does not follow the paths of others. He does not even follow his own if he finds them too unproblematic and they have too few thorns. He then fears them or gets bored with them and throws himself off to the side—where there are neither roads nor paths. There he enjoys himself and can let down his hair in a literary solo dance, at times unfathomable but always in dazzling colors" (*R* 30 Oct. 1930). Other reviewers, in particular D.G. Ristad, J.O. Sæter, and Georg Strandvold, had faith in the ultimate value of Norstog's work, even though they, too, were forced to admit occasional frustration. It is difficult to assess how the reading public of *Vesterheimen* responded to the many volumes produced on the Norstog homestead. They were apparently sold. When Rølvaag wrote to Norstog in 1929 requesting copies of his work for the archives of the Norwegian-American Historical Association, he responded that there were none left except for a few copies of the recently published *Exodus* and the poetry volumes *Livshorpa* and *Fraa Audni*. All the others, he wrote, were out of print (undated, OERP).

NOTES

1. Inga Norstog lived a more social life. A graduate of the University of Minnesota, she was superintendent of schools in McKenzie county. After Jon's death in 1942 she worked for the Department of the Navy in Washington and became director of the museum at Luther College, later Vesterheim Museum, in Decorah (Williamson 74, 78).

2. Correspondence on these attempts in Luther College.

3. See Mengshoel's review of *Paa heklemogen* in *Gaa Paa* (clipping in Norstog papers, NAHA). Norstog responded with a review of Mengshoel's *Øen Salvavida* in the last issue of *Dølen*. Norstog's small handpress is on display at Vesterheim Museum.

4. Although the place of publication on the title page of his North Dakota books after 1910 may vary, they were all published from his homestead near Watford City. One of his brothers, Bjørgulv, wrote the play *Syndens sold* (1917, The wages of sin).

5. One difficulty in reading Norstog is his Telemark-based vocabulary. Norstog's title, *Paa heklemogen*, suggests a desert-like place, a place of desolation. Williamson (67) mistranslates it "To Seagull Heights," but does not appear to have read it, and believes that it anthologizes the "best" pieces from *Dølen*, probably misled by the legend at the bottom of the title page, "Hjaa 'Dølen,'" meaning that the book is available from *Dølen*.

6. The suffix—rud in the title identifies it as the name of a farm. It may be translated as the place of eagles.

7. See letters (in LC) to Norstog from Olaf Norli (27 Jan. 1931), Det norske samlaget (29 Sep. 1931), and Lunde & Co. (23 June 1936).

8. See undated letter to Rølvaag (OERP) and letters to Norstog from Georg Strandvold (15 Jan 1932, LC) and Richard Beck (30 March and 21 June 1937, LC).

9. Ruth's article is one of many suggestions that Norstog identified himself with Sigbjørn: before marrying Norstog, Inga Bredesen had an article about him in *Poet Lore* (1919).

Johannes B. Wist:
Bemused Spector

Coming to the fiction of Johannes Benjaminsen Wist (1864–1923), or Johs. B. Wist as he signed himself when not hiding behind the pseudonym "Arnljot," can be a refreshing experience after spending time with Johnson and Norstog, who, for all their differences, shared a sense of the elevated nature of literature and their own calling.[1] In his reluctance to acknowledge authorship of his own work or make much of his position as editor of *Decorah-Posten*, which vied with *Skandinaven* for the largest circulation among the newspapers in *Vesterheimen*, Wist may appear self-effacingly modest. But he lacked neither ambition nor the drive to realize it. He had had some experience of free-lance journalism before immigrating in 1884, and after short stints of work in a lumberyard, a grocery store, and a parochial school he began his journalistic career publishing and editing *Fakkelen*, a weekly newspaper in a small Minnesota town in the fall of 1885. *Fakkelen* ceased to appear after a few months, and before he became co-editor of *Nordvesten* in St. Paul in 1889, Wist was involved in two other short-lived newspaper ventures in Minneapolis and Madison. *Nordvesten* was a relatively large newspaper and at various times employed such prominent journalists as Ole S. Hervin, Nicolay Grevstad, and Svein Nilsson. Wist's eight years there, in particular his year as editor-in-chief, gave him valuable experience and visibility. In 1900 he accepted an editorial position with *Decorah-Posten* and became chief editor the following year. There he loyally continued the policy of the founder and publisher, Brynild Anundsen, of avoiding political controversy, promoting the interests of *Vesterheimen*, and providing both news and entertainment.

Given the instability of his early years in America and his responsibilities

Johannes B. Wist (1864–1923).

as provider for a growing family it is not surprising that the little pamphlet of 1888 was all that came of the ambitious history project that Wist took over from David Schøyen. But he continued to collect material, especially on the press, and his study of Norwegian-American newspapers and publishing after the Civil War (1914) remains the best source of information on this aspect of Norwegian-American history. Under the editorship of Wist, moreover, *Decorah-Posten* became an important repository of historical material, an editorial tradition that was continued by his successor, Kristian Prestgard. Memoirs as well as historical studies were solicited and prominently displayed, as for instance in the 1922–1923 series on "the lives of our immigrants." Wist's first contact with *Decorah-Posten* had been as a writer of fiction in 1897 with a slight sketch of the hardships of pioneer life, "Paa prærien" (On the prairie). The narrator is caught in a snowstorm and saved by stumbling on the doorstep of a pioneer cabin where an elderly couple and their daughter-in-law are anxiously waiting for their son and husband. When the narrator revisits the settlement two months later he learns of the funeral services of the young man, recently found after the thaw in spring. The young widow is beyond comfort: "Her hope in life had been broken for ever. Later I heard that she had become a patient in a mental hospital. Terrible nature!"

In the years that followed, Wist's literary interests found expression in criticism rather than in fiction. Although few labored as diligently as Wist for *Vesterheimen*, his realistic outlook and his refusal to give voice to what he thought was a romantic dream made him an adversary of cultural preservationists like Buslett, Ager, and Rølvaag. But he differed from his preservationist colleagues in manner more than in substance. For while Ager and Buslett proclaimed their vision of a viable Norwegian-American culture, Wist soberly spoke of the necessarily transitory and transitional nature of such a culture. That Wist should become one of the finest contributors to the literature of *Vesterheimen* further compounds the irony of his position. When Wist, Ager, and Buslett argued about the future of a Norwegian-American literature in 1904–1905, they agreed on the importance of cultural and literary work among the inhabitants of *Vesterheimen*. In a literary debate in *Decorah-Posten* twelve years later, the tone had become more acrimonious. One reason may have been an awareness of the challenge of a diminishing stream of immigrants, but the more immediate reason was no doubt the satirical style Wist in the meantime had developed in his column "Mellemmad" (Snacks). There "Arnljot" presented his observations on the current affairs of *Vesterheimen* or let them be voiced in dialogue between characters in the invented Iowa towns of "Salt Grove" and "Lone Crossing" or in equally fictitious correspondence from a farmer in Montana.

Always ready to perforate inflated sentiments, Wist reacted to Simon Johnson's bombastically filiopietist poem "Det nye vikingetog" (*Kv* July 1916, The new Viking expedition). Johnson had written with pride about the material progress of the Norwegian pioneers in the Midwest and, as "one who has listened to the voice of the blood," he admonishes them in conclusion "not to forget / The past that for centuries across the ocean / Cut the foundation for the New Kingdom in rock." In "Mellemmad" Wist observed that while it was true that Norwegian-American settlements had prospered, it was equally true that with material success the immigrants lost interest in their past and their cultural heritage. "Do Ager and Buslett, for instance, believe that there is a more fertile soil today for the Norwegian-American literature they have dreamed of than there was 20 or 25 years ago?" he asked (*DP* 13 Oct. 1916). Wist spoke for realism, and he knew all too well whereof he spoke. With Prestgard he had labored for years with the most ambitious journal in *Vesterheimen*, *Symra*, which had ceased publication after ten volumes in 1914. He suggested that this was an indication of what could be expected in the future and observed that Norwegian Americans increasingly preferred to subscribe to journals in English and that it had been stupid to believe that it could have been otherwise.

Rather than respond encouragingly with reference to his significant contributions, one after another of his friends and colleagues berated Wist for his pessimism, forgetting that his point of departure, the sad lack of correspondence between material progress and cultural interest, was also a central theme in the fiction of Johnson, Ager, and other cultural preservationists. This controversy lasted over several months and the final word, from Rølvaag, who by then had already won recognition as the most promising writer in *Vesterheimen*, was one of reconciliation (*DP* 9 Jan. 1917). Although Rølvaag readily admits that all arguments favor Wist's pessimistic position, he points to the apparent paradox that a Norwegian-American literature is nevertheless a fact and that to continue to write "is a sacred duty." But although his language may be that of idealism, the literary program he proclaims in his concluding paragraph is one of realism: "And here is the task of our authors: to draw images of our own life that we can see and understand. Yes, this above all. The beautiful castle of literature has many towers, wings and facades, and the wing that we must build first is the one facing our daily life. Could we only get a wide view from that position then we would be so strongly moved that we would also be able to move others. For this is what the literature of a people does: it both mirrors life and transcends it." Wist made no response and thus let these words of reason conclude the debate, turning it away from the rather epistemological question of the existence of a literature to the more pragmatic one of its function. Indeed, Wist seems to have tired of the controversy long before it had run its course. Beginning in 1911, he had shown increasing interest in writing fiction himself, and he may have been struck by the anomaly of arguing for the impossibility of what he was actually doing. In the period 1911–1913, while he was responsible for the bi-weekly *Decorah-Posten* and the weekly *Ved Arnen* and was both co-publisher and co-editor of *Symra*, Wist found time not only to do the research for his long article on the history of the Norwegian-American press (for which there were no archives or collections), but to begin to write stories. And, as the two he published in *Symra* in 1912 and 1913 demonstrate, Wist was in practice already following Rølvaag's program for a literature that would show the daily life of a people.

As indicated by his titles, "Blade av en nybyggersaga" (Pages of a pioneer saga) and "Da Bjørnson kom til La Crosse" (When Bjørnson came to La Crosse), Wist regarded fiction as a way of writing history, the first suggest-

ing that the story is a representative part of a larger history, the second referring to a well-known episode in the history of *Vesterheimen*, the lecture tour
of Bjørnstjerne Bjørnson. By taking off where *Husmands-gutten* ends, with
the marriage of the poor *husmannsgutt* to the daughter of the prosperous
farmer, "Blade av en nybyggersaga" is a response to the simplistic glorifica-
tion of material success in the popular Foss novel. Kari and Mons come to
America to realize their dream of "finding happiness," but from the very
beginning it is clear that Kari, who has known material comfort in Europe,
is not convinced that happiness is to be found in prosperity. Indeed, for her,
immigration means the loss of "something that she would never be able to
regain" (1912, 21). As the years go by their success is indisputable; they own
two sections of land and their home looks more like "a Norwegian manor
than a farm in a relatively new settlement on the Dakota prairies" (27). But
the price has been high—spiritual poverty and an apparently insurmount-
able gap between the parents and their three college-educated children.
Moreover, with his hard-earned wealth Mons has taken over the social attitudes that had forced him and Kari to leave Norway: he will not give their
daughter permission to marry the hired hand. As a writer of social comedy,
however, Wist provides a happy ending.

Buslett, Johnson, Dahl, and many others explored the coexistence of material success and spiritual poverty in their fiction, but Wist had an eye for
the comedy of life rather than for its tragedy and his basic fondness for his
characters comes through even when he satirizes their foibles, as in the story
about Bjørnson in La Crosse. Here he uses fiction as history in a more specific sense than in the story of how Mons and Kari eventually found happiness in America: characterizations of newspapers and other aspects of the
cultural life of *Vesterheimen* are woven into the story in a way that is characteristic of his main work, the trilogy about Jonas Olsen. The trilogy grew
out of Wist's "Mellemmad" column, which from 1917 gradually took on
the character of fiction, moving from satirical sketches and short stories to
the first installment of the series "Nykommerbilleder fra otti'erne" (4 Nov.
1919), which was published in 1920 as *Nykommerbilleder. Jonas Olsens første aar
i Amerika* (Newcomer sketches: Jonas Olsen's first year in America), a book
produced, as so often in *Vesterheimen*, from the original newspaper plates.

Nykommerbilleder is a satire of immigrant society in Minneapolis in the
mid 1880s. As is common in historical novels, many background characters
bear the names of actual people of the time (for example, Kristofer Janson,
Sven Oftedal, and Lars M. Rand) and others are recognizable behind thin
disguises. As is also common in historical novels, the hero is a character who

moves between classes, entering at the bottom but making it to the top as
he constantly wavers between the sumptuous drawing room and the favors
of the enticing daughter of his business partner and the plain and undistin-
guished boardinghouse presided over by the American-born housemaid,
Ragna. Much of the satire depends on the author's excellent ear for how
people speak. Jonas Olsen arrives in Minneapolis with expectations of immediate and spectacular success but with no knowledge of English beyond a
few phrases like "yes sir," "don't know," and "goodness," all learned on the
ship coming over (1920, 6). His cousin, supposedly the holder of an influential political office, but actually an assistant janitor in the courthouse, speaks
in such a mixture of English and Norwegian that Jonas is unable to understand him: "'Well sørri, in dis' her' kontri'e er vi alle læborers, ju 'no,' his cousin
replied. 'No læbor is simpelt in Amerika, og all offic'holdera tek sin tørn med
at kline op.' But then he suddenly remembered that Jonas of course could
not understand English, and he continued in Norwegian: 'Amerika er en
demokratisk kontry, ju 'no! 'Onest arbe' er det, som kounter.'" Realizing that Jonas
still does not understand much of this, Mr. Salmon (Salomonsen before he
changed his name) explains, "'Jeg har getta saa jused te' aa speak English, at jeg
forgetter mig right 'long, naar jeg juser norsk . . . Det tek tid for en nykommer at faa
saapas hæng af languagen, at han kan kætche on te de most komment English, men
det kjem saa'n bey and bey.'"[2] Such extreme use of the linguistic phenomenon known as code switching is mainly found in the early chapters where it
serves to caricature the hodgepodge of English and Norwegian used among
uneducated immigrants.

Jonas, who had placed his hopes for instant advancement on his powerful
cousin, is puzzled rather than crushed by his confrontation with reality, and
climbs rapidly, from digger of ditches for the municipal sewer system to
grocery clerk, to partner in the grocery business and a tenuous position in
the immigrant middle class. He is eager to learn and his liberal-populist political views and his opportunistic pragmatism predispose him to embrace a
shoddy version of the American dream. When Jonas is urged to join the
temperance movement, he appears a parody of Franklin: "These ideas of
moral and intellectual values were foreign to Jonas' nature, but he fully understood the notion that from a worldly point of view it was profitable to
be proper and that virtue was essentially the same as success. Consequently
he was willing to make any reasonable sacrifice. In his view he would be re-
warded for his sacrifice in cash, power, and comfort" (75–76). Clearly, this
anti-hero is no European innocent corrupted by American materialism: his
less endearing traits are all part of his character formed in Norway. Indeed,

apart from some of the historical characters in the background, the only principled and morally upright characters in the first volume are American-born Ragna and some Swedes, whom Jonas is duty-bound to regard as either rascals or reactionary imperialists.

He has an eye open for opportunity and quickly learns both that appearances are important and that "business is business," his favorite saying. So he seeks membership in the most conservative of the three main synods and judges his own actions solely by their success, as when he hires the novelist Bolwarius Lyvenfelt, modeled on Lars Andreas Stenholt, to write a scandalous *roman à clef* about his competitor in the grocery business.[3] Jonas's hopes of rising in society by marrying his partner's daughter are defeated when she marries an officer from Fort Snelling, but a yet greater blow awaits him: his partner has placed all their capital in his own shoddy bank and when the bank closes and his partner disappears, Jonas is again penniless. But when all is lost and he is humiliated, Ragna, who had been repelled by the bragging and amoral Jonas, now takes him in her arms and reminds him of the quarter section of land he had purchased in the Red River Valley. Married, they leave the city for a new life.

As the book about Jonas's first year in America was being distributed, his adventures on the prairie, where he settles on his quarter section in O'Brien's Grove, began serialization. The novel was published the next year as *Hjemmet paa prærien. Jonas Olsens første aar i nybygget* (The home on the prairie: Jonas Olsen's first year in the settlement). While a broad social satire takes precedence in the first volume, plot and character are at the center of *Hjemmet paa prærien*. The main plot grows out of the machinations of Elihu Ward, a political boss and speculator in Normanville, the seat of Garfield county, and his attempts to secure land where the H&B Railroad plans to have a station. Through good luck, complicated transactions, and the help of neighbors in battle with Ward's henchmen, Jonas thwarts his adversary and acquires the valuable land, where he establishes and names the town of Johnsville, pronounced Jonasville by all except Yankees.

Jonas is no more likeable in the second volume than in the first as he continues his rise to wealth and power. Two dominant traits are his opportunism and his jealousy, the latter, enhanced by his inability to speak openly with Ragna, triggering several sub-plots. His opportunistic lack of interest in moral distinctions is contrasted with his insistence on rigid orthodoxy in the church. While the community of Norwegian settlers is not as negatively portrayed as in the first volume, these are, after all, homesteaders, not businessmen and aspiring society women, Wist does not idealize his rural char-

acters or setting. Jonas's shoddy urban past follows him to the western garden when the thief, con man, and blackmailer Ludvig Napoleon Stomhoff
arrives from Minneapolis to teach parochial school and preach in the absence of an ordained pastor, but soon feels too uncomfortable in this role
and enters into the service of the boss of neighboring Arrowtown. Two of
the three most likeable characters, and certainly the most honest ones, represent ethnic groups seldom praised in the fiction of *Vesterheimen*: the unlucky yet ever optimistic Irishman Jim O'Brien and his Swedish son-in-law
Gust Nyblom, who had been one of Ragna's many suitors at the Minneapolis boardinghouse. Nor does Wist idealize his Yankees. The third contender for most likeable minor character, the intellectual yet slovenly Mrs.
O'Brien, a Presbyterian and a "Southern Yankee," may, with her warm hos-
pitality and upright moral character, be seen as a parody of the idealized
New Englanders in the novels of Foss and Johnson. The main contenders
for power in Garfield county before Jonas enters the ring are "Seff"
Thompson, the Americanized Norwegian-American Republican boss of
Arrowtown, and Elihu Ward, the Republican boss of Normanville, who
traces his New England family back to the Mayflower.

The second volume is a novel of homesteading, but a very different one
from the sentimental accounts of Johnson and Dahl or the starkly monumental trilogy of Rølvaag. Frontier virtues are mainly represented by the
O'Briens, while the Norwegian settlers are often preoccupied with fault-
finding, envy, and theological squabbles. As the fight for the future railroad
site comes to its fast-paced climax, Wist employs elements of the dime-
novel western, the attempts of the old boss to hold on to power, the uprising of honest homesteaders, the activities of a corrupt sheriff and his
deputies, and the use of deception as well as force on both sides. Jonas, however, is hardly fit for the role of white-hatted hero, and in the third volume,
Jonasville, subtitled "A Social Portrait" (1922), he is as much the undisputed
boss of his town as Thompson and Ward are of theirs.

In the first volume of the trilogy Jonas goes with Ragna to a political
meeting in Harmonia Hall, presided over by Lars Rand and with the Minneapolis mayor Albert Alonzo Ames as main speaker. Jonas is impressed by
the latter, who seems to appreciate the common man in quite a different
way from the more aristocratically inclined politicians in Norway (1920,
44). But as a newcomer, Jonas has no notion of a role in politics for himself.
In the second volume Jonas gets involved in local politics, but his introduction to American politics is to a rough-and-tumble not described in idealiz-
ing textbooks. Actually, it is Ragna who first exercises political leverage

when she refuses to sign over their tornado-ravaged homestead to boss
Ward, who has been misled to believe that this is the land selected for a railroad depot, until he has reluctantly ensured Mrs. O'Brien's nomination as
county school superintendent on the Republican ticket. In the third volume
politics is at the center. Formally, the issue is the location of the county seat.
Actually, the issue is the struggle between Ward and Jonas for power over
the county machine.

At the end of the second volume Johnsville is merely the dream of Jonas
Olsen. The third volume begins on a winter morning in 1909, some twenty
years later, and Johnsville is now a considerable town, with many businesses
and three class-defined residential districts. While the second half of the
novel (Chapters 16–29) is as plot-centered as the preceding volume, the first
half is, as the subtitle announces, a social portrait of a prairie town at the beginning of the twentieth century. Business and finance, social structures and
class divisions, cultural and religious institutions, and local and state politics
are all scrutinized. Presiding over Johnsville is its virtual proprietor, Jonas
Olsen, who tries by any means available to control everything in "his town"
while maintaining a facade of democratic principles, theological purity, and
ethnic pride. Like his rival, the boss of Normanville, Jonas does not seek political office. His source of power is control over finance and real estate. Even
though he has found it prudent to allow the establishment of other businesses, he is, in secrecy, the main shareholder in the competing bank and also
has interests in several other ostensibly competing businesses, just as he is the
owner of all three newspapers, Democratic, Republican, and Norwegian.

Wist avoids the parochially narrow concerns of much Norwegian-
American literature, both by never suggesting that a Norwegian heritage is
superior to any other heritage and by showing his Norwegian-American
characters as much in interaction with the outside world as with their own
kind. While it may seem natural that Norwegian Americans should play a
dominant role in fiction set in the Red River Valley, since they were the
largest ethnic group in the region, neither they nor other demographically
dominant immigrant groups are allowed center stage in mainstream western fiction. From the point of view of the immigrants and in particular of
their offspring, it is difficult to accept such invisibility. But, Wist explains,
this is only natural from the Yankee point of view: "If you asked these
young people of Norwegian descent what nationality they were, they
would immediately answer—not without some indignation at being asked
such a question—that they naturally were Americans. What else could they
be? But if you asked a Yankee what kind of people these immigrant chil-

dren were, they would always answer without hesitation that they were foreigners or Norwegians. It was not unusual to hear more or less cultivated Americans use expressions such as 'half-civilized foreigners' or 'dirty Norwegians' about the native-born American descendants of Norwegian immigrants of the second or third generation." Consequently, "while it was your duty to be an American, you did not really have permission to be one" (1922, 113–114).

Until the rise of Jonas Olsen, Garfield county is controlled by a Yankee boss. Although this is fully in keeping with the history of the region, Wist, in his second volume, finds it necessary to explain why a Yankee minority played such a dominant role on the agricultural frontier of the Red River Valley: "Elihu Ward was a well-educated, well-tailored, and well-mannered man. He was an 'Eastern Yankee' and without doubt the only person in the county who knew the name of his great-great-grandfather. The prairie had no tradition for the settler and the tradition of the country was not his, for in nine out of ten instances he was an immigrant and had his roots in another tradition and another culture. This is what has given the Yankee his great advantage over the others in the making of those traits that are characteristic of the American West. This made it possible for his kind above all others to become an upper class in the many-hued society that has been created in this part of the country. The Yankee brought the country's own tradition to the settlement." Elihu Ward had been brought up to venerate his tradition as well as to regard the West "as an undiscovered, rich hunting field" to which his kind came "and found it, figuratively speaking, full of game — immigrants from Europe who had just had time to make the land inhabitable for the more or less civilized American." He "was the first to settle in Normanville. He had not come as those who before and after him had come to settle on the land as homesteaders and pioneers. He had come as a capitalist and an entrepreneur. He had not come to sow but to reap" (1921, 98–99). Consequently, the struggle between Ward and the Norwegian upstart Jonas Olsen is not only a personal battle, but a war with historical dimensions: where should the power lie? With the established minority or with the immigrant majority? It is this perspective rather than the sprinkling of historical background characters and specific historical issues that makes the trilogy a historical novel.

The outcome of this war is in keeping with Wist's historical vision in his polemics on the nature and future of Norwegian-American culture in 1904–1905 and 1916. There he had tried to take a realistic middle ground, unacceptable to the more idealistically inclined Ager, Buslett, and Baumann. For Wist it was natural both to live the main part of his American life in *Vesterheimen* and to accept its eventual demise without regret. The immigrant neither could nor should attempt to escape from what he, in spite of the transatlantic journey, inescapably remained, nor should he see it as his mission to remain untouched by the American experience and to create a cultural ghetto. Johnson, with his idealized versions of the Norwegian and the New England American, concluded his novels either with the vindication of Norwegian-American values, as in *The Home of Freedom*, or with the mutual recognition of Yankee and Norwegian American, as in *Lonea*. Wist needed another equally emblematic ending.

The struggle for the control of Garfield county is fierce, but Jonas has history on his side; not only is Johnsville a burgeoning prairie town because of its railroad depot, while Elihu Ward's Normanville has become a backwater, but the Norwegians are coming into their own as the largest ethnic group and beginning to learn how to play the American game of politics. Jonas plays his cards with mastery and is not hampered by any political or moral vision beyond the simple one of power. He consolidates his own forces, buys an important ally in "Seff" Thompson, the boss of Arrowtown, and turns some of the dirty tricks Ward has played on him back on his adversary. The first time the question of moving the county seat is put to a vote, Ward narrowly wins, but four years later there is a landslide in favor of Johnsville. As Jonas is busy paying off his allies and using force as well as trickery to thwart a last-ditch attempt by Ward to annul the election results, Ward is bedridden by a heart attack. Their offspring, Miles Standish Ward, the only son of his widowed father, and Signe Marie, the pampered and vivacious daughter of the Olsens, meet, fall in love, and are married in Chicago. The fallen Ward sends a telegram giving his son the permission he requests and when Jonas and Ragna on the last page receive Signe Marie's telegram that she and Miles Standish have married, their resignation, too, readily gives way to acceptance: "Well, there isn't much to be done about it . . . And the boy is supposed to be quite okay, I've heard." As Ragna ponders Signe Marie's information that they "have Ward's blessing," Jonas explains, "Well sir, these Wards are smart people. They know a good thing when they see it. And this will add up to about half a million altogether." Even before the final reconciliation, Jonas has shown himself magnanimous in victory by providing for Ward's henchmen. He has also turned from his position of dogmatic rigidity and decided to take the side of church unity. The American future, however, is not for this unreconstructed Norwegian opportunist, nor is it for the Yankee supremacist Ward. It is Miles Standish

Ward, to whom none of their squabbles makes sense, and Signe Marie, for whom the larger American world holds more excitement than the narrow and parochial one of her father, who together represent a new America, neither Yankee nor Norwegian, but a union of both. By becoming a Ward, the Olsen daughter does not disappear but merely takes on a new role in the performance of which she is informed by her Olsen past. Wist's conclusion is an eloquent response to Johnson's and Ager's and Rølvaag's fear of the melting pot.

Wist's trilogy is not merely his best work, unique in the literature of *Vesterheimen*, but it is also a portrait of the late nineteenth and early twentieth century Upper Midwest that deserves a place in American literature along with the other fiction of this region from the 1920s. His trilogy should be compared not so much with the works of Willa Cather and Rølvaag as with the satirical novels of the Minnesotan Sinclair Lewis. Nevertheless, an important difference between these two writers affects the tone of their writing and should be kept in mind by readers of a later period: while Lewis was writing for a largely eastern urban middle class about a Midwest on which he had turned his back, Wist was writing for the largely rural and small-town subscribers to *Decorah-Posten*, among whom were Jonas Olsen, who, on the penultimate page of the trilogy, reads in his author's newspaper about his own exploits: "Would you believe that they have already got the news about the election of Floen and 'Seff' Thompson and everything! They are pretty good at getting the news down there in Decorah, don't you think!" In *Minneapolis Tidende* the reviewer of *Jonasville* compared it with *Main Street*, fearing that the novel would give rise to protests similar to those "that came from the inhabitants of various 'Gopher Prairies'" (1 Oct. 1922). In *Duluth Skandinav* "Bjarne Blehr" took Wist's novels as an affront to all Norwegian Americans, suggesting that a book without "a single honest person" could hardly have a honest author (16 Oct. 1922). Wist, not the only humorist who voiced his pessimism in private, commented on the negative reception of his trilogy some days later to his friend Ager, revealing that while all 1,200 copies of the first volume had been sold, only half that number had been distributed of the second. He feared that there would be even less interest in the third; now that the public had realized his pernicious intentions they would "defend themselves against his false doctrines" (2 Nov. 1922, WAP).

Wist spent long hours at his desk during the last years of his life. A few days after the first installment of the third volume had appeared in *Decorah-Posten*, a very different kind of narrative by "Arnljot" began to appear. It was published some months later by Augsburg as *Reisen til Rochester* (The journey to Rochester), a low-keyed humorous account of an automobile excursion by the narrator and the retired gardener Bonifacius to Rochester, where Bonifacius hopes to get help for his arthritis at the Mayo Clinic. The ancient Ford, inclement weather, and the wilful and irascible character of Bonifacius conspire to make a five-day journey of the few miles north across the state line to the renowned city of medicine, ending with the anti-climactic total wreck of the Ford, the purchase of some worthless quack medicine, and the return by train to Lone Crossing just outside Decorah.

The other five serialized novels Wist completed in the less than two years before his death at the age of 59 on 1 December 1923, after several months of declining health, are slight pieces compared to his trilogy. Three, *Reisen til Montana* (The journey to Montana), "Housecleaning" and "Sommerferie" (Summer vacation) are in the mode of *Reisen til Rochester*. The other two are novels of immigrant life but without the scope or the compelling central character of the trilogy. The less interesting of the two, "Aslak farlaus" (1922, Aslak fatherless), seems a parody of Foss's incredible plots. In "Hvorledes Lars Bakka blev akklimatiseret" (1923, How Lars Bakka was acclimatized), the Americanization of Lars Bakka consists of the realization that he is free to follow his heart, marry, and move back to his farm, rather than be governed by the dictates of his old-world prejudices or the whims of his urbanized and Americanized daughter.

Social comedy and satire were not genres with which Norwegian-American writers felt comfortable. Ager demonstrated a comic talent in some of his best stories, but he was too personally involved in his characters and themes to achieve the distance necessary for comedy. Rølvaag, too, wrote social comedy in some of his short stories and in parts of *Pure Gold*. The writer who comes closest to Wist in using fiction to expose the foibles of his people is Knut Teigen. While Teigen's satire became increasingly vicious, however, Wist remained a friendly observer. Teigen's emotional dependence on *Vesterheimen* gradually led to a hate relationship and his isolation from the community that had nourished him. Wist chose a very different and more accommodating path. Satirizing the successful Norwegian American and questioning the validity of a Norwegian-American culture, he also served as editor of the most successful and most culturally and politically bland of all Norwegian-American newspapers. Neither hypocrisy nor deceit was involved in filling these two roles: Wist seems truly to have enjoyed the company of the Jonas Olsens and Bonifaciuses that he exposed in his fiction. He also remained the good friend of those

colleagues he occasionally disagreed with in public. His use of the pseudonym "Arnljot" was not merely a literary device but an expression of a deep-
rooted modesty. Although journalism was his profession, he was a true literary amateur. Kristian Prestgard, in the obituary he wrote for his friend and
fellow editor, suggested that literature was the area of his greatest gifts, even
though "circumstances did not permit these gifts to develop until late—
perhaps too late—in life. For him literature became a little private garden
that he cultivated only in spare moments" (*DP* 4 Dec. 1923). It is only natural that his work is uneven and that his best work suffers from being written for serialization. But it is no mean achievement to have written the
Jonas Olsen trilogy, one of the most interesting and entertaining literary
products of *Vesterheimen*.

NOTES

1. Wist 1914 and Imbsen 1977 provide biographical information as does the obituary in *DP* 4 Dec. 1923. Zempel 1980 is a study of Wist's language and style.

2. The italicized words are in the original. In plain English: "Well sir, in this here
country we are all laborers, you know. No labor is inferior in America and all office-
holders take their turn in cleaning up." . . . "America is a democratic country, you
know! Honest work is what counts . . . I have gotten so used to speaking English that
I forget myself right along when I use Norwegian. It takes time for a newcomer to
get enough hang of the language that he can catch on to the most common English,
but it comes by and by."

3. The author's name begins with the verb *lyve* = to lie. Lyvenfelt's publisher is
Franz Jeppesen, obviously a Dane, as was Stenholt's publisher, Waldemar Kriedt. Another recognizable person satirized by Wist is the journalist Tom Overland, who appears as Nersjøen ("Nethersea").

Waldemar Ager:
Untiring Crusader

As nativist hysteria was reaching new heights after the United States had entered the First World War, Waldemar Ager (1869–1941), editor of the weekly newspaper *Reform*, received a letter from the chairman of Wisconsin's State Council of Defense, Magnus Swenson, questioning his loyalty: "I can hardly believe that it is true that you and your paper are so unpatriotic as to assume a critical and unfriendly attitude toward our government in the present crisis, but I have received so many complaints . . . that I cannot but take notice and write you to find out the truth" (11 Sept. 1917, WAP).[1] Unmentioned in the letter, but nevertheless at the heart of the issue, was Ager's persistent use of Norwegian in an American publication. To Ager, the cultivation of the language of the old country by loyal citizens of the new was essential to the ethnic survival that he was convinced would contribute to the greatness of the United States. But to increasing numbers of his fellow citizens, among them Theodore Roosevelt and Woodrow Wilson, any vestige of old-world culture (except that of Britain) among the country's immigrant citizens was tantamount to betrayal.

In May 1915 Wilson told a group of recently naturalized Americans: "You cannot dedicate yourself to America unless you become in every respect and with every purpose of your will thorough Americans . . . A man who thinks of himself as belonging to a particular national group in America has not yet become an American . . . " Roosevelt, speaking later that year to the Knights of Columbus, echoed his views, but in stronger and more threatening language: "The men who do not become Americans and nothing else are hyphenated Americans; and there ought to be no room for them in this country" (Lovoll 1977, 25). Ager, however, could not accept

Waldemar Ager (1869–1941).

that Americans of British origin could celebrate their linguistic and cultural heritage while the heritage of Americans of other backgrounds was foreign to the United States. "There are no definite rules for what is truly 'American,'" he wrote in an essay on "Smeltedigelen" ("The Melting Pot") in 1916. "We encounter a culture which is regarded as being American, but on closer examination we find that it is 'English' and that it has no more valid claim to be native here than the Norwegians' *norskdom* [Norwegianness] or the Germans' Germanness" (Lovoll 1977, 79). American meant Anglo-American and the melting pot was not intended for those who claimed that epithet: "It is its function to denationalize those who are not of English descent" (85). This is what Ager in another essay in 1917 called "Den store udjævning" ("The Great Leveling"), a kind of cultural genocide, "the killing of the creativity of whole nations" (102). But the strongest argument against the melting-pot ideology was not that it was a disservice to the immigrant groups of America but that it was a disservice to the United States. To enter the melting pot was ultimately an act of disloyalty: "If we are to contribute anything, it must be on the basis of our Norwegian heritage. We do not say that it is greater, for that it is not; nor do we say that it is better. But we must say that it is ours, and we must make our cultural contribution on the basis of it, if we are to offer anything at all of value to make the country richer" (111–112). And, "what we do not preserve, we cannot contribute to the culture here" (113).

When Ager wrote his reply to Swenson, who was as Norwegian as Ager, these views would have been on his mind, but he concentrated on the immediate issue of disloyalty, pointing out that as a longtime supporter of the Prohibition Party, *Reform* "has always been for peace and against war." Nevertheless, the newspaper had consistently supported the war effort. Ager's conclusion is an expression of midwestern isolationism, couched in an English with a distinctly foreign flavor: "But we do not rejoice over the war and are neither proud nor glad that we were mixed into it . . . We are and have been opposed to mixing up into foreign alliances or to tie up with 'foreign princes, potentates, states or sovereignties' which some of us under oath consented to abjure and renounce when we became citizens" (13 Sep. WAP).

In very different ways the First World War signaled the eventual defeat of the two major causes to which Ager was devoted: prohibition and an American literature in Norwegian. With ratification of the Eighteenth Amendment in 1918 prohibition became law. But what at first seemed a victory proved such a failure that prohibition as a national policy became a dead issue with its repeal in 1933. While the pressure towards cultural and linguistic conformity born of wartime nativism hastened the decline of other European languages than English, the most important factor in the rapid decline of the use of Norwegian was the sudden drop in immigration. *I Sit Alone*, the title of the English translation in 1931 of Ager's last novel *Hundeøine* (1929, literally Dog's eyes), was an apt characterization of his own lonely position in the last decade of his life, aware that neither prohibition nor a Norwegian-American literature had a future.

The world had appeared very different when Ager immigrated at the age of 16 in 1885. Before he was out of his teens he made two career decisions that influenced the shape and direction of his life: he became an apprentice printer for a Norwegian-American newspaper in Chicago and a member and secretary of a Templar lodge. The print shop was often the first step in a career in journalism or publishing for those without the advantage of a formal education. This was as true for Waldemar Ager in late nineteenth-century Chicago as it had been for Benjamin Franklin in colonial Philadelphia. Since he had some experience in making newspapers, Ager was the natural choice to be editor when a new association of Norwe-

In the office of Reform *about 1914. Note, on the shelves, the packaged works of Waldemar Ager. Courtesy Norwegian-American Historical Association.*

gian Templar lodges in Chicago decided to publish a monthly. The two other members of the publishing committee knew nothing about "the business," he explains in an undated autobiographical letter to Rølvaag (OERP). The following year, in 1892, he came to Eau Claire to work as printer for the prohibition newspaper, *Reform.*

It is important to recognize that when Ager made prohibition his cause in the 1890s, he was taking a place on the center stage of American reform politics, not in the wings, and that he was, moreover, to all appearances on the winning side. As temperance agitator and editor of *Reform* he traveled extensively in *Vesterheimen*, from the eastern reaches of the Midwest to the West Coast, and got to know its people and their changing conditions. Lecturing and writing against the blight of the saloon, Ager soon discovered that he had a special knack with words. Apparently, the Templar lodges were unable to pay him for his editorial work, and in his autobiographical letter to Rølvaag Ager claims that his first book was an attempt to get some of the money he was due. He took the didactic pieces he had contributed and wrote some additional texts to fill out a volume with the stirring title *På drikkeondets konto* (1894, Charged to the account of the scourge of drink). The book proved popular and, if we may believe Ager's account, brought him from the print shop to the editorial offices of *Reform*. Two years later he was business manager and co-editor, and when the editor, Ole Brun Olsen, died in 1903, Ager became editor and publisher, a position he held until his death in 1941. Ager had no literary ambitions when he wrote sentimental propaganda pieces with titles like "Little Johnny's Christmas Eve" and "The Death of a Drunkard." He was engaged in the war against alcohol and what he wrote was a weapon in that war. But as he continued to write didactic temperance fiction in between his work as editor, business manager, and temperance agitator and his duties as father of a growing family, Ager began to regard himself as a writer, independent of the causes he continued to devote himself to.

Five years after his first book, in 1899, the year of his marriage, he published the novel *I strømmen* (In the current), set in a Norwegian town modeled on his birthplace. It, too, is essentially a temperance tract and is marred by the excessive melodrama typical of this genre. But in the symbolically suggestive opening description of the river that eventually finds its death as it empties into the sea, in the competent plot that weaves the lives of several families on their different steps on the social ladder into one convincing story, and in the portraits of childhood, Ager demonstrated literary skills and an artistic maturity that had been all too rarely seen in *Vesterheimen*. "The author is a young man," Peer Strømme observed in *Minneapolis Times*, "and it seems probable that he is destined to take a place in the front rank among Norwegian writers of fiction."[2] The veteran Ole Buslett claimed that *I strømmen* was "the best book written on this side of the Atlantic" (Haugen 1989, 38).

Ager's many obligations continued to take most of his time. His second novel appeared eleven years after his first, while stories and essays, more easily written during moments of respite, appeared regularly. Except for those published in *Afholdssmuler fra boghylden* (1901, Temperance crumbs from the bookshelf), his critical and polemical essays did not reappear in book form. His stories, however, were regularly recycled. Their first appearance would be in *Reform* or *Kvartalskrift* or, usually in response to an editor's request, in journals like *Symra, Jul i Vesterheimen,* and *Norsk Ungdom*. Stories published elsewhere would make a second appearance in *Reform* before most eventually were collected in one of Ager's many volumes of short fiction, each dedicated to one of his children: *Stories for Eyvind* (1904; translated in 1907 as *When You Are Tired of Playing*), *Hverdagsfolk* (1908, Common people), *Fortællinger og skisser* (1913, Stories and sketches), *Ny samling fortællinger og skisser* (1921, New stories and sketches), *Under forvandlingens tegn* (1930, Under the sign of change), and *Skyldfolk og andre* (1938, Kin and others).

The 1904 volume is still essentially a tract, with fables, allegories, and moral tales that demonstrate that prohibition is the only solution to the evil of alcohol. But there are also stories of the kind that characterize his 1908 volume, where, as he explained to Buslett, his aim was simply "to describe different kinds of people, [each story] making its own point" (21 May 1908, OABP). As a novelist Ager explored new themes and new forms from book to book, but there is little to distinguish one collection of short stories from another. Nor would it seem that he approached a story with the same seriousness as he did a novel: the two main modes of his stories about "common people" are the comic and the sentimental. At his best, Ager can be as entertainingly funny as Wist, as for instance in "Naar Græker møder Græker" (1908, When Greek meets Greek) in which two friends, who unexpectedly meet each other by the lake on a Sunday morning fishing out of season, engage in sanctimonious sophistry. Another humorous story of fishing and tobacco is "Ellefson og Ingvold" (1921) where two friends who have vowed to break their smoking habit gladly admit defeat and give in to their shared vice. A more serious vice that appealed to Ager's sense of humor is greed, especially in confrontation with frustrated expectations of an inheritance, as in "Det fandtes ikke Ondt i ham" (1921, There was no evil in him), an entertaining story of a sickly husband who outlives the woman who had married him for his money. Ager is at his best when he successfully gives humorous treatment to a serious theme, as in "Hvorledes ægteparret fik nattero" (1921, How the married couple got their sleep) where a clergyman finally succeeds in finding a home for an infant orphan, as he has promised its unwed mother on her deathbed.

These stories could have had other American settings; they are about immigrants and their descendants but not about immigration. Ager's stories about the consequences of immigration are in the sentimental rather than in the comic mode. In essays he argued that the immigrant generation was creating a widening gap between themselves and the next one by neglecting to pass on their traditions to the young. His short-story volumes all have tales about the consequences of abandoning the past. In "Han saa liden og uanselig ud" (1908, He looked small and insignificant) an aging immigrant couple are despised by their educated adult children. The visiting narrator has "heard the farm spoken of as one of the largest and oldest in the settlement" but finds that the fine home is spoiled by "a small and crooked wreck of an old house that was clinging to it" (83). When the narrator leaves the company in the living room and wanders by mistake into the kitchen in the old part of the house, he comes upon an old man and woman. At first there is embarrassment—evidently the old couple are kept out of sight when the young have guests—but the narrator's friendly attitude gives them confidence, and as the old man speaks of pioneer times his narrative is ironically juxtaposed to snatches of popular tunes heard from the living room. Other stories on this theme are "En mor" (1930, A mother), in which the title character is neglected by her adult children, and "Juledrømmen som brast" (1938, The Christmas dream that was shattered), where the aging parents are strangers to their sons who have come home for Christmas.

Writing on request for Christmas publications, Ager and his colleagues tended to write immigrant variations on the "home-for-Christmas" story. Some examples are "Johan Arndt og hans mor" (1913), about the old mother in Norway who has had no letter from her son in the United States and their miraculous reunion at Christmas, and "John McEstees vugge-sang" (1921, lullaby), about a successful immigrant who has turned his back on his past and his culture but is moved by music to decide to visit his old home in Norway for Christmas.[3] In order to appreciate such stories it may be helpful to realize their impact on contemporaries. For Rølvaag, reviewing Ager's selected stories (1918) in *Lutheraneren,* his main theme was "For what shall it profit a man, if he shall gain the whole world, and lose his own soul." His favorite stories were "He Looked Small and Insignificant" and "John McEstee's Lullaby" (*Sk* 19 Dec. 1923). One reason for his praise of the latter may be his classroom experience of students who sometimes "cried on reading that story, really burst into tears. I think it was because the image that was enfolded there caused anguish in their conscience as they acknowledged their own guilt" (*DP* 5 Jan. 1917). Stories that seem sentimental from one point of view may have the ring of truth from another.

Ager's novels deal with his main themes and motifs not only in greater depth, which would follow naturally from the longer form, but with more seriousness than his stories. "En teddy-bjørn" (1908, A teddy bear), in which the clergyman protagonist is an early version of the protagonist in *Christ Before Pilate* (1910/1924), is a case in point: while the novel explores the character's ironic and tragic potentials, the short story is a comedy, as is "Hvorledes ægteparret fik nattero," with a similar protagonist. A sentimental version is given in "Den gamle prest" (1913, The old clergyman), where the protagonist, who fears retirement since he has been unable to save money, dies as his letter of resignation is being discussed by a congregation already looking forward to a younger replacement. *Kristus for Pilatus (Christ Before Pilate)*, however, is a disturbing study of the ironically self-destructive consequences of a selfless life. It has humor—the account of the congregation's *lutefisk* supper is fine social comedy—but neither the sentimentality nor the didacticism so typical of his early work.

The title refers to an image well known to the contemporary public, "Ecce Homo," the painting by Mihály Munkáczy of Christ standing before Pilate and an unruly flock of accusing elders, priests, and scribes. A reproduction of this "most expensive painting in the world" had been advertised by *Skandinaven* as a premium in 1889–1890 and adorned many Norwegian-American homes.[4] The painting also had personal significance for Ager, who had contemplated it in a Liverpool art gallery in 1900 and, like his clergyman protagonist Conrad Walther Welde, had a reproduction in his office (Haugen 1989, 41, 66). Throughout the novel Welde ponders the significance of the painting, in particular the contrasting roles of Christ and Pilate. Welde is himself a Christlike figure, who always strives to serve others. By endeavoring to do good, however, he creates situations where gradually all members of his congregation turn against him. Indeed, since he is never ostentatious in his good deeds, even those who are helped by Welde innocently believe that he has unsuccessfully tried to thwart them. Welde is Christlike also in hating sin but never the sinner. But for most members of his congregation it is difficult to appreciate this distinction and to them it appears that their pastor is more ready to support and help obvious sinners than the faithful. Welde, the meekest and least aggressive character imaginable, has enormous physical strength. This irony is further compounded by a hidden flaw: he dies because of a weak heart. Implied is a parallel flaw in his character: his moral or spiritual strength is undermined by a lack of understanding of the world and of human nature, and it is this innocence that turns so many of his good deeds into events that tear apart the congregation he has been set to serve.

The novel opens and closes with a clergyman passing judgment on the protagonist. Welde is first seen through the prejudiced eyes of Mosevig, the pietistic and narrow-minded pastor of the town's other Norwegian Lutheran congregation, as a man with book learning but without true inspiration. In the end, pacing back and forth preparing his funeral oration, a senior pastor reflects on Welde's wasted life: "The young man was gifted; had been brought up in a good home, was exemplary in his conduct, was conscientious in the execution of his duties—but—he had been given one of the best parishes in the church, and altho he had discharged his clerical duties faithfully, there was really nothing of importance about his work that could be pointed out" (1924, 276). Thus irony frames the portrait of an imitator of Christ, "despised and rejected of men."

The novel is as much a social study of a late nineteenth-century urban and ethnic congregation as a psychological study of its pastor. The opening paragraph presents the two competing congregations: "There were two Norwegian churches in town. One was a large and beautiful edifice in a desirable locality, while the other was a small wooden structure whose steeple scarcely rose above the neighboring chimneys" (5). The novel focuses on the former, on Welde's congregation, which, since immigrant churches had an ethnic rather than a social base, realistically includes the entire social spectrum of the urban ethnic community from the lowly unskilled laborer to the bank director. Ager shows great skill in describing the social, cultural, and political contrasts and conflicts in this community. *Christ Before Pilate* compares favorably with a better known novel about a clergyman in a similar setting, Harold Frederic's *The Damnation of Theron Ware* (1896). An important difference between the two novels—and a distinguishing difference between Norwegian-American and mainstream American fiction—is that while Frederic gives an outsider's view of Theron Ware and his congregation, Ager identifies with Welde and his world.

In the seven years between his second novel and his third, *Paa veien til smeltepotten* (1917, *On the Way to the Melting Pot*), Ager spent many late nights at his desk. His essays, articles, and stories speak of his confidence as spokesman as well as writer. While *Christ Before Pilate* and most stories are free from the didacticism of his early work, his essays are among the best argued statements on the culture of *Vesterheimen*. In 1910, four years before the centennial celebrations of Norwegian independence, Ager wrote two companion pieces that may be regarded as his declaration of cultural independence for *Vesterheimen*. An essay on contemporary Norwegian literature in *Kvartalskrift* and *Reform*, expanded and revised on request for *Symra* the following year, insisted that the literatures in Norwegian on each side of the Atlantic had developed so differently that the literature of Norway was foreign to Norwegian Americans. A companion essay on Norwegian-American literature in *Kvartalskrift*, expanded and revised for Wist's *Festskrift* in 1914, outlined the history and character of this literature: "There is a yawning chasm between contemporary Norwegian and Norwegian-American literature" (1914, 304). This confident view of an American culture in Norwegian is the tenor of most of Ager's literary and critical essays, culminating with his visit to Norway in 1914 (as official representative of Wisconsin) for the centennial celebrations. But in response to the crusades against the hyphen, Ager became more aggressively polemic, as in his essays on "The Great Leveling" (Lovoll 1977). Moreover, he could no longer separate his function as agitator from that of novelist: his 1917 novel on the melting pot is as much a polemical tract as his first one on the evils of alcohol. As a consequence, not only does the novel suffer, but the author's message is correspondingly weakened. Anger takes the place of understanding, spite crowds out compassion, and the characters are not given sufficient life to fulfill their function as illustrations of the author's cultural and linguistic theories.

Paa veien til smeltepotten is Ager's fictional response to the popularity of Israel Zangwill's drama *The Melting-Pot* "among those individuals in our population who above all others consider themselves true Americans," as Ager put it in the opening sentence of his essay on "The Melting Pot" in 1916 (Lovoll 1977, 77). The novel illustrates his view that the melting pot was a threat, not only to the immigrant's identity but to the American nation. While the ideal aim of the melting pot was to create a new American identity on the basis of all the diverse elements that went into the melting process, it would "as an equalizer . . . destroy the best qualities in all metals and thus also end their useful values." It was, in fact, never intended for "Anglo-Americans": "It is its function to denationalize those who are not of English descent." In Ager's analysis of the melting-pot ideology of Americanization, "the taking on of the character of the 'new man' is of secondary importance. Discarding the 'old man' is by far the more significant issue" (Lovoll 1977, 78, 84, 85). In his novel, the road to the melting pot is one on which the immigrant discards all distinguishing traits, all vestiges of the culture of the old country, and becomes an empty shell, good for little else than extinction in the melting pot. His central thesis, that the melting pot is for those who have gone down this road, is expressed through the extended metaphor of an industrial process involving a melting of useless scraps and wrecked parts to make new patented machines. The manager of the factory where this work is done explains that "He could not recall having seen a single typewriter, an electric motor, a usable sewing machine or piece of farm machinery wander into the melting pot." Even though the particular machine produced by the factory is an improvement on existing products, other machines are never purchased to be melted down. Only useless scrap metal is used because it is the cheapest available raw material. The message is clear: it does not make economic sense to melt down products, even inferior products, that have a function and still can serve a purpose. To make the implication even more explicit, we are told that the manager, who did not hold the masses of new immigrants in high regard, was particularly suspicious of those who appeared to have Americanized themselves. It is not only his factory that depends on immigrant labor: "A French cook prepared his food, a Belgian kept his garden in order, his clothes were sewn by a Swedish tailor, and a Norwegian girl cared for his children; but at his club, he sought to associate with people of his own kind" (1995, 173). Regardless of our lowly social status, the author admonishes his fellow immigrants, it is we, the immigrants of America, who are crucial to the machinery of the nation as well as to the creation of that variety that is the essence of being American.

The road to the melting pot can be a painful one: "The inner pain he experienced made him feel as if his insides had been ripped apart and the pieces were trying to put themselves together again" (35). Once immigrants have pulled loose from their accustomed soil, they do not easily take root in the new, and the only remedy is "to take enough soil with them from home to cover over the most tender roots" (180). The rootless losers "were like ships adrift; they bumped into kitchen doors, and now and then ran into a police officer . . . They washed in and out of the saloon doors to be swept off to another skerry full of breakers, only later to turn up again in the same waters as before. They were neither living nor dead, they neither wholly floated nor wholly sank. They were typical Norwegian wrecks" (38). In addition to such imagery and some explicit comments by characters who serve as mouthpieces for the author, the critique of the melting pot is expressed through social satire involving a large gallery of minor characters as well as in the contrasting stories of the two protagonists, Lars Olsen and Karoline Huseby. A comparison with Wist's trilogy may demonstrate the failure of Ager's satire and character portrayal, for where Wist smiles at the foibles of his characters, Ager snarls at the stupidity of his; where Wist notes the vagaries of code switching with the detachment of a linguist, Ager places ludicrous locutions in the mouths of his characters to expose their ignorance and lack of culture. While Wist's Jonas and Ragna are contrasting characters, the down-to-earth Ragna is far from an idealized angel and Jonas is as likable as he is venal. Ager's Karoline, on the other hand, embodies her author's lofty ideals, while Lars is a pitiful illustration of the dire consequences of walking down the road to the melting pot.

The opening dinner party at the Omleys' sets the satirical tone. Before the party Mrs. Omley is nervous and flustered. This experienced housewife, who knows little English but peppers her Norwegian dialect with the few words and phrases she has picked up, has to consult every now and then with her daughter Sophy, who is able to read the cookbook and who pretends to know very little Norwegian: "She was preparing an American-style dinner, and that was no simple task" (1). After the meal the men gather on the porch to discuss politics and compare the United States with backward Norway while the women sit in the living room and talk with pride about the Americanization of their children. Much of the satire and some of the subplots are concerned with how the rush to the melting pot creates an unbridgeable gap between the generations, as for instance in the case of the mother who is unable to communicate with her English-speaking children and slowly declines into mental illness. Present at the dinner and impressed by all he sees and hears is the newly arrived Lars Olsen. After most have left, he chats with another guest and observes that "It's strange that more Norwegians don't make the journey to America." "It's just as strange that more Norwegians don't make the journey back to Norway," the older immigrant responds. "You have to pay for what you get here too, and some things get plenty expensive, and what you pay with you don't get back again." Lars believes he is speaking of higher prices and is confident that this will be compensated by a higher income (21). Lars illustrates Ager's thesis that Americanization is primarily a process of "discarding the 'old man.'" When Karoline, the girl he has left behind, eventually comes to join him they soon drift apart as she shies away from the changed Lars and he reacts to her lowly status as a maid and her stubborn refusal to admire and aspire to the superficial world of the Americanized second generation. In demonstrating that Karoline's way is an *American* alternative to the road to the melting pot, Ager resorts to one of the clichés of Norwegian-American fiction, introduced by Foss and used by writers as different as Johnson, Dahl, and Norstog: she is met with approval by the family of her employer, "a New Englander of the old school" (110). On the 17th of May she wears her Norwegian ribbons of red, white, and blue while serving at a party and is chastised by one of the guests, who turns out to be "some kind of Scandinavian" (114), for not appreciating her new country. Her employers respond by asking for pieces of her ribbons and hoist the American flag in recognition of her holiday.

Lars continues to climb, marries the daughter of his employer, and takes over the business. Karoline returns to Norway where she discovers that she has become an American. She often dreams "about the big country on the other side of the ocean"; like Jacob Riis, she could not hold back "a great outburst of joy one day when she saw a steamship sail past bearing the American flag" (179). Back in the United States she discovers that the Lars she "had known and loved no longer existed." But his fate is a common one: "First they stripped away their love for their parents, then they sacrificed their love for the one they held most dear, then the language they had learned from their mother, then their love for their childhood upbringing, for God and man, then the songs they learned as children, then their memories, then the ideals of their youth—tore their heritage asunder little by little—and when one had hurled from his heart and mind everything which he had been fond of earlier, then there was a great empty void to be filled with love of self, selfishness, greed, and the like ... Thus they readied themselves for the melting pot's last great test ... the melting pot was precisely for the spiritually stunted, those who no longer had qualities that let people see what they were or what they had been" (192–195). Although *Paa veien til smeltepotten* suffers from the author's anger, it remains an important comment on the melting-pot ideology of Americanization.

In his next novel Ager departs from the realism of his earlier work. *Det vældige navn* (1923, The mighty name) is subtitled "A dream vision from the World War" and, as in Ambrose Bierce's "An Occurrence at Owl Creek Bridge," the ending reveals that most of the preceding narrative, set in Europe during the First World War, has been imagined by the protagonist, a capitalist magnate, as he dies in a car accident on a country road in England.[5] Instead of his belief in the absolute power of gold "beyond evil and good" (24) the protagonist discovers the greater power in the secret name of God, and instead of his cold insensitivity to human suffering he comes to realize that "Life is the greatest of all blessings, that all other blessings have meaning in life alone, and that war, the destruction of living human beings for the acquisition of lifeless and dead things, is a rebellion against life" (77). To Rølvaag, *Det vældige navn* was "a sermon on the sacredness of life" (*Sk* 26 Dec. 1923).

In 1911, with the Kristiania edition of *Christ Before Pilate*, Ager had been introduced in Norway. He was not the first writer in *Vesterheimen* to be published there, but Foss and Stenholt had been sponsored by popular publishers whose products were never recognized by reviewers. An equally peripheral status was achieved by Norstog, who had placed a few books with provincial publishers. Ager's Norwegian publisher, however, was the prestigious firm of Aschehoug. Although recognition in the country of his childhood was important to Ager, he wrote for *Vesterheimen*, not only for its readers but also as a record of its culture. But when Ager completed *Gamle-*

Ager's study at home. The flag draped on bookcase is the flag of the 15th Wisconsin Volunteers during the Civil War. On the wall the central picture is Munkasy's "Christ before Pilate." Courtesy Norwegian-American Historical Association.

landets sønner (*Sons of the Old Country*) in 1926 *Vesterheimen* was on its way to extinction. The only substantial publisher of fiction, Augsburg, could hardly be expected to accept a novel that not only took its readers to saloons and a whorehouse, but did so without moralizing comment. By the time he wrote his last chapter, Ager seems to have made up his mind to publish in Norway, probably encouraged by Rølvaag's success with the Norwegian two-volume edition of *Giants in the Earth.* Ager's decision had an impact on his novel, its title as well as its ending. For while *Christ Before Pilate* and most of his short stories had been about Americans of Norwegian origin, the title *Sons of the Old Country* suggests that his intended readers, those who had stayed behind, should regard the characters of the novel as their siblings, as emigrated Norwegians.

The title's plural form indicates a novel about a group of characters rather than a single protagonist. Some of them are first seen on the deck of a paddle steamer making its way against the current of the Chippewa River in the mid 1850s. They are bound for Eau Claire, where they hope to get work in the sawmills in summer and the lumber camps in winter; they represent a wide social spectrum, from the patrician Frederik Berg to the impoverished Evan Evanson, and an equally wide range of motives for emigration. In Eau Claire the gallery of characters is enlarged to include not only more Norwegians from a variety of social and geographical backgrounds, but also Irishmen, Yankees, and a Frenchman. Among them they represent the people who built this Wisconsin city, the Irish and the Norwegians through their labor, the Yankees with their capital and positions of power.

Sons of the Old Country is a historical novel in the sense that it gives an account of the growth of an urban community, life in the lumber camps and sawmills of Wisconsin, and the cultural, social, and psychological impact of the American experience on European immigrants at the middle of the nineteenth century. And Ager proves himself an excellent historian. Unobtrusively, he describes the working processes and the labor conditions at the mills, in the camps, and on the river. The accounts of individual characters are also accounts of the growth of the community: homes are built, families established, institutions formed. The prohibitionist does not interfere with the historian: saloons and boardinghouses are among the institutions central to the lives of his characters. Nor does he neglect the multiethnic character of the growing town. A dominant group in the labor force is Irish and in the town's makeshift hospital Norwegian Lutherans are in the good hands of nuns. On two critical occasions the immigrants rally to save the society they have built. On the local level the Irish and Norwegian laborers join hands in averting a flood that threatens to destroy their homes and workplaces. On the national level the immigrants go to war to save the Union, most of the Norwegians joining the Wisconsin 15th where Norwegian was the language of command.

Several characters illustrate the Americanization process, a process that involves positive changes in character and in social perceptions, not the destructive transformation of the melting pot. There is the young boy, Karinius, whose first English words are "I'll be damned!" (1983, 23) and who through his initiative and willingness to work at the mill and his bravery in the war seems destined for success.[6] There is the socially ambitious Ole Brekke, who in Norway has been turned away by the aristocratic father of the girl he loves because of his plebeian origin, but whose engineering skills and ingenuity make him invaluable in the lumber industry and whose non-commissioned officer's training places him on the first rung of the ladder he climbs to the rank of colonel in the Union army. There is the mill hand, Greger Gregersen, who as a labor spokesman in Norway had been stamped as a troublemaker and had to leave in order to avoid prison in the aftermath of the reaction that swept most of Europe after the unrest of 1848. In America he dedicates himself to the security and well-being of his family and again becomes a leader, now solidly middle-class, as "chairman of the building committee" and sexton of the new congregation (87).[7]

Most importantly, there is Frederik Berg, scion of a landowning merchant family, and *primus inter pares* in this collective novel, who is dismissed by his furious father in the opening sentence: "Get out!—I never want to see you again!" While the first chapter describes his break with his father and his family background, the second presents a wayward and recalcitrant log: "If the log had had eyes, it could have learned its own fate from that of other logs that had gone astray. Many lay along the shores, rotting partially; others lay high on dry land, rotting completely—hollowed, worm-eaten, crumbling; some had sunk to the bottom and were buried in sand; some had become deadheads, with one end above water and the other below, waiting for a chance to cause trouble before sinking completely" (10). The log that stubbornly refuses to obey the booms and pikes and follows the current to a final resting place seems an allegory of the fate in store for young men who break away from authority. But the narrative demonstrates that Frederik has other and more positive qualities than mere obstinacy. As the other characters prove that they, as so often in immigrant fiction, can do well for themselves in a society that rewards them for their labor, Frederik proves to himself that he, who could have had a fortune in the Old World, can provide for himself with his own two hands in the New. Moreover, he eventually marries the daughter of Gregersen, the one-time rebellious laborer in his father's employ.

Meanwhile, the many plots involving the wide range of characters have included brawls, love stories, labor conflict, ethnic conflict, a near catastrophe that threatens the entire town, raucous comedy, and sentimental romance. The threads in Ager's narrative come together in the Civil War, in which most of the male characters take part. After some realistic battle and prison-camp episodes and a mawkishly melodramatic hospital romance, Ager brings his story to a close. The immigrant community is firmly established in modest prosperity; families have been formed, wounds healed, and the foundation laid for a promising future for the city and the nation. And at this point Waldemar Ager's novel and his son Trygve's translation part company. Ager wrote a conclusion suited for his intended Norwegian audi-

ence by sending a handful of the characters back to Norway. A woman returning after the deaths of her husband and only child is a reminder of the
high cost of immigration. Ole Brekke, who in democratic America
achieved a military rank that in Europe was reserved for those of better
families, has received word from the crusty father of his beloved that he is
now welcome as a suitor. Frederik, the young upper-class rebel who has
proved his mettle in the land of opportunity, now has the confidence, together with his working-class wife, Gunda, to take up relations with his father and accept his inheritance. The message was of course not that the immigrant should return to the Old World. Such a notion would be foreign to
the novel's American author. Rather, the message to readers on either side
of the Atlantic was that Norway would have to look to America in order to
create a society without the class distinctions that kept people in their places
and did not encourage them to fulfill their potential.

Trygve Ager, however, seems to have found this conclusion artificial for
an American novel, and made two subtle changes in a sentence in the last
chapter. Where his father had written " . . . they had been married before
they left, so this was also their wedding trip" (1926, 286), the son substituted
"they had been married quietly back home in Wisconsin and this was their
wedding trip" (1983, 253). In the translation their home is in Wisconsin, not
Norway, and their visit to Norway *is* a wedding journey, not a return that
also functions as a wedding journey.[8] These slight but significant changes are
in keeping with the spirit of the novel. Had he been asked, Ager surely
would have enjoyed having the descendants of Frederik and Gunda as his
neighbors in Eau Claire.

In achieving access to a prestigious Norwegian publisher, Ager had succeeded where many of his colleagues had tried and failed. Success with the
English-reading American public, however, eluded him. His friend J. J.
Skordalsvold, who had translated one of Foss's novels into English in 1899,
translated a volume of Ager's short stories and *Christ Before Pilate*, but publication in Eau Claire and Minneapolis hardly made the English editions
more visible to the readers who counted than those in Norwegian. The national recognition won by his friend Rølvaag in 1927, when *Giants in the
Earth* was published by Harper in New York, gave Ager hope of a similar
success.

Rølvaag did his best to see the hopes of his friend realized. In December
1927 he tried to interest his publisher in *Christ Before Pilate*, but Harper was
reluctant to take a book that had already been published in English. His
next attempt was with Simon and Schuster, to whom he recommended

both *Christ before Pilate* and *Det vældige navn*. "Do not say anything about the translation of C.B.P.," he somewhat naively advised his friend. "If he writes to you, you should send him the original."[9] Nothing seems to have come of this either, but Rølvaag continued his efforts. In January 1929 Rølvaag suggested *Sons of the Old Country* to Doubleday, who immediately wrote to Ager, evidently hoping that he would prove as hot a property for them as Rølvaag was for Harper. Ager responded eagerly, but again he was frustrated. Doubleday expressed concern with finding a good translator, but after a few months Ager was convinced that Doubleday had not been sincere but had hoped all along they would be able to publish it with Rølvaag's name on the title page as translator or author of a preface.[10] But by this time Ager was more interested in a new novel and 10 September 1929 he wrote to Rølvaag that *Hundeøine* had been accepted by Aschehoug in Oslo. Again Rølvaag set about trying to awaken interest in New York for Ager's work and this time he succeeded: as *I Sit Alone*, Ager's last novel was published by Harper in 1931.

At first the novel may seem a negation not only of the collective experience of *Sons of the Old Country* but of the life lived by the author. For the opening sentence is written by a man who has given up on life and feels intensely sorry for himself: "I sit alone in a little shack out here on the prairie, and the time seems long to me. There are many others around here in the same situation, but they are pioneers and have great hopes for getting ahead. I am merely a fugitive, whose business is to dig himself down; the others are digging to raise themselves up—most of them" (1931, 1). Christian Pedersen, the forty-year old narrator, has fled from some calamity in his life and has assumed the name Inslee, an anglicized spelling, he explains, of "einsli," a Norwegian word that may be translated as "the solitary" (353). He is a writer, but his manuscripts pile up in the space behind his wardrobe: "What makes it especially dismal is that in it lie poems which no one has read, poems which were to have made their author famous but which, instead, lie there, becoming ever more yellow and brittle. There, too, lie letters written but never sent." Such a space is a "capital publisher": "No ceremony, no advisers, no humiliation. There will be no critics . . . no one to be annoyed at the over-use of the pronoun 'I'—I may fill a whole ream of paper with 'I's,' as many as I choose" (3, 7). The reviewer in the *Herald Tribune* did not distinguish between the narrator and the author, who could not see "through the haze of his own self-pity" (15 March 1931), but neither a careful reading of the text nor a consideration of the situation and character of the author will bear out such a reading. Christian is an anti-hero, whose responses to adversity ironically are not approved by his own narrative, where he is surrounded by characters, all inhabitants of a little town on the Dakota prairie, who serve as foils to his self-absorbed and self-pitying self. These characters represent alternative responses to adversity and the narrator's "conversion" to a more active life on the concluding pages may seem less sudden and contrived than Rølvaag found it to be (*N* Jan. 1930, 15–16) if seen as a response to the many positive role models he has been studying throughout the novel.

"There is first and foremost 'the minister,' as we call him" (15). Now an elderly man, he has also been driven out on to the plains by defeat, but rather than sit self-absorbed in his cabin, he lives a life of service, tending the ill as an amateur physician and giving occasional sermons on Sundays in the schoolhouse. "And then we have Egidius—an odd name and an odd man." He is not given to much speculation and does not lament his lonely plight after he has spent his youth and manhood caring for his mother and younger siblings. "Egidius seems very well satisfied with what he has done, for there is no more healthy and radiant face in all the prairies of Dakota than his . . . It's his specialty to volunteer in helping others" (16, 18). Then there is the Civil War veteran whose mind seems shattered by his war experience, but who still is able to help others. "There is also an elderly man who is now clearing land for a home the third time. Two splendid farms he has had and lost. The first he himself made away with; for the second his children were responsible. Now he's at it again. 'All good things come in threes,' he says, and, smiles confidently at a halfscore years' toil and moil ahead of him, he with sixty years on his shoulders." (19). And then there are "young fellows," some sent by "parents because they couldn't make men of them, and one at least come voluntarily to make a man of himself" (19). And finally there are the families who live "in shacks no bigger than mine" (20).

When the narrator finally begins to see himself in perspective, he realizes that with his newly acquired point of view he probably would not have written these memoirs. All he has done is make up excuses for himself instead of taking responsibility for his own life: "In that case," he concludes, "I've got what I deserved" (259). In the end he breaks out of his cocoon of self-pity and is ready to take up his life, indeed, to begin anew without regret for the past and without blaming others for his failures. The ending may be contrived, but the message is clear: by placing blame elsewhere you also avoid taking responsibility for your own life. Only by taking such responsibility can you be someone for yourself and for others.

It may be that Ager needed to remind himself of such trite truths as he saw that both causes to which he had dedicated his life had failed. In this sense *I Sit Alone* may have been a kind of whistling in the dark for the author. Not only had prohibition proved to be a failure, but *Vesterheimen*—the fact and the dream—had lost its vitality. Assimilation had in practice carried the day. There was no denying that there had been a Norwegian-American literature, or that Waldemar Ager had been an important contributor, but by the time he wrote *I Sit Alone* it was already of the past. The writers were there, but they had no audience. Ager never gave in. That was not his nature. But he sat more and more alone. He kept *Reform* alive as long as he himself lived and he continued to write short stories—two more volumes were published in Eau Claire after his last novel. A portrait of a lonely man contemplating his failed dreams, however, would hardly do justice to Waldemar Ager. Nor should his lifelong resistance to the pull of the melting pot be equated with a resistance to adapting to the land of his choice. On the contrary, he saw his work as a contribution to the Americanization of his people. Contemplating the coming celebrations of the centennial of Norwegian immigration in 1925, Ager began his prize-winning essay, "The most essential effect of a great and successful celebration of the centennial . . . would naturally be that Americans of Norwegian origin felt more at home, were more secure in their rights as citizens, and felt more the equals of the descendants of the Anglo-Saxon immigrants who commonly and in a distinctly different degree than all others are regarded as true Americans." The most important element in such domestication was a sense of a shared history, and Ager points to the many similarities in the experiences of the nineteenth-century Norwegian settler in Wisconsin and the seventeenth-century English settler in New England (1925, 12).

Norwegian Americans had not only made as much as they could of Leif Erikson and the early Viking discoveries and settlements, but had developed myths of the medieval Norse influence on England and English institutions and a Scandinavian presence in Minnesota in the fourteenth century. Rather than contemplate such flimsy claims to roots in America, Ager turned to the more recent past for the right won by his people to the name American: the Norwegian blood shed in the nation's greatest crisis, the Civil War. There Ager could find "the most obvious evidence that the most nationalistically minded Norwegians over here are also actually the best Americans—that is the most self-sacrificing—the first to report for duty when the war alarm sounds and their new country is in danger."[11] Hence his interest in the history of the Fifteenth Wisconsin Regiment (1916) and the importance given the Civil War in *Sons of the Old Country* ten years later. Looking back on his life, Ager saw his greatest achievement to be not his work for prohibition, nor yet his many literary works, but his successful effort to have a monument to Colonel Hans Christian Heg raised on the grounds of the Wisconsin State Capitol in Madison with legends that noted his Norwegian birth and American death and the fact that "Norwegian Americans gave this memorial to the State of Wisconsin."[12] The monument is unique, as both the only monument in honor of an individual in the park area surrounding the state capitol and the only one bearing the name of a specific American ethnic group.

Ager's work in and for *Vesterheimen* was all of a piece. In his writing and in his organizational and political efforts his aim was one he shared with Knud Langeland and so many other contributors to the literature of *Vesterheimen*: to leave behind lasting traces of the history of his people on their way into America. As early as 19 August 1900 he wrote to his friend Ole Buslett about why their literary work was so important: "Should it be that the Norwegian population here is to be swallowed up, then our literary efforts will prove to have the longest life and be our best witnesses. Wherever conditions are new and a culture emerges, literature—because it is both art and history—will be the gauge ... If we as an immigrant people are unable to bring forth *major* prophets this is no reason for the *minor* ones to be slain. The future will place literature in the first rank. The dust will be removed from whatever is published here, journals will be searched, and what has been forgotten will be brought to light" (OABP). To regard his efforts as misdirected or his life as a failure would be to misread Waldemar Ager's view of *Vesterheimen* as a transitional culture as well as to disregard the continuing importance of ethnicity in American society.

NOTES

1. Excellent for an understanding of the restrictions placed on the foreign-language press and of Norwegian-American responses to nativism are Chrislock 1981 and his introduction to Lovoll 1977. Haugen 1989 is particularly useful for its biographical information and summaries of Ager's fiction.

2. Extracts of several reviews in *Reform* 13 Nov. 1900.

3. Ager had attended a concert of the Minneapolis Symphony Orchestra in Eau Claire earlier that year with his son Eyvind and had been deeply moved when the solo cellist played a Norwegian lullaby as an encore. When a letter came that fall from Sundheim requesting a story for *Jul i Vesterheimen*, Ager used this experience as his point of departure (Letter to author from Eyvind Ager 12 Dec. 1991).

4. See, for example, 25 Dec. 1889 and 23 April 1890. For $2.00, subscribers could acquire the painting that John Wanamaker had purchased for more than $100,000, ap-

parently the highest price ever paid for a painting until the same artist's "Christ on Golgotha" fetched an even higher price and was offered as a new premium (29 Oct. 1890). In 1895 the first issue of the monthly journal *Skirnir* had a black and white reproduction of "Ecce Homo" as frontispiece. Ager's novel has a reproduction, in color, on the front cover.

5. Haugen is disturbed by "the element of anti-Semitism" (113) in the novel, but the protagonist, though a Russian Jew by birth, has cut himself off from his cultural and religious roots and serves Gold and its power in the world. The voice that comes closest to that of the implied author belongs to an old English Jew who speaks for the traditions of his people. For Ager, as for Rølvaag, the Jews exemplify a people who despite centuries of life in the Diaspora have been able to withstand the melting pot and maintain their racial, religious, and cultural identity.

6. As a comment on the success story cliché, Ager has Karinius dive off the deck of the paddle steamer to save the daughter of a mill owner without in this manner proving his right to her hand and her father's fortune.

7. Gulliksen 1987 gives an interesting analysis of Gregersen.

8. Eyvind Ager, the author's oldest son, informs me that he is unaware of "any discussion or reference made to any changes in the text" between his father and his brother. "In the early 1970s some of us . . . including my brother Trygve discussed a possible translation effort. Trygve did not particularly like the ending in the final chapter and thought that in translating a change would be an advantage. We encouraged him to try . . . Thus the change you refer to must be credited to Trygve as well as any other revisions that occur" (20 July 1991). As early as January 1929, Waldemar Ager was considering the possibility of having Trygve, then in his last year at St. Olaf College, assist him in revising a projected translation (Letter to Rølvaag 19 Jan., OERP).

9. Rølvaag to Harper 6 Dec. 1927 (WAP). Rølvaag wrote 11 March 1928 that prior publication in English was Harper's reason for turning it down. Ager felt that Augsburg had "strangled" his favorite novel (to Rølvaag, 23 Jan. 1929, OERP). Rølvaag's advice is on the margin of a letter from Simon and Schuster, 19 March 1928 (WAP).

10. Doubleday to Rølvaag 12 Jan., to Ager 14 Jan., Ager to Rølvaag 19, 23 Jan., 12, 16 March (OERP). The Norwegian novelist Peter Egge was on Doubleday's list.

11. Ager's preface to his 1916 book on the Fifteenth Wisconsin Regiment.

12. Eyvind Ager in conversation, 25 Nov. 1990. The monument was the work of the Norwegian-American sculptor Paul Fjelde. Ager's account of the work to raise money for the monument is in *JiV* 1927.

The Four Lives of
Ole Edvart Rølvaag

"It is as if I have already lived two lives here on earth: the first was in Smeviken, and that lasted almost twenty-one years. The second one I lived through on the trip from Smeviken in Helgeland to Clarkfield, South Dakota. Now I am about to begin a third." Thus the young narrator of Ole Edvart Rølvaag's first novel writes home to his father shortly after his arrival in South Dakota, and wonders whether he "will ever experience a fourth life" (1912/1971, 1). As the only author from *Vesterheimen* to gain access to the American slope of Parnassus, Rølvaag (1876–1931) did experience a brief fourth life as an American writer after the publication of *Giants in the Earth* in 1927. His recognition marks him as essentially different from the other characters in this history, who share the common trait of invisibility. Although Rølvaag may not be a household name in university departments of English, and most college courses in American literature may not study his work, this is as much due to the regional bias in canon construction as to Rølvaag's home in *Vesterheimen*.

The story of Rølvaag's childhood and youth on the northern island of Dønna, his emigration at the age of twenty to South Dakota and his education at Augustana Academy and St. Olaf College has been well told by his biographers.[1] In his early work the idealized figure of the potential artist, unappreciated by family and a materialistic community, is a central character. While there is a weakness at the core of the unnamed protagonist of his first published story, "Forviklinger" (1907, Entanglements), and in Nils Vaag in *Længselens baat* (1921, *The Boat of Longing*), Rølvaag's aspirations were matched by his dedication and will.

His first serious literary attempt is the unpublished novel "Nils og Astri"

Ole Edvart Rølvaag (1876–1931).

that he wrote during his senior year at St. Olaf College and took with him when he went to study for a year at the university in Kristiania in 1905. After it was turned down by Aschehoug, he wrote of his despondency to his fiancée in South Dakota. But Rølvaag's despondency was never long-lasting and after he had returned to the United States to begin his teaching career at St. Olaf he submitted a story to *Vor Tid,* where it appeared in 1907. Even judged by the literary standards of *Vesterheimen* this sentimental story holds little promise. Read as an allegory of immigration, however, "Forviklinger" takes on more interest as the starting point of Rølvaag's literary career. In the story of two lovers who are separated by a series of misunderstandings and who in the evening of their lives recognize that in spite of their lasting love they have grown apart is the larger story, as Rølvaag saw it, of the immigrant's tragic loss and his recognition that the act of immigration had forever separated him from the people to which he once belonged. This insight, born of his sense of alienation on his first return to Norway in 1905, is at the heart of his first novel, *Amerika-breve, fra P. A. Smevik til hans far og bror i Norge* (1912, America letters from P.A. Smevik to his father and brother in Norway, translated as *The Third Life of Per Smevik*, 1971).

While Rølvaag had had no qualms about publishing his first story under his own name, the college professor, who by 1912 had put his name to a textbook and was a well-known contributer to newspapers, hid behind the pseudonym Paal Mørck. Mørck, meaning dark, was a fitting disguise, while Paal, the standard name of one of the two elder and unsuccessful brothers of the Norwegian fairy-tale hero Espen Askeladden (the Ashlad), who in tale after tale wins the princess and half the kingdom, was a no less suitably modest cover for one whose early aspirations had been dashed. The cover-up of the author's identity in the introduction to the novel is elaborate and an integral part of the book. "Paal Mørck" presents himself as the editor of the letters "Peder Smeviken" sent to his father and brother on an island in northern Norway before they, too, came to South Dakota. The letters, covering the period August 1896 to July 1901, tell the story of the education and acculturation of an immigrant: the narrator arrives in the United States on a ticket sent to him by his farm-laborer uncle and the letters to his father and brother come to a natural conclusion with practical advice for their journey to "Clarkfield," where Paal Mørck later meets them and acquires the letters written by the now eminent clergyman Peder Smeviken. Rølvaag's choice of the epistolary mode for his first novel was as natural as it was brilliant. The letter is the ur-genre of Norwegian-American literature; not only were "America-letters" the earliest instances of writing in the Norwegian language in the United States, they also established the basic narrative patterns and major themes of much of the later fiction of *Vesterheimen*. In the letters of his fictional immigrant, Rølvaag was repeating the real-life narrative act of the immigrants of many nations.

Although his first royalty slip from Augsburg reported a sale of no more than 471 copies in the first four months (OERP), the reception of *Amerikabreve* was encouraging. In *Decorah-Posten, Skandinaven, Lutheraneren, Kvartalskrift, Eidsvold,* and other newspapers and journals the book was hailed as a significant contribution to Norwegian-American literature by an unknown but promising writer. And it soon became obvious that Paal Mørck had ambitions beyond setting his name to a single book. A few weeks after the appearance of *Amerika-breve,* Augsburg's Christmas annual, *Jul i Vesterheimen,* brought Paal Mørck's impressionistic "Stemninger fra prærien" (Prairie moods) into many Norwegian-American homes. The style of these sketches of the prairie and its seasons has a refreshingly oral quality and they are an implicit statement about an important aspect of Rølvaag's literary program: writing should be yet another way of making a home for the immigrant in the New World. An even larger audience was reached when *Decorah-Posten* (15 May 1914) published the story "Gammel arv" (An ancient legacy).

The promise of these sketches is renewed but hardly fulfilled with Paal Mørck's second novel, *Paa glemte veie* (1914, On forgotten paths). It is a strangely uneven work. Compared to his epistolary novel and later work, it seems parochial. Religious concerns are central in Rølvaag's fiction as they were in his life; but *Paa glemte veie* is the only novel where he preaches and where, moreover, his sermon is narrow-mindedly pietistic. Talking of his earlier effort a decade later to his friend and colleague C.A. Clausen while they were both spending a sabbatical year in Oslo, Rølvaag called it "rather meagre material."[2] Yet it has descriptions of the land and accounts of man pitted against the land as powerful as any in American fiction of the West. The setting is the same imaginary South Dakota township as in *Amerikabreve*. The antagonist "Chris Larsen was the wealthiest farmer in the entire Clarkfield settlement" (5). Buslett found him "a rather typical Norwegian prairie farmer. He is hard as flint and avaricious and without extenuating characteristics such as the luxurious desires that frequently overwhelm these people at a more advanced age" (*Kv* Jan. 1915). Later, Rølvaag was often accused of presenting a negative image of Norwegian Americans. The reason reviewers of *Paa glemte veie* did not engage in the critical closing of ranks so common in an ethnic culture is no doubt that the novel's idealistic norm is represented by Larsen's daughter, the protagonist Mabel Larsen. The conflict between them is the result of Mabel's determined struggle to save the soul of her father, an inveterate materialist and sinner.

The turning point comes three years after the widowed Larsen and Mabel have moved to Saskatchewan to make use of the opportunities offered by the undeveloped Canadian West. Here Chris's hubris brings on his downfall. Sitting helpless in a full-loaded wagon behind a runaway team of horses heading across the plains, "his rage suddenly flooded him; it came over him as an enormous uncontrollable tidal wave, the mad rage of a powerless human being confronted with a stronger power" (46). Before long he lies unconscious, his back broken, beside his wrecked wagon, never more to stand on his feet. Chris is defeated in his attempt to subdue the plains, and he and his daughter return to South Dakota after a lonely winter in their homesteader's cabin. Now begins Mabel's struggle for the salvation of her father, a struggle ironically paralleled by her father's constant scheming to keep his daughter from running out on him. The battle for Chris Larsen's soul is set geographically and socially in the marginal ethnic community of Clarkfield. Ideologically, however, its setting is one of the central intellectual and theological conflicts of turn-of-the-century America. In making the evangelical beliefs and practices of pietistic Lutheranism the moral and ideological norm of his novel and the salvation of Chris Larsen the center of his plot, Rølvaag takes issue with the current social gospel of American Protestantism. Rølvaag caricatures the views of such prominent theologians as Washington Gladden, Walter Rauschenbusch, and George Herron in the bland and self-important young theological student, Harry Haugland, whose favored theme on all occasions is "Social Service" (141), and whose favored language is English. Mabel, who at a youth church social stands up and speaks for the old pietistic values, speaks in Norwegian. Thus Rølvaag presents the immigrant group's language and heritage as one with a conservative Lutheran view of the function of religion and the role of the church, both under pressure from popular trends of the time. It would be a misreading, however, to see Rølvaag speaking for an immigrant culture hermetically closed to outside influence. The novel is after all a response to a national cultural and theological debate and its norm is as much midwestern as it is Norwegian. Moreover, the character who voices the ideal that Mabel attempts to live by is a Scottish Presbyterian clergyman on the plains of Saskatchewan. The novel ends, as the genre requires, with the deathbed conversion of Chris Larsen. And Mabel, now graying, can finally write to the pious clergyman whose earlier proposal she had turned down because of her filial and Christian duty to her father. Reviewers, with the exception of Ager (*R* 22 Dec.), praised the novel and it sold well enough to encourage Augsburg to venture a second printing in 1918.

The fictional addressees of Rølvaag's epistolary novel reside in Europe. His second novel addresses itself to the immigrant community, pointing a warning finger at questionable tendencies in the larger world of which they had become a part. But in placing the conflict between Lutheran piety and the more intellectually attractive theology of the social gospel at the thematic center of his novel, Rølvaag was mediating between his ethnic group and a larger America. Indeed, the many weaknesses in the novel's plot and characterization suggest that the writer may not have been entirely convinced of the validity of his novel's ethnocentric message. Rølvaag's third novel, *To tullinger* (Two fools), published by Augsburg in 1920, is an American novel with an ethnic setting. It was not warmly welcomed in *Vesterheimen*.

In the six years between his second and his third novel, Rølvaag continued to publish short stories, poems, and essays, and worked on a three-volume anthology of Norwegian and Norwegian-American literature with his senior colleague at St. Olaf, P.J. Eikeland. The first volume, a joint effort, appeared in 1919. The second, for which Rølvaag was responsible, was devoted to American texts and it may be that his attempt to create a Norwegian-American literary canon helped give him the confidence not only to publish under his own name but to break out of the claustrophobic ethnicity of his first two books and simply write an American novel in Norwegian. The challenge to ethnicity by the nativist attacks on hyphenism and "foreign" languages during and after the First World War had led Rølvaag to think through his position and develop a theoretical and ideological basis for an ethnic minority culture. In a review in 1920 occasioned by a second printing of Simon Johnson's volume of short stories, he explained that he disliked the term Norwegian-American literature: "It would be more correct to call it American literature in the Norwegian language." Look at the books that have been written among us, he suggested, and "see if you can find anything Norwegian about them. I read them and find nothing but the language they are dressed in. This literature is about American life as we have experienced it on the plains and forest claim, in small towns and in prairie homes." In *Omkring fædrearven* (On our ancestral heritage) he insisted that the novels and poetry he and his colleagues wrote were neither a Norwegian "provincial literature nor immigrant literature" but simply "American literature in Norwegian" (1922, 60). Rølvaag later acknowledged that his career as an American writer had begun with his third novel by selecting it as the earliest of his books to be published in English, as *Pure Gold*, in 1930.[3]

At about the time Rølvaag was writing his tale of greed, another European immigrant, Erich von Stroheim in Hollywood, decided to make a major statement on his new country, taking his story from Frank Norris's *McTeague* (1899). This naturalistic classic, demonstrating the destructive and dehumanizing force of avarice, has a multi-ethnic urban setting, and Stroheim, a German immigrant thinking of images rather than sound, may not have been aware of the irony of the German accents on the silently moving lips of several of the characters he had borrowed from Norris for his film *Greed* (1924). Rølvaag, however, was deliberate in his choice of an ethnic setting for his novel. He saw the perversity of extreme avarice as an effect of a life without cultural roots. Like so many of his contemporaries among American authors, Rølvaag explored the consequences of the loss of identity. In 1930 Rølvaag explained that a specific experience as well as a more general one had gone into the making of *Pure Gold*. While waiting for a

train in the summer of 1919 he had come upon a notice in a local newspaper about a man who had found two crocks of gold while building a new
house. The image of the persons who had hidden the gold stayed with him.
"To me it seemed beyond all measure insane that people could find pleasure
in saving up good money for no better purpose than digging it down into
the cold ground." But Rølvaag's novel is not simply about how two characters develop a mania. As he also explained, "other experiences have gone
into the making of the story. I have observed what might happen, and what,
in many cases, actually does happen, to an individual who has no tradition
and no cultural background—we have plenty of them in America! I chose
two such people to carry the story" (Jorgensen 1939, 255–256). Rootlessness
and the isolation of individuals without a strong sense of community—neither in time, that is tradition, nor in space, that is social bonds—is the theme
that gives Rølvaag's story of greed a perspective beyond that of a case history of perversity. And it is this quintessential American theme, a theme expressed through such diverse characters as Henry Sutpen, Jay Gatsby, and
Bigger Thomas, that also gives *Pure Gold* its compelling power.

The novel opens around 1890, at threshing time on a farm in fictitious
Greenfield, Minnesota, the setting of several of Rølvaag's short stories. A
strong sensual attraction is kindled between Lizzie, the farmer's daughter,
and Lars (soon Americanized to Louis), co-owner of the threshing machine: "Through the screen door Lizzie watched him. Heaving the heavy
sledge above his head, his muscular body bending gracefully under the
weight, he struck the peg squarely every time. As she watched, the rhythmic
motion of his body and the sound of the impact changed into music. Never
had Lizzie witnessed anything so beautiful" (1930, 2). After a friendly
wrestling match between the two as the rest of the crew cheer them on,
"Strange emotions were astir within him, feelings that made him want to be
alone and to sing" (8). Such is the beginning of their happy courtship. But,
as the style reveals, naturalism rather than the idealism of *Paa glemte veie* is
the mode of *Pure Gold*, and from here on the story has the downward
movement to be expected in naturalistic fiction. For the story that has such
an earthy and sensual opening set to joyful music is one of how avarice
turns these two good country people into grotesques with hardly a vestige
of humanity left when they eventually freeze to death one on each side of a
locked door in lonely desperation and terror. They are buried as paupers
and their ragged and dirty clothes and belongings, including their homemade canvas money belts packed with $72,000, are thrown on a bonfire:
"The paper which had been wrapped around the clothes and the clothes

themselves gave a cheerful flame. The belts went more slowly. But gradually they too changed into slender columns of blue smoke which mingled with the calm, deep night and was gone" (346). The story that begins with the music of sensuous and youthful dreams ends in a vast and silent emptiness.

Their development from a young farmer couple to two elderly misers is narrated against a backdrop of community life as well as national and international events. At first their attitude toward money is one of youthful infatuation. On evenings when new bills and gold coins had been added to their growing hoard "they pulled the shades low, and then counted the money, sorting it and playing with it, happy as two lovers, until far into the night" (83). But with time their childish delight turns into a "mystic devotion [that] could only be held during the dark, secret hours of the night; then they could give themselves up with undivided hearts [. . .] Love was slowly changing into unquenchable desire. Their faces bore marks of the change, Their features grew sharper, thinner—somehow, longer; their eyes were uneasy and roving" (114).[4] They are exposed to a series of trials that serve to confirm them in their conviction that they must protect their money themselves: bank failure, a charming confidence man representing the Arizona Pure Gold company, and the constant demands on their purse from their church. The greatest crisis in their lives comes with the First World War and the Liberty Loan drives that follow in its wake. Their harrowing experience of persecution is given apocalyptic overtones in the subtitle "The Day of the Great Beast." At first the war seems a godsend, driving up the price of produce, and Lizzie and Louis are so unaware of the world beyond the limits of their own land that they declare that if indeed Kaiser Bill was responsible for the war, "his picture, beautifully framed, ought to hang in every farm home in America!" (195). The United States' declaration of war makes the prices soar yet higher and now Louis is full of praise of the Democrats who have brought such blessings on the land. "But then, like a bolt out of a clear sky, came the first Liberty Loan drive" (212) and the beginning of a reign of terror for Lizzie and Louis. They whine and wheedle, they rage and cry bitter tears, but against them stand not only the government, but popular opinion. The climax of their battle with the Great Beast comes one night when a drunken mob of young men—all Norwegian American—drive up to their farm with the aim of scaring them out of their wits. When they find the house empty, they set fire to it by accident and drive off, suddenly sobered by the realization of what they have done. Hiding in the barn, Lizzie and Louis are unscathed by the fire but confirmed in their paranoia. With their savings—augmented by insurance money and a good price for their farm—secured in the money belts they wear day and night, they move into cheap rooms above a store in town. They miss the farm, the work and the animals, but find comfort in their money, the soft-worn $1,000 bills in their money belts. Lizzie "might lock the door securely, bracing a chair against it for further protection; then she would sit down on the bed, remove her clothes so that she could get the belt off, and play with the bills. Usually her features would soften . . . Fine boys they were! When they had first arrived they had been stubborn and naughty, with no tenderness in them . . . but under her heart, where they had lain these many years, they had softened—tears dimmed her eyes—yes, so they had! She laid them against her cheek; there was a silken tenderness in them; she could feel how fond they were of her and how they snuggled close to her" (283–284). The naked sixty-year-old Lizzie in bed with her $1,000 bills, fondling them one after the other, remembering when she had acquired each and every one of them, speaking to them, scolding, fretting, and cooing, is as powerful an image of human degradation as any in American literature.

Ager could be a perceptive reader, and in his review of *To tullinger* he noted that Rølvaag had taken a new direction with his third novel, that it was "not a Norwegian-American book except in its language and the names of its characters." He recognized Rølvaag's theme of rootlessness and its consequences: "We are a transitional people, pulled up by the roots and taken far away to be planted in foreign soil . . . Generations will pass before the other races are as rooted as the English. For a long period much that concerns the life of the soul will be adrift . . . But in all this drifting, cut off from an ancient culture and placed in a new that has not been grasped, 'gold' offers a fixed point for gravitation. To a greater or lesser degree property—money—was the immigrant's first and main goal . . . Why wonder that these two simpletons should find the meaning of life in the possession of gold?" (Kv 1920, 21). While some reviewers, notably Simon Johnson, praised Rølvaag's novel, the more common reaction was to regard it as "an insult to Norwegian immigrants" (*Sk*, clipping OERP). Augsburg was criticized for publishing *To tullinger* and the church publisher's readiness to take on Rølvaag's next novel in spite of this criticism is yet another instance of the dedication of the managing director, A.M. Sundheim, to his ethnic publishing policy.

Rølvaag seems to have conceived *The Boat of Longing* (1921/1933) as a series of images, much as a film director conceives a film. The Norwegian subtitle is "Movie Scenes," and the 1933 "Foreword" calls the novel a "series of moving pictures." There are four such sets of pictures and in the first, "The Cove Under the Hill," set on an island off the coast of northern Norway, much like the author's Dønna, the dominant image is that of "a boat said from time to tme to have shown itself out in the open sea" (1933, 2). All accounts of this legendary boat share the theme of longing for what lies beyond life and they foreshadow the longing for a larger life in the land to the west of the sea that leads many a young man and woman on the path to the steamship landing and the long journey to America. The protagonist, Nils Vaag, "was not exactly like other young folk" (17) and his story is the oft-told one of the artist as a young man. Not only does Nils learn to play the violin as a child; he also explores the world through the books in the local library. Attracted by stories of the many wonders of "a tremendously large city by the name of Minneapolis" (49) that come back to the island from those who have gone before, he decides to immigrate. He has to go, he tries to explain to his parents, Jo and Anna, "Because life is not in this place . . . not for me [. . .] That's why I must go out after it. For it is that which one must find" (69–70).

Then follow two sets of scenes of Minnesota, of Minneapolis and the forests to the north. The protagonist's two guides in the New World are an alcoholic elderly poet who shows him the challenge of Soria Moria, the fairy-tale castle from one of the many adventures of the fabled Ashlad, and Kristine Dahl, a woman from his own northern region of Norway who leaves him the violin once owned by her long-dead betrothed. But Nils, in spite of his dreams and visions, proves too weak for a life dedicated to art and is last seen working for the Great Northern Railway, wandering "from bridge to bridge, and city to city. Happening to get into a city of a Saturday night, he would immediately seek out the city's busiest corner; and there he would stand searching and searching, like a lone gull perched watchful on some bold headland round which the ocean current runs swift" (243). Those who became aware of the "sad and weary look" on his face wondered what "dreadful wrong" he must have committed. In 1921 the novel was presented as the first of two volumes, but Rølvaag never got around to writing the second one. The result is a novel that leaves the protagonist at large in America, much like Jimmy Herf at the end of Dos Passos's *Manhattan Transfer* (1925), yet another character of the 1920s too weak to realize his ideals and dreams.

Meanwhile his parents long for their lost son, who has ceased to write, and Jo sets off for America to search for him. But at Ellis Island he is turned away as an aging pauper, his only consolation coming from an elderly woman on the return voyage who believes she may indeed have "seen a young man in Minneapolis who was medium tall, light-complexioned, and had broad shoulders and blue eyes" (294–295). But Jo cannot live with his intense longing and one day he goes out to sea, rowing "farther and farther into the skyline, out to the Great Ocean itself" (304). His boat is never found.

The nineteen reviews in Rølvaag's scrapbook range from positive to superlative. In *Reform* Ager proclaimed: "Now we have a literature!" (3 Jan. 1922). With *The Boat of Longing* Rølvaag had completed his long apprenticeship. He had taken the original immigrant genre, the letter, and made art of it. He had taken the pious novel, a genre practiced by so many amateurs, and used it to explore new American themes. He had turned from idealism to naturalism and created anti-heroes of his own "race" in an American ethnic novel. He had explored the themes, images, and style he was making his own and demonstrated that the traditional on-both-sides-of-the-ocean story could be turned to new uses. Above all, as contributor of verse, short fiction, and articles to the numerous journals and newspapers of *Vesterheimen* and as a popular speaker at gatherings indoors and out in the Midwest, he had become a spokesman for Norwegian America. All this is what Lincoln Colcord, Rølvaag's co-translator of *Giants in the Earth*, called the "formidable background to the present picture," when he wrote to Harper & Brothers 9 March 1926 about the "new" author he had discovered in Northfield, Minnesota (OERP). Rølvaag was ready to write his great novel on the immigrant in America.

He might not have written it had he not been goaded into action by the news that Johan Bojer, then "the most widely-read foreign author in America" (Simonson 1987, 49), planned to visit the Midwest in preparation for a novel about Norwegian immigrants, a timely subject now that the 1925 centennial of Norwegian migration to the United States was drawing near. Rølvaag reacted as an American: a European could not write truly about so quintessentially American an experience. As it turned out, there was no competition between their two novels. Bojer's title may be translated "Our Own Tribe" (1924), demonstrating that he was more interested in the immigrants' origin than in the land of their choice, a point also underscored in the title of the translation, *The Emigrants* (1925). Bojer's novel not only focuses on the social conditions in Norway that brought about mass migration, but concludes with a lament on Norway's loss of so many of its young. Rølvaag, taking his cue from the Book of Genesis and the medieval Icelandic sagas, called his novel *Giants in the Earth: A Saga of the Prairie* and opened it with the bright sun above a covered wagon on a western plain stretching from horizon to horizon. It is soon apparent that Per Hansa, one of the two main characters, is an American in all but his northern dialect. Rølvaag's language, too, was Norwegian, and in order to reach a wider audience than the dwindling one of *Vesterheimen* he went to Oslo rather than to New York to find a publisher. Ironically, it was his Norwegian success with *I de dage* (1924, In those days) and its sequel *Riket grundlægges* (1925, The founding of the kingdom), that eventually made Americans aware of their "new" author. Rølvaag's initial attempts to establish a working relationship with a translator failed, as did his attempts to gain the attention of the Century Co. and Alfred A. Knopf.[5] Then came the serendipitous meeting with Lincoln Colcord that resulted in a contract with Harper & Brothers and their cooperative translation of the two Norwegian volumes into the American *Giants in the Earth*, published in 1927.[6] The next year the sequel, *Peder Seier*, appeared in Oslo and was published in New York in 1929 as *Peder Victorious*. In 1931, the year Rølvaag died, the trilogy was concluded with *Den signede dag*, translated as *Their Fathers' God*.

The trilogy spans the years from 1873, when Per Hansa and Beret Holm[7] are first seen crossing the prairies on their way from Fillmore county in southeastern Minnesota to the present Minnehaha county in South Dakota, to 1896, when their youngest son, Peder, runs for local office on the Republican ticket and is defeated and disillusioned. Earlier criticism sees Per Hansa as the hero of the first volume and his son Peder as the center of the other two. More recently, critics have recognized the importance of Beret. The most penetrating and profound reading has been offered by Harold Simonson, who by bringing the religious dimension of the trilogy to the fore makes a better book of the third volume than do critics who have primarily seen it as a didactic statement on cultural retention. Simonson suggests that in Beret, the woman with a troubled soul who nevertheless was said to be "the ablest farmer in the town of Spring Creek" (1929, 174), "Rølvaag mirrored his private self" (1987, 50). Although Simonson gives a compelling reading of the trilogy, it may be argued that there are problems in seeing Beret as the self-portrait of an author who gave his projected autobiography the title "Romance of a Life" (OERP). But while there is little that may qualify as romance in the bitter struggles of Beret or the broken dreams of her husband and her youngest son, the context of their misspent lives is the constantly growing settlement. The trilogy also tells the story of the territory that became a state. The land is built at great cost, "much more than money can ever pay," as Beret says on her deathbed

"The fullest, finest, and most powerful novel that has been written about pioneer life in America." —*The Nation*

GIANTS in the EARTH

O. E. RÖLVAAG

Cover of a recent paperback reprint of Giants in the Earth.
Courtesy of HarperCollins Publishers.

cost, "much more than money can ever pay," as Beret says on her deathbed (1931, 253), but it is built.

From beginning to end Per Hansa has his eyes on the West, metaphorically toward the future and also quite literally, whether searching the horizon on his way to his new land or, in death, staring emptily from a haystack where he has made a futile attempt to find protection against the raging snowstorm that takes his life. He is an American Adam: "A divine restlessness ran in his blood; he strode forward with outstretched arms toward the wonders of the future, already partly realized" (1927, 112). Per enters a land of opportunity; Beret is traveling "to the end of the world . . . beyond the end of the world" (8). As the coming night fills Beret's landscape "with terror" (10), the end of day simply brings the future that much closer for Per: "the sooner the day's over, the sooner the next day comes" (13). Arriving at the place they and their friends have selected, Beret is struck with the sense "that *here something was about to go wrong*" (28). Per, who sees not the untilled plain but "the new kingdom which they were about to found," is impatient to realize his dream: "Come on, woman, let's go over to our new home!" (32–33). Eventually, Per comes to recognize that his wife "has never felt at home here in America . . . There are some people, I know now, who never should emigrate, because, you see, they can't take pleasure in what is to come—they simply can't see it!" he confides to an itinerant minister (385). But his insight is at best a limited one, for he never comes to realize the dehumanizing consequences of living without history, of accepting the "spirit of America" voiced by his son's elementary-school teacher in the second volume, "that mighty force which had brought their parents out of bondage in the Old World, had flung wide the doors to this great land, and thereupon had invited the poor and the downtrodden to come and be happy in the beauty and promise of the New World [. . .] All previous history was finished, worn out like an old garment and discarded because no longer usable" (1929, 85–86). In the concluding volume a character uses the metaphor of the lotus-eaters when speaking to an uncomprehending Peder of a life without history: "they ate and ate, and just slept and ate [. . .] Until they forgot they were human beings. After that they lived in bliss and contentment all their days. But it was a sad sort of happiness, because they could never become human again!" (1931, 158).

At first, life seems bright for Per Hansa; all he touches is blessed by success. He is a man of luck, a *hamingjumadr*, to use a term from the saga literature of medieval Iceland, while his unhappy wife is burdened with *ógæfa*, un-luck or misfortune.[8] Per succeeds even when failure seems unavoidable, as when he is sure that the frost has taken his wheat. Not only does he find one Sunday morning that "over the whole field tiny green shoots were quivering in the warm sunshine" (1927, 306) but his precipitous early sowing makes it possible for him to harvest his wheat before the arrival of the devastating grasshoppers. But "how and why?" he reflects: "Hadn't they worked just as faithfully, hadn't they struggled just as hard—and with a great deal more common sense than he had shown? Why should they have to suffer this terrible calamity while he went scot-free?" (346). Ironically, however, the calamity does strike in his own home where the terror of the grasshopper-blackened skies leaves Beret in a psychotic state, hiding in a chest with one of their children. "Hasn't the devil got you yet?" she asks her husband when he finds her. "He has been all around here today" (348).

As the main public actor Per tends to upstage his wife. Moreover, he is a likable fellow, with an optimism that keeps his friends and neighbors from giving up in the face of adversity. Indeed, he has the *hamingjumadr*'s knack of turning adversity into opportunity, as when he not only succeeds in getting the Irish homesteaders to desist from claiming the land the Norwegians have settled on but sells "them more than ten dollars' worth of potatoes" (149). But there are serious flaws in his character, two of which are highlighted in the conflict with the Irish. When Per discovers stakes revealing that strangers had already claimed the land of one of his neighbors he decides to solve the problem by pulling them up and burning them, demonstrating an ethic that is at best utilitarian. When the crisis is over, the Irish have come and gone, and Per has revealed his secret to his friends, Beret puts a stop to their celebration with a biting comment: "Where I come from, it was always considered a shameful sin to destroy another man's landmarks. . . . But here, I see, people are proud of such doings" (154). Per had kept his knowledge of the stakes to himself, as he keeps his worries to himself from the very beginning: "You might have told me" (21), his wife reproaches him. Per, who has the potential for leadership, is too set on getting ahead to give service to his community priority. When he discovers new ways of building a sod house and then of whitewashing walls and ceiling, or when he makes money by trading with the Indians or invents a use of nets to catch ducks, he keeps it to himself. Hans Olsa is made uneasy by his friend's egocentric behavior: "When he had learned how a black earthen wall could be made shining white at so small a cost, why hadn't he told the others? There was so little cheer out here; they all sorely needed to share whatever they found." Later, congratulating his friend on his fine sod house, Hans Olsa admonishes him: "You shouldn't be vain in your own strength, you know!" Per, as has become his wont, merely makes fun of the warning (202–203). Beret, however, pines for spiritual nourishment in the sod house Per, to her dismay, has built for both man and beast and fears that "Everything human in them would gradually be blotted out" (188). For Per it is a practical matter, for Beret it is one of principle—of ethics and religion. God-fearing and guilt-ridden, Beret's concern is with eternity rather than with the future. Thus the relationship between these two who have so much love for each other comes to a standstill—Per fearing for Beret's mind, she for his soul.

A turning point comes with the visit of one of the unsung heroes of the frontier, the itinerant pastor or "buggy minister," as Kristofer Janson called him in one of his short stories. This unnamed clergyman, who in spite of misgivings of his own efficacy brings solace to the community at Spring Creek, is the most sympathetically portrayed of the many clergymen in Rølvaag's fiction. Implicit in his appearance is also the message that the period of isolation for the frontier settlement is drawing to a close and that the institutions they had left behind are catching up with them. The sod house of the Holms is the largest structure in the settlement and the natural place for divine service: "The minister stood in the corner next to the window, arrayed in full canonicals" (370), and he conducted "the full service just as if it had been in a real church." His sermon takes as its point of departure "the coming of the Israelites into the Land of Canaan" (372), which he applies to the migration of his congregation, giving a vision of their venture that transcends both Per's material and egocentric dream and Beret's bleak repudiation. When time comes for the baptism of the children born in the new settlement and the Holms's youngest child, Peder Victorious, is brought forth, "something extraordinary happened. From out that pale face over in the corner came a sound of anguish" and Beret suffers a breakdown, screaming that "This sin shall not happen! How can a man be *victorious* out here, where the evil one gets us all!" (378)

Two weeks and separate conversations with the Holms later, the minister returns to give a communion service but is weighed down by the awareness of his own frailty and lack of faith. Throughout his sermon he senses his inadequacy: "He had talked himself into complete bankruptcy respecting all things great and beautiful, without finding a message that seemed to apply here. [. . .] And all at once he did something that he had never done before in a Communion sermon—he told a story . . . " The story is of the immigrant widow Kari and her nine children who arrive in New York, ignorant of the language and without "a single friend in all America. When she landed, and saw the great throngs of people, and looked at the whirlpool of traffic, she got terribly frightened, poor soul! She had been told that in this foreign metropolis almost anything might happen to a mother coming alone with nine children; and so she had prepared herself in her own way. Around her waist was wound a long rope; this she now unrolled, tying all nine children to it in single file, but keeping the end still securely fastened around her waist. In this fashion Kari plodded through the streets of the great city, a laughingstock to all passers-by. But just the same, she reached her destination at last, with all her nine children safe and sound!" (405–406).[9] The more direct message to Beret as well as to Per is of their responsibility for each other as well as for their community.

Beret, cured of her illness though she is never to experience lightness of heart, and Per, his dream tarnished but intact, take up their lives and might have grown old and prosperous together had it not been for the crisis of their good friend Hans Olsa's illness and his appeal for help. Beret, fearing for his soul, convinces him that he must have a minister before he dies and there is no one in the settlement but Per who could possibly go the many miles through a Dakota snowstorm to fetch one. If it may seem that Beret sends her husband to his death, it should be remembered that Per has created an image of himself as invincible: had he not earlier driven many miles through an even more violent snowstorm until his oxen came to a stop right at the door of his destination? Hans's wife pleads for his help, insisting "we all have a feeling that nothing is ever impossible for you" (457). Hans, however, has earlier warned him of his *hubris*: "You shouldn't be vain in your own strength, you know!" It may even be suggested that Per deliberately chooses the path of destruction: before taking off he explains to his sons how the farm should be managed and how their barn should be designed. Be that as it may, he skis to his death and is not found until spring, sitting in a haystack as if "resting while he waited for better skiing . . . His face was ashen and drawn. His eyes were set toward the west" (465).

The author's manuscript in the University Library, Oslo, suggests that it was when he was revising his text that he became aware that the story was not to end with the death of Per Hansa. Harsh as the parting may seem between Beret and Per, Rølvaag added indications of reconciliation in the process of revision and deleted a passage proclaiming that "Here the record of these people of the West at Spring Creek and of their participation in the greatest settling in history comes to an end." Per, who "never would take help from any man," and who has been warned not to be vain in his "own strength," is cut out for the role of tragic hero in the first volume.

Beret has lived in the shadow of her charismatic husband and only after his death can the author explore her potential as a character.

Eternity remains Beret's main concern but two others emerge: history and community. The child Peder has little patience with his mother's Norwegian ways and is increasingly reluctant to use her language, but her most dramatic action for community values catches his attention. The setting is a meeting of the congregation, the issue is how to handle a minority who wish to withdraw and form a new one. Women do not have a vote, yet Beret asks permission to speak. "Never before had a woman talked at a congregational meeting" and many are convinced that her madness has returned. She speaks words of healing, of letting those who wish to leave do so in peace and friendship, and "she stood there admonishing them like a devoted mother." Peder is full of admiration:"when he was grown up he would preach so ... so ... well, so that every Mother's son of them would have to go the way he pointed!" (1929, 75–77). Neither his motive nor his attitude are those of his mother, however, and in spite of his oratorical and intellectual gifts he never achieves his youthful goal. As he unsuccessfully tries to convince a town meeting of the folly of paying a self-proclaimed rainmaker to end the long drought, he thinks that it is "Great sport to stand here teasing the monster" and his sarcasms hardly endear him to the desperate farmers (1931, 42). Nor would his final defeat after his bid for political office move the most softhearted of readers to tears. Peder seeks office less in order to serve his community than to further his own ambitions: he sides with the party he is advised will win, not the one he is inclined to support.

As a child Peder lives "in three rooms. Moving freely among them, he scarcely realized when he left the one and went into the other. Yet only in the one did he feel really at home and dare to let himself go [...] here he dreamed the future, built it; here he planned how he would do this thing and that, and how he would be the boss and set things to rights when he got to be a man [...] In this room he lived everything in English." The second room is the room of tradition that he shared with his family and where "he lived everything in Norwegian," while the third was "a dim, shadowy place, mysterious and secret, into which only God and he could come" (1929, 1–3). Peder's story is the story of how the third room atrophies, and the second becomes more and more sparse and poorly furnished, while the first comes to dominate to such a degree that his inner life as well as his relations with his wife and his mother suffer irreparable damage.

In the second volume the struggle for Peder's mind and soul is between Beret and, ironically, both school and church. That she would have to do battle with the great assimilator, the public school, is only natural. By one teacher Beret is urged to "send him to college" and to use only English at home so that Peder may learn to speak without an accent: "She had arisen and said, in broken English, that she considered it more important that the boy should learn to understand his own mother than that he should learn to talk nice!" (1929, 138) At a school dominated by the children of Norwegian settlers and taught by a Norwegian American, Peder faces a blackboard with the message: *"This is an American school; in work and play alike we speak English only!"* (155) Their pastor becomes deeply interested in Peder and he too tries to arrange for him to go to college. But he is an assimilationist who not only uses English as much as possible but even provides Peder with an English Bible. For Beret, religion and language are inseparable and she cannot but see the pastor's work to awaken Peder to his calling as yet another attempt to cut him off from his roots and take him away from her. While Beret may be able to hold her own against the institutions of church and school, she is helpless when confronted with the maturing sexuality of her son, who eventually settles his emotions on the Irish-American Susie Doheny, sister of his childhood friend Charley. In a powerful conclusion to the second volume Beret suffers a brief spell of her former psychosis and tries to set fire to the schoolhouse where she has seen her son and Susie embrace while rehearsing their roles as characters in a melodrama. She then becomes convinced that her main duty is to save Peder from her own youthful sin of premarital sex and let him marry the girl he loves: "Go and get yourself ready," she says to her bewildered son, "don't you hear me? . . . Later in the day they may not be home at Doheny's . . . I must see him at once!" (350). Thus Beret herself, however reluctantly, hastens a marriage that in claustrophobic self-destruction may be compared to that of Jim and Ella in O'Neill's *All God's Chillun Got Wings* (1924).

The omens for the married life of Susie and Peder are hardly favorable. Beret had warned her uncomprehending twelve-year-old against being too friendly with their Irish neighbors "Because you are Norwegian and they are Irish!" When Peder insists that "They are *people* just the same," his mother explains: "But they are of another kind. They have another faith. And that is dangerous. [. . .] And it is no better for them than it is for us. We should never have had the school together—you can't mix wheat and potatoes in the same bin" (113–114). As a child he is blithely innocent of ethnic or religious prejudice. As an adult his attitude is more programmatic: "You and I are Americans, Charley," he says to his brother-in-law. "Popes and kings don't mean a darn to us" (1931, 11). The question of whether being Americans is a sufficient basis for a shared identity is not the only doubt raised about the marriage of Peder and Susie. From one of his childhood sweethearts Peder picks up the Norwegian folktale image of "the end of the world" (1929, 297) as his way of thinking of his grand goals. When he joyously tells Susie that they are heading for "the end of the world," she is not ready to set out on such an adventure: "'I'd rather be here with you!' she begged timidly" (325). Peder is as full of schemes for the future as was his father, and as reticent. Neither his mother nor his wife is taken into his confidence and in his increasingly naturalistic and rationalistic speculations Peder isolates himself further from the women in his family.

Both Beret and Susie hold up family, tradition, and religion as counter-values to Peder's increasingly frenzied and self-absorbed pursuit of the future. But since their traditions and religions have different roots, they are opponents rather than allies in their struggle for Peder as well as for his son. Peder can see no reason to have his child baptized and always finds an excuse for delay when he is urged by either Beret or Susie. As a result, both have it done, according to their different rites, in secrecy. And baptism, a ritual of entry into the Christian community, becomes a divisive force, driving the two guilt-ridden women to mutual suspicion as well as to an increasingly desperate struggle for possession of the child. Fearing for the soul of their husband and son, and striving by their different lights to keep the family together, both Beret and Susie fall short of providing Peder with the spiritual nourishment his parched soul needs. In spite of her powerful sense of tradition, Beret knows little beyond her beloved language and her narrow Lutheranism, and Susie's religion is as narrow-minded as that of her mother-in-law.

The novel presents Peder with a third carrier of tradition, Nikoline, a character with a function similar to that of the Nigerian Asagai in Lorraine Hansberry's *A Raisin in the Sun* (1959). A newcomer from Rølvaag's own northern coast of Norway, Nikoline makes her entry midway in the third volume. She speaks not only of a Norway that is absent in Beret's traditions but of an America of which the American Peder is unaware: "She knew many of Mark Twain's stories by heart; when she began relating one of them and realized that Peder did not know who he was, she clapped her hands in surprise: 'Good heavens! You an American and haven't even heard of Mark Twain! What in the world do you learn in your schools over here?' Peder had tried to conceal his embarrassment by laughing it off, and had succeeded only moderately. . . . He was sure she was exaggerating; if this fellow Mark Twain was half as much as she said, he'd certainly have heard of

him!" (1931, 157)[10] Peder, whose marriage by this time is foundering, tells
Nikoline she "should have come sooner." "Why didn't you come and get
me?" she teasingly responds, and when Peder keeps up the flirtatious tone
and explains that he could not have known "there was such a lovely, lonely
little rose waiting for" him in Norway, there is an accusatory edge to Nikoline's counter question: "Why didn't you come and look? It's your father's
country" (158).

As Peder's life becomes more barren and as he compensates with schemes
of material and political success, a clergyman, the Reverend Kaldahl, whose
"English was downright terrible" (205), also points to a way in which pride
in origin may be combined with pride in America. He dominates conversation at a Christmas party on the Holm farm, lecturing on the greatness of
Norwegian history and exhorting his listeners to hold on to their traditions
if they want to take part in the building of the nation and not merely go
into the building like "dead timber." Peder is increasingly irritated and
rudely exclaims: "We're Americans here!" But the pastor insists that it is as
Norwegians that they must be Americans, holding up the Jews as example.
Then he lectures on the most potent of the homemaking myths of *Vester-
heimen*, explaining how American institutions and American ideals have
Norwegian roots, either via the Puritans, who came from that part of
England where the Norwegians "exerted their greatest influence," or via
Normandy, where the lords came from who created the Magna Charta
(207–211).[11]

But all of this comes too late for Peder, who is set on his path to "the
end of the world" and who a few days later accepts the call to enter politics
and take a place on the Republican ticket: "To-night the Call had laid a
hand on his shoulder and spoken clearly, unmistakably, determining his
course from now on. . . . And this was only the beginning! Hereafter he
would be thinking and planning for the welfare of a whole county. . . . Sit in
council with older men and show them ways and means that they themselves had never thought of [. . .] Did he possess the gift to lead others? The
loud *yes* that rose from his soul forced him to drive faster" (214). Allowing
his choice of party to be guided by expediency is his *hamartia*; assuming he
will come out on top is his *hubris*. Surely the reader may expect this hero's
fall! Indeed, Peder's fall is private as well as public and in the end he sits
alone, deserted by his wife and with his political career shattered before it
gets started.

Beret dies before all falls apart and on her deathbed she thinks of the future of their farm as had her husband on the day he set off into the snow-

storm. Her overriding concern is that the farm they had created should remain in the family. But she also has to unburden her soul of her sense of guilt for having baptized her grandson in secrecy: "Oh, oh, Susie . . . have you . . . forgiveness for me?" she asks in anguish, and as her last living word is "Susie!" her daughter-in-law lies upstairs in a rage. Afterward the gulf widens between Peder, whose basic premise is "what difference did it make," and Susie, who believes her child's soul has been stolen (258–262). Peder's attempts at reconciliation are as charged with expediency as is his entry into politics, where he gets to see the folly in believing that being Americans together is more meaningful than ethnic solidarity. Forced to choose between loyalty to her Norwegian-American husband and her Irish-American family, Susie casts her lot with her own blood and reveals the most intimate details of their troubled marriage to the Democratic opposition. Peder has heard rumors of a campaign slogan that "no self-respecting Irish Catholic would ever disgrace himself by voting for a Norwegian Lutheran," but turning up at a Democratic campaign meeting, he is totally unprepared for the mudslinging oratory of his opponent, whose revelations could only have had Susie as their source: "He had dragged himself over to the wall so that he could lean against it; he had to steady himself because his knees would no longer carry him. A feeling of nausea had come over him, he wanted to vomit but could not; worst of all was the dizziness, everything inside his head was whirling around and around; he saw things and heard things which he knew were impossible . . . they were not there, couldn't be there, and it bothered him that he couldn't get rid of them" (333). At home he himself commits an act which is even more despicable than his wife's, and her reaction is no less traumatic than his had been. After Peder "slowly, deliberately" and with a "cold grin" on his face has broken and crushed Susie's crucifix and rosary with his boot heel, he leaves his wife alone in their room: "Dumb-faced, Susie sat staring at the door; her eyes were unnaturally big; but there was a silly grin on her face as if she had seen into horror itself, was seeing it yet and could not believe it; from her throat rose gurglings, as if she were trying to laugh, had to laugh, and could not get the laughter out. Her head began to droop and she sank over in a swoon" (336–337). When Peder awakens the next morning Susie and their son have left: "I've been to the End of the World and have found out what it looks like," reads her note. "I'll never go near there again, because it is an accursed place" (338).

The *Vesterheimen* experienced by Peder Victorious, the childhood "second room he shared with his mother" and his family where "he lived everything in Norwegian," was too confined and too sparsely furnished a space for his growth and development. Even as a child he was not happy there "because all was so ordinary" (1929, 1–3). With the environment and role models provided in *Peder Victorious* and the first half of *Their Fathers' God,* Peder can hardly be expected to feel at home in *Vesterheimen,* the ethnic culture of which his creator was a driving force. Not only does his road to the Golden Gate lead to spiritual and intellectual bankruptcy, but an America without ethnicity also proves an illusion. Before she returns to Norway, Nikoline tries to explain to Peder the difference between what she calls *hilder,* "the magic mirror" of the imagination, and a blinding illusion: "We know when we see *hilder;* we can tell it and make allowance. You Americans believe all you see until you run your heads against a stone wall; then you don't believe anything any more" (235). But Peder understands this as little as he does her parting admonition "that Success and Happiness don't live on the same road! Why don't you use your magic mirror? If you want the one, give up seeking the other" (313). Peder wants both and is left with emptiness.

Nikoline speaks of her home, but Norway is not a home for the American Peder. The Reverend Kaldahl speaks of a Norwegian America with much the same fervor as did Rølvaag when he wrote the essays that went into his 1922 book *On Our Ancestral Heritage.* But less than a decade later it would seem that Rølvaag no longer believed in the viability of the culture whose prophet he had been: his main efforts are aimed at a national rather than an ethnic audience. Indeed, in the last year of his life he toyed with the idea of making English his language as a writer and the fragments he completed of his autobiography, "Romance of a Life," are in English (Haugen 1983, 117). Although Ole Edvart Rølvaag may be seen as breaking out of the narrow confines of *Vesterheimen* with *Giants in the Earth* in 1927, he never, as did his ironically named anti-hero Peder Victorious, turned his back on it. His work is the most valuable literary contribution of *Vesterheimen,* its main offering to the multi-ethnic national literature of the United States.

NOTES

1. Jorgenson and Solum (1939), Gvåle (1962), Reigstad (1972), and Haugen (1983). Valuable critical studies are Thorson (1957 and 1975) and Simonson (1987).

2. Written in a copy of *Paa glemte veie* in this author's possession.

3. *Pure Gold* is not merely a translation but a revised text. The Oslo edition, *Rent guld*, is a translation of *Pure Gold*, making it the only Rølvaag novel in Norwegian translation.

4. Ellipses in Rølvaag quotations are indicated [...], since " ... " is frequently used as punctuation by Rølvaag.

5. See correspondence in OERP, for example from the American-Scandinavian Foundation 14 Oct. 1924, from Jessie Muir 6 April and 11 Sept. 1925, and from Knopf 14 Sept. 1925.

6. Accounts of Rølvaag's response to Bojer, his sabbatical, his use of his wife's family for information on the pioneer experience, his visit to Norway and acceptance by Aschehoug, his meeting with Colcord and the resulting translation may be found in Jorgensen 1939, Gvåle 1962, Reigstad 1972, Paulson 1977, and Haugen 1983. Reigstad's introduction to the 1978 reprint of Bojer's *The Emigrants* compares it with Rølvaag's novel. *The Emigrants* is a sequel to *Dyrendal* (1919), which has emigration as a subsidiary theme.

7. Hansa is a dialect patronymic. Holm, a place name, is their shared family name.

8. For a discussion of these Old Norse terms see Sveinsson 1959.

9. Rølvaag may have remembered this anecdote from one of the novels of H.A. Foss, *Den amerikanske saloon*, or it may have circulated in various versions in *Vesterheimen*. Early in the Foss novel the protagonist, on arriving in New York, takes a rope and ties it around the waists of his children and then of himself before venturing with his wife into the city.

10. Rølvaag had surely read R.B. Anderson's account of his embarrassing confrontation with Bjørnson, when he, an American, had to admit ignorance of Whitman (1915, 160–161).

11. This was a favorite topic of the author, who spoke in a similar vein to his students as well as to audiences throughout *Vesterheimen* (see Kristine Haugen on Rølvaag's 17 May speech in Sioux City, *NU* June 1926, 95). Early expressions of this myth are in R.B. Anderson's *America Not Discovered By Columbus* (1877) and Foss's *Hvite slaver* (1892).

Coda

Carl M. Roan, a physician who had published popular books on health care, wrote a book about his visit to the country of his parents in 1921. Here he explains the strange attraction of this country that he had never seen: "Born in America of Norwegian parents, growing up with the powerful influence of Norwegian immigration and educated at schools strongly influenced by the culture and civilization of the Old World . . . and having lived most of my days among immigrants . . . all this has had a part in creating this longing" (93). Roan still writes in Norwegian. Nevertheless, it is his visit to Norway that has made him come to the realization that the immigrant culture he has depended on has kept him from setting down his roots in his own country. Accepting the value of the immigrant culture and its necessary function in the past, he has now come to the conclusion that its period of usefulness is over and that "as a good and faithful servant who can no longer continue to serve," it should now retire (129, 131). But *Vesterheimen* was not quite ready for retirement in 1921. Indeed, its greatest achievements were yet to come.

The following year Waldemar Ager saw the publication of Rølvaag's *Boat of Longing* as a cause for celebration: "Now we have a literature!" he proudly announced to the readers of *Reform* on 3 January 1922. But as the literature of *Vesterheimen* was reaching maturity in the second and third decades of the twentieth century, outside events were laying down the conditions for its rapid decline and termination. Immigration from Europe came to a virtual stop with the First World War. In the years after the war a political process that John Higham (1963) has called "closing the gates," was concluded with Coolidge's signing of the Johnson-Reed Act 26 May 1924.

A quota law based on the 1890 census may indeed have been the "Nordic victory" announced by the Los Angeles *Times* (Higham 300), but Norway's share of immigrants to the United States could probably not have been sustained regardless of restrictions at the high level of the first fourteen years of the century, when an average of about 15,000 entered the country. While "the quota laws of 1921 and 1924 greatly reduced the flow" of immigrants from Norway, economic factors in Norway "produced a radical decline" in the 1930s (Lovoll 1984, 29). Immigration statistics alone, however, do not explain the drastic reduction in the use of the Norwegian language in publications as well as in the largest of all Norwegian immigrant institutions, their churches, in the course of the 1920s. For while the United States Bureau of Statistics figures show a gradual decline in the number of Norwegian-born Americans from 403,877 in 1910 to 363,863 in 1920 and 347,852 in 1930, the statistics of the Norwegian Lutheran Church in America show a far more rapid decline in the use of Norwegian for church services after the First World War. In 1917, 73.1 percent of all services were in Norwegian, by 1925 more than half the services were in English, and in 1930 only 37.1 percent were in Norwegian. The use of Norwegian for the instruction of the young declined even more rapidly and had "practically ceased" by 1928 (Haugen 1953, 262–263).

The natural process of Americanization was taking its toll on *Vesterheimen*. *Reform* continued publication with a dwindling number of subscribers until Ager's death in 1941. *Skandinaven* in Chicago gave up its daily edition in 1930, while the weekly survived another eleven years. *Minneapolis Tidende* closed its daily edition in 1932 and ceased to exist as a weekly three years later. Of the larger publications founded in the 1870s and 1890s *Decorah-Posten* was a lone survivor when it published its last issue in 1972, merging with *Western Viking,* which at the moment of writing still appears weekly in Seattle.

As they experienced a loss of audience through decreasing immigration and increasing Anglicization, Norwegian-American writers were also becoming acutely aware that their medium, the language itself, was in a process of disintegration. This linguistic disintegration took many forms, most of them unavoidable aspects of the transitional nature of immigrant cultures, one of them peculiar to the history of the Norwegian language. With Norwegian independence from Denmark in 1814, the written language of the new country remained Danish. As the national confidence grew and found expression in politics, scholarship, the arts, and literature, the need for a written language more related to the Norwegian vernacular

than the Danish that had served Ibsen and other nineteenth-century writers (who had continued to publish in Copenhagen) found two different responses in the second half of the nineteenth century. One was through the
work of the autodidact Ivar Aasen, who created the grammar and the first
dictionary for a written norm based on rural dialects, the other through the
language reforms of Knud Knudsen, who urged spelling reforms that
would bring the originally Danish written language closer to the speech of
educated urban Norwegians (Haugen 1953, 104–108, 154–155). It was in
particular the consequences of the latter, a series of language reforms that
gradually changed the character of written Norwegian, that caused problems in *Vesterheimen*.

After the success of the Norwegian edition of Rølvaag's *Giants in the
Earth* it was only natural that *Decorah-Posten* should secure serialization
rights. But as he began editing the book for serialization in January 1927,
Kristian Prestgard realized that he had a problem on his hands. For not only
had the St. Olaf professor written his novel with full awareness of current
usage in Norway, he had shown himself to be in the vanguard of Norwegian authors who sought to flavor their written language with the vocabulary and constructions of dialect and colloquial Norwegian. Prestgard feared
that an unedited version would cause an uproar among his subscribers, who
had protested a proposed switch from black letter to Roman type just a few
months earlier. Would Rølvaag object, Prestgard asked, to some changes in
his spelling? (3 Feb. LC).

Rølvaag was one of the few writers of *Vesterheimen* whose language was
not out of touch with current usage in Norway. As professor of Norwegian
he was not only well read in contemporary Norwegian literature but had,
with his elder colleague P.J. Eikeland, written a handbook for students on
spelling and pronunciation (1916) based on the officially adopted standard
of 1907. The language of his contemporaries, Dahl, Johnson, Wist, and others, follows the norm of an earlier generation. The capitalization of nouns
was for instance abandoned in 1877, but is still the norm in Simon Johnson's *I et nyt Rige* in 1914. While church publications adopted the 1907 reforms in 1916 (*Jul i Vesterheimen*) and 1917 (*Lutheraneren*), the major secular
newspapers held to the older spelling, more afraid of offending their old
subscribers than of not appealing to the decreasing number of new immigrants (Haugen 142–145). In 1929 Nicolay A. Grevstad, editor of *Skandinaven*, wrote in English to Kristian Prestgard of *Decorah-Posten*: "Do you believe the time is come for the three leading Norwegian papers in this
country to get a little more in line with the common usage in Norway in

the matter of spelling and types? As it is they are way behind the times in this respect. If they were to agree upon making the same changes simultaneously, no one of them would run any risks on this account, while all of them would stand to gain. Would you favor a discussion of this matter at a meeting of representatives of Decorah-Posten, Skandinaven and Minneapolis Tidende, at Chicago or some other convenient place? Kindly favor me with a few lines on this subject, to be considered as confidential if you please . . . " (7 Jan. KPP) Nothing came of this, and Grevstad's extreme caution in even suggesting the possibility of change speaks of how strongly the majority of the inhabitants of *Vesterheimen* identified themselves with a language that would strike most of their Norwegian contemporaries as quaintly old-fashioned. Language conservation, which many had regarded as the *sine qua non* of a Norwegian-American identity, had become one of the many factors that marginalized *Vesterheimen*, making it seem irrelevant from the perspective of Norway.

But while such external features as spelling, capitalization, and black-letter type were retained, the language of *Vesterheimen* was as naturally prone to change and development as any other language. To varying degrees American speakers of Norwegian were influenced by the dominant language of their environment in syntax, vocabulary, and idiom, and this was a far more important factor than antiquated spelling in distancing their language from that of their European relatives. For while their linguistic conservatism made them appear quaint, their Americanisms or Anglicisms made them appear ridiculously ignorant, unable to speak their own language correctly. From another point of view, the use of loan words and new idioms may be considered an indication of linguistic flexibility and an adaptation to new surroundings necessary for linguistic survival. But the standards of correct language and good style are set in the centers of a culture, not on its margins.

Even the best writers were influenced by this development. Wist, reflecting on the language of Norwegian-American literature in 1921, reminded his readers that this was "not primarily a *Norwegian* literature, but an *American* one—admittedly in Norwegian, as literary Norwegian may be written outside of Norway, but nevertheless essentially American." His concern was that this literature was becoming more and more isolated and that it would disappear from sight, forgotten along with the Norwegian language in the United States and disregarded in Norway: "These books are adapted to the needs of an immigrant people, a people in transition from one nation to another. The literary needs of such a people and their standard of style and narrative are naturally different from those of an older and more literary culture" (*DP* 4 Oct.).

The following year, Buslett wrote an article on "Literatur og 'Mixing'" in *Decorah-Posten* on the occasion of the completion of Wist's trilogy: "Of course we mix [languages]. How can intelligent people who understand the nature of literature imagine that real people may be portrayed accurately in print without the use of the language they speak?" As if to underline his point, he uses the English word "mixing," the standard Norwegian-American term for code switching. Buslett's essay is informed by his sense of the rapidly approaching end of the literature he has devoted so much of his life to creating and his recognition that his work would disappear along with American readers of Norwegian. As so often in these years, Buslett is urging the establishment of an author-owned publishing agency in Norway as a way of ensuring the survival of Norwegian-American literature. Wist, too much the realist to have much faith in such a venture, nevertheless shared Buslett's concern with Norwegian attitudes to the language of *Vesterheimen*: "Our mixed language has developed quite naturally." But even though there is a tendency in Norway to look down on this phenomenon, "we have no right to insist that this mixed language is Norwegian." Moreover, he adds, "it should not surprise us that Norwegian reviewers at times find that Norwegian-American Norwegian is impoverished, awkward, and abundant in Anglicisms, even when we try not to mix languages. It is regrettably all too true that much of the Norwegian written here is not the spontaneous and living Norwegian spoken and written in Norway today. This said with all respect for our own writers. What else should we expect? We live far away from the Norwegian-speaking society and are constantly exposed to influences that lead us away from the essence of a Norwegian national culture" (*DP* 26 Dec. 1922). Much the same point had been made by Eikeland and Rølvaag in their 1916 textbook on Norwegian spelling in a note to a chapter "On Anglicisms": "In the Norwegian spoken and written in this country, Anglicisms are naturally becoming more and more frequent with every passing year" (94). It should not surprise us that writers, many of whom had come to the United States as young children and who had little or no formal education in Norwegian, should not be exempt from this development. In 1917 an editor at Augsburg Publishing House had written to Dorthea Dahl accepting her first book for publication but insisting that the many errors in language "in particular in the use of prepositions" would have to be corrected. Ironically, his typewriter did not have the Norwegian characters "æ" and "ø" (Ole Glesne Papers, NAHA). Wist had thought that

Rølvaag was an exception to the rule, but, as Haugen observes, even he "certainly did not escape" Americanisms (153).

As political, social, and economic factors were closing the gates on the influx of new inhabitants necessary for the transitional *Vesterheimen* to make up for the constant stream that from the beginning had left it for more permanent homes in the larger American society, the language itself, the vital center of this culture, was suffering from atrophy and erosion. In spite of this development, however, *Vesterheimen* in the 1920s still appeared so vital and interesting that a relatively new type of immigrant, the young educated man and woman in search of further education or employment in a profession, could be attracted to playing an active role in its literature. A group of such immigrants were behind the last and most interesting of the many Norwegian-American literary journals, *Norden*, published from December 1928 to May 1933 by the Norwegian Literary Society of Chicago. It could have been expected that they would go the way of Karsten Roedder in New York, who in 1926 had launched the literary magazine *Symra* as an alternative to the culture of *Vesterheimen* for the sophisticated and urbanized post-World War One immigrant. Instead, the ambitious group of young Chicagoans deliberately placed themselves in a Norwegian-American rather than a Norwegian and American tradition and created an outlet not only for themselves but for Gundersen, Ager, Dahl, Norstog, Johnson, Bratager, Rølvaag, and others. Considering the question of what language the journal should use (Nov. 1930, 10), the editor takes a pragmatic view, observing that for immigrants whose main concern is business, English will very soon become the natural language, while those whose interests are of a cultural and literary nature will be spiritually crippled if the transition is too rapid. Consequently, the editor concludes both that *Norden* for many years will have to use Norwegian as its main language and that it would be best "that Norwegian-American literature have as independent a development as possible." It was in the penultimate issue of *Norden* that Waldemar Ager—of all people—announced "The Last Chapter" (Dec. 1932, 11–12) of the literature he ten years earlier had declared had arrived.

Norwegian-American culture, wrote Ager, was in its third and last phase. It was the aging middle generation, who had been inspired by the nineteenth-century national cultural renaissance of the old country and had brought with them a sense of pride in their heritage, that had built the institutions of *Vesterheimen*. Ager saw three main reasons for the decline of Norwegian-American culture in the third phase: improved communications that had brought settlements out of their isolation, immigration re-

Vesterheim, the Norwegian-American Museum, Decorah, Iowa.
Courtesy Vesterheim, the Norwegian-American Museum.

strictions, and the nativist hysteria in the wake of the First World War. To
the embittered Ager, who had been critical of the Norwegian-American
Historical Association, this phase is characterized by "an academic national
movement": "While the first generation of American-born Norwegian
Americans were primarily concerned with the making of history, the second and third seem satisfied with writing down the exploits of their fathers.
This, then, seems to be the completion of the chapter the Norwegians
wrote or sought to write in the history of the United States. We have
packed our bags and prepared ourselves for the melting pot and our extinction in the motley mass." Although Ager is not willing to admit to the
necessity of this development and points to ways in which the Norwegian
language may yet be preserved in the United States, he has obviously lost
faith in the cause for which he worked all his life. His essay concludes with
observations on crowded old-people's homes and an Americanized generation of Norwegian Americans who no longer can fit the old into their
lives. "Old-people's homes and nameless graves will then perhaps become
the concluding chapter of the greatest Norwegian adventure — our massive
participation in the conquest of the Northwest."[1]

But even had Ager's dream of linguistic survival beyond his own genera-

Nordic Heritage Museum, Seattle, Washington. Vesterheimen must now be sought in museums and archives. Courtesy Nordic Heritage Museum.

tion been realizable, language alone would not have been sufficient to sustain a viable literary culture. Rølvaag's spelling was not the only problem Prestgard had in editing the Norwegian version of *Giants in the Earth* for serialization in *Decorah-Posten*. The language of his characters was not at all times delicate enough for the tastes—real or imagined—of the newspaper's readers; nor did these characters always behave in ways to demonstrate the superior attributes and achievements of the race. A degree of bowdlerization was required for serialization. Prestgard, an enlightened journalist and literary critic, was not free to follow his own tastes and inclinations. As the editor of one of the major newspapers of *Vesterheimen* and, moreover, the only one with fiction as a regular and substantial feature, Prestgard often had to perform a delicate balancing act, making necessary compromises between what was required to keep the newspaper going and what was required to make this worth the effort. In 1926, the year before he edited *Giants in the Earth* for serialization, he had written to Antonette Tovsen regretting that he could not accept her "Nordens sommernat" for serialization, not because he did not think highly of her work, but because it would not suit the conservative taste of his subscribers. Unable to place her story in his own newspaper, he offered to help her place it in *Nordisk Tidende* in New York or in some other journal (10 Sept. LC).

Prestgard's cosmetics, however, could not make Rølvaag palatable to the many who were striving for the acceptance of their ethnic group by living up to the cultural doctrines of midwestern towns and churches. That a writer who demonstrated an awareness of the procreative process and whose characters used swear words should also be professor at a Lutheran college was both an added affront and an opportunity for action. The last few years of Rølvaag's life were not only crowned by success, they were also clouded by attacks questioning his moral integrity and his fitness for service as a teacher of the young in a church institution. Such attacks came to a head in the spring of 1930 and when it seemed that they would be given voice at the church council Rølvaag offered his resignation to the college president, the Reverend Lars Wilhelm Boe. Boe, however, who though he admitted that he himself was still "a child of the training I have had, both in regard to introducing 'cuss' words and the sex proposition," made it clear to Rølvaag, who had ceased to teach for reasons of health and was spending the winter and early spring in Biloxi, Mississippi, that he, too, would have to resign should Rølvaag feel pressured to do so: "The issue will have to be fought out and if the day should come that the Church says that you and I will have to go, you because of what you write, I because of the fact that I stand for a freedom which they do not understand, we should go."[2] They both weathered the attack.

But Rølvaag remained unacceptable to the augurs of taste in the last phase of *Vesterheimen*. A few months after his death a meeting of the Twin City Norwegian Literary Society denounced him for misrepresenting Norwegian Americans. The speaker on this occasion was, as so often, a clergyman, Gustav Marius Bruce, who "observed that there is a tendency among some of our Norwegian-American authors to sully their characters and . . . find a boyish pleasure in doing this. Then they defend themselves by calling themselves 'realists.' . . . In particular, the speaker regretted that Norwegian men and women in America for all time, whether they wished it or not, were sentenced to be represented by such paper men and women as Per Hansa and Beret, whose saga had been presented as the Saga of Norwegian Americans." In the discussion that followed, at the meeting as well as in the columns of *Minneapolis Tidende* and *Skandinaven*, most agreed with Bruce, and the secretary of the society questioned whether a lone defender of the author would have been willing to read some passages from Rølvaag's work "in mixed company."[3]

"So what?" one might legitimately ask. A handful of philistines and conservative clergy do not make or break a culture. The storm around Rølvaag was on a small scale compared to the storm that surrounded another Minnesota writer, Sinclair Lewis, in particular when his portrait of life in the Midwest was given the stamp of international approval with the Nobel Prize in 1930. But while such attacks hardly mattered to a writer who had turned his back on the people he portrayed and who looked for approval among the liberal urban intelligentsia, they could be crippling to writers who had dedicated their life's work to the very people who were unable to appreciate them and whose cultural centers were on the margins of the mainstream literary culture. And this marginal culture could be no less crippling to writers who more or less adopted its premises and points of view. In his last years Rølvaag was attempting the impossible: to follow the dictates of his creative conscience and to serve his marginalized ethnic culture. In *Norden* he criticized the prejudice and ignorance of those who had cried out against awarding the Nobel Prize to Lewis: "One thing they have achieved: to demonstrate for the entire world that Lewis has given an accurate satirical portrait of America as a society of Babbitts." Who else among living American authors may match his achievement, he rhetorically asked, suggesting some runners-up, in particular "Ernest Hemingway: but he is yet too young and has not written enough to be considered" for the prize (Feb. 1931, 4–5).

He did not mention any writer of *Vesterheimen* as worthy of such international recognition (although he did find the Swedish-American Carl Sandburg a worthy candidate). As *Vesterheimen* was losing its language and shrinking in size year by year, no new writers appeared who could pick up the mantles worn with varying degrees of elegance and dignity by Johnson, Dahl, Norstog, Wist, Ager, and Rølvaag. Had they appeared, moreover, they would have had to seek their readership outside *Vesterheimen*, either in Norway or in the United States itself. The literature of the Western Home had become a closed chapter that has yet to become accepted as a chapter in the literary history of their chosen home.

These writers were in a sense as transitional as the culture that defined them and that they also had helped to create. This does not, however, diminish their achievement. Nor does it diminish the significance of their work. In the course of a few generations the writers of *Vesterheimen* made of their native Norwegian an American literary language, a language in which they could express American experience to an American audience. In so doing they collectively created a record of the emotional and social life of one ethnic group on its way from being migrant Europeans to integrated, indeed largely indistinguishable members of American society. The literature of *Vesterheimen* may be a closed chapter in the sense that the transition has been completed, and "Vesterheim" survives as the name of a museum. But not only is this transition at the very heart of American history, it is a history that continues to be written as immigrants continue to enter the United States seeking better lives and in the process create their transitional cultures in their American languages. The literary history of the "Western Home" of one group may thus enter into and inform our understanding of a larger American pattern.

Without the literary histories of the many western or eastern homes of immigrants and their descendants the literary history of the United States will remain partial and incomplete.

NOTES

1. *Vesterheimen* was of course as dependent on the American economy as the rest of the country. *Norden* did not survive the depression of the early 1930s. The necessary advertisements ceased to appear, subscribers, in particular in Chicago itself, were unable to pay, and the editor, whose own salary in the outside world where he made his living had been reduced by 45 percent, could no longer take the financial responsibility for continued publication. See *DP* 19 May 1933 and letter from the editor, C.F. Berg, to Prestgard 14 June 1933, KPP.

2. The correspondence in March 1930 (OERP) on ecclesiastical attacks on Rølvaag that surfaced at a church meeting in Milwaukee has not been referred to by Rølvaag's biographers. Boe writes in English. The first quotation is from a letter to D.G. Ristad 21 March, the second from a letter to Rølvaag 26 March.

3. The report is in *Sk* 15 March 1932. It was also printed in *MT* where the issue was debated 9 and 16 June. Further correspondence on this debate, clippings, and information on the Literary Society are in the G.M. Bruce Papers, NAHA.

References

A. Abbreviations and Usage

A—*Aftenposten* (Oslo).

Anderson; The John Anderson Publishing Co.—See *Sk*.

Anundsen; The B. Anundsen Publishing Co.—See *DP*.

AP—Author's Publisher.

Aschehoug—H. Aschehoug & Co.

Augsburg—Augsburg Publishing House.

B—*Budstikken* (Minneapolis).

DGRP—Ditlef Georgson Ristad Papers, NAHA.

DP—*Decorah-Posten* (Decorah, Iowa), including its literary supplement *Ved Arnen*. Also used to indicate the newspaper's publisher, The B. Anundsen Publishing Co.

DS—*Duluth Skandinav* (Duluth, Minnesota).

E—*Emigranten* (Inmansville and Madison, Wisconsin).

Ei—*Eidsvold* (Grand Forks and Fargo, North Dakota).

ELK—*Evangelisk Luthersk Kirketidende* (Decorah, Iowa).

F—*Fædrelandet* (La Crosse, Wisconsin).

FB—*Folkebladet* (Minneapolis).

FM—*Familiens Magasin* (Minneapolis). On superseding *UV* in 1916, *FM* began with Vol. 1, but from 1921 volumes were counted as a continuation of *UV*.

FogE—*Fædrelandet og Emigranten* (La Crosse, Wisconsin, and Minneapolis).

Fremad—Fremad Publishing Company.

H—*Husbibliothek*, a supplement to *Sk*.

Holter—K.C. Holter Publishing Co.

HT—*Herald Tribune*.

IF—*Illustreret familieblad* (Chicago).

IU—*Illustreret ugeblad* (Chicago and Minneapolis).

JAJP—John A. Johnson Papers, NAHA.

JBBP—Julius B. Baumann Papers, NAHA.

JiV—Jul i Vesterheimen (Minneapolis). No pagination before 1939.

KGP—Knut Gjerset Papers, NAHA.

KM—Kirkelig Maanedstidende (Inmansville and Madison, Wisconsin, and Decorah, Iowa).

KPP—Kristian Prestgard Papers, NAHA.

Kriedt—Waldemar Kriedt Publishing Company.

Kv—Kvartalskrift (Eau Claire, Wisconsin).

KvM—Kvindens Magasin (Minneapolis).

L—Lutheraneren (Minneapolis).

LC—Luther College Library.

M—Morgenbladet (Oslo).

MT—Minneapolis Tidende (including *Daglig Tidende* and *Søndag Tidende*.

MTCP—*Minneapolis Tidende* Clipping File, NAHA.

N—Normanden (Fargo, North Dakota).

NAHA—Norwegian-American Historical Association.

NAS—Norwegian-American Studies.

NF—Nordmanns-Forbundet (Oslo).

No—Norden (a newspaper, Chicago 1874–1897; a literary journal, Chicago 1928–1933).

NSP—Det norske selskab Papers, NAHA.

NT—Nordisk Tidende (NY).

NU—Norsk Ungdom (Chicago).

OABP—Ole Amundsen Buslett Papers, NAHA.

OERP—Ole Edvart Rølvaag Papers, NAHA.

OGP—Oscar Gundersen Papers, NAHA.

OJSP—Ola Johann Særvold Papers, NAHA.

POSP—Peer O. Strømme Papers, NAHA.

R:—Reviews

R—Reform (Eau Claire, Wisconsin).

Rasmussen—C. Rasmussen Forlagsboghandel.

RBAP—Rasmus B. Anderson Papers, Wisconsin Historical Society.

Relling—I.T. Relling & Co.

SJP—Simon Johnson Papers, NAHA.

Sk—Skandinaven (Chicago). References are to the weekly/semi-weekly edition. Also used to indicate the newspaper's publisher, The John Anderson Publishing Company.

UV—Ungdommens Ven (Minneapolis).

VT—Vor Tid (Minneapolis).

WAP—Waldemar Ager Papers, NAHA.

WP—Washington-Posten (Seattle, Washington).

Genres are indicated in parenthesis at the end of each entry in the bibliography:

A—anthology

B—biography

E—essay(s)/arcticle(s)/non-fiction
F—fiction
G—guide
H—history
HB—handbook
J—juvenile fiction
M—memoirs, autobiography
N—novel
P—play
S—story/stories
SF—serialized fiction
T—travel
Text—text book
V—verse

/ separates the two years of publication for the original and the translation: 1924/1926.

* indicates that the book has not been located.

For reviews published the same year as the text the year is not repeated in the bibliographical entry.

A pseudonym is given in parentheses immediately after the date of publication.

Æ,æ—alphabetized as "ae"

Ø,ø—alphabetized as "o"

Å,å—alphabetized as "a"

B. Selected Bibliography of Norwegian-American Texts

A., J. 1852. "For Emigranten." *E* 30 April. (V)
Aabak, Iver. n.d. *Sigurd Solvatn.* Decorah: AP. 75pp. (N)
Aanrud, Mona. 1947. "Jul er jul." *JiV*, 7–11. (S)
——. 1948. "Glade jul." *JiV*, 28–32. (S)
Ager, Waldemar. 1894. *Paa drikkeondets konto.* Eau Claire: AP. 126pp. Illustrated by Ben Blessum. Also 1897, 1898, and as *Blade af en dagbog. Fortællinger og vers,* 1909. R: *R* 27 Nov. (Skordalsvold); *Normannen* 30 Nov. (Buslett); 7 Dec. (Iversen); *Sk* 19 Dec.; *B* 26 Dec. (Gundersen); *R* 16 Jan., 5 March 1895 (extracts from reviews); *DP* 31 Dec. 1897. (S&V)
——. 1899. *I strømmen.* Eau Claire: Fremad. 190pp. Also 1908. Serialized in *R* 12 Oct. 1907–24 March 1908. R: *R* 27 March 1900 (Buslett); 13 Nov. (extracts from reviews). (N)

———. 1901. *Afholdssmuler fra boghylden.* Eau Claire: AP. R: *Smuler* Jan. 1902: 20–23 (Hervin). (E)

———. [1904]/1907. *Fortællinger for Eyvind.* Eau Claire: Fremad. 123pp. Also 1906, 1907, 1909, and Trondheim, Norway, 1911. Trans. by J.J. Skordalsvold, *When You Are Tired of Playing.* Eau Claire: Fremad. R: *DP* 30 Sept. (Wist); *Smuler* Oct.: 2–5 (Hervin); *R* 4 Oct. (Møst). (S)

———. 1904. "Løst fra alt." *VT* 1 (No.2): 81–85. In 1908 and 1918. (S)

———. 1905. "Han saa liden og uanselig ud." *VT* 1 (No.4): 195–198. In 1908 and 1918. (S)

———. 1905. "Vore kulturelle muligheder." *Kv* 1 (April): 2–10. In *VT* 1 (No. 12, 1905): 595–600. Trans. Lovoll 1977. (E)

———. 1905. "'Os sjøl' og det store 'ja'et'." *Kv* 1 (July): 1–4. (E)

———. 1905. "Om at bevare vort modersmaal." *Kv* 1 (Oct.): 14–29. As a pamphlet 1907. Trans. Lovoll 1977. (E)

———. 1905. "Norskie." *Symra* 1: 168–172. In 1908 and 1918. (S)

———. 1906. "Vore Frænder hinsides havet." *Kv* 2 (Jan.): 2–30. (E)

———. 1906. "Vore religionsskoler." *Kv* 2 (April): 22–24. (E)

———. 1906. "Naar græker møder græker." *Symra* 2: 145–50. In 1908 and 1918. (S)

———. 1907. "Den anden side." *Kv* 3 (April): 6–12. (E)

———. 1907. "Da sneen gik bort." *Kv* 3 (Jan.): 4–7. (S)

———. 1908. *Hverdagsfolk.* Eau Claire: Fremad. 86pp. R: *NT* 7 May (Stavnheim); *Ny Tid* 1 (May): 423 (Stavnheim); *Idun* 1 (Oct.): 26 (Hanson); *Kv* 5 (Jan. 1909): 16–19. (S)

———. 1908. "Det vigtigste." *Kv* 4 (Jan.): 4–12. Trans. Lovoll 1977. (E)

———. 1908. "Norsk–amerikanske forfattere. Wilhelm Mauritz Pettersen." *Symra* 4: 67–78. (E)

———. 1909. "Norsk-Amerikaneren Peer Gynt." *Kv* 5 (July): 4–13. In 1930 and *No* 1 (Jan. 1929): 4–6. (E)

———. 1910/1924. *Kristus for Pilatus. En norsk-amerikansk fortælling.* Eau Claire: Fremad. 282pp. As *Presten Conrad Walther Welde,* Kristiania: Aschehoug, 1911. Serialized in *R* 7 Jan.–1 July 1926. Trans. by J.J. Skordalsvold, *Christ Before Pilate: An American Story.* Minneapolis: Augsburg. R: *DP* 12 May (Ristad), 13 Dec. (Wist); *Sk* 14 December (Hanson); *Smuler* Jan. 1911: 26–29 (Hervin); *Kv* 7 (April 1911): 9–11 (Gundersen); *L* 17 (1911): 307; *Symra* 8 (1912): 125–127 (Josephsen); other reviews reprinted in *R* 9 Jan., 20 Feb., 23 April, 25 June 1912. (N)

———. 1910. "Moderne norsk literatur." *Kv* 6 (Jan.): 2–8, (April): 3–15, (July): 11–20. In *R* and, revised, in *Symra* 7 (No.3, 1911): 166–192. (E)

———. 1910. "Norsk-amerikansk skjønliteratur." *Kv* 6 (Oct.): 16–25. Revised in Wist 1914 and *Kv* 10 (April 1914): 43–55, and *NF* 7 (Oct. 1914): 658–674. (E)

———. 1911. "Norsk-amerikanske forfattere. O.S. Sneve." *Symra* 7: 214–224. (E)

———. 1911. "Den gamle prest." *JiV.* In 1913. (S)

———. 1912. "Norske bøger fra ifjor." *Kv* 8 (Oct.): 113–124. (E)

———. 1912. "Ole Amundsen Buslett." *Symra* 8: 214–224. (E)

———. 1912. "Lars." *Ei* 3 (Sept.-Oct.): 3–9. In 1913. (S)

———. 1913. *Fortællinger og skisser.* Eau Claire: Fremad. 86pp. R: *DP* 8 Jan. (Wist). (S)

———. 1913. "En norsk-amerikansk kunstner. Gulbrand Sether." *Kv* 9 (Jan.): 27–29. (E)

———. 1914. "To tomme hænder." *Kv* 10 (April): 35–39. In 1913. (S)

——. 1915. "Dr. Agnes Mathilde Wergeland." *Kv* 11 (Jan.): 12–17. (E)

——. 1915. "Hvorledes ægteparret fik nattero." *JiV*. In 1921. (S)

——. 1916. *Oberst Heg og hans gutter*. Eau Claire: Fremad. 327pp. R: *MT* 10 Sept. (H)

——. 1916. "Smeltedigelen." *Kv* 12 (April): 33–42. Trans. Lovoll 1977. (E)

——. 1917/1995. *Paa veien til smeltepotten*. Eau Claire: Fremad. 270pp. Serialized in *R* 9 Jan.–24 July 1917. Trans. by Harry T. Cleven. *On the Way to the Melting Pot*. Madison. Prairie Oak Press. R: *MT* 11 Nov. (Hansen); *DP* 16 Nov., 20 Nov. (Ager), 27 Nov. (Buslett, Wist), 30 Nov.; *FB* 28 Nov. (Skordalsvold); *L* 1: 753–754 (Johnsen); *NF* 12 (1919): 363–364 (Gade). (N)

——. 1917. "Julius B. Baumann." *Kv* 13 (Oct.): 116–120. (E)

——. 1917. "Da graagaasen trak mot syd." *JiV*. In 1921. (S)

——. 1917–1920. "Den store udjævning." I. *Kv* 13 (July 1917): 73–89 (Trans. Lovoll 1977); II. *Kv* 13 (Oct. 1917): 100–15; III. 15 (April, July, Oct. 1919): 37–50 (Trans. Lovoll 1977); IV. *Kv* 16 (1920): 9–16. (E)

——. 1918. *Udvalgte fortællinger*. Minneapolis: Holter. 128pp. R: *MT* 12 Jan. 1919. (S)

——. 1918. "Sigurd Folkestad." *Kv* 14: 14–20. (E)

——. 1919. "Miss Dorthea Dahl." *Kv* 15: 55–58. (E)

——. 1920. "Der fandtes ikke ondt i ham." *Jul i Vesterland*. In 1921. (S)

——. 1921. *Ny samling fortællinger og skisser*. Eau Claire: Fremad. 88pp. R: *DP* 31 Jan. 1922 (Wist); *R* 28 March (Skordalsvold); *L* 6: 179 (Eastvold), 1166–1167 (Trønsdal). (S)

——. 1922. "Det gamle Muskego." *JiV*. (V)

——. 1922. "Aaffer kommer du'nte da, jaala!" *JiV*. (S)

——. 1923. *Det vældige navn. Et drømmebillede fra verdenskrigen*. Eau Claire: AP. 82pp. R: *MT* 16 Dec.; *Sk* 26 Dec. (Rølvaag); *R* 27 Dec. (Buslett), 3 Jan. 1924 (Rølvaag), 24 Jan. (Skordalsvold); *DP* 4 Jan. (Dørrum); *WP* 7 March (Storseth); *L* 8 (1924): 882 (Skordalsvold). (N)

——. 1925. "Omkring hundreaarsfesten." Pp. 12–13 in *Norse-American Centennial 1825–1925*. Minneapolis 1925. Many reprints, e.g. *DP* 3 Feb. (E)

——. 1925. "Norsk-amerikansk literatur. En sammenligning med norsk literatur." *Sk* 5 June. (E)

——. 1925. "Norskhetsbevægelsen i Amerika." *NF* 18 (April): 211–219. (E)

——. 1925. "Et barndomsminde." *JiV*. (S)

——. 1925. "Den norske nissen." *Sønner av Norge* Christmas issue, 38–41. In 1930. (S)

——. 1925. "Et barndomsminde." *JiV*. (S)

——. 1926/1983. *Gamlelandets sønner*. Oslo: Aschehoug. 288pp. Serialized in *DP* 18 Oct. 1927–3 Jan. 1928. Trans. by Trygve M. Ager, *Sons of the Old Country*. 255pp. Lincoln: University of Nebraska Press. R: *Sk* 12 Jan. (Ristad); 24 Nov. (Rølvaag); *NT* 23 Sep. (Petersen), 7 Oct. (Olav); *NF* 19 (Nov.): 494–6 (Kildal); *MT* 21 Nov.; *M* 30 Nov. (Hambro); *Skandia* 2 April 1927 (Nilsen). (N)

——. 1927. "Oberst Hegs Monument." *JiV*. (E)

——. 1928. "Bare mor." *JiV*. (S)

——. 1929/1931. *Hundeøine*. Oslo: Aschehoug. 232pp. Trans. by Charles W. Stork, *I Sit Alone*. NY: Harper. R: *DP* 12 Nov. (Strandvold); *NT* 28 Nov. (Olav); *MT* 12 Dec. (Hambro); *N* Dec. (Wefald); *A* 2 Nov.; *Morgenposten* 12 Nov.; *No* 1 (Dec.): 31 (S.B.), 2 (Jan. 1930): 15–6 (Rølvaag), 3 (April-May 1931): 18 (Heitmann); *R* 9 Jan. 1930

(Heitmann, from *DS*), 6 Feb. (Rodning); *NYT* 12 April 1931; *HT* 15 March 1931; *R* 28 May 1931 has reviews from several newspapers. (N)

———. 1929. "Norsk-amerikanske reisebeskrivelser." *No* 1 (Nov.): 5–6. (E)

———. 1929. "Et nutidseventyr." *JiV.* In 1930. (S)

———. 1930. *Under forvandlingens tegn.* Eau Claire: Fremad. 87pp. R: *MT* 28 Sept.; *No* 2 (Dec.): 29 (Nelson). (S)

———. 1931. "Det hvite kors i skogen." *JiV.* (S)

———. 1931. "Det blev en råd til sist." *NF* Christmas issue. In 1938. (S)

———. 1932. "Siste kapitel." *No* 4 (Dec.): 11–12. (E)

———. 1932. "Stjernen." *NU* 20 (Dec.): 3. (E)

———. 1933. "Arven." *JiV.* In 1938. (S)

———. 1935. "Sjel til slags." *JiV.* In 1938. (S)

———. 1937. "Det kunde slompe." *JiV.* In 1938. (S)

———. 1938/1982. *Skyldfolk og andre.* Eau Claire: Fremad. 90pp. Trans. by Hildur Ager Nicolai, *The White Cross in the Woods.* R: *R* 3 Nov. (Skordalsvold). (S)

Alsaker, Bertha. 1914. *Eivinds prøvetid. En fortælling fra fjeldbygden i Norge.* Winnipeg, Canada: Norwegian Canadian Publishing Co. 209p. (N)

Amble, Ole. 1877 (Samuel Sommer). *Et sognebud.* Boston: AP. 25pp. R: *Sk* 2 Oct.; 16 Oct.; *FogE* 28 Nov. (Petersen). (P)

Amundsen, Helge. 1910. *Hjemløse fugle.* Brooklyn, NY: A.G. Gulliksen. (N)

Andersen, Paul. 1854. *En røst fra Chicago.* Chicago.* R: *E* 18 Aug. (E)

Anderson, Johan Peter. 1927. *Om fire lykkelige ægtepar i England.* Superior, Wisconsin: AP. (N)

Anderson, Marie Sundheim. 1933. "Black Hawk Bessies besøk." *JiV.* (S)

———. 1935. "Hvorledes Jim Towler atter kom på rett kjøl." *JiV.* (S)

Anderson, Mrs. O.A. [1934]. *Ho Marit.* Roosevelt, Minnesota: AP. 43pp. (S&V)

Anderson, Rasmus Bjørn. 1872. ed. *Julegave.* Chicago: *Amerika.* 170pp. 8th and last edition, 1900. R: *FogE* 26 Dec. (A)

———. [1875]. *Den norske maalsag.* Chicago: Sk. R: *Sk* 18 May (B.T.); *B* 25 May; *No* 20 May. (E)

———. 1875. "En tur ikring Vesterheimen." *Sk* 23 Feb. (E)

———. 1877/1878. *America Not Discovered By Columbus.* Chicago: S.C. Griggs. Also 1883 and 1891. In Norwegian, *Amerika ikke opdaget af Columbus.* Chicago: *Sk.* (H)

———. 1903. ed. *Bygdejævning. Artikler af repræsentanter fra de forskjellige bygder i Norge, om hvad deres sambygdinger har udrettet i Vesterheimen.* Madison: *Amerika.* 415pp. (A)

Andreassen, Ola. 1912. "Guldet i dødsdalen." *Symra* 8: 160–162. (S)

Anker-Midling, Julius. 1875. *Under Election; eller Valglivets mysterier. Komedie med sange og kor i tre akter.* Chicago: *Sk.* 108pp. R: *Sk* 30 Nov. (Play, first performed Chicago, 27 June 1875.)

Anonymous. 1847. *Norsk-nord-amerikansk-almanak for 1848,* Muskego: *Nordlyset.**

———. 1847. "Emigrantens tilbageblik." *Nordlyset* 19 Aug. (V)

———. 1848. *Slaveriet foraarsager haarde tider.** (E)

———. 1858. "Brudstykker af Jens og Oles hændelser paa vestsiden af Mississippi." *E* 22 Nov. (F)

———. 1865. *En ny og rørende sang om krigens slutning og Præsident Lincolns mord af den forvorpne skuespiller Wilkes Booth.* Madison: Ole Monsen.* (V)

———. 1866. *Den norske Amerikaner.* Chicago: Ole Trøan.* (A)

———. 1866. *Sex maaneders fangenskab i Andersonville fængsel.* Chicago: Ole Tröan.* (Translation.)

———. 1870. *Aarsager hvorfor Jens Jensen og hans familie udvandrede til Amerika, indeholdende mange nyttige raad, angaaende, hvorledes man forlader hjemmet og reisen til de Forenede Stater og oplysninger til personer, der agte at bosætte sig der.* Chicago: Anchor Line. 66pp. Second edition: Chicago, 1871. (N)

———. 1873. *Formularbog for breve og dokumenter samt hver mands skrive- og regnemester.* La Crosse: *FogE.* 84pp. (HB)

———. 1876. *Beskrivelse af Holden, Goodhue Co. Minn. læst ved hundred-aarsfesten den fjerde juli 1876.* Holden, Minnesota. (H)

———. 1876. *Ny norsk-engelsk brevbog med formularer til udfærdigelse af forretnings — og andre legale dokumenter tilligemed retskrivningslære for norsk og engelsk samt anvisning til affattelsen af alle slags breve . . .* Chicago: Relling. 170pp. Also 1878. (HB)

———. 1876 (Ajax). "To Søstre; en fortælling fra en norsk fjeldbygd." *For Hjemmet,* 3–14, 33–44, 65–76, 97–108. (SF)

———. 1882. "Gengangere." *Sk* 30 May (Review of a production of Ibsen's *Ghosts*).

———. 1887. "Farvel du Moder Norge." *B* 11 May. (V)

———. 1888. *Fagerlierne.* Minneapolis: *FogE.* 284pp. Serialized in *FogE* 21 Dec. 1887–11 April 1888. (N)

———. 1888. "Stina. En novelle fra Sigdal i Norge." *FogE* 1 Feb.–29 Feb. (SF)

———. 1890 (Erling). *Bohêmen i sidste akt. Indlæg mod bohême-literaturen.* Chicago: N.J. Deichmann. 15pp. (F)

———. 1906. "I ferien. Skildringer fra livet i et norsk settlement." *VT* 2: 722–737, 777–788, 825–837. (SF)

———. 1908 (Olav Uræd). *Rivalinderne; eller Heltene fra Kamphaug. En roman fra vestens prærier.* Minneapolis: Kriedt. 96pp. Also Capital Publishing Co. bound with Stenholt, *Minnesotabibelen.* (N)

———. 1916 (Elisabet—en norsk prestekone). "Smaastubber om 'Vesle-Lars.'" *KvM* 11 (No. 7, April): 19–20. (M)

———. 1919 (Herman Seckler). "Kløver tre." *DP* 4 Nov.–20 Jan. 1920. (SF)

———. 1926–1928 (Elisabeth). "Kaffekjelen." *NU* 14 (Sept. 1926)–16 (Sept. 1928). (SF)

———. 1928 (Elisabeth). "Juleengelen." *NU* 16 (Dec.): 182–184. (S)

———. 1929–1930 (Elisabeth). "Opalkjeden." *NU* 17 (March)–18 (Jan.). (SF)

———. 1938. "Nybyggerliv paa prærien." *DP* Feb. 22–May 24. (SF)

Ash, Hans. 1931. "Tante Mina." *JiV.* (S)

———. 1935. "God jul, partner." *JiV.* (S)

Askevold, Bernt. 1874. Fiction and verse in *For Hjemmet* 5: "En ny livsgaade," 204–205; "Historien om Kraake og Ragnar Lodbrok," 216–219, 234–236, 247–249; "Tilbageblik og haab," 177–178; "Naar livet er skjønt," 273; "Frierstenene," 294–295; "Hun slap ei haabet," 305.

———. 1876. *Hun Ragnhild eller Billeder fra Søndfjord.* Chicago: *Sk.* 162pp. Promotion and polemics in *Sk* 1875: 17 Aug. (Askevold), 31 Aug. (Anderson), 21 Sep., 5 Oct. (Anderson). (N)

———. 1876. "Norsk-amerikansk literatur." *B* 14, 21 Nov. (E)

———. 1876. "Min mening om sagen." *Sk* 21 November. (E)

——. 1888. *Familien paa Skovseth*. St. Paul: AP. 96pp. Bergen, Norway, 1889. (N)

——. 1893. *I den gamles sted*. Bergen, Norway: Nygaard. 216pp. (N)

——. 1899. *Et barns død*. Fergus Falls: AP. 15pp. (S)

——. 1899. *Trang vei*. Fergus Falls: AP. 106pp. (N)

——. 1912. "Julefortælling." *JiV*. (S)

Aslagsson, Olai. 1918/1923. *Under vestens himmel*. Minneapolis: Augsburg. 252pp. As *Under præriens himmel*, Kristiania: Aschehoug, 1918. Trans. by Peer Strømme, *Under Western Skies*. Minneapolis: Augsburg. R: *L* 2: 1562 (Rølvaag); *Kv* 15 (Jan. 1919): 32; *MT* 23 Dec. 1923. (N)

——. 1918. "Coyoten." *JiV*. Included in 1918/1923. (S)

——. 1919. "Den nye norske forfatter. Et interview." *Skandia* 15 Feb.

Baalson, Herman. 1929. *Brødrene Svingen. Et glimt fra hverdagslivet*. Sunborg, Minnesota: Hallinglaget. (P)

Bache, Søren. 1847(MS)/1951. "Søren Baches dagbogsoptegnelser under sit ophold i Amerika aarene 1839 til 1847." Serialized in *NU* 15 (1927). Trans. and Ed. by Clarence A. Clausen and Andreas Elviken, *A Chronicle of Old Muskego: The Diary of Søren Bache, 1839–1847*, Northfield: NAHA. (M)

Baker, Mons. nd. (Monssini). *"Strilevisen — Fiskevisen med Nogle sandheds sange."* Minneapolis: AP. 31pp. (V)

Bakke, Thorvald Martinus. 1927. *Et tomt hus*. Thorsby, Alabama: AP. 79pp. R: *Sk* 4 Jan. 1928 (Ristad). (N)

Bakken, J.P. 1889. *Smaa*.* Referred to in *B* 25 Sep. 1889, advertised 19 Feb. 1890.

Bang, Marie. 1901. *Livets alvor*. Warren, Minnesota: AP. 262pp. (N)

Bangsberg, John. 1929. *Louise Enerby: Fortælling fra folkelivet*. Minneapolis: AP. 311pp. R: *No* 2 (Feb. 1930): 15 (Nelson). (N)

Baumann, Julius Berg. 1897. "Lap Jon." *R* 4 Jan. (S)

——. 1905 (Julius). "Blind tro." *Smuler* (Jan.): 1. (V)

——. 1906 (Julius Apostata). Contributions to *Smuler*: "Mefistofeles" (April): 28–30 (E); "Splitternøgne sandheder" (May): 23–25 (Aphorisms); "Dyret i Mennesket" (June): 15–16 (E); "Splitternøgne sandheder" (July): 11–3, (Sept.): 24–25, (Oct.): 2–3, (Nov.): 17–18, (Dec.): 24–26. (E)

——. 1907 (Julius Apostata). Contributions to *Smuler*: "Splitternøgne sandheder" (Jan.): 14–15, (Feb.): 20–21; "Til Tom" (March): 1–3 (V); "Voltaire — 'Peter Olsen!'" (Sept.): 2–3 (E); "Kvelve og døden" (Nov.): 1 (V), "Voltaire" 25–7, "Djævelens herkomst" (Dec.): 23–28 (E).

——. 1908. "Literære hilsninger fra Norge." *Kv* 4 (April): 23–27. (E)

——. 1908 (Julius Apostata). "Skovbrand." *Smuler* (Oct.): 4–6. (E)

——. 1909. *Digte*. Eau Claire: Fremad. 78pp. R: *Kv* 5 (Oct.): 28–30; *Ei* 2 (Feb. 1910): 65–66 (Norstog); *Smuler* (April 1910): 17–18 (Hervin). (V)

——. 1909 (Julius Apostata). Contributions to *Smuler*: "Kirken og usædeligheden" (Jan.): 18–22 (E); "Præstens omvendelse" (April): 1–2 (V).

——. 1910 (Julius Apostata). "Rettelser af det hellige(?) og ufeilbarlige(?) Guds ord." *Smuler* (July): 17–19. (E)

——. 1913. "Død." *Kv* 9 (Jan.): 3–5. (E)

——. 1913. "Julefortælling." *JiV*. (S)

——. 1915. *Fra vidderne. Nye digte.* Minneapolis: Augsburg. 136pp. R: *Smuler* (Aug. 1916): 26–27 (Hervin); *DP* 1 Aug. 1916 (Pettersen); *Kv* 13 (Oct. 1917): 116–120 (Ager). (V)

——. 1915. "Pioneeren." *JiV.* (V)

——. 1919. "Storskogen." *JiV.* (S)

——. 1920. "Matti Savo. Et billede fra skogslivet." *JiV.* (S)

——. 1922. "Mit folk i Vesterheimen! Hjertelig Tak!" *DS* [late Dec.] clipping in JBBP. (E)

——. 1922. "Den sidste akt." *JiV.* (S)

——. 1924. *Samlede digte.* Minneapolis: Augsburg. 250pp. R: *L* 8: 1105 (Christensen); *MSP* 20 July; *DP* 9 Dec. (V)

Benson, John. 1889. *Ved gry og kveld.* Chicago: Markus & Kalheim. 44pp. R: *Sk* 25 Dec. (V)

——. 1891. "En af de faa." *B* 21 Jan. Also in Straaberg 1921 (V); "Gule og grønne Blade." *B* 28 Jan. (S)

——. 1926. "Vandrerens Bethlehems færd" *JiV.* (V)

——. 1931. "Turid Gran." *No* 3 (April–May): 6. (V)

——. 1932. "Barnas 17de maitog." *No* 4 (May): 1. (V)

Bentsen, Christian. 1926. *Guld og kjærlighed.* Brooklyn, NY: Knudsen Printing & Publishing Co. 51pp. (P)

——. n.d. *Aktiv og passiv. Versificeret drama.* Brooklyn, NY: Norwegian News Co. 24pp. (P)

——. n.d. *Uleilighets rim og dikte.* Brooklyn, NY: Norwegian News Co. 20pp. (V)

Berg, Karin Benedicte Andersen. 1922–1923. "Bare en bonde." *DP* 28 Nov.–2 Jan. (SF)

——. 1923–1924. "Kaptein Id." *DP* 11 Dec.-5 Feb. (SF)

——. 1924–1925. "I bakkehuset." *DP* 16 Dec.–17 March. (SF)

——. 1929. *Oberstindens pleiedatter.* Cedar Rapids: N.Fr. Hansen. 160pp. (N)

——. 1929. "Kaare Mehl. Fortælling fra Nordfjord." *DP* 9 April–28 May. (SF)

Berge, J.J. 1897. *Haabets vinger. Nogle religiøse sange.* Minneapolis. (V)

Berger, Aaslaug, Yngvar Grythfeldt, Sigrid Hakstad, eds. 1926. *Forum. Det litterære samfunds årbok.* Chicago: Det litterære samfund. 110pp. (A)

Bergh, Johan Arndt. 1888. ed. *I ledige stunder.* Chicago: Lutherforeningen. 199pp. Also 1891, 1891, 1898. (S)

——. 1891. ed. *I sidste øieblik og andre fortællinger fra livet.* Oxfordville Rock, Wisconsin: Kirken og Hjemmet. 159pp. (S)

Bergum, Ingerid. 1893. *Familien af Stjerneklip.* Chicago: AP. 341pp. (N)

Berild, Olaf. 1917. *Spredte tanker.* Seattle: AP. 51pp. (E)

——. 1918/1924. *Kast den første sten.* Seattle: AP. Trans. by S. Garberg, *Cast the First Stone.* (N)

——. 1923. *Glimt av Norge og Amerika.* Seattle: AP. 259pp. (N)

——. 1931. *De nye ideer. Skuespil i to akter.* Tacoma: Puget Sound Publ. Co. 24pp. (P)

Bernhart, Iver. [1933]. *Nyveien til Fevatn.* Decorah: DP. 97pp. Serialized in *DP* 14–28 Feb. 1933. (N)

Berven, Jacob Amundsen. 1916. *Reisebreve og digte.* Radcliffe, Iowa: AP. 206pp. R: *L* 23: 467 (Lundeberg). (T&V)

Birkeland, Knut Bergesen. 1895. *Han kommer. Fortælling i to dele.* Minneapolis: AP. 186p. R: *Sk* 27 Feb. (N)

——. 1896. *Farlige mænd.* Minneapolis: AP. 192pp. (N)

——. 1900. *Lysglimt i mørket; eller Kristendom og hedenskab. Optegnelser fra en reise rundt jorden gjennem Europa, Asia og Amerika.* Minneapolis: Minnehaha Publ. Co. 626pp. (T)

——. 1924. *Paa hvalfangst. Fire aar paa jagt efter verdens største dyr.* Minneapolis: Augsburg. R: *L* 8: 818–819 (Skordalsvold). (T)

——. N.d. *En menneskeven. Hans Peter Børresens liv og arbeide.* Minneapolis: Minnehaha Publ. Co. 200pp. (B)

Blegen, Johan. 1891. *Blegen's veileder og verdens-atlas.* Chicago: AP. 468pp. R: *Sk* 9 Nov. 1892; *B* 28 Dec. 1892. (HB)

Blehr, Bjarne. See Heitmann, John.

Bøhmer, Olav. 1905. "Gudbrand Sæther" [sic]. *DP* 21 March 1905. (E)

——. 1922. *Min første bog. Digte og skisser.* Chicago: Twilight Publ. Co. 24pp. (V)

——. 1924. *Fra fremmede strande.* Chicago: Twilight Publ. Co. 29pp. (T&V)

Bonhus, Emma Quie. 1943. "Trekløverblade." *DP* 22 April–3 June. (SF)

——. 1944. "Usynlige tråder." *JiV*, 7–13. (S)

——. 1947. "Det skjer noe i det som skjer." *JiV*, 38–43. (S)

——. 1953. "En nittiårig prestekone forteller." *JiV*, 44–48. (M)

Borchsenius, J. Valdemar. 1874. *Ved Øresund og Mississippi.* Chicago: AP. R: *FogE* 5 Nov.; *Sk* 10 Nov.; *B* 1 Dec. (Arctander); 14 May 1879 (Petersen). (V, Danish American.)

Bothum, L.M. 1915. *En historie fra nybyggerlivet.* Dalton, Minnesota: AP. 117pp. (N)

Braatelien, Syver. 1896. *Samlede smaastykker.* Fergus Falls, Minnesota: AP. 36pp. (S)

Branborg, A. 1866. "Reisen fra Norge til Amerika." *F* 1 Feb. (V)

Brandt, Nils. 1907. "Pastor Nils Brandts erindringer fra aarene 1851 til 1855." *Symra* 3: 97–122. (M)

Bratager, Laura Ringdal. 1910. *Digte og smaafortællinger.* Minneapolis: AP. Also 1914, 1916, 1918. R: *Smuler* (Jan. 1911): 29–30; *DP* 24 April 1914. (S&V)

——. 1912. *Sange.* Minneapolis: AP. 31pp. Also 1918 and 1927. (V)

——. 1921. *Før og nu. Reiseskildringer m.m.* Minneapolis: AP. 128pp. R: *MT* 2 Oct., 18 Dec. (Egilsrud). (T)

——. 1925. *Over hav og land. Lyngblomstens historie. Pionerliv i Minneapolis med flere skildringer.* Minneapolis: AP. 128pp. (H)

——. 1925. "Det var juleaften." *NU,* Christmas. (S)

——. 1926. "Gjenforening." *NU,* Christmas. (S)

——. 1932. "Julesangen." *No* 4 (Dec.): 4. (S)

Brekhus, Edward. 1897. *En kortfattet levnetsbeskrivelse. Fortalt af ham selv.* Minneapolis: AP. 28pp. (M)

Brekke, J.J. 1895. *Synderens ven.* Minneapolis: AP. 40pp. (V)

——. 1895. *Hyrdelokking.* Minneapolis: AP. 191pp. (V)

Brohaugh, Chr.O. and J. Eisteinsen. 1883. *Kortfattet beretning om Elling Eielsens liv og virksomhed.* Chicago, AP. 208pp. R: *No* 19 Sep.; *Sk* 13 Nov. (B)

Bru, Ingomar. 1921. "Dagsbogsoptegnelser." *Norsk-amerikansk julebog,* 65–77. (S)

Bruflot, Arnfinn. 1969. *Juni-båten.* Oslo: Det norske samlaget. 61pp. (V)

———. 1970. *Det storkna havet.* Oslo: Det norske samlaget. 48pp. (V)

———. 1973. *Præriekveld.* Oslo: Det norske samlaget. 48pp. (V)

———. 1975. *Dei kom til Amerika.* Oslo: Det norske samlaget. 47pp. (V)

———. 1980. *Inn i Amerika.* Oslo: Det norske samlaget. 148pp. (N)

———. 1986. *På andre sida av havet.* Oslo: Cappelen. 54pp. (V)

Brun, Nils Christian. 1881. *Et minde; eller Elen Bruns liv og død.* Chicago: AP. 68pp. R: *Sk* 16, 30 Aug. (M)

Bruun, Ulrikka R. Feldtman. 1879. *Menneskets største fiende; eller drukkenskabslastens skrækkelige følger.* Kristiansund, Norway: Petrine Hasselø. 8opp. R: *IF* 1 (July-Aug. 1879): 71; *Sk* 5 Dec. 1881. (N)

———. 1880. *Lykkens nøgle.* Chicago: AP.* R: *IF* 2 (Jan. 1880): 7; *Sk* 5 Dec. 1881. (N)

———. 1884. *Fjendens faldgruber.* Chicago: Rasmussen. 198pp. (N)

———. 1886. "Farvel til Amerika." *Sk* 1 Sep. (V)

———. 1891. *Gamle og nye sange. Oversatte fra engelsk.* Chicago: AP. 228pp. (A)

———. 1902. *Den syngende evangelist.* Chicago: AP. Also 1909. (V)

———. 1914. *Norge 1814 og 1914. En Mindekrans til Moder Norge.* Fargo: AP. In 1920. (V)

———. 1920. *Sange, digte og rim.* Chicago: AP. 442pp. 2nd edition, 1921. 503pp. (V)

———. [1928]. *Tilæg til Sange—digte og rim.* Chicago: Hope Mission. 30pp. (V)

Buan, Bertha. 1937. *Stevneminne.* [Duluth]: AP. 16pp. (V)

———. 1941. "Vestfjorden." *JiV*, 51–52. (S)

———. 1947. See Johnsrud, Rosanna Gutterud.

———. 1949. "Et hverdagsminne hjemmefra." *JiV*, 48–49. (S)

———. 1950. "Sol over Superior-sjøen." *JiV*, 19–21. (S)

———. 1956. "De var rike." *JiV*, 46–48. (S)

Buslett, Ole Amundsen. 1882. *Fram!* Chicago: AP. 75pp. In *Buslett's* 2–3 (April 1922–Oct. 1922). R: *Sk* 9 Jan. (Anderson); 16 Jan. (Hago); *B* 21 Feb. 1883 (Petersen). (V)

———. 1882. *Leiligheds digte,* Chicago: AP. 24pp. (V)

———. 1882. "Julefortælling." *Sk* 19 Dec. (S)

———. 1883. *Skaars skjæbne. Billeder fra borgerkrigen.* Chicago: AP. 21pp. Also serialized in *No* 17, 24 Sept., 1 Oct. 1889, and included in Johan Bøgh, *Fra Bergenskanten.* Chicago: *Sk,* 1889, 1892. R: *Sk* 25 March 1884 (Hago). (V)

———. 1884. *Øistein og Nora.* Madison: AP. 47pp. (V)

———. 1885. *De to veivisere. Et dramatisk digt i seks handlinger.* Chicago: AP. 167pp. R: *B* 18 Aug. (Petersen); *No* 16 Sept. (Hande); *Sk* 19 Aug. (J. A. Johnson), *Sk* 30 Sept. (Anderson); Lange 1887, 120. (P)

———. 1890. *Et dødens døgn. Sørgespil.* Chicago: AP. 40pp. (The catalogue of the University Library, Oslo, has *døgn* corrected to *tegn,* and this is the version given in other bibliographies. However, the copy in this library has the title as given here). (P)

———. [1890]. *Snip-Snap-Snude. Lystspil.* Chicago: AP. 40pp. (P)

———. [1891]. *Digte og sange.* Chicago: AP. 279pp. (V)

———. 1893. *Rolf Hagen.* LaCrosse: AP. 108pp. (N)

———. 1894. ed. *Det femtende Wisconsin frivillige.* Decorah: AP. 696pp. First serialized in *DP.* (H)

———. 1897. *Torstein i Nybygden. Virkelighedsfortælling fra det norske Nord-Amerika.* Fergus Falls, Minnesota: *Rodhuggeren.* 86p. Serialized in *Rodhuggeren.* First publication of material for this book: "Tunge tanker, Olav Busterud." *Normannen* 17 Jan. 1896. (N)

———. 1904. "Om betingelserne for en norsk-amerikansk skjønliteratur." *VT* 1 (Nov.): 101–105. (E)

———. 1905. "I Bygdom." *R* 2 May–23 May. In 1908. (S)

———. 1905. "Julebrev." *Kv* (Oct.): 7–13. (S)

———. 1905–1907. "Frelserne." *Smuler* (Most issues, Nov. 1905–Aug. 1907). (V)

———. 1906–1907 (Hans Rundtom). "Et og andet fra nybyggerlivet." *VT* 2 (Nov.): 1157–1166; (Dec.): 1211–1128; 3 (Jan.): 16–34; (Feb.): 73–79. (F)

———. 1908. *Sagastolen. Fortælling fra det norske Nord-Amerika.* Chicago: Sk. 237pp. Incorporates 1897. Partly serialized in *R* in 1905 and then serialized in *Sk.* R: *Kv* 5 (April 1909): 29–30 (Ager); *Sk* 5 May 1909 (Oftelie); *Idun* I (May 1910): 162–165. (N)

———. 1908. "Atvaa" [Atpaa?]. *Smuler* (Jan.): 19–20. (E)

———. 1909. "Dr. Koht i Madison; lidt om landsmaalet." *Sk* 7 May. (E)

———. 1911. *I Parnassets lunde. Dramatisk eventyrdigt.* Northland, Wisconsin: AP. 101pp. R: *Kv* 7 (April): 32 (Ager); *DP* 14 March (Wist); *Sk* 15 March (H. Hanson). (P)

———. 1912. *Glans-om-Sol og hans folks historie.* Northland: AP. 250pp. R: *R* 4 June (Johnson); *Ei* 4 (April 1913): 56 (Norstog). (N)

———. 1913. "Amerika-Paul." *Kv* 9 (Oct.): 97–132. (P)

———. 1913. " —Og de solgte ut." *Ji V.* (S)

———. [1915]/1978. *Veien til Golden Gate.* [Minneapolis]: AP. 27pp. Trans. by Myrtle Christenson Buslett et al, *The Road to Golden Gate and a Funeral in Pioneer Times.* Oshkosh, Wisconsin: Winchester Academy. Trans. by Orm Øverland, "The Road to the Golden Gate," in a forthcoming anthology ed. by Marc Shell and Werner Sollors. R: *DP* 29 Oct. (Ristad); *R* 16 Nov., 23 Nov. (Rølvaag); *Kv* 12 (Jan. 1916): 19–20 (Ager). (S)

———. 1915. "Butt og Bøle." *Ji V.* (S)

———. 1916. "En drøm i marmor." *Kv* 12 (Oct.): 97–107. (V)

———. 1917. "To brødre." *Kv* 13 (July): [65]–69. (V)

———. 1918. *Fra min ungdoms nabolag. Norsk-amerikansk prosa med et eventyr i.* Eau Claire: Fremad. 121pp. R: *MT* 3 Nov. (Hansen); *Skandia* 26 Oct. (N)

———. 1920. *Benedictus og Jacobus. Fortælling om nogle norske Wisconsin-borgere, som har sat mærker i det private og offentlige liv, dikterisk belyst.* Eau Claire: Fremad. R: *Sk* 18 Nov.; *Visergutten* (clipping in OABP); *L* 4: 1550; *NF* 14 (1921): 553; *MT* 27 March 1921. (N)

———. 1922. "Literatur og 'Mixing.'" *DP* 26 Dec. (E)

———. 1922–1923. *Buslett's* 1–4. R: *MT* 9 Dec. 1923; *Fergus Falls Ugeblad* (clipping in OABP, Oftelie), *R* (clipping in OABP, Ager), *DS* (clipping in JBBP, Baumann).

———. 1923. "Emmeline." *Gudbrandsdølenes Julehilsen,* 51–61. (S)

———. 1923. "Norsk Literatur i Amerika." *Sk* 28 Sept. (E)

Carlsen, Berntine Stover. 1948. *Hverdagsfolk.* Duluth: Fuhr. One of these stories, "Grubebyens hvite engel," serialized in *DP* 21 Feb.–7 March. (S)

———. 1956. "Endelig den rette." *Ji V,* 36–40. (S)

Christensen, C.B. 1898. *Fra Amerikas kultur. Et aandslivs historie.* Minneapolis: Oscar W. Lund. 196pp. (E)

Christiansen, Christian. 1886. *Morgenstjernen.* Chicago: *Sk.* 151pp. Also 1897, 1926. R: *Sk* 19 May. (V)

———. 1917. *Udvandringen eller En norsk immigrants oplevelse.* Chicago: *Sk.* R: *L* 23: 371 (Guldseth). (Allegory.)

Christopherson, John. 1928. *Nybyggerlivet og den tabte og gjenfundne.* Devils Lake, North Dakota: AP. 50pp. (N)

Dahl, Borghild. 1944–1945. "Marit." *DP* 16 Nov.–1 March. (SF)

Dahl, Dorthea. 1901 (Dorthea). "Missionærens hustru." *UV* 12 (15 March): 148. (S)

———. 1912 (D.D.). "Jul i Idaho." *UV* 23 (15 Dec.): 746–748. (S)

———. 1914 (D.D.). "Hun ville dele med glæde deres kaar." *UV* 25 (1 Aug.): 454–458. (S)

———. 1915. "Hjem til jul." *UV* 26 (15 Dec.): 761–764, 802. (S)

———. 1915. *Fra hverdagslivet.* Minneapolis: Augsburg. 116pp. One story trans. as "Grandmother" in 1920. R: *L* 22: 1692; *Sk* 19 Jan. 1916 (Sundheim); *R* 25 Jan. 1916 (Ager), 1 Feb. 1916 (Rølvaag); *KvM* 11 (Feb. 1916), (April 1916) (Rølvaag); *N* 14 Feb. 1916 (Redal); *MT* 26 March 1916 (Hansen); *DP* 11 Aug. 1916 (Josephson). (S)

———. 1917. Two stories in *FM* 2: "Bedstestuen" (trans. "The Best Room," *The Friend* Feb. 1938) and "Bækkens sang." (Nov.): 22–23 and (Dec.): 8–11.

———. 1917. "Sangkoret i Hancock." *JiV.* Trans. "The Choir in Hancock" in 1920. (S)

———. 1918. Four related serialized stories in *L* 2: "Ungdomsforeningen paa Wauka Ridge," 806–809, 872–874, 883–884, 932–933; "Kirkeindvielsen," 965–966, 996–998, 1026–1028 (trans. "The Dedication" in 1920); "Rotfæstet," 1161–1162, 1170, 1187–1189, 1224–1225 (trans. "Rooted," *JiV,* 1929); "Søster Hannah," 1549–1554, 1562–1563. (S)

———. 1918. "Mors jul. Hvad familien lærte mens mor var paa hospitalet." *FM* 3 (Dec.): 23–25, 52–53. (S)

———. 1919. "Det gamle bokskap." *JiV.* Trans. "The Old Bookcase" in 1920. (S)

———. 1920. *Returning Home.* Minneapolis: Augsburg. 133pp. R: *MT* 14 Nov. (Hansen); *L* 4: 1518 (Johnsen); *R* 30 Nov. (Ager); *Sk* 1 Dec. (Buslett). (S)

———. 1920. "The Story That Was Never Written." *JiV.* (S)

———. 1921. "Prestens motorbaad." *FM* 32 (Jan.): 10–14, 21. (S)

———. 1921. "The Seventeenth of May." *The North Star* No.4, May–June, 221–228. In *Sturdy Folks and Other Stories by Norwegian Authors.* Minneapolis: Holter. n.d. (S)

———. 1922. "Julegranen." *FM* 34 (Dec.): 23–25. (S)

———. 1922. "The Holy Day." *JiV.* (S)

———. 1925. *Byen paa berget.* Minneapolis: Augsburg. 255pp. Part of Ch.5 and Ch.6 in *FM* 36 (Jan.): 12–5. R: *MT* 6 Sept. (Hansen); *DS* 25 Sept. (Anna Dahl), 18 Dec. (Heitmann); *L* 9: 1141 (Mellbye), 1152–1153 (Christensen); *R* 8 Oct. (Ager); *Nord-Norge* No. 39, 15–16. (N)

———. 1926. "Bedstemors rok." *FM* 38 (Nov.): 9–11. (S)

———. 1926. "The Beckoning Distance." *JiV.* (S)

———. 1930. "Kopper-kjelen." *No* 2. Discontinued serialization May, 13–14; complete Dec., 18–19, 27–28, 31. Trans. by Orm Øverland, "The Copper Kettle," in a forthcoming anthology ed. by Marc Shell and Werner Sollors. (S)

———. 1931. "Julekvad." *No* 3 (Dec.): 3–5. (S)

——. 1932. "Forgaarden." *JiV.* (S)

——. 1934. "Grovær." *JiV.* (S)

——. 1935. "Jul hjemme." *JiV.* (S)

——. 1942. "The Heart's Desires." *The Friend*, Feb., 12–14. (S)

Dalager, Kristofer. 1903. *I kirken.* Minneapolis: AP. 62pp. (V)

——. 1925. *Jordens skjød.* Lake Park, Minnesota: AP. 29pp. R: *DP* 25 Dec. (Høverstad). (S)

Dalen, Anna. n.d. *Det største.* Chicago: *Sk.* 32pp. (S)

Danielson, Peter Clavian. 1920. *Læg og lærd.* Minneapolis: Augsburg. 125pp. R: *MT* 14 Nov. (N)

Dieserud, Juul. 1893. *Sagaens Leif Erikson.* Chicago: *Sk.* 19pp. (H)

Dietrichson, Peter G. 1884. *En kortfattet skildring af Det femtende Wisconsin regiments historie og virksomhed under borgerkrigen samt nogle korte træk af fangernes ophold i Andersonville.* Chicago: *Sk.* 32pp. (H)

Døving, Carl. 1892. *Billeder fra Syd-Afrika.* Decorah: AP. 120pp. R: *ELK* 19: 218; *Sk* 9 March. (T)

Dundas, Johan C. 1868. "Ved at høre Ole Bull." *Sk* 9 Dec. (V)

——. 1870. "Til Ole Bull." *Sk* 23 March. (V)

——. 1882. *Tre digte.* Cambridge, Wisconsin: AP. 16pp. (V)

Egilsrud, Helen Storjohann. 1932. *Ny dag.* Minneapolis: AP. 391pp. R: *No* 4 (Dec.): 31 (Hakstad). (N)

Egilsrud, Johan Storjohann. 1926. *Dikte.* Minneapolis: Augsburg. R: *R* (Rølvaag, Scrapbook OERP); *No* 3 (Dec. 1931): 28 (Hammer). (V)

Ellenson, Ellen. 1934. *Storbuslektens saga. Anden del.* Grand Forks, North Dakota: AP. (N)

Erickson, Chas. 1858. ed. *Norsk folke calender for aaret efter Christi byrd 1858.* Madison: AP. 48pp. (Almanac.)

Erikson, Johannes A. 1938. *Det forjættede land.* Decorah: DP. 430pp. Serialized in *DP* 9 Nov. 1937–8 March 1938. (N)

——. 1939. "Større end det største." *DP* 14 Feb.–30 May. (SF)

——. 1940. "Den trofaste Jon." *DP* 27 Feb.–26 March. (SF)

——. 1943. "Gunhild og Jørgen." *DP* 25 March–13 May. (SF)

——. 1944. "Eremitten." *DP* 27 Jan.–20 April. (SF)

——. 1944. "Det er forskjel paa Henning og Haakon." *DP* 21 Dec. (S)

——. 1945. "Præriedronningen, eller træet kjendes paa frugten." *DP* 15 Feb.–24 May. (SF)

——. 1945–1946. "Et forlis." *DP* 15 Nov.–17 Jan. (SF)

Evanger, Nils O. 1929. "Da Ole Marius Geitmyrstua vant prisen." *No* 1 (Dec.): 15–19. (S)

——. 1930. "Paa ski." *No* 2 (Jan.): 10. (V)

——. 1930. "Bernt Paa-Timen." *No* 2 (Feb.): 4–6. (S)

——. 1930. "Land forut." *No* 2 (March): 8. (V)

——. 1930. "Vår." *No* 2 (April): 3. (V)

——. 1931. "Petter Sjøgutt." *No* 3 (Feb.): 8–10. (S)

——. 1931. "Syn mig en stjerne." *No* 3 (March): 3. (V)

———. 1931. "Kor blir det med han far." *No* 3 (Dec.): 29, 39. (S)

Evans, Eyvind J. 1947. "Jeg synger julekvad." *JiV*, 18–22. (S)

———. 1947. "Guds vegar." *JiV*, 46–51. (S)

———. 1948. "Nykommerens juleaften." *NU* 36 (Dec.): 7–8. (S)

———. 1949. "Kjærlighetens gjenskapermakt." *JiV*, 23–28. (S)

———. 1951. "Prest eller 'løyert'?" *JiV*, 7–13. (S)

———. 1953. "Den sterkeste vant." *JiV*, 28–34. (S)

———. 1955. "Et minne fra skogslivet." *JiV*, 24–29. (S)

Evanson, Aileen Berger. 1926. See Berger, Aslaug.

———. 1930. "Bumpens land." *No* 2 (Feb.): 13–14. (S)

———. 1930. "Min trylleverden." *No* 2 (April: 4. (S)

———. 1930. "Nedlagte kjøtkaker." *No* 2 (Nov.): 9, 23. (S)

———. n.d. *Slekt i Amerika. Chicago fortælling.* Duluth: Fuhr. 87pp. (N)

Fjeldsaa, Ruth L. 1924 (Jutta). "Guld og glans." *DP* 24 Oct.–9 Dec. In *R* 1929–1930. (SF)

———. 1927 (Jutta). "Stækkede vinger." *DP* 15 March–3 May. (SF)

———. 1933–1934 (Jutta). "Hans ungdoms borg." *DP* 28 Nov. 1933–20 Feb. 1934. (SF)

———. 1939. "Julens rene toner." *JiV*, 51–54. (S)

———. 1940. "Julebakkels i palmelund." *JiV*, 28–31. (S)

———. 1942. "I stille kveld." *JiV*, 34. (V)

———. 1942. "Norsk jul sydpå." *JiV*, 50–53. (S)

———. 1943. "Antonette Tovsen død." *DP* 11 Feb. 1943. (M)

———. n.d. *Blomster i høst.* [Miami]: AP. 74pp. (V)

Folkestad, Sigurd. 1907. "To digte." *Symra* 3: 123–126. (V)

———. 1909. "Naar vi længter." *Symra* 5: 1. (V)

———. 1910. "Herre, herre, hvad er jeg?" *Kv* 6 (April): 2. (V)

———. 1911. *Paa kongevei.* Strum, Wisconsin: AP. 141pp. R: *Kv* 7 (April): 11–15 (Ager); (July): 26–29 (W. Pettersen); *Smuler* (June): 21–25 (Hervin); *R* 16 Jan. 1912 (Trønsdal). (V)

———. 1916. *Flytfugl.* Eau Claire: AP. 144pp. R: *L* 23: 163; *Sk* 10 Jan. 1917 (Doe), 9 Feb. 1917 (Buslett), 28 Feb. 1917 (Eikjarud); *DP* 6 Feb. 1917, 11 May 1917 (Skagen); *MT* 9 Sep. 1917. (V)

———. 1917. "Muslingen." *Kv* 13 (Oct.): 120–3. (V)

———. [1919]. *Fra utflytter-kampen.* Chicago: *Sk.* 61pp. R: *NF* 20 July. (V)

———. 1920. "O Herre, dit ord." *JiV.* (V)

[Førde, Jno. A.] [1924?] *Paa sporet. Af Mississippi-guttens fortællinger.* 200pp. (N)

Foss, Hans Anderson. 1884. "Drikkeondet." *No* 18 March. (V)

———. 1885/1963. *Husmands-gutten. En fortælling fra Sigdal.* Decorah: *DP.* 278pp. At least 9 printings of this edition. Serialized in *DP* 3 Dec. 1884–22 April 1885. Minneapolis: J. Leachman, 1903; Kristiania: Omtvedt, 1886, with 9 printings by 1913; later Norwegian editions: Oslo 1936 (12th edition), 1950, 1957, 1958, 1984; Trans. by Joel J. Winkjer, *The Cotter's Son,* Alexandria, Minnesota: Park Region Publ. Co., 1963. (N)

———. 1886. *Livet i Vesterheimen.* Decorah: AP. 192pp. Some copies have *Livet i Vesterhejmen.* Also 1891, 1896; Kristiania: Omtvedt, 1887. Dramatization reviewed in *B* 9 Feb. (N)

——. 1886. *Kristine. En fortælling fra Valders.* Decorah: *DP.* Serialized in *DP* 16 Dec. 1885–21 July 1886. As *Kristine Valdrisdatter.* Minneapolis: Leachman, 1901. (N)

——. 1889/1899. *Den amerikanske saloon.* Grand Forks: AP. 302pp. Also Grand Forks: *N*, 1890; Minneapolis: AP, 1897; *DP*, 1897; as Vol.1, No.2 in *Nye Normandens Reform Bibliothek*, Minneapolis: Foss & Lund, 1897; as *Fisker-Tobias*, Kristiania: Omtvedt, 1892. Trans. by J.J. Skordalsvold, *Tobias, a Story of the Northwest*, Minneapolis: Petersen. R: *No* 10 April (Strømme), 23 April (Houkom); *Saamanden* April: 217 (Janson); *DP* 26 Nov. 1897 (Trønsdal). (N)

——. 1892. *Hvide slaver. En social-politisk skildring.* Grand Forks: *N.* 251pp. Christiania: Omtvedt, 1893. (N)

——. 1894. "4000 bushels hvede. Billede fra farmen." *Skandinavisk illustrert folkekalender*, 1894. In Bjørnstjerne Bjørnson, *En livsgaade, samt andre fortællinger af norske forfattere.* Minneapolis and Chicago: Rasmussen, 1906. (S)

——. 1904. "Skomager, bliv ved din læst." *VT* 1 (No.2): 91–97. (S)

——. 1906. "Fra nybyggerlivet. En sandfærdig tildragelse." In Kristofer Janson, *Ungdomsminder samt andre fortællinger af norske forfattere.* Minneapolis and Chicago: Rasmussen. (S)

——. 1907. *Allehaande.* Minneapolis: Scandinavian-American Publishing Association. 128pp. R: *Ny Tid* 1 (March 1908): 304 (Stavnheim). (S)

——. 1909. "Minder fra gamle dage. Traill County." *Ei* 1 (No. 1, May): 15–18. (M)

——. 1916/1986. "Nybyggerens jul." *Norsk-amerikaneren* 1 (No.2, Oct.-Dec.): 85–86. Trans. by Sigvald Stoylen, "The Pioneer's Christmas," *The Sons of Norway Viking* (Dec. 1986): 484–485. (S)

——. 1921. "Gamle minder." Pp. 307–321 in Ole S. Johnson, Vol.2. (M)

——. 1921–1922. "Saamænd paa vidderne." *NF* 14: 281–287 (on Buslett), 382–383 (on Strømme), 453–455 (on Ager), 523–525 (on Folkestad); 15: 317–319 (on Baumann), 471–473 (on Norstog). (H)

——. 1922. Ed. with Simon Johnson and B. Olson. *Trediveaarskrigen mod drikkeondet: Kort oversigt over avholds — og forbudsarbeidet, særlig blandt skandinaver i Nord Dakota.* [Minot, ND]: Nord Dakota Totalavholdsselskab. 278pp. R: *L* 8 (1924): 368; *MT* 24 Feb. 1924. (H)

——. 1924. "Nogle gamle lyse minder." *DP* 5 Sep. (M)

——. 1927. *Valborg.* Decorah: DP. 208pp. Oslo, 1928. R: *DP* 19 Aug. (Rølvaag), 23 Aug. (Oftelie), 9 Sep. (Garnaas), 4 Oct. (Johnson); *NT* 23 Aug. (Olav); *MT* 11 Aug.; *L* 11: 1093. (N)

Fuhr, Anna Dahl. 1922. "Da juleklokkene kimte." *JiV.* (S.)

——. 1923. "Stemninger." *JiV.* (S)

——. 1926. "To nyaarsnætter." *JiV.* (S)

——. 1930. "Maakene." *JiV.* (S)

——. 1935. "Severine and Company." *JiV.* (S)

Galtung, Hans. 1888. *Aften-læsning for ældre og yngre farmere.* Chicago: *Sk.* 37pp. (E&S)

Gimmestad, Lars M. 1940. *Nordfjordingernes historie i Amerika.* Minneapolis: AP. 510pp. (H)

Gjerde, Mons Pedersen. 1900. *Kamp og seier.* Minneapolis: *AP.* 163pp. (N)

Gjertsen, Melchior Falk. 1877. ed. *Hjemlandssange.* Minneapolis: Konferentsen. (A)

———. 1914. *Harald Hegg. Billeder fra prærien med skildringer af norsk-amerikansk folkeliv.* Minneapolis: Augsburg. 188pp. R: *DP* 17 Nov.; *Symra* 10: 274 (Josephson); *R* 5 Jan. 1915 (Heiberg); *UV* 25: 698; *Kv* 11 (Jan. 1915): 17–19; *L* 21 (1915): 135. (N)

Granli, Alf. 1919. "Fortællinger fra krigen." *DP* 1 July–23 Sept. (S)

Gransted, Thorvald. 1901. "Beist?—Natyrligvis!" *H* 5 May 1901. (S)

———. 1901. "Varslet." *H* 9 Aug. (S)

———. 1902. "Kjærlighed og træsko." *H* 7 Feb. (S)

Grønfur, P. 1912. *Hilsen fra Norge. En samling jagtfortællinger, reisebeskrivelser, naturskildringer, og digte, m.m.* . . . Wheelock, North Dakota. 234pp. (T)

Grundeland, Lasse C. 1920. *Blanda eller snurrige greier* . . . Chicago: AP. 190pp. (F)

Grundysen, Tellef. 1877. *Fra begge sider af havet.* Chicago: *Sk.* 204pp. Also 1882, 1885, 1896. R: *Sk* 10 Sept. (Romland); 1 Oct. (Lien); 19 Nov. (Romland); 31 Dec. 1878 (Lien); 29 April (Romland); 29 July 1879 (Lien). (N)

Guldseth, Olaf. 1916. "Da en 'Mayflower' bar trøstebud til presten." *JiV.* (S)

Gulliksen, Anders. 1865. *Haandbog, eller Hver mands brev-, skrive-, og regnemester.* La Crosse: AP. 240pp. (HB)

Gundersen, Oscar. 1887. Contributions to *B* : "Mennesket i evolutionslærens lys," 4 May; "Darwinismen i et nøddeskal," 1, 8 June (E); "Fiskerens Historie." 20 July. (S)

———. [1891]. *Stemningsbilder.* Chicago: AP. R: *Sk* 25 Nov. (V)

———. 1910. *Ralph Waldo Emerson: En fremstilling.* Chicago: *Sk.* 156pp. R: *Kv* 7 (July 1911): 29–31 (Johnson). (E)

———. 1929. "Litteraturen og livet" *No* 1 (April–May): 8–9. (E)

———. 1930. "Vorten." *No* 2 (March): 6–7. (S)

———. 1930. "Romance." *No* 2 (Dec.): 8–9. (S, English)

———. 1931. "The Immigrant." *No* 3 (Dec. 1931): 6–7. (E, English.)

———. 1932. "Bjørnstjerne Bjørnson," *No* 4 (May 1932): 2–5. (E)

Gundersen–Storhøi, A. 1914. *Fra Stillehavet til Jesu grav.* Seattle: AP. 202pp. (T)

Gunderson, L.L. 1886. *Amerikanske skildringer eller korte fremstillinger af love og forhold i De for. stater, Amerika.* Chicago: AP. 148pp. (E)

Guttersen, Alma A. and Regina Hilleboe Christensen. 1926. eds. *Souvenir: "Norse-American Women" 1825–1925. A Symposium of Prose and Poetry, Newspaper Articles, and Biographies, Contributed by One Hundred Prominent Women.* Minneapolis: Lutheran Free Church. (A)

Haaeim, Sjur Jørgensen. 1842/1928. *Oplysninger om forholdene i Nordamerika,* Christiania: Chr. Grøndahl. Trans. and ed. by Gunnar J. Malmin, "The Disillusionment of an Immigrant: Sjur Jørgensen Haaeim's 'Information on Conditions in North America,'" *NAS* 3: 1–12. (G)

Hagen, Eiliv. 1928. "En farmers datter." *R* 12 April–17 May. (SF)

———. 1937. "Lykkebarnet. Norsk-amerikansk fortælling." *DP* 30 March–18 May. (SF)

Hagen, Gudbrand Torsteinson. 1898. *Bruden fra fjeldet.* Mayville, North Dakota: *Vesterheimen.* 47pp. (N)

———. 1898. ed. *Fra snelandets hytter. Fortællinger og gamle sagn fra Norge.* Mayville: *Vesterheimen.* 104pp. (Folklore.)

———. 1903. *Per Kjølseth, eller "Manden til Marit."* Crookston, Minnesota: *Vesterheimen.* 179pp. R: *Smuler* (Nov. 1903): 14–15 (Hervin). (N)

Hagen, Ole Eriksson. 1881. *En kort skildring af Wisconsins statsuniversitet og skandinavernes forhold til samme.* Chicago: AP. R: *B* 23 Aug. (Petersen). (E)

———. 1885. *Stenspranget.* Minneapolis: Samband. 32pp. (V)

———. 1904. *Tilfjelds.* Crookston, Minnesota: AP. 119pp. This is the 4th ed. R: *Smuler* Sep., 14–19. (N)

———. 1909. *Erik O. Hagen. Kort omrids af hans liv og virksomhed i Norge og Amerika. Et haugiansk livsbillede.* Madison: *Amerika.* 93pp. (B)

———. 1909. *Sylvester Sivertsen. Literærhistorisk afhandling i andledning af reisningen af hans minde-bauta.* Eau Claire: AP. (E)

Hakstad, Sigrid. 1927. "Vort sprog." *NU* 15 (May): 65. (V)

———. 1929. "Om nordmennerne og norskheten i Amerika." *No* 1 (June): 7. (E)

———. 1930. "Et aktuelt spørsmål." *No* 2 (Feb.): 11–12. (E)

Hammerstrøm, Leiv. 1942. "Et stykke julekake." *JiV*, 17–19. (S)

Hansen, Angell Watland. 1911. *Min Gud og jeg. En samling digte for kristendom og afhold.* Minneapolis: AP. 72pp. (V)

Hansen, Carl. 1896. *Præriens børn. Tre fortællinger.* Cedar Rapids: N. Fr. Hansen. 77pp. (S, Danish)

Hansen, Peter. 1923. *Friske vindpust.* Sheboygan, Wisconsin: AP. 46pp. (V)

Hansen, Søren Johan. 1861. *Menneskelighed og orthodoxi casuelt afhandlede i aabne breve til norske præster i Nord-Amerika . . .* Madison: AP. 80pp. (E)

Hanson, Eldor Mikal. 1918. *Gjensvar og varsko.* (V)

———. 1921. *Antikristen.* 16pp. (V)

———. 1926 (E.H.V.). *Bjarne. Et dramatisk digt.* Eau Claire: AP. 197pp. R: *Sk* 13 Jan. 1928 (Reierson). (P)

Harildstad, John A. 1919. *Bondegutten Hastad under asylbehandling i den nye verden.* Minneapolis: AP. 124pp. (N)

Hasberg, K. 1871. *Trapperens veileder. En nøiagtig beskrivelse og undervisning om maaden at fange alle værdifulle pels-dyr . . .* LaCrosse: *FogE.* 94pp. (HB)

Hassel, Nicolai Severin. 1874. "Alf Brage; eller skolelæreren i Minnesota." *For Hjemmet* 5 (Nos. 1–11). (SF)

———. 1874. "Rædselsdagene; et norsk billede fra indianerkrigen i Minnesota." *For Hjemmet* 5 (Nos. 12–19). (SF)

———. 1876. "Den gamle sjøulk." *FogE.* 10, 17 Feb. (SF)

———. 1897. *Juletanker og julefortællinger for gamle og unge.* Decorah: Den norske Synode. 111pp. (A)

Hatlestad, Ole J. 1887. *Historiske meddelelser om Den norske augustana-synode samt nogle oplysninger om andre samfund i Amerika.* Decorah: AP. 254pp. R: *No* 24 April 1888. (H)

Haugan, Bernt Benjaminsen. 1895. *Et besøg hos presten.* Faribault, Minnesota: O.A. Østby. 64pp. (N)

———. 1897. *Over land og bølge. Reiseskildringer fra Orienten og de europeiske lande.* Minneapolis: *UV.* 238pp. (T)

———. 1901. *De syv djævle.* Eau Claire: Fremad. 48pp. (E)

Haugan, Reidar Rye. nd. *Norge venter.* Chicago: AP. 29pp. (P)

Haugen, A.J. 1913. *Sol bag sky.* Vernon, South Dakota: AP. 76pp. (N)

Haugen, Kristine. 1929. "Da Lars Berg skulde under kirketukt." *No* 1 (Oct.): 8. (S)

——. 1932. "Dr. O.E. Rølvaag." *NU* 20 (Jan.): 3–4, (March): 7–8, (April): 7–8, (May): 9–11. (E)

——. 1938. "En aandens stormann—Pastor Ristad." *NU* 26 (Nov.): 1–2. (E)

Heiberg, Lars. 1893. *Brogede blade. Et socialt-kristeligt agitationsskrift.* Minneapolis: AP. 246pp. R: *Saamanden* 6 (No. 12, Aug.): 336. (V&E)

——. 1925. "Kommer han til jul?" *JiV.* (S)

Heinse, John. 1875. *Lidt forstyrrelse paa farmen. Vaudeville i 1 akt.* Chicago: *Sk.* 54pp. R: *Sk* 30 Nov. (P, first performed Chicago, 4 July 1874.)

Heir, Martin. 1906. "Slavens befrielse." *VT* 2 (Jan.): 681–694. (S)

——. 1906. "Da Tore Gundersen Speilberg kom til Amerika." *VT* 2 (May): 883–895. (S)

Heitmann, John. 1922. "Hvor kræfter ulmer." *JiV.* (V)

——. 1922–1923 (Bjarne Blehr). Critical essays on Norwegian-American literature in *DS* 2 Dec. 1922–16 Feb. 1923, most titled "Vore forfattere."

——. 1923 (Bjarne Blehr). "Simple svar paa professor Rølvaags simple spørsmaal." *DS* 1 Dec. (E)

——. 1923 (Bjarne Blehr). "Julius B. Baumann." *JiV.* (E&V)

——. 1924. [Anonymous.] "Julius B. Baumann." Introduction to Baumann 1924. (E)

——. 1934. "Jul i skogen." *JiV.* (S)

——. 1937. "Røsten i skogen." *JiV.* (S)

——. 1938. "Hvad var det?" *JiV.* (S)

——. 1941. "Omkring Ole Edvart Rølvaag." *DP* 15, 22, 29 Aug. (E)

Helgeson, Thor. [1915]. *Fra "Indianernes lande." Nogle minder om Indilandets første beboere og de første rydningsfolk . . . Første samling.* Minneapolis: AP. 333pp. R: *Kv* 13 (April 1917): 47 (Iverslie). (H)

——. [1918]. *Fra "Indianernes lande" og andre steder i Wisconsin. Nogle minder om de første rydningsfolk—træk fra nybyggerlivet . . . Anden Samling.* Minneapolis: AP. 242pp. (H)

——. 1919. *Bibelhistoriske fortællinger . . . .* Minneapolis: AP. 282pp. (V)

——. 1923. *Folkesagn og folketro, fortalt av de første nybyggere paa Indilandet.* Eau Claire: Fremad. 8opp. (Folklore)

——. 1924–1928. "Gamle minder fra Indielandet og andre steder." *R* 27 Nov. 1924–19 March 1925; 18 Nov. 1926–14 April 1927; 9 Feb.–5 April 1928. (H)

——. 1926. "Minder fra Indilandet, Wis," "Den norske arven hans Amund," "Johan og Marte Øygarn." *Gudbrandsdølenes julehilsen,* 33–40. (H)

——. 1928. "Gamle minder." *R* 9 Feb.–5 April. (M)

Hellesnes, Lars. 1934. *I onkel Sams land. En utvandrers ungdomssaga.* Kragerø, Norway: *Vestmar.* Serialized in *DP* 17 Aug.–21 Sep. 1937. (Novel, written around 1900 and published posthumously).

Henderson, Knud. 1865. *Koral-bog.* Many editions, the seventh: *Koral-bog, indeholdende melodier for salmer og aandelige sange, tilligemed et udvalg af "anthems." Samt musikskole som veiledning til sangøvelser.* Chicago: *Sk,* 1887. 172pp. R: *Sk* 24 April 1877; 20 Nov. 1897 (of 10th ed. by Eggen). (Music)

——. 1876. *National- og selskabs-sange med musik.* Chicago: *Sk.* R: *FogE* 28 Dec. (Erik Jensen?). (Music)

——. 1928. *Digte om hjemlige tanker.* Cambridge, Wisconsin: AP. 8opp. (V)

Hendrickson, Peter. 1885. *Farming med hoved og hænder; eller Praktisk veiledning for farmeren*. Chicago: *Sk*. 312pp. Several reprints: 10,000 copies by 1886, 15,000 by 1898. R: *B* 8 Dec. (Petersen). (HB&S)

——. 1887. *Afhandlinger om meieri og kvægavl* . . . . Chicago: *Sk*. 351pp. (HB)

Hervin, Ole S. 1904. *Ved hovedkirken*. St. Paul: AP. 40pp. Serialized in *Smuler*. R: *R* 8 Nov. (M&V)

Hetle, Erik. 1938. "Gamlepresten." *JiV*. (S)

——. 1940. "Kem sin son er du?" *JiV*, 24–27. (S)

——. 1951. "Det ble jul lel." *JiV*, 42–43. (S)

Hilsen, Einar. 1911/1915. *Strengelek*. Fargo: Ulsaker. 192pp. Two editions. Trans. by Bergliot Caspary, *Love Songs and Other Poems*, 1915. (V)

——. [1916]. *Stjerneglimt*. Sioux Falls, South Dakota: *Fremad*. 48pp. (V)

——. 1928. "Norsk læsning." *MT* 29 Oct. (E)

Hirsch, E. 1883. "Om Montana." *B* 8, 15 Aug. (E)

——. 1886. *Jagt og rejseeventyr i Montana*. Chicago: Relling. 102pp. Serialized in *R* 1906. (N)

Hjelmeseth, Eilert. 1934. *Vinlandsgaaten*. Chicago: *Sk*. 206pp. Serialized in *NU* July 1932–March 1934. (N)

Hjelt, Ole. 1920. *Nybyggerliv paa prærien*. Instow, Saskatchewan: AP. Also Winnipeg, 1921. (S)

Hofstad, Jno. A. nd. *Ungdomsdigte*. Minneapolis: AP. 70pp. (V)

Høifjeld, Johannes. 1913. *Unge spirer*. Minneapolis: AP. 63pp. R: *R* 11 Nov. (V&S)

——. 1922. *Julebluss. Digt for julen*. Minneapolis: AP. R: *L* 6: 1621 (Johnsen). (V)

——. 1923. "Der stormen raser." *JiV*. (S)

Holand, Hjalmar Rued. 1908. *De norske settlementers historie* . . . Ephraim, Wisconsin: AP. 603pp. Third edition, 9,000 copies, 1909. Fourth edition, Chicago: *Sk*, 1912. R: *Ny Tid* 2 (Nov. 1908): 45 (Stavnheim); *Kv* 5 (April 1909): 21–26 (Skordalsvold). (H)

——. 1921. " 'The Married Buck.' " *JiV*. (S)

——. 1927. *Coon Prairie. En historisk beretning om Den norske evangeliske lutherske menighet paa Coon Prairie*. Minneapolis: Augsburg. 236pp. (H)

——. 1928. *Coon Valley. En historisk beretning om de norske menigheter i Coon Valley*. Minneapolis: Augsburg. 272pp. R: *MT* 26 Aug. (H)

——. 1930/1978. *Den siste folkevandring. Sagastubber fra nybyggerlivet i Amerika*. Oslo: Aschehoug. 331pp. Trans. by H.M. Blegen, *Norwegians in America: The Last Migration*. Sioux Falls, South Dakota: Augustana College. R: *No* 2 (Oct.): 5 (Hakstad); *No* 2 (Nov.): 3–5 (Rølvaag); *Tidens Tegn* 13 Dec. (Rølvaag). (H)

——. 1957. *My First Eighty Years*. NY: Twayne. 256pp. (M)

Holter, Anna Marie. 1904. *Minder og stemninger i poesi og prosa*. Minneapolis: AP. 44pp. R: *DP* 23 Dec.; *Smuler* (Jan. 1905): 9–10; *VT* 1 (No. 6 1905): 327.

Holvik, J.A. 1920. "Da bykarene kom hjem." *JiV*. (S)

——. 1924. "En aften med Peer Strømme." *JiV*. (M)

——. 1930. "Et juleminde." *JiV*. (S)

Hommefoss, Lise B. Henning. 1916/1917. *Lille Humør. Allegorie*. Minneapolis: AP. 56pp. 2nd ed., 1918. Trans., *Little Cheer-up. Allegory*. R: *MT* 26 March 1916. (V)

——. 1917. *Markblomster*. Minneapolis: AP. 61pp. At least 5 editions. (V)

——. 1920. *Solglimt*. Minneapolis: AP. 32pp. (V&F)

Houeland, Albert. 1917. *Stavangergutten. Hans oplevelser tillands og tilvands.* Minneapolis: AP. 99pp. R: *MT* 9 Dec. R: *DP* 14 Dec. (T)

Hougen, John Olai. 1906. *1814–1905. 17de mai og 7de juni.* Minneapolis: Augsburg. 37pp. (E)

Houkom, Aslak Olavson. 1911 (Alf). *Sæterliv og solskin.* Eau Claire: Fremad. 117pp. R: *Smuler* (June): 31 (Hervin). (N)

Hoyme, Gjermund. 1902. *I hvilestunder.* Minneapolis: Augsburg. 120pp. (A)

Huglen, Reinert Johannessen. 1914. *Blomsterknoppe.* Minneapolis: AP. 11pp. (V)

———. 1914. *Mindekranse.* Minneapolis: AP. 32pp. (V)

———. 1930. *Olavsfest 1030–1930 og Lutherfest 1530–1930.* Wildrose, North Dakota: AP. 32pp. (V)

Hustad, Nicolai. *Opgjør. Skuespil i fem akter. Første del.* Minneapolis: Oscar W. Lund. 177pp. (P)

Hustoft, Ole. 1916. *Taktmesteren og andre eventyr.* Minneapolis: AP. 99pp. R: *MT* 9 Sept. 1917. (S)

Ihme, Olaf Jarl. 1929. *3 skuespil. Badegjesterne. Stammekurset. Da unge Olsen kom hjem.* Tacoma: Sønner av Norge. 115pp. (P)

———. nd. *To skuespil for amatører. "Hjem til Norge" og "To friere."* 30pp. (P)

———. nd. *Turisterne. Farce i 2 akter.* Los Angeles: Viking. 31pp. (P)

Iverslie, Peter P. 1899. *Events Leading to the Separation of Norway and Denmark.* Minneapolis: AP. 122pp. (H)

———. 1902. *Nogle af verdenshistoriens vigtigste begivenheder i den hellige skrifts belysning.* Minneapolis: AP. 126pp. (H)

———. 1912. *Gustav Storms studier over Vinlandsreisene.* Minneapolis: AP. 122pp. (H)

———. 1914. "Kensingtonsteinen og Vinlands beliggenhed." Kv 10 (Jan.): 3–10. (E)

———. 1917. "I sukkerskogen." JiV. (M)

Jaastad, Iver J. 1861. "Et stev. Blik tilbage til Norge." *E* 21 Jan. (V)

Jacobson, Abraham. 1908. "Fra gamle dage." *Symra* 4: 146–156. (M)

Jacobson, Adolph. 1920. *Stridstoner.* Racine: AP. 168pp. (V)

Jacobson, Albert. 1896. *Fremskridtets kamp. Eller, Indgangen til "det tusindaarige rige".* Minneapolis: AP. 200pp. (N)

Janson, Drude Krog. 1889 (1887). *En saloonkeepers datter.* Minneapolis and Chicago: Rasmussen. 229pp. Serialized in *IU*, beginning 4 Oct. 1888. 4th ed. 1894. First published in Copenhagen 1887 as *En ung Pige*, with a preface by K. Janson. R: *B* 6 Dec. 1887. (N)

———. 1894. *Tore. Fortælling fra prærien.* Kristiania: *Verdens Gang.* 74pp. Minneapolis, 1914. (N)

Janson, Kristofer. 1876. *Amerikanske fantasier.* Chicago: *Sk.* R: *Sk* 7 March (Anderson); *FogE* 16 March; *No* 6 April; *B* 11 April; *IF* 1 (Jan. 1879): 23. (P)

———. 1881. *Amerikanske forholde. Fem foredrag.* Copenhagen: Gyldendal. R: *B* 2 May 1882 (Petersen). (E)

———. 1883. *Sande og falske liberale. Prædiken.* Minneapolis: AP. 15pp. (E)

———. 1883. *Vogter eder for de falske profeter. Prædiken.* Minneapolis: AP. 16pp. (E)

——. 1884. *Helvedes børn: Prædiken i dramaform.* Chicago: Rasmussen. 55pp. R: *B* 10 Feb. 1885 (Petersen). (E)

——. 1885. *Præriens saga.* Chicago: AP. Three volumes. I: "Kvinden skal være manden underdanig" and "Kjærlighed paa Kofangeren." II: "En Buggy-Præst." III: "Folkets Fiender" and "En Bygdekonge." 77 + 83 + 69pp. Copenhagen: Gyldendal, 1904. Trans. by Aubertine Woodward (Auber Forestier): "Wives Submit Yourselves unto Your Husbands," *Scandinavia* 2 (Jan.-April 1885); trans. by Oscar Christensen, *A Buggy Priest*, Minneapolis, n.d. R: *Minneapolis Evening Tribune* 10 Dec. 1884 ("A Pathetic Story"); *FB* 23 Dec. 1884 (Oftedal); *B* 21 April 1885; 26 Jan., 27 April 1886; *No* 26 Jan., 16 Feb., 29 June 1886 (S)

——. 1886. *Har ortodoksien ret?* Chicago: AP. 66pp. R: *No* 25 Jan. 1887 (Iverslie). (E)

——. 1886. "The Savior of Yorkville." *Scandinavia* 3 (No. 1, Jan.): 15–16. Norwegian version in 1890. (S)

——. 1887. *Femtende Wisconsin.* Minneapolis and Chicago: Rasmussen. 148pp. Serialized in *IU* beginning 8 Dec. Also 1890, 1891. In *Normænd i Amerika.* Copenhagen, 1887. (N)

——. 1887. *Vildrose. Fortælling fra indianerudbruddet i 1862.* Minneapolis and Chicago: Rasmussen. Serialized in *IU* 6 Oct.–1 Dec. In *Nordmænd i Amerika.* Copenhagen, 1887 and *Juuls store nordiske bibliotek* 1. Chicago: N. Juul & Co, 1891. (N)

——. 1887. *Svar paa spørgsmaal af en farmergut.* Minneapolis: AP. 48pp. (E)

——. 1889. *Et arbeidsdyr.* Minneapolis: AP. 64pp. R: *B* 24 April; *No* 14 May. (N)

——. 1889. *Bag gardinet.* Minneapolis: AP. 247pp. R: *B* 12 Feb.; 19 Feb. 1890 (Janson); March 5 1890 (Knutson); March 26, 1890 (Jensen). (N)

——. 1890. *Fra begge sider havet.* Kristiania & Copenhagen: Cammermeyer. 226pp. (S)

——. 1891. *Sara.* Kristiania and Copenhagen: Cammermeyer. 402pp. (N)

——. 1893. *Jesus-sangene.* Minneapolis: AP. 129pp. R: *B* 18 Oct. (Gundersen). (V)

——. 1913. *Hvad jeg har oplevet.* Kristiania and Copenhagen: Gyldendal. (M)

Jensen, Amund. [ca 1890]. *Kommersraaden. Greven. To livskildringer fra Hedemarken.* Elizabeth, Minnesota: AP. 32pp. (S)

Jensen, Erik. 1878. *Sangbog for børn og ungdom. Samling af to-, tre-, og firstemmige sange, for mandskor og blandet kor. Til brug for hjemmet, skolen, kirken og sangforeninger, samt ved festlige anledninger. Tilligemed en praktisk sanglære.* Decorah, Iowa: Den norske Synodes Forlag. 205pp. R: *Sk* 11 June; 30 July (Jensen); 8 Oct; 19 Nov. (Jensen); *B* 13 March (E.L. Petersen). (M)

Jensenius, Bertram. 1929. "Adel i odel." *No* 1 (Jan.): 13–14; and "Til Amerika." *No* 1 (Feb.–March): 27–28. (S)

Jervell, Hans. 1916. *Nordmænd og norske hjem i Amerika* . . . Fargo: AP. 208pp. R: *DP* 27 April 1917 (Ødegaard). (H)

Johnsen, Erik Kristian. 1918. *Paa reise gjennom England, Norge, Danmark, Tyskland, Schweitz og Italien.* Minneapolis: Holter. 160pp. (T)

Johnson, John A. 1869. ed. *Det skandinaviske regiments historie.* LaCrosse: AP. 151pp. (H)

——. 1869. "Om udvandringen." *Billed-Magazin* 1: 58–59, 66–67, 78–79, 86–88, 114–115, 123–124. As a book, Chicago, 1869, and Christiania, 1870. (E)

——. 1888. *Det store stridspunkt. En afhandling om toldspørgsmaalet.* Minneapolis: AP. 16pp. (Political pamphlet, in English, *The Great Issue.*)

Johnson, Ole S. 1906. *Socialismen.* Spring Grove, Minnesota: AP. 80pp. (E)

———. 1919–1930. *Utvandringshistorie fra Ringerikesbygderne* 1–4. Minneapolis: Ringerik-slaget. 404+442+309+312pp. R: *MT* 27 Sept. 1919. (H)

———. 1920. *Nybyggerhistorie fra Spring Grove og omegn, Minnesota.* Minneapolis: AP. 450pp. Trans. by Aagot Svanøe as *The Pioneer Story of Spring Grove and the Surrounding Area, Minnesota.* La Crescent, Minnesota, n.d. (H)

Johnson, Osmun. 1887/1890. *Johnson's Journey Around the World . . .* Chicago: AP. 400pp. Norwegian edition, *Johnson's reise rundt jorden . . .* Chicago: AP. (T)

Johnson, Simon. 1901. "Efter sjøslaget ved Santiago." *R* 4 June. (V)

———. 1904. "En stille aften." *R* 26 April. (V)

———. 1906. "De nye hjem." *Kv* 2 (July): 12. (V)

———. 1906. "Sommerkveld paa prærien." *VT* 2: 944. (V)

———. 1907. *Et geni.* Eau Claire: AP. R: *Kv* (Oct.): 26–31 (Ager); *Ny Tid* (Dec.): 110–112 (Stavnheim). (N)

———. 1909. *Lonea.* Eau Claire: Fremad. 190pp. R: *Kv* (Oct.): 26–29 (Ager); *R* 1 Feb. 1910 (Mason); *Idun* 1 (May 1910): 164; *Ei* 2 (Feb. 1910): 82 (Strømme), 4 (April 1913): 56–57 (Norstog); *UV* 25 (Dec. 1914): 710–711 (Rønning). (N)

———. 1911. "Udflytterens sang." *Kv* 7 (April): 3–4. (V)

———. 1912. "Vort nye rige." *Kv* 8 (1912): 127–128. (V)

———. 1913. "I seildugsvognen." *R* 23 Dec. (S)

———. 1914/1916. *I et nyt rige.* Minneapolis: Augsburg. 248pp. Also 1915, 1919. Serialized in *DP* 24 Dec. 1953–18 Feb. 1954. Trans. by C.O. Solberg, *From Fjord to Prairie; or In the New Kingdom.* Minneapolis: Augsburg. R: *MT* 27 Dec.; *DP* 1 Jan. 1915; *R* 12 Jan. 1915 and *Kv* (April 1915): 54–59 (Ager); *Norrøna* 4 (Jan.-Feb. 1915): 19–20; *MT* 28 Jan. 1917; *Sk* 7 March 1917 (Eikjarud), 8 April 1927. (N)

———. 1914. "Den første førstefødte." *Symra* 10: 226–231. In *Vesterland* 1 (1915). (S)

———. 1914. "Det skal ikke meget til for at dræbe sligt." *Norrøna* 3 (June-July): 78–79. (Obituary: A.M. Wergeland.)

———. 1914. "Med 'salt til Bukken.'" *Smuler* (March): 1. (V)

———. 1914. "Blaa øine." *JiV.* (S)

———. 1916. "Det nye vikingetog." *Kv* 12 (July): 66–67. (V)

———. 1916. "En forpostfegtning." *JiV.* (S)

———. 1917. *Fire fortællinger.* Minneapolis: Augsburg. 253pp. Also 1919. R: *DP* 8 Jan.; *MT* 20 Jan. 1918 (Hansen); *L* 2 (1918): 114–115 (Rølvaag); *FB* 6 March 1918 (Skordalsvold); *Kv* 16 (1920): 16–18 (Rølvaag). (S)

———. n.d. [1917?]. "Da isslæden løp løpsk." *Julebud. Illustrert julehefte for barn* 2. (S)

———. 1918. "Jims sidste dag." *JiV.* (S)

———. 1919. "Den graa prest." *JiV.* (S)

———. 1921. "Naar livet bærer slør." *JiV.* (S)

———. 1922. *Falitten paa Braastad.* Minneapolis: Augsburg. 456pp. R: *DP* 19 Dec. (Wist); *MT* 21 Dec.; *Sk* 22 Dec. (Skordalsvold); *L* 6: 1514; *DS* Dec. (Baumann, clipping in JBBP). (N)

———. 1922. "Prærien min." *JiV.* (V)

———. 1924. "Julius B. Baumann." *Scandinavia* 1 (Jan.): 41–42. (E)

———. 1924. "Den langveisfarende." *JiV.* (V)

———. 1924. "Borgere." *JiV.* (S)

———. 1925. *Frihetens hjem*. Minneapolis: Augsburg. 361pp. R: *L* 9: 1421–1422 (Skordalsvold); *DS* 11 Dec. (Heitmann); *Sk* 11 Dec. (Rølvaag); *DP* 16 March 1926 (Foss). (N)

———. 1925. "Glimt av norsk foreningsliv i Amerika." *NF* 18 (April): 189–197. (E)

———. 1925. "Mit hjem er paradiset." *JiV*. (V)

———. 1926. "Det vaakende øie." *JiV*. (S)

———. 1928. "Havfuglen." *JiV*. (S)

———. 1929. "Alene." *No* 1 (Oct.): 5. (V)

———. 1931. "Ungdom." *No* 3 (April-May): 5. In *DP* 14 June. (V)

———. 1931. "Hos den gamle mester." *No* 3 (Dec.): 14–15. (V)

———. 1931. "Mor Norge." *JiV*. (V)

———. 1932. "Karantænen." *JiV*. (S)

———. 1934. "En idyl fra nybyggertiden." *JiV*. (S)

———. 1935. "Jon og Ragnhild." *JiV*. (S)

———. 1936. "En vinterdag." *JiV*. (V)

———. 1939. "Skjønlitterære sysler blandt norsk-amerikanere." *DP* 2 Feb., 3, 10 March. (E)

———. 1940. "Paul Olson sitt land." *JiV*, 21–23, 27. (S)

———. 1943. "Indre og ytre." *JiV*, 34. (V)

———. 1948. "I utferdens spor." *JiV*, 8–12. (S)

Johnsrud, Rosanna Gutterud, Bertha Buan and Marcus Tellevik. [1947.] *Tre-kløver-hjørnet*. Duluth: Fuhr. (V)

Jonsrud, Johan P. 1888. *Et minde. Af en benaadet synder*. Keyser, Wisconsin: AP. 32pp. (V)

Jørgensen, Herman E. 1930. "Bare en bare er middels." *JiV*. (S)

———. 1931. "Det kvelder paa Sunnyvale." *JiV*. (S)

———. 1933. "Efter skoletid en fredagskveld." *JiV*. (S)

———. 1936. "Skiftende tider." *JiV*. (S)

———. 1941. "Varg fra Vendland." *JiV*, 9–14. (S)

Jørgensen, S.E. 1893. *Sydmadagaskar*. Minneapolis: AP. (T)

Jørgensen, Theodore. 1937. "Min bror Jørund." *JiV*. (S)

———. 1938. "På forklarelsens berg." *JiV*. (S)

Josephsen, Einar. 1921. "Har vi en norsk-amerikansk literatur?" *Scandia* 4, 18, 25 June. (E)

Juul, Ole. 1902. *Erindringer*. Decorah: AP. R: *Sk* 24 Dec. (A. Johnson). (M)

Kildahl, John Nathan. 1906/1917. *Naar Jesus kommer ind i huset*. Minneapolis: Augsburg. 201pp. Trans., *When Jesus Enters the Home*. R: *R* 8 Jan. 1907. (N)

———. 1911. "Skystøtten." *JiV*. (S)

Kirkeberg, Ole Larson. 1919. *Minder fra Valdres*. [Decorah, Iowa]: AP. 160pp. (M)

Kleven, Gunnar. 1898. *De splidagtige. Eller, Den ældre søns fortælling. Nutidsroman fra begge sider af havet*. Minneapolis: AP. 172pp. (N)

Knudsen, Hedvig. 1914. *Solstreif*. Brooklyn, NY: AP. 125p. R: *R* 16 March 1915; *Kv* 11 (April 1915): 61 (Ager). (V)

Knudsen, Knud. 1840/1967. *Beretning om en reise fra Drammen i Norge til New York i Nord-America*. Drammen. Trans. by Beulah Folkedahl, "Knud Knudsen and His America Book," *NAS* 23: 108–125. (G)

Kolkin, Nils. 1878. *Winona*. Chicago: *Sk*. 106pp. Title poem in *H* 1 (1879): 328. R: *Sk* 31 Dec. (Anderson); 18 March 1879 (Johnson); *B* 1879: 26 Feb. (Petersen); 5 March (Kolkin); 12 March (A.); 19 March (Petersen); 2 April (Johnson and Petersen); 23 April (O.O. Lien and A.); 30 April (Petersen). (V)

———. 1883. "Ogsaa noget om ønskekvisten." *Sk* 11 Sept. (E)

Koren, Elisabeth. 1914/1955. *Fra pioneertiden*. Decorah: AP. 210pp. Trans. and ed. by David T. Nelson, *The Diary of Elisabeth Koren*. Northfield: NAHA. R: *UV* 25: 801; *R* 16 March 1915. (Diary)

Koren, Vilhelm. 1905. "Nogle erindringer fra min ungdom og fra min første tid i Amerika." *Symra* 1: 11–37. (M)

Krug, Christian. 1859. *Dyrlægebog* . . . Madison: *Nordstjernen*. 100pp. 2nd ed.: Grand Forks: *Nordstjernen*, 1881. 96pp. (HB)

Kvam, Olaf Th. 1892. *En fremsynt. Fortælling fra Alaska*. San Francisco: AP. 162pp. (N)

Lang, N. P. 1868. "Opmuntring til at læse gode bøger og blade." *F* 5 March. (E)

[Lange, Anthon B.?] 1885. *Republiken og det arvelige monarki*. Chicago: Agitations-Samfundet "Den norske Republik." 64pp. (E)

Lange, Anton B. 1887. *Amerika og amerikanerne*. Chicago: AP. 232pp. R: *B* 29 Feb. 1888. (E)

Langeland, Knud. 1888. *Nordmændene i Amerika. Nogle optegnelser om de norskes udvandring til Amerika*. Chicago: *Sk*. 224pp. R: *Sk* 11, 18 Jan., 1 Feb. (Knute Nelson); *B* 29 Feb. (H&M)

———. nd. "Lidt skandinavisk-amerikansk literaturhistorie." In *Fortællinger for folket*. Minneapolis and Chicago: Rasmussen.

Larsen, Hanna Astrup. 1905. *Skisser fra Zululand*. Decorah: Lutheran Publ. House. 213pp. R: *ELK* 32: 714–715; *DP* 27 June; *Sk* 2 Aug.; *WP* 18 Aug. (T)

Larsen, Laur. 1913. "Nogle gamle minder," "Atter nogle gamle minder." *Symra* 9: 162–170, 241–250. (M)

Larsen, Valborg Rønne. 1947. "Drømme og virkelighed." *DP* 30 Oct.–27 Nov. (SF)

Larssen, Edward. 1885. *Politiske røvere, eller "Hvor David kjøbte øllet". Lystspill med sange i tre akter*. Chicago: AP. 132pp. R: *B* 18 Aug. (Petersen); *No* 16 Sept.) (P)

Lee, Edward O. 1897. *Lov — og pris-sange*. Chicago: AP. 201pp. (V)

Lee, Jakobine. 1920. *Hyrderøsten*. Erickson, Manitoba: AP. (V)

Lee, John O. 1914. *Nogle smaastubber*. St. Paul: AP. 30pp. (F)

Liabøe, Johannes O. 1893. *Udvælgelsen. Et forsøg paa en harmonisk løsning af dette omtvistede spørgsmaal*. Chicago: AP. 75pp. Also 1910. (E)

———. 1896. *Redningsbøien; eller fra tvil til tro*. Chicago: AP. Also Minneapolis, 1910: AP. R: *Sk* 24 Feb. 1897 (Gundersen); *DP* 21 May 1897 (Eckermann). (E)

———. 1910–1916. *Religionshistorie* 1–4. Chicago: AP. 1. *Asalæren eller de gamle norboeres gudetro i historiske foredrag*. 1910. 319pp. 2. *Oprindelsen til afguder og afgudstro. En ny afsløring af myter og mysterier*. 1912. 336pp. 3. *De kristnes religionshistorie om Gud og Israel fra Adam til David i foredragsform med kronologiske tabeller*. 1913. 367pp. 4. *Kristendommens kilder*. 1916. 349pp. R: *R* 17 Sept. 1912 (Ager), 22 July 1913 (Trønsdal), 6 Jan. 1914 (Ager); *Kv* 9 (Jan. 1913): 14 (Ager). (E)

Lillehei, Lars. 1917. *Erindringer. 92 kortfattede religiøse fortællinger om svar paa bønner, guds aands veiledning, guddommelig helbredelse* . . . Minneapolis: AP. (S)

———. 1928. *Med Leif Erikson paa Vinlandsreise. Eller, Torleif fra Eikaas.* Minneapolis: Augsburg. 55pp. R: *MT* 11 Nov. (J)

Lima, Ludvig. 1903. ed. *Norsk-amerikanske digte i udvalg.* Minneapolis: UV. 355pp. R: *R* 9 Feb. (Buslett), 1 March 1904 (Ager); *DP* 5 Jan. 1904 (Wist). (A)

Lind, Martin. 1891. *Frenologi; eller Efter hjerneskallens form at kunne bedømme menneskets karakter . . .* Chicago: *Sk.* 166pp. (E)

Løbeck, Engebret E. 1894. *Forglemmigei.* Eau Claire: AP. 26pp. (V)

———. 1899. *Billeder fra dødens dal.* Eau Claire: Fremad. Also Alexandria, Minnesota. 1907. (N)

Lock, Otto. 1909. *Syndens sold.* Eau Claire: Fremad. 48pp. R: *Kv* 6 (Jan. 1910): 28. (F)

———. [1913]. *Der var engang.* Patterson, California: AP. 16pp. (V)

———. 1920. *I bunden stil.* Patterson: AP. 35pp. (V)

Lund, Einar. 1945. "Solstrålen i nybygget." *JiV*, 25–29. (S)

Lund, L.H. [1916] (Ohlsen). *Vesterlandiana og andre historier.* Chicago: L.H. Lunds Forlag. 64pp. Previously published as a series in *Skandia.* R: *DP* 24 Nov. 1916. (S)

Lunde, Fridthjof. 1904. "Langveis julegjester." *VT* 1 (No. 3): 129–132. (S)

———. 1905. "Julenat." *Kv* 1 (Oct.): 1. (V)

———. 1906. "Det som hjalp, da mor var syg." *VT* 2: 677–680. As "For det hun forstod norsk" in *Varden* 1 (Nov. 1910): 5–7. (S)

———. 1908. *Døgnfluer.* Eau Claire: Fremad. 77pp. R: *Smuler* (Jan. 1909): 29 (Hervin). (S)

———. 1915. "En størrelse." *Kv* 11 (April): 59–60. (V)

———. 1919. "Fra eneboerne i Jakobsbugta." *Kv* 15 (April, July, Oct.): 34–37. (S)

Malmin, C.K. 1939. "Hitchhiking." *JiV*, 23–28. (S)

———. 1942. "Storfangst." *JiV*, 35–40. (S)

———. 1946. "Landlocked Salmon." *JiV*, 31–34. (S)

———. 1949. 1949. "Berre ein hund." *JiV*, 33–37. (S)

———. 1953. "Han ble på ættegården." *JiV*, 7–10. (S)

———. 1955. "Ut av mørjen." *JiV*, 7–10. (S)

Martinson, Embret. 1895. *Sigmund Framnæs.* Tacoma: AP. 176pp. (N)

Mason, A.H. 1907. *I ørneskyggen.* Eau Claire: Fremad. Serialized in *R.* 240pp. R: *Ny Tid* 1 (June 1908): 483 (Stavnheim); *Kv* 4 (July 1908): 13–19 (Ager); *Smuler* (July 1908): 6 (Hervin). (N)

———. 1907. "Grundskaden." *Kv* 3 (April): 13–19. (V)

———. 1907. "Nu og da." *VT* 3 (1907): 59. (V)

———. 1909. "Hyrekaren kvæder." *Kv* 5 (Jan.): 9–11. (V)

Mathison, Olaf. 1907. *Et budskab til verden.* Everett, Washington: AP. 147pp. R: *Kv* 4 (July 1908): 28–29 (Ager). (V)

Meelberg, Theo. O. 1916. *Kristelige sange.* Fargo: AP. (V)

Meidell, Frithjof A. 1857 (Et træmenneske). "Running for æn office." *E* 23 Sep. (S)

———. 1858 (Et træmenneske). "Amerikanske reiseskizzer. Onkel 'Jim.'" *E* 24 Feb. In *Skilling-Magazin* (Kristiania) 6 April 1861: 214–218. (S)

———. 1858 (Terje Terjesen Terjeland). "Terjes brev fra Kansas." *E* 4 Oct. (S)

———. 1869 (Terje Terjesen Terjeland). "Ansøkning om professor post." *FogE* 15 July. (E)

———. 1874 (Terje Terjesen Terjeland). "Uplysning! Ny uplysning! Stor uplysning." *FogE* 10 Dec. (E)

———. 1876 (Terje Terjesen Terjeland). "Om professorpost." *FogE*. 18 May. (E)

Melbye, Gustav. 1892. *Vildblomsten*. Seattle: AP. (V)

Mengshoel, Emil Lauritz. 1898. Trans. of Frederick Upham Adams. *President John Smith, eller Amerikas redning* . . . Minneapolis: Foss & Lund. 296pp.

———. 1904. *Øen Salvavida: Et samfunnsbillede*. Girard, Kansas: "Gaa Paa." 97pp. R: *R* 9 Dec.; *Smuler* Jan. 1905: 6–9 (Hervin); *Dølen* 2 (No.1): 16 (Norstog). (N)

———. 1919. *Mené Tekél: Norsk-amerikansk arbeiderfortælling fra slutten af det 19. aarhundrede*. Minneapolis: AP. 416pp. R: *MT* 4 Jan. 1920; *DP* 16 January 1920. (N)

Michelet, Maren. 1916. *Glimt fra Agnes Mathilde Wergelands liv*. Minneapolis: AP. Author's trans. *Glimpses from Agnes Mathilde Wergeland's Life*. (B)

———. 1930. "Et aktuelt spørsmål." *No* 2 (March): 22–23. (E)

Minne, Nils Monson. 1892. *Santhalistan*. Minneapolis: AP. 47pp. (E)

———. 1900. *Sange og digte*. Madison, South Dakota: AP. 69pp. (V)

———. 1912. *Nye sange. I-II*. Canton, South Dakota: AP. (V)

———. 1926. *Den gamle pakts folk. Jødene og jødemissionen*. AP. 31pp. (E)

———. 1931. *Liv og virke*. Menominee, Michigan: AP. 61pp. (M)

Moe, P. 1899. *Immanuels ø og omkringliggende øer og øgrupper*. Coon Valley, Wisconsin: AP. 190pp. (N)

Moen, Carl J. 1926. *Religiøse sange til veiledning og trøst for frelsesøgende sjæle*. Minneapolis: AP. 50pp. (V)

Moen, J.K. 1926. *Knut Langaas. Et kapitel fra emigranternes, pioneerenes og præriens saga*. Minneapolis: Rudie. 112pp. R: *MT* 27 June. (N)

———. 1929. "Latter." *No* 1 (Jan.): 25. (V)

———. 1929. "Lars Haug Kaasa." *No* 1 (Feb.-March): 19–20, (June-July): 6–7. (SF)

Mohn, Fredrik. 1890. *Før doktoren kommer. Letvint lægehjelp og sundhedspleie*. Decorah: DP. 151pp. 3rd ed., 1892. (HB)

Monsen, Ole. 1866. *Navne-kalender indeholdende adresser for den skandinaviske befolkning i Amerika, samt underholdende læsestof*. Madison: Ole Monsen.*

Monson, Christie. 1947. "Hvorledes en sognebygd i midtre Iowa ble til." *JiV*. (M)

———. 1952. "En bolig har du vært oss." *JiV*, 37–40. (M)

———. 1956. "Den gamle emigrantkisten." *JiV*, 33–35. (M)

———. 1957. "Bestemors tekanne." *JiV*, 29–32. (S)

Monson, Julius C. 1867. "Pleiedatteren." *F* 31 Oct.–28 Nov. (SF)

Mortensen, John. 1914. *Nogle blade*. Eau Claire: Fremad. 56pp. R: *Kv* 11 (Jan. 1915): 25–26; *R* 16 Feb. 1915 (Ødegaard). (V)

Mossin, P. L. 1852. "Emigrantens udvandring." *E* 4 June. Revised as "Udvandringen." *Sk* 30 March 1870. (V)

———. 1852. "Skulle vi gaae for principer eller partier?" *E* 24 Sept. (E)

———. 1852. "Ei blot at synes men være." *E* 3 Dec. (E)

———. 1856. "En erindring fra reisen." *E* 7 March. (T)

———. 1856. "Den nordiske folkeaand." *E* 4 April. (E)

———. 1856. "Frihedens sande væsen og betydning." *E* 2 May. (E)

Munson, Martha. 1888. *En troende sjæls tanker under korset*. Chicago: Christina Munson. 32pp. (V)

Næstegaard, O.S. 1895. *En missionærs oplevelser i Mongoliet*. Minneapolis: AP. (T)

Nattestad, Ole Knudsen. 1839/1917. *Beskrivelse over en reise til Nordamerika begyndt den 8de April 1837 og skrevet paa skibet Hilda samt siden fortsatt paa reisen op igjennem de Forenede Stater i Nordamerica*. Drammen: J. Wulfsbergs Bogtrykkerie. Trans. by R.B. Anderson, "Description of a Journey to North America." *Wisconsin Magazine of History* 1 (No.2, Dec. 1917): 149–186. (G)

Nelson, Hilda. 1955. "Vesle-Annes første jul i Amerika." *JiV*, 30–34. (S)

Nelson, Luther. 1917. *Omkring Verdun. En norsk-amerikansk students oplevelser i ambulancetjenesten*. Chicago: Sk. 167pp. 2nd ed. 1918. (M)

Nelson, Peder H. 1930. "Da Per Nerigar'n slaktet julegrisen," *No* 2 (Jan.): 4–5; "Ollerudsblakken," (March): 15–16, 24; "Haldor Holters frierferd," (Nov.): 16–17, 23. (S)

——. 1931. "Jul på Elvestad," *No* 3 (Jan.): 5–6; "Svartpurka til Nils Olsa," (April-May): 21, 26. (S)

——. 1932. "Da Bjørnson var ung," *No* 4 (May): 33–34; "Et nasjonalhistorisk minne," (May): 34–35. (E)

Neppelberg, Anders. 1911. *Kjære minder*. Minneapolis: AP. 24pp.

——. 1911. *Drivende skyer*. Minneapolis: AP. 152pp. (V)

Nilsen, Karl G,. 1938. *Østerdølenes saga*. Duluth, Minnesota: Fuhr. 517pp. (H)

Nilsen, Ole. 1892. *Taale Tangen. En historie for børn og ungdom*. Minneapolis: Augsburg. 63pp. (J)

——. 1928. *Dalrosen. Fra virkelighetens verden paa begge sider av havet*. Minneapolis: AP. 76pp. Also Augsburg, 1949. R: *NU* 17 (April 1929): 62. (N)

Nilsson, Svein. 1868–1870/1982. *A Chronicler of Immigrant Life: Svein Nilsson's Articles in Billed-Magazin, 1868–1870*. Trans. and Intro. by C.A. Clausen. Northfield: NAHA. (H)

Njus, L.J. 1952. "Såre hjertestrenger." *JiV*, 7–10. (S)

——. 1955. "Fra en landsens prestegård." *JiV*, 46–48. (S)

Nordberg, Carl Edin. 1922. *Presten som ikke kunde brukes, og andre skisser*. Minneapolis: AP. 93pp. (S)

——. 1923. *Indremissionspresten i storbyen. En videreutvikling av fortællingen "Presten som ikke kunde brukes," samt to andre fortællinger* .... Minneapolis: Lutheran Free Church. 108pp. (S)

——. 1924. *Nykommeren som blev diakon, eller Et ret menighetsmedlem*. Minneapolis: AP. 80pp. (N)

Norgaard, Sofie. 1913. *En norsk familie i Sydafrika*. Minneapolis: Holter. R: *UV* 24: 94. (T)

Norman, Amandus. 1922. *Nordmændene i Amerika*. Hanska Minnesota: AP. 30pp. (H)

Norse-American Centennial 1825–1925. 1925. Minneapolis.

Norske selskab i Amerika, Det. 1904. *Aarbog for Det norske selskab i Amerika 1903*. Minneapolis: The Vineyard Press. 158pp. R: *DP* 14 June. (E)

Norstog, Bjørgulv. 1917. *Syndens sold. Drama i fem akter*. Watford City, North Dakota: AP. 97pp. R: *Kv* 13 (April): 63; *MT* 9 Sept. (P)

Norstog, Jon. 1902. *Yggdrasil*. Kristiania: Thuessen Christensen. (V)

——. 1903–1904. *Dølen. Tidsskrift paa norsk maal*. 1 (Nos. 1–5, 1903), Joice, Iowa. 2 (No.1, 1904), Minneapolis. R: *Smuler* (Dec. 1904): 27–28 (Hervin). (Journal)

——. 1903. *Paa heklemogen.* Joice, Iowa: *Dølen.* 77pp. (N)

——. 1906. *Haakon Sollid.* Minot, North Dakota: AP. 115pp. R: *R* 19 June (Ager); *DP* 26 June (Reynolds); *Smuler* Aug.: 30–32 (Hervin). (N)

——. 1907. *Ørnerud.* Grand Forks, North Dakota: AP. 169pp. (N)

——. 1908. *Tornekronen. Drama i fem Akter.* Minot: AP. 156pp. R: *Ny Tid* 2 (Jan. 1909): 138–139 (Stavnheim); *Kv* 5 (Jan.): 19–22 (Ager). (P)

——. 1909. *Glitretind.* Minot: AP. 76pp. R: *Ny Tid* 2 (March 1909): 237 (Leirfall); *Kv* 5 (April): 30–31 (Ager). (V)

——. 1909. *Svein.* Minot: AP. 117pp. R: *Ei* 2 (Jan. 1910): 41–42 (Strømme); *Kv* 6 (Jan.): 31 (Ager). (V)

——. 1912. *Kain. Eit dramatisk dikt.* Farland, North Dakota: AP. 324pp. R: *R* 12 Nov. (Ager), 7 Jan. 1913 (Buslett); 4 Feb. 1913; *N* Dec. 1912 (Kirkeberg), 17 Sep. 1913 (Lindelie); *Kv* 9 (Jan. 1913): 16–18. (Verse drama)

——. 1913. *Tone.* Farland: AP. 277pp. 2nd ed. Minneapolis: Augsburg, 1920. R: *R* 7 Oct. (Buslett), 14 Oct. (Wergeland), 21 Oct. (Ager); *DP* 28 Oct.; 12 Dec. (Xavier); *N* 29 Oct. (Lone), 24 Dec. (Kirkeberg); *L* 4: 1618 (Johnsen); *Symra* 9: 255–257 (Wergeland); *UV* 24: 792–793; *Ei* 5 (Jan. 1914): 38–40 (Voldal); *Kv* 10 (Jan. 1914): 26–27 (Ager); *Norrøna* 4 (Jan.-Feb. 1915): 18 (C.O.); *MT* 14 Nov. 1920. (V)

——. 1914. *Moses. Drama i fem vendingar.* Cherry, North Dakota: AP. 531pp. R: *DP* 29 Dec. (Ristad); *Kv* 11 (Jan.): 92–96 (Ager); *R* 9 Feb. 1915 (Ager); *MT* 19 April 1915. (Verse drama)

——. 1915. *Natten. Drama i fem akter.* Watford City, North Dakota: AP. 135pp. R: *DP* 16 Nov. (Ristad); *R* 7 Dec. (Ager), 28 Dec. (Buslett); *L* 21: 1610; *Kv* 12 (Jan. 1915) 17–19 (Ager). (P)

——. 1916. *Josva. Drama i fem vendingar.* Watford City: AP. 204pp. (Verse drama)

——. 1917. *Israel. Drama i tolv vendingar.* Watford City: AP. 885pp. R: *Sk* 4 April (Ristad), 18 April; *DP* 19 June. (Verse drama)

——. 1918. *Josef. Eit episk dikt.* Watford City: AP. 135pp. R: *DP* 8 Feb.; *MT* 24 Feb. (Hansen); *L* 2: 309. (V)

——. 1919. "Fyrsten." *JiV.* (S)

——. 1920. *Kong Saul. Drama i fem vendingar.* Risør, Norway: Erik Gunleikson. 208pp. (Verse drama)

——. 1920. "Simeon." *JiV.* (V)

——. 1921. *Kong David. Drama i fem vendingar.* Risør: Erik Gunleikson. 148pp. R: *L* 6: 147; *DP* 31 March 1922. (Verse drama)

——. 1923. *Kong David. Andre bolken. Drama i fem vendingar.* Watford City: AP. 181pp. R: *Sk* 2 Feb. (Ristad); *DP* 9 March (Gjerset); *MT* 2 Nov. (Verse drama)

——. 1923. *Fraa Audni.* Watford City: AP. 196pp. R: *Sk* 9 May (Ristad); *L* 7: 789. (V)

——. 1923. *Golgatariket. Drama i 6 Vendingar.* Watford City: AP. 152pp. R: *MT* 16 Dec.; *Sk* 19 Dec. (Ristad). (P)

——. 1924. "Mundharpen." *JiV.* (S)

——. 1927. *Livshorpa.* Watford City: AP. 205pp. R: *Sk* 16 March 1927 (Ristad). (V)

——. 1928. *Exodus I.* Watford City: AP. 413pp. R: *DP* 9 March (Strandvold); *Sk* 6 March (Ristad), 24 April (Sæter); *R* 19 April. (N)

——. 1928. "Jol i øydemorki." *JiV.* (V)

——. 1929. "Gjesten." *JiV.* (V)

——. 1930. *Exodus II.* Watford City: AP. 319pp. R: *R* 23 Oct.–27 Nov. (Ager). (N)

——. 1931. *Exodus III.* Watford City: AP. 247pp. R: *Sk* 8 Dec. (Sæter). *DP* 15 Dec. (Strandvold); *No* 3 (Dec.): 35–36 (Evanger), 4 (Dec. 1932): 15–17 (Gundersen); *Western Viking* 15 Jan. 1932 (Redal). (N)

——. 1931. "Mr. Kari." *JiV.* (S)

——. 1933. "Kristofer Pilgrim." *JiV.* (S)

——. 1934. *Når elvane møtest.* Bergen, Norway: Lunde. 287pp. R: *DP* 15 Nov.; *Sk* 1 Jan. 1935 (Sæter). (N)

——. 1935. "Landet som er burte—." *JiV.* (V)

——. 1936. "Han talde—." *JiV.* (V)

——. 1937. "Torgrim Kvisl." *JiV.* (S)

——. 1938. *Havet.* Watford City: AP. 182pp. (V)

——. 1938. "Jolekveld hjaa tussane." *JiV.* (V)

——. 1948. "To dikt." *JiV*, 50–51. (V)

Nybroten, Anton A. 1922. *Fra en Norgestur i 1919.* Minneapolis: AP. 160pp. (T)

Nystuen, John C. 1917. *Erindringer.* [New London, Minnesota]: AP. 39pp. (M)

Odden, Halvor Gunnarson. 1910. *Bygaks, samlede langs med veien.* Minneapolis: AP. Also Decorah: *DP*, n.d. (V)

Ødegaard, Oscar Olson. 1911. *Martin Huldre-Bakken. En fortælling fra Romerike.* Homestead, North Dakota: AP. 82pp. R: *Vesterheimen* 5 June 1912. (N)

——. 1914/1915. *Naar det blomstrer i husmandsstuen.* Grand Forks: AP. 46pp. At least 5 editions. Trans. by H. Thorersen, *Camilla.* Wyndmere, North Dakota: 1915. R: *DP* 22 Jan. 1915. (N)

——. 1917. *Fra visergutt til millionær.* Fargo: AP. 31pp. (N)

——. [1923]. *Kirken paa Kvam.* Wyndmere: AP. 16pp. R: *Sk* 25 May (Nielsen). (V)

——. 1924. *Fortællinger og digte.* Wyndmere: AP. 24pp. *MT* 8 Jan. (Ellenson). (S&V)

——. 1925. *Naar man er tilfreds.* Grand Forks: AP. 30pp. (N)

——. 1930. *Kjærlighet og penger. En fortælling fra prærien.* Wyndmere: AP. 65pp. 2nd ed. R: *R* 20 Feb. (Hilsen). (N)

——. 1932. *Skyttsengelen.* Pekin, ND: AP. 28pp. (N)

——. 1947. *Barndomsminner.* Grand Forks, North Dakota: AP. 6th edition. (Music set to one of his poems.)

Ødegaard, Zacharias. 1907. *Ungdomstanker. En samling smaa digte.* Beloit, Wisconsin: AP. 40pp. (V)

Odson, O. 1896. "Gik fra forstanden. Hvordan det gik til, at en norsk farmerkone gik fra forstanden." *H* 19 Feb. 1896: 122–124. (S)

Oftedal, Sven. 1875. "Nordmændenes opgave i det amerikanske statssamfund." *Kvartalskrift for Den norsk lutherske kirke i Amerika* 1: 10–20, 116–128. (E)

Oftedal, Sven and August Wenaas. 1874. "Aaben erklæring." *Sk* 20 Jan. Polemics in *Sk*: Oftedal 10 March; R. B. Anderson 14 April; Carl Rasmussen 12 May; Jørgen Jensen 9 June; "A," 30 June; P. P. Iverslie 21, 28 July; Jensen 18 Aug.

Oftelie, Torkel. 1915. "Jon Norstog." *Telesoga* (No. 25, Sept.): 14–23. (E)

Olsen, Arthur E. [1914?]. *En morsom Norgesreise.* Minneapolis: Holter. 207pp. Trans. *The Land of the Norsemen.* Minneapolis: Holter. (T)

Olsen, B. Tobias. 1864. *Noget om den christelige børneopdragelse og undervisning.* Madison: AP. 120pp. (E)

Olsen, Gideon J. [1914]. *Solvending.* Minneapolis: AP. 80pp. R: *R* 16 Nov. 1915. (V)

———. *Dybe rødder. Fortælling fra Norge.* Decorah: *DP.* 106pp. (N)

Olsen, J. 1906. *Nogle salmer og leilighedssange.* Minneapolis: AP. 114pp. R: *DP* 11 May; 23 May (O. Nilsen). (V)

Olson, O. 1848. "Tag dig iagt for slemme bøger." *Nordlyset* 2 March. (E)

Østrem, O.O. 1858. *Erindringer fra min reise over Atlanterhavet, fremstillet i korthed.* Leland, Illinois: AP. 7pp. (M)

Ottesen, Jacob Aall. 1871. "For hjemmet." *KM* 16 (15 Sept.), 277–283. (E)

Ovren, Johan. 1915. *Vinlandske digte.* Madison: *Amerika.* 48pp. (V)

———. 1926. "Svein i Nebraska." *Gudbrandsdølernes julehilsen:* 21–29. (S)

Paulson, Ole. 1907. *Erindringer.* Minneapolis: The Free Church. 245pp. (M)

Pedersen, Anders Braatelien. 1900. *Mor Hansen. Et romantisk billede fra livet, tilegnet alle aldre.* Rothsay, Minnesota: AP. 309pp. (N)

Pedersen, Carl J.P. 1867. *Hvad jeg oplevde under de 6 første aar af min virksomhed i Amerika.* Chicago: AP. 224pp. (E)

Pedersen, Palma. 1911. *Syrener.* LaCrosse: AP. 64pp. R: *Smuler* (Aug.): 29–32 (Hervin); *Norrøna* 3 (March-April 1914): 59 (Norstog). (V)

———. 1923 (Palma). *Under ansvarets svøbe.* Eau Claire: Fremad. 122pp. Serialized in *N,* 1919. R: *MT* 9 Dec.; 14 Dec. (Sæter). (N)

———. 1924 (Palma). *Ragna.* Eau Claire: Fremad. 136pp. R: *DP* 9 Dec.; 27 Jan. 1925 (Oftelie); *DS* 27 Feb. 1925 (Rølvaag). (N)

———. 1925 (Palma). *Genier.* Eau Claire: Fremad. 206pp. R: *MT* 21 June; *Sk* 10 July (Rølvaag); *DP* 7 Aug. (Prestgard); 25 Sept. (Egilsrud); *Nord-Norge* 39: 16. (N)

———. 1935. "Det rette valg." *DP* 19 Feb.–12 March. (SF)

Petersen, Erik L. 1888. *Det Kristiania, som svinder. Erindringer.* LaCrosse and Minneapolis: *FogE.* Also Chicago: Relling, 1889. Serialized in *FogE* 23 May–20 June. R: *No* 24 July. (M)

Petersen, Franklin. 1900. *Ensomme frivagtstunde.* Brooklyn: AP. 94p. (V)

———. 1907. *Siv i strømmen.* Brooklyn: AP. (V)

———. 1907. "En navnløs grav." *H* 30 Sep. 1904. (V)

———. 1907. "De faderløses jul." *Norsk-amerikansk almanak for 1907,* 66. (V)

———. 1917. "Julenatten." *Kv* 13 (Jan.): 19–20. Also in *R.* (V)

———. 1924. "Norsk-amerikansk literatur." *NT* 16, 23 Oct. (E)

———. 1934. "Naar kjærligheten trækker." *JiV.* (S)

———. 1938. "Kallebas første reise tilsjøs." *DP* 15–29 March. (F)

Peterson, O.M. 1872. *100 timer i engelsk.* Chicago: AP. R: *FogE* 29 Aug.; *No* 23 Dec. (Hvistendahl), 21 Jan. 1875 (OMP). (HB)

———. 1875. *Fuldstændig norsk-amerikansk brev—og formularbog.* Chicago: AP. 168pp. Two expanded editions in 1876. In 1882 published by *Sk* (224p.), which has new editions and reprints at least as late as 1921. R: *No* 24 June. (HB)

———. 1885. *Gen. U.S. Grants liv og virksomhed.* Chicago: *Sk.* 380pp. Also 1886, 1900. R: *Sk* 16 Dec. (H)

———. 1885. *Første læsebog i norsk.* Chicago: *Sk.* 160pp. Also 1889, 1895. R: *B* Dec. 18 (Petersen). (Text)

———. 1889. *Abraham Lincoln og hans samtid* 3 vols. Chicago: *Sk.* Vol.1: *Abraham Lincolns barndom og ungdom* . . . . 245pp. Vol.2: *Abraham Lincoln og negerslaveriet* . . . . 253pp. Vol.3: *Abraham Lincoln som præsident* . . . . 208pp. Another edition the same year, using the same plates, but with different pagination and cheaper paper. R: *Sk* 15 Oct. 1890. (H)

———. 1892. *Billed-ABC-bog med stave—og læseøvelser.* Chicago: *Sk.* 40pp. This is the fourth edition. (Text)

———. 1894. *Florida: Den evige sommers land.** R: *Sk* 13 Dec.

Peterson, Otis S. 1941. "Hjemveien er lang." *JiV*, 36–41. (S)

———. 1944. "Han kom som venn." *JiV*, 46–52. (S)

———. 1949. "Veien tilbake." *JiV*, 9–15. (S)

Pettersen, Wilhelm M. 1891. *Digte.* Minneapolis: Rasmussen. 276pp. R: *Sk* 5 Aug.; *Illustrert Husbibliotek* 18 (Sept.): 425 (Peterson). (V)

———. 1894. *Festdigt i anledning Augsburg Seminariums 25aars jubilæum oktober 1894.* Minneapolis: *UV.* (V)

———. 1895. *En ny slægt.* Minneapolis: AP. 132pp. R: *Normannen* 21 Jan. 1896 (Buslett); *Skirnir* 1 (April 1896): 131–132. (Verse drama)

———. 1907. "Fire digte." *Symra* 3: 43–47. (V)

———. 1908. *The Pilot's Christmas and Other Poems.* Minneapolis: Holter. 80pp. (V)

———. 1908. "Nils." *Kv* 4 (April): 3–5. (S)

———. 1911. *Fra bjørkeskog og granholt.* Chicago: *Sk.* 256pp. R: *MT* Aug. (T)

———. 1912. "Kantate til Norges hundredaars fest." *Kv* 8 (Oct.): 125–126. (V)

———. 1913. "Snip snap snude." *JiV.* (S)

———. 1921. *The Light in the Prison-Window. The Life Story of Hans Nielsen Hauge.* Minneapolis: Holter. R: *MT* 22 Jan. 1922. (B)

———. 1922. *Naar juleklokkene ringer.* Minneapolis: Augsburg. 237pp. Some poems have previously been published in *Kv, Symra* and *JiV.* R: *L* 6: 1621 (Johnsen); *DP* 12 Dec.; *MT* 21 Dec. (V)

———. 1926. "Da lillegut drømte" and "Et nyt aar-Herrens aar." *JiV.* (S&V)

———. 1927. *Fire avhandlinger.* Minneapolis: AP. 121pp. (E)

———. 1927. *Slegten i Vaagefjorden. En saga fra Norges Sørland.* Minneapolis: Augsburg. 341pp. R: *Sk* 28 Feb. 1928 (Bruce). (N)

———. 1927. "Julekveld" and "Saa blev det jul." *JiV.* (V&S)

———. 1930. "The Brintons." *JiV.* (S)

———. 1932. "Ralph Roemer." *JiV.* (S)

Prestgard, Kristian. 1896. *Nansenfærden. Et omrids.* Minneapolis: Rasmussen. 96pp. (E)

———. Editor. 1906. *Norske kvad.* Decorah: *DP.* 720pp. Serialized in *DP* July 1902–Dec. 1903. (A)

———. 1913. "Et sommerminde fra landet uten navn." *JiV.* (T)

———. 1928/1938. *En sommer i Norge.* Vol.1: *Fra den gamle heimbygd,* Vol.2: *Bladmandsferden.* Minneapolis: Augsburg. 210+216pp. Vol.1 trans., *Fjords and Faces.* Minneapolis: Augsburg. *Tilbake til heimbygda,* Oslo: Blix forlag, 1944, is a pirated translation from the English edition. R: *DP* 30 Nov. 1928 (Rølvaag). (T)

———. 1937. *Streiftog. Stemninger og skildringer.* Minneapolis: Augsburg. 172pp. Two editions. (S&E)

Preus, Adolph Carl. 1853. (A) "Den skandinaviske presse i Amerika." *E* 20 May. (H)

———. 1854 (A). "Hvad skulle vi norske læsere ønske og vente af vort norske blad 'Emigranten'?" *E* 5, 12 May. (E)

———. 1854 (A). "Om historien og de kilder hvorfra den haves." *E* 21 Sept. (E)

———. 1857. *ABC eller første begyndelsesgrunde til læsning, for børn.* Madison: Den skandinaviske presseforening. 16pp. (Text)

———. 1857. "Nogle ord angaaende min ABC." *E* 26 Aug. (E)

Preus, Christian Keyser. 1906. "Minder fra Spring Prairie prestegaard." *Symra* 2: 18–30. (M)

Preus, Lulla. 1911. "Minder fra den gamle Paint Creek præstegaard." *Symra* 7: 1–15. (M)

Quam, Erik Tobias. 1905. "Aasmund Kvalstads ottiende fødselsdag." *VT* 1 (No.7 April): 349–353. (S)

Redal, Olav. 1917. *En norsk bygds historie. Nordre Bottineau County North Dakota.* Stanley, North Dakota: AP. 240pp. Trans., *A History of the Norwegian Settlement,* n.d. R: *MT* 9 Dec. (H)

Refsdal, Olav. 1902. *To konfirmanter. Fortælling for børn.* Minneapolis: The Free Church Book Concern. 89pp. (J)

———. 1912. *Fagerliens tvillinger; eller Hverdagslivet.* Chetek, Wisconsin: AP. 90pp. R: *Samband* 54 (Oct.): 488; *Kv* 9 (Jan. 1913): 15; *Norrøna* 3 (March-April 1914): 60; *R* 24 Sept. (Ager). (V)

———. 1916. *Elias.* Eau Claire: Fremad. 43pp. R: *DP* 27 Oct. (Thoresen). (V)

———. 1916. *Samuel.* Eau Claire: Fremad. 48pp. (V)

———. 1916. *Sange.* Deer Park, Wisconsin: AP. 16pp. (V)

Reiersen, Johan Reinert. 1844/1981. *Veiviser for norske emigranter til De forenede nordamerikanske stater og Texas.* Christiania. O. Reiersen. Trans. by Frank G. Nelson, *Pathfinder for Norwegian Immigrants.* Northfield: NAHA. (G)

Reine, Rasmus O. 1868. "Opfyld ei begeret for mig." *F* 12 March. (V)

———. 1868. "Foraarei." *F* 21 May. (V)

———. 1868. "Hurra for Grant." *F og E* 24 Sept. (V)

———. 1868. "En kristens kamp og seier." *F og E* 3 Dec. (V)

———. 1871. *En liden samling af psalmer og religiøse digte.* La Crosse: FogE. 104pp. R: *FogE* 11 May; *KM* 16 (15 Sept.): 273–277 and *FogE* 12 Oct. (Mikkelsen). (V)

Reite, Peter Thoresen. 1912. ed. *Fra det amerikanske Normandi.* Moorhead, Minnesota: Concordia College. 119pp. (A)

Rene, Knut Arneson. 1930. *Historie om udvandringen fra Voss og Vossingerne i Amerika.* Madison: AP. 830pp. (H)

Rinde, Olaus. 1934. *Forandringen paa Stone Hill.* Minneapolis: AP. 207pp. (N)

Rise, Ola J. 1908. *Lasarus Geistus.* Minneapolis: AP. 32pp. R: *Ny Tid* 2 (Jan. 1909): 139–140 (Stavnheim). (V)

———. 1909. *Snø. Forteljingar fraa nybyggjarlive paa dei villaste vidder i Vesterheimen.* Kristiania: AP. 48pp. Some of these poems had appeared earlier in *Kv*: "Snø. Ei soga fraa nybyggjarlivet paa Nord Amerikas præricidder," 3 (Jan. 1907): 7–12, "Præri-natt," 4 (April 1908): 2. (V)

Ristad, Ditlef Georgson. 1922. *Fra det nye Normandie. Kvad.* Edgerton, Wisconsin: AP. 64pp. R: *MT* 26 Nov.; *L* 6: 1651 (H. Bjørnson); *DS* Dec. 1922 (Baumann, clipping in JBBP). (V)

———. 1930. *Kvad. Fra det norske Amerika.* Minneapolis: Augsburg. 90pp. R: *R* 1 Jan. 1931 (Rølvaag); *No* 3 (Jan. 1931): 13 (Norstog), (July 1931): 17–18 (Hakstad). (V)

Rivedal, Jacob J. 1893. *Friheim.* Minneapolis: AP. 206pp. (N)

———. 1920. *Verdens larm. Billeder fra livets komedie.* Spokane: Western Publishing Co. 219pp. (N)

Roan, Carl M. 1921. *Paa tur hit og dit. Reiseskildringer og litt til.* Minneapolis: AP. 140pp. These essays were originally published in *FB.* R: *MT* 27 March. (T)

———. 1924. *Sygdom, sundhet og velvære. En populær fremstilling av medicinsk-videnskabelige emner.* Minneapolis: Augsburg. 340pp. Part of book (79pp) first published with same title, Minneapolis: *KvM.* 1916. R: *MT* 1 Feb. 1925 (HB)

Rodning, Syver Stensen. 1907. *Digt og drama.* Eau Claire: AP. 56pp. R: *R* 16 July. (V&P)

———. 1926. *Nyhusfamilien. Norsk-amerikansk skuespil i 3 akter. Første spil.* Minnewaukan, North Dakota: AP. 32p. (P)

Rødvik, Sigvald. 1921. *Fortællinger fra Canada. Optegnelser fra nybyggerlivet i norske settlementer i Saskatchewan.* St. Paul: *Fremtiden.* 160pp. R: *MT* 27 March. (S)

Roeberg, Jim. 1905. *Blandt norske farmere.* Minneapolis: Kriedt. 128pp. (S&V)

Rogne, Thorstein. nd. *Ole paa prærien.* Millet, Alberta: AP. 65pp. (V)

Rølvaag, Ole Edvart. 1907. "Forviklinger." *VT* 3: 35–39. In *Varden* Sept. 1910. (S)

———. 1909. *Ordforklaringer til Nordahl Rolfsens læsebok for folkeskolen. II.* Minneapolis: Augsburg. (Text)

———. 1911. "Hvor staar vi idag med hensyn til norsken?" *Sk* (daily edition) 24, 25, 27 May 1911. (E)

———. 1912/1971 (Paal Mørck). *Amerika-breve, fra P.A. Smevik til hans far og bror i Norge.* Minneapolis: Augsburg. 184pp. Trans. by Ella Valborg Tweet and Solveig Zempel, *The Third Life of Per Smevik.* Minneapolis: Dillon Press. R: *L* 11 June; *DP* 29 Nov. (Prestgard); *Sk* Dec. (Clipping, OERP); *R* 31 Dec. (Thorkveen); *Kv* 9 (Jan. 1913): 14; *Ei* 4 (Jan. 1913): 38–39 (Volldal); several unidentified clippings in Scrapbook, OERP. (N)

———. 1912 (Paal Mørck). "Stemninger fra prærien." *JiV.* (S)

———. 1914 (Paal Mørck). *Paa glemte veie.* Minneapolis: Augsburg. 286pp. Also 1918. R: *UV* 25: 800; *Sk* 23 Dec.; *R* 22 Dec. (Ager), 12 Jan. 1915 (Ager); *DP* 22 Jan. 1915 (Wist); *L* 21 (1915): 64 (Holvik), 467 (Johnsen); *Kv* 11 (Jan. 1915): 22–25 (Ager); *Samband* No. 85, Feb. 1915, 217–220 and *NF* March 1915, 137–140 (Dieserud); *Tidsskrift for kirke og samfund* Oct. 1915, 221–223 (Wee); several unidentified clippings in Scrapbook, OERP. (N)

———. 1914 (Paal Mørck). "Gammel arv." *DP* 15 mai. (S)

———. 1914 (Paal Mørck). "Sommernat ved præriesjøen." *JiV.* (V)

———. 1914 (Paal Mørck). "Naar sneen daler ved juletide." *JiV.* (S)

———. 1914. "One of those who came across." *JiV.* (S)

———. 1916. With P.J. Eikeland. *Haandbog i norsk retskrivning og uttale.* Minneapolis:

Augsburg. 126pp. Also 1918, 1922. A summary by Rølvaag: "Om den nye ret-skrivning." *L* 1: 611–613. (Text)

——. 1917. "Gutten som ikke hadde lommekniv." *JiV*. In 1932. (S)

——. 1918. ed. *Deklamationsboken*. Minneapolis: Augsburg. 302pp. (A)

——. 1919. ed. with P.J. Eikeland. *Norsk læsebok. 1. For barneskolen og hjemmet*. Minneapolis: Augsburg. 339pp. (Text)

——. 1920. ed. with P.J. Eikeland. *Norsk læsebok. 2. For akademiene, høiskolen og hjemmet*. Minneapolis: Augsburg. 461pp. R: *L* 4: 1331; 1490 (Johnsen). (Text)

——. 1920/1930. *To tullinger. Et bilde fra idag*. Minneapolis: Augsburg. 240pp. Revised version trans. by Sivert Erdahl and Rølvaag, *Pure Gold*. NY: Harper & Row. R: *Kv* 16: 19–22 and *R* 4 June 1921 (Ager); *Sk* (clippings, OERP); *V* 30 Dec. (Løkens-gaard); *DP* (Wist), *DS* (Baumann, clippings, OERP); *N* 18 Dec. (Johnson); *L* 4 (1920): 1578 (Johnsen); *MT* 26 Dec. 1920; *FM* June 1921 (Rønning); *No* 2 (April 1930): 17–18 (Witt), (May 1930): 17–18 (Gundersen), 4 (Dec. 1932): 31 (Gundersen); *Manitou Messenger* 17 Jan. (Spohn); *NY Evening Post* 7 Feb. (Soskin); *NY Times* 9 Feb. 1930 (Hutchison); *Saturday Review* 22 March 1930; *M* 11 Oct. 1930 (Hambro); *Morgenposten* 27 Oct. 1932. (N)

——. 1920. "Julestjernen." *JiV*. (V)

——. 1921/1933. *Længselens baat. Film-billeder. Første bok*. Minneapolis: Augsburg. 368pp. Trans. by Nora O. Solum, *The Boat of Longing*. NY: Harper & Brothers. R: *MT* 29 Dec.; *Sk* Dec. (Ristad, clipping, OERP), 28 Dec.; *R* 3 Jan. 1921 (Ager); *DS*, also in *L* 6 (1922): 1479–1480; *Nord-Norge* (No.23, Spring 1921): 17–18 (Heitmann), (No. 24, Dec. 1921): 28 (Johnsen), (Nos. 25–27, 1922): 26–28 (Baumann); *DP* (Wist, clipping, OERP); *V* (Thompson, clipping, OERP); *FM* Jan. 1923 (Rønning); *NY Times* 22 Jan. 1933 (Hutchison); *NY Herald–Tribune* 22 Jan. 1933 (Marsh); *Boston Evening Transcript* 28 Jan.; *MT* 9 Feb. 1933 (Hansen). (N)

——. 1921. "Klare morgen og vaate kveld." *JiV*. In 1932. (S)

——. 1922. *Omkring fædrearven*. Northfield: St. Olaf College Press. 200pp. R: *DS* Dec. 1922 (Baumann, clipping, JBBP); *DP* 12 Dec.; *MT* 18 Dec.; *MT* 21 Dec.; *Sk* 23 Feb. 1923 (Granskou). (E)

——. 1924. "Det Norge jeg fandt." Serialized in *DP* 4 Nov. 1924–6 Jan. 1925. (E)

——. 1924/1927. *I de dage*. Oslo: Aschehoug. 237pp. Serialized (bowdlerized), *DP* 6 March–8 May 1928. R: *A* 8 Nov. (Elster); *M* 17 Nov. (Hambro); *MT* 30 Nov.; *DP* 9 Dec. (Prestgard); *Broderbaandet* 1 Feb. 1925. (N)

——. 1925/1927. *Riket grundlægges*. Oslo: Aschehoug. 206pp. Serialized (bowdlerized), *DP* 15 May–10 July 1928. Trans. with *I de dage* by Lincoln Colcord and Rølvaag, *Giants in the Earth*. NY: Harper & Row. R: *M* 31 Oct. (Hambro); *DP* 24 Nov. (Prestgard); *NU* (Christmas 1925): 24–25 (K. Haugen); *Chicago Daily News* 11 Feb. 1927 (Sandburg); *NY Times* 29 May 1927 (Hutchison); *Saturday Review of Literature* 11 June 1927 (Nevins); *Independent* 9 July (Walker); *Nation* 125 (13 July 1927) (Vodges); *Boston Transcript* 13 Aug. (Mann); *Atlantic* Sept. 1927 (Gay). (N)

——. 1925. ed. with P.J. Eikeland. *Norsk læsebog. 3. For de høiere skoler og hjemmet*. Minneapolis: Augsburg. 589pp. (Text)

——. 1925. "Trønderjenten som fik hjertefeil." *JiV*. In 1932. (S)

——. 1925–1926. "Det Norge jeg fandt." *DP* 4, 11, 18, 25 Nov., 2, 9, 16, 23, 30 Dec., 1925; 6 Jan. 1926. (T)

———. 1926. ed. *Mindebok om Hans Nielsen Hauge.* Minneapolis: Augsburg. (B)

———. 1928/1929. *Peder Seier.* Oslo: Aschehoug. 361pp. Trans. by Nora O. Solum and the author, *Peder Victorious.* NY: Harper & Row. R: *Morgenposten* 29 Oct. (Kielland); *R* 15 Nov. (Ager), 6 Dec. (Undstad); *M* 18 Nov. (Hambro); *MT* 18 Nov.; *No* 1 (Jan. 1929): 21 (Gundersen); *NY Evening Post* 5 Jan.; *NY Telegram* 5 Jan.; *NY Times* 6 Jan. 1929; *Brooklyn Eagle* 16 Jan.; *Forum* 81 (March 1929) (Fadiman). (N)

———. 1928. "Smørkrigen i Greenfield." *JiV.* In 1932. (S)

———. 1931/1931. *Den signede dag.* Oslo: Aschehoug. 315pp. Trans. by Trygve M. Ager, *Their Fathers' God.* NY: Harper & Row. R: *NY Herald-Tribune* 18 Oct. (Parsons); *NY Sun* 23 Oct. (Marsh); *Nationen* 28 Oct. (Ring); *Buffalo News* 31 Oct.; *MT* 1 Nov.;*NYT* 1 Nov.; *Tidens Tegn* 25 Nov.; *M* 8 Dec. (Hambro); *Boston Transcript* 30 Dec.; *Sk* 22 Dec.; *No* 3 (Dec.): 35 (Gundersen); *Nation* 27 Jan. 1932. (N)

———. 1931. "Omkring Sinclair Lewis og Nobelprisen." *No* 3 (Feb.): 4–5. (E)

———. 1931. "Ogsaa et juleoffer." *JiV.* (S)

———. 1932. *Fortællinger og skildringer.* Minneapolis: Augsburg. 128pp. (S)

Rønnevik, Hans. 1923. "Livet." *DP* 6 April. (S)

———. 1926. *100 procent.* Carlisle, Minnesota: AP. 208pp. R: *Sk* Nov. (Rølvaag, clipping, OERP). (N)

———. 1931. "En vise." *JiV.* (S)

———. 1932. "Det gaar saa underlig til." *JiV.* (S)

———. 1956. "Slik ble det jul hos Nils Vassvik." *JiV,* 42–44. (S)

Rønning, Nils Nilsen. 1903/1904. *A Summer in Telemarken.* Minneapolis: Northland Press. 117pp. In Norwegian, *En sommer i Telemarken.* Minneapolis: Holter. 155pp. Also 1906. R: *DP* 16 Feb. 1904, 23 Dec. 1904. (T)

———. 1907. *Abraham Lincoln.* Minneapolis: Holter. 128pp. (B)

———. 1913. *Bare for moro.* Minneapolis: Holter. 48pp. The first of these sketches is based on an earlier version in *JiV* 1912. R: *R* 11 Nov.; *DP* 14 Nov. (Pettersen); *UV* 25 (1914): 93; *Kv* 10 (Jan. 1914): 23–24; *Ei* 5 (Jan. 1914): 400 (Ager); *Norrøna* 3 (March-April 1914): 59 (Norstog). (M)

———. 1918. "Naar døren aapnes." *JiV.* (S)

———. 1922. "Der sto kvinder bak os." *JiV.* (S)

———. 1924/1928. *Gutten fra Norge.* Minneapolis: Holter. 212pp. Trans., *Lars Lee: The Boy from Norway.* Minneapolis: The Christian Literature Co. R: *L* 8: 594 (Ristad); 803 (Smedal); *MT* 27 April (Bratager). (N)

———. 1925. *Gutten fra Norge—Anden del.* Minneapolis: Holter. pp. 212–284. (Continues 1924.)

———. 1925. *Da stjernene sang.* Minneapolis: Augsburg. 56pp. R: *MT* 3 May. (N)

———. 1933. *The Boy from Telemark.* Minneapolis: The Friend. 150pp. (M)

———. 1943. "Når et folk mister sitt morsmål." *JiV,* 35–37. (E)

Rosendahl, Peter J. 1918–1935. "Han Ola og han Per." *DP.* A comic strip. Republished: Joan N. Buckley and Einar Haugen, eds. *Han Ola og Han Per: A Norwegian-American Comic Strip.* Oslo: Universitetsforlaget, 1984; *More Han Ola og Han Per: A Norwegian-American Comic Strip.* Iowa City: University of Iowa Press, 1988.

Rudie, K.K. 1903. *Sol og skygge.* Minneapolis: AP. 207pp. R: *Smuler* (Oct.): 24–26. (V)

———. 1903. *Valdris-Sambandet.* Minneapolis: AP. (V)

———. 1910. *Mindekrans om Bjørnstjerne Bjørnson.* Minneapolis: AP. (V)

――. 1912. *Johnsons merkelige drømme om himmel og helvede*. [Minneapolis]: AP. In *NU* July, Oct. 1926. R: *UV* 24: 285. (V)

――. 1914. *Norge. En mindekrans. 1814–1914*. Minneapolis: AP. (V)

――. 1916. *Til minde om min gjæve ven John Lie*. Minneapolis: AP. (V)

Rygh, George Alfred Taylor. 1909. *Morgenrødens vinger*. Minneapolis: Augsburg. 147pp. Trans., *The Shadow of a Wrong*. Augsburg, 1909. R: *Idun* 1 (May 1910): 163–164. (N)

Rynning, Ole. 1838/1926. *Sandfærdig beretning om Amerika, til oplysning og nytte for bonde og menigmand. Forfattet af en norsk, som kom derover i juni maaned 1837*. Christiania: P.T. Malling. 40pp. Trans. and ed. by Theodore C. Blegen, *Ole Rynning's True Account of America*. Minneapolis: NAHA. (G)

Særvold, Ola Johan. 1926. *Reisebreve 1–3*. Minneapolis: AP. 379+350+336pp. (Vol.1: *Fra de nordiske lande og Mellem-Europa*, Vol.2: *Fra Østerlandene*, Vol.3: *Fra Italien og den franske riviera*.) R: *MT*, *Sk* (Ristad), *DS, R* (Ager), *V* (Rølvaag and Bruce), *WP*—clippings, OJSP; *FM* Feb., 1927 (Rønning); *L* 11 (2 March 1927); *NT* 10 March 1927 (Dieserud); *FB* 7 Dec. 1927. (T)

――. 1926. *Det store stævne i Camrose, Canada*. Chicago: *Sk*. (E)

Sæter, Johannes Olavson. 1927. *Naar samvitet vaknar*. Minneapolis: Augsburg. 63pp. (V)

――. 1929. *Reisebreve fra en Norgestur*. Fosston, Minnesota: AP. 150pp. R: *No* 2 (Feb. 1930): 15 (P. Nelson). (T)

――. 1944. "En sang om livet." *JiV*, 16. (V)

Sæterlie, Hans Martin. 1912. *Madagaskar. oversigt over Den forenede kirkes missionsmark paa øen* . . . Minneapolis: Augsburg. 266pp. (T)

――. 1916. *Minder og indtryk fra reisen til Kina*. Minneapolis: Augsburg. 216pp. R: *L* 23 (1917): 323; 515 (Stolee), 4 (1920): 339–340 (Tangjerd); *DP* 8 June 1917. (T)

Sætre, Allan. 1882. *English and Scandinavian Conversationalist. A Collection of Familiar Words, Phrases, Sayings, Dialogues &c. Especially Adapted to the Use of the American Housewife and the Scandinavian Servant as a Book of Reference*. Chicago: *Sk*. A bilingual edition with two title pages. (HB)

――. 1883. *Bondekonen Marit Kjølseths erfaringer i Chicago. En skildring af en med bylivets mysterier ukjendt kvindes oplevelser under et kort ophold i havestaden*. Chicago: *Sk*. 108pp. 24 editions by 1918. (N)

Sand, Gustav. 1918. *Adam*. Tacoma: AP. 92pp. (V)

[Sandbakken], Embret Martinson. 1895. *Sigmund Framnæs*. Tacoma: AP. 176pp. R: *Skirnir* 1 (Dec.): 19. (N)

Schack, Thor. 1925. *Nordmannernes sidste gæstebud samt andre digte*. Chicago: AP. 94pp. (V)

Schilbred, Gustav. nd. *Stemninger*. 35pp. (V)

Schmarling, B.A. 1876. "Folket og literaturen" and "Blick paa det norske folk og dets literære udvikling." *B* 6 June, 5 July.

Schøyen, David Monrad. 1874, 1875, 1876. *Amerikas forenede staters historie*. Chicago: *Sk*. Vol.1: *Tidsrummet indtil unionen*. 204pp. Vol.2: *Unionen indtil borgerkrigen*. 207pp. Vol.3: *Den amerikanske borgerkrigs historie*. 200pp. Many later editions. R: *Sk* 12 Jan. 1875 (Hjelm Hansen); 2 Jan. 1877 (Anderson). (H)

――. 1878. *Lovbog for hvermand. En oversigt over den amerikanske civil- og privatrett*. Chicago: *Sk*. 320pp. R: *FogE* 1 Jan. 1879. (HB)

———. 1879. *Norsk-amerikansk haandbog. En fuldstændig haandbog for farmere, kjøbmænd, haandverkere, arbeidere o. a.* Chicago: *Sk.* 233pp. Fourth ed. 1899. (HB)

———. 1879. "To af den norske emigrations fædre." *Sk* 30 Sept. (H)

———. 1879. "Om et skandinavisk-amerikansk historisk selskab." *IF* 1 (Sep.): 78. In *B* 28 Oct. Rejoinders: Luth Jæger, *B* 28 Oct., as "Mere om et skandinavisk-amerikansk historisk selskab," *IF* 1 (Oct.-Nov.): 86; Andersen "Endnu mere om et skand.-amer. historisk selskab," *IF* 1 (Dec.): 95. (E)

———. 1880. *Præsident Lincolns snigmord.* Chicago: Nels Sampson. 166pp. R: *Sk* 3 Nov.; *B* 4 Jan. 1881 (Petersen). (H)

———. 1881. *Præsident Garfield. Hans liv og snigmord, samt en interessant beretning om hans mærkelige bane fra hans ungdomsliv paa farmen til hans ende som nationens første mand.* Chicago: *Verdens Gang* [Nels Sampson]. 163pp. R: *Sk* 17 Jan. 1882; *B* 2 May 1882 (Petersen). (H)

———. 1890. *Bennett-loven.* Stoughton, Wisconsin: Allberg, Swan & Co. R: *B* 20 Aug. (E)

Schrøder, Johan. 1863/1989. "En bog for nordboerne hjemme og i Amerika. Af Schrøders dagbog i Amerika." *E* 5–19 Oct. Trans. in Øverland 1989. (T)

———. 1867/1989. *Skandinaverne i de Forenede Stater og Canada med indberetninger og oplysninger fra 200 skandinaviske settlementer. En ledetraad for emigranten fra det gamle land og for nybyggeren i Amerika.* La Crosse: AP. 292pp. Christiania, 1867 and Stockholm, 1868. The section on Canada trans. with an intro. in Øverland 1989. Promotion by Schrøder in *F* 1866: "Til de norske, svenske og danske geistlige i de Forenede Stater og Canada," 11 Jan.; "Emigrantredaktøren Solbergs selvmodsigelser og opspind," 1 Feb.; "Til det norske folk i Amerika," 22 Feb. (T&G)

Selfors, N. nd. *Digte.* Fargo: AP. 40pp. (V)

Selnes, Johan. 1915. "Vi lovet at komme -." *JiV.* (S)

———. 1917. "Ole Petter og norsk-amerikanerinden." *JiV* (S)

———. 1918. *Vestlandstoner.* Minneapolis: Holter. 150pp. 4 editions by 1919. R: *MT* 2 June (Hansen). (S&V)

Sether, Gulbrand. 1912. *Stræv.* Chicago: AP. 120pp. R: *R* 21 Jan. 1913 (Ager), 29 April 1913 (Baumann). (N)

———. 1915. *Fjeldbygdens datter.* Chicago: AP. 260pp. R: *R* 16 Nov. (Ager); *DP* 16 Nov.; *N* 6 Oct. 1916. (N)

———. 1917. *Sønnen paa Hofstad. Norsk-amerikansk fortælling.* Chicago: *Sk.* 220pp. Also 1917 (twice), 1918. R: *Sk* 24 Jan. (Buslett). (N)

———. 1920. *Bernt Myrstua.* Chicago: *Sk.* 249pp. (N)

———. 1938. "Et underlig syn." *NU* 26 (Dec.): 7–8. (M)

Severson, Sever H. 1892. *Dei møttes ved Utica. En paa personlige iagtagelser grundet skildring af livet i ældre norsk-amerikanske settlementer.* Stoughton, Wisconsin: AP. 176pp. Serialized in *Normannen.* (N)

Shawhem, K.O. 1917. *Nordmændenes opdagelse af Amerika i det ellefte aarhundrede og deres erobringer i Europa.* Grand Forks: AP. 128pp. (H)

Shefveland, Ole. 1899. *Pastor Gram.* Minneapolis: AP. 185pp. (N)

———. 1924. *Marit Gjeldaker.* West Union, Iowa: AP. 179pp. (N)

Shol, Herman O. 1899. *Fra begge sider.* Fargo, North Dakota: AP. (N)

Sieverts, Sverre. 1925. *Dessa byfolka.* Minneapolis: Norrøna. 55pp. R: *MT* 3 May. (P)

Siljan, Lars J. 1919. "Palma Pedersen." *N* 12 Aug. (E)

Skordalsvold, J.J. 1923. "Stor-Jo hørte Kristina Nilsson." *JiV.* (S)

Skugrud, G.A. 1899. *En banebryter. En norsk guts levnedsløb.* Seattle: AP. (N)

Smedsrud, Peder. 1899. *I ensomme stunder.* Hillsboro, North Dakota: AP. 32pp. (V)

Sneve, Ole Svendsen. 1896. *Sange og digte tilegnet afholdssagens venner.* Eau Claire: AP. 86pp. 2nd ed. 1899; 3rd ed. 1904. (V)

———. 1912. *Samlede sange og digte.* Silvana, Washington: AP. 424pp. R: *Kv* 9 (Jan. 1913): 15–16 (Ager); *R* 14 Jan. 1913 (Buslett), 21 Jan. (Ager), 15 April (Reimestad); *Ei* 4 (April 1913): 57–58 (Ristad). (V)

Solheim, Signe. 1939. "Gull, røkelse og myrra." *JiV.* (S)

———. 1941. "Den rette." *JiV,* 43–50. (S)

———. 1942. "Paa andre veie." *DP* 7 April–28 April. (SF)

———. 1943. "Ardis." *JiV,* 39–46. (S)

Sorensen, M. 1912. "De fire bomuldstrær. En saga fra Minnesota River dalen." *Symra* 8: 113–116. (S)

———. 1912. "En taksigelsesdag. En historie om, hvorledes en nordmand kom frem." *Symra* 8: 169–175. (S)

Steensland, Halle. 1898. *Bibelens lande.* Madison: AP. 211pp. Two other editions in 1898. Revised edition: Minneapolis: Augsburg. 1900. 557pp. R: *Sk* 12 Dec. 1900. (T)

———. 1899. *Trange tider og hvorledes de kan forebygges. Et foredrag.* Madison: AP. (E)

———. 1909. "Erindringer fra min Amerika–reise og mine første aar i Amerika." *Symra* 5: 80–89. (M)

Stenersen, Gina. 1949. "Nils og Signe." *DP* 27 Jan.–17 Feb. (SF)

Stenholt, Lars A. 1880. *Olaf.* Ålesund, Norway: AP. 31pp. (N)

———. 1881. *Sivert Aarflots minde.* Ålesund: AP. 32pp. (B)

———. 1882. "Fra Norge til Amerika." *Sk* 5, 12 Dec. (T)

———. 1883. "Advokat W.S. Dahl." *Sk* 18 Dec. (B)

———. 1887. *Mod drik. To foredrag.* Decorah: AP. 40pp. (E)

———. 1887. *Bjørnstjerne Bjørnson.* Minneapolis: Kriedt. 24pp. (B)

———. 1888. *"Chicago anarkisterne." Historisk skildring.* Minneapolis: Kriedt & Kristiania: Omtvedt, 80pp. (H)

———. 1889. *Fra trælle til folk.* Minneapolis: Kriedt. 128pp. (N)

———. 1889. *Præsten Erik: Fortælling.* LaCrosse: AP. (N)

———. 1890. *Dr. Cronins mord. Kortfattet historisk skildring.* LaCrosse: AP. 79pp. (E)

———. 1892. *Lars Oftedal. I hans storhed og i hans fald. En karakterskildring.* Minneapolis: Kriedt. 2nd ed. 1895. 100pp. 3rd ed. 1904. (B)

———. 1893. *Fra farmergut til millionær. En biografi-skildring af Jay Gould.* Minneapolis: Kriedt. 105pp. Several editions. (B)

———. 1893. *Normændenes opdagelse af Amerika. Historiske skildringer.* Minneapolis: Kriedt. 144pp. (H)

———. 1893. *Præste-historier. Skildringer af nordmændenes aandsliv i Nordamerika.* Minneapolis: Kriedt. 132pp. (Satire)

———. 1893. ed. *Gjest Baardsen. En forbryders livsroman. Fortælling fra aarhundredets begyndelse* 1–2. Minneapolis: Kriedt. 177+171pp. (N)

———. 1894. *Moderne vikinger. Historisk skildring af kapt. Magnus Andersens fredelige vikingefærd.* Minneapolis: Kriedt. 100pp. (E)

——. 1894. ed. *Blus. En samling af lystige historier, fortællinger og anekdoter.* Minneapolis: Kriedt. 116pp. Several later editions. (A)

——. 1894. ed. Hans Jæger, *Fra Kristiania bohemen* 1–2. Minneapolis: Kriedt. 250+268pp.

——. 1895. *Pullman, Debs og Coxey. Nutidsroman.* Minneapolis: Kriedt. 114pp. (H)

——. 1896. *Harry Høyward.* [sic].*En historisk berettelse om Hayward og Blixts mord paa Katharina Ging.* title varies: *Hayward og Blixt. En historisk berettelse om mordet paa Katharina Ging.* Minneapolis: Kriedt. (E)

——. 1896. *Harry Haywards bekjendelser, nedskrevne og dikteret af ham selv kort før hans hængning.* Minneapolis: Kriedt. Both books on Hayward and *Durrant* (1897, below) were published in Swedish (1896) and Norwegian (1897) editions in one volume by Kriedt. (E)

——. 1896. *Knute Nelson. En studie.* Minneapolis: Kriedt. 116pp. (B)

——. 1896. *Massemorderen Holmes, alias Mudgett m.fl. En historisk berettelse om denne store forbryders misgjærninger.* Minneapolis: Kriedt. 131pp. Also 1899 and 1903. (E)

——. 1897. *Durrant. En sandfærdig beskrivelse af det skrækkellige dobbeltmord i Emanuelskirken i San Francisco.* (Also bound with *Farlige folk*, 1897). Minneapolis: Kriedt. 17pp. (E)

——. 1897. *Farlige folk.Fortællinger og skitser.* Minneapolis: Kriedt. 116pp. (Satire)

——. 1897. *Norge i Amerika. Skildringer af nordmændenes liv i Amerika.* Also 1898. Minneapolis: Kriedt. 152pp. Kristiania: Sophus Kriedt. R: *DP* 31 Dec. (H)

——. 1897. *Dr. Fridtjof Nansen. Billeder fra Nordishavet.* Also 1908. Minneapolis: Kriedt. (B)

——. 1897. *Sitting Bull. Billeder fra den sidste indianerkrig.* Minneapolis: Kriedt. 162pp. Kristiania: Sophus Kriedt. Also St. Paul, 1917. (H)

——. 1897. *To banditter. James og Younger brødrenes bedrifter. Novellistisk fremstillet.* Minneapolis: Kriedt. 123pp. With varying titles, 1898, 1901, 1905 and 1906. The 1905 edition has an addition (53pp.) with a separate title page: *Younger beødrenes bedrifter.* (F)

——. 1898. *America's kamp med Spanien.* Also 1899. Minneapolis: Kriedt. 180pp. (E)

——. 1899. *De sidste indianeruroligheder i Minnesota.* Minneapolis: Kriedt. (E)

——. 1900. *Fangen paa Djevleøen. Alfred Dreyfus. Et billede af nutidens største sørgespil.* Minneapolis: Kriedt. Also 1906. (H)

——. 1900. *Prest Erik Jensen.Den forenede kirkes arvefiende.* Minneapolis: Kriedt. 17pp. (Satire)

——. 1901. *Falk og jødinden. Fortælling fra Norge og Amerika.* Minneapolis: Kriedt. 140pp. (Satire)

——. 1901. *President Wm. McKinley. En historisk beretning om hans liv og død, et kort omrids af President Roosevelts liv, samt en udsigt over Czolgozs's ugjerning og domfældelse.* Minneapolis: Kriedt. 160pp. (E)

——. 1901. *Minnesota-bibelen for 1901. En fortsættelse af Wisconsin-Bibelen.* Minneapolis: Kriedt. 104pp. Two imprints on 1908 edition: Kriedt and Capital. (Satire)

——. 1903. With John Ring. *Norske og amerikanske kriminal-historier.* 3rd enlarged edition, Minneapolis: Kriedt. 143pp. (Satire)

——. 1903. *Harry Tracy og Merrill. Pacifiklandenes svøbe.* Minneapolis: Kriedt.*

———. 1903. *L.A. Stenholts politihistorier. Billeder af Minneapolis bystyre* . . . . Minneapolis: Kriedt. 158pp. (Satire)

———. 1905. *Det frie Norge. En historisk beretning om Norges frigjørelse fra Sverige.* Minneapolis: Kriedt. 190pp. Also 1907. (H)

———. 1905. *Kvaksalvere og halvgalninger. Skildringer af lægevæsenet her i Nordvesten.* Minneapolis: Kriedt. 48pp. (Satire)

———. 1905. *Tyve aar paa farten efter lykken. En interessant og belærende beretning om Karl Johnsons mærkverdige hændelser paa hans stormfulle løbebane i hans higen efter lykken.* Minneapolis: Kriedt. 352pp. (N)

———. 1907. *Paul O. Stensland og hans hjælpere, eller Milliontyvene i Chicago.* Minneapolis: Kriedt. 189pp. (Satire)

———. 1908. *Arbeidets martyrer, Moyer, Hayward og Pettibone, samt deres bødler James McParland and Orchard & Co. En historisk fremstilling af sørgespillet i Boise, Idaho.* Minneapolis: Kriedt. 192pp. (H)

———. 1908. *Paven i Madison. Eller, Rasmus Kvelves mærkværdige liv og hændelser.* Minneapolis: Kriedt. R: *Smuler* (Nov. 1907): 30–31. (Satire)

———. 1908. *Mrs. Bella Gunness.* Minneapolis: Kriedt. (E)

———. 1912. *John F. Deitz. Deitz's og hans families kampe mod tømmerkongerne for eiendomsretten til Cameron Dam paa Thornapple-elven i Wisconsin. Et nutidsdrama fra Wisconsin.* Minneapolis: Kriedt.*

Storm, Eilert. 1907. *Alene i urskogen. Fortælling fra Amerika.* Chicago: *Sk.* 379pp. First published in Kristiania: Stenersen. 1899. (N)

Storseth, John. 1933. *Djævelskap.* Tacoma: Puget Sound Publ. Co. 188pp. R: *No 5* (May): 26–30 (Gundersen). (E)

Straaberg, Josef. 1910. "Ondt med godt." *Varden* (Dec.): 12–14. (S)

———. 1921. *Norma Holm og andre skildringer.* Salt Lake City: Bikuben. 163pp. (S)

Strandvold, Georg. 1932. "Paa vei til julen." *JiV.* (S)

———. 1933. "Mors gut." *JiV.* (S)

———. 1935. "Fra sommer til høst." *JiV.* (S)

———. 1938. "Maleriet." *JiV.* (S)

Strømme, Peer Olsen. 1893/1960. *Hvorledes Halvor blev Prest.* Decorah: *DP.* 220pp. Grand Forks, 1910. Serialized in *Superior Posten* 24 Nov. 1892–8 June 1893 and in *N* 18 May–31 Aug. 1910. Trans. by Inga Norstog, *How Halvor Became a Minister.* Minneapolis, 1936; trans. by Inga Norstog and David Nelson, *Halvor: A Story of Pioneer Youth.* Decorah: Luther College Press. R: *Sk* 20 Dec. (N)

———. 1902. *Compend of Church History for Lutheran Young People.* Chicago: *Sk.* 154pp. (Text)

———. 1904. "Hvad vi vil." *VT* 1 (No.1): 1–3. (E)

———. 1904. *Det norske selskab i Amerika. Beretning om selskabets 2det aarsmøde i Minneapolis* . . . Minneapolis. (E)

———. 1905. "Mark Twain." *Symra* 1: 102–108. (E)

———. 1909. Two stories in *Symra* 5: "Lars Tobiason" (25–34) and "Dengang det spøgte for Sjur Grinde" (90–95). The latter trans. by Gerald Thorson, "The Time a Ghost Appeared to Sjur Grinde," *Peer Strømme's Noraville Stories*, Winchester Academy Ethnic Heritage Monograph No. 2. (S)

———. 1910 (Halfdan Moe). *Den vonde ivold. Oversat fra Engelsk af Peer Strømme*. Grand Forks: AP. 141pp. First chapter in *Ei* 2 (February 1910): 50–56. (N)

———. [1911]. *Breve fra Peer Strømme paa reise rundt verden som "Normanden"s korrespondent*. Grand Forks: *N*. 96pp. (Serialized in *N* from June 1911.) (T)

———. 1911. *Unge Helgesen*. Grand Forks: AP. 160pp. (Serialized in *VT* 2 (1906) and *N* 26 Oct. 1910–15 March 1911. Selections trans. in *Peer Strømme's Noraville Stories*, Winchester Academy Ethnic Heritage Monograph No. 2. (N)

———. 1915. "En juleaften i Bethlehem." *JiV*. (T)

———. 1917. "Norsk-amerikansk bogavl." *N* 1 May. (E)

———. 1918. "Two poets of Finland." *JiV*. (E)

———. 1920. *Digte*. Minneapolis: Augsburg. 84pp. R: *L* 4: 1585 (E.Kr. Johnsen); *MT* 12 Dec. (V)

———. 1921. "Verdens mest interessante by." *JiV*. (T)

———. 1923. *Erindringer*. Minneapolis: Augsburg. 431pp. An earlier version serialized in *N* 1915. Extracts trans. by Neil T. Eckstein, "Peer Strømme's Memoirs." *The Round Table* 1 (1975) and following issues and collected in *Peer Strømme's Memoirs of a Winchester Childhood*, Winchester Academy Ethnic Heritage monograph No. 1. R: *L* 7: 105; 395–396 (Christensen); *MT* 27 Feb.; *DP* 2 March (Christensen). (M)

Sunde, Hjalmar Olsen. 1903. *Vagabonden. Skildringer og egne oplevelser fra alle dele af verden*. Minneapolis: *Nye Nordmanden*. 320pp. (T)

Sundheim, Anders M. 1923. "Paa eventyr i vildmarken." *JiV*. (S)

———. 1924. "Der skogene suser." *JiV*. (S)

———. 1927. "Kuno den heldige." *JiV*. (S)

———. 1934. "En tapper liten kriger." *JiV*. (S)

———. 1937. "Den siste fisker ved Kabekona-vannet." *JiV*. (S)

———. 1942. "Ute på viddene." *JiV*, 29–33. (S)

———. 1944. "Skiftende horisonter." *DP* 6 Jan.–30 March. (E)

———. 1944. "Den kongelige Missinaibi." *JiV*, 17–20. (E)

———. 1945. "Stølen, stølslivet og Jotunheimen." *JiV*, 35–42. (E)

Swanes, J. 1934. *Blandt kveitefiskerne paa nordvestkysten*. Eau Claire, Wisconsin: Fremad. 164pp. (E)

Syversen, Henry. 1862. "17 de Mai paa 10de Eiland, Tennessee." *E* 28 July. (V)

Tangen, Anders. 1918. *Skjulte kræfter*. Tacoma: AP. 128pp. (N)

Teigen, Knut Martin Olson. 1899. *Ligt og uligt i vers, skisser, humoresker og smaaskildringer fra livet blandt de norske i Amerika*. Minneapolis: Berner Loftfjeld. Expanded 2nd edition: *Ligt og uligt i skisser, humorekser, eventyr og pennebilleder fra livet blandt vestens vikinger*. Minneapolis: Kriedt, 1907. (S)

———. 1901. *Amnor. Et fragmentært, serio-komisk heltedigt, med nogle kortere smaating i vers*. St. Paul: AP. 47pp. Revised version in 1905. (V)

———. 1901 (Jeremias Pederson Jammerdalen). "Brev fra Jeremias." *Smuler* No.1, May: 7–12, No.2, June: 8–22, July: 13–23, Aug.: 15–26, Sep.: 9–28, Oct.: 7–29. (Satire)

———. 1901–1903 (Lars Lægmand). "Sermoner til vor geistlighed." *Smuler* Nov.: 8–11, Dec.: 14–19, Jan. 1902: 12–18, Feb.: 10–16, March: 9–15, April: 11–16, May: 16–24, ("Nogle ord fra klokkeren," June 1902: 6–8, may not be by Teigen,) July: 12–15, Sept.: 12–13, Jan. 1903: 10–19, Feb.: 10–21, March: 11–29, May: 5–18.

——. 1903. Prose in *Smuler:* "En menighedsbeslutning," Aug.: 12–15; "Johan Olais forargelser," Sept.: 10–15; "Griseliteratur," Nov.: 9–11; "Kamp altid misforståelse," Dec.: 4–11.

——. 1903. "Epigrammer." *Smuler* April: 32; Nov.: 30–32. (V)

——. 1903. "Half-Breeds," "Numedøler." Pp. 129–132, 182–189 in Anderson 1903.

——. 1903–1905. "Hickory-Nødder." *Smuler* Dec. 1903–Oct. 1905. The poems in this series are included in 1905. (V&E)

——. 1905. *Vesterlandske digte.* Minneapolis: Gode Venners Forlag. 208pp. R: *Smuler* Oct.: 1–4 (Hervin), Nov.: 9–12 (Baumann); *DP* 7 Nov. (Wist). (V)

——. 1905 ("Oversat af Tom") "Dooley om Brokvelvninger." *Smuler* Nov.: 7–9.

——. 1906 (Tom). "Til J. Apostata." *Smuler* (Dec.): 31–32. (V)

——. 1907. *Blandt vestens vikinger. Skisser, humoresker, norsk-amerikanske folkelivsbilleder.* Minneapolis: Kriedt. 46pp. Also as addenda to some copies of 1907 ed. of *Ligt og uligt.* (S)

——. 1907 (Tom). Contributions to *Smuler:* "Til J. Apostata," (Jan.): 31–32 (V); "Dooley om Socialismen," (April): 10–11; "Micae Panis," (May): 15–18, "Friheden," (July): 19–21, "Om kirkelige fonografer," (Nov.): 20–24 (Satire).

——. 1908. "I slaatten østom Svartekulpen: Fra 'Dugstadgutten,' Dr. Teigens nye fortælling." *Kv* 4 (April): 6–18. (S)

——. 1908. Prose in *Smuler:* "Om grov kjæft og pen kjæft," (Jan.): 11–15; "Kuriko og 'den rene lære,'" (March): 15–19; "Hurra for 'Norges samvittighed,'" (April): 10–14; "Atter om Bibelfusk," (June): 5–13; "Naar vore kirker blir theatre," (July): 10–15; "Syltelabber," (Sept.): 14–17; "Lidt om socialismen," "I tusmørket," (Oct.): 14–19; "Lefseklining og sildesalat," (Dec.): 3–7.

——. 1908. Verse in *Smuler:* "Visnede figentrær." (March): 1–2.

——. 1909. Prose in *Smuler:* "En amnorsk forklaring til enfoldiges brug og nytte," Feb.: 4–11 — April: 17–24; "De mortuis nil nisi veritas," Dec.: 13–15.

——. 1909. *Om hjernefeil og sindsvagheter.* Minneapolis: Forskaren. 14pp. (E)

——. 1909. "Usonas vikingestamme." *Forskaren* March: 100–104, "1. Norsk sjælefrelseri"; April: 134–141, "2. Journalistik og bogfabrikation"; May: 170–174, "3. Naar vikinger faar vondt"; June: 244–250, "4. Ved valgurnen"; Aug.: 337–342, "5. I Usonas smeltedigel." (E)

——. 1910. Contributions to *Smuler:* "Fingerpeg," (July): 1–2 (V); "Honning kager fra 'Mot.'" (July): 20–23. (E)

——. 1911. *Some Popular American Paranoias at Large: A Psychiatric Compendium on Modern Brain Spots and Their Results on American Mentality* . . . Minneapolis: Evolution. 90pp. (E)

——. 1912. "A Norwegian Paine. Marcus Thrane Tried to bring Daylight to his Benighted Countrymen, Here and at Home." *The Truth Seeker* 16 March. (E)

——. 1913. *Amnorske digte. En fortsettelse af vesterlandske digte.* Minneapolis: Evolution. Some of these poems had earlier appeared in *Smuler.* (V)

Tellevik, Marcus. 1938. *Uro.* Fargo: N. 36pp. (V)

——. 1947. See Johnsrud, Rosanna Gutterud.

Testman, Peter. 1839/1927. *Kort beskrivelse over de vigtigste erfaringer under et ophold i Nord-Amerika og paa flere dermed forbundne reiser.* Stavanger: L.C. Kielland. Trans.

and ed. by Theodore C. Blegen, *Peter Testman's Account of his Experiences in North America*. Northfield: NAHA. (G)

Thrane, Marcus. 1867. "Skydsskiftet i Hallingdal." MS: Oslo University Library. R: *Sk* 14 Feb. (Play performed in Chicago 1867.)

——. 1867. "Syttende Mai." No extant MS. R: *Sk* 23 May; *E* 25 May (Solberg). (P)*

——. 1880. "Holden; eller Smør deg med taalmodighed. Synode-opera i tre akter af Tubalkin." Typescript trans. by Henriette Naeseth, NAHA. (Play, performed in Chicago 1880.)

——. 1882/1955. *Wisconsin-Bibelen. (24 Kapitler) af Profeten Tubalcain*. Chicago: Den nye Tid. 65pp. Several later editions: Minneapolis: Kriedt, 1908; Chicago: Scandia, 1938. Trans. and ed. by Linsie Caroline Krook and F. Hilding Krook, *The Wisconsin Bible*. New Ulm, Minnesota. (Satire)

Throndsen, Knud. 1890. *Ørkenblomster. En samling digte og salme*. Decorah: *DP*. R: *Sk* 24 Dec. (V)

——. 1893. *Bibel og geologi. Et indlæg mod de falske geologiske theorier*. Decorah: AP. 352pp. R: *Sk* 27 Dec. (Ottesen). (E)

——. 1896. *Bibel og astronomi. Et populært foredrag*. Decorah: AP. 24pp. (E)

Thuland, Conrad M. 1910. *Leif Erikson. Historisk drama i 3 handlinger*. Seattle: AP. 58pp. (P)

Thvedt, Ragnhild Thinn. 1917 (R. Th.). Stories in *Kv* 13. "En forfulgt," (Jan.): 2–7; "Da jeg fridde. (En prestefrues optegnelser)," (April): 51–54; "Lige børn leger bedst," (July): 69–73. (S)

——. 1923. "Det syvende bud." *JiV*. (S)

——. 1936. "Bønnhørt." *JiV*. (S)

——. 1940. *Nogle minder fra en norsk-amerikansk prestegaard*. Eau Claire, Wisconsin: Fremad. 60pp. (M)

Tjernagel, Nehemias. 1897. *Fodture i Ægypten og Palæstina*. Randall, Iowa: AP. Second edition, Minneapolis: Augsburg, 1919. 318pp. (T)

Tovsen, Antonette. 1920. "Blaaveis." *DP* 30 Nov.–7 Dec. (SF)

——. 1923. "Herdis." *DP* 6 March–24 April. (SF)

——. 1923. "For tidlig ude." *DP* 18 Dec. (S)

——. 1925. "Naar strengene brister." *DP* 24 March–12 May. (SF)

——. 1929–1930 "Rebecca." *DP* 5 Nov. 1929–21 Jan. 1930. (SF)

——. 1930. "Anstalten." *DP* 11 March–6 May. (SF)

——. 1934–1935. "Markens trælle." *DP* 2 Oct. 1934–1 Jan. 1935. (SF)

——. 1935. "Det siste forsøk." *JiV*. (S)

——. 1936. "Toner." *DP* 10 March–2 June. (SF)

——. 1936. "Hvite seil." *JiV*. (S)

——. 1937. "Spøkelset." *JiV*. (S)

——. 1938. "Hvite seil." *JiV*. (S)

——. 1941. "Da kronprinsparret kom." *JiV*. (S)

——. 1943. "Dybe hjulspor." *DP* 21 Jan.–15 April. (SF)

Travaas, Erik Arnesen. 1925. *Norske digte og fortællinger*. Minneapolis: AP. (V&S)

Trovatten, Ole Knudsen. 1842(MS)/1956. Trans. and ed. by Clarence A. Clausen, "The Trials of an Immigrant: The Journal of Ole K. Trovatten." *NAS* 19: 142–159.

——. 1854. *Nogle ord til de norske i America*. Buffalo.* (E)

Ulvestad, Martin. 1895. *Engelsk-dansk-norsk ordbog*. Minneapolis: AP. Several printings, one claiming a total of 20,000 copies. 730pp. An undated dictionary: *Selvhjælp i engelsk. Engelsk-norsk ordbog med fuldstændig udtalebetegnelse*. 624pp.

——. 1901. *Norge i Amerika med kart*. . . . 2nd edition 1902 with slightly different title. R: *Sk* 5 Oct. 1900; *No* 26 Feb. 1901. (H)

——. 1907 and 1913. *Nordmændene i Amerika: Deres historie og rekord*. Volume 1, Minneapolis 1907. Volume 2, Tacoma 1913. 1008pp. R: *ELK* 34 (1907): 494; *Kv* 3 (April 1907): 31–32; *R* 21 May 1907, 21 Oct. 1913; *DP* 14 Oct. 1913; *Kv* 10 (Jan. 1914): 27–28. (H)

——. 1916–1926. *Norsk-Amerikaneren*. Seattle: AP. R: *Kv* 13 (April 1917): 46–47 (Iverslie). (H)

Vangsnes, O.P. 1914. "Jeg glemmer aldrig den første jul." *JiV*. (S)

Vetlesen, Thomas F.C. 1906. "Havarerede eksistenser." *VT* 2: 990–993. (S)

Voldal, Henrik. 1914. "Sigrid-Sjur, som ikke kunde forlade Norge." *JiV*. (S)

——. 1920. "For Fædrearven." *L* 4: 1640–1642. (E)

Wærenskjold, J.M.C.W. 1856. "En normands hjemve." *E* 19 March. (V)

——. 1856. "Graven." *E* 4 April (V)

Wee, Mary Nelson. 1939. "Vinger." *JiV*, 31–5. (S)

——. 1943. "I Guds hånd." *JiV*, 26–33. (S)

——. 1948. "Bestemors vindu." *JiV*, 39–41. (S)

——. 1953. "Prestekone blir jeg aldri." *JiV*, 24–7. (S)

Wefald, Knut. 1932. "Prærien." *JiV*. (V)

Werenskjold, Frithjof. [1925]. *Potpourri. (Humanum est errare.)*. Seattle: AP. 91pp. R: *Nord-Norge* 39: 16. (E)

——. nd. *Halmstrå*. 64pp. (V&E)

Wergeland, Agnes Mathilde. 1911. "De stød verden gir." *Symra* 7: 225–229. (E)

——. 1912. "Tre digte." *Symra* 8: 88–91. (V)

——. 1912. *Amerika og andre digte*. Decorah: DP. 260pp. R: *R* 17 Dec. (Ager); *Kv* 9 (Jan. 1913): 14–15 (Ager). (V)

——. 1913. "Camilla Collett." *Symra* 9: 1–8. (E)

——. 1914. *Efterladte digte*. Minneapolis: The Free Church. 175pp. R: *DP* 15 Dec. (Wist); *R* 29 Dec. (Ager); *UV* 25: 731; *Kv* 11 (Jan. 1915) 20–22 (Ager). (V)

Westheim, D.J.O. 1910. *Fra aandens slagmark*. Minneapolis: Augsburg. 214pp. (N)

Wigeland, R. 1847. "Til Nordlysets ven." *Nordlyset* 23 Sept. (V)

Winslow, Ferdinand S. 1854. "Udvandreren og hans stilling i det nye hjem." *E* 13 Oct. (E)

——. 1854. "Et glædeligt nytaar." *E* 29 Dec. (E)

——. 1855. "Sproget." *E* 12 Jan. (E)

——. 1855. "Dannet og udannet." *E* 13 April. (E)

Wist, Johannes B. [1888]. *Den norske indvandring til 1850* . . . . Madison: AP. Revised and abbreviated, "Brudstykker af Indvandringens Historie," *Skandinavens illustreret folke-kalender* 8 (1894): 24–35; and Bjørnstjerne Bjørnson, *En livsgaade samt andre fortællinger af norske forfattere*. Minneapolis and Chicago: Rasmussen, 1906. R: *Sk* 26 Aug. 1891. (H)

——. 1897. "Paa prærien." *DP* 16 Nov. (S)

——. 1904. "Norsk amerikansk literatur." Norske selskab, 1904, 72–87. (E)

——. 1904. "Norsk literatur i Amerika." *DP* 10 May. (E)

——. 1905. "Norsk-amerikanske forfattere. Peer Strømme." *Symra* 1: 144–158. (E)

——. 1905. "Vor kulturelle stilling." *Kv* 1 (Jan.): 1–10; and *DP* 7 March. Trans. Lovoll 1977. (E)

——. 1906. "Norge i 1905." *Kv* 2 (Jan.): 1–8. (E)

——. 1907. "Under jul." *Symra* 3: 186. (V)

——. 1909. "Vor historiske literatur." *Symra* 5 127–143. (E)

——. 1909. "Edgar Allan Poe." *Symra* 5: 214. (E)

——. 1911. "Smadra." *Familielæsning* 17 (No. 36): 47–52. Decorah: *DP*. (S)

——. 1912. "Blade av en nybyggersaga." *Symra* 8: 19–49. (S)

——. 1912. "En ferieudflugt." *DP* 13 Aug. (T)

——. 1913. "Da Bjørnson kom til La Crosse." *Symra* 9: 55–68. (S)

——. 1914. ed. *Norsk-amerikanernes festskrift 1914*. Decorah: Symra. 352pp. (H)

——. 1920 (Arnljot). *Nykommerbilleder. Jonas Olsens første aar i Amerika*. Decorah: *DP*. 152pp. Serialized in *DP*, "Nykommerbilleder fra otti'erne," 4 Nov. 1919–18 May 1920. R: *MT* 25 July; *DP* 5 Nov. (Norstog). (N)

——. 1921 (Arnljot). *Hjemmet paa prærien. Jonas Olsens første aar i nybygget*. Decorah: *DP*. 322pp. Serialized in *DP* 1 Oct. 1920–13 May 1921. R: *DP* 27 Sept. (Prestgard), 4 Nov. (Bothne) *MT* 2 Oct. (N)

——. 1921. "Et mindeord." *DP* 23 Sept. (Obituary: Strømme.)

——. 1922 (Arnljot). *Jonasville (Et kulturbillede)*. Decorah: *DP*. 325pp. Serialized in *DP* 7 Oct. 1921–21 April 1922. R: *DP* 19 May (Oftelie), 24 Oct. (Ristad), 26 Dec. (Buslett); *L* 6: 1297; *MT* 1 Oct.; *DS* 16 Oct. (Heitmann). (N)

——. 1922 (Arnljot). *Reisen til Rochester*. Minneapolis: Augsburg. 136pp. Serialized in *DP* 11 Oct. 1921–10 Jan. 1922. R: *L* 6: 1621 (Johnsen); *DP* 19 Dec. (Ristad); *MT* 21 Dec. (N)

——. 1922 (Arnljot). "Reisen til Montana."*DP* 31 Jan.–14 March. (SF)

——. 1922 (Arnljot). "Housecleaning." *DP* 28 May–11 July. (SF)

——. 1922 (Arnljot). "Aslak farlaus. En fortælling fra Norge og nordlige Wisconsin." *DP* 27 Oct.–22 Dec. (SF)

——. 1923 (Arnljot). "Hvorledes Lars Bakka blev akklimatiseret." *DP* 20 Feb.–8 May. (SF)

——. 1923–1924 (Arnljot). "Sommerferie." *DP* 30 Oct.–12 Feb. (SF)

[Wist.] 1924. *In memoriam Johannes B. Wist*. Decorah: Symra.

Woldhagen, M.H. 1909. *Fortællinger og digte*. Walworth, Minnesota: AP. (S&V)

——. [1911?] *Folkesnak*. [Chicago]: AP. (S&V)

Woll, Carsten. 1885. *"Lærken". En liden samling kristelige sange*. La Crosse: AP. 47pp. (V)

——. 1894. *En julefest i Chicago 1881*. Stoughton: AP. 32pp.

Wright, Andreas. 1867. "Hvad jeg syntes om bladene." *Sk* 14 March. (V)

——. 1877. *Turtelduen*. La Crosse: *FogE*. 160pp. (A)

——. 1881. *Gjenløser blandt syndere; eller Rettergang i tid og evighed. En Allegori*. Rushford, Minnesota: AP. (N)

C: Secondary

Aaron, Daniel. 1964. "The Hyphenate Writer and American Letters." *Smith Alumnae Quarterly* (July): 213–217.

Aikio, Matti. 1919. "Norsk-amerikansk skjønlitteratur; hvorfor den ikke er til." *Nationen* (Oslo) 19 June.

Alnæs, Barbara Ann. 1978. "Borghild M. Dahl: Second-Generation Norwegian-American Author." Unpublished thesis. Oslo: University of Oslo.

Amundsen, Svein Schrøder and Reimund Kvideland. 1975. *Emigrantviser* (Norsk Folkeminnelags Skrifter No. 115). Oslo: Universitetsforlaget.

Andersen, Arlow W. 1953. *The Immigrant Takes His Stand: The Norwegian-American Press and Public Affairs, 1847–1872.* Northfield: NAHA.

——. 1975. *The Norwegian-Americans.* Boston: Twayne.

——. 1990. *Rough Road to Glory: The Norwegian-American Press Speaks Out on Public Affairs, 1875 to 1925.* Philadelphia: Balch Institute.

Andersen, Thor M. 1982. *Norway in America: Bibliographical Collections.* Oslo: American Institute, University of Oslo. (A "pilot" pamphlet including entries under "A" of a projected bibliography of Norwegian-American literature.)

Anderson, Rasmus Bjørn. 1895. *First Chapter of Norwegian Immigration.* Madison: AP.

——. 1915. *Life Story.* Madison: AP.

Andreassen, Odd Gunnar. 1977. "Lars Andreas Stenholt: Norwegian-American Author." Unpublished thesis. Oslo: University of Oslo.

——. 1986. "Lars Andreas Stenholt: Popular Author and Radical." *Essays on Norwegian-American Literature and History* 1: 61–72.

Bagley, Clarence. 1916. *History of Seattle from the Earliest Settlement to the Present Time.* Chicago: S.J. Clarke.

Bahr, Ingeborg. 1981. "Generational Conflict in Immigrant Families in Five Norwegian-American Novels." Unpublished thesis. Oslo: University of Oslo.

Baron, Dennis. 1990. *The English-Only Question: An Official Language for Americans?* New Haven: Yale University Press.

Barstad, Johanna. 1975. *Litteratur om utvandringen fra Norge til Nord-Amerika: En bibliografi basert på katalogen over Norsk-amerikansk Samling.* Oslo: Universitetsbiblioteket i Oslo.

Barton, A.O. 1928. "Norwegian-American Emigration Societies in the Forties and Fifties." *NAS* 3: 23–42.

Barton, H. Arnold. 1975. *Letters from the Promised Land: Swedes in America, 1840–1914.* Minneapolis: University of Minnesota Press.

Baym, Nina. 1981. "Melodramas of Beset Manhood: How Theories of American Fiction Exclude Woman Authors." *American Quarterly* 33 (Summer, No. 2): 123–139.

Beck, Richard. 1938. "Norwegian-American Literature." Pp. 74–84 in Frederika Blankner, *The History of the Scandinavian Literatures.* New York: Dial.

Berner, Robert L. 1986. "Peer Stømme in Two Worlds." *Essays on Norwegian-American Literature and History* 1: 73–84.

Bjork, Kenneth. 1940. "The Unknown Rølvaag: Secretary in the Norwegian-American Historical Association." *NAS* 11: 114–149.

Blegen, Theodore C. 1931. *Norwegian Migration to America 1825–1860*. Northfield: NAHA.

——. 1940. *Norwegian Migration to America: The American Transition*. Northfield: NAHA.

——. 1955. *Land of Their Choice: The Immigrants Write Home*. Minneapolis: University of Minnesota Press.

Boelhower, William. 1987. *Through a Glass Darkly: Ethnic Semiosis in American Literature*. New York: Oxford.

Bojer, Johan. 1924/1925. *Vor egen stamme*. Oslo: Gyldendal. Trans. by A.G. Jayne as *The Emigrants*. New York: Grosset & Dunlap. Reprinted with an Introduction by Paul Reigstad. Lincoln: University of Nebraska Press, 1978.

Boyesen, Hjalmar Hjorth. 1892. "The Scandinavians in the United States." *North American Review* 155 (November): 526–535.

Brandt, Nils O. 1907. "Pastor Nils Brandts Erindringer fra Aarene 1851 til 1855," as told to Adolf Bredesen. *Symra* 3: 97–122.

Bredesen, Inga M. 1919. "Jon Norstog, the Bookmaker." *Poet Lore* 30 (Spring): 112–126.

Brungot, Hilde Petra. 1977. "Dorthea Dahl: Norwegian-American Author of Everyday Experience." Unpublished thesis. Oslo: University of Oslo.

——. 1986. "Dorthea Dahl: Norwegian-American Author of Everyday Life." *Essays on Norwegian-American Literature and History* 1: 175–185.

Buenker, John D. and Lorman A. Ratner, eds. 1992. *Multiculturalism in the United States: A Comparative Guide to Acculturation and Ethnicity*. New York: Greenwood Press.

Chametzky, Jules. 1972. "Our Decentralized Literature: A Consideration of Regional, Ethnic, Racial, and Sexual Factors." *Jahrbuch für Amerikastudien* 17: 56–72.

Chrislock, Carl H. 1977. "Name Change and the Church 1918–1920." *NAS* 27: 194–223.

——. 1981. *Ethnicity Challenged. The Upper Midwest Norwegian-American Experience in World War I*. Northfield: NAHA.

Christianson, John R. 1985. Ed. *Scandinavians in America: Literary Life*. Decorah, Iowa: Symra.

Di Pietro, Robert J. and Edward Ifkovic, eds. 1983. *Ethnic Perspectives in American Literature: Selected Essays on the European Contribution*. New York: MLA.

Draxten, Nina. 1966. "Oscar Gundersen and his Daughter." *Minnesota Posten* 18 August 1966.

——. 1976. *Kristofer Janson in America*. Boston: Twayne.

——. 1988. *The Testing of M. Falck Gjertsen*. Northfield: NAHA.

Erickson, Rolf H. 1990. Musical Compositions by Norwegian Americans. Evanston, Illinois: Unfinished MS.

Fletre, Lars. 1979. "The Vossing Correspondence Society and the Report of Adam Løvenskjold," *NAS* 28: 245–273.

——. 1986. "Det Litterære Samfund (The Literary Society of Chicago)." *Essays on Norwegian-American Literature and Society* 1: 365–372.

Folkestad, Sigure. 1925. "Den norsk-amerikanske skjønlitteratur." *Nordmanns-Forbundet* 18: 219–227.

Free Passage: A Journal of Prose and Poetry (No. 9, Spring). [An issue on Simon Johnson.]

Granhus, Odd-Stein. 1988. "A Socialist Among Norwegian-Americans: Emil Lauritz Mengshoel, Newspaper Publisher and Editor." Unpublished thesis. Oslo: University of Oslo.

———. 1992. "Socialist Dissent among Norwegian-Americans: Emil Lauritz Mengshoel, Newspaper Publisher and Author." *NAS* 33: 27–71.

Gulliksen, Øyvind T. 1987. "In Defense of a Norwegian-American Culture: Waldemar Ager's *Sons of the Old Country.*" *American Studies in Scandinavia* 19: 39–52.

Gulmoen, Sissel Marie. 1980. "Immigrant Experience and the West as Depicted in the Works of the Norwegian-American Author Olai Aslagsson." Unpublished thesis. Oslo: University of Oslo.

Gvåle, Gudrun Hovde. 1962. *O.E. Rølvaag: Nordmann og amerikanar.* Oslo: Universitetsforlaget.

Hale, Frederick. 1984. *Danes in North America.* Seattle: University of Washington Press.

Halvorsen, H. 1903. Ed. *Festskrift til Den norske synodes jubiæum 1853–1903*, Decorah: Den norske synodes forlag.

Hansen, Carl G.O. 1956. *My Minneapolis: A Chronicle of What Has Been Learned and Observed about the Norwegians in Minneapolis Through One Hundred Years.* Minneapolis: AP.

Hansen, Jean Skogerboe. 1972. "History of the John Anderson Publishing Company of Chicago, Illinois." Unpublished MA Thesis, Graduate Library School, University of Chicago.

———. 1979. "*Skandinaven* and the John Anderson Publishing Company." *NAS* 28: 35–68.

Hanson, Haldor. 1909. "Lidt om norsk-amerikansk bokavl i de første 20 aar - eller ned til 1870." *Idun* 1 (April–May): 108–110.

———. 1925. "Vor første Bogavl. Spredte Bemerkninger om Amerikanernes Medvirken til Fremhjælp af norsk-dansk Bogavl her i Landet i og omkring 50-Aarene." *DP* 13 February.

Hart, James D. 1950. *The Popular Book: A History of America's Literary Taste.* New York: Oxford University Press.

Haugen, Einar. 1949. "A Norwegian-American Pioneer Ballad." *NAS* 15: 1–19.

———. 1953. *The Norwegian Language in America: A Study in Bilingual Behavior* 1–2. Philadelphia: University of Pennsylvania Press.

———. 1970. "Thor Helgeson: Schoolmaster and Raconteur." *NAS* 24: 3–28.

———. 1977. "Symra: A Memoir." *NAS* 27: 101–110.

———. 1983. *Ole Edvart Rølvaag.* Boston: Twayne Publishers.

———. 1989. *Immigrant Idealist: A Literary Biography of Waldemar Ager, Norwegian-American.* Northfield: NAHA.

Haugen, Eva Lund and Einar Haugen (1978) eds. *Land of the Free: Bjørnstjerne Bjørnson's America Letters, 1880–1881.* Northfield: NAHA.

Hausberg, Sv. 1977. "Presten Bernt Askevold 1846–1926." *Jul i Sunnfjord.* Førde, Norway: Sunnfjord Sogelag, 6–10.

Heitmann, John. 1941. "Ole Edvart Rølvaag." *NAS* 12: 144–166.

———. 1949. "Julius B. Baumann: A Biographical Sketch." *NAS* 15: 140–175.

Helland, Andreas. 1920. *Augsburg Seminar gjennem femti aar 1869–1919*. Minneapolis: AP.

Higham, John. 1963. *Strangers in the Land: Patterns of American Nativism 1860–1925*. Second edition. New York: Atheneum.

Hodnefield, Jacob. 1949. "Erik L. Petersen." *NAS* 15: 176–184.

Hoidahl, Aagot D. 1930. "Norwegian-American Fiction Since 1880." *NAS* 5: 61–83.

Hovde, Oivind M. and Martha E. Henzler. 1975. *Norwegian-American Newspapers in Luther College Library*. Decorah: Luther College Press.

Hove, Haldor L. 1962. "Five Norwegian Newspapers, 1870–1890: Purveyors of Literary Taste and Culture." Unpublished dissertation. Chicago: University of Chicago.

Huseboe, Arthur R. and William Geyer. 1978. Eds. *Where the West Begins: Essays on Middle Border and Siouxland Writing, in Honor of Herbert Krause*. Sioux Falls, South Dakota: Center for Western Studies Press.

Hustvedt, Lloyd. 1966. *Rasmus Bjørn Anderson: Pioneer Scholar*. Northfield: NAHA.

———. 1971. "The Norwegian-American Historical Association and its Antecedents." *Americana Norvegica* 3: 294–306.

———. 1976. "The Simon Johnson – Ole Edvart Rølvaag Correspondence." Pp. 54–58 in Harald S. Naess, ed. *Norwegian Influence on the Upper Midwest*. Duluth: University of Minnesota.

———. 1979. *Guide to Manuscript Collections of the Norwegian-American Historical Association*. Northfield: NAHA.

———. 1980. "Ole Amundsen Buslett, 1855–1924." Pp. 131–158 in Lovoll (1980).

———. 1984. "Immigrant Letters and Diaries." Pp. 38–51 in Sandra Looney et al. eds., *The Prairies Frontier*. Sioux Falls, South Dakota: The Nordland Heritage Foundation.

———. 1990. "Images of the Minister in Norwegian-American Literature." *Essays on Norwegian-American Literature and History* 2: 201–210.

Hustvedt, Sigurd Bernhard. 1925. "An American Manifesto by Norwegian Immigrants." *American-Scandinavian* Review 13 (October): 619–622.

Imbsen, Jan-Erik. 1977. "Johannes B. Wist: Norwegian-American Leader." Unpublished thesis. Oslo: University of Oslo.

Jonassen, Jorun Marie. 1988. "Arbeiderlederen Marcus Thrane som teatermann og dramatiker. Teaterhistorisk plassering av Marcus Thranes skuespill og teaterdrift i Amerika, sett i lys av hans livhistorie og hans åndelige og politiske samtid." Unpublished thesis. Trondheim: University of Trondheim.

Jorgenson, Theodore. 1964. "*Decorah-Posten* og norsk litteratur." *DP* 3 September.

Josephsen, Einar. 1924. "An Outline of Norwegian-American Literature." *Scandinavia* 1 (April): 50–55.

Kilde, Clarence. 1979. "Dark Decade: The Declining Years of Waldemar Ager." *NAS* 28: 157–191.

Kongslien, Ingeborg R. 1989. *Draumen om fridom og jord: Ein studie i skandinaviske emigrantromanar*. Oslo: Det norske samlaget.

Lægdene, Anne-Marie. 1981. "Laura Ringdal Bratager: Norwegian-American Author." Unpublished thesis. Oslo: University of Oslo.

Larsen, Karen. 1929. "The Adjustment of a Pioneer Pastor to American Conditions: Laur. Larsen, 1857–1880." *NAS* 4: 1–14.

Larson, Agnes M. 1934. "The Editorial Policy of *Skandinaven*, 1900–1903." *NAS* 8: 112–135.

———. 1969. *John A. Johnson: An Uncommon American*. Northfield: NAHA.

Larson, Laurence M. 1934. "Tellef Grundysen and the Beginnings of Norwegian-American Fiction." *NAS* 8: 1–17.

Leiren, Terje. 1987. *Marcus Thrane: A Norwegian Radical in America*. Northfield: NAHA.

Lindberg, Duane R. 1979. "Norwegian-American Pastors in Immigrant Fiction, 1870–1920." *NAS* 28: 290–308.

Lovoll, Odd S. 1970. "The Norwegian Press in North Dakota." *NAS* 24: 78–101.

———. 1975. *A Folk Epic: The Bygdelag in America*. Boston: Twayne.

———. 1977. Ed. *Cultural Pluralism versus Assimilation: The Views of Waldemar Ager*. Introduction by Carl H. Chrislock. Northfield: NAHA.

———. 1977. "*Decorah-Posten*: The Story of an Immigrant Newspaper." *NAS* 28: 77–100.

———1980. Ed. *Makers of an American Immigrant Legacy: Essays in Honor of Kenneth O. Bjork*. Northfield: NAHA.

———. 1980. "Simon Johnson and the Ku Klux Klan in Grand Forks." *North Dakota Quarterly* 49 (autumn): 9–20.

———. 1984. *The Promise of America: A History of the Norwegian-American People*. Minneapolis: University of Minnesota Press.

———. 1988. *A Century of Urban Life: The Norwegians in Chicago Before 1930*. Northfield: NAHA.

———. 1990. "*Gaa Paa*: A Scandinavian Voice of Dissent." *Minnesota History* 52 (No.3 Fall): 86–99.

Mossberg, Christer Lennart. 1979. "The Immigrant Voice as American Literature: Scandinavian Immigrant Fiction of the American West." Unpublished dissertation. Indiana University.

———. 1981. *Scandinavian Immigrant literature*. Boise State University Western Writers Series No. 47. Boise: Boise State University Press.

Munch, Peter A. 1970. *The Strange American Way: Letters of Caja Munch from Wiota, Wisconsin, 1855–1859 with An American Adventure: Excerpts from "Vita Mea" an Autobiography Written in 1903 for His Children by Johan Storm Munch* . . . Carbondale: Southern Illinois University Press.

Naeseth, Henriette C.K. 1949. "Kristian Prestgard: An Appreciation." *NAS* 15: 131–139.

———. 1951. *The Swedish Theatre of Chicago 1868–1950*. Rock Island: Augustana Historical Society.

Nelson, David T. 1961. *Luther College 1861–1961*. Decorah: Luther College Press.

Nelson, E. Clifford and Eugene L. Fevold. 1960. *The Lutheran Church Among Norwegian-Americans: A History of the Evangelical Lutheran Church*. Vol. 1: 1825–1890. Vol. 2: 1890–1959. Minneapolis: Augsburg.

Nelson, James P. 1990. "The Problem of Cultural Identity in the Works of Waldemar Ager, Simon Johnson, and Johannes B. Wist." Unpublished dissertation. Seattle: University of Washington.

Nelson, O.N. 1893. *History of the Scandinavians and Successful Scandinavians in the United States*. Minneapolis: AP. Second rev. ed. 2 Vols., Minneapolis: AP. 1900.

Neumann, Jacob. 1837. *Varselsord til de udvandringslystne bønder i Bergens Stift. Et hyrdebrev fra Stiftets Biskob.* Bergen, Norway. Trans. and ed. by Gunnar J. Malmin, "Bishop Jacob Neumann's Word of Admonition to the Peasants," *NAS* 1: 95–109.

Nilsen, Evelyn Nilsen. 1941. "Buslett's Editorship of *Normannen* from 1894 to 1896." *NAS* 12: 128–143.

Norlie, Olaf M. et al, eds. (1922). *Luther College Through Sixty Years 1861–1921.* Minneapolis: Augsburg.

———. 1925. *History of the Norwegian People in America.* Minneapolis: Augsburg.

Omenaas, Veslemøy Steensnæs. 1978. "Nicolai Severin Hassel: The First Norwegian-American Novelist." Unpublished thesis. Oslo: University of Oslo.

———. 1986. "Nicolai Severin Hassel: Early Norwegian-American Novelist." *Essays on Norwegian-American Literature and History* 1: 11–21.

Øverland, Orm. 1968. "Americans Debate Ibsen, 1889–1910." *Americana Norvegica* 2: 135–159.

———. 1979. "Ole Edvart Rølvaag and *Giants in the Earth:* A Writer Between Two Countries." *Hungarian Studies in English* 12: 77–87. Reprinted in *American Studies in Scandinavia* 13 (No. 1, 1981): 35–45.

———. 1981. *Ole Edvart Rølvaag og den norske kulturen i Amerika.* Vinstra, Norway: Per Gynt nemnda.

———. 1986. "*Skandinaven* and the Beginnings of Professional Publishing." *NAS* 31: 187–214.

———. 1986. "Da embetsmannsklassen tok seg til rette i Vesterheimen." *Nytt norsk tidsskrift.* No.2: 49–61.

———. 1986. "Norwegian-American Theater and Drama 1865–1885." Pp. 189–200 in Peter Bilton et al, eds. *Essays in Honour of Kristian Smidt.* Oslo: Institute of English Studies.

———. 1986. "The Fiction of H.A. Foss: From Norwegian to American Populism." In Sven H. Rossel and Birgitta Steene, eds. *Scandinavian Literature in a Transcultural Context.* Seattle: University of Washington.

———. 1989. *Johan Schrøder's Travels in Canada 1863.* Montreal: McGill-Queen's University Press.

———. 1989. "History as Prerequisite for an Ethnic Identity: The Roots of Organized Historical Research and Publishing Among the Norwegian-Americans." In Hans Storhaug et al, eds. *Norse Heritage – 1989 Yearbook.* Stavanger: Norwegian Emigration Center.

———. 1993. "Augsburg Publishing House: The Penultimate Chapter of Norwegian-American Literature." In Knut Djupedal et al, eds. *Norwegian-American Essays,* 11–27. Oslo: NAHA-Norway.

———. 1995. "Fra norsk emigrant til amerikansk forfatter. Amerikaniseringen av Ole Edvart Rølvaag." Ole Karlsen and Renee Waara, eds. " . . . etter Rølvaag har problema har stridde med vorte til verdsproblem," 55–71. Nesna: Høgskolen.

———. 1996. *Home-Making Myths: Immigrants' Claims to a Special Status in their New Land.* Odease American Studies International Series. Working Paper No. 20. Odease: Center for American Studies.

———. 1996. "Learning to Read Immigrant Letters: Reflections Toward a Textual Theory." Øyvind T. Gulliksen et al., eds. *Norwegian-American Essays 1996*, 207–228. Oslo: NAHA-Norway and the Norwegian Immigrant Museum.

Øverland, Orm and Steinar Kjærheim. 1992. Eds. *Fra Amerika til Norge 1: Norske utvandrerbrev 1838–1857*. Oslo: Solum.

———. 1992. Eds. *Fra Amerika til Norge 2: Norske utvandrerbrev 1858–1868*. Oslo: Solum

———. 1993. Eds. *Fra Amerika til Norge III: Norske utvandrerbrev 1869–1874*. Oslo: Solum.

Ozolius, Karlis Lotars. 1960. "A History of Augsburg Publishing House." Unpublished thesis. Minneapolis: University of Minnesota.

———. 1972. "Book Publishing Trends in the American Lutheran Church and its Antecedent Bodies, 1917–1967." Unpublished dissertation. Ann Arbor: University of Michigan.

Paulson, Arthur C. 1930. "Bjørnson and the Norwegian Americans, 1880–81." *NAS* 5: 84109.

———. 1932. "Bjørnson and the Norwegian-Americans, 1855–75." *Norden* 4 (May): 23–25.

Paulson, Arthur C. and Kenneth Björk. 1938. "A School and Language Controversy in 1858: A Documentary Study." *NAS* 10: 76–106.

———. 1940. "*A Doll's House* on the Prairie: The First Ibsen Controversy in America." *NAS* 11: 1–16.

Paulson. Kristoffer F. 1977. "Berdahl Family History and Rølvaag's Immigrant Trilogy." *NAS* 27: 55–76.

Pochmann, Henry A. 1963. "The Mingling of Tongues." In Robert E. Spiller et al, *Literary History of the United States*. Third edition, revised. New York: Macmillan.

Ræder, Ole Munch. 1929. Translated and Edited by Gunnar J. Malmin. *America in the Forties: The Letters of Ole Munch Raeder*. Minneapolis: University of Minnesota Press.

Reigstad, Paul. 1972. *Rølvaag: His Life and Art*. Lincoln: University OF Nebraska Press.

———. 1978. See Boyer, Johan.

Ristad, Ditlef Georgson. 1936. "Svein Nilsson, Pioneer Norwegian-American Historian." *NAS* 9: 29–37.

Robinson, Elwyn B. 1966. *History of North Dakota*. Lincoln: University of Nebraska Press.

Rodgers, Drew. 1979. *The Norwegian Immigrant Experience as Depicted in the Fiction of Simon Johnson*. Bø: Telemark Regional College.

———. 1986. "The Americanization of Two Norwegian-American Institutions as Depicted in the Works of Simon Johnson." *Essays on Norwegian-American Literature and History* 1: 111–124.

Rolfsen, Nordahl. 1915. *Norge i Amerika: Livsbilleder fra nordmændenes liv og historie i De forenede stater*. Oslo: Jacob Dybwad.

Røssbø, Sigrun. 1983. "Drude Krog Janson: Norwegian-American and Norwegian Author." Unpublished thesis. Oslo: University of Oslo.

———. 1986. "Drude Krog Janson: Norwegian-American and Norwegian Writer." *Essays on Norwegian-American Literature and History* 1: 49–60.

Ruoff, A., LaVonne Brown and Jerry W. Ward, Jr. 1990. *Redefining American Literary History*. New York: The Modern Language Association of America.

Sandvik, Svein Ove. 1977. "H.A. Foss: Norwegian-American Author and Editor." Unpublished thesis. Oslo: University of Oslo.

———. 1986. "H.A. Foss: Norwegian-American Author and Editor," *Essays in Norwegian-American Literature and History* 1: 23–35.

Schultz, April. 1991. "'The Pride of the Race Had Been Touched': Norse-American Immigration Centennial and Ethnic Identity." *The Journal of American History* 77 (March): 1265–1295.

Semmingsen, Ingrid. 1941. *Veien mot vest: Utvandringen fra Norge til Amerika 1825–1865.* Oslo: Aschehoug.

———. 1950. *Veien mot vest: Utvandringen fra Norge til Amerika 1865–1915.* Oslo: Aschehoug.

———. 1980. "A Pioneer: Agnes Mathilde Wergeland, 1857–1914. In Lovoll 1980.

———. 1986. "Who Was Herm. Wang?" *NAS* 31: 215–243.

Simonson, Harold P. 1987. *Prairies Within: The Tragic Trilogy of Ole Rølvaag.* Seattle: University of Washington Press.

Skårdal, Dorothy Burton. 1962. "The Scandinavian Immigrant Writer in America." *NAS* 21: 14–53.

—. 1974. *The Divided Heart: Scandinavian Immigrant Experience Through Literary Sources.* Lincoln: University of Nebraska Press and Oslo: Universitetsforlaget.

———. 1977. "Scandinavian-American Literature: A Frontier for Research." *The Swedish Pioneer Historical Quarterly* 28 (October): 237–251.

Skarstedt, Ernst. 1914. *Vagabond och redaktør. Lefnadsøden och tidsbilder.* Seattle: AP.

Skordalsvold, Johannes Jensen. [1931]. "History of Augsburg Publishing House 1841–1931." Typescript in Archives of Augsburg Publishing House.

Smemo, Kenneth. 1986. "Waldemar Ager: Norwegian-American Sisyphus." *Essays on Norwegian-American Literature and History* 1: 141–157.

Smith, Liv. 1978. "Ole Amundsen Buslett: Norwegian-American Author." Unpublished thesis. Oslo: University of Oslo.

———. 1986. "Ole Amundsen Buslett: Norwegian-American Author." *Essays in Norwegian-American Literature and History* 1: 37–47.

Söderström, Alfred. 1899. *Minneapolis minnen: kulturhistoriskt axplockning från qvarnstaden vid Mississippi.* Minneapolis: AP.

Solensten, John. 1985. *There Lies a Fair Land: An Anthology of Norwegian-American Writing.* St. Paul: New Rivers Press.

Sollors, Werner. 1986. *Beyond Ethnicity: Consent and Descent in American Culture.* New York and Oxford: Oxford University Press.

———. 1989. Ed. *The Invention of Ethnicity.* New York and Oxford: Oxford University Press.

Søyland, Carl. 1954. *Skrift i sand. Bruddstykker av utvandrersagaen . . .* Oslo: Gyldendal.

Stegner, Wallace and Richard W. Etulain. 1990. *Conversations With Wallace Stegner on Western History and Historians.* Salt Lake City: University of Utah Press. Revised Edition.

Støylen, Sigvald. 1965. "Marcus Thrane i Amerika." *Syn og Segn* 71: 176–182.

Sunde, Arne. 1984. "Heime, men borte: Ein analyse av 7 norsk-amerikanske romanar." Unpublished thesis. Bergen: University of Bergen.

———. 1986. "Jon Norstog: A Problematic Author?" *Essays in Norwegian-American Literature and History* 1: 99–110.

———. 1990. "Arnfinn Bruflot: Norsk-amerikansk etterkrigsforfattar." *Essays on Norwegian-American Literature and History* 2: 49–56.

Sundheim, Borghild K. and Marie Sundheim Anderson. 1957. "Vår far – Anders M. Sundheim." *JiV*: 7–10.

Sveino, Per. 1971. "Kristofer Janson and his American Experience." *Americana Norvegica* 3: 88–104.

Sveinsson, Einar Ol. 1959. *Njåls saga: Kunstverket.* Bergen & Oslo: Universitetsforlaget.

Thernstrom, Stephan. 1980. Ed. *Harvard Encyclopedia of American Ethnic Groups.* Cambridge: Harvard University Press.

Thorson, Gerald Howard. 1954. "The Novels of Peer Stømme." *NAS* 18: 141–162.

———. 1957. "America is Not Norway: The Story of the Norwegian-American Novel." Unpublished dissertation. New York: Columbia University.

———. 1975. Ed. *Ole Rølvaag: Artist and Cultural Leader.* Northfield: St. Olaf College Press.

———. 1977. "Tinsel and Dust: Disenchantment in Two Minneapolis Novels from the 1880's." *Minneapolis History* 45 (No. 6, Summer): 211–222.

———. 1978. "Pressed Flowers and Still-Running Brooks: Norwegian-American Literature." Pp. 375–94 in Wlodomyr T. Zyla and Wendell M. Aycock, eds. *Ethnic Literature Since 1776: The Many Voices of America.* Lubbock: Texas Tech Press.

Torvik, Ingvald. 1952. "Jon Norstog, landsmålsdiktaren på prærien i Nord-Dakota." *Syn og Segn* 58: 165–174.

Torvik, Judith Ann. 1982. "Eyvind J. Evans: Norwegian-American Lumberjack, Farmer, and Writer." Unpublished thesis. Oslo: University of Oslo.

———. 1986. "Eyvind Johnson Evans: Norwegian Immigrant Writer." *Essays on Norwegian-American Literature and History* 1: 199–209.

Trommler, Frank and Joseph McVeigh, eds. 1985. *America and the Germans: An Assessment of a Three-Hundred-Year History. Volume One: Immigration, Language, Ethnicity.* Philadelphia: University of Pennsylvania Press.

[Tweet]. Ella Valborg Rølvaag. 1941. "Norwegian Folk Narrative in America." *NAS* 12: 33–59.

Ueland, Andreas. 1929. *Recollections of an Immigrant.* New York: Minton, Balch.

U.S. Bureau of the Census. 1975. *Historical Statistics of the United States: Colonial Times to 1970* 1–2. Washington, D.C.

Vossler, Ronald J. 1979. "Writing in the Sand: The Enigma of Jon Norstog." *Horizons* 9 (No. 3 Fall): 67.

Wærenskjold, Elise. 1961. C.A. Clausen, ed., *The Lady with a Pen: Elise Wærenskjold in Texas.* Northfield: NAHA.

Weber, Brom. 1975. "Our Multi-Ethnic Origins and American Literary Studies." *M.E.L.U.S.* 2 (March): 5–19.

Wiers-Jenssen, H. and J. Nordahl-Olsen. 1926. *Den nationale scene: De første 25 aar.* Bergen.

Williamson, Erik Luther. 1981. "Jon Norstog: North Dakota's Norwegian Poet." *North Dakota Quarterly* 49 (No.4 Autumn): 65–78.

Wilt, Napier and Henriette C. Koren Naeseth. 1938. "Two Early Norwegian Dramatic Societies in Chicago." *NAS* 10: 44–75.

Zempel, Solveig Pauline Tweet. 1980. "Language Use In the Novels of Johannes B. Wist: A Study of Bilingualism in Literature." Unpublished dissertation. Minneapolis: University of Minnesota.

———. 1986. "Johannes B. Wist." *Essays in Norwegian-American Literature and History* 1: 125–140.

———. 1991. *In Their Own Words: Letters from Norwegian Immigrants.* Minneapolis and Oxford: University of Minnesota Press.

Index

Aasen, Ivar, 198, 372
Ager, Trygve, 339–340
Ager, Waldemar, 325, 327 (ills.); on
  Stenholt, 120–121; and Buslett, 133,
  135, 136, 139, 140; on Teigen and
  Strømme, 181; on Norwegian litera-
  ture, 191; as editor, 194; and Norwe-
  gian-American culture, 194–196,
  375–376; on NAHA, 208; and his
  works, 208, 284–285, 324–344; as reviewer, 211, 235, 246, 253, 254; and
  Norwegian-American literature,
  215, 222, 229, 231, 312; and Simon
  Johnson, 268, 270; and Jon Norstog,
  293, 296, 298, 308; on Rølvaag, 354,
  356, 370. Also numerous mentions.
Aikio, Matti, 13
Amble, Ole, 92, 96
Amundsen, Helge, 198
Anderson, John, 57 (ill.); 56–57, 74, 179
Anderson, Rasmus B., 54 (ill.); introduced term *Vesterheimen*, 5; and
  Bjørnson, 12; his influence in Norwegian America, 54, 62–63, 65, 109;
  and his works, 57, 61; as reviewer, 61;
  as mentor, 82, 83–84, 94, 137, 248; as
  champion of Norwegian-American
  literature, 102–103, 114, 159; Stenholt on, 117, 119; and the *bygdelag*

movement, 190. Also numerous
  mentions.
Anderson, Sherwood, 13
Andreassen, Ola, 244
Andrewson, Ole, 48
Anker-Midling, Julius, 87, 92
Anundsen, Brynild, 63 (ill.); 55, 104,
  143–144, 199, 310
Askevold, Bernt, 62, 65, 103–106,
  109–110, 121, 182
Aslagsson, Olai, 254

Bache, Søren, 260
Bakke, Thorvald, 254
Bang, Marie, 122
Bangsberg, John, 254–255
Baumann, Julius Berg, 231 (ill.); 141,
  171, 181–182, 196, 206, 216,
  230–234, 319
Bellamy, Edward, 149, 152
Benson, John, 225, 262
Berg, Karin, 258–259
Berild, Olaf, 253
Berven, Jacob, 221
Bierce, Ambrose, 336
Birkeland, Knut, 122
"Bjarne Blehr." See Heitmann, John.
Bjørnson, Bjørnstjerne, 12, 44, 50, 94,
  114, 129, 162, 191, 314